Master Apache JMeter – From Testing to DevOps

Master performance testing with JMeter

Antonio Gomes Rodrigues

Bruno Demion (Milamber)

Philippe Mouawad

Packt

Master Apache JMeter – From Load Testing to DevOps

Copyright © 2019 Packt Publishing

All rights reserved. No part of this book may be reproduced, stored in a retrieval system, or transmitted in any form or by any means, without the prior written permission of the publisher, except in the case of brief quotations embedded in critical articles or reviews.

Every effort has been made in the preparation of this book to ensure the accuracy of the information presented. However, the information contained in this book is sold without warranty, either express or implied. Neither the authors, nor Packt Publishing, and its dealers and distributors will be held liable for any damages caused or alleged to be caused directly or indirectly by this book.

Packt Publishing has endeavored to provide trademark information about all of the companies and products mentioned in this book by the appropriate use of capitals. However, Packt Publishing cannot guarantee the accuracy of this information.

Authors: Antonio Gomes Rodrigues, Bruno Demion (Milamber), and Philippe Mouawad

Managing Editor: Anush Kumar Mehalavarunan

Acquisitions Editor: Bridget Neale

Production Editor: Samita Warang

Editorial Board: David Barnes, Mayank Bhardwaj, Ewan Buckingham, Simon Cox, Mahesh Dhyani, Taabish Khan, Manasa Kumar, Alex Mazonowicz, Pramod Menon, Douglas Paterson, Dominic Pereira, Shiny Poojary, Erol Staveley, Ankita Thakur, and Jonathan Wray

First Published: August 2019

Production Reference: 3200919

ISBN: 978-1-83921-764-7

Published by Packt Publishing Ltd.

Livery Place, 35 Livery Street

Birmingham B3 2PB, UK

Table of Contents

Preface i

Quick Start with JMeter 1

Our Process 1
Setup JMeter to Record Our Browsing Session 2
Configure Your Browser 5
Save Our Script 7
Validate Our Script with Only One User 15
Setup Our Load Test and Launch It 15
Run Our Load Test and Analyze It 18

JMeter Overview 23

JMeter Overview 23
Types of Load Tests Supported 27
Supported Test Protocols 28
Reporting 29

Designing a Test Case 31

Introduction 31
Warning 31
Type of Load Test 32
    Performance/Load Test 33
    Stress Test 33
    Soak/Endurance Test 35
    Failover/Resilience Test 35

Spike Test 36

Other 36

Load Model 36

Concurrency User (Closed Model) 38

Throughput (Open Model) 42

Arrivals Rate (Open Model) 45

Structure of a Test Case 49

Ramp-Up 50

Plateau/Step 51

Ramp-Down 51

Example: Step Load Test 51

Identify Critical Business Scenarios to Script 54

Frequent 54

Vital 54

Risky 55

How Many Virtual Users Do I Need? 55

Parameters to Take into Account when Creating a Scenario 57

Vary User Input 57

Reuse the Same Values 57

Vary the Types of Users 58

Vary and Adjust Think Times 58

Adjust the Ramp-Up Time 59

Adjust the Test Duration 59

Error Handling 59

User Connection Type 60

Size of the Scenarios 60

Meeting Point/Rendezvous 61

Cookie Management 61

Cache Management 62
Conclusion 62

Important Concepts in JMeter   65

Scoping 65
Elements' Execution Order 67
How Timer Scope Works 69
Rule 1: Timers Are Executed before Each Sampler in Their Scope 69
Rule 2: If There Is More Than One Timer in the Scope, All the Timers Will Be Processed before the Sampler 70
Controlling the Execution Order of Timers 71
How Assertion Scope Works 72
Rule 1: Assertions Are Executed after Each Sampler in Their Scope or to Parent Samplers 73
Rule 2: Failed Assertions Cause the Failure of the Entire Transaction Controller 74
Rule 3: Assertions Can Validate the Main Sample and/or the Sub-Samples 75
Rule 4: Be Careful with Low-Performing Assertions 76
Our Advice 77
How Properties Differ from Variables 77
How Properties Are Created 77
How Variables Are Created 78
How ${} Differs from ${_P} 78

Preparing the Test Environment
(Injectors and Tested Systems)   81

Introduction 81
Setting Up the Injectors 81
Never Host Injectors on the Same Server as the Tested System 82

Calibrating Your Test 83

Monitoring Injectors 83

IP Spoofing 84

Using the Latest Version 87

JMeter Memory Configuration 88

Avoiding Load Testing behind a Proxy 88

Preparation of the System under Test 88

A Testing Environment 88

An Environment Consistent with the Target 89

Datasets 90

Take into Account Calls to Third-Party Services 90

Disabling Protection Systems 91

Using Isolated Environments 91

License Management 92

Monitoring 92

Conclusion 92

Being Productive with JMeter   95

Introduction 95

Good Practices When Recording a Script 96

Use the HTTP(S) Test Script Recorder Element 96

BlazeMeter Chrome Extension 96

Pre-Populating HTTP Request Defaults before Recording the Script 98

Use Tools / Import from cURL 99

Static Resources 101

Using Timeouts 103

Applying a Naming Convention to Transactions/Requests 104

  Global Assertion 106
  Reusing Script Parts 107
  Recording an HTTPS website 108
  Keyboard Shortcuts 109

Debugging a script 109
  Using View Results Tree 110
  Capturing Errors 112
  Debug Sampler 113
  jp@gc - Dummy Sampler 114
  Log Viewer 117
  BlazeMeter's Step-by-Step Debugger 119
  The Old-Fashioned Way in the Console 120
  Using a Third-Party Tool 120

Finalizing a Script 121
  Changing the Name of a Transaction According to a Parameter 121
  Sharing an Object between Different Thread Groups 121
  Getting the Most out of CSV Files 125
  Marking a Response as an Error 131
  Using a Regular Expression Extractor on Content
  with Spaces and Multiple Lines 132
  Executing an Action Based on the Status of the Previous One 133
  Adding Headers to Our HTTP Requests 135
  Waiting with While Controller 136
  The Right Extractor at the Right Time 142
  Handle Cookies 143

Conclusion 145

Load Testing a Website — 147

A Bit of Theory — 147
Setup with JMeter — 152
Methodology — 157
Put into Practice with JMeter — 162
Example 1: Simulate Realistic Load — 162
Example 2: Technical Tests with Byteman — 189
Example 3: Technical Tests with JProfiler — 202
Example 4: Tricking CAPTCHAs with a Java Request — 208
Conclusion — 213

Load Testing Web Services — 215

A Few Concepts — 215
REST (REpresentational State Transfer) Web Services — 216
WS-* Web Services — 216
Setup with JMeter — 217
Methodology — 219
Practice with JMeter — 219
SOAP/XML-RPC Web Services — 219
REST Web Service: Discussion Forum — 224
REST Web Service: Customer Database — 229
Conclusion — 240

Load Testinga Database Server — 243

A Bit of Theory — 245
Methodology — 246
Setup with JMeter — 248
Putting Theory into Practice with JMeter — 251

Example 1: Load Test of a Database	251
Example 2: Studying the Impact of Indexes on Performance	268
Example 3: ETL	275

Conclusion 279

Load TestingMessage-Oriented Middleware (MOM) via JMS — 281

A Bit of Theory 281
Asynchronous Messages 282
Decoupling 283
Back Pressure 284
Communication Models 285
What is a Message Composed of? 287

Setup with JMeter 287
Installing the MOM libraries 288
The JMS Point-to-Point Element 288
JMS Resources and JNDI Properties 289
Publish/Subscribe 297

Methodology 303

Putting It into Practice with JMeter 303
Example 1: Testing the Configuration of an MOM server with Point-to-Point Messaging 304
Example 2: Testing the Performance of Our Consumer with JMS Publish/Subscribe 309
Example 3: Testing the Configuration of an MOM Server with Publish/Subscribe 313
Example 4: Testing Any MOM 322

Conclusion 324

Performing a Load Test — 327

Introduction — 327
Methodology — 328
Testing Your Script with the Graphical User Interface — 328
Running Your Test from the Command Line — 329
Running Your Test on the Command Line with Taurus — 331
Running Your Test from Apache Maven — 335
Running Your Test from Jenkins — 338
Running Your Test from Apache Ant — 338
Best Practices — 340
Have Well-Prepared Injectors — 340
Generating Reports at the End of the Test — 340

Visualizing and Analyzing the Load Testing Results — 347

Introduction — 347
Visualizing the Results with Listeners — 348
View Results Tree — 348
Summary Report — 351
Aggregate Report — 352
Backend Listener — 352
Report Dashboard — 355
Particularities of the Visualization of Results a Distributed Load Test before JMeter 5.0 — 356
Visualizing the Results with Third Party Visualizing Tools — 356
Visualizing the Results with PaaS Load Testing tools — 357
Redline13 — 357
BlazeMeter — 358

Some Tips to Read the Results 358
Prefer Percentiles over Average 359
Be Careful with Downsampling and Data Retention 361
Be Careful with Metric Definition 362
Be Careful with Response Time at the Beginning of the Load Test 364
Don't Rely on the Metrics of a Short Load Test 366
Check Response Time Distribution 366
Some Tips to Present the Results 368
Don't Average Percentiles 368
Define the Number of Metrics to Display in a Time Series Line Graph ... 369
Define the Resolution/Granularity of the Measures 370
Don't Forget to Add Labels, Legends, and Units in Graphs 372
Axis Forced 0 372
Don't Use Pie Charts 374
Prefer Bar Graphs When We Have Sparse Metrics 375
Present Errors with Toplist 376
Time Series Graphs and Single-Value Summaries 377
Conclusion 378

Integration of JMeter in the DevOpsTool Chain   381

Introduction 381
Organization/Team Topology 382
Load Testing Team in Its Ivory Tower 382
DevOps and Load Test Team Collaboration 383
One Performance Tester Integrated on DevOps Team 383
No Performance Tester 384
Team of Evangelists Performance Testers 385

Setting Up Shift-Left Strategy 385
   Modification in JMeter Script to Implement Shift-Left Strategy 387
Integrating JMeter in Our Software Factory 390
   Example 1: Integrating with Jenkins Using Maven 391
   Example 2: Enhancing Integration with Jenkins Using
   Performance Plugin 402
Automation 410
   Example 3: Non-Regression Testing of Memory Consumption
   with EJ JProfiler 410
   Example 4: Detecting a Memory Leak during an Endurance
   Test with EJ JProfiler 416
   Example 5: Retrieving SQL Queries Executed during a Load
   Test with YourKit Java Profiler 419
   Example 6: Analysis of the Garbage Collector (GC) Log File
   with GCViewer 425
   Example 7: Non-Regression Testing of Web APIs
   with Dynatrace AppMon 432
Conclusion 437

Index   439

Preface

About

This section briefly introduces the authors and what the book covers.

About the Book

Preface by Alexander Podelko

An important event, directly related to this book, happened recently and probably went unnoticed. It appears that Apache JMeter has become the most popular load testing tool. In 2014, I was preparing a presentation about load testing tools and the criteria for their selection. One criterion was the existence of an ecosystem (documents, expertise, people, services, and so on). It may be not the defining factor, but it is an important factor to consider. To evaluate such ecosystems, in the absence of more sophisticated data, I used the number of web pages returned by Google and the number of jobs that Monster finds that mention each product.

LoadRunner (then an HP product) clearly held first place in both categories, with JMeter following not too far behind. Silk Performer (then owned by Borland) trailed far behind in third place. But now, in 2018, JMeter appears to be well ahead of LoadRunner (now owned by Micro Focus) in both the number of documents and the number of jobs mentioning it, apparently becoming the most popular load testing tool. Of course, it doesn't mean that JMeter became the best tool for every task, but its popularity, in addition to being an open-source tool, definitely earns it a high place in the list of options to consider. It is also very important for an open-source project to attract people who will work to improve it, thus ensuring the future development of the product.

Another interesting trend is that JMeter scripts have become a de facto standard, and many SaaS tools are built on top of JMeter or at least support JMeter scripts. These tools complement JMeter in many important ways and elevate its functionality and services to a new level, allowing it to compete with commercial products in more sophisticated environments.

Several books about JMeter have been published before, but this one is the first by JMeter contributors who know it inside out and are renowned experts in this area. JMeter is not a trivial product. It has a lot of functionality, but this can be implemented in many different ways and it is not always easy to figure out the best way to do it. While, as we have already mentioned, there is an enormous number of posts on the internet discussing different aspects of JMeter, the problem is that most of them are for beginners. And while there is more advanced stuff too, if you want to use it, you'd better know exactly what you're looking for as it may be hard to find it by searching just for generic terms. This is where this book will be invaluable in establishing a framework of knowledge and familiarity with the basic concepts, so you will at least understand what you should be looking for.

This book, with all the aforementioned valuable information in one place, is a must for anybody who is working seriously with JMeter. It may be a little too condensed for absolute beginners (although, as already mentioned, there are lots of introductory materials on the internet that can help here), but it is the best resource that you can find for JMeter if you already have some performance-testing experience and need to go further. In particular, it will be invaluable to people who want to expand their JMeter knowledge into advanced topics or switch to JMeter from other load testing tools.

In particular, JMeter has many integrations with other popular tools and a large number of plugins. It is quite possible that somebody has already solved the problem you are confronting, so you may save a lot of effort by simply reusing their solution. It is fortunate that this book is not limited to the core JMeter functionality and discusses available components and integrations when appropriate. While it is impossible to cover everything that is available in detail, the advantage of this book is that it puts everything into a system, allowing the reader to understand the relations between different parts and technologies.

Load testing is an important part of the performance-engineering process. However, the industry is changing and load testing needs to adjust to these changes. A stereotypical, last-minute performance check is not enough anymore. Performance testing should be interwoven into the development process, starting early and continuing throughout the whole life cycle of the product. The importance of this transformation is stressed in the title of the book itself, **From Load Testing to DevOps**, moving from standalone load testing as a mere step at the end of the software development cycle, to performance testing fully integrated into DevOps. And while we are not fully there yet, the *Chapter 13, Integration of JMeter in the DevOps Tool Chain* dives directly into what can be done right now.

DevOps, putting together the development and operations sides, is supposed to drastically improve feedback from production to development, and the free flow of performance information in both directions. So, a holistic approach to performance should be one of its main advantages. Unfortunately, it doesn't look like such a holistic approach happens often. Rather, it looks like DevOps teams just drop the more sophisticated parts of performance engineering (and performance testing usually gets into that category) and rely on a more reactive approach to performance issues, concentrating more on quick fixes for issues than on their prevention. Still, load testing is a very important method of risk mitigation and can't be fully replaced by other performance-engineering activities. Let's have a quick look at the benefits delivered by load testing.

First, there are always the risks of crashing a system or experiencing performance issues under heavy load, and the only way to mitigate them is to actually test the system. Even stellar performance in production and a highly scalable architecture don't guarantee that it won't crash under a slightly heavier load.

It is important to note that load testing doesn't completely guarantee that the system won't crash: this would be the case if, for example, the real-life workload was different from what was tested. So, you need to monitor the production system to verify that your test workload is close enough. That said, load tests do considerably reduce the risk if they are carried out correctly (and, of course, can be completely useless and misleading if they are not).

Another important benefit of load testing is in verifying how changes affect multi-user performance. The impact of changes on multi-user performance is generally not proportional to what is observed with single-user performance and can often be counterintuitive. Sometimes, improving single-user performance can lead to a degradation of multiuser performance. The more complex the system, the more exotic the multiuser performance problems that can occur are.

Another value of load testing is to provide a reliable and reproducible way to apply a multiuser load necessary for performance optimization and troubleshooting. You apply exactly the same workload and see if the change makes a difference. In most cases, you cannot do this in production when the workload changes, so you never know if the result is due to a change in the code or a change in the workload (except, perhaps, the rather rare case of very homogeneous and manageable workloads, where you can apply a very precisely measured portion of the actual workload). And, of course, a reproducible workload greatly simplifies the debugging and checking of multiuser problems.

In addition, given current trends in system self-regulation (such as auto-scaling or load-dependent service level changes), load tests are required to verify this functionality. You must apply a heavy load to see how auto-scaling will work. Load testing thus becomes a means of testing the functionality of the system, blurring the traditional division between functional and non-functional testing.

You will find further examples of different types of performance tests and their links to different aspects of DevOps in the book. Although the book does not focus on the theoretical aspects of performance testing, it provides sufficient theoretical information to understand the concepts discussed and their practical applications in JMeter. Practical examples of integrating performance testing with DevOps are all the more important as this is a rather new field of expertise and is probably the main challenge of performance testing at the moment.

This book leads the reader through the basics of working with today's most popular load testing tool, JMeter, through more advanced aspects of the tool, and performance testing in general, through to its complete integration into DevOps.

Alexander Podelko Bio

Over the last 20 years, Alex Podelko has supported major performance initiatives for Oracle, Hyperion, Aetna, and Intel in different roles, including as a performance tester, a performance analyst, a performance architect, and a performance engineer. Currently, he is a consulting member of technical staff at Oracle, responsible for the performance testing and tuning of Hyperion (that is, Enterprise Performance Management and Business Intelligence) products. Before specializing in performance, Alex led software development for Rodnik Software. Having more than 30 years of overall experience in the software industry, he holds a Ph.D. in computer science from Gubkin University and an MBA from Bellevue University.

Alex periodically talks and writes about performance-related topics, advocating tearing down silo walls between different groups of performance professionals. He currently serves as a board director for the Computer Measurement Group (CMG), a worldwide organization of performance and capacity management professionals.

About the Authors

Antonio Gomes Rodrigues

Antonio Gomes Rodrigues is an expert in the field of application performance for more than 10 years.

His missions led him to work:

- On the performance of high traffic websites
- On the performance of an application for brokers
- On the performance of rich clients, cloud applications, WEB applications, and so on
- With various profilers: *JProfiler*, *Yourkit*, *PerfView*, and so on
- With various APM: *Dynatrace*, *AppDynamics*, *Introscope*, *NewRelic*, and so on
- With various load testing tools: *JMeter*, *LoadRunner*, and so on
- In various missions: load tests, implementation of performance strategies, training, performance audits, troubleshooting, and so on

He shares his knowledge of application performance at conferences, on his blog (http://arodrigues.developpez.com/) and during technical book reviews.

He is currently a committer and a PMC member of the JMeter project (http://jmeter.apache.org/) within the Apache Software Foundation (http://www.apache.org/foundation/how-it-works.html#what).

Bruno Demion (Milamber)

Bruno Demion, better known in the JMeter community under the pseudonym **Milamber** is a French computer scientist living in Morocco since 2002, currently living in Temara (near Rabat).

He works in a technology consulting company, as a partner, architect and senior technical expert on web and cloud technologies.

Thanks to his work and passion, IT, Milamber has strong skills in the field of performance, troubleshooting, IT security as well as technical architectures for web and cloud solutions.

Since December 2003, he has been working with JMeter to perform load tests in various performance missions and also gives training on this topic. He contributes as much as possible to the JMeter project on his free time, especially on the French translation of the graphical interface, bug fixes and some changes (proxy https, new results tree, icon bar, and so on).

He is currently a committer and a PMC member of the JMeter project (http://jmeter.apache.org/) within the Apache Software Foundation (http://www.apache.org/foundation/how-it-works.html#what). He is also an official ASF member (http://www.apache.org/foundation/how-it-works.html#roles). His Apache ID is milamber (http://people.apache.org/~milamber/).

Milamber also has a personal blog (http://blog.milamberspace.net/) with many articles and tutorials about JMeter, some of which inspired this book.

Philippe Mouawad

Philippe Mouawad is a technical expert and architect in JEE and Web environments within the company Ubik-Ingenierie. He has been using JMeter since 2009 as part of performance improvements missions, load testing of intranet or e-commerce websites and training on JMeter.

He has been contributing to JMeter since 2009, first through patches and then as a committer and member of Project Management Committee at Apache. Among his main contributions are the **CSS selector Extractor**, the **Boundary Extractor**, the **Backend Listener** (allowing to interface among others *Graphite*, *InfluxDB* or *ElasticSearch*), part of the Web reporting feature and the optimization of the performances of the core and its stabilization and various ergonomic improvements, to his credit more than 400 bugs/improvements.

He also contributes to the JMeter-Plugins (https://jmeter-plugins.org/) project, among his contributions are **Redis DataSet**, **Graphs Generator Listener** and various patches to different plugins.

He also manages the JMeter Maven Plugin (https://github.com/jmeter-maven-plugin/jmeter-maven-plugin) project, he has been managing it since version 2.3.0 ensuring its compatibility with last JMeter releases and improving its dependencies management and reporting mechanism.

He is currently a committer and a PMC member of the JMeter project (https://jmeter.apache.org/) within the Apache Software Foundation (http://www.apache.org/foundation/how-it-works.html#what). His Apache ID is pmouawad (http://people.apache.org/~pmouawad/).

He is also a lead developer of the Ubik Load Pack (https://ubikloadpack.com) solution, a set of Enterprise Plugins which provides support for protocols that are not natively supported by JMeter. Finally, he contributes to the Ubik-Ingenierie blog (https://www.ubik-ingenierie.com/blog/).

About the Reviewer

Felix Schumacher

Felix is a committer to the JMeter project since October 2014 and a PMC member since February 2015. He is also a committer on Apache Tomcat. He has a diploma in mathematics but found working in IT more appealing. Since he became a developer for JMeter, he has been active in all fields, from bug fixing to designing multiple enhancements, tests, documentation, and quality improvements.

Learning Objectives

- Explore various JMeter concepts, including Timers scope and Assertion scope
- Discover the types of test protocols and load tests that JMeter supports
- Design a realistic test scenario using various tips and best practices
- Prepare your test environment with injectors and the system under test
- Learn and apply good practices when recording a script
- Integrate JMeter with Jenkins using Maven

Audience

This book contains all the valuable information you need in one place and is a must for everybody who is seriously working with JMeter. It might be a little condensed for absolute beginners, but this book is the best you can find if you already have some performance testing experience and want to get further. In particular, it would be invaluable to developers who want to expand their JMeter knowledge into advanced topics or switch to JMeter from other load testing tools.

Approach

This book explains concepts through real-world examples. You will find examples of different types of performance tests and their links to different aspects of DevOps. You will also be provided with sufficient theoretical information to understand the concepts discussed and their practical applications in JMeter.

Acknowledgment

In no particular order.

Thanks to Vladimir Sitnikov for his feedback.

Thanks to Mark Tomlinson for his feedback.

Copyright

No part of the contents of this book may be reproduced or transmitted in any form or by any means without the written permission of the authors.

Apache, Apache JMeter, JMeter, the Apache feather, and the Apache JMeter logo are registered trademarks of the Apache Software Foundation (ASF).

Dynatrace and PurePath are registered trademarks of Dynatrace.

UbikLoadPack is a registered trademark of Ubik-Ingénierie.

Tricentis Flood is a registered trademark of Tricentis.

OctoPerf is a registered trademark of OctoPerf.

BlazeMeter is a registered trademark of CA Technologies.

Byteman is a registered trademark of Red Hat.

JProfiler is a registered trademark of ej-technologies GmbH.

Firefox is a registered trademark of Mozilla.

Spring is a registered trademark of Pivotal Software. NetBeans is a registered trademark of Oracle Corporation.

Apache Netbeans is a registered trademark of the ASF.

Oracle and MySQL are registered trademarks of Oracle Corporation.

Apache ActiveMQ and Apache ActiveMQ Artemis are trademarks of the ASF.

Apache Ant and Apache Maven are registered trademarks of the ASF.

JMeter Plugins is a registered trademark of Andrey Pokhilko.

RedLine13 is a registered trademark of RedLine13.

1

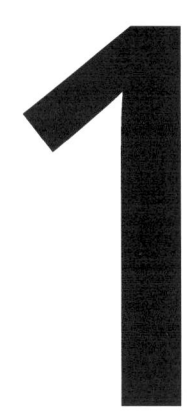

Quick Start with JMeter

With JMeter, you can quickly run your first load test. This chapter will show you how to set up a simple test case with JMeter and its **HTTP(S) Test Script Recorder** element.

Our Process

Here are the steps to set up our test:

1. Launch JMeter and prepare the recording of our script
2. Configure the browser to use the **HTTP(S) Test Script Recorder** of JMeter
3. Record the script
4. Customize our script (add assertions, rename transactions, add think time…)
5. Validate our script with a single user
6. Configure the load test (define the number of users, number of iterations, warm-up duration, and load test duration…)
7. Run and analyze the load test

Setup JMeter to Record Our Browsing Session

1. Launch JMeter:

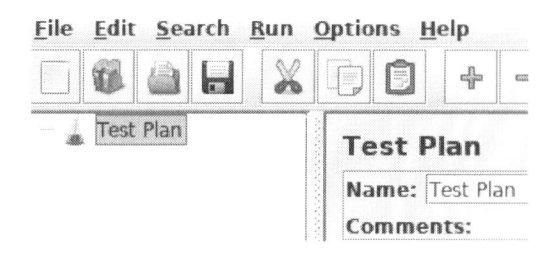

Figure 1.1: JMeter

2. Use the **Templates...** feature of JMeter:

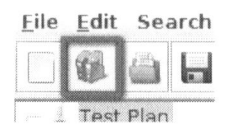

Figure 1.2: JMeter Templates... feature

3. Choose **Recording with Think Time** model and click **Create**:

Template showing how to record with think time

JMeter Configuration

- JMeter Server Proxy port is set to 8888, you may want to change this

Browser Configuration

Configure your browser so that it uses the JMeter proxy, set:
- the host of the machine that runs JMeter
- the port you setup in JMeter Server Proxy

Useful links

- http://jmeter.apache.org/usermanual/jmeter_proxy_step_by_step.pdf
- http://jmeter.apache.org/usermanual/component_reference.html#HTTP_Proxy_Server

Figure 1.3: Recording template

4. The test plan is ready:

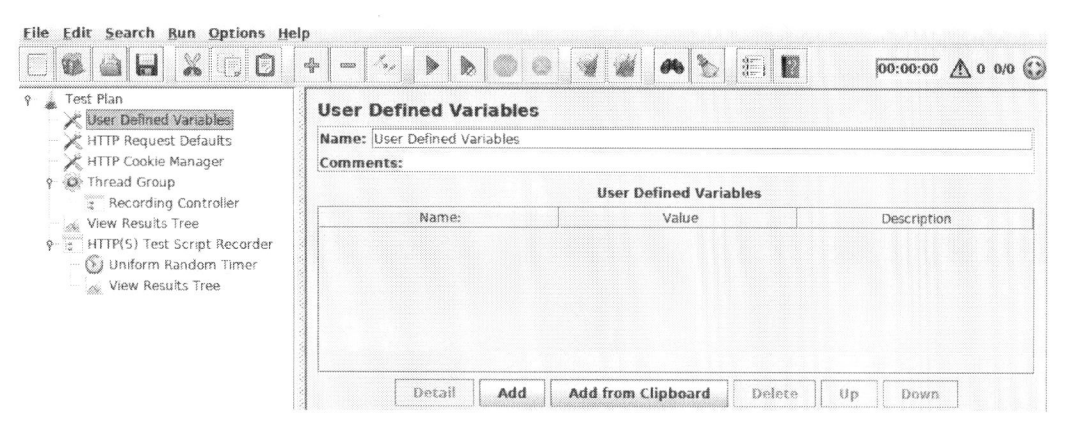

Figure 1.4: Result of Recording template

5. To save time in the future, we will select the **HTTP Request Defaults** element and fill in the **Server Name or IP** and **Port Number** sections:

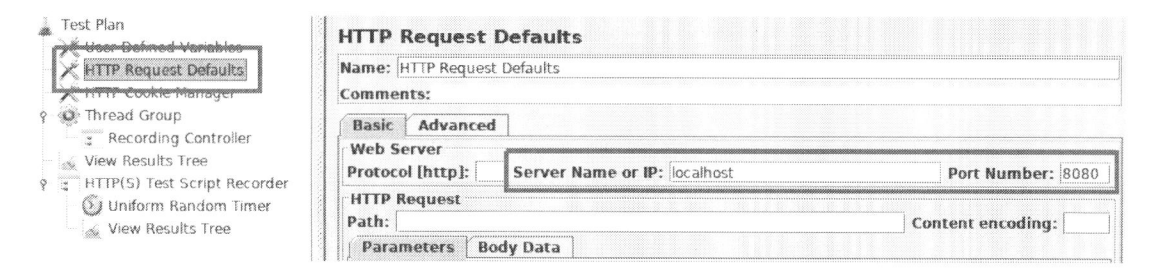

Figure 1.5: Result of Recording template

> **Note**
> With this trick, we will share these two fields in every element **HTTP Request Defaults** and JMeter will not put them in each **HTTP Request** during recording.

> **Caution**
> During the load test, you should avoid having the injector (JMeter) on the same server as the application under test.
>
> Otherwise, the injected load will be impacted by the application's bad performance, and the application could be impacted by the injector's bad performance.

Our tree is ready; we must now start the proxy server of JMeter.

But before doing that, let's look at the **HTTP(S) Test Script Recorder** element.

6. For the name of recorded transactions, we have two options in Recorder:

   Transaction name, which allows you to fully name them as you wish.

   Prefix, which will just prepend the prefix to the default name given by JMeter, which is usually the URL path.

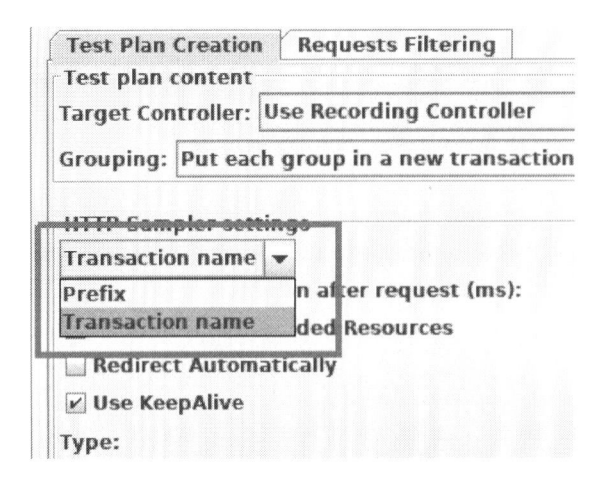

   Figure 1.6: Transaction naming strategy

7. Note that with the default configuration of the template, static resources (image, CSS file, JS file...) are not recorded:

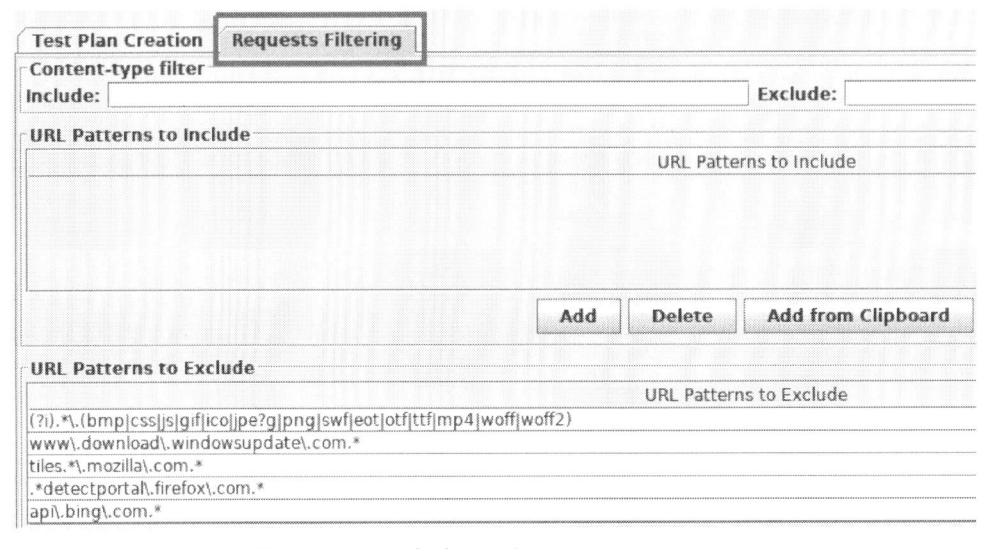

   Figure 1.7: Exclude static resource capture

JMeter is now ready to record our navigation session.

Configure Your Browser

1. In order for JMeter to record the navigation session, we must configure our browser to use the proxy server that JMeter launched.

2. For example, with Firefox, choose the menu **Edit** > **Preferences**:

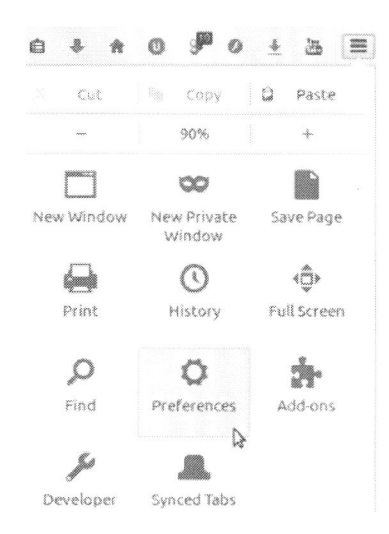

Figure 1.8: Proxy selection in Firefox

3. Then select the **Advanced** tab and then the **Network** sub-tab. Let's click on **Settings...**:

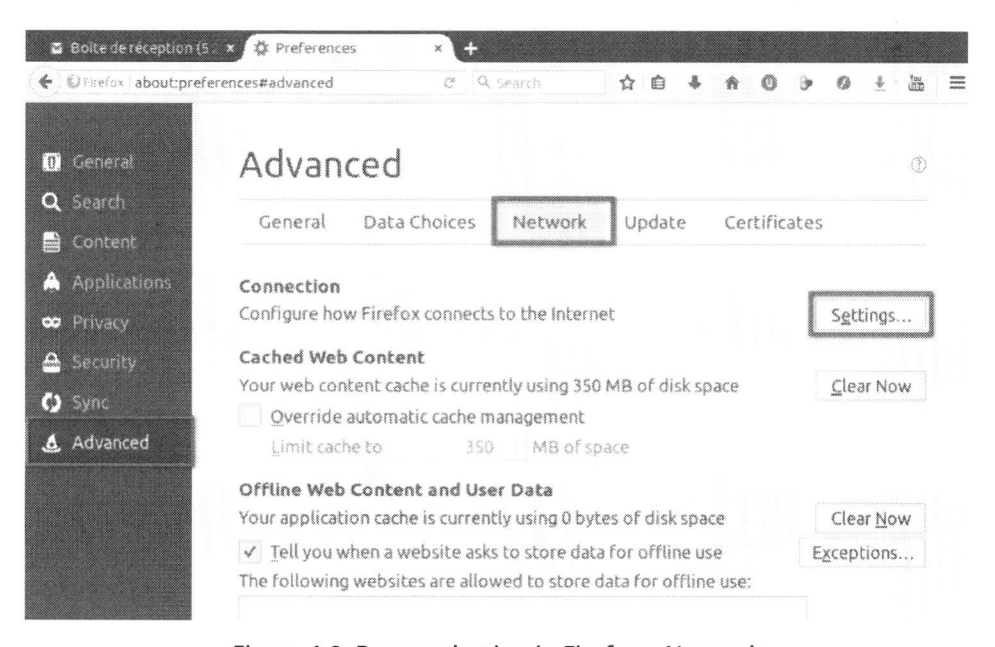

Figure 1.9: Proxy selection in Firefox – Network

4. In the new window, select the **Manual proxy configuration** option, then fill in the **HTTP Proxy** field with the following IP address: **127.0.0.1** (corresponding to the local IP address (**localhost**)), and fill in the **Port** field with **8888** (corresponding to the default listening port of the JMeter proxy server).

> **Caution**
> When recording a local application, be careful to delete **localhost** and **127.0.0.1** from the **No Proxy for:** field.

5. Finally, check the **Use this proxy server for all protocols** box.
6. Let's save the modifications by clicking on the **OK** button in the Firefox window:

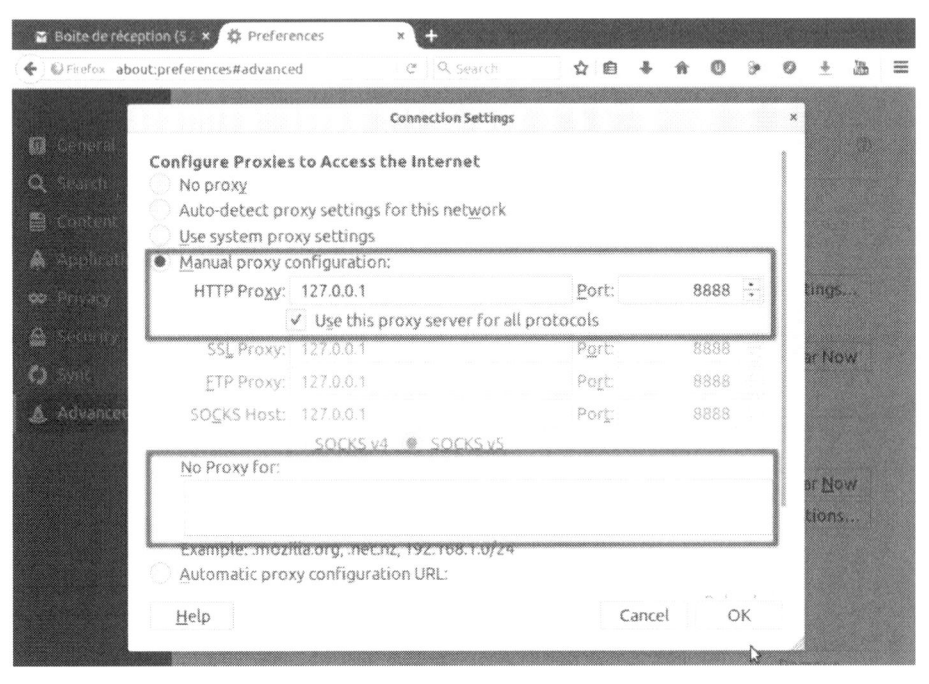

Figure 1.10: Proxy selection in Firefox – configuration

Save Our Script

Now, let's start our navigation session.

1. To do this, simply click the **Start** button on the **HTTP(S) Test Script Recorder** element:

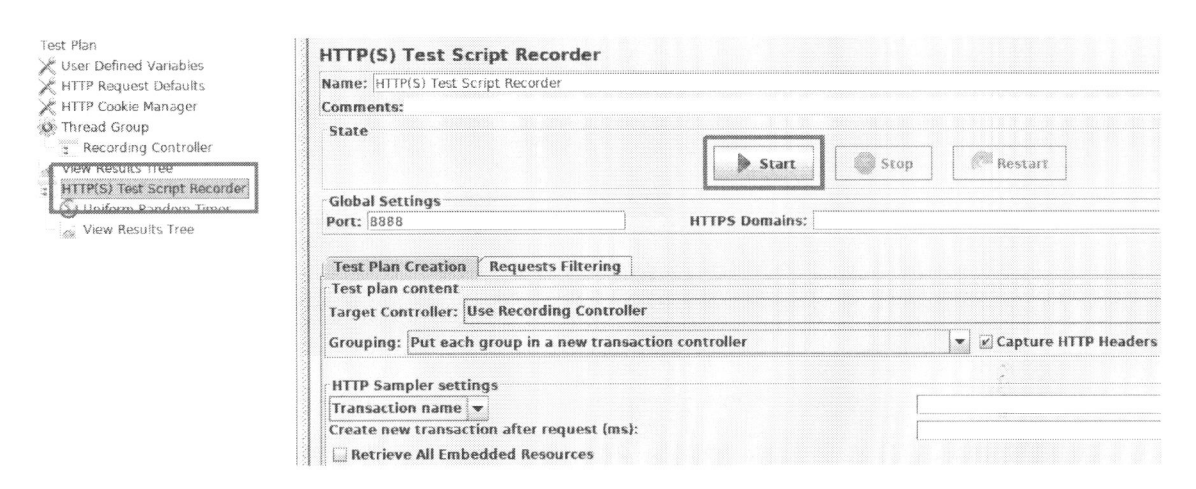

Figure 1.11: HTTP(S) Test Script Recorder

> **Note**
> Note that the default listening port of JMeter proxy server is 8888.
>
> Note the first time you start the recorder, it takes more time as it generates a Certificate Authority that you can use to intercept HTTPS traffic.

2. This will open a **Recorder: Transactions Control** window, allowing us to set in real time the name of each recorded step transactions and their grouping based on time:

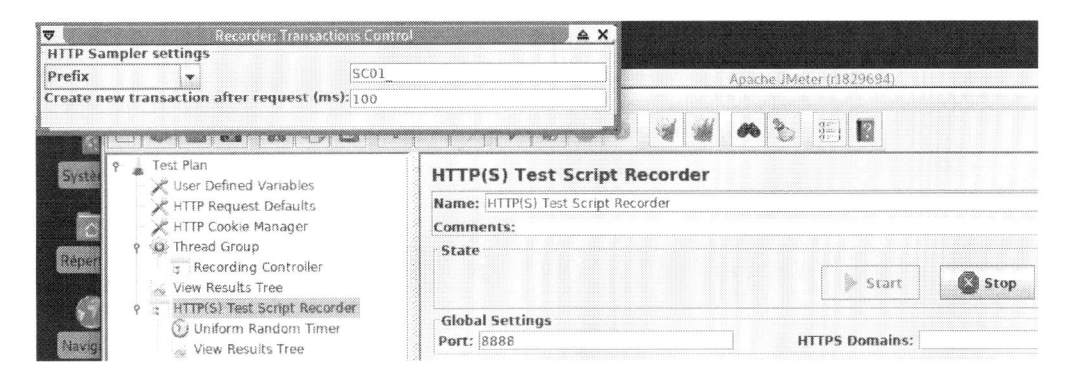

Figure 1.12: Recorder: Transactions Control

3. In this chapter, we will use the **Request Parameters** example delivered with **Apache Tomcat**.

   From the browser, navigate to the website:

   http://server:8080/examples/servlets/

   In our case, it will be:

   http://localhost:8080/examples/servlets/

   Here is the first page:

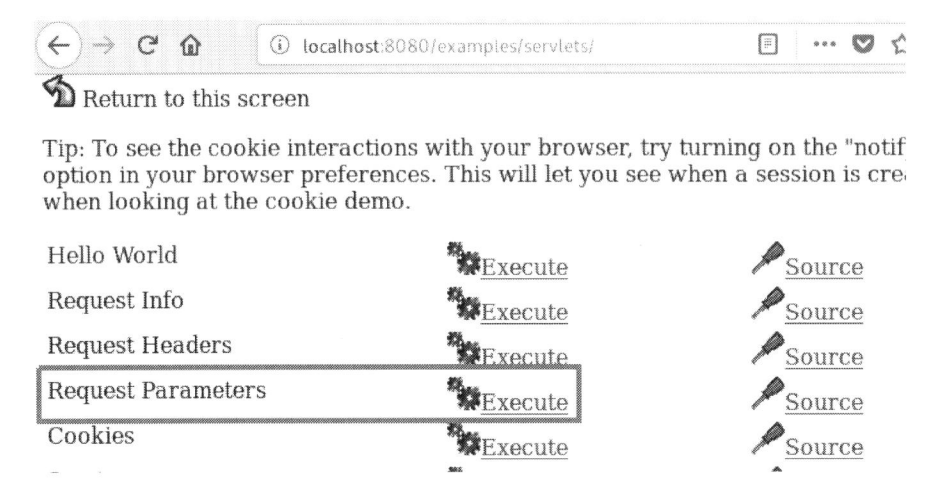

   Figure 1.13: First page of our scenario

4. Then, click on the **Execute** link of the **Required** test servlet:

Figure 1.14: Request Parameters Example with no entries

Enter first and last name and click on **Submit Query**:

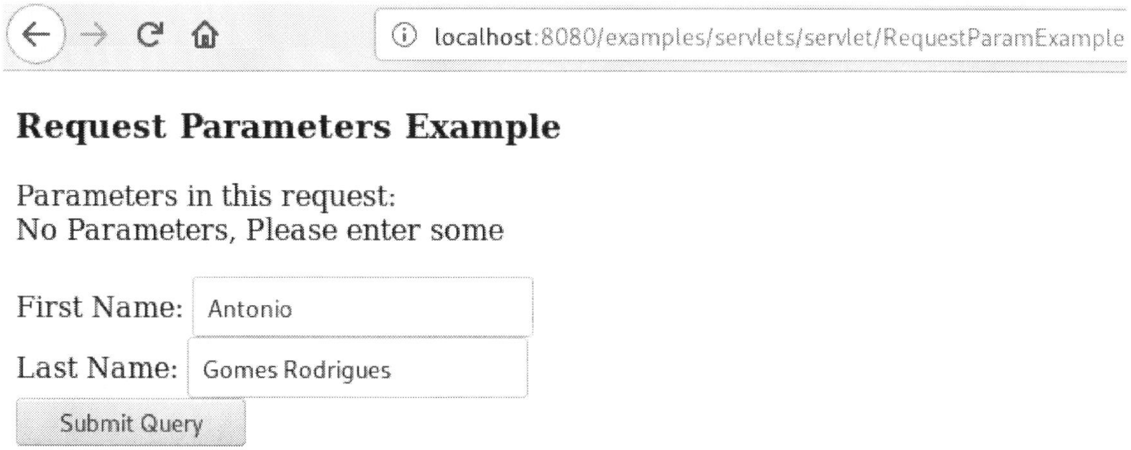

Request Parameters Example

Parameters in this request:
No Parameters, Please enter some

First Name: Antonio
Last Name: Gomes Rodrigues
Submit Query

Figure 1.15: Request Parameters Example before submitting query

When the result appears, we can stop our navigation session:

Request Parameters Example

Parameters in this request:
First Name: = Antonio
Last Name: = Gomes Rodrigues

First Name:
Last Name:
Submit Query

Figure 1.16: Request Parameters Example after submitting query

5. In JMeter, the scenario tree is the following:

```
Test Plan
    User Defined Variables
    HTTP Request Defaults
    HTTP Cookie Manager
    Thread Group
        Recording Controller
            SC01_2 /examples/servlets/
                SC01_2 /examples/servlets/
                    Uniform Random Timer
                    HTTP Header Manager
            SC01_7 /examples/servlets/servlet/RequestParamExample
                SC01_7 /examples/servlets/servlet/RequestParamExample
                    Uniform Random Timer
                    HTTP Header Manager
            SC01_8 /examples/servlets/servlet/RequestParamExample
                SC01_8 /examples/servlets/servlet/RequestParamExample
                    Uniform Random Timer
                    HTTP Header Manager
        View Results Tree
    HTTP(S) Test Script Recorder
        Uniform Random Timer
        View Results Tree
```

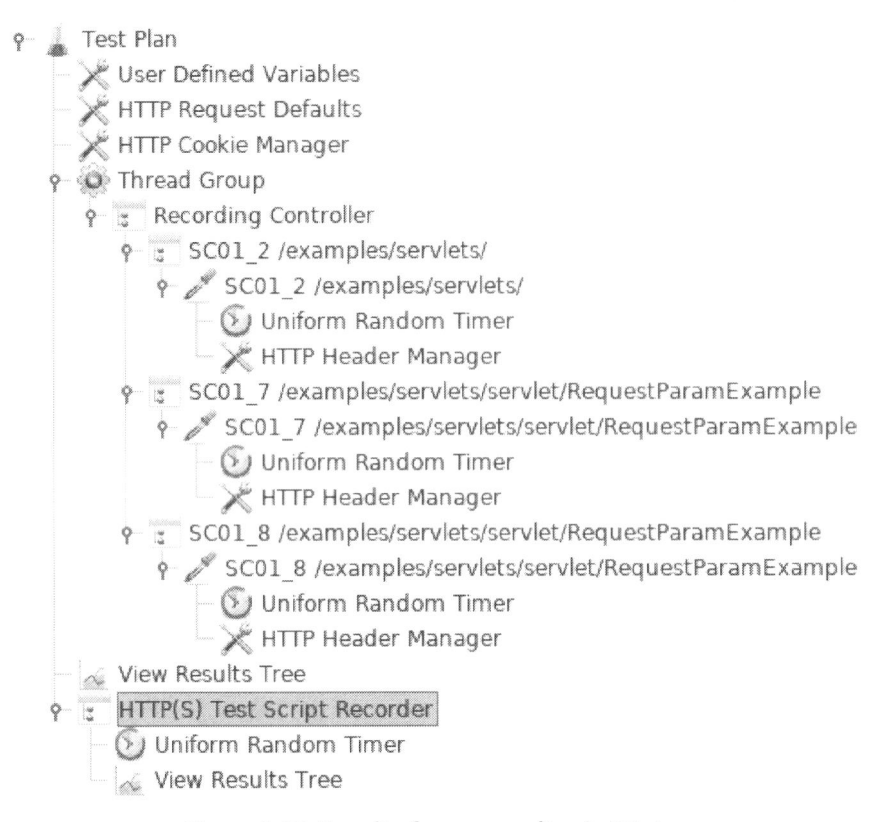

Figure 1.17: Result of our recording in JMeter

6. Let us observe what has been recorded:

URI	Corresponding to
/examples/servlets	The home page (Note prefix as been added)
.../servlet/RequestParamExample	First call (in GET) of the servlet (Note prefix as been changed and added)
.../servlet/RequestParamExample	Second call (POST) of the servlet (Note prefix as been changed and added)

Figure 1.18: Observation table

7. As we can see, thanks to the trick of filling the **Server Name or IP** and **Port Number** sections of the **HTTP Request Defaults** element, these fields remain empty in the **HTTP Request** elements.

This will allow us to change the URL and port of the tested site in only one location (**HTTP Request Defaults**) if necessary (for example, if the script was run on a development environment, and the final test will run on the pre-production environment):

Figure 1.19: Result of filling in the Server Name or IP and Port Number sections of the HTTP Request Defaults element

8. Similarly, the waiting time between each action (**Think time**) was recorded:

Figure 1.20: Recorded think time

9. To make it easier to read the results, it is preferable to rename HTTP requests. The automatically chosen name, by default, corresponds to the called URI, but you can control it in the little popup and give it a meaningful name before clicking on the button that will issue the request(s).

The result of the renaming:

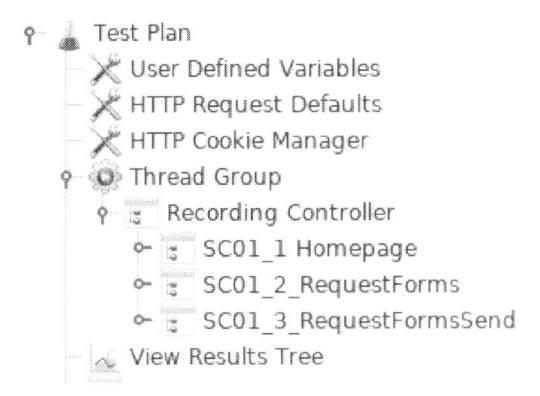

Figure 1.21: Renaming result

10. As the last step to the development of the scenario, we are going to add assertions to each HTTP request. These will make it possible to verify that the response received is indeed the expected one.

11. To do this, select the HTTP request that will receive the assertion, then, via the context menu, choose **Add** > **Assertions** > **Response Assertion**:

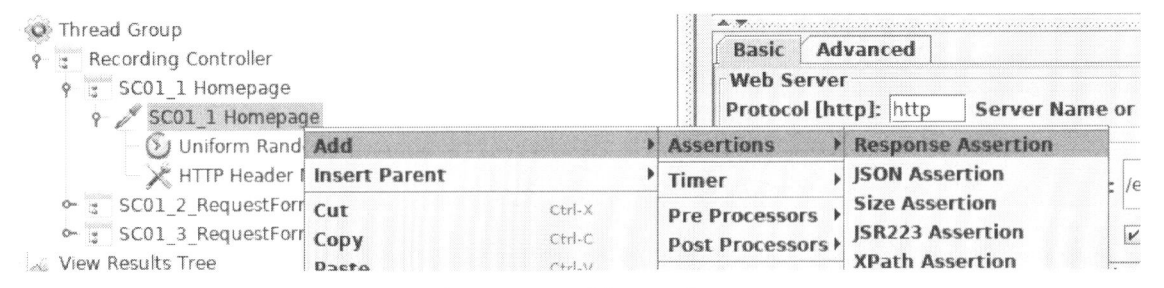

Figure 1.22: Add assertion

12. A new **Response Assertion** element has been added as a child to the **SC01_1 Homepage** request.

13. Let's select the following options:

    Field to Test: **Text Response**

    Pattern Matching Rules: **Substring** (default)

Patterns to Test: Let's click on the **Add** button, then insert text contained in the answer:

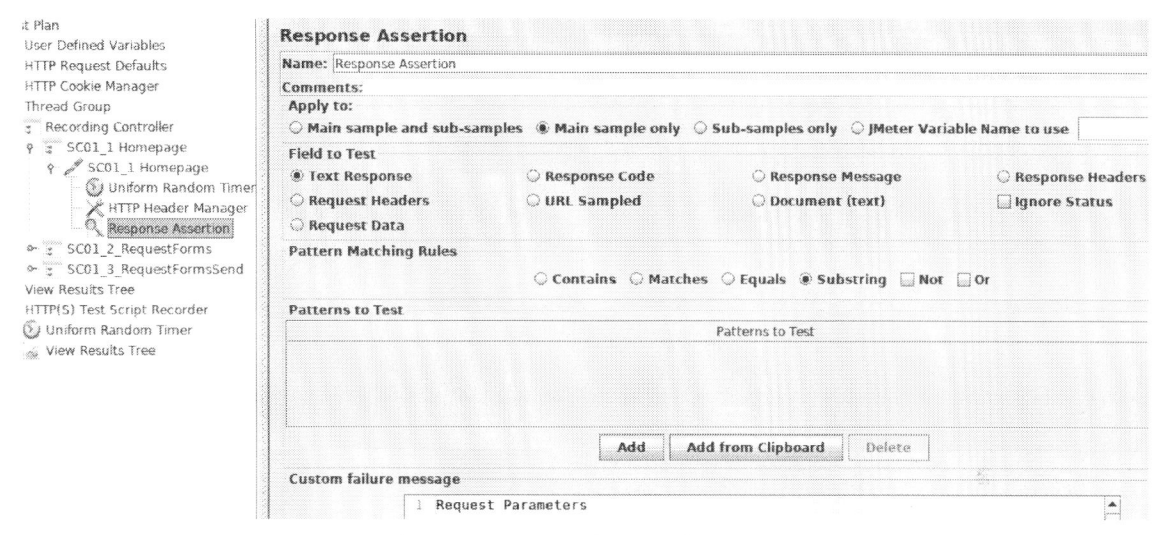

Figure 1.23: Assertion configuration

14. To find what data we need to check in response, the trick is to use the **View Results Tree** element, located under our **HTTP(S) Test Script Recorder**, by choosing the desired request and then by selecting the tab **Response data** > **Response Body**.

15. We can then copy the text and use **Add from clipboard** button in the **Response Assertion**:

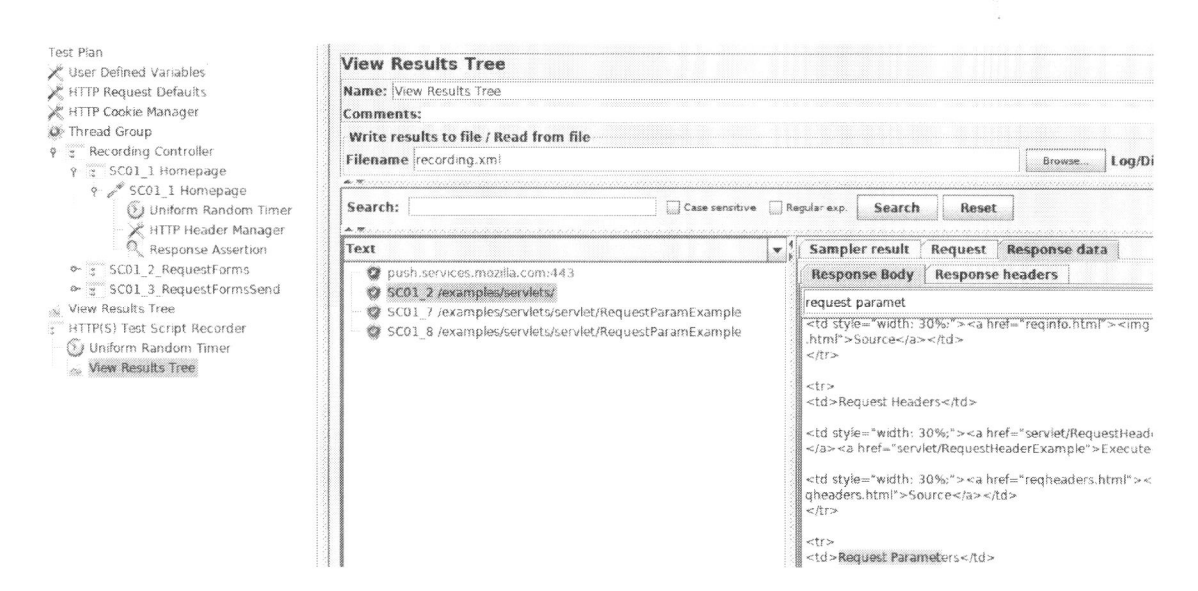

Figure 1.24: Result in Results Tree

16. Repeat the operation for all the requests in the same way as you did for the home page.

    In the end, we get this JMeter scenario tree:

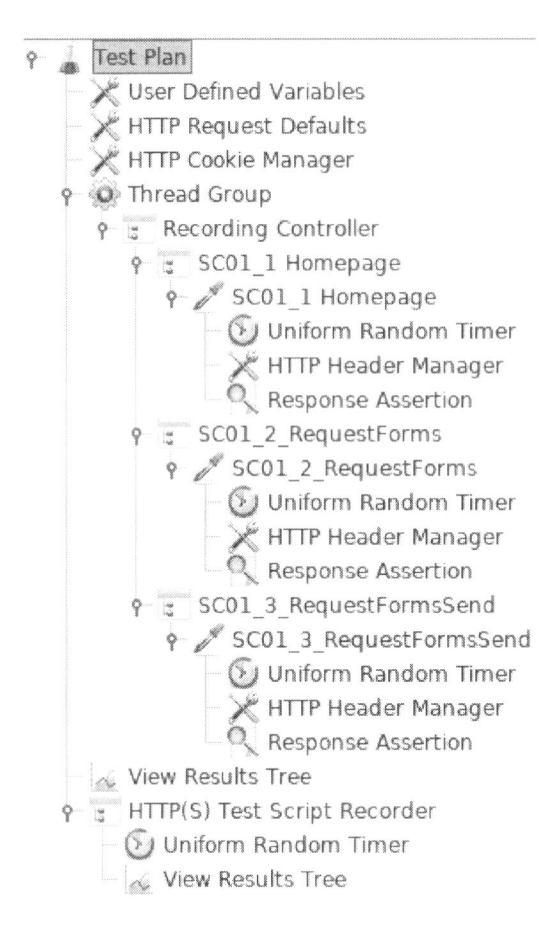

```
Test Plan
    User Defined Variables
    HTTP Request Defaults
    HTTP Cookie Manager
    Thread Group
        Recording Controller
            SC01_1_Homepage
                SC01_1_Homepage
                    Uniform Random Timer
                    HTTP Header Manager
                    Response Assertion
            SC01_2_RequestForms
                SC01_2_RequestForms
                    Uniform Random Timer
                    HTTP Header Manager
                    Response Assertion
            SC01_3_RequestFormsSend
                SC01_3_RequestFormsSend
                    Uniform Random Timer
                    HTTP Header Manager
                    Response Assertion
        View Results Tree
        HTTP(S) Test Script Recorder
            Uniform Random Timer
            View Results Tree
```

Figure 1.25: Our JMeter scenario

Now our scenario is ready, let's proceed to the validation of our script.

Validate Our Script with Only One User

1. It's easy with the validation mode, as it allows us to execute our script with only one user, one iteration, and without pause time.

2. To do this, let's select the **Thread Group** that we want to test, right-click, and select **Validate**:

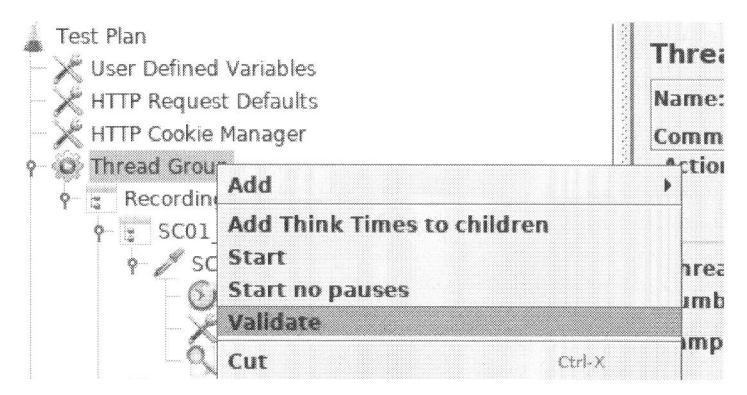

Figure 1.26: Validation of our script

3. Validate in the **View Results Tree** element that all Sample Results are green. If that is the case, we can proceed to the configuration step of our load test.

Setup Our Load Test and Launch It

1. To set up our load test, select the **Thread Group** element in order to change the following values:

   Number of Threads (users): 10

   Ramp-Up Period (in seconds): 10

   Loop Count: 100

This gives **10** virtual users (**VU**) who arrive in 10 seconds (1 per second), and each one will make **100** executions of the query sequence.

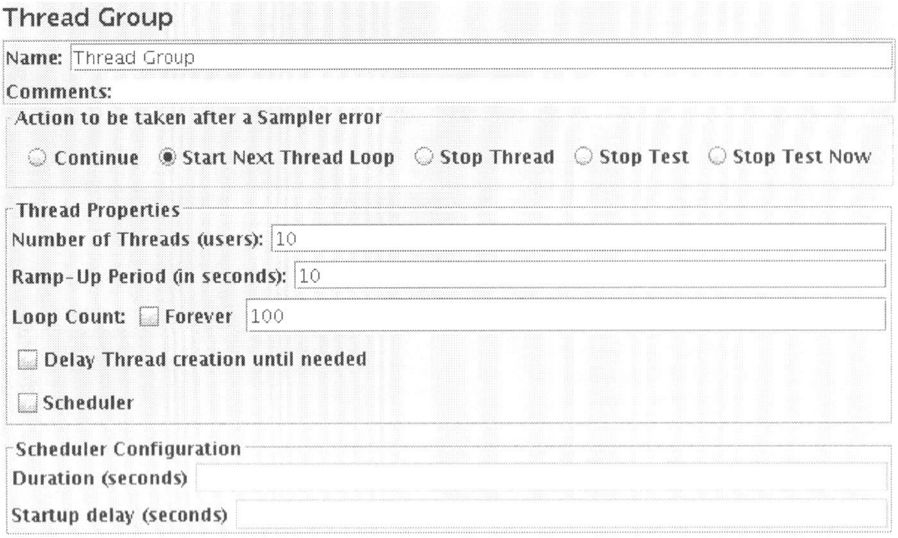

Figure 1.27: Load test parameters

> **Caution**
> Several strategies for setting the load test exists. This point will be discussed deeply in *Chapter 2, JMeter Overview*.

2. We could run our load test directly from the JMeter GUI, but this is not recommended as it would not be optimal for performances of injection (although, in our case, with only 10 users, it shouldn't be a problem).

3. When load testing, it is advisable to monitor the injectors (servers where JMeter runs) at least during the first test at full load to validate the correct behavior of the injectors.

   This ensures that if we get bad response times, the cause is the application being tested and not JMeter.

   Note that this is not specific to JMeter but should be done regardless of the tool you use.

> **Note**
> An easy and quick solution to monitor JMeter can be to use the **Servers Performance Monitoring** plugin from the JMeter Plugins (https://jmeter-plugins.org/wiki/PerfMon/).

4. So, let's use best practices directly and run our test from the command line in CLI mode (also called Non-GUI mode in JMeter).

5. But before that, to follow our test in real time, we will add the **Backend Listener** element to enable live monitoring of the progress of the test with Grafana (https://grafana.com/).

6. To do this, right-click on **Test Plan** -> **Add** -> **Listener** -> **Backend Listener**:

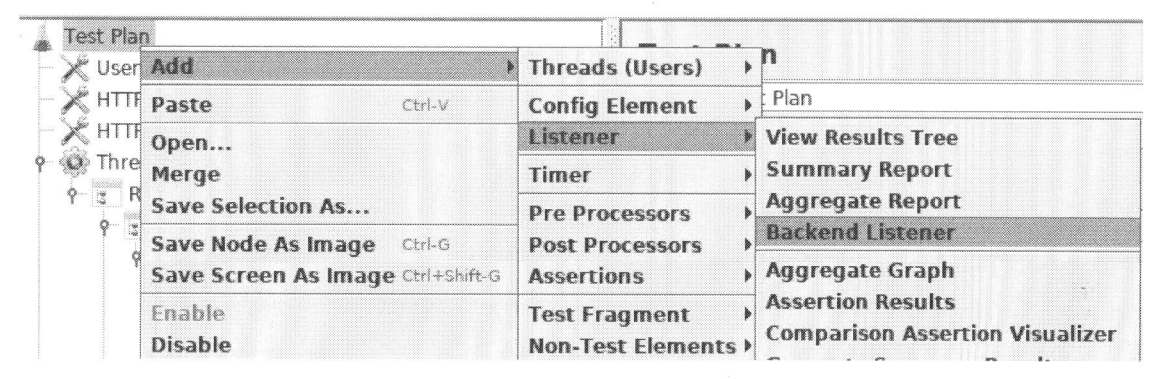

Figure 1.28: Add Backend Listener

7. Let's configure it to send the test results to our InfluxDB database (https://www.influxdata.com/):

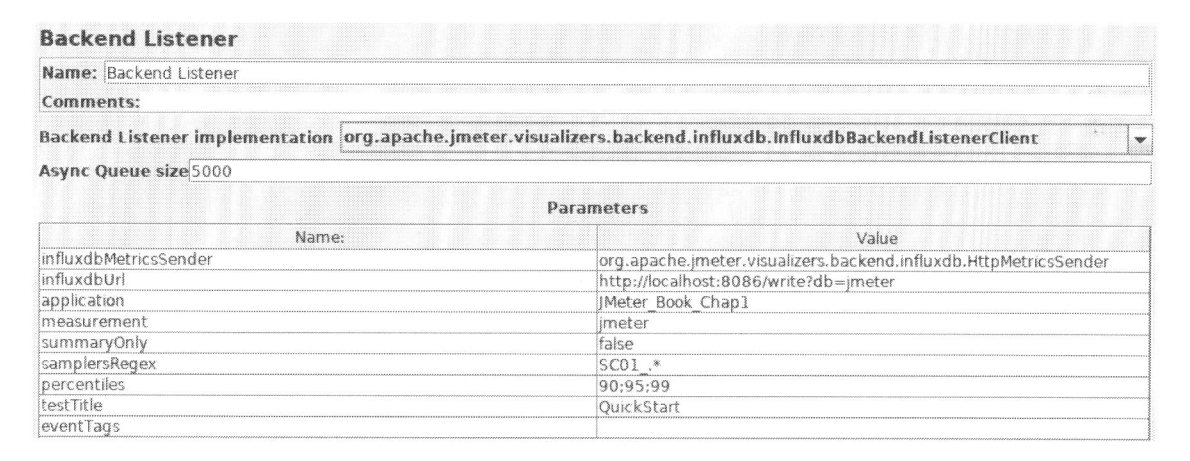

Figure 1.29: Backend Listener configuration

> **Note**
> In the **samplersRegex** field, we can use a regular expression to keep only the queries that were recorded by the **HTTP(S) Test Script Recorder** element (thanks to **Prefix:** field).

Run Our Load Test and Analyze It

1. Before launching our test, one last tip is to ask JMeter to generate an HTML report at the end.

   For this, we will use the following command line:

   ```
   <JMETER_HOME>/bin/jmeter -n -t [jmx file] -l [results file] -e -o [Path\ to output folder]
   ```

2. Let's run our test and see what happens.

   In our terminal:

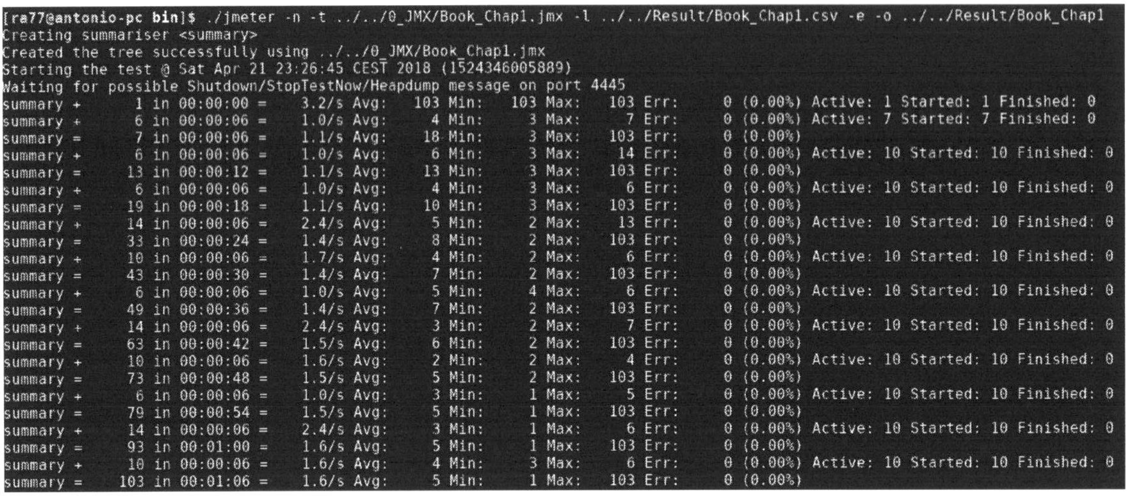

```
[ra77@antonio-pc bin]$ ./jmeter -n -t ../../0_JMX/Book_Chap1.jmx -l ../../Result/Book_Chap1.csv -e -o ../../Result/Book_Chap1
Creating summariser <summary>
Created the tree successfully using ../../0_JMX/Book_Chap1.jmx
Starting the test @ Sat Apr 21 23:26:45 CEST 2018 (1524346005889)
Waiting for possible Shutdown/StopTestNow/Heapdump message on port 4445
summary +      1 in 00:00:00 =    3.2/s Avg:   103 Min:   103 Max:   103 Err:     0 (0.00%) Active: 1 Started: 1 Finished: 0
summary +      6 in 00:00:06 =    1.0/s Avg:     4 Min:     3 Max:     7 Err:     0 (0.00%) Active: 7 Started: 7 Finished: 0
summary =      7 in 00:00:06 =    1.1/s Avg:    18 Min:     3 Max:   103 Err:     0 (0.00%)
summary +      6 in 00:00:06 =    1.0/s Avg:     6 Min:     3 Max:    14 Err:     0 (0.00%) Active: 10 Started: 10 Finished: 0
summary =     13 in 00:00:12 =    1.1/s Avg:    13 Min:     3 Max:   103 Err:     0 (0.00%)
summary +      6 in 00:00:06 =    1.0/s Avg:     4 Min:     3 Max:     6 Err:     0 (0.00%) Active: 10 Started: 10 Finished: 0
summary =     19 in 00:00:18 =    1.1/s Avg:    10 Min:     3 Max:   103 Err:     0 (0.00%)
summary +     14 in 00:00:06 =    2.4/s Avg:     5 Min:     2 Max:    13 Err:     0 (0.00%) Active: 10 Started: 10 Finished: 0
summary =     33 in 00:00:24 =    1.4/s Avg:     8 Min:     2 Max:   103 Err:     0 (0.00%)
summary +     10 in 00:00:06 =    1.7/s Avg:     4 Min:     2 Max:     6 Err:     0 (0.00%) Active: 10 Started: 10 Finished: 0
summary =     43 in 00:00:30 =    1.4/s Avg:     7 Min:     2 Max:   103 Err:     0 (0.00%)
summary +      6 in 00:00:06 =    1.0/s Avg:     5 Min:     4 Max:     6 Err:     0 (0.00%) Active: 10 Started: 10 Finished: 0
summary =     49 in 00:00:36 =    1.4/s Avg:     7 Min:     2 Max:   103 Err:     0 (0.00%)
summary +     14 in 00:00:06 =    2.4/s Avg:     3 Min:     2 Max:     7 Err:     0 (0.00%) Active: 10 Started: 10 Finished: 0
summary =     63 in 00:00:42 =    1.5/s Avg:     6 Min:     2 Max:   103 Err:     0 (0.00%)
summary +     10 in 00:00:06 =    1.6/s Avg:     2 Min:     2 Max:     4 Err:     0 (0.00%) Active: 10 Started: 10 Finished: 0
summary =     73 in 00:00:48 =    1.5/s Avg:     5 Min:     2 Max:   103 Err:     0 (0.00%)
summary +      6 in 00:00:06 =    1.0/s Avg:     3 Min:     1 Max:     5 Err:     0 (0.00%) Active: 10 Started: 10 Finished: 0
summary =     79 in 00:00:54 =    1.5/s Avg:     5 Min:     1 Max:   103 Err:     0 (0.00%)
summary +     14 in 00:00:06 =    2.4/s Avg:     3 Min:     1 Max:     6 Err:     0 (0.00%) Active: 10 Started: 10 Finished: 0
summary =     93 in 00:01:00 =    1.6/s Avg:     5 Min:     1 Max:   103 Err:     0 (0.00%)
summary +     10 in 00:00:06 =    1.6/s Avg:     4 Min:     3 Max:     6 Err:     0 (0.00%) Active: 10 Started: 10 Finished: 0
summary =    103 in 00:01:06 =    1.6/s Avg:     5 Min:     1 Max:   103 Err:     0 (0.00%)
```

Figure 1.30: Follows a load test in the terminal

3. In Grafana (the dashboard used is one of those proposed in the Grafana website (https://grafana.com/dashboards/3351)):

> **Note**
> We can use this dashboard, too: https://grafana.com/dashboards/5496.

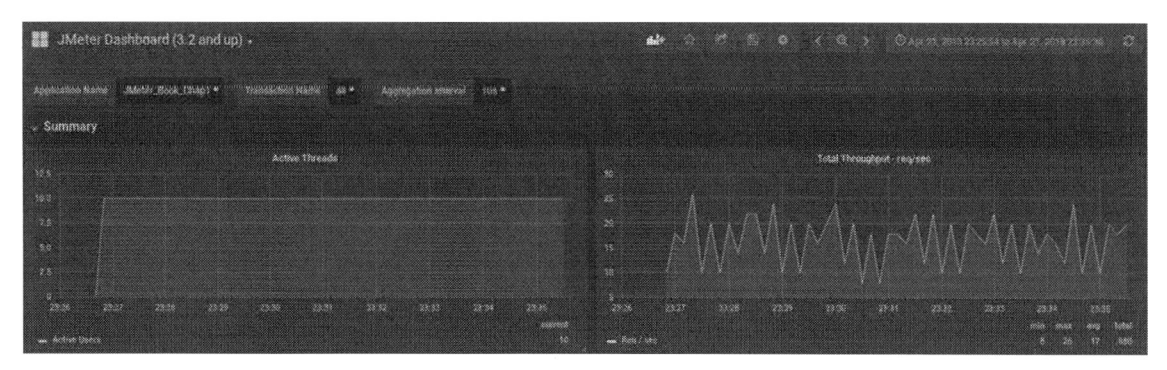

Figure 1.31: Real-time monitoring in Grafana

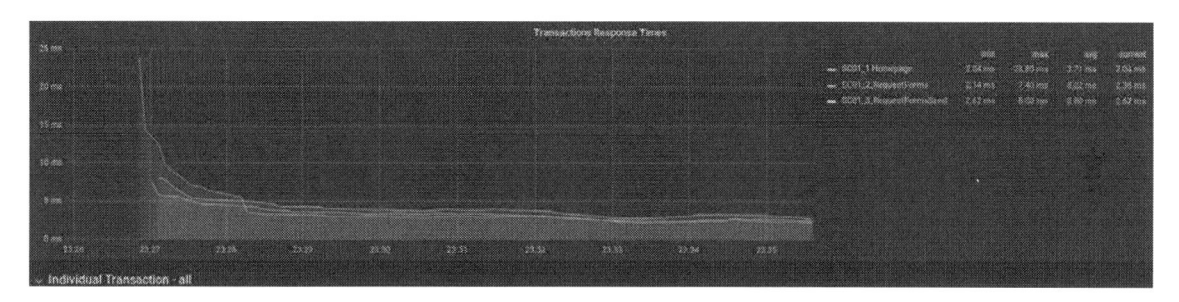

Figure 1.32: Real-time monitoring in Grafana

4. At the end of our test, we get the HTML dynamic Web Report with 17 graphs, an APDEX (https://en.wikipedia.org/wiki/Apdex) table, a statistics table (showing response times, error rates, network metrics...), a table with an errors summary, and a table with Top5errors per sampler. So, you get everything you need to analyze your load test:

Figure 1.33: HTML report

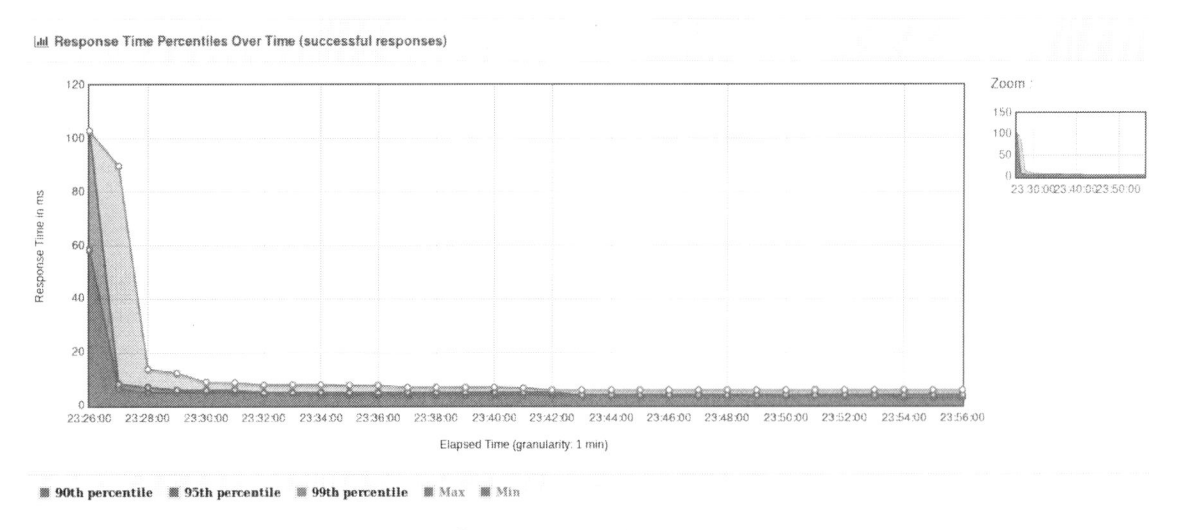

Figure 1.34: HTML report

The icing on the cake is a CSV file we get at the end of our test; this format is usable by many tools to visualize the results differently.

In this chapter, we have seen how to quickly get started with JMeter to perform a simple load test.

2

JMeter Overview

JMeter Overview

Apache JMeter is a software that allows you to perform load tests on various protocols and technologies.

It was developed by the Apache Software Foundation (https://apache.org/).

Figure 2.1: Apache JMeter logo

JMeter is an application written in Java and offers an integrated development environment (IDE) for load test development.

This IDE has multiple looks and feels (LAFs), the default one shown here is based on Darcula LAF. Later in this book, we'll use the cross-platform LAF for presentation purposes because it is white.

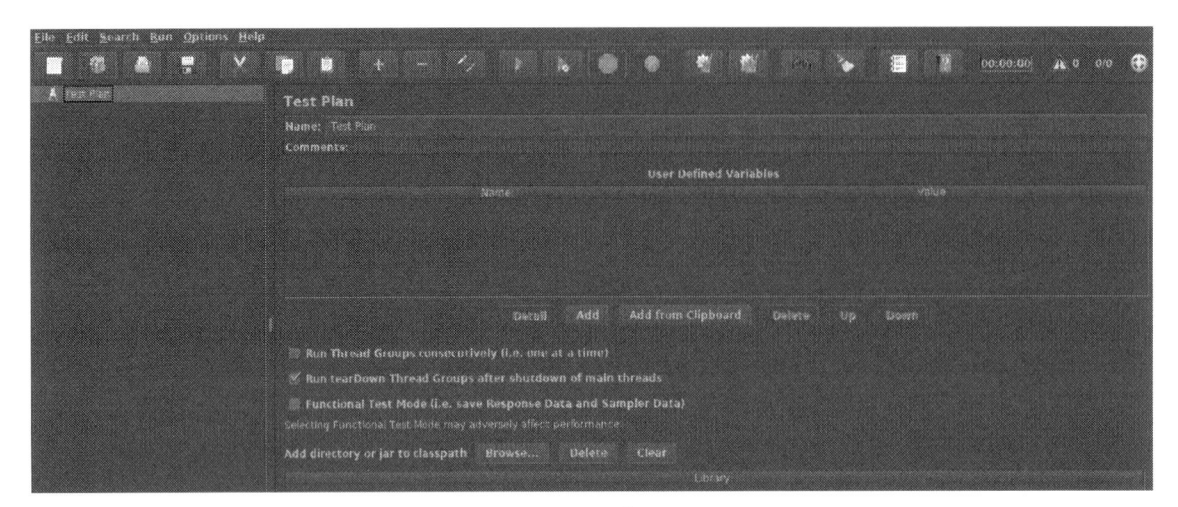

Figure 2.2: Apache JMeter

JMeter runs on any Java-compatible OS (including *Linux*, *Microsoft Windows*, *macOS*, and so on).

The application can also be used on the command line, in other words, without a graphical interface, which is the mode that should be used systematically during your load tests.

JMeter is multithreaded and can simulate a lot of virtual users (**VU**s).

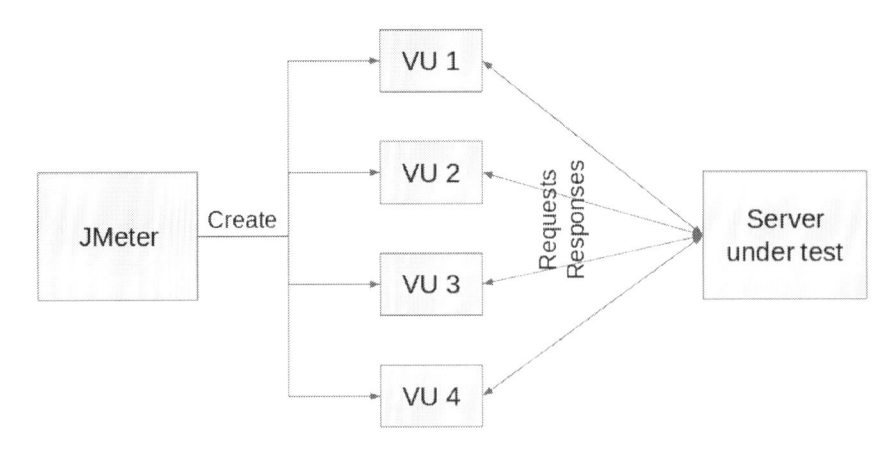

Figure 2.3: Multithreading in JMeter

JMeter may be used to test performance both on static and dynamic resources by modifying the inputs during the load test.

For very large loads, JMeter has a distributed mode (horizontally scaling injectors over several machines).

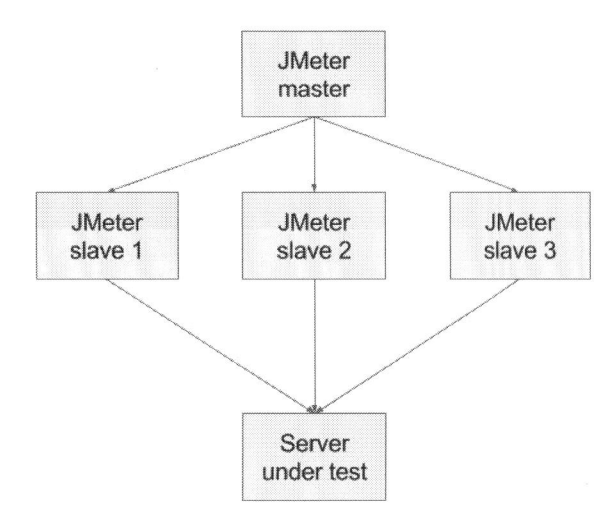

Figure 2.4: Distributed load test

JMeter is highly extensible, through multiple options:

- Scriptable samplers (*JSR223-compatible* languages, such as *Groovy*, *Kotlin*, *JRuby*, *Jython*, *JavaScript*...)
- Simple and custom plugins based on *Java Request*
- Plugins for functions, protocols, and elements as provided by JMeter plugins (https://jmeter-plugins.org/) and UbikLoadPack (https://ubikloadpack.com)

JMeter is also available on the cloud through multiple enterprise Platform-as-a-Service (PaaS) solutions:

- BlazeMeter (https://www.blazemeter.com/)
- RedLine13 (https://www.redline13.com/blog/)
- Tricentis Flood (https://flood.io/)
- XMeter (https://www.xmeter.net)
- OctoPerf (https://octoperf.com/)
- Loadium (https://loadium.com/)

Finally, JMeter provides out-of-the-box (OOTB) rich reporting through its native HTML Report.

This reporting can be enhanced through multiple options:

- Sending metrics to InfluxDB for graphing with Grafana (Core BackendListener)
- Sending metrics to Elasticsearch for graphing with Grafana or Kibana (free open source software (OSS) plugin)
- Exporting CSV or XML to allow personalized visualizations

In the case of web applications, JMeter has the **HTTP(S) Test Script Recorder** element to record scripts for HTTP and HTTPS.

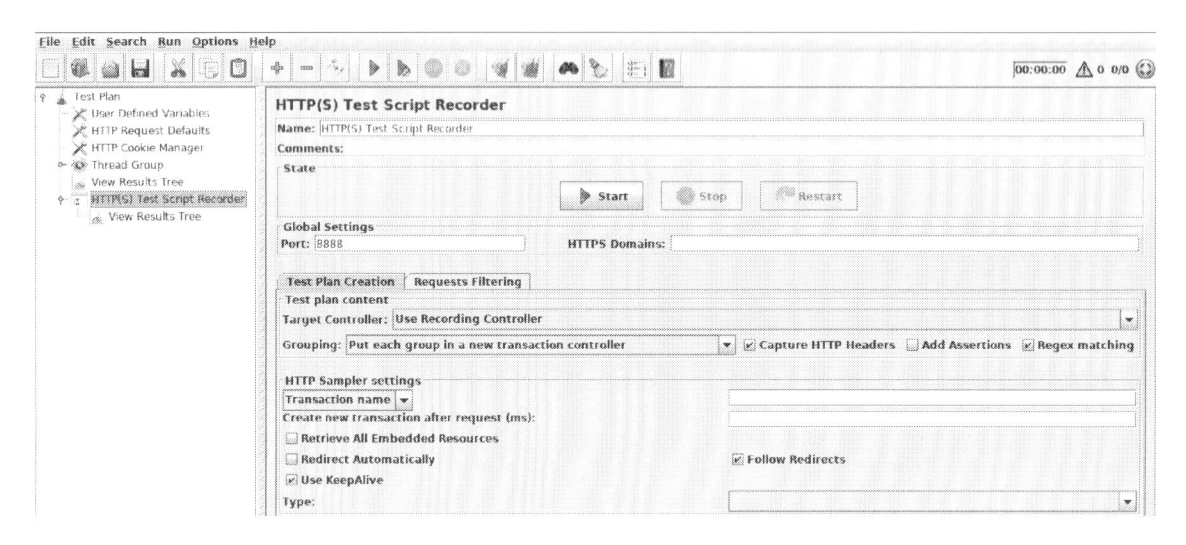

Figure 2.5: HTTP(S) Test Script Recorder

This acts as a proxy to automatically record a load test script during a model scenario session performed by a real user. This speeds up the preparation of the scripting.

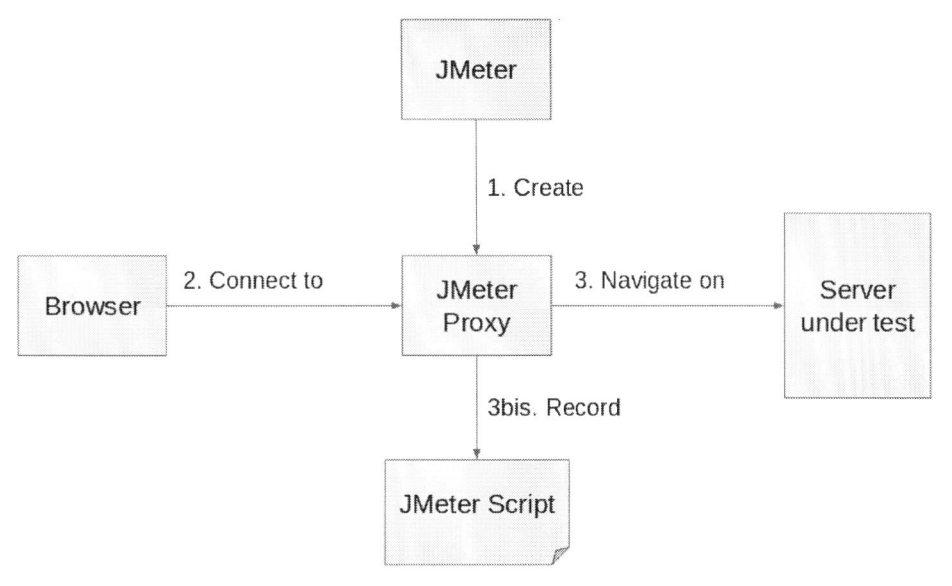

Figure 2.6: Use of the HTTP(S) Test Script Recorder

To summarize, JMeter is a load testing tool that can test the performance of an application by simulating users (qualified as "virtual") and recording information (time, success/failure, size, network usage...) on responses to allow their analysis.

Types of Load Tests Supported

JMeter is a generic test tool that has great flexibility and adaptability to meet multiple scenario requirements.

Specifically, here are some examples of possible load tests:

- Check the response times of a web application, according to the number of virtual users
- Test differences in the behavior of the same application on two (or more) different runtime environments (for example, clustered environment versus non-clustered environment, or configuration 1 versus configuration 2)
- Test the limits of an application (the number of users the application can accommodate before it crashes)

- Functionally test an application automatically (with non-regression tests, functional validity tests, and so on), often coupled with a continuous integration tool

- Reproduce a load-related production bug in a QA environment

- Automate load testing in the continuous integration (CI) process

- Test a database, a lightweight directory access protocol (LDAP) (or Active Directory) server, a mail server (SMTP or POP/IMAP), a message-oriented middleware (MOM) server, an FTP server, or a network service

These are only some of the possibilities on offer. It is up to you to imagine others.

Supported Test Protocols

JMeter natively manages the following protocols:

Protocol	Description	Example(s)
HTTP, HTTPS	Web server	Apache, Microsoft IIS, Nginx, Apache Tomcat
SOAP, XML-RPC, REST	Web Service	Axis2, WebSphere
JDBC	Database	Oracle, MySQL, MS-SQL, DB2, Postgresql
SMTP, SMTP/TLS, SMTP/SSL	Mail server for sending messages	Exchange, Postfix, Sendmail
POP3, POP3S, IMAP, IMAPS	Inbox Mail Server	Exchange, Cyrus, Dovecot, Courier
LDAP, LDAPS	Directory	OpenLDAP, ActiveDirectory
JMS	Message-Oriented Messaging	IBM MQ, Apache ActiveMQ, Tuxedo, RabbitMQ
FTP	File Transfer Server	proftpd, vsftpd, war-ftpd
TCP	Miscellaneous Network Services	Telnetd, DNS

Figure 2.7: JMeter-managed protocols

> **Note**
> This already-high number of supported protocols can be extended using plugins.

Let's name a few protocols that can be installed through Plugin Manager (https://jmeter-plugins.org/install/Install/):

Protocol	Plugin	Website
HTTP 2	Open Source plugin contributed and supported by Blazemeter/Computer Associates	HTTP2 Plugin for Jmeter (https://github.com/Blazemeter/jmeter-http2-plugin/blob/master/README.md)
Websocket	Open Source plugin by Peter Doornbosch	WebSocket Samplers by Peter Doornbosch (https://bitbucket.org/pjtr/jmeter-websocket-samplers)
Mainframe RTE	Open Source plugin contributed and supported by Blazemeter/Computer Associates	JMeter-RTE-Plugin (https://github.com/Blazemeter/RTEPlugin/blob/master/README.md)

Figure 2.8: Website links for JMeter protocols

Reporting

JMeter allows you to analyze the results of a test at the following times:

- At the end of the test using the OOTB HTML report, which can be generated automatically

- In real time, using the **Backend Listener** element combined with a time series database such as InfluxDB and Grafana as a dashboard creation tool

- At the end of the test using the XML or CSV file created by JMeter and with the help of any visualization tool supporting this file format, such as *Microsoft Excel*, *LibreOffice Calc*, *QlikView*, *Jupyter*, *Apache Zeppelin*, and so on

- At the end of the test within continuous integration solutions such as *Jenkins* using *Performance Plugin*

3

Designing a Test Case

Introduction

It is important to perform load tests, but it is even more important to test with the right scenarios. In this chapter, we will see some tips for designing the most realistic test scenario.

Warning

It's important to understand that a load test is only a simulation. This implies that despite all the possible and imaginable tests, you don't have a 100% guarantee that everything will proceed smoothly in production. There will always be an unplanned case (failure of a part of the system, unanticipated customer action, and so on).

To increase the chances of success, it's important to also work on the architecture (*design for failure* and so on) and the deployment process (*canary release* and so on).

Despite this, a load test is important to:

- Put into production the healthiest application
- Fine-tune as much as possible the architecture and application
- Reproduce a performance or multithreading issue detected in production to fix it
- Give business an idea of future response times when a new application goes live
- Anticipate Sales period
- Understand the weak points of the application
- Validate/improve monitoring (metrics, tools, dashboards, and so on)
- Compare two versions of the same application
- Validate/tune autoscaling
- Validate/tune the mechanisms of *design for failure*
- Confirm/tune the alarming system
- Find the *soft limits* (https://docs.aws.amazon.com/general/latest/gr/aws_service_limits.html) of the AWS infrastructure and so on

Let's start by explaining some concepts.

Type of Load Test

The type of test often depends on the goals. You have to answer the question, "What should I check?"

Performance/Load Test

Validate the target performance of the application (for example, the response time represented by a target percentile is always less than two seconds).

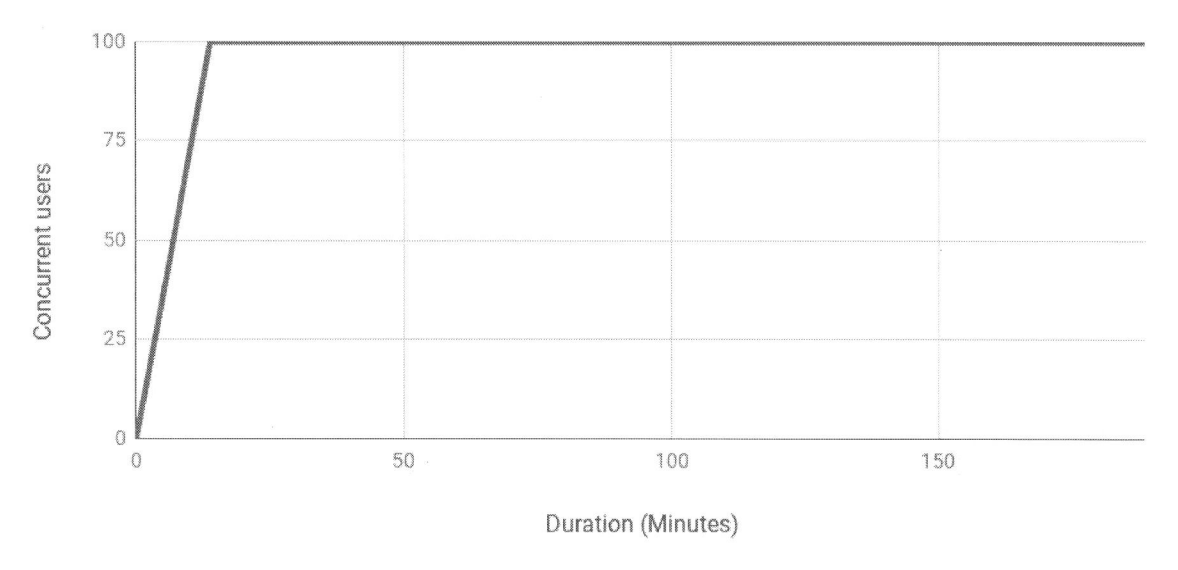

Figure 3.1: Performance/load test

Stress Test

Know the response times during peak periods.

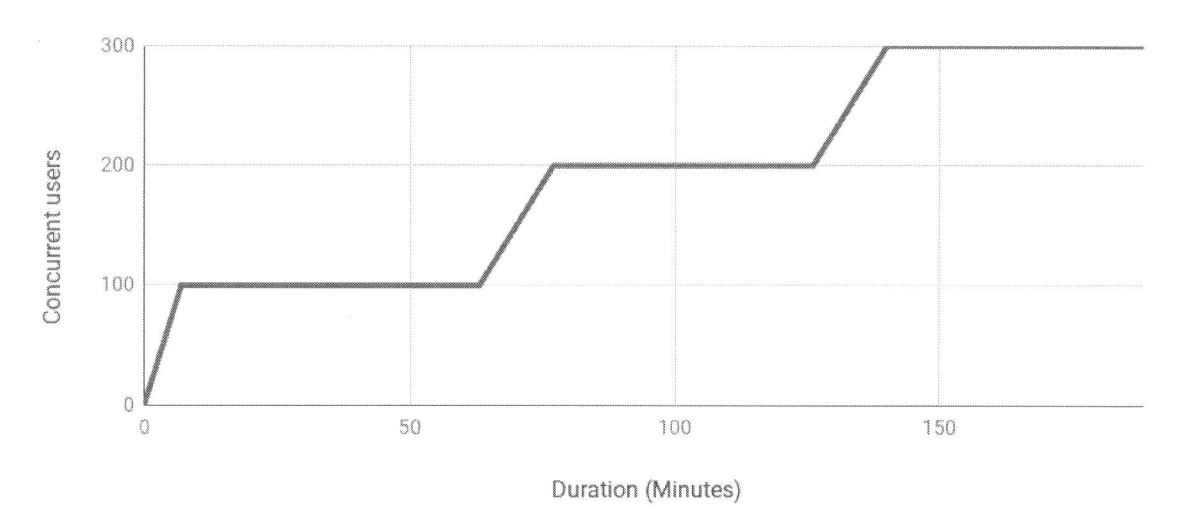

Figure 3.2: Stress test

The language I've been using in recent years for a 1x, 2x, 3x test workload I'm calling a "scale test" to indicate a particular scale for handling load.

It's helped me to more clearly communicate with PMs and business people the value of doing such a test:

- *If we pass a 1x phase, everyone here doesn't get fired, customers are happy, and we can stay in business*
- *If we pass a 2x phase, we're able to handle the upcoming holiday season/increased load as we have some headroom in the system*
- *If we can pass a 3x phase, we show that business can triple the volume of transactions, and is prepared for growth/future acquisitions*

— Mark Tomlinson's quote

Alternatively, be aware of the performance limits of the application.

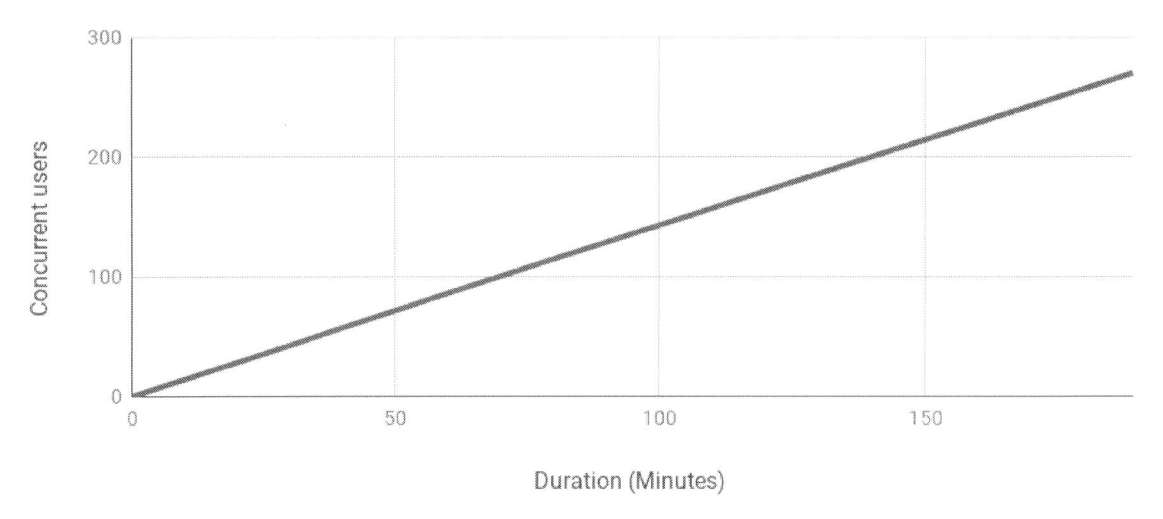

Figure 3.3: Stress test

Soak/Endurance Test

Check the application during a long period to detect stability problems (for example, memory leak).

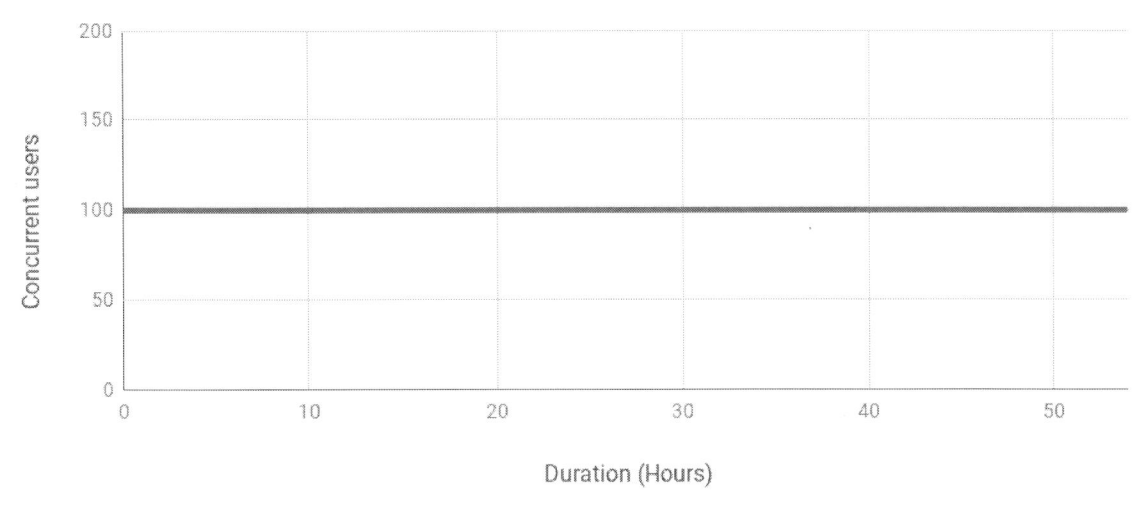

Figure 3.4: Soak/endurance test

Failover/Resilience Test

Simulate a failure during a load test to check robustness.

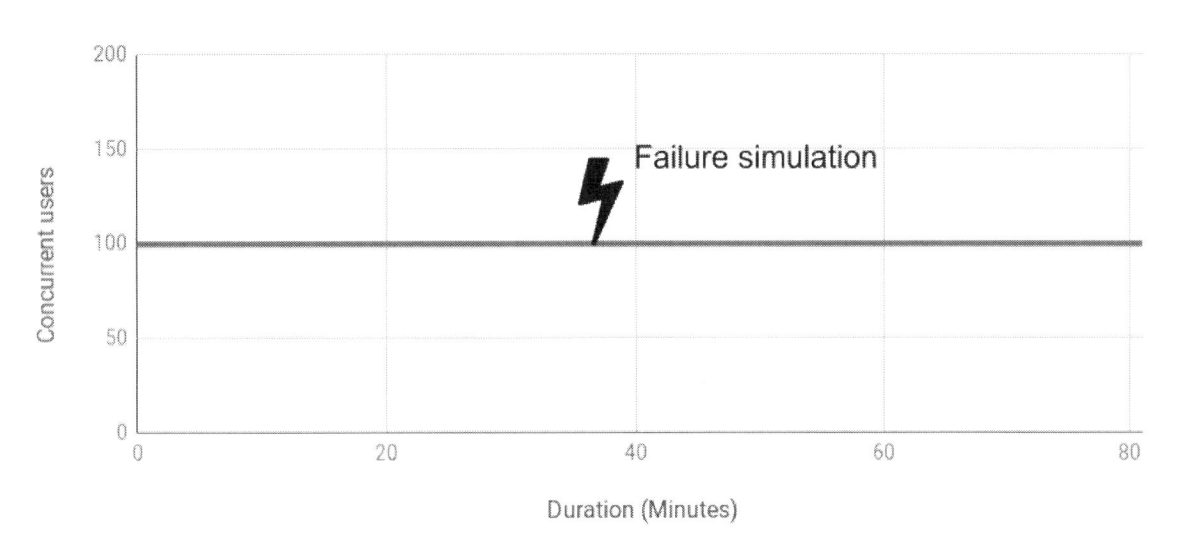

Figure 3.5: Failover/resilience test

Spike Test

Observe the behavior of the server(s) during a sudden change of load.

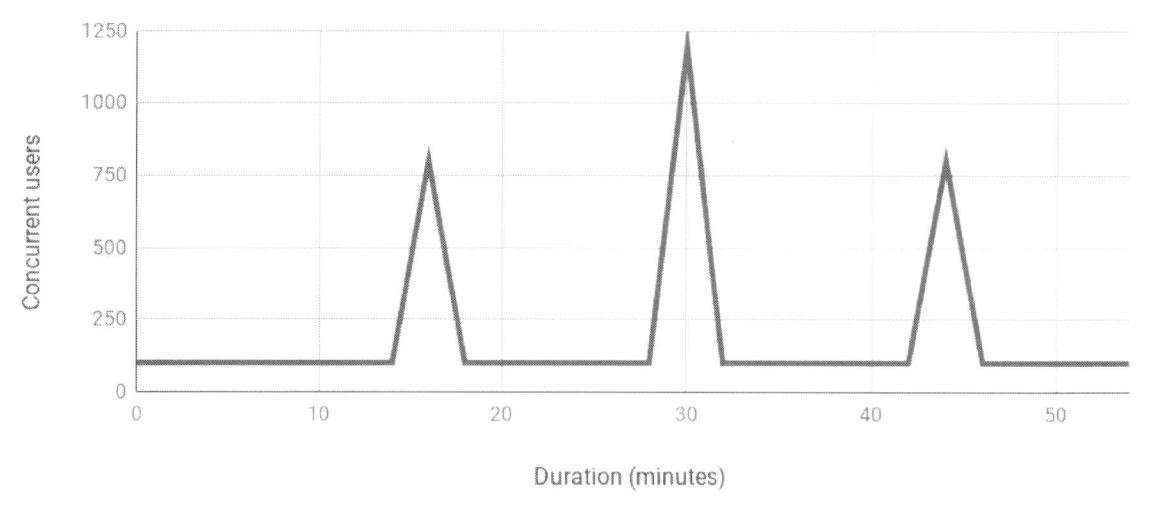

Figure 3.6: Spike test

Other

Other types of tests are possible. You can, for example, see how your application behaves with users under a certain bandwidth. JMeter makes it possible to meet this requirement thanks to a mechanism that limits the network speed of a virtual user.

JMeter is not limited, and it is possible to imagine other types of tests by arranging the elements of JMeter differently or by setting up different test scenarios.

Load Model

Choosing the correct load model is very important and depends on:

- What we want to test (the type of application and so on)
- The goal of the test (comparison between two versions and so on)

Let's look at the main load models.

There are two main models:

- *Closed model*: There are only a given number of users in our system, and a new user cannot enter the system before the end of another one.

    This model is used in some ticketing websites to limit the number of concurrent users. The limit is made to prevent the website from crashing and customers from going to a competitor's site to buy their tickets.

This model is also used in call center applications because the number of concurrent calls is limited by the number of operators.

This model can be used in closed user groups (groups of employees in an intranet, private forums…) where we know the maximum number of users. In this case, we will simulate the maximum number of possible users.

In this model, each **VU** depends on the previous user, so users are not independent of one another. So, if the *System Under Test* (SUT) slows down, the injector will stop creating new VUs.

For example, say we simulate nine users with three **Thread**s:

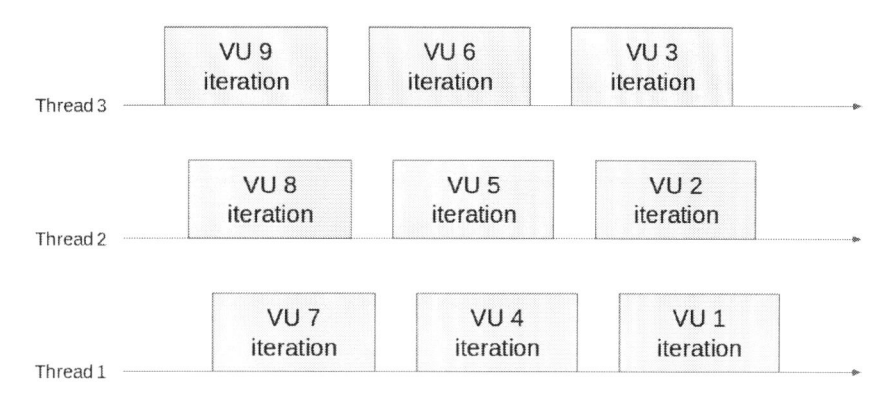

Figure 3.7: Closed model

User 10 will only arrive when a user has finished.

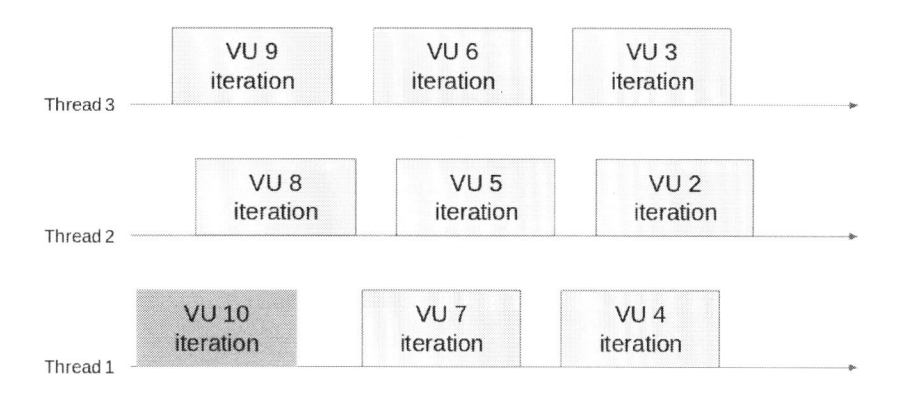

Figure 3.8: Closed model – VUs depend on each other

- *Open model*: Whatever happens on the tested system, the injector keeps the flow of the arrival of VUs.

  This model is used in the majority of e-commerce websites.

  In this case, the *virtual users* are independent of each other, and if the SUT slows down, the injector will continue to create new *virtual users*.

So, compared to the example above, user 10 will arrive even if no other user has finished their iteration.

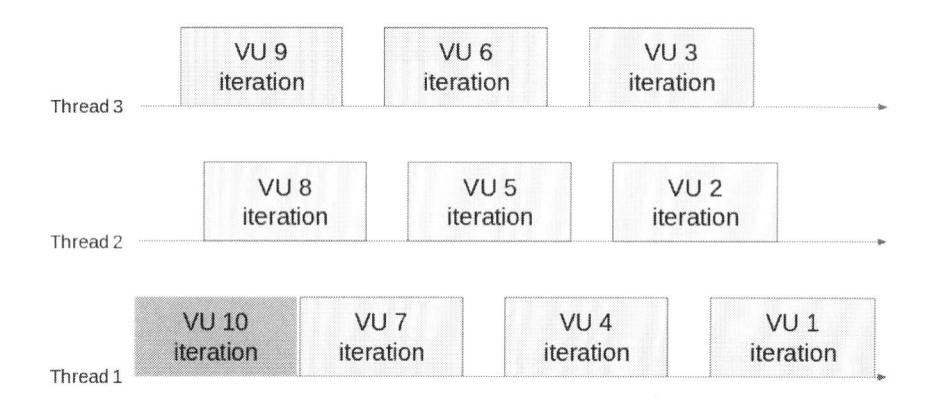

Figure 3.9: Open model – VUs are independent of one another

Now let's look at how this applies to JMeter.

Concurrency User (Closed Model)

In this model, we control the number of VUs.

With JMeter, it is quite simple to implement this load model by setting the number of VUs in a **Thread Group**.

For example:

Thread Group

Name: Thread Group
Comments:

Action to be taken after a Sampler error
- ● Continue ○ Start Next Thread Loop ○ Stop Thread ○ Stop Test ○ Stop Test Now

Thread Properties
Number of Threads (users): 100
Ramp-Up Period (in seconds): 120
Loop Count: ☑ Forever
☐ Delay Thread creation until needed
☑ Scheduler

Scheduler Configuration
Duration (seconds) 3600
Startup delay (seconds)

Figure 3.10: Controlling the number of VUs with a Thread Group

Will give:

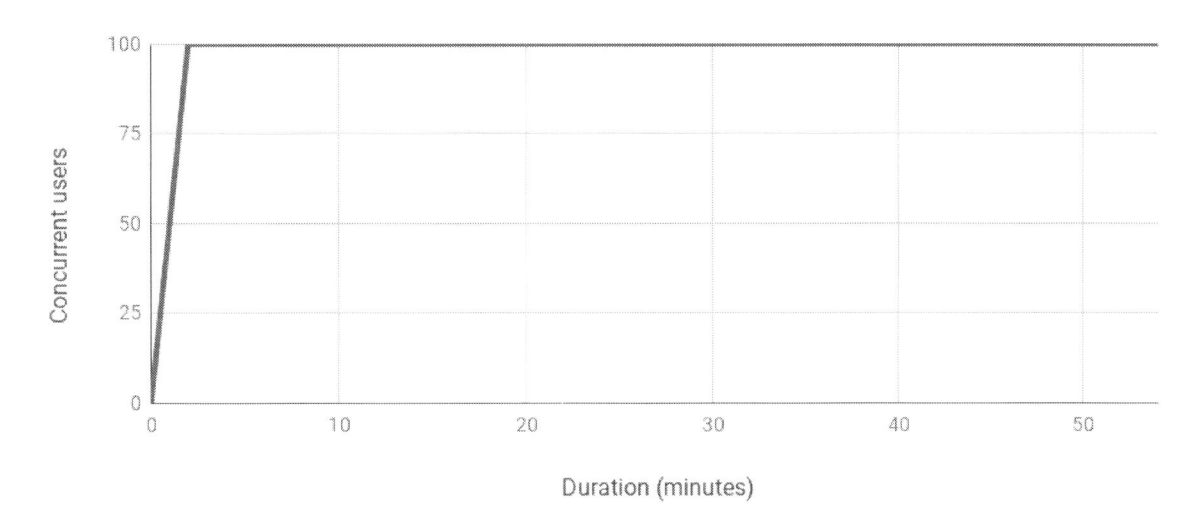

Figure 3.11: Controlling the number of VUs with a Thread Group – outcome

40 | Designing a Test Case

Alternatively, we can use the *Thread Groups* shipped with JMeter plugins (https://jmeter-plugins.org/). They allow you to visualize the configuration while setting it up.

For example, with **bzm - Concurrency Thread Group** (https://jmeter-plugins.org/wiki/ConcurrencyThreadGroup/):

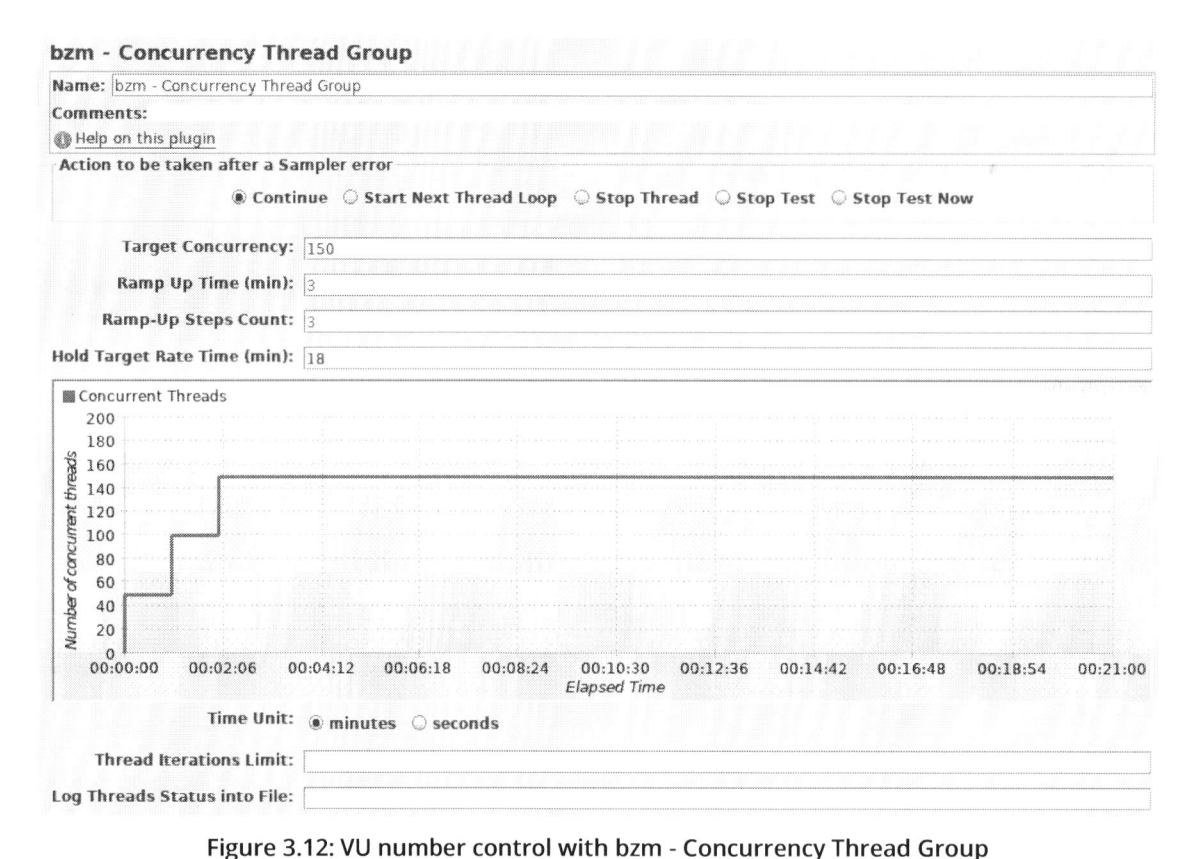

Figure 3.12: VU number control with bzm - Concurrency Thread Group

Or, with **jp@gc - Ultimate Thread Group** (https://jmeter-plugins.org/wiki/UltimateThreadGroup/):

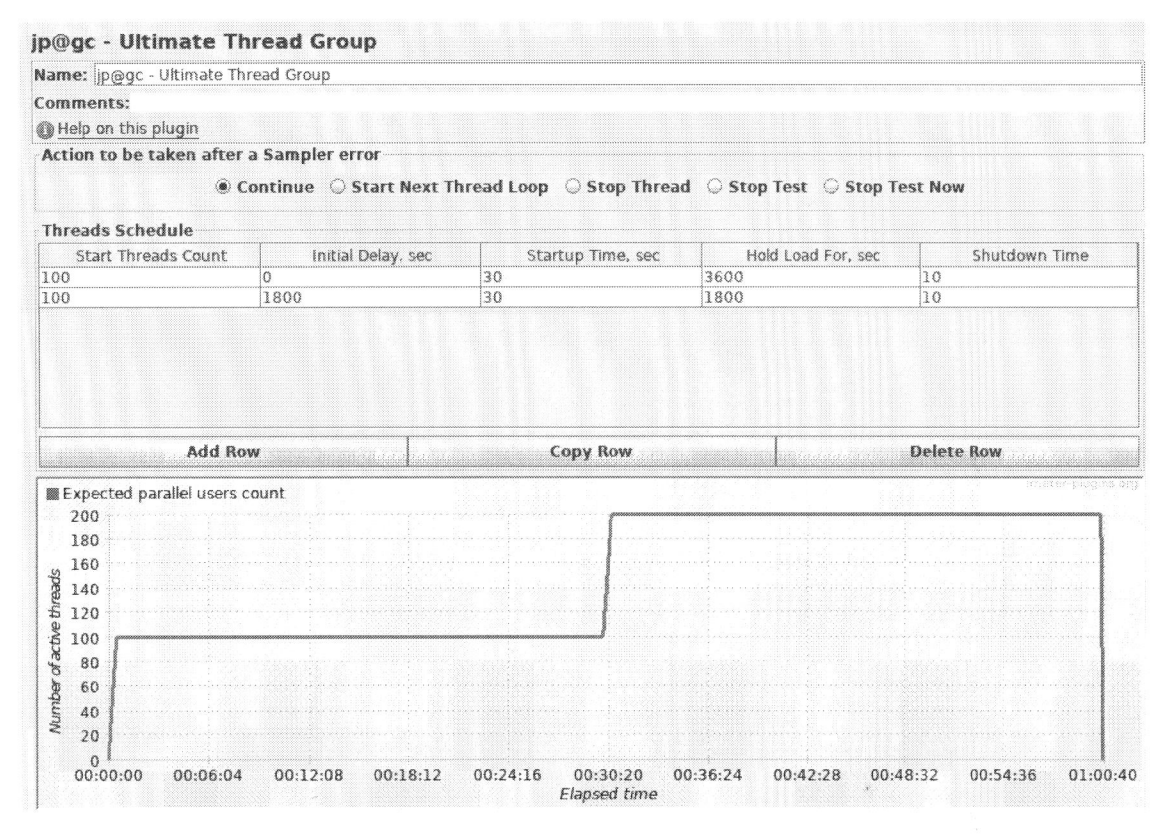

Figure 3.13: Control of the number of VUs with jp@gc - Ultimate Thread Group

Throughput (Open Model)

Here, we let JMeter handle the number of VUs while we control the number of transactions. In this model, whatever happens to the SUT, the injector maintains the throughput provided we have setup enough VUs.

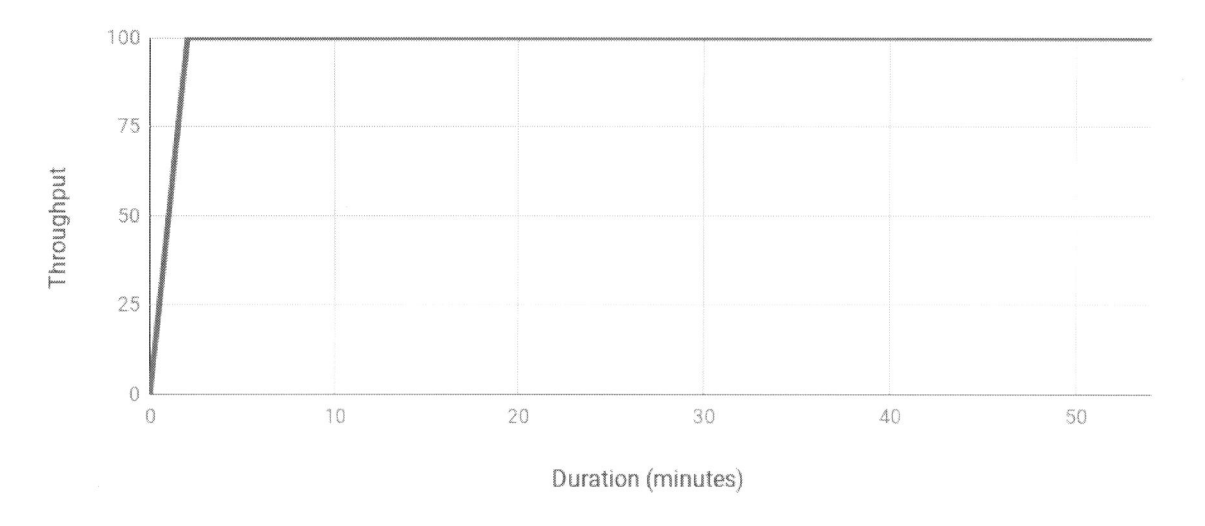

Figure 3.14: Throughput

This makes it easy to:

- Compare two tests
- Transform business needs into a goal for our tests

For this, there are several solutions:

- **Constant Throughput Timer**

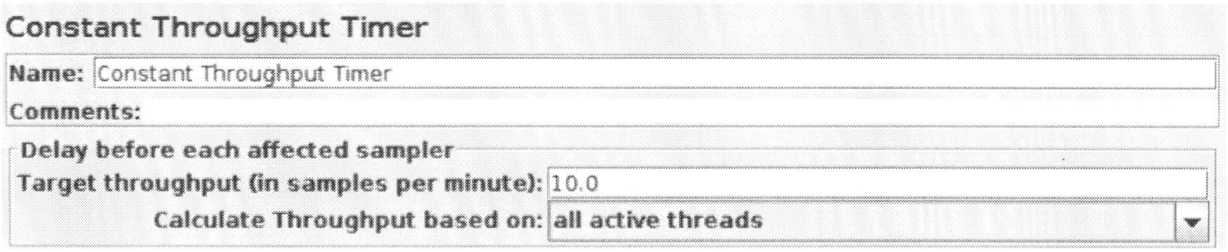

Figure 3.15: Constant Throughput Timer

- **Precise Throughput Timer**

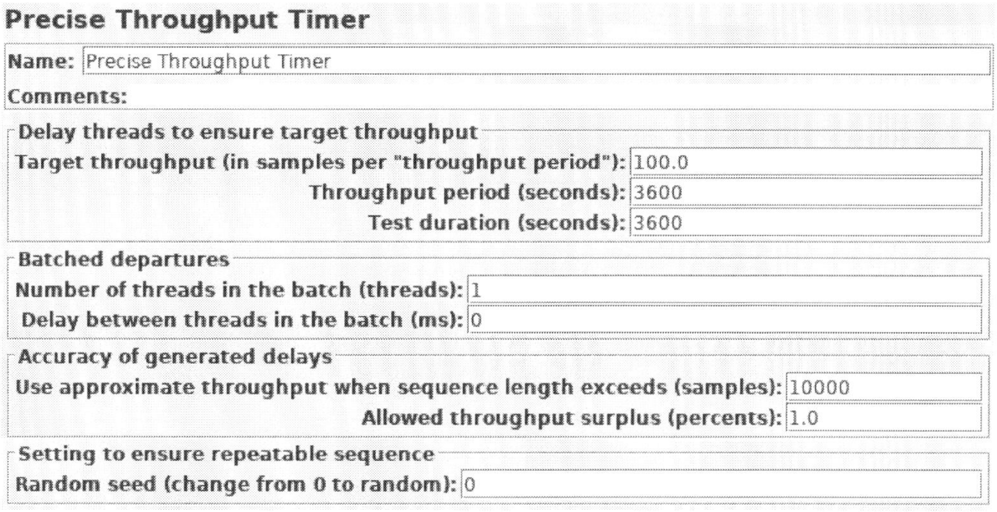

Figure 3.16: Precise Throughput Timer

- The use of plugins such as JMeter Plugins (https://jmeter-plugins.org/)
- Also provided by JMeter Plugins, we have the Throughput Shaping Timer plugin (https://jmeter-plugins.org/wiki/ThroughputShapingTimer/)

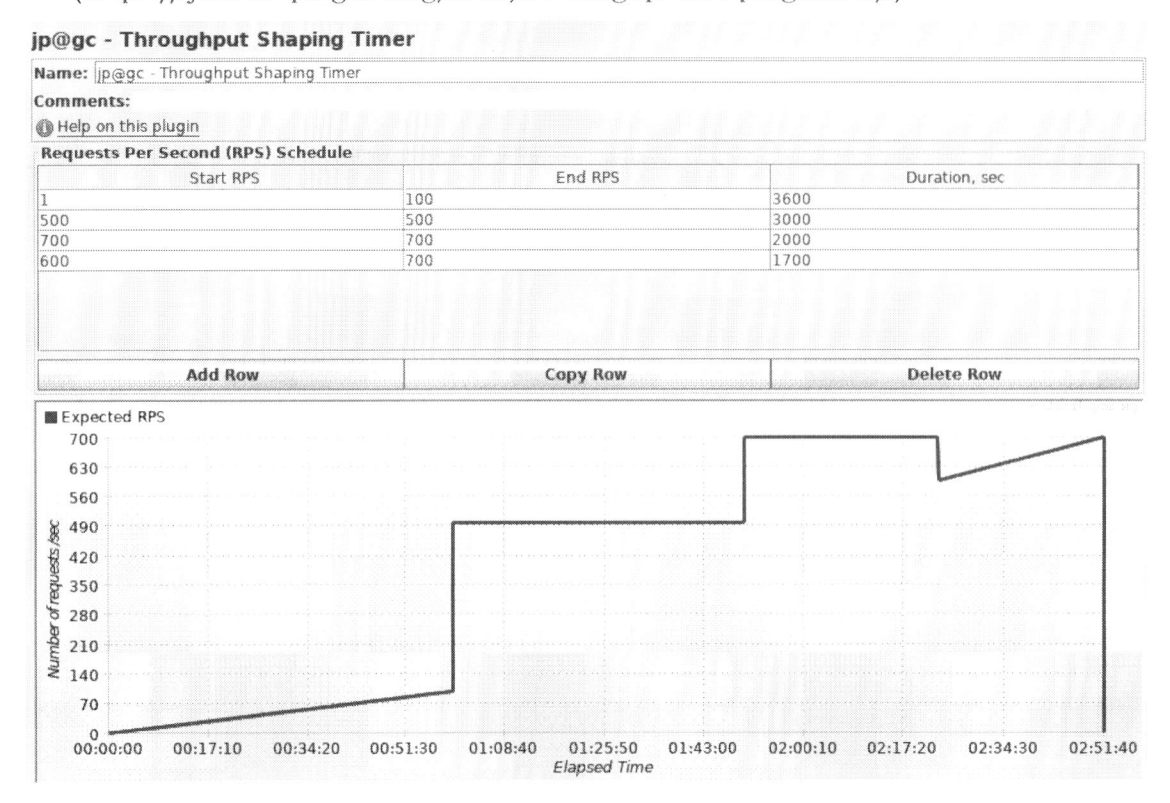

Figure 3.17: Throughput Shaping Timer

To allow JMeter to create VUs during the test (and not all at the beginning), do not forget to enable the **Delay Thread creation until needed** option under **Thread Group**.

Load Model | 45

Figure 3.18: Thread Group

Arrivals Rate (Open Model)

In this model, irrespective of what happens to the SUT, the injector maintains the arrival rate of VUs. For example, this is what happens on a customer-facing website. Customers will connect without waiting for other users to be disconnected, even if the site is crashing or has slow response times.

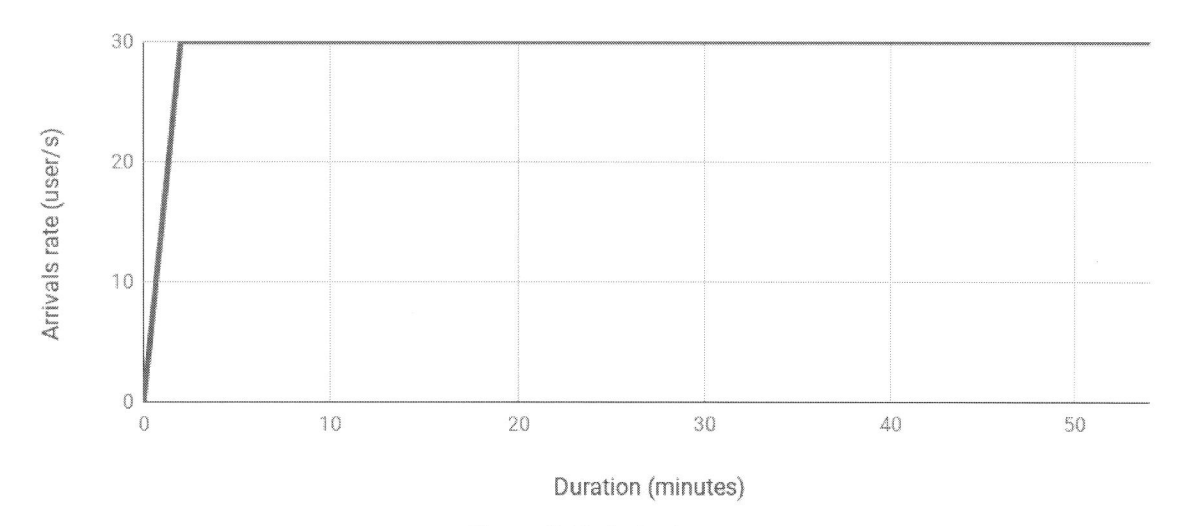

Figure 3.19: Arrival rate

46 | Designing a Test Case

To simulate an unhappy customer who abandons their navigation because of very slow response times, we can use:

- **Duration Assertion**, which can be added to **Thread Group** to apply to all requests in our script

Figure 3.20: Duration Assertion to simulate the exit of a client

- In the **Advanced** -> **Timeout (milliseconds)** -> **Connect** + **Response** option of **HTTP Request**

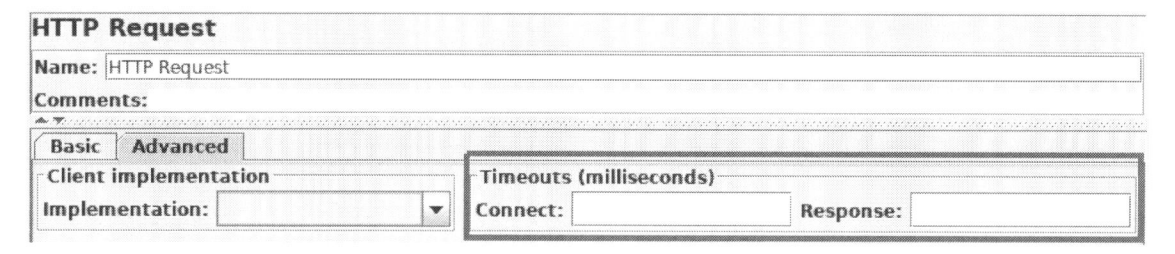

Figure 3.21: Timeout (milliseconds) to simulate a client leaving the website

With JMeter, there are several solutions:

- The **bzm - Arrivals Thread Group** plugin (https://jmeter-plugins.org/wiki/ArrivalsThreadGroup/)

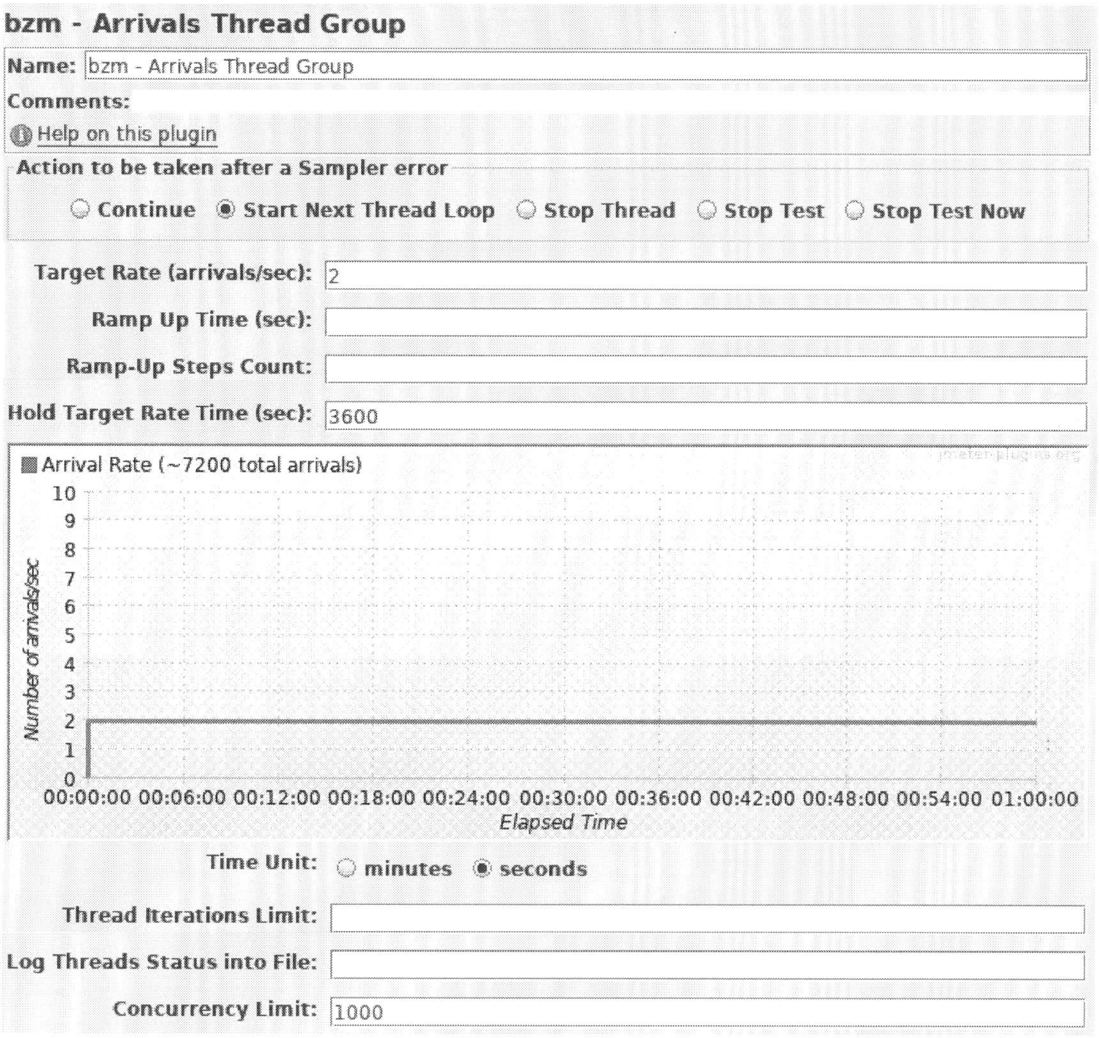

Figure 3.22: bzm - Arrivals Thread Group: 2 VUs/s for 1h

- The **bzm - Free-Form Arrivals Thread Group** plugin (https://jmeter-plugins.org/wiki/FreeFormArrivalsThreadGroup/)

Figure 3.23: bzm - Free-Form Arrivals Thread Group: 2 VUs/s for 1h

- In **Thread Group**: disable iterations (**Loop Count** to **1**), adjust the duration of **Ramp-Up Period (in seconds)** to be equal to the duration of the test, set the correct value to **Number of Threads (users)**, and enable **Delay Thread creation until needed**

Figure 3.24: Thread Group: 2 VUs/s for 1h

Structure of a Test Case

A test case can be divided into three parts.

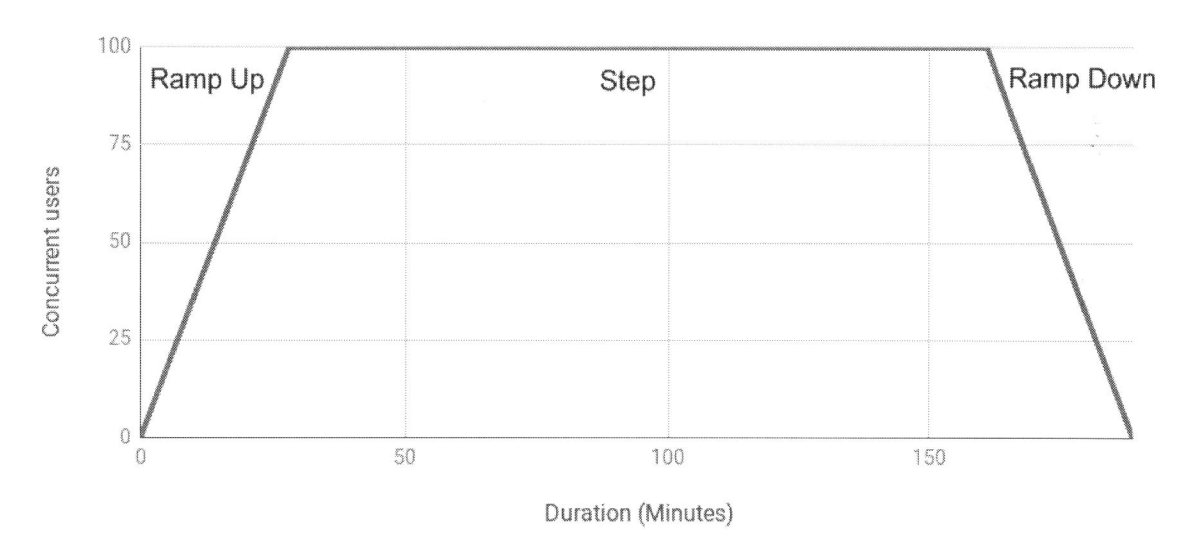

Figure 3.25: Structure of a test case

Ramp-Up

A load test often has a so-called "ramp-up" period.

This period corresponds to the gradual arrival of virtual users on the target system.

A warm-up period allows both the target server and the injectors to:

- Warm up the just in time (JIT) compiler of the java virtual machine (JVM) injectors
- Warm up the JIT of the (JVM)/common language runtime (CLR) of the tested application
- Retrieve/initiate resources (database connections, brokers queues, and so on)
- Fill caches
- Initiate the mechanism of *autoscaling*
- Distribute loads in a uniform manner (load balancer and so on) and so on

Ramp-up is configured with the **Thread Group** parameters.

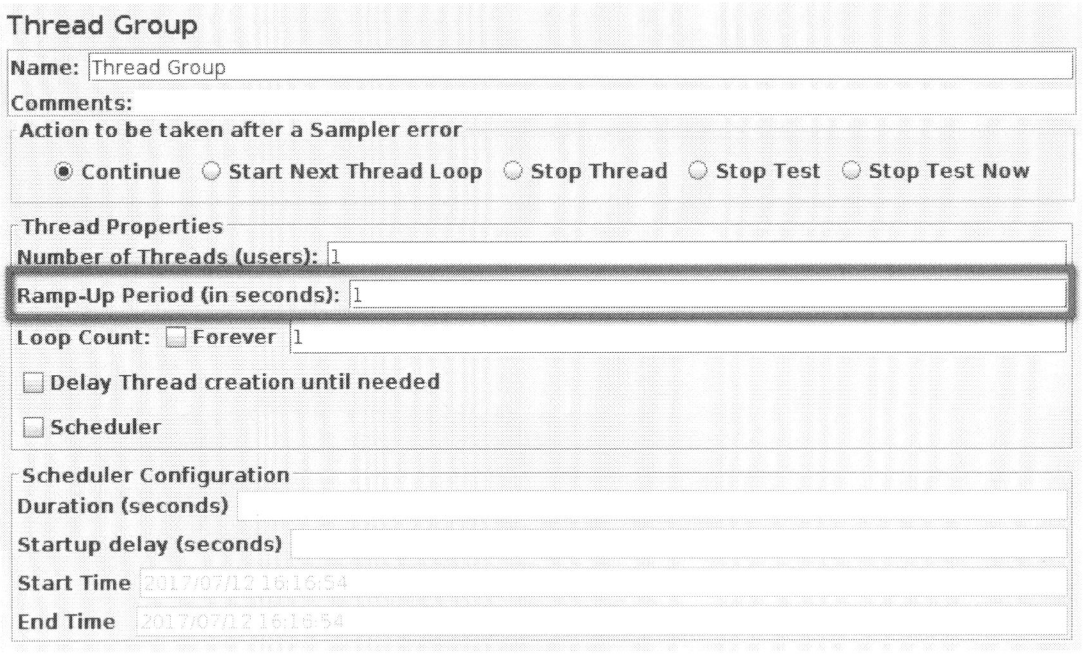

Figure 3.26: Ramp-Up

The arrival rate of users is calculated as follows:

- The ramp-up time divided by the number of units (VUs)

Example for 300 seconds duration with 100 users:

- Frequency: 300/100 = 3 users every second

Plateau/Step

Following ramp-up, we arrive at a step. Its duration should be long enough (at least several tens of minutes) to allow a relevant analysis of the results.

If we want to test multiple target loads, it is possible to have multiple steps (refer to the *Example: Step Load Test* section of this chapter).

Ramp-Down

Ramp-down is the opposite of *ramp-up*. This is the part of the scenario where the number of VUs decreases.

> **Note**
> At the moment, JMeter does not allow the duration of ramp-down to be set.
>
> However, thanks to JMeter's rich ecosystem, just add the JMeter Plugins plugin called Ultimate Thread Group (https://jmeter-plugins.org/wiki/UltimateThreadGroup/) to incorporate this feature.

Example: Step Load Test

In this example, we will divide the test into multiple steps.

Each step is characterized by the number of users and/or types of transactions performed on the tested server.

- This allows us to compare: 1,000 VUs versus 2,000 VUs
- It also allows us to simulate different periods of use of the application: Current month versus end of the month (for example, the closing of accounts, the billing period)

In JMeter, a step load test relies on using multiple **Thread Group** and scheduling their execution.

Each Thread Group defines a certain number of users/threads executing functional scenarios during a given period.

- Thread Group 1 starts first and lasts for the entire duration of the test
- Thread Group 2 starts after a delay and stops earlier

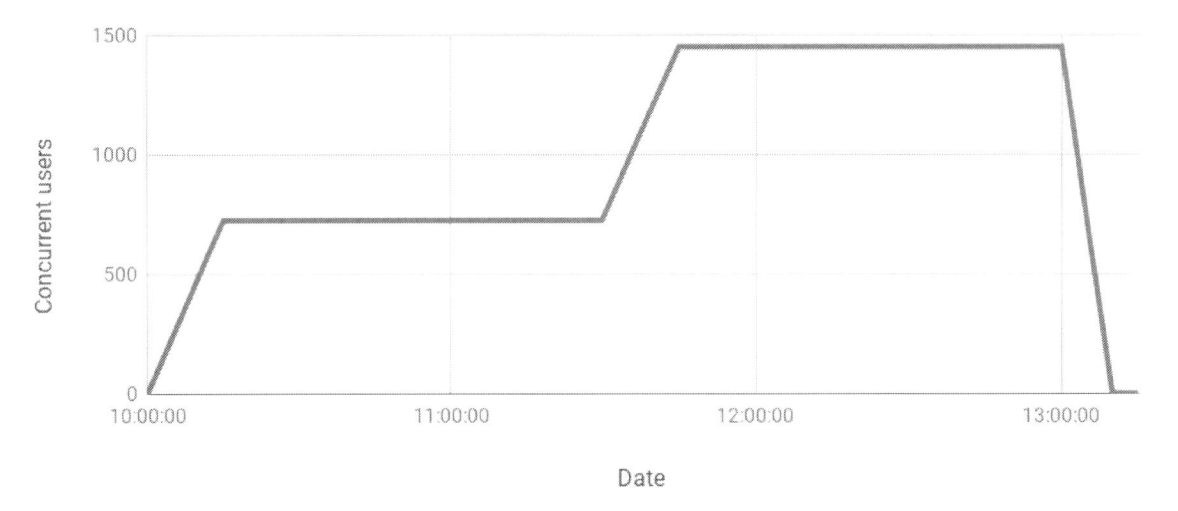

Figure 3.27: Step load tests

For a load test with two steps:

- The first **Thread group** represents the **regular** load
- The second **Thread group** represents the **peak** load

Since the only difference between the **Thread Group**s is just this Thread Group scheduling and number of threads configuration:

Figure 3.28: Peak Thread Group configuration

To avoid copy/paste, we would use a **Module Controller** in the second **Thread Group**, referencing the **scenario** of the first **Thread Group**.

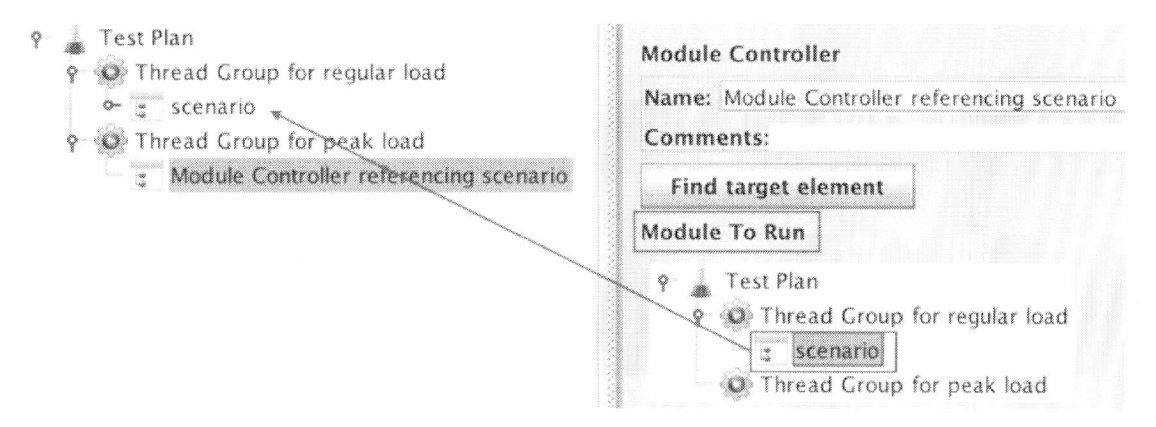

Figure 3.29: Module controller

At startup, JMeter launches both (or all) **Thread Group**s at the same time.

Use **Startup delay (seconds)** to allow a **Thread Group** to start later.

> Note
> Another easier way to create steps is to use JMeter Plugins.

Identify Critical Business Scenarios to Script

If the business scenarios are not identified well, the tests will not conform to what will happen during production, and will therefore be useless, or even dangerous, giving the false impression that the targeted platform handles the load without problems.

It is therefore critical to identify the relevant business scenarios and weight them.

To define these scenarios, we can:

- Retrieve the statistics of the application if they exist (for example, the daily or monthly number of business transactions, an analysis of web statistics (access log, analytics tools...), and so on)
- Define them with Users/Business User/Product Owner

For the number of scenarios, it is advisable to apply the Pareto Principle (https://en.wikipedia.org/wiki/Pareto_principle), also called the 80/20 rule, and therefore to take (at least as a first step) only the 20% of scenarios that cover 80% of the scope of the application – for example, by not simulating different connection speeds, and suchlike.

The second recommendation is to undertake a risk study to prioritize the tests. This will enable tests to be chosen in the case of a tight schedule (application delivered later than expected, servers unavailable, and so on).

During this identification phase, there are three types of scenarios to take into account.

Frequent

Those scenarios that happen every day.

For example, in the case of an e-commerce site:

- Product sheet consultations
- The addition of items to the shopping cart
- Search engine use

Vital

Those scenarios that are vital.

For example:

- Payroll triggering for a human resources management application
- Cart checkout for an e-commerce application

Risky

Those scenarios that are risky from a performance point of view for the application.

For example:

- Complex research
- Document generation (Excel, Word, PDF...)

This identification work will lead to:

- A validated list of business scenarios to script
- For each business scenario, a document indicating the screens consulted, fields entered in the forms, the time between each action, business rules for entries, and so on
- A sharing of the test perimeter with all the teams

How Many Virtual Users Do I Need?

Once the number of users/transactions has been validated in the previous step, we only have to transform this number into virtual users (Threads) in JMeter.

> **Caution**
> Do not forget to take into account the requests made by bots (Qwantify (Qwant Bot), Google Bot, Bing Bot, and so on) in the calculation of the number of users.

The maximum number of virtual users configurable per injector depends on:

- The test plan (simple or complex, well or badly written)
- The number of *listeners* and their nature (some require more resources, so if we set too many virtual users, we run the risk of having a performance problem at the level of the injector, thereby distorting the results)
- The JMeter execution type (GUI or CLI mode (also called Non-GUI mode in JMeter))
- The resources made available for the test (number of servers, processor, memory, network, and so on)

The maximum number of virtual users is therefore limited by the available resources (injector's power, network resources, and so on).

But since the target load is not necessarily equal to the maximum, there are two possible strategies:

- One virtual user (simulated) = one user
- One virtual user (simulated) = n users

In the first case, there is no need for calculations to find the number of virtual users, and it may be wise to use the **Delay Thread creation until needed** option of the **Thread Group**.

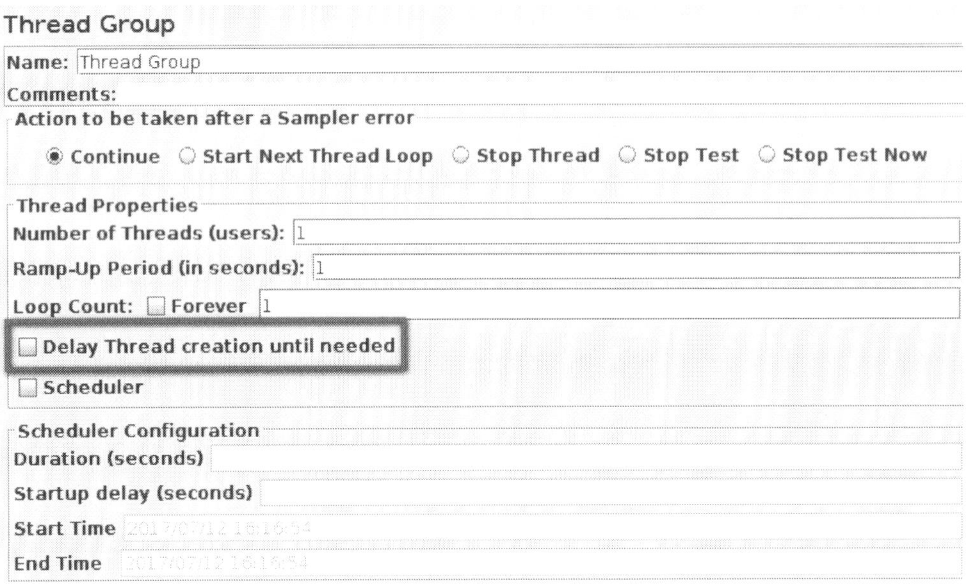

Figure 3.30: Thread Group

In the second case, it will be necessary to calculate the number of iterations that a virtual user can execute over a given period, and then divide the target load by that number.

For example, on an e-commerce site, we need to simulate 50 purchases per hour.

We know that a virtual user can make 10 purchases per hour (because we have limited the throughput using the **Constant Throughput Timer** element or by means of a calculation in a previous test).

We will need at least 50/10 = 5 virtual users to reach our target load.

In all cases, it is possible to use a calculator that will perform the calculation for us, such as the online one provided by the Virtual Users' Calculator on the Ubik Load Pack website (https://ubikloadpack.com/virtual-users-computer.php).

Parameters to Take into Account when Creating a Scenario

Our list of scenarios is defined, but there are still many challenges in order to implement them in the most realistic way.

Here is a non-exhaustive list of important parameters for the implementation of our scenarios.

Vary User Input

In order to avoid testing only the performance of the cache of the targeted solution, it is necessary to vary the user inputs (values in the forms, login/password, and so on).

On the other hand, do make sure that you don't overly diversify the user input values at the risk of ending up with an application cache that appears to be inefficient because of an unrealistically wide data range.

> **Note**
> Monitor the metric cache hit ratio delivered by cache servers to validate the fact that the inputs chosen reflect reality.
>
> If the hit ratio is too high, and higher than the production cache hit ratio, the dataset is not large enough.
>
> If the hit ratio is too low, and lower than the production cache hit ratio, the dataset is too large.

Reuse the Same Values

In some cases, however, it may be useful to regularly use the same values to test a possible contention. But, of course, in doing so, ensure you don't diverge too much from the real use cases.

For example, on an e-commerce site, the purchase of the same product can allow us to check whether there is a contention in the database when several virtual users try to buy the same product. This can happen if a lock is set when writing to a table, slowing down concurrent access to this table.

Vary the Types of Users

For each scenario, it is necessary to identify the types of users and their ratio within the entire load test.

For example, for an e-commerce site, there are buyers, and there are visitors who will not buy anything.

Similarly, it can be useful to differentiate between new and returning users, as this impacts the server and web browser cache.

By way of a final example, a user with administrator access will have a different use for the application compared to other users.

Vary and Adjust Think Times

Think time is the time between two actions executed by the user. This time generally includes the screen reading time, the reflection period, and the time taken by the user to input some data on the screen.

You have to find the right balance for its duration to reflect reality. A different and bounded duration for each think time is a good solution.

Ensure that think times are not too short, because the results of the test could be impacted negatively, showing a non-existent problem.

> **Note**
> Using the Recording with Think Time template in the **Templates...** feature automatically saves think times.

In JMeter, a long list of elements facilitates the simulation of these think times.

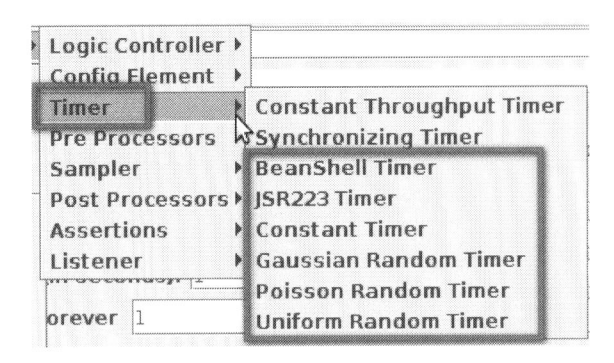

Figure 3.31: Think time

Adjust the Ramp-Up Time

This must be sufficiently long so that the server does not collapse under a load peak from the beginning unless it is the use case.

Indeed, during this period, "heavy" processing on the tested platform side will probably happen (pool size increase, JIT compilation by the JVM, and so on) over a short period, whereas, in reality, the server would surely have more time to process this extra work.

Another reason for adjusting the ramp-up time, at least when starting the tests, is to establish the failure point or the point at which response times start to degrade.

Adjust the Test Duration

In order to give caches time to initialize and to detect memory/thread/connection leaks more easily, it may be wise in some tests to have a long test time (depending on the architecture and up to several days).

Short-term load tests (less than 30 minutes) are to be avoided as they do not enable the behavior of the targeted solution to be tested in terms of robustness and under continuous load.

Error Handling

It is important to take the number of errors returned by the application into account in order to avoid an incorrect interpretation of the load test.

For example, for the response time of a web page:

Iteration	response time
1	10 ms
2	8 ms
3	7 ms
4	error
5	error
6	error
7	error

Figure 3.32: Table of Iteration-response times for a web page

If we do not take the errors into account, we obtain an average response time of 8.33 ms, whereas, in reality, if the errors were due to a timeout and/or the inability of the application to respond because it is overloaded, we could conclude that the application does not hold the load.

We're going to miss a problem revealed by the load test.

To solve this problem, JMeter provides **Assertions** that will check whether the response received is the expected one.

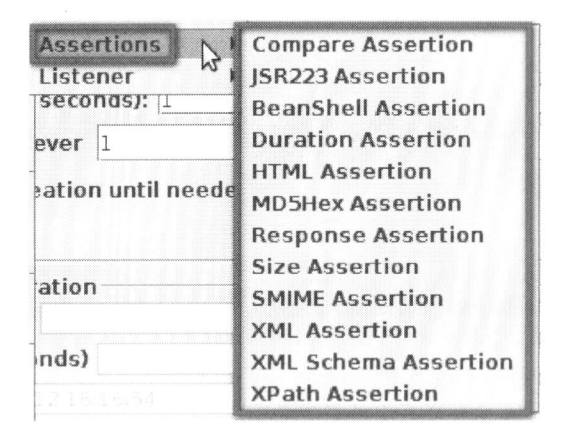

Figure 3.33: Assertions

User Connection Type

If a majority of users have the same connection type (for example, 3G on a phone), it may be a good idea to test the application with this bandwidth.

Size of the Scenarios

It is important to have medium-sized scenarios in terms of the number of elements to ease their maintenance.

For that, JMeter offers many options. These include:

- **CSV Data Set Config** and **Random Variable**: To have different values on each iteration of the scenario
- **Include Controller** or **Module Controller**: To share parts of scripts between several scenarios
- Control elements (**Interleave Controller**, **If Controller**, and so on): To modify the navigation flow

Meeting Point/Rendezvous

In some cases, to make sure that there is concurrency in some steps of the scenario, it may be useful to use a **Synchronizing Timer**.

Figure 3.34: Synchronizing Timer

> **Note**
> This component only makes the appointment within one injector. Therefore, make sure that the number of users set is less than, or equal to, the number of **Thread Group** users of one injector.

Cookie Management

If we want to manage cookies, add **HTTP Cookie Manager**.

This will:

- Make JMeter manage (store and send) the cookies for us
- Simulate a new user without cookies at each iteration with the *Clear cookies each iteration?* option
- Add our own cookies with the *User-Defined Cookies* option
- Allow us to manipulate cookies as variables by adding the `CookieManager.save.cookies = true` property to the `user.properties` file
- Make JMeter take into account cookies that are not bound to the tested host by adding the `CookieManager.check.cookies = false` property to the `user.properties` file

Cache Management

Depending on the requirements of the test, enable or disable the cache with **HTTP Cache Manager**.

A mix of both types of users is possible.

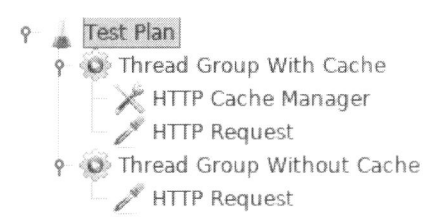

Figure 3.35: User simulation with and without cache

Conclusion

As we have seen, it is not easy to design a load test scenario. However, it is an important task to execute the right load test, with the right business scenarios, the right frequency, the right duration, and so on with the goal of making a load test that will actually validate the performance of the targeted platform.

These tips will help you to perform realistic load tests and not just "simulate a big load on your applications" that does not correspond to any reality.

Important Concepts in JMeter

All tools have their own specific concepts, and JMeter is no exception to this.

It is important to understand these concepts in order to use JMeter properly.

Scoping

In JMeter, elements are organized in a tree, where each node has parents and children, which can be branches or leaves.

The scope of an element is based on where the element is located in the tree branch.

Simply defined, the scope of an element is composed of the elements that are children of its own parent.

66 | Important Concepts in JMeter

In the following screenshot, the scope of **Response Assertion,** highlighted in red, includes the elements contained in the yellow rectangle; namely, all the child elements of the parent, **Test Plan**:

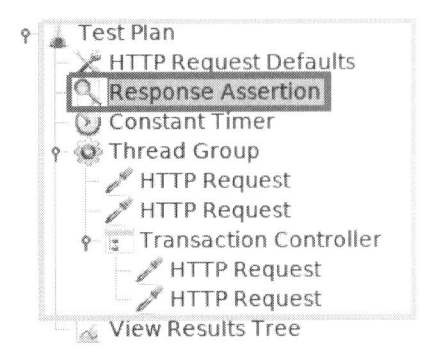

Figure 4.1: Scope

As a consequence, when the test is run, it will execute the assertion for every **HTTP Request**:

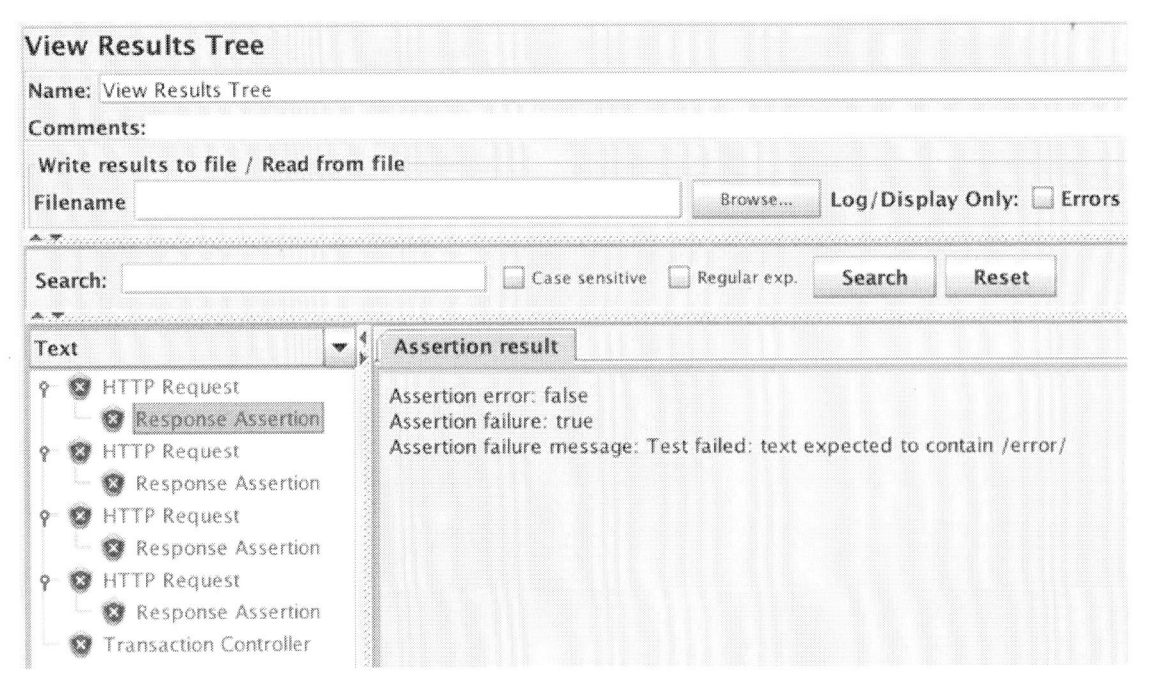

Figure 4.2: Scope of Assertion

Elements' Execution Order

The execution of elements in JMeter depends on their type and their scope:

- **Samplers** and **Controllers** are not scoped elements – they are executed where they are located.
- **Pre-Processor**, **Post-Processor**, **Timer**, **Assertion**, and **Listener** are scoped elements – they are executed where their scope applies AND their execution order depends both on their type and their position if two elements of the same type apply.
- **Config Elements** are also scoped elements, but their execution depends on their type.

The first rule for execution order is the following:

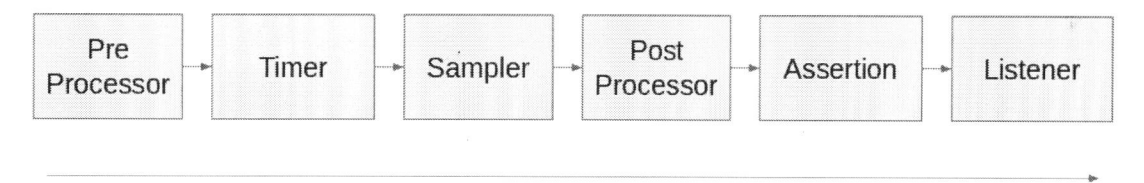

Pre Processor → Timer → Sampler → Post Processor → Assertion → Listener

Execution order for Sampler within a JMeter Thread

Figure 4.3: Execution order based on type

68 | Important Concepts in JMeter

As you can see in the following screenshot, the positions of different elements do not impact the execution order:

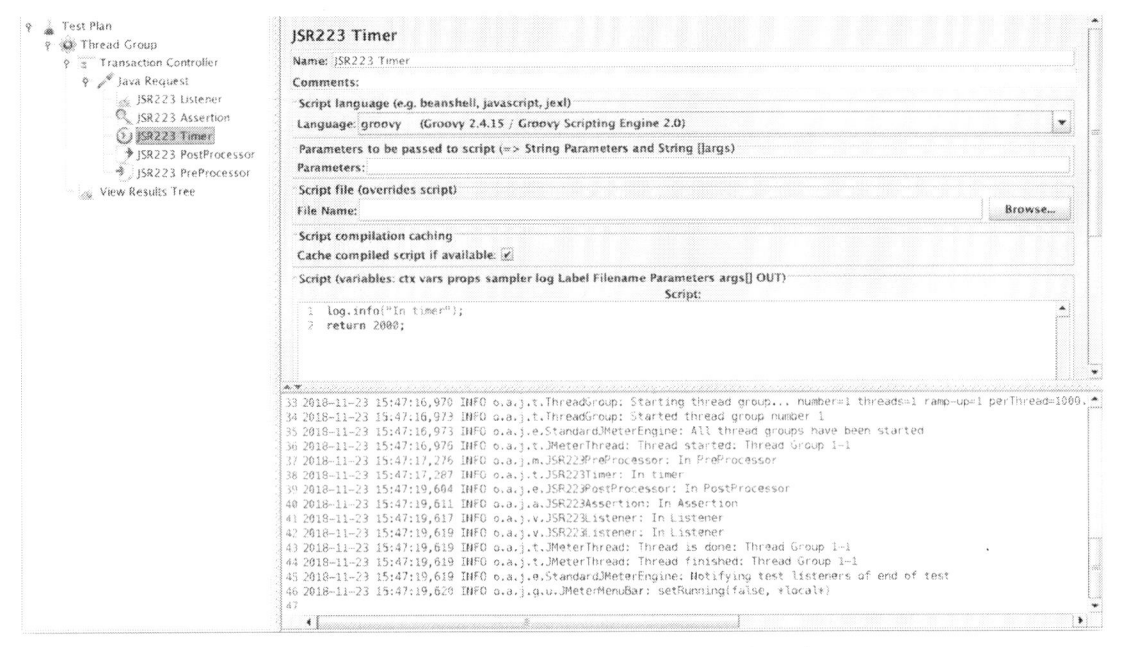

Figure 4.4: Type and not position, impacts the order of execution

The second rule is that outer elements are executed before inner elements of the same type:

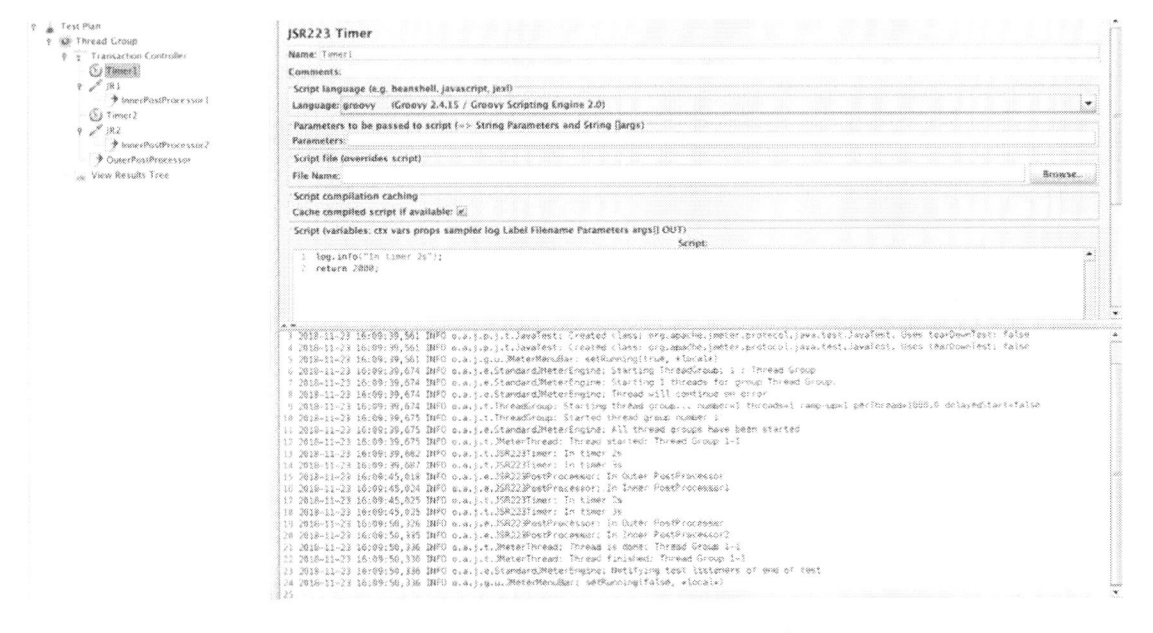

Figure 4.5: Same elements execution order

In the preceding example, **OuterPostProcessor** is executed before **InnerPostProcessor1** for **JR1** and before **InnerPostProcessor1** for **JR2**.

How Timer Scope Works

Timers are important to simulate *think time* in our script. Think time is the time a user takes between two interactions with the application to do things such as the following:

- Read screen content
- Enter login and password
- Enter order form data

To avoid unexpected behavior, it's critical to understand how and when **Timers** are executed.

There are two rules, and these rules apply regardless of the location of the timer.

Rule 1: Timers Are Executed before Each Sampler in Their Scope

For example, consider the following script:

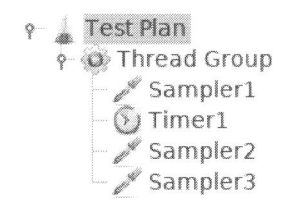

```
Test Plan
  Thread Group
    Sampler1
    Timer1
    Sampler2
    Sampler3
```

Figure 4.6: Our script with one timer

This script will be executed in the following order:

Timer1 → Sampler1 → Timer1 → Sampler2 → Timer1 → Sampler3

Execution order

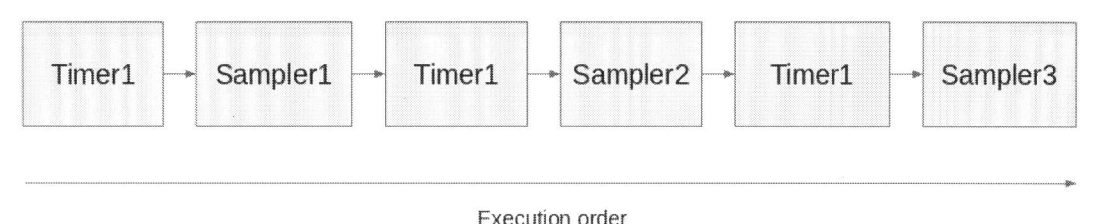

Figure 4.7: Execution order of our script with one timer

70 | Important Concepts in JMeter

As we can see, **Timer1** is:

- Executed three times because of the scoping rule
- Executed once before **Sampler1**
- Executed once before **Sampler2**
- Executed once before **Sampler3**

Rule 2: If There Is More Than One Timer in the Scope, All the Timers Will Be Processed before the Sampler

Consider the following script:

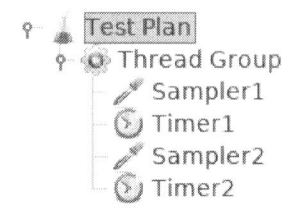

```
Test Plan
  Thread Group
    Sampler1
    Timer1
    Sampler2
    Timer2
```

Figure 4.8: Our script with two timers

This script will be executed in this order:

Timer1 → Timer2 → Sampler1 → Timer1 → Timer2 → Sampler2

Execution order

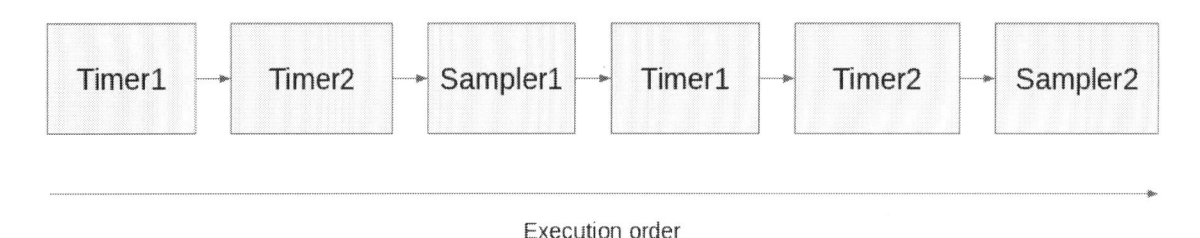

Figure 4.9: Execution order for our script with two timers

As we can see, **Timer1** and **Timer2** are:

- *Grouped*, because all timers in the scope are executed before every sampler
- Executed twice because they are applied to every sampler in the scope
- Executed once before **Sampler1**
- Executed once before **Sampler2**

Controlling the Execution Order of Timers

Let's say that we want the following execution order for our script:

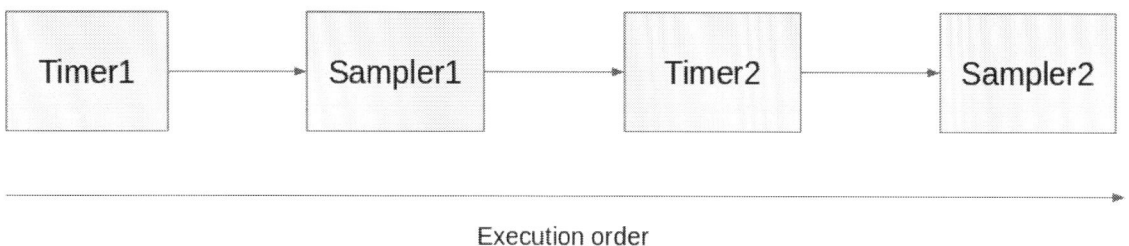

Figure 4.10: Our desired execution order

We can achieve this using the **Add Think Times to children** feature, as shown in the following screenshot:

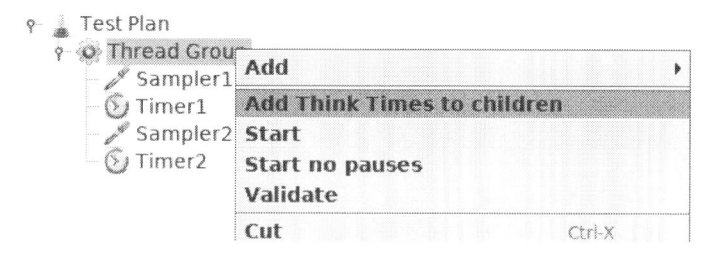

Figure 4.11: The Add Think Times to children feature

Using this feature will give us the following result:

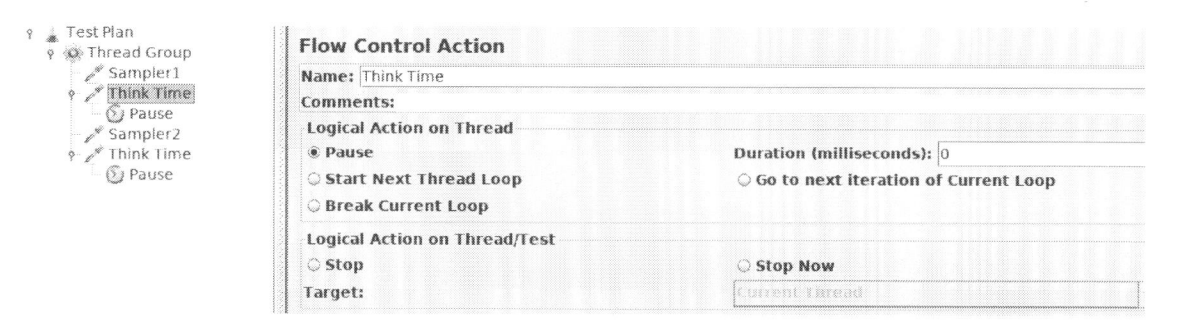

Figure 4.12: The result of the Add Think Times to children feature

> **Note**
> This feature allows us to have different think times for each element.

72 | Important Concepts in JMeter

Without this feature, we could have a similar result, with the difference that the timer is executed before the sampler:

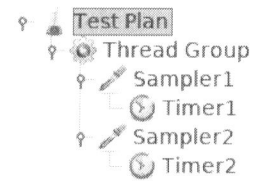

Figure 4.13: Timers as children

> **Note**
> Nesting timers as children of samplers is less readable since timers are executed before the Sampler.

Or, if we have a **random timer** and we put it at the same level as the **Sampler**, then thanks to our scoping rules, it would run before each **Sampler**:

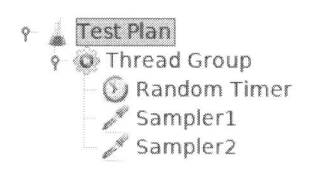

Figure 4.14: Random Timer

> **Note**
> If think times are very similar, using one timer element scoped correctly can be a more maintainable way to achieve this.

How Assertion Scope Works

Assertions are used to validate a response.

> **Note**
> Out of the box, JMeter considers all 4xx and 5xx responses as failures.

Like **Timers**, assertions have rules, too.

These rules apply regardless of the location of the assertion.

Rule 1: Assertions Are Executed after Each Sampler in Their Scope or to Parent Samplers

Example 1:

- **Assertion** will validate the responses from **Sampler1** and **Sampler2**:

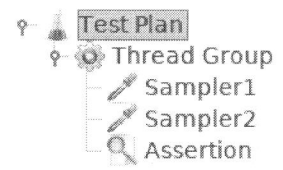

Figure 4.15: Example 1

Example 2:

- **Assertion1** will validate the response from **Sampler1**:
- **Assertion2** will validate the response from **Sampler2**:

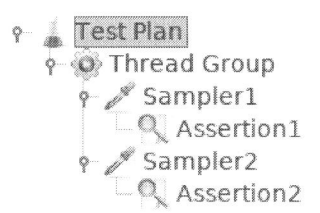

Figure 4.16: Example 2

Example 3:

- **Assertion1** will validate the response from **Sampler1**:
- **Assertion2** will validate the responses from **Sampler1** and **Sampler2**:

```
Test Plan
  Thread Group
    Sampler1
      Assertion1
    Sampler2
    Assertion2
```

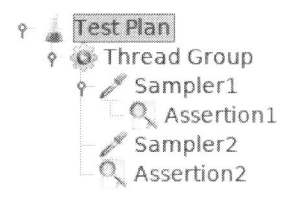

Figure 4.17: Example 3

Example 4:

- Here, **Assertion1** will validate the responses of **Sampler1** and **Sampler2**:

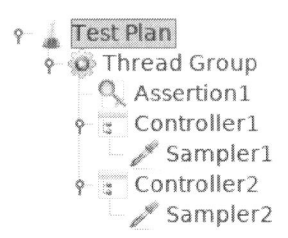

```
Test Plan
  Thread Group
    Assertion1
    Controller1
      Sampler1
    Controller2
      Sampler2
```

Figure 4.18: Example 4

Rule 2: Failed Assertions Cause the Failure of the Entire Transaction Controller

Example 5:

All samplers will be validated by the **Assertion1** assertion.

Controller1 will be marked as failed because of the failure of **Sampler2**:

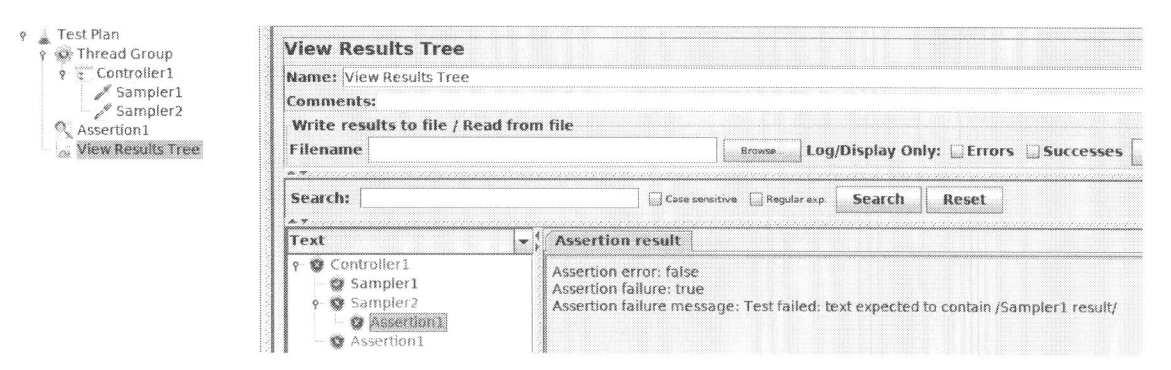

Figure 4.19: Example 5

Rule 3: Assertions Can Validate the Main Sample and/or the Sub-Samples

For some **Assertions**, we can select whether we want to apply the assertion to the main sample and/or the sub-samples.

For example, with **Response Assertion**, we have the following options:

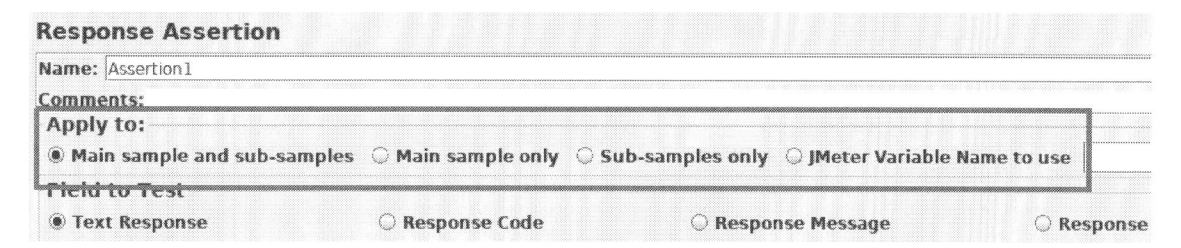

Figure 4.20: Defining what our Response Assertion applies to

Validating sub-samples can be useful when *Retrieve all Embedded resources* is checked in an **HTTP Request**.

76 | Important Concepts in JMeter

Example 6:

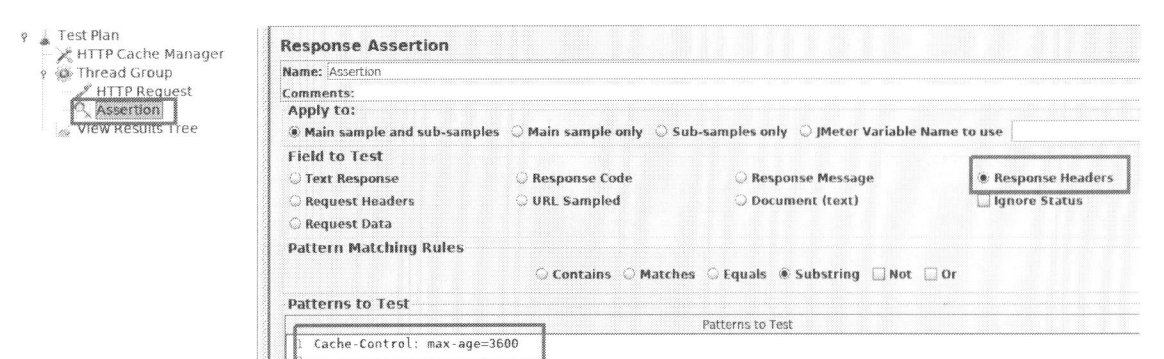

Figure 4.21: Validate Cache-Control: max-age=3600

We want to validate that all Embedded resources have a **Cache-Control** response header equal to **max-age=3600**:

Figure 4.22: Validation of Cache-Control failed

Rule 4: Be Careful with Low-Performing Assertions

Some **assertions** consume a lot of resources. These assertions include the following:

- **XPath Assertion**
- **XML Assertion**
- **XML Schema Assertion**
- **HTML Assertion**

We advise you to limit the number of assertions for these types and possibly only use the first one – **XPath Assertion** – which has a real benefit.

Our Advice

The easiest way to use **Assertions** is to add them as children of samplers.

How Properties Differ from Variables

Properties and variables allow you to make data dynamic in JMeter. So, their purposes are very similar:

- Variables are tightly bound to their threads, meaning that every thread has its own copy and can manipulate their own version of a variable.
- Properties are shared among all threads, so changing a property during a test should be avoided. If you really need to change it, ensure that the value is not corrupted by simultaneous access. You can do this by synchronizing this access.

In summary, variables and properties differ in that properties are global and variables are local with respect to threads.

Based on this, we can define two rules:

- Properties should be used for environment-related data.
- Variables should be used for user-related data and correlation rules. That's why, for example, extractors in JMeter will create variables.

How Properties Are Created

Properties are created by JMeter, which reads them from:

- jmeter.properties
- user.properties
- The command line, using the `-J` option, as in `-JpropName=propValue`
- The command line, using the `-G` option, as in `-GpropName=propValue`
- Any file referenced through the command line using the `-p` option or `--propfile`
- Any file referenced through the command line using the `-q` option or `--addprop`
- Any file passed using a command-line option

You can also create properties in JMeter using the following function:

    ${__setProperty(propName, propValue)}

And finally, you can use scripting elements such as JSR223 Test Elements:

```
props.put("propName", "propValue");
```

Or, you could use the following syntax:

```
props.setProperty("propName", "propValue");
```

How Variables Are Created

Variables are created by JMeter using different elements:

- **User-Defined Variables**, such as a config element
- **User Parameters**, such as a preprocessor
- JMeter functions (https://jmeter.apache.org/usermanual/functions.html), which accept a variable as the last argument
- JMeter extractors (https://jmeter.apache.org/usermanual/component_reference.html#postprocessors), which create variables from response excerpts

You can also create variables using scripting elements such as JSR223 Test Elements:

```
vars.put("varName", "varValue");
```

Or, you could use the following syntax:

```
vars.putObject("varName", objectToBeUsed);
```

How ${} Differs from ${_P}

Since we know the difference between variables and properties, let's see how to use them.

> **Note**
> Variables are accessed using **${varName}**.

> **Note**
> Properties are accessed using the **__P** function, so to read the **propA** property, you would use **${__P(propA)}**.

5

Preparing the Test Environment (Injectors and Tested Systems)

Introduction

Now that we have finished our scripts, it is important to prepare the test environment. This consists of the injectors and the system under test. If these two tasks are not performed properly, the accuracy of the load test results will degrade.

Setting Up the Injectors

Without a good injection, our load tests would be meaningless.

Never Host Injectors on the Same Server as the Tested System

Let's say that you think the installation of dedicated injectors takes too much time, so you decide to install JMeter on one of the servers of the system being tested. In your script, you replace the host with **localhost** and you launch your load test.

What seemed to be a good idea at the start will turn into a waste of time afterward!

Having the injector on one of the servers of the system being tested is *strongly discouraged* for several reasons:

- The load consumed by the tested application can have a negative impact on JMeter.
- The load consumed by JMeter can negatively impact the tested application.
- You'll be testing with a network profile that does not exist in real life (meaning no *load balancer*, minimal network latency, no packet loss, and so on).

Regarding the last point here, on my laptop I have no packet loss and a maximum latency of 0.102 ms:

```
ping -c 4 localhost
PING localhost(localhost (::1)) 56 data bytes
64 bytes from localhost (::1): icmp_seq=1 ttl=64 time=0.053 ms
64 bytes from localhost (::1): icmp_seq=2 ttl=64 time=0.096 ms
64 bytes from localhost (::1): icmp_seq=3 ttl=64 time=0.098 ms
64 bytes from localhost (::1): icmp_seq=4 ttl=64 time=0.102 ms
--- localhost ping statistics ---
4 packets transmitted, 4 received, 0% packet loss, time 3048ms
rtt min/avg/max/mdev = 0.053/0.087/0.102/0.020 ms
```

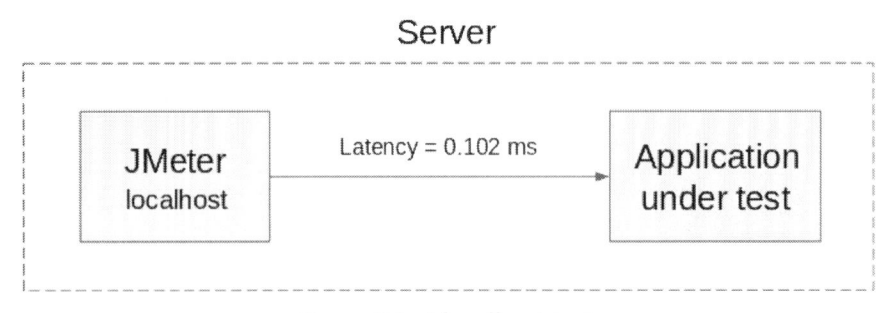

Figure 5.1: A localhost test

No real customer will have these conditions. In real life, it would look more like this:

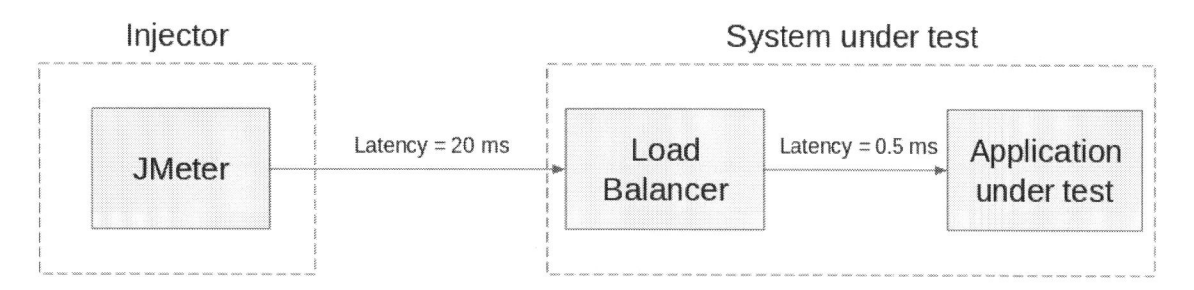

```
Injector                              System under test
┌─────────────┐                    ┌──────────────────────────────────┐
│   JMeter    │──Latency = 20 ms──▶│  Load    ──Latency = 0.5 ms──▶ Application │
│             │                    │  Balancer                      under test  │
└─────────────┘                    └──────────────────────────────────┘
```

Figure 5.2: A test with a realistic network profile

Calibrating Your Test

Before launching a "big" load test with a large number of users, it is best to ensure that the test is properly calibrated.

For this, we will make a "small" load test with a reduced number of users; for example, with only 10% of targeted users.

This allows us to:

- Check the script with multiple VUs
- Check the configuration of think times and script throughput
- Check the assertions
- Obtain a baseline response time

We will save time if we discover performance problems with this reduced load.

From an organizational point of view, this also allows us to:

- Check the organization (that is, the role of every person involved in the load test)
- Check the monitoring (are all components monitored?)
- Get a result quickly and check we have everything that we expect in our report

Monitoring Injectors

It is important to avoid overloaded injectors so that the interpretation of the results of our tests is not distorted. You should monitor injectors with a monitoring tool to ensure that bad response times are not due to injector saturation.

This saturation can have several sources:

- The server configuration (such as an undersized machine)
- The system configuration (such as an untuned TCP stack or misconfigured Linux virtual machine)
- Too narrow a network bandwidth
- Disruptive intermediate components (such as a proxy or firewall)

This rule is not specific to JMeter and must be applied regardless of the tool used.

IP Spoofing

IP spoofing allows the injector to simulate requests with multiple IPs.

This avoids targeting only one part of the target environment if the system being tested has a load balancer configured with an *IP affinity*.

This feature is also very useful when you need to bypass protection systems that block massive requests coming from the same IP (such as an anti-bot protection system).

For example, in an environment with IP affinity and without *IP Spoofing* for our injectors, JMeter will inject four queries with a source **IP** address of **192.168.1.10**:

Figure 5.3: Testing without IP spoofing

The **Load Balancer** configured with **IP stickiness** (that is, IP affinity) will redirect all requests to **Instance 1**:

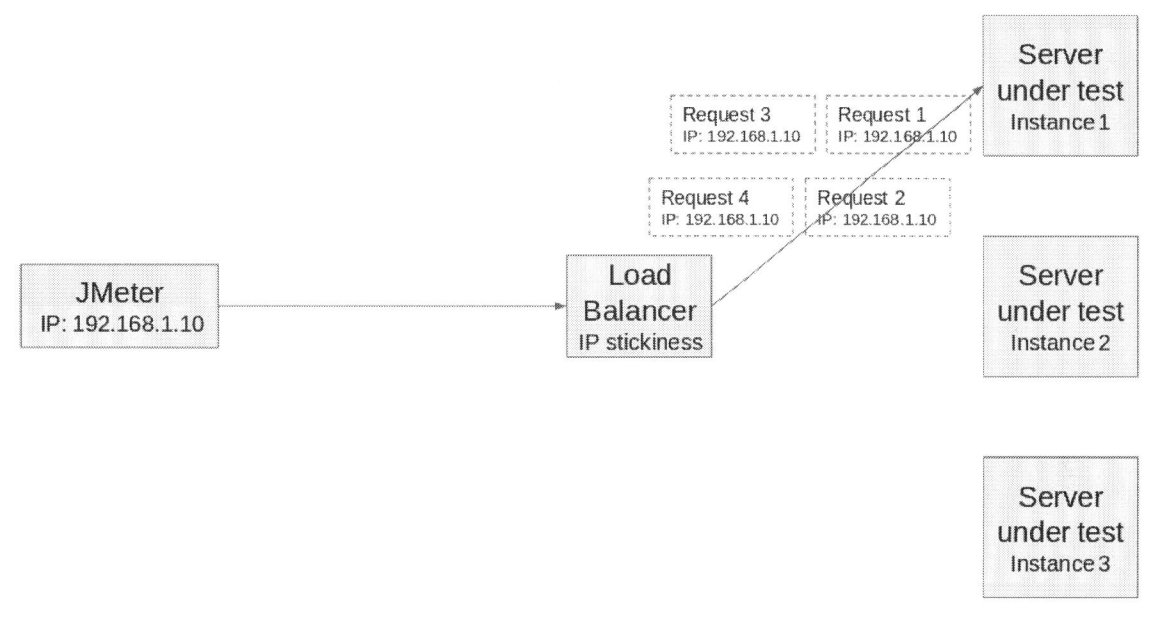

Figure 5.4: Testing without IP spoofing continued

For the same test with *IP spoofing*, JMeter will inject four queries with the source **IP** addresses of **192.168.1.10**, **192.168.1.11**, and **192.168.1.12**:

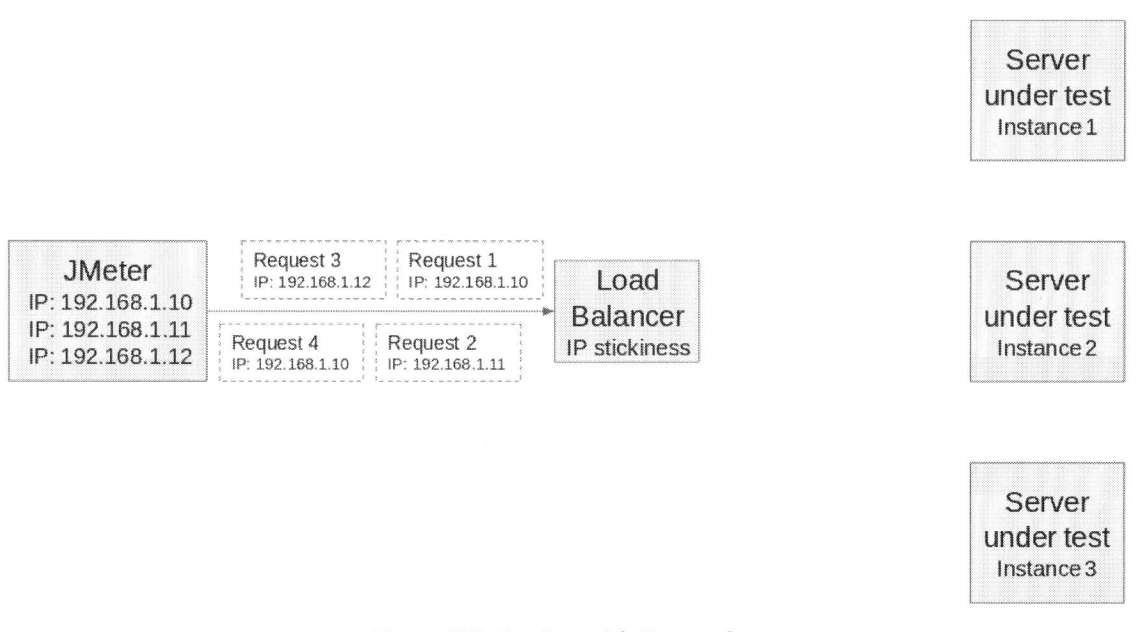

Figure 5.5: Testing with IP spoofing

The **Load Balancer** configured with **IP stickiness** will dispatch requests to all three instances:

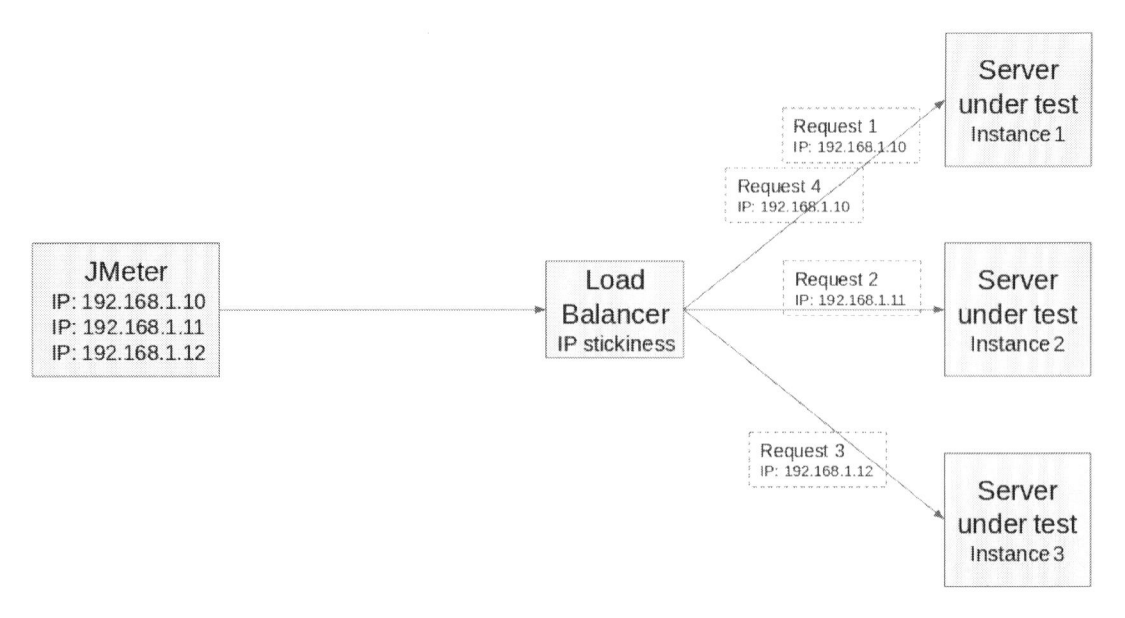

Figure 5.6: Testing with IP spoofing continued

If the **Load Balancer** is not configured with the **IP stickiness** option, the load will normally be distributed to all instances, but there is still the risk of the requests being blocked by a protection system.

> **Caution**
>
> In some cases, the IP affinity part of the test may be in the application code, and in such a case, setting up IP spoofing is mandatory.

Setting up IP spoofing:

- Attach several IP addresses to the network cards of our injectors.
- Put them in a CSV file:

	A	B
1	Ip_source	
2	192.168.1.10	
3	192.168.1.11	
4	192.168.1.12	
5		

Figure 5.7: A CSV file with IP addresses

- Use the **CSV Data Set Config** options in our script:

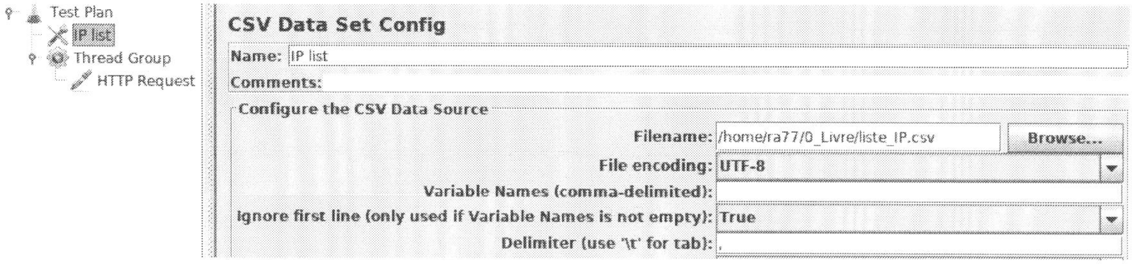

Figure 5.8: CSV Data Set Config

- Use the CSV file values in the **Advanced** -> **Source address** option of **HTTP Request**:

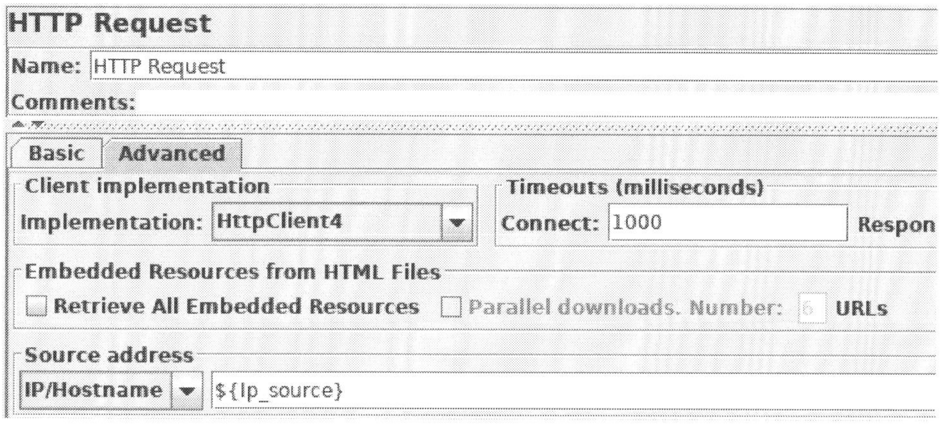

Figure 5.9: HTTP Request with IP spoofing

Using the Latest Version

As with many tools, using the latest version is recommended.

You can read the release notes (https://jmeter.apache.org/changes.html) to:

- See the performance improvement between each release
- See the new features introduced with each new version
- See the bugs that have been fixed and read about known problems
- See the productivity gains you can get by upgrading your version

JMeter Memory Configuration

By default, JMeter will use 1 GB for the JVM heap. But in some cases (such as when using a very complex script, or working with large datasets that require the downloading of very large files), this may not be enough.

If this is the case, create a **setenv.sh** file for Linux in the JMeter bin folder and adjust the values as follows (in our case, we use 2 GB for Xmx):

```
export HEAP="-Xms2g -Xmx2g -XX:MaxMetaspaceSize=256m"
```

Or, for Windows systems, create a **setenv.bat** file with the following values:

```
set HEAP="-Xms2g -Xmx2g -XX:MaxMetaspaceSize=256m"
```

Avoiding Load Testing behind a Proxy

In this case, you would be testing the proxy and not necessarily the target application.

Indeed, a proxy can be a bottleneck when testing. Do not forget that it might be used elsewhere by other employees in the company, introducing uncontrollable variables to the test, so we are not operating in reproducible and known conditions.

Preparation of the System under Test

The preparation of the system under test is just as important as that of the injectors.

A Testing Environment

To avoid wasting time finding bugs that are not related to performance, it is important to have a stable application that has been thoroughly tested.

If the load tests are written just before production deployment, there will be little time left for the tests.

This means that if the application has not been functionally and technically tested (for example, with unit and integration testing), every bug detected during the load tests will jeopardize the planned date for the start of production and under good conditions.

Load testing (even if it can be automated with continuous integration) should not be used to replace Non Regression testing.

Follow the *Testing Pyramid*:

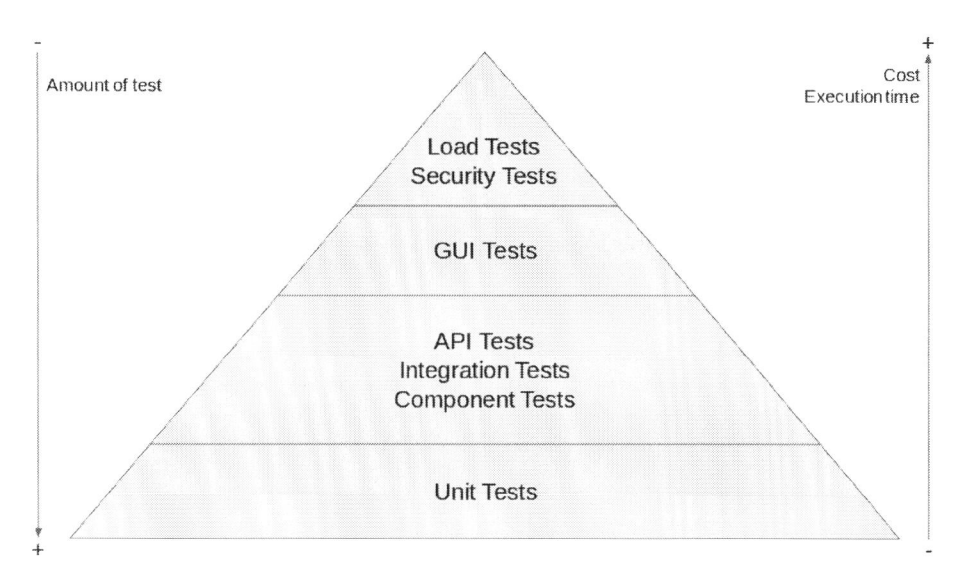

Figure 5.10: The testing pyramid

An Environment Consistent with the Target

Ideally, you should have an environment that is equivalent to the production environment.

By equivalent to the production environment, we mean using:

- The same hardware
- The same software
- The same configuration
- The same dataset
- The same application mapping

If this is not possible, focus on reducing the number of servers or their power, but maintain the same application architecture.

For example, if we have a cluster of four nodes in production and it is impossible to reproduce this for testing, then it is important to do either of the following:

- Keep a cluster of four nodes, but with less power
- Reduce the number of nodes in the cluster without removing the cluster functionality

Datasets

As for the data, it is important to have a sufficient volume of data and a good-quality dataset.

If data does not exist, it should be created (for example, via replication of the production database using a dataset creation tool such as Talend – note that databases also provide such tools).

If data already exists, ensure that it matches future needs. For example, if data for the first version exists, and we will test a future version, we must check that this new version will have the same volume of data as the first version).

Also, pay attention to the possibility of data exhaustion. If the script modifies data (for example, by simulating the purchase of a product), then there is a risk that after a number of iterations, you will run out of data, leading to a lot of errors.

If this happens, your results will contain a lot of false-positive results that have no relation to application stability or performance.

Take into Account Calls to Third-Party Services

> **Caution**
>
> Be careful if the application that will be tested uses an external service (such as a map server, an address validation service, or a Blue Card number validation server).

The external services must be informed, coordinated, and emulated before the load test.

This is for many reasons:
- To avoid being banned by the service, because it thinks it is under attack
- To avoid saturating the external service, because it is not the same size as the production system
- To avoid increasing costs if the service is licensed per call

If we want to test these calls, two solutions are possible:

- Ask the partners to provide an environment that has been sized and configured for the load test.
- Use mocks that will simulate these external services if possible.

Disabling Protection Systems

Many applications or infrastructures nowadays have DDoS protection or similar systems.

These systems are made to block bots or floods of requests coming from one machine. A JMeter instance is a **BOT** that floods the system from one machine, and as a consequence, there is a big chance that your load test will be blocked unless those protection systems are misconfigured.

If you don't disable these systems, your load test will probably fail and you'll spend a lot of time trying to investigate the root cause. As such, it is critical to disable protection systems, including:

- *Web Application Firewall*
- Bot detection
- CAPTCHA
- Load balancer protection

Using Isolated Environments

The main advantage of an isolated environment is the ability to analyze test results by eliminating external and unexpected causes.

For example, let's say that when analyzing results, we notice that for 10 minutes, our response times deteriorated.

Several hypotheses that could explain this come to mind:

- It may be because of the other users who were working on the application, such as someone from the QA team starting a nightly batch.
- It may be because we used a production image of the database (to avoid having to recreate one for the test) and there was something scheduled at that period (such as a maintenance batch, or peak usage).

It is critical that our load test does not impact other environments. Indeed, since we used a production image of the database, if we don't use a dedicated mail server, we might end up sending emails to real customers.

License Management

In some cases, the tested environment will use a service/product with a per-use license price (this is common, for example, with cloud services). To avoid any unwanted surprises, ensure that you know every component of the environment and check each of their licenses.

Monitoring

If the test results are not as expected, we will have to investigate the cause. So, the more accurate and relevant the monitoring is, the easier the analysis will be. Ensure that you set up monitoring from the beginning if possible, so as not to be *blind*.

Conclusion

As we have seen, controlling our environment (both the injectors and the system under test) will allow us to perform our tests under good conditions and to safely analyze the results.

6

Being Productive with JMeter

Introduction

We have seen how to prepare environments and choose the correct use cases to load test. Now it's time to move on to scripting.

The scripting process can take a lot of time without:

- Good preparation
- Knowledge of best practices (recording and debugging)
- An understanding of the JMeter ecosystem

Good Practices When Recording a Script

Use the HTTP(S) Test Script Recorder Element

We saw in *Chapter 1, Quick start with Jmeter*, the use of **HTTP(S) Test Script Recorder** for the recording of our script by navigating on the target application. But we can go even further if a test script (whether it be for integration or functional) has already been created with tools such as:

- Postman (https://www.getpostman.com/)
- SoapUI (https://www.soapui.org/)
- Selenium (https://www.seleniumhq.org/)
- Swagger (https://swagger.io/)

All you need to do is:

- Configure the test tool to use a JMeter proxy (here's an example of this using Postman: https://www.getpostman.com/docs/v6/postman/sending_api_requests/proxy)
- Launch **HTTP(S) Test Script Recorder**
- Run the test script
- Finalize the script saved in JMeter

BlazeMeter Chrome Extension

If the preceding solution does not suit you, you can use the BlazeMeter Chrome extension (https://chrome.google.com/webstore/detail/blazemeter-the-continuous/mbopgmdnpcbohhpnfglgohlbhfongabi).

Once the extension is installed, you end up with an interface to configure and launch the recording:

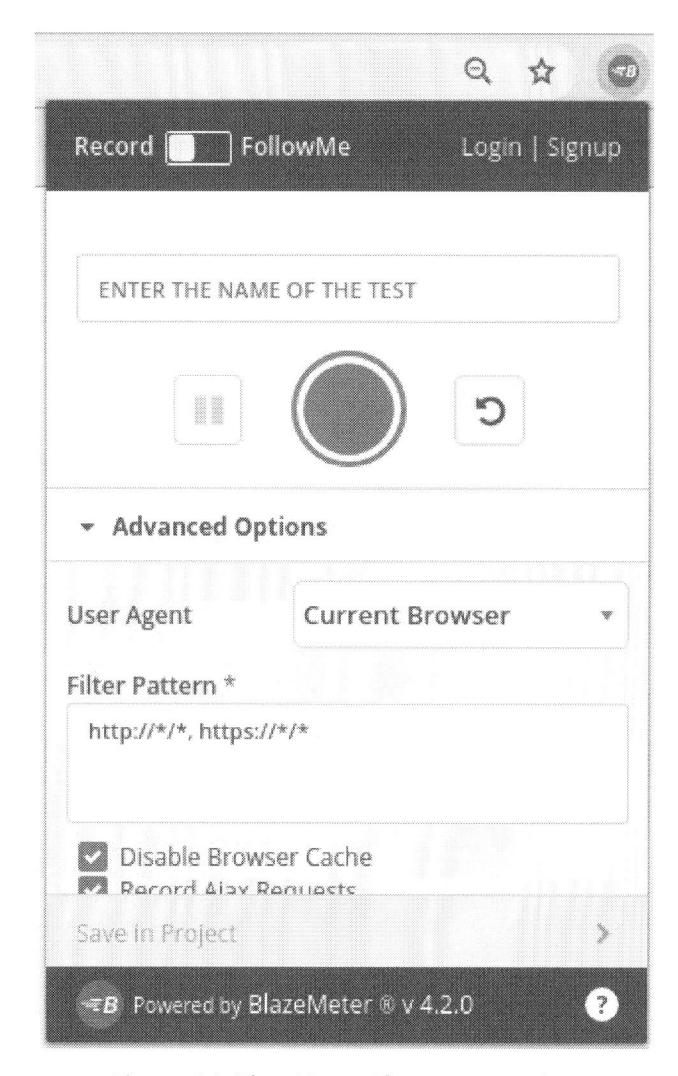

Figure 6.1: BlazeMeter Chrome extension

Once the recording is done, we can export to JMeter format (JMX).

The benefit of this extension is that it eases the proxy configuration if you use an Enterprise proxy when hitting your target application.

The drawback is that if your data needs to remain confidential, you may not be allowed to use it.

Figure 6.2: Export in JMX format

Pre-Populating HTTP Request Defaults before Recording the Script

Another trick already discussed in *Chapter 1, Quick start with Jmeter* is to pre-fill the **HTTP Request Defaults** element.

For example, if we fill in the *host*, it will not be filled in any of the **HTTP Request** that composes the script and has the same value as the one set in **HTTP Request Defaults**. As such, the modification of this *host* will only be necessary for **HTTP Request Defaults** and no longer in each HTTP request. This makes the script more robust to environment changes.

Use Tools / Import from cURL

The JMeter 5.1 release integrated a new tool called **Import from cURL**. The JMeter 5.2 release (not yet released but you can use a nightly build) has improved this feature a lot. In the next example, we will use this release.

> **Note**
>
> Swagger can generate curl command.

We will use httpbin.org (http://httpbin.org/) to have some `curl` commands.

curl -X GET "http://httpbin.org/user-agent" -H "accept: application/json"

curl -X GET "http://httpbin.org/get" -H "accept: application/json"

Now we can go to **Tools | Import from cURL** and use the previous two `curl` commands:

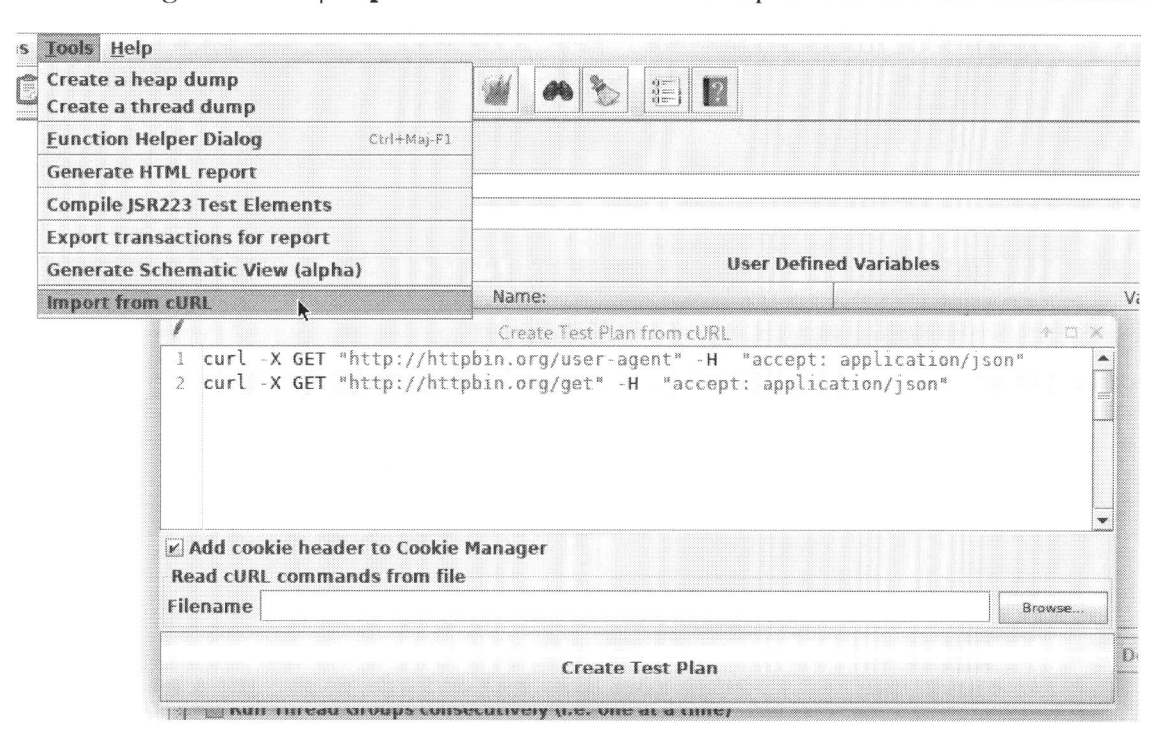

Figure 6.3: Tools | Import from cURL

As we can see, we have a preconfigured *test plan*.

Figure 6.4: Test plan generated by cURL

We can execute it without a problem.

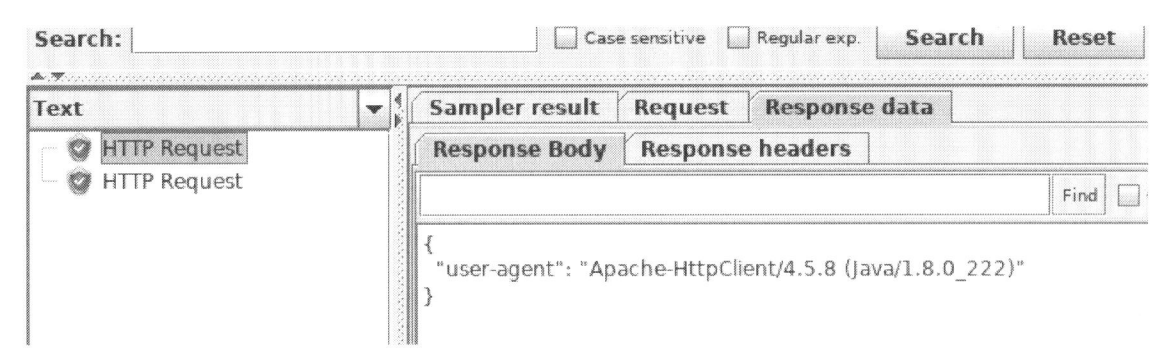

Figure 6.5: Execution of the test plan

We still need to add **Assertions**, **Timer**, **Post processors**, and more, but we have saved a lot of time.

Static Resources

Do not forget that JMeter is not a browser; the management of static resources may differ from how it would be in a real browser.

There are several possibilities for managing static resources in our tests.

Solution 1: Do Not Take Them into Account

This solution is useful in cases where static resources are not hosted on the tested server (that is, where a **Content Delivery Network (CDN)** is used instead) and/or we want to test only the *backend*.

In JMeter, when saving, remember to disable their recording by using **Requests Filtering** -> **URL Patterns to Exclude** option of **HTTP(S) Test Script Recorder**:

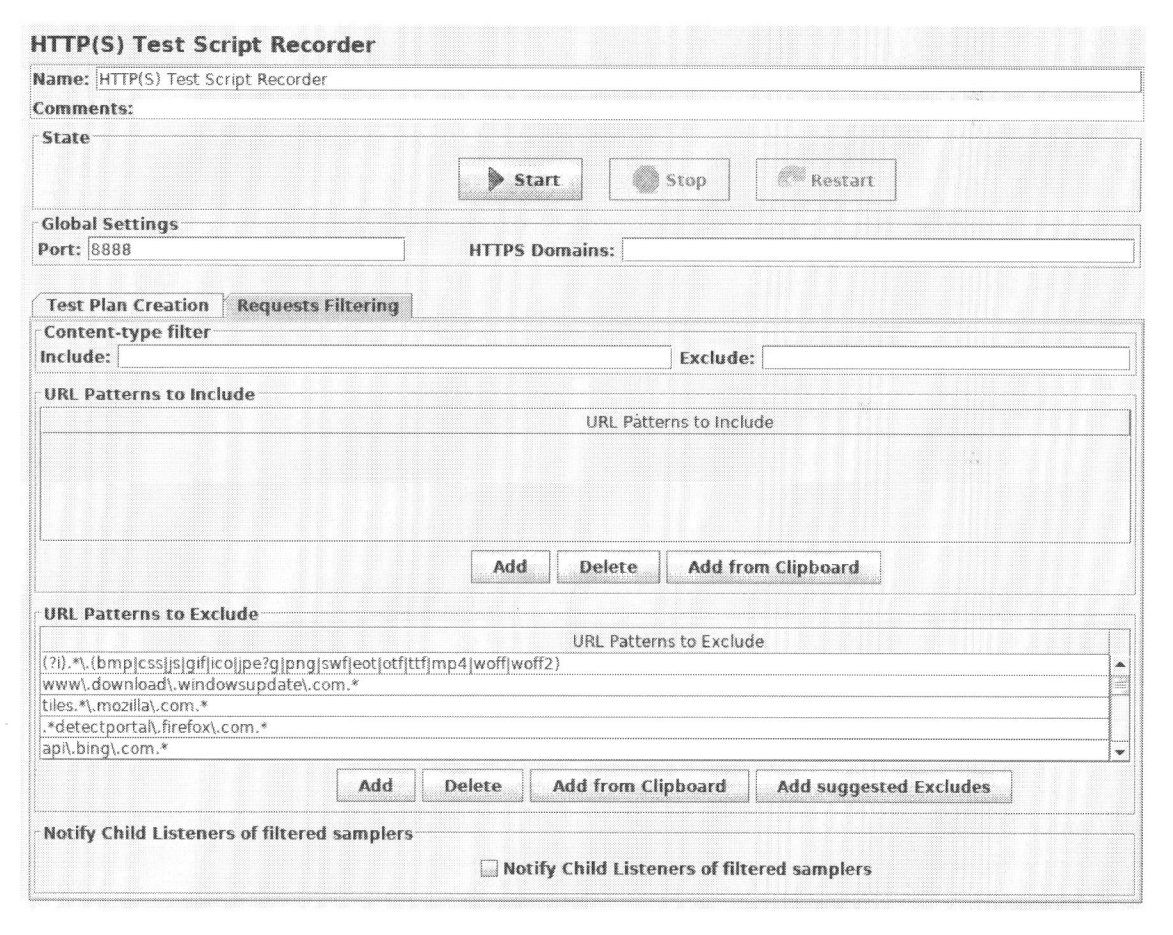

Figure 6.6: Filtering the static resources

Solution 2: Let JMeter Manage the Static Resources

The second solution is to ask JMeter to dynamically load the static resources when running the script.

JMeter allows this in the **Advanced -> Embedded Resources from HTML Files** option of **HTTP Request Defaults**:

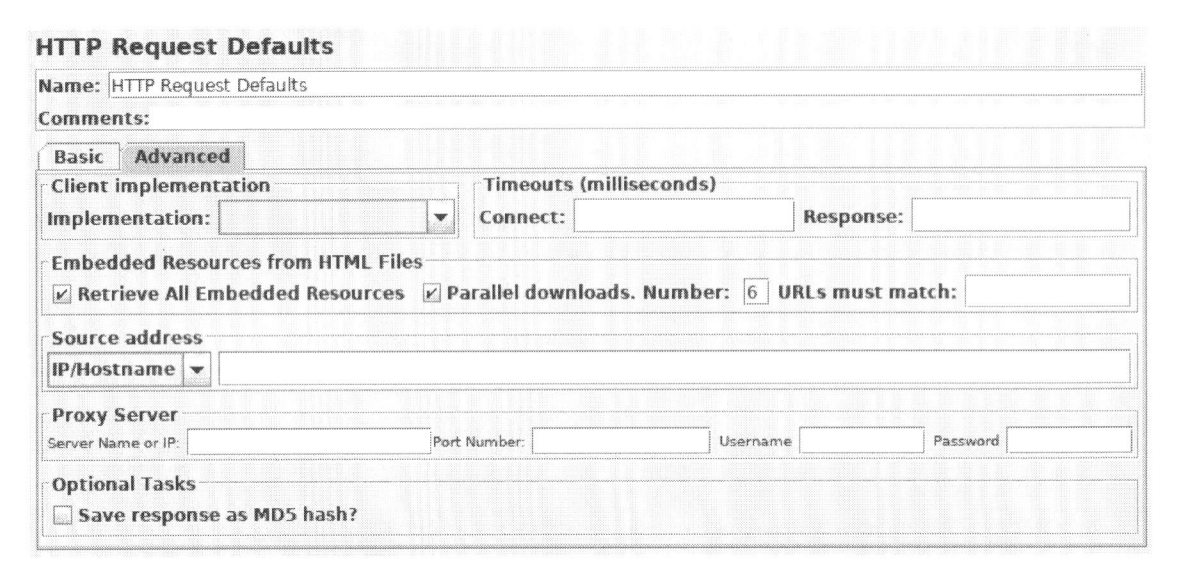

Figure 6.7: Dynamic discovery of static resources

At first sight, this seems to be the ideal solution:

- You can record the script on any environment (even in the development environment without the final static resources).
- If the static resources change during the test campaign, there is no need to modify the script.
- If the static resources change during the execution of the test (and/or change with each load), there is no need to modify the script.
- The script is made less complex.
- You can load static resources in parallel (otherwise, you would need to use the Parallel Controller plugin: https://github.com/Blazemeter/jmeter-bzm-plugins/blob/master/parallel/Parallel.md).

Unfortunately, JMeter is not a browser, and a number of webperf rules may not be taken into account:

Lazy loading of images

- Loading the right size image according to the resolution of the screen
- Loading the correct image format according to the browser (for example, WebP (https://en.wikipedia.org/wiki/WebP) needs to be used for Chrome)
- Loading any resource that would be loaded by some JavaScript code

Solution 3: Manage the Static Resources Ourselves

The third possibility is to capture static resources directly when recording.

This solution avoids the problems of solution 2; unfortunately, we lose the benefits of it at the same time, particularly the ability to load static resources in parallel, which will make our script unrealistic compared to that of a real browser.

Using Timeouts

Filling out the *Timeouts (milliseconds)* option of **HTTP Request** means you don't have to wait for an SUT response indefinitely.

This will provide the following benefits:

- Allow JMeter to stop at the end of the test without waiting indefinitely for hanging requests. By default, the timeout is infinite in HTTP Request.
- Avoid lowering the load whenever SUT slows down. This might be considered Coordinated Omission.
- No *unreadable* HTML reports at the end of the test.

During one of our tests, we did not use timeout – this is the result:

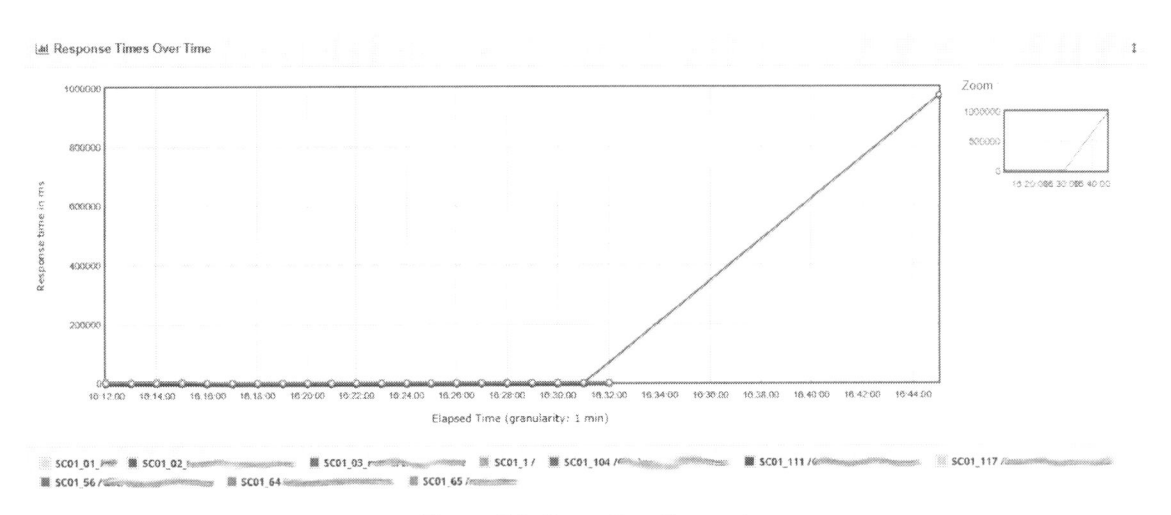

Figure 6.8: Forgotten timeout

Applying a Naming Convention to Transactions/Requests

As you will see throughout this book, I always use a naming convention to facilitate the analysis of results (HTML report, simplified use of filters/regex, and so on).

During recording, the **HTTP sampler settings** option of **HTTP(S) Test Script Recorder** greatly simplifies this task:

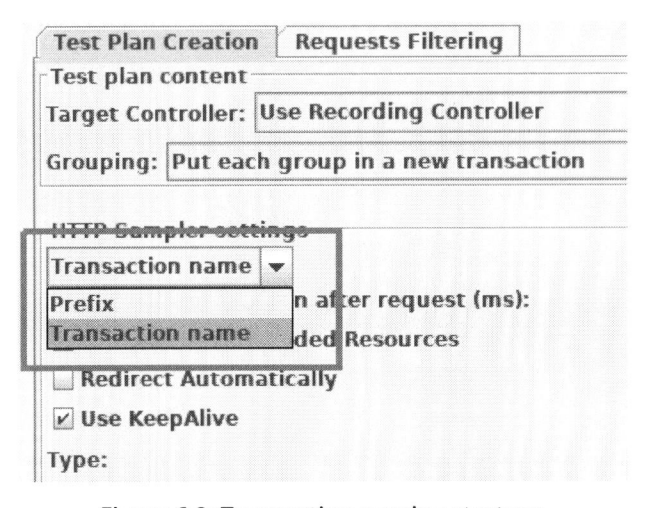

Figure 6.9: Transaction naming strategy

After recording, you can name the requests of business transactions using the **Apply naming policy** pop-up menu:

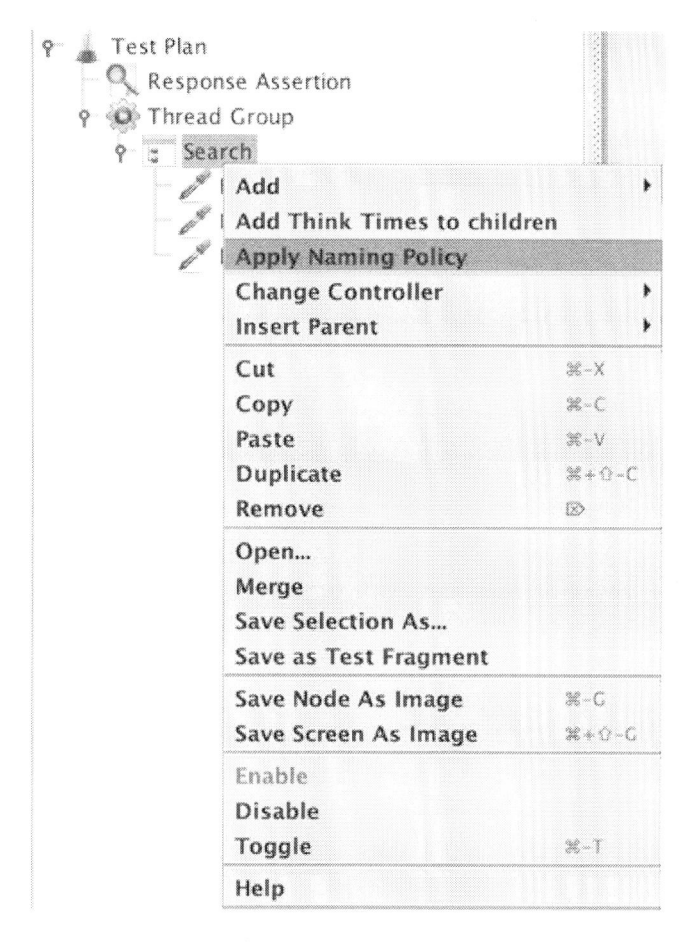

Figure 6.10: Before applying the naming strategy

After applying the renaming strategy, you end up with:

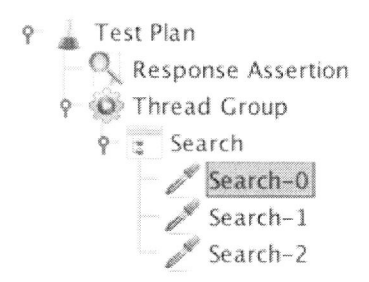

Figure 6.11: After applying the naming strategy

Thanks to this, when generating the report, JMeter will be able to understand that the three HTTP requests under the **Search** transaction are related and will only mention **Search** while keeping the details about subrequests' errors.

Global Assertion

If we need to check the result of all our queries with the same assertion, you might think we need to duplicate it for each query. Thanks to JMeter's **scoping rules**, it is possible to add only one query at the highest level, making the scope global.

For example, if we want to check that our requests on the *Oracle database* do not return an error, it will be enough in our **Assertion** to test for the absence of ORA-:

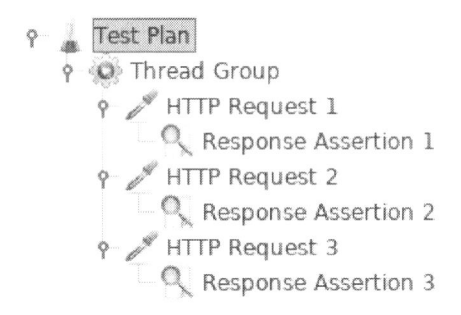

```
Test Plan
 Thread Group
  HTTP Request 1
   Response Assertion 1
  HTTP Request 2
   Response Assertion 2
  HTTP Request 3
   Response Assertion 3
```

Figure 6.12: Duplication of assertions

```
Test Plan
 Thread Group
  HTTP Request 1
  HTTP Request 2
  HTTP Request 3
  Response Assertion Global
```

Figure 6.13: The equivalent with a single assertion

Understanding scoping rules (https://jmeter.apache.org/usermanual/test_plan.html#scoping_rules) is critical to using JMeter properly.

Reusing Script Parts

Always try to avoid the duplication of code (for example, login step on different scripts). To achieve this goal, we can use:

- **Include Controller** to include external scripts
- **Module Controller** if we're reusing parts of the same script

To use **Include Controller**, the first step is to save the part of the script that we want to reuse with **Save Selection As...**:

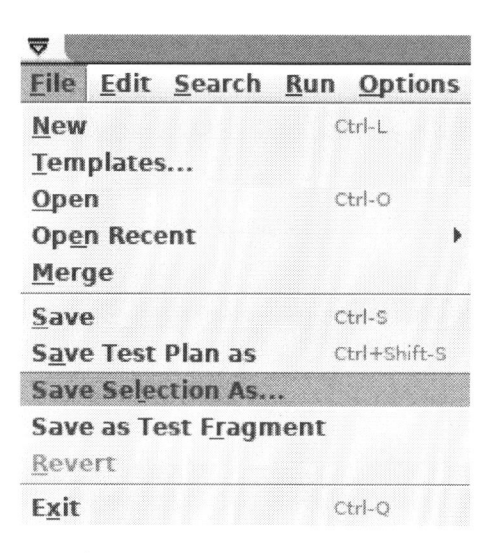

Figure 6.14: Save Selection As...

Then use **Include Controller** to import this part of the script:

Figure 6.15: Include Controller

Recording an HTTPS website

To be able to record an HTTPS site, JMeter uses a **Root CA certificate**. JMeter creates this certificate when we first start **HTTP(S) Test Script Recorder**; you then need to import it into your browser.

By default, this certificate is valid for 7 days. In order to increase the validity period, we must add the `proxy.cert.validity= property` with the desired value in days to the `/bin/user.properties` file.

Once we start **HTTP(S) Test Script Recorder**, a popup appears with the details of the **Root CA certificate**:

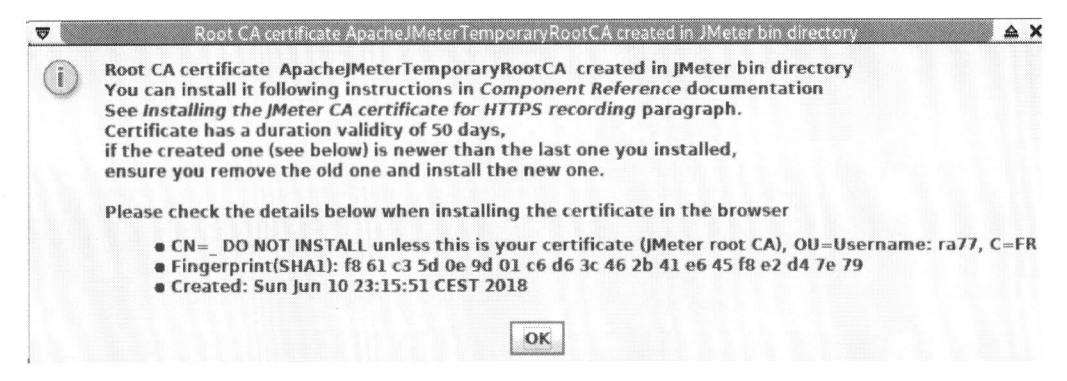

Figure 6.16: Root CA certificate

Ensure you import it as an authority and not as a user or server certificate:

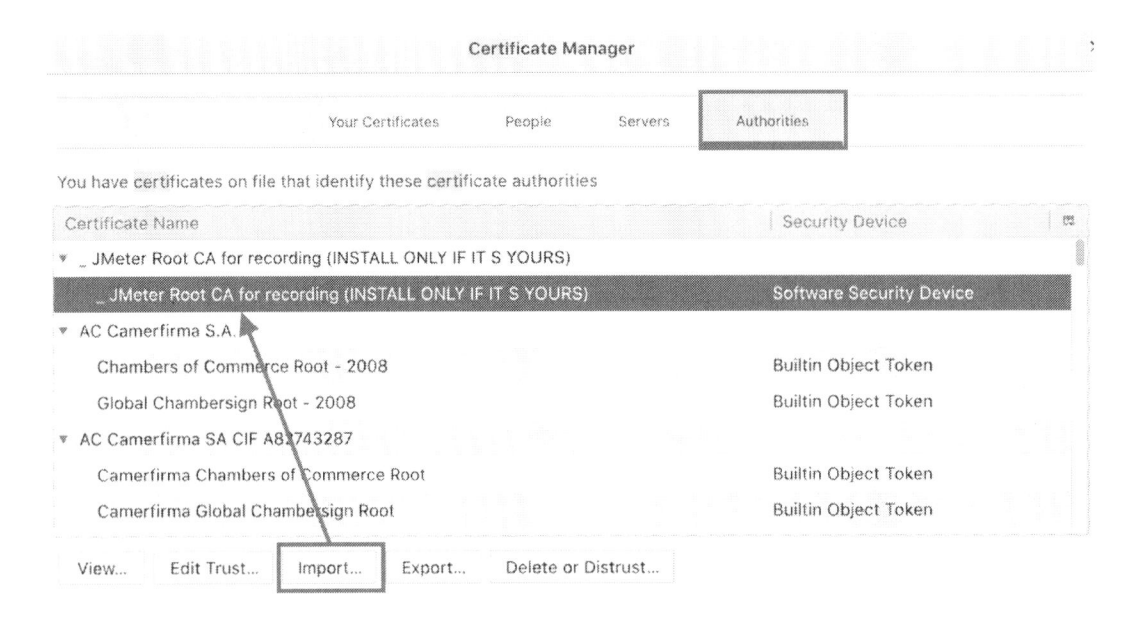

Figure 6.17: Importing the JMeter certificate as an authority certificate

Keyboard Shortcuts

JMeter has several keyboard shortcuts for common actions (such as saving and copying). In addition to these shortcuts, 10 customizable shortcuts allow us to add elements to our script. These shortcuts can be modified, if they do not suit your needs, using the following options in the **jmeter.properties** file:

```
# Hotkeys to add JMeter components, will add elements when you press Ctrl+0
.. Ctrl+9 (Command+0 .. Command+9 on Mac)
gui.quick_0=ThreadGroupGui
gui.quick_1=HttpTestSampleGui
gui.quick_2=RegexExtractorGui
gui.quick_3=AssertionGui
gui.quick_4=ConstantTimerGui
gui.quick_5=TestActionGui
gui.quick_6=JSR223PostProcessor
gui.quick_7=JSR223PreProcessor
gui.quick_8=DebugSampler
gui.quick_9=ViewResultsFullVisualizer
```

Debugging a script

It can be difficult to debug a simulation script, whatever tool you use. Fortunately, JMeter offers a powerful IDE for debugging these scripts. It is also possible to use plugins.

Using View Results Tree

The easiest way is to use **View Results Tree** to get the content of queries and responses:

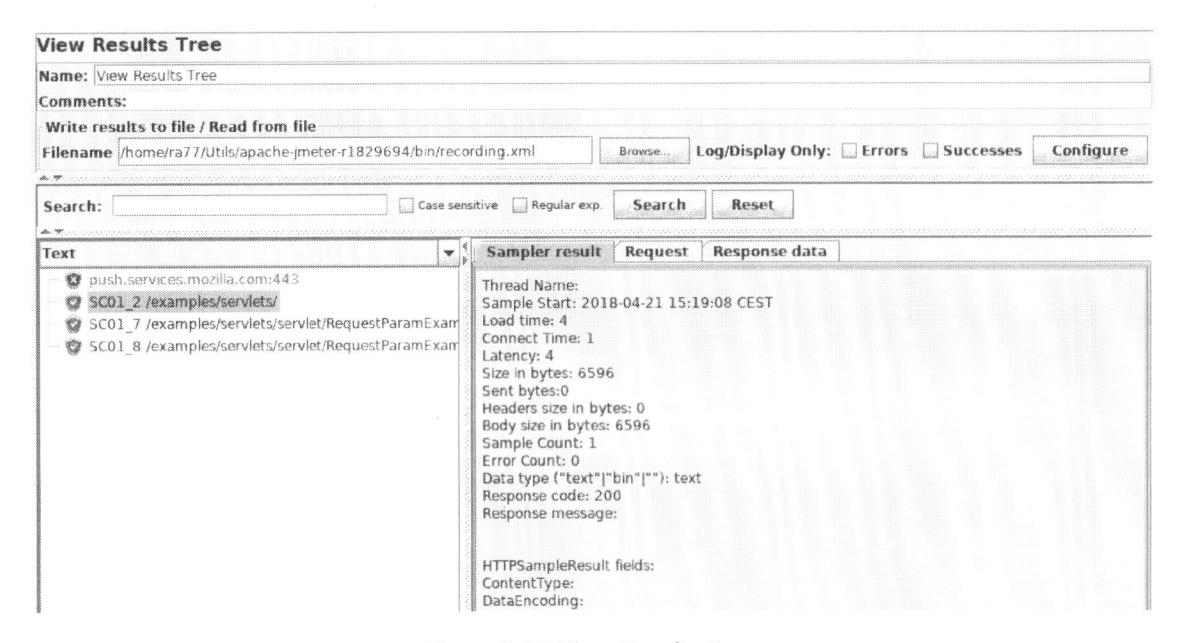

Figure 6.18: View Results Tree

In addition to seeing the content, we can use all the **testers** available in JMeter.

For every extractor, there is a tester available:

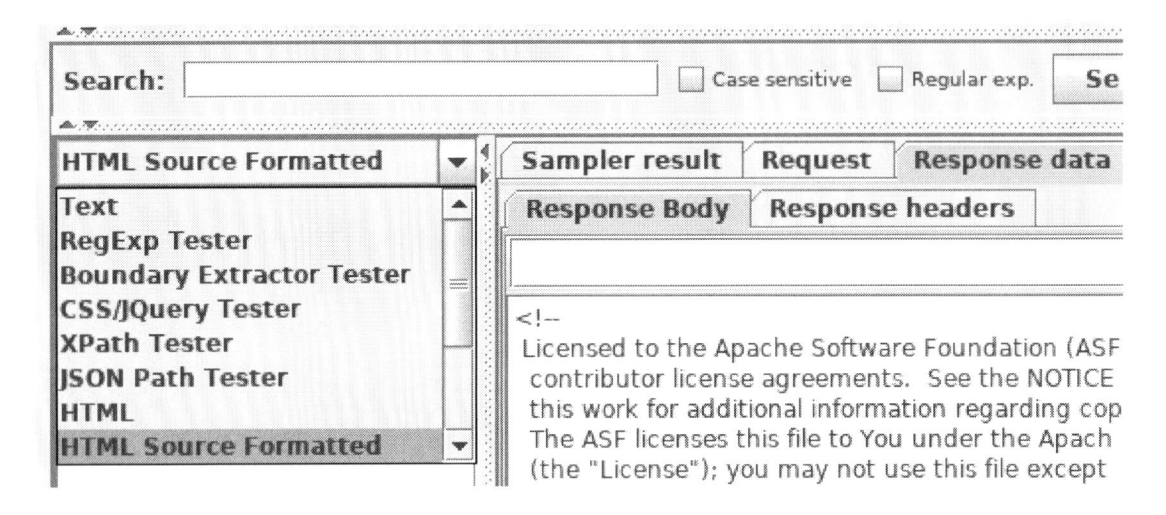

Figure 6.19: List of testers

We can find:

- **CSS Selector Tester**
- **JSON Path Tester**
- **RegExp Tester**
- **Boundary Extractor Tester**
- **XPath2 Tester**
- **XPath Tester**

This allows us to validate our *Extractor* configuration:

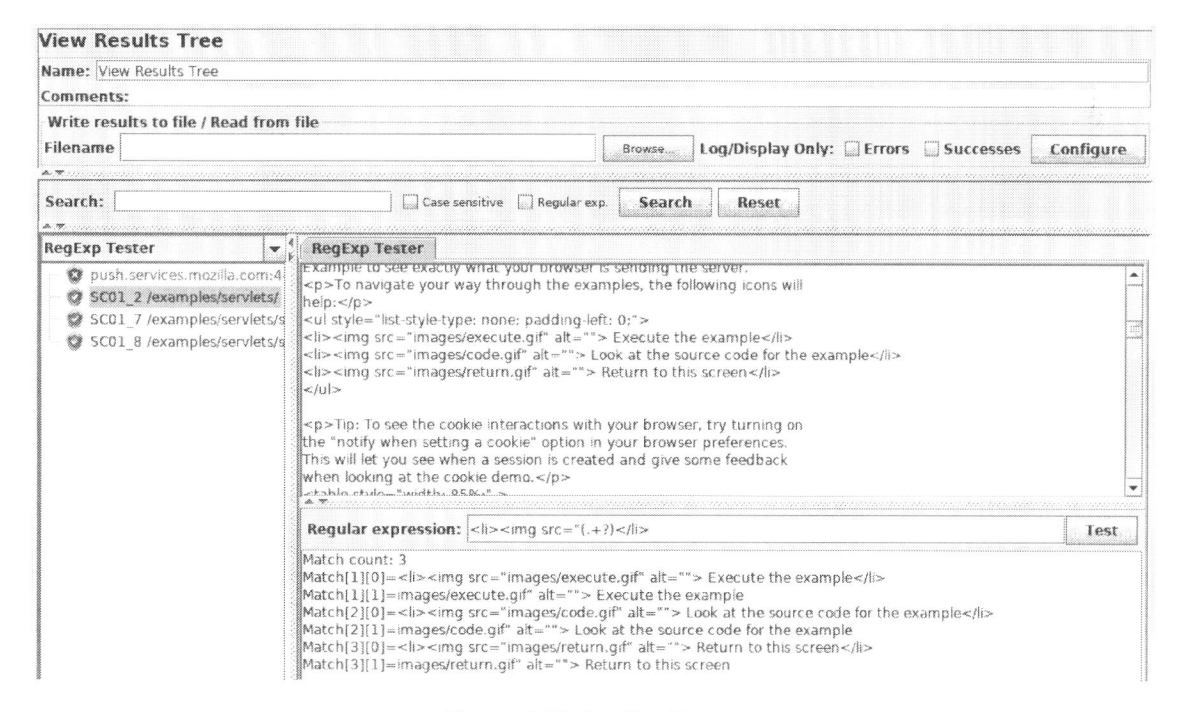

Figure 6.20: RegExp Tester

Capturing Errors

The trick of using the **View Results Tree** element is useful, but it would be even better if we only recorded samples that were in error.

This is possible with the **Log/Display Only** -> **Errors** option:

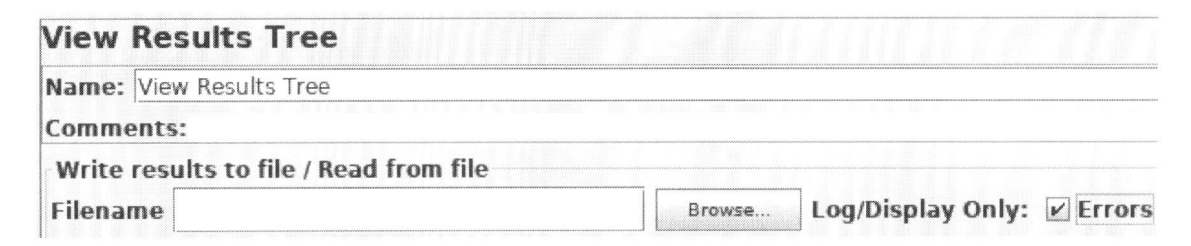

Figure 6.21: Save only samples in error

If we associate this option with viewers, such as the following, then we can quickly see the root cause of errors:

- **HTML**
- **HTML Source Formatted**
- **HTML (download resources)**
- **Browser** (requires JavaFX; we have to install this library if not using Oracle JDK 8):

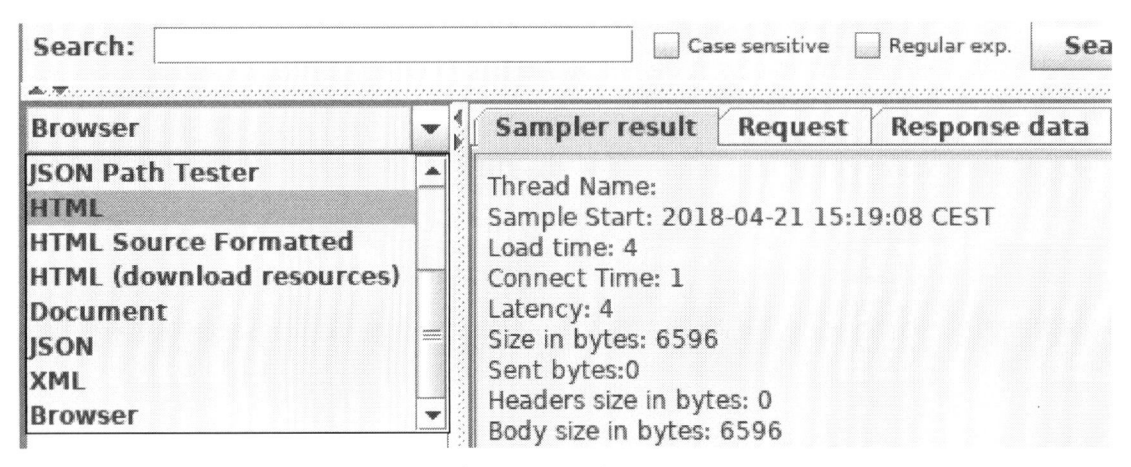

Figure 6.22: Viewers

Debug Sampler

Debug Sampler allows you to take a snapshot of the following values to visualize them at the time of the sampler's execution:

- **JMeter properties**
- **JMeter variables**
- **System properties**:

Figure 6.23: Debug Sampler

In the following example, we display the value of **JMeterBookDebug**, which we retrieved using a **Boundary Extractor** element in our **Debug Sampler**:

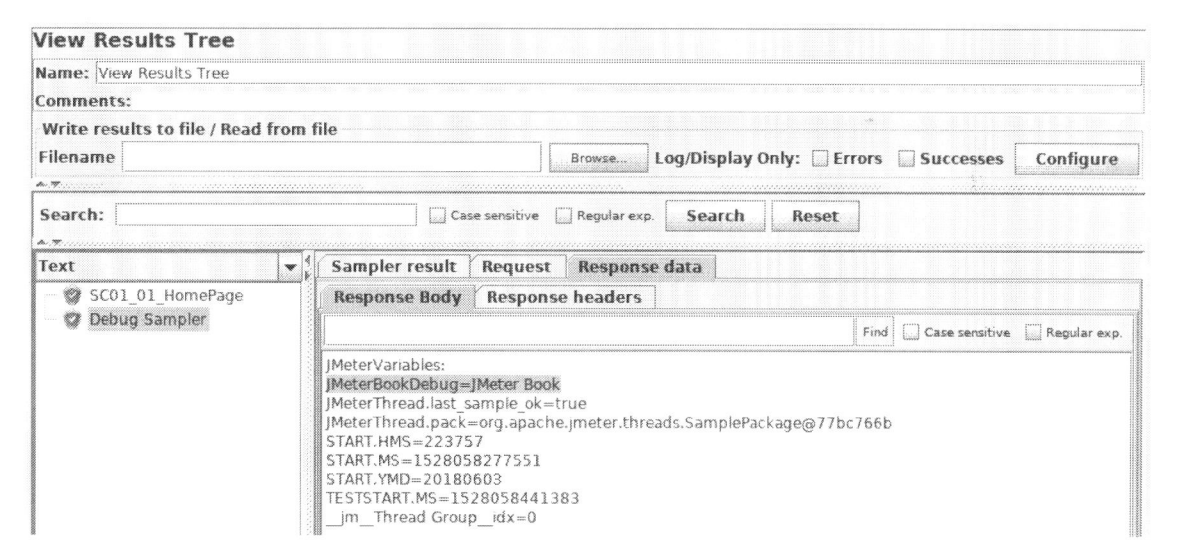

Figure 6.24: Result of our Debug Sampler

jp@gc - Dummy Sampler

jp@gc - Dummy Sampler is part of the JMeter plugins (https://jmeter-plugins.org/wiki/DummySampler/) and simulates a query and its response:

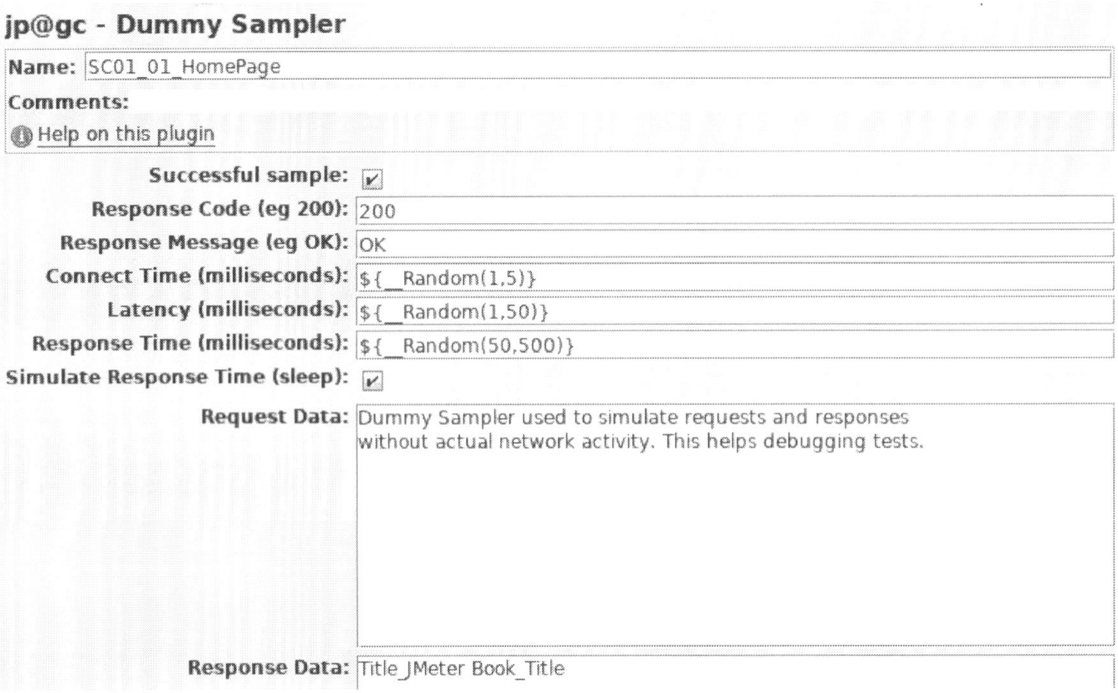

Figure 6.25: jp@gc - Dummy Sampler

A built-in alternative is to use **Java Request**, selecting `Classname org.apache.jmeter.protocol.java.test.JavaTest` and filling in the `ResponseCode`, `ResponseMessage`, and `SamplerData` or `ResultData` parameters.

With these benefits:

- There is no need to wait until the target application is tested and operational to test your script.
- It is possible to compare the performance/adaptability of JMeter elements (such as **Pre Processors**, **Post Processors**, and **Config Element**).
- You can test an item on a particular response that does not often occur.
- You can debug a test item without having to run the preceding steps.
- You can validate assertions.

Debugging a script | 115

For example, we want to validate that JMeter does not count a **404** response as an error:

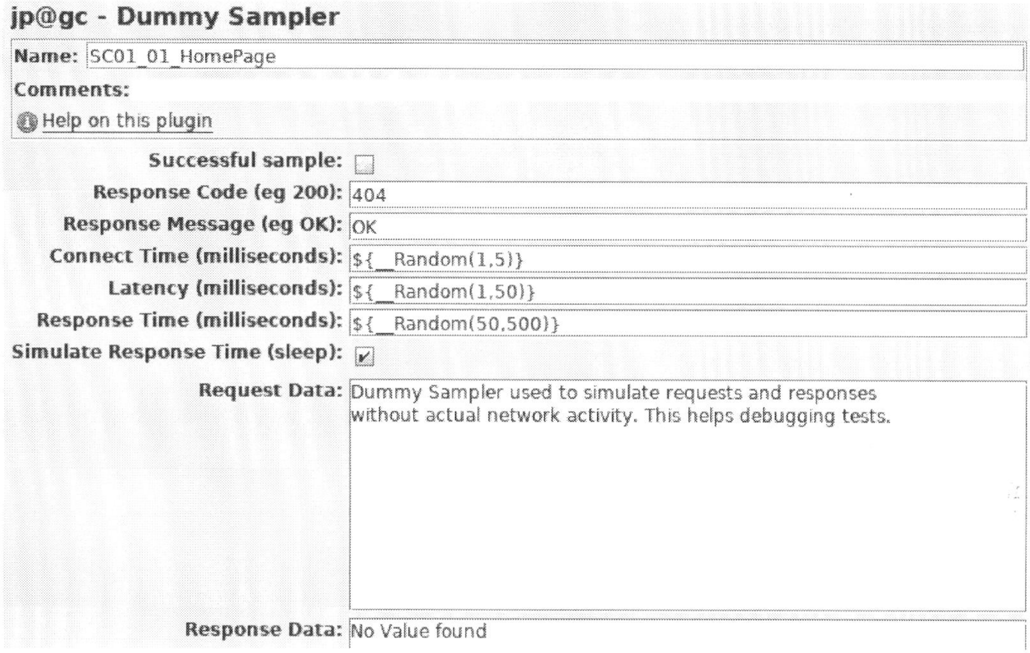

Figure 6.26: Dummy Sampler - 404 response

In our **Response Assertion**, we check the **Ignore Status** option and test the **No Value found** string:

Figure 6.27: Response Assertion using Ignore Status

With a **View Results Tree**, we validate that our **Response Assertion** is valid:

Figure 6.28: Validation of our Response Assertion with Ignore Status

Without the **Ignore Status** option, the sample fails:

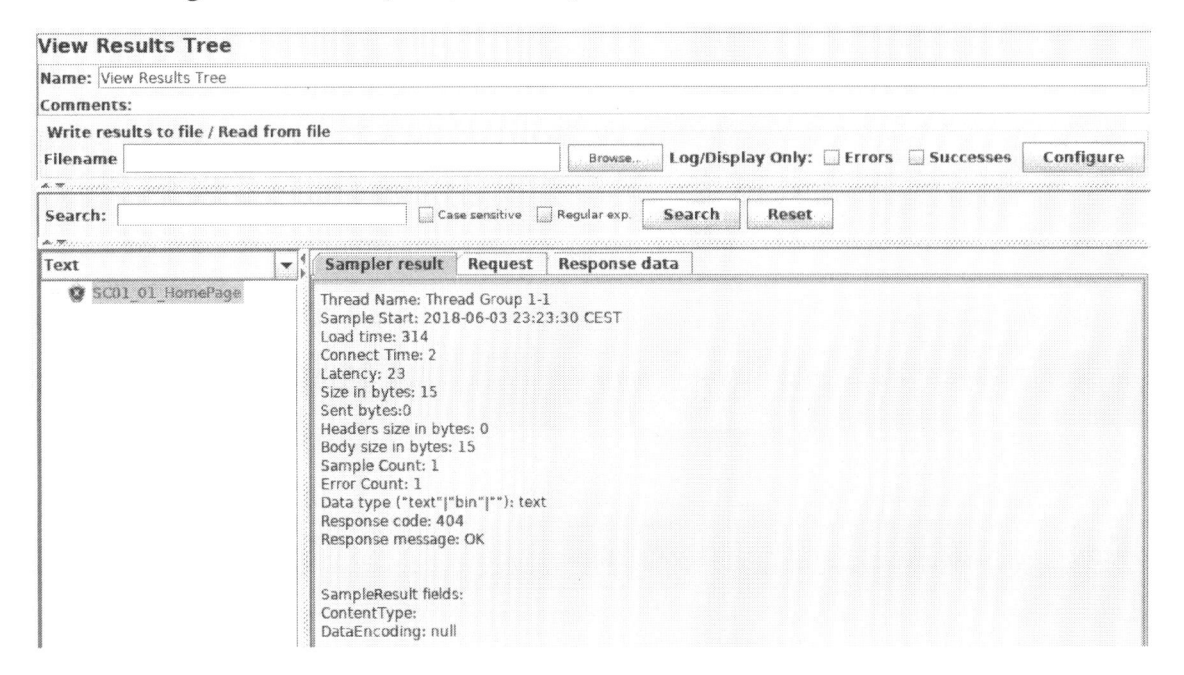

Figure 6.29: Response Assertion without the Ignore Status option

Log Viewer

There are a number of interesting log entries (such as CSV *file not present*) that can be seen in **Log Viewer**.

Log entries can be generated with our custom logs using `log.error`, `log.warn`, `log.info`, and so on in **JSR223 Sampler**. JMeter actually uses SLF4J as a log framework:

```
log.info("This is an INFO level log")
log.warn("This is a WARNING level log")
log.error("This is an ERROR level log")
```

To access **Log Viewer**, there are two options:

- Access through the GUI at the top right:

Figure 6.30: Access Log Viewer by GUI

- Access via the menu:

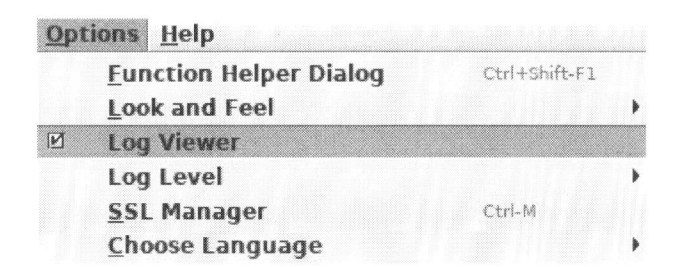

Figure 6.31: Access Log Viewer via the menu

Here is an example of an error message triggered by **CSV Data Set Config** elements when a CSV file is not found:

```
11  2018-06-03 23:29:53,593 INFO o.a.j.s.FileServer: Stored: /home/ra77/O_Livre/O_jmx/Chap8.csv
12  2018-06-03 23:29:53,594 ERROR o.a.j.t.JMeterThread: Test failed!
13  java.lang.IllegalArgumentException: Could not read file header line for file /home/ra77/O_Livre/O_jmx/Chap8.csv
14      at org.apache.jmeter.services.FileServer.reserveFile(FileServer.java:283) ~[ApacheJMeter_core.jar:r1832778]
15      at org.apache.jmeter.config.CSVDataSet.iterationStart(CSVDataSet.java:183) ~[ApacheJMeter_components.jar:r1832778]
16      at org.apache.jmeter.control.GenericController.fireIterationStart(GenericController.java:399) ~[ApacheJMeter_core.jar
17      at org.apache.jmeter.control.GenericController.fireIterEvents(GenericController.java:391) ~[ApacheJMeter_core.jar:r18
18      at org.apache.jmeter.control.GenericController.next(GenericController.java:160) ~[ApacheJMeter_core.jar:r1832778]
19      at org.apache.jmeter.control.LoopController.next(LoopController.java:130) ~[ApacheJMeter_core.jar:r1832778]
20      at org.apache.jmeter.threads.AbstractThreadGroup.next(AbstractThreadGroup.java:87) ~[ApacheJMeter_core.jar:r1832778]
21      at org.apache.jmeter.threads.JMeterThread.run(JMeterThread.java:251) [ApacheJMeter_core.jar:r1832778]
22      at java.lang.Thread.run(Thread.java:748) [?:1.8.0_172]
23  Caused by: java.lang.IllegalArgumentException: File Chap8.csv must exist and be readable
24      at org.apache.jmeter.services.FileServer.createBufferedReader(FileServer.java:424) ~[ApacheJMeter_core.jar:r1832778]
25      at org.apache.jmeter.services.FileServer.readLine(FileServer.java:340) ~[ApacheJMeter_core.jar:r1832778]
26      at org.apache.jmeter.services.FileServer.readLine(FileServer.java:324) ~[ApacheJMeter_core.jar:r1832778]
27      at org.apache.jmeter.services.FileServer.reserveFile(FileServer.java:272) ~[ApacheJMeter_core.jar:r1832778]
```

Figure 6.32: Log Viewer and CSV file not found

Note that at the top right of our GUI, the number of errors (here, there is one) appears in red:

Figure 6.33: GUI and CSV file not found

If necessary, we can change the log level to be more verbose in the JMeter GUI by going to **Option** -> **Log Level**:

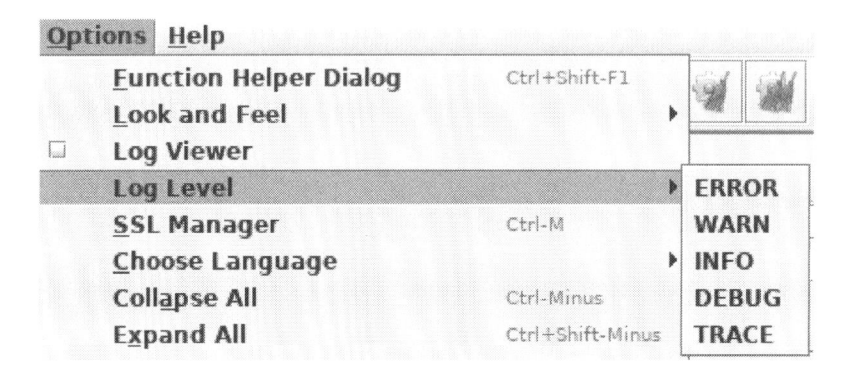

Figure 6.34: Changing the log level

BlazeMeter's Step-by-Step Debugger

Step-by-Step Debugger (https://github.com/Blazemeter/jmeter-debugger) is a debugger created by BlazeMeter (https://www.blazemeter.com/).

As with an IDE debugger (such as one for Eclipse, NetBeans, or IntelliJ), it allows you to:

- Run the script step by step
- Set breakpoints
- Evaluate expressions
- View JMeter variables/properties/logs

As for the vast majority of JMeter plugins, installation is made easy by JMeter Plugins Manager (https://jmeter-plugins.org/wiki/PluginsManager/).

Once installed, it appears in the **Run** menu:

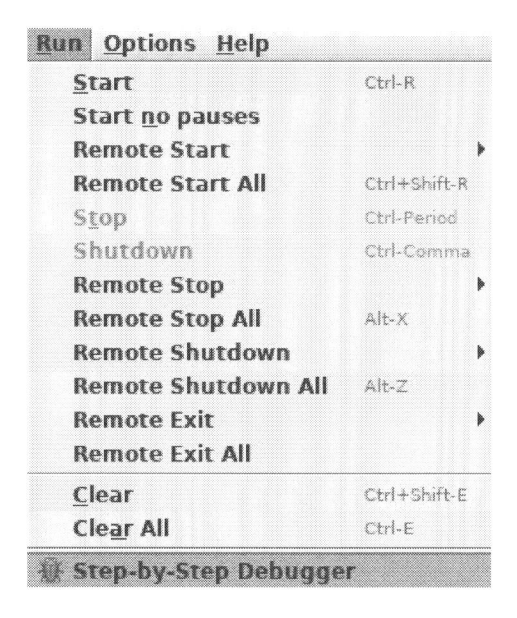

Figure 6.35: Access to Step-by-Step Debugger

We end up with a window that opens with a fairly simple GUI:

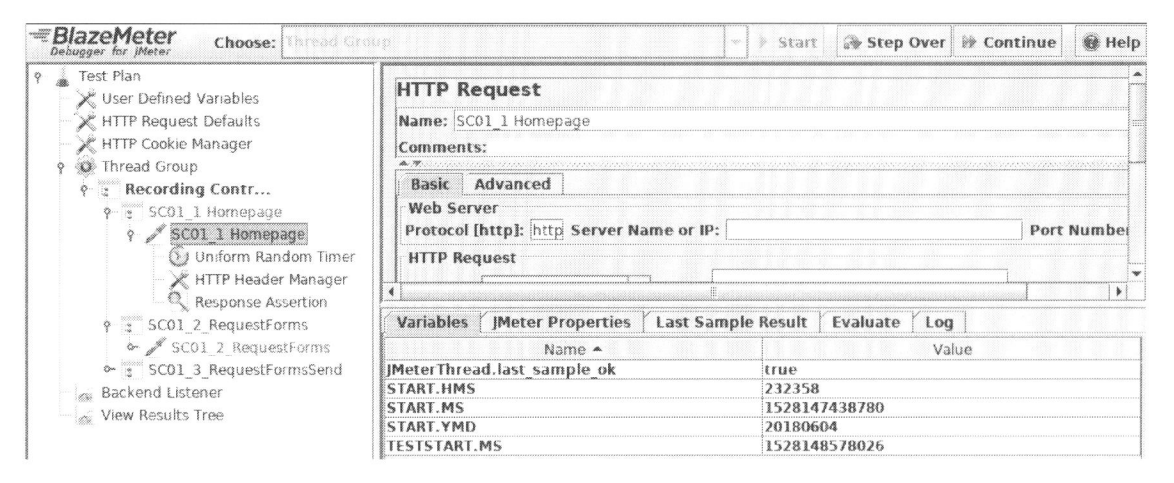

Figure 6.36: Step-by-Step Debugger

Still, this plugin can be rather intrusive upon JMeter behavior and can sometimes trigger issues that would not occur without it, so be aware of this when using it.

The Old-Fashioned Way in the Console

In **JSR223 Sampler**, we have OUT, which allows writing to the console:

```
OUT.println("My console message");
```

> **Note**
>
> For performance reasons, it is better to use the logging mechanism!

Using a Third-Party Tool

Alternatively, we can use a third-party tool that allows us to sniff/capture network packets:

- Wireshark (https://www.wireshark.org/)
- Fiddler (https://www.telerik.com/fiddler)
- Charles (https://www.charlesproxy.com/)

Then we can check whether the exchanged packets are the ones that are expected.

Finalizing a Script

We'll see in this section some nice tips to save time during scripting and to not end up with too-complex scripts due to a lack of knowledge of JMeter features.

Changing the Name of a Transaction According to a Parameter

In some cases, it is useful to be able to change the name of a transaction during *runtime* and not during scripting, such as when:

- Comparing the performance of the same query with different parameters
- Numerating the request to validate that none are lost
- Changing the name according to the answer

As often, several solutions are available:

- Use a value from a CSV file field using **CSV Data Set Config**.
- Use a JMeter function such as **__counter**, **__RandomDate**, or **__Random**.
- Use **JSR223 Listener** and the `prev.setSampleLabel` function; for example, to change the name to *VerySlow* for responses that take more than 400ms:

```
if (prev.getTime() > 400) {
    prev.setSampleLabel("VerySlow")
}
```

Sharing an Object between Different Thread Groups

In some cases, it is necessary to be able to share a variable between different **Thread Groups**, such as when:

- Retrieving a variable to use in a **Thread Group**
- Importing data from a source for use in a **Thread Group**
- Creating accounts in a **setUp Thread Group**
- Cleaning up these same accounts in a **tearDown Thread Group**

For this, you need to use *JMeter properties*, which are global to the instance of JMeter, and not *JMeter variables*, which are local to each thread of a **Thread Group**.

The implementation is quite simple:

- We initialize the property using the `__setProperty()` or `props.put()` function in a *Thread Group*.
- We use this property in another **Thread Group** using the `__P()`, `__property`, or `props.get()` function.

For our example, we will use the **jp@gc - Dummy Sampler** element seen previously:

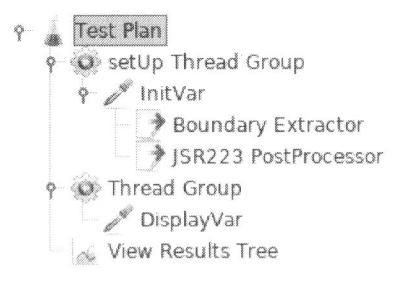

Figure 6.37: Our script

Our script will consist of:

- A **setUp Thread Group** where our property will be initialized
- A **jp@gc - Dummy Sampler** instance to simulate an HTTP request

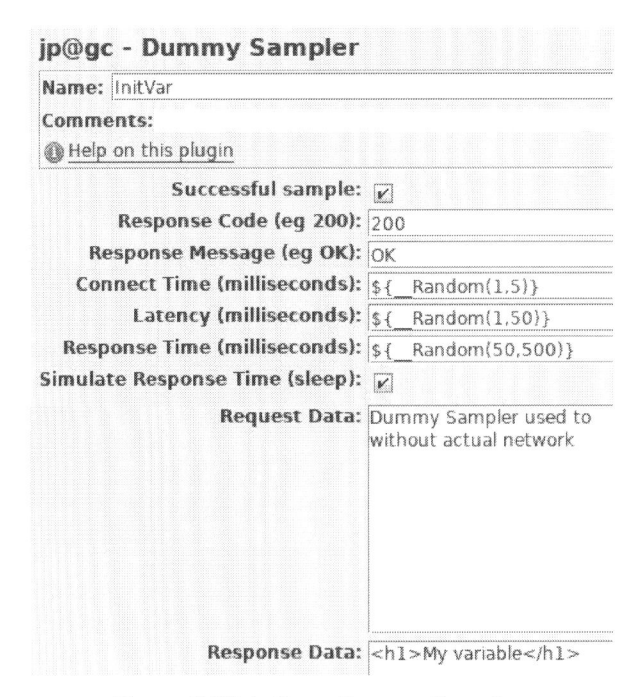

Figure 6.38: jp@gc - Dummy Sampler

- A **Boundary Extractor** instance to extract our variable from the HTTP request:

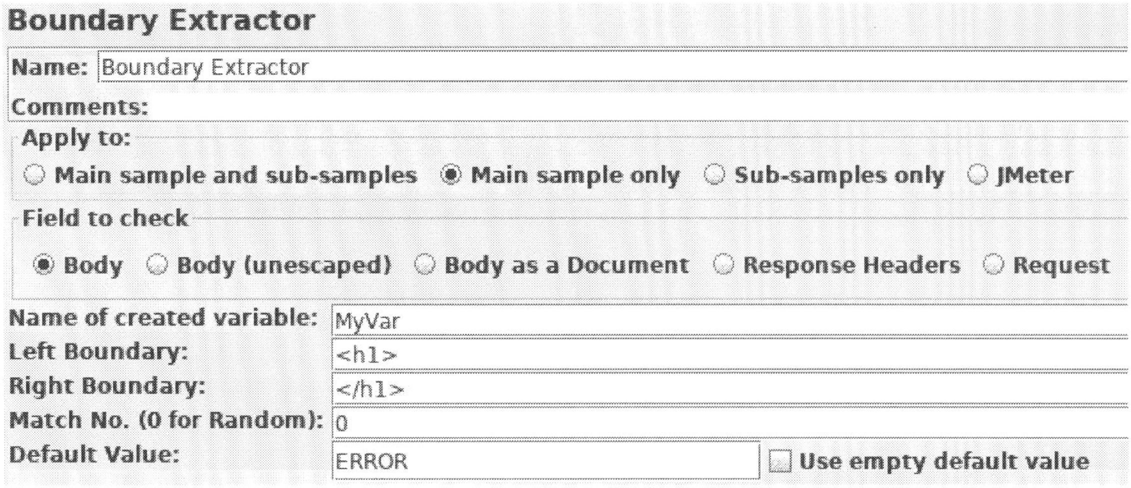

Figure 6.39: Boundary Extractor

- **JSR223 PostProcessor** to save the property using `props.put()`:

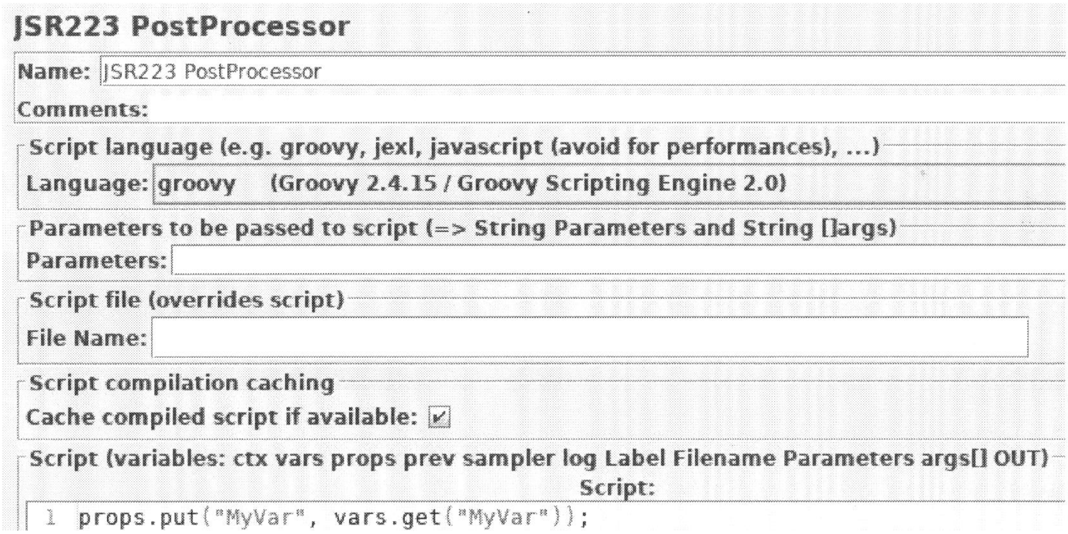

Figure 6.40: Using props.put()

- A **Thread Group** where the previously initialized property will be used

- A **jp@gc - Dummy Sampler** instance that will use the property using __P():

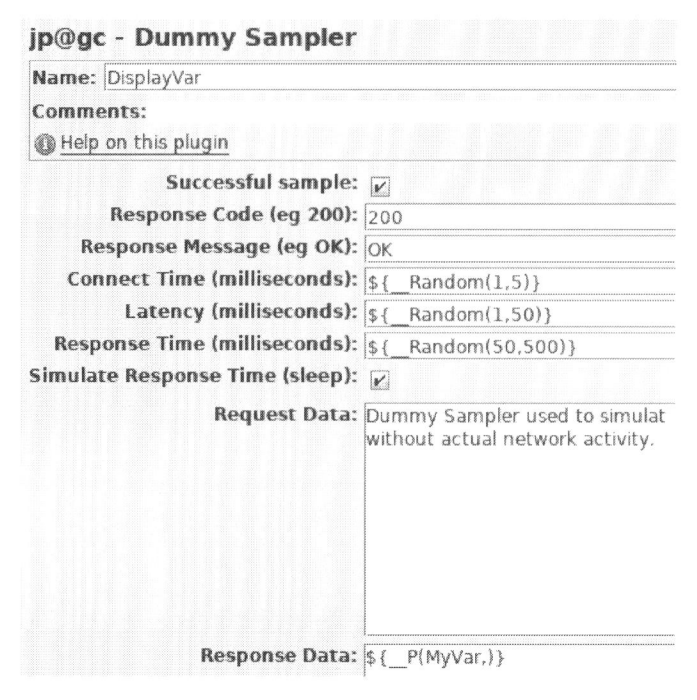

Figure 6.41: Using __P()

The result or Dummy Sampler:

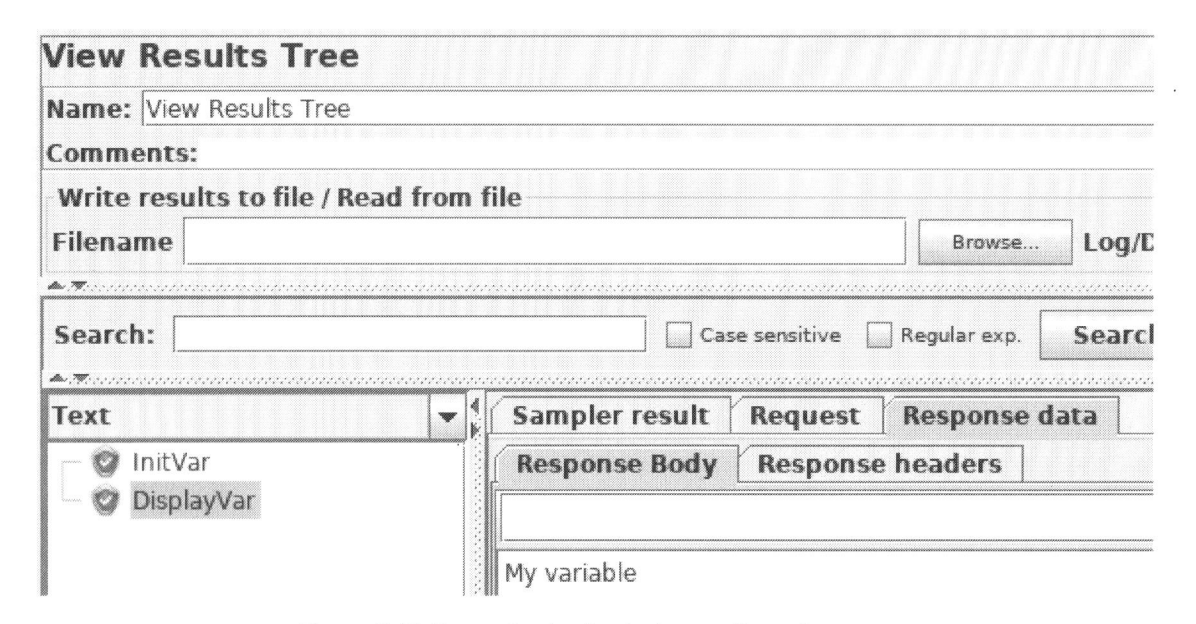

Figure 6.42: Property sharing between thread groups

Note that it is usually a bad idea to try to share data between thread groups. Whenever you end up doing it, reconsider your script architecture.

Alternatively, use the Inter-Thread Communication (https://jmeter-plugins.org/wiki/InterThreadCommunication/) plugin, which provides a FIFO queue to ease communication between threads.

Getting the Most out of CSV Files

The **CSV Data Set Config** element is feature-rich and allows the following:

- Using existing data (search keywords, URL, assertions, and more)
- Having a separate login/password for each VU
- Avoiding the duplication of elements for one or more different variables
- Stopping the test at the end of the CSV file with the *Stop thread on EOF?* option

The different modes/options of CSV reader

It is important to understand the combination of the *Sharing mode*, *Recycle on EOF?*, and *Stop thread on EOF?* options to avoid unexpected side effects.

For example, if, in our CSV file, we have credentials that should be used only once during all the tests, we must have:

- *Sharing mode* equal to *All threads*
- *Stop thread on EOF?* equal to *true*
- *Recycle on EOF?* equal to *false*:

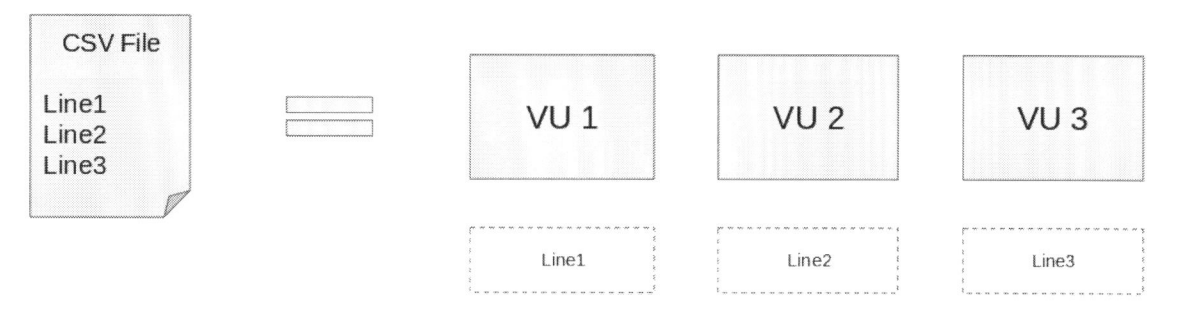

Figure 6.43: No duplication possible

In another case, duplicates are possible (for example, search keywords used on an e-commerce site) and we want to loop over the values contained in the CSV file. We set the following:

- *Stop thread on EOF?* equal to *false*
- *Recycle on EOF?* equal to *true*:

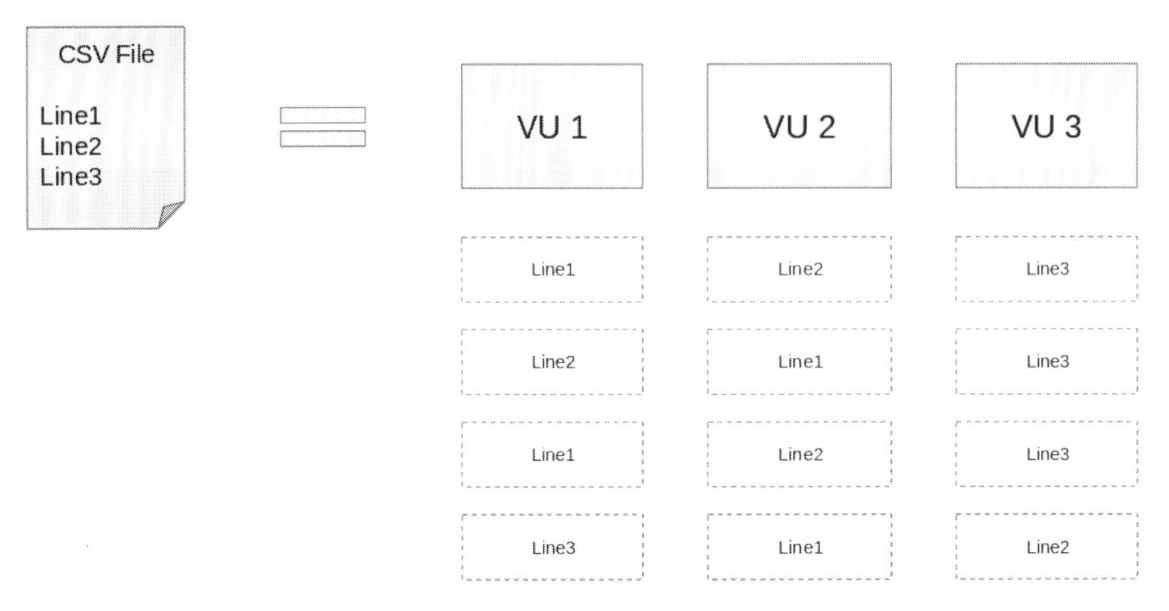

Figure 6.44: Possible duplicates – note that the order of the lines will probably look different for each run, as we can't guarantee the order of the threads

We will end our list of common use cases with a case where each thread will be consuming the same set of data. We set the following:

- *Sharing mode* equal to *Current thread*
- *Stop thread on EOF?* equal to *true*:

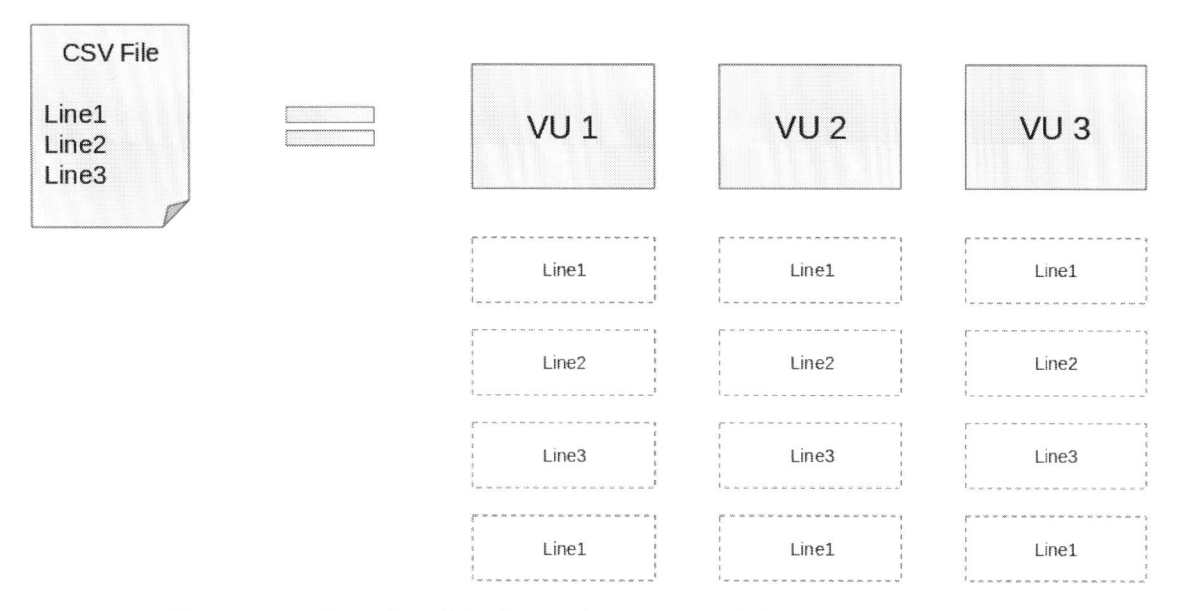

Figure 6.45: The order of the lines is important and duplicates are possible

CSV file and JSON content

The issue, in this case, is how to retrieve JSON content from the CSV file; for example, we may want to get JSON content:

```
{
    "name":"Master Apache JMeter",
    "pages":500,
    "buzword":["devops","cloud","chaos"]
}
```

An easy solution is to put everything on one line and use **CSV Data Set Config** with the **Delimiter** option equal to **\n**:

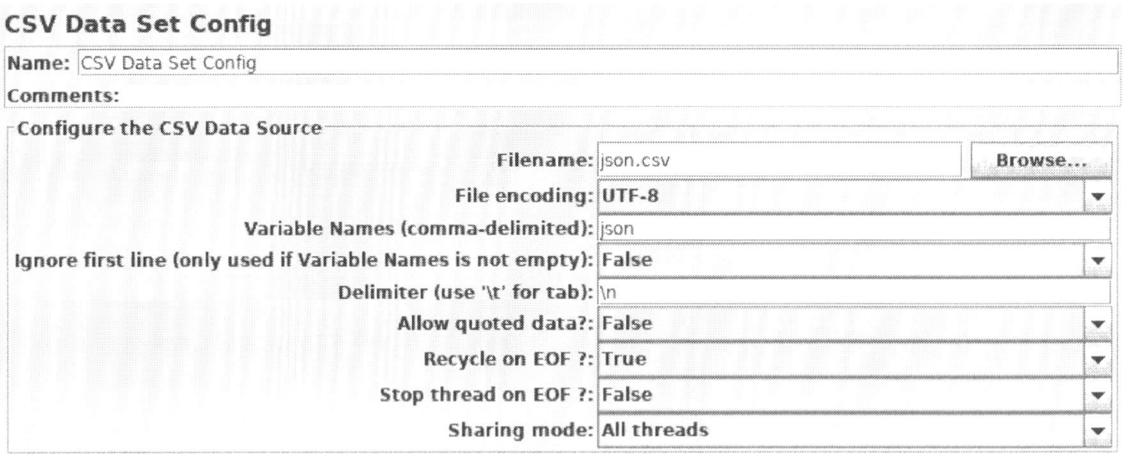

Figure 6.46: Loading a JSON content from a CSV file

Data coming from several CSV files

A limitation of **CSV Data Set Config** is that it can only import data from one file. To work around this limitation, we can use the **__StringFromFile()** function.

The following example loads data from the **Data1.csv**, **Data2.csv**, **Data3.csv**, **Data4.csv**, and **Data5.csv** files:

```
${__StringFromFile(/home/ra77/Utils/'0'_JMX/Data/Data#'.'csv,,1,5)}
```

> **Note**
>
> In the file path, there are special characters (https://docs.oracle.com/javase/6/docs/api/java/text/DecimalFormat.html), **0** and **.**, which need to be escaped with the **'** character.

However, when using the **__StringFromFile()** function, you should be aware of the performance penalty it incurs – limits its use to initializations in a **setUp Thread Group**, for example.

CSV and Groovy

The last example of using **CSV Data Set Config** involved retrieving a variable number of HTTP parameters.

For example, say we want to send several parameters (here, *param1*, *param2*, and *param3*) in our HTTP request:

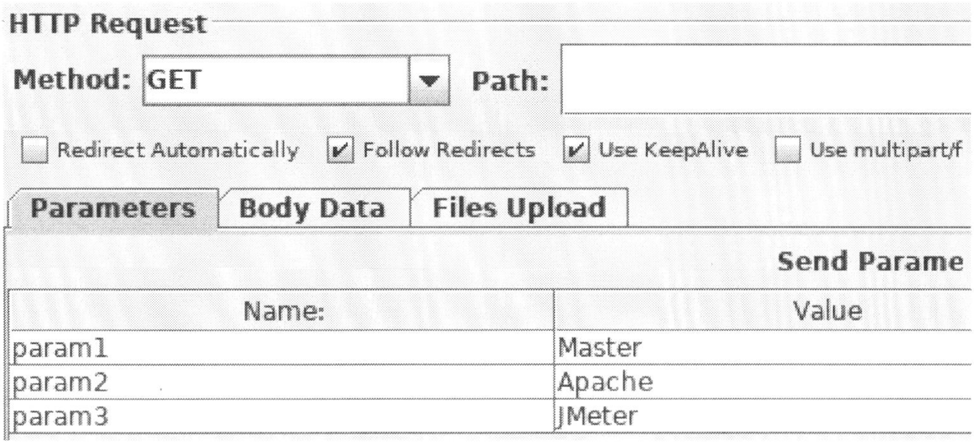

Figure 6.47: HTTP request with three parameters

We cannot store the three values in three columns of our CSV file, because the number of parameters can vary from one request to another.

The solution is to concatenate all the parameters of a query in the same column of the CSV file and use **JSR223 PreProcessor** to cut and insert the parameters one by one.

Our CSV file becomes:

    Master Apache JMeter

    My favorite holiday book

    The best IT book ever

We load it with **CSV Data Set Config**:

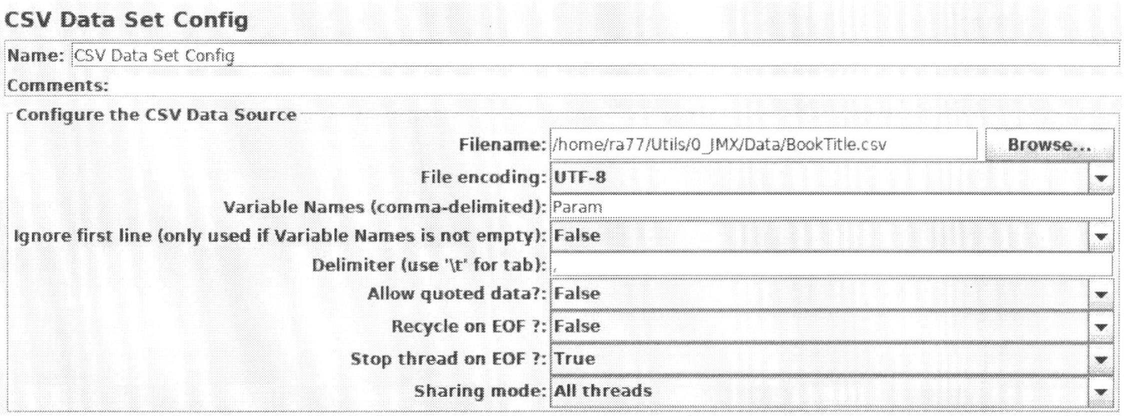

Figure 6.48: Loading parameters

We use a **JSR223 PreProcessor** instance, which we place as a child of our **HTTP Request**:

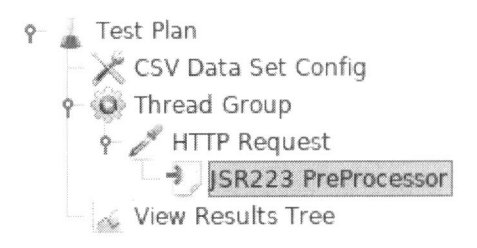

Figure 6.49: Adding JSR223 PreProcessor

We leave the parameters of our HTTP request empty, as they will be filled by our *Groovy* script:

Figure 6.50: Empty parameter list

In **JSR223 PreProcessor**, we write the script that will split the string and add the parameters to the HTTP request:

```
String[] str = vars.get('Param').split(' ');
int paramNumber = 1;
for( String values : str ) {
```

```
        sampler.addArgument('param' + paramNumber,values);
    paramNumber++
}
```

JSR223 PreProcessor

Name: JSR223 PreProcessor
Comments:
Script language (e.g. beanshell, javascript, jexl)
Language: groovy   (Groovy 2.4.15 / Groovy Scripting Engine 2.0)
Parameters to be passed to script (=> String Parameters and String
Parameters:
Script file (overrides script)
File Name:
Script compilation caching
Cache compiled script if available: ☑
Script (variables: ctx vars props sampler log Label Filename Parameter
Script:
```
1  String[] str = vars.get('Param').split(' ');
2  int paramNumber = 1;
3
4  for( String values : str ) {
5      sampler.addArgument('param' + paramNumber,values);
6      paramNumber++
7  }
```

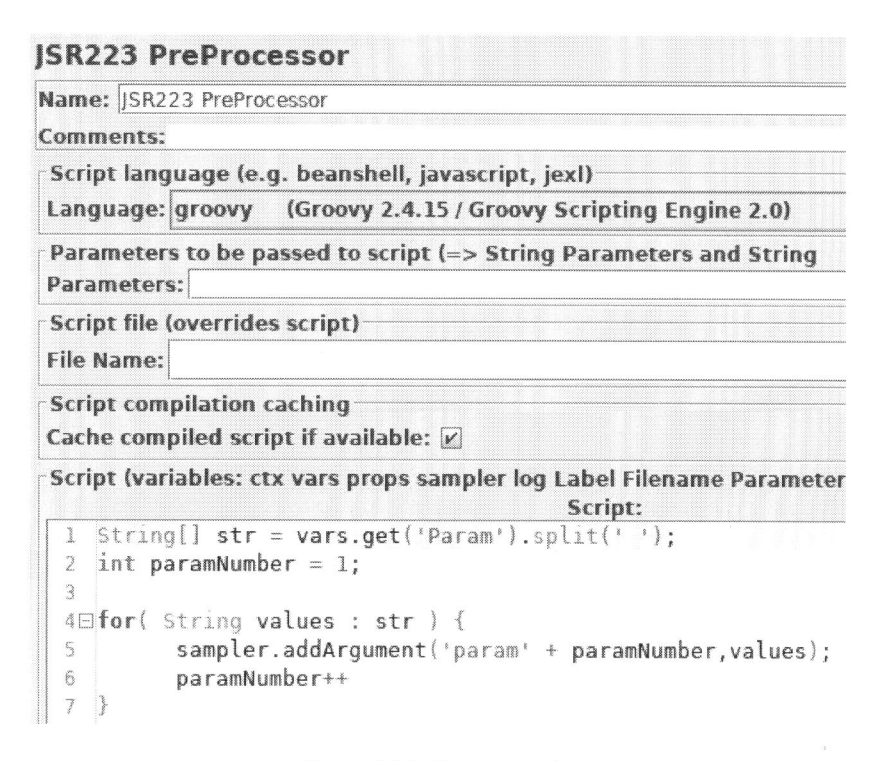

Figure 6.51: Groovy script

The result of the script will be:

  GET http://foo.com/?param1=Master&param2=Apache&param3=JMeter

  GET http://foo.com/?param1=My&param2=favorite&param3=holiday&param4=book

  GET http://foo.com/?param1=The&param2=best&param3=IT&param4=book&param5=ever

As you can see, the number of parameters is no longer a problem.

Marking a Response as an Error

During a load test, a built-in assertion (such as a **Response Assertion**) might not fit. It is then possible to use **Groovy**.

For example, you could use **JSR223 Assertion** or **JSR223 Sampler** combined with the `SampleResult.setSuccessful(true/false)` function:

  `prev.setSuccessful(false)`

Using a Regular Expression Extractor on Content with Spaces and Multiple Lines

It can be painful to find the right regular expression for this type of content which has spaces and multiple lines.

For example:

```
<script id="MyScript">
            setupVars = {
                var1:2
                var2:8
            }
</script>
```

We can use **\s+** to take into account one or more spaces.

Our regular expression becomes:

```
<script id="MyScript">\s+setupVars = {\s+var1:([0-9])\s+var2
```

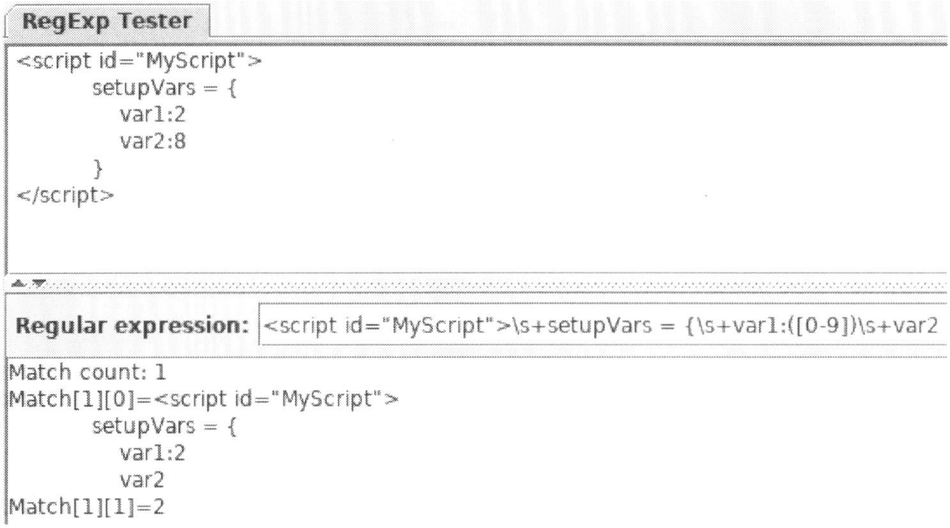

```
RegExp Tester
<script id="MyScript">
        setupVars = {
            var1:2
            var2:8
        }
</script>

Regular expression: <script id="MyScript">\s+setupVars = {\s+var1:([0-9])\s+var2
Match count: 1
Match[1][0]=<script id="MyScript">
        setupVars = {
            var1:2
            var2
Match[1][1]=2
```

Figure 6.52: Using \s+

Another way is to use **(?s)** to ignore line breaks:

```
(?s)<script id="MyScript">.+?setupVars = {.+?var1:([0-9]).+?var2
```

```
RegExp Tester
<script id="MyScript">
        setupVars = {
            var1:2
            var2:8
        }
</script>

Regular expression: (?s)<script id="MyScript">.+?setupVars = {.+?var1:([0-9]).+?var2
Match count: 1
Match[1][0]=<script id="MyScript">
        setupVars = {
            var1:2
            var2
Match[1][1]=2
```

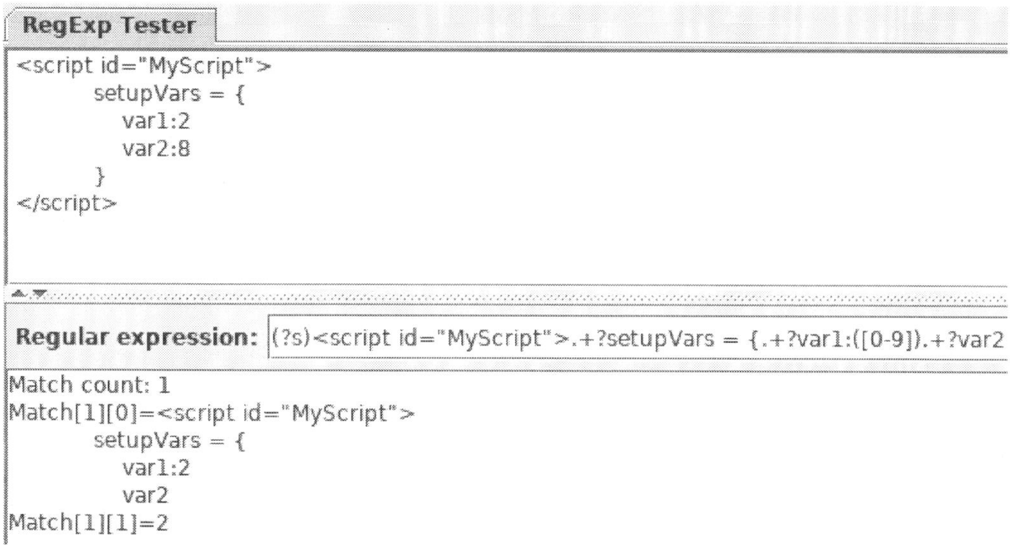

Figure 6.53: Using (?s)

In any case, we can test those regular expressions with online regular expression test websites, such as regular expressions 101 (https://regex101.com/).

> **Note**
>
> You should use regular expressions as a last resort – XML or JSON parsing with regular expressions is really tricky and hard to get right.

Executing an Action Based on the Status of the Previous One

If Controller allows you to execute elements according to the result of the **Expression (must evaluate to true or false)** option.

To find out the status (success or failure) of the previous action, we can use the `${JMeterThread.last_sample_ok}` condition:

Figure 6.54: Testing the status of the last action

Our script and the result of its execution will look like this:

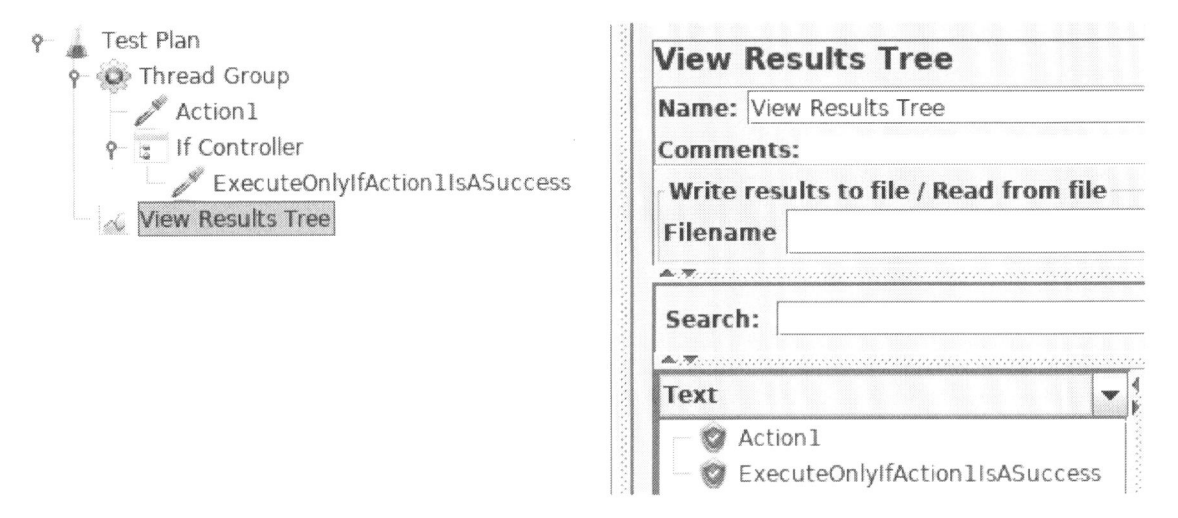

Figure 6.55: Our script

If you need to test a more complex condition, don't uncheck **Interpret condition as Variable Expression?**. Unchecking that means JMeter will use JavaScript to interpret your condition, leading to performance issues as JavaScript implementations (such as Rhino and Nashorn) do not scale at high load. Instead, you can use the __jexl3 function and put your condition code inside it:

```
${__jexl3(vars.get("recordsFiltered") != "nv_recordsFiltered"
    && vars.get("recordsFiltered") > 0,)}
```

In the preceding example, we check whether the **recordsFiltered** variable differs from **nv_recordsFiltered** (the default value we have set for when extraction fails) and whether its value is strictly higher than 0.

Adding Headers to Our HTTP Requests

In order to find our HTTP requests in the logs and/or in a monitoring tool, it may be useful to add a specific header to help us filter them.

We are going to:

- Access the methods (**removeHeaderNamed** and **add**) of **HTTP Header Manager**
- Use **JSR223 PreProcessor** to run our *Groovy* script to add HTTP headers

Here is our *Groovy* script:

```
import org.apache.jmeter.protocol.http.sampler.HTTPSamplerBase;
import org.apache.jmeter.protocol.http.control.HeaderManager;
import org.apache.jmeter.protocol.http.control.Header;


if (sampler instanceof HTTPSamplerBase) {
    HeaderManager hm = sampler.getHeaderManager();
    hm.removeHeaderNamed("X-JMeter");
    Header myHeader = new Header("X-JMeter","My Load Test");
    hm.add(myHeader);
}
```

Our script and the result of its execution will look like this:

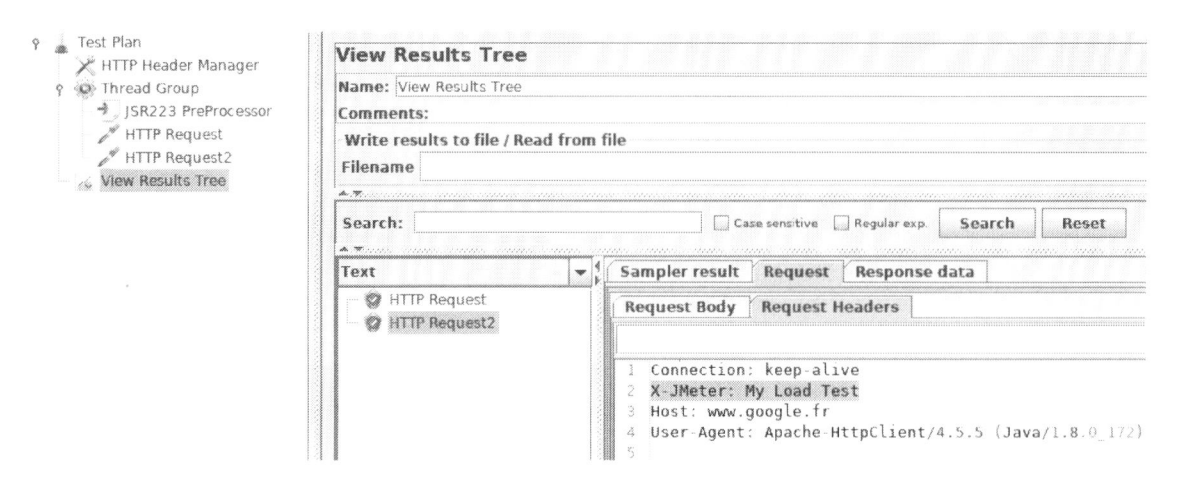

Figure 6.56: Our script

Waiting with While Controller

This element combined with the other features of JMeter can be of great help.

Waiting for the end of execution: example 1

Imagine that we have to wait in our script for the end of a process that writes to the database. This background processing is asynchronous, so it is impossible to predict its end.

The solution is this:

- Use the **JDBC Request** and **JDBC Connection Configuration** items to check the end of processing:

JDBC Request

Name: IsItOK
Comments:

Variable Name Bound to Pool
Variable Name of Pool declared in JDBC Connection Configuration: MyJDBCPool

SQL Query
Query Type: Select Statement

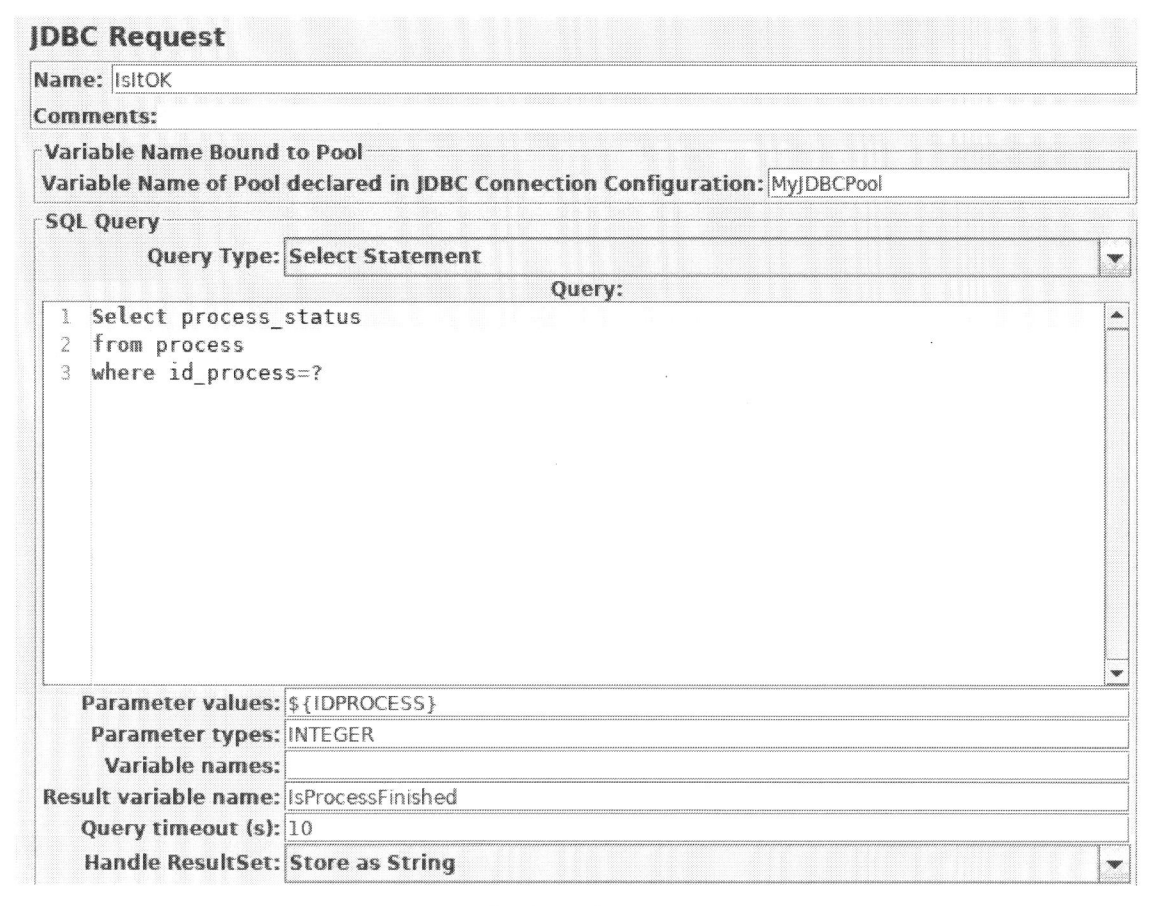

Query:
```
1  Select process_status
2  from process
3  where id_process=?
```

Parameter values: ${IDPROCESS}
Parameter types: INTEGER
Variable names:
Result variable name: IsProcessFinished
Query timeout (s): 10
Handle ResultSet: Store as String

Figure 6.57: Checking the execution status

- Use **While Controller** to loop as long as the execution is not finished:

While Controller

Name: While Controller
Comments:

Condition (function or variable)
```
1  ${__jexl3("${IsProcessFinished}" != "1",)}
```

Figure 6.58: Waiting for the end of the execution

Be careful not to forget to make pauses with a **Timer** between each SQL query to avoid overloading the database.

We end up with:

```
Test Plan
    JDBC Connection Configuration
    Thread Group
        ExecuteProcess
            GetProcessID
        While Controller
            IsItOK
                Constant Timer
        NextActionAfterProcessFinished
```

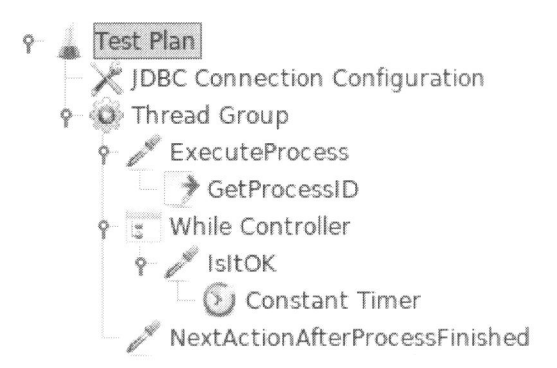

Figure 6.59: Our script

Waiting for the end of execution: example 2

Now we'll look at an easier case than the previous one. This time, the status of the external process is visible on the tested site (in returned pages) and no longer in the database.

Our script will consist of:

- A **JSR223 Sampler** element to initialize our `IsProcessFinished` and `MyCounter` variables:

    ```
    vars.put("IsProcessFinished","")
    vars.put("MyCounter","1")
    ```

- A **While Controller** element that will check our conditions:

    ```
    ${__jexl3((vars.get("IsProcessFinished").indexOf("Finished") == -1
        && vars.get("MyCounter").toInteger() < 10),)}
    ```

- Our HTTP request with an **Extractor** element that will retrieve the part of the answer we're interested in in the `IsProcessFinished` variable.
- A **Counter** element that will increment `MyCounter` to avoid waiting for an answer indefinitely.

This gives us:

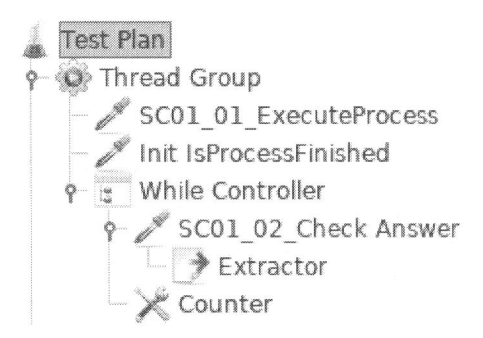

```
Test Plan
└── Thread Group
    ├── SC01_01_ExecuteProcess
    ├── Init IsProcessFinished
    └── While Controller
        ├── SC01_02_Check Answer
        │   └── Extractor
        └── Counter
```

Figure 6.60: Our script

Waiting for three products to be added to the cart

This time, we have an e-commerce site and we want to simulate customers who go to the shopping cart validation stage only when it contains three products.

One solution would be to use the **Loop Controller** element; unfortunately, we cannot do this, because we don't know the number of loops to make:

- Some additions to the cart are impossible for business reasons.
- Products may be sold out
- Some searches may have no matching products.

We decide to use:

- A **JSR223 Sampler** item to initialize the number of products in the basket at 1:

Figure 6.61: Initializing our number of products to 1

- A **While Controller** item to loop as long as we do not have three products in our cart:

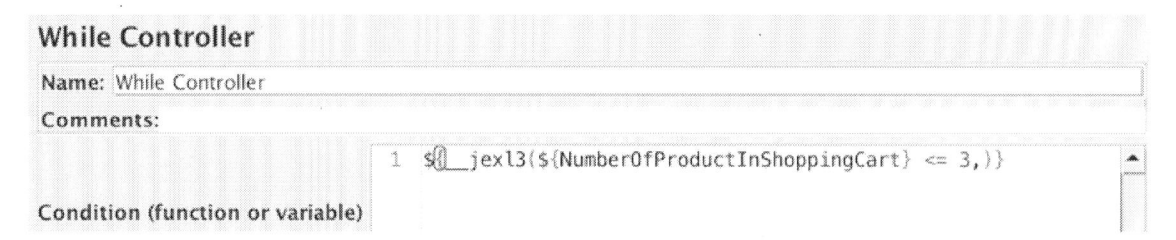

Figure 6.62: Expecting three products in the cart

- An **If Controller** item to verify that our search returns products that we can put in the cart.

- A **JSR223 Sampler** element to increment the number of products in the cart with each addition:

```
JSR223 Sampler
Name: Inc NumberOfProductInShoppingCart
Comments:
Script language (e.g. Groovy, beanshell, javascript, jexl ...)
Language: groovy     (Groovy 2.4.15 / Groovy Scripting Engine 2.0)
Parameters to be passed to script (=> String Parameters and String []args)
Parameters:
Script file (overrides script)
File Name:
Script compilation caching
Cache compiled script if available: ☑
Script (variables: ctx vars props SampleResult sampler log Label Filename Parameters args[] OUT)
                                          Script:
1  int counter = Integer.parseInt(vars.get("NumberOfProductInShoppingCart")) + 1
2  vars.put("NumberOfProductInShoppingCart",Integer.toString(counter))
```

Figure 6.63: Increasing the number of products in the cart

This gives us:

```
Test Plan
  CSV Data Set Config
  Thread Group
    Init NumberOfProductInShoppingCart
    SC01_00_Login
    While Controller
      SC01_01_Search
        Regular Expression Extractor
      If product is available
        SC01_02_Put in shopping cart
        Inc NumberOfProductInShoppingCart
    SC01_03_Checkout
```

Figure 6.64: Our script

Exiting from While if the last action returns an error

Doing this is easy in JMeter. For the condition field of the **While Controller**, do either of the following:

- Leave it empty
- Enter LAST (LAST has a particular meaning here used by JMeter)

The Right Extractor at the Right Time

There are several *extractors* in JMeter:

Extractor	Source Format
CSS Selector Extractor	HTML body
JSON Extractor	JSON body
XPath2 Extractor	XML body
Boundary Extractor	Any text format in headers or body
Regular Expression Extractor	Any text format in headers or body

Figure 6.65: Extractors

Choosing the right *extractor* depends on three criteria:

- Suitability to the type of response (**JSON Extractor** for JSON, **XPath2 Extractor** for XML, **CSS Selector Extractor** for HTML, and so on)
- Power in terms of extraction (especially true for big tests)
- Resilience to changes in response (there is nothing more painful than having to modify an *extractor* with every change to the expected response)

The advantages of choosing the most suited extractor based on the type of response are:

- A solid test that is less sensitive to changes
- Easier configuration of the *extractor* compared to **Regular Expression Extractor**

Regarding performance and ease of use, **Boundary Extractor** is the best choice if data allows it.

The most versatile and *battle-tested* is **Regular Expression Extractor**.

Handle Cookies

In the same way that we can handle HTTP headers, it is possible to handle cookies as well. Note that HTTP Cookie Manager handles the cookies returned by the server for you already.

The tips we describe here are needed for cookies set by some JSR223 and Groovy code.

For this, we have several possibilities:

- Having **User-Defined Cookies** in **HTTP Cookie Manager**:

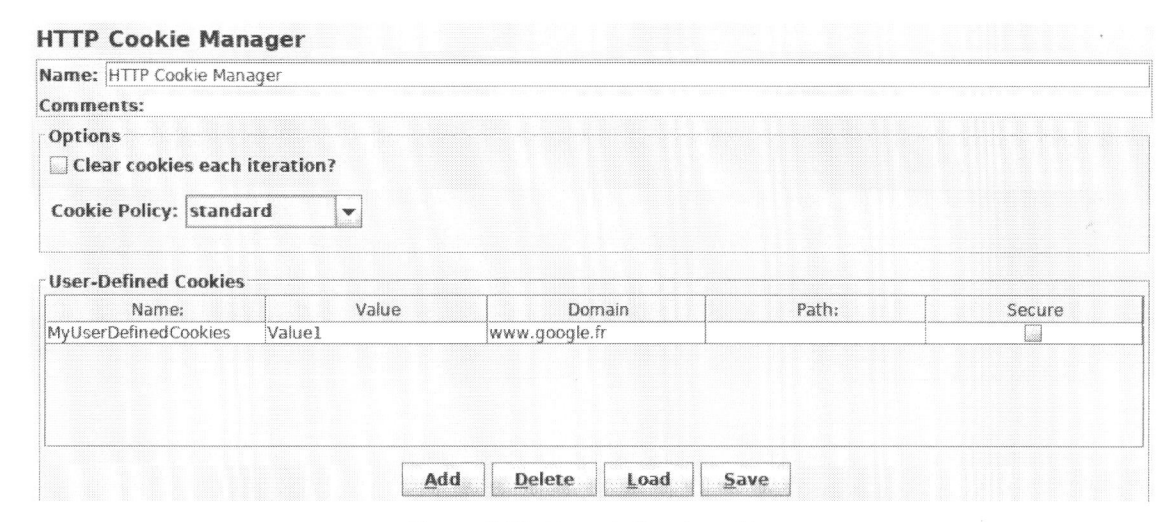

Figure 6.66: User-defined cookies

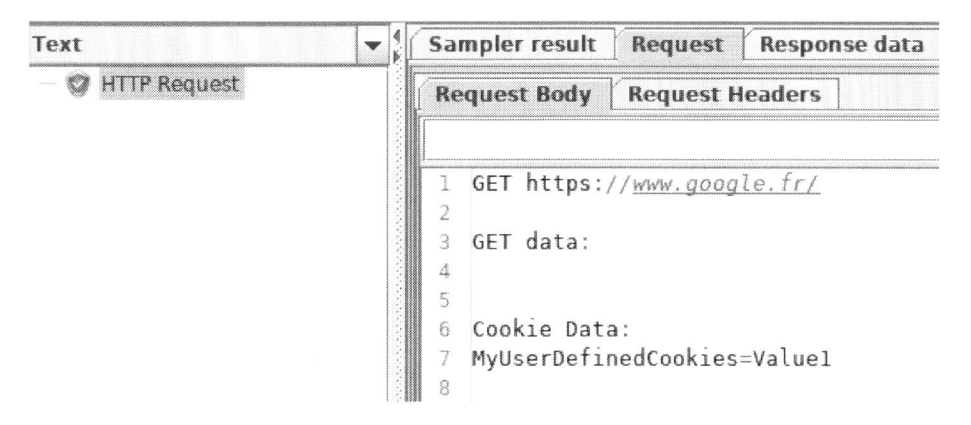

Figure 6.67: User-defined cookies – the result

- Adding a cookie using a **JSR223 PreProcessor** element with the following code:

  ```
  import org.apache.jmeter.protocol.http.control.CookieManager
  import org.apache.jmeter.protocol.http.control.Cookie
  Cookie cookie = new Cookie("MyCookie","TheValueOfCookie","www.qwant.com","",false,-1)
  CookieManager manager = sampler.getCookieManager();
  manager.add(cookie)
  ```

Figure 6.68: Adding a cookie with a JSR223 PreProcessor element

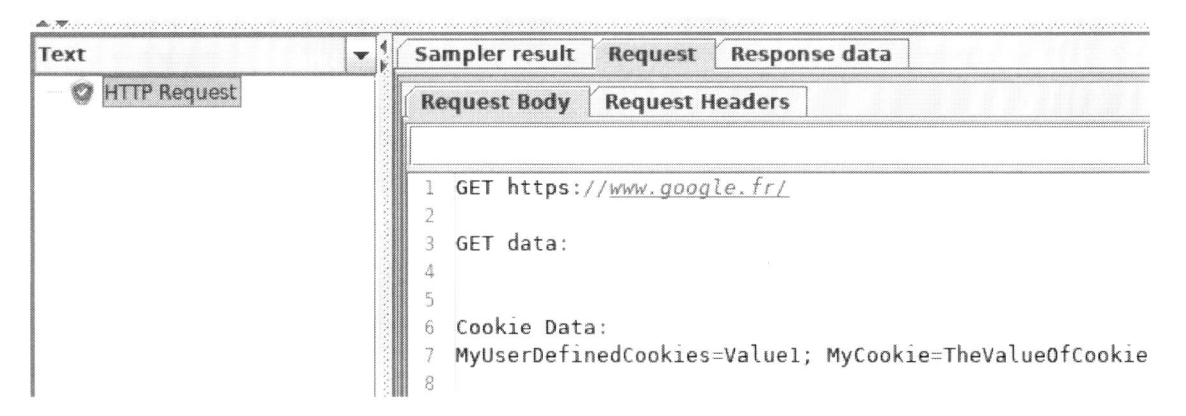

Figure 6.69: Adding a cookie with a JSR223 PreProcessor element – the result

- Deleting a cookie using a **JSR223 PreProcessor** element with the following code:

    ```
    import org.apache.jmeter.protocol.http.control.CookieManager
    import org.apache.jmeter.protocol.http.control.Cookie
    sampler.getCookieManager().
        getCookies().remove('MyUserDefinedCookies')
    ```

- Deleting all cookies using a **JSR223 PreProcessor** element with the following code:

    ```
    sampler.getCookieManager().clear()
    ```

In cases where we use a **JSR223 PreProcessor** element, we must put it in the thread of our HTTP request and add an **HTTP Cookie Manager** element in our script:

Figure 6.70: Our script

Conclusion

In this chapter, we have seen some best practices for the three steps of creating a script:

- The recording part
- The debugging part
- The variabilization and finalization part

We did not limit ourselves to JMeter, but we picked good ideas to explore from the JMeter ecosystem. Indeed, it is important to know about the whole ecosystem of JMeter to get the most out of JMeter.

These tips are generic and valid for whatever type of application you want to test. In the following chapters, we will study and deepen our knowledge of the protocols supported by JMeter, examining the specifics of each one.

7
Load Testing a Website

A Bit of Theory

In *Chapter 1, Quick Start with JMeter*, we saw how to create and run a simple test case on a web application. In this chapter, we're going to go deeper into this part.

In order to access your web application, users will use the *Hypertext Transfer Protocol* (HTTP) protocol through their web browser.

The HTTP protocol is rather simple, and understanding it is of great help when writing a test script with JMeter. The role of HTTP is to exchange information between the client and the server.

As a picture says a thousand words:

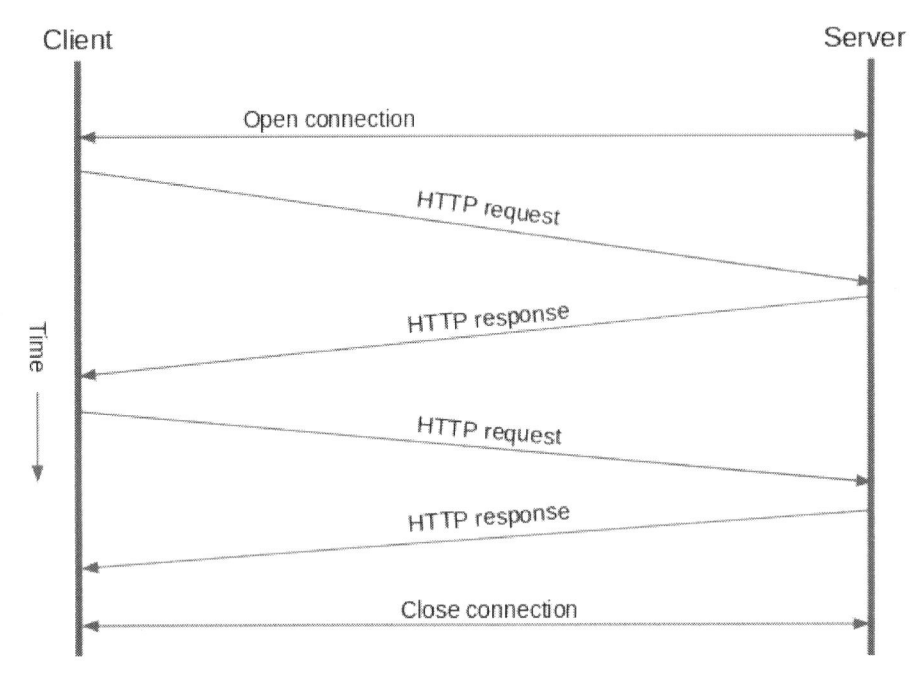

Figure 7.1: A simplified view of the HTTP protocol

An HTTP request will have the following form:

- One, and only one, HTTP method line in the form **HTTPMETHOD URI Protocol/Version**
- Zero or more lines of headers in the form **Header: Value**
- Possibly an empty line, if the body is not empty
- Possibly the body of the request (the content)

For example, when accessing the European search engine www.qwant.com:

```
GET / HTTP/1.1
Host: www.qwant.com
User-Agent: Mozilla/5.0 (X11; Ubuntu; Linux x86_64; rv:20.0) Gecko/20100101 Firefox/20.0
Accept: text/html,application/xhtml+xml,application/xml;q=0.9,*/*;q=0.8
Accept-Language: fr,fr-fr;q=0.8,en-us;q=0.5,en;q=0.3
Accept-Encoding: gzip, deflate
Connection: keep-alive
```

The HTTP response will have:

- One, and only one, status line in the form **Protocol/Version Response_status_code Message_of_the_response**
- Zero or more lines of headers in the form **Header: Value**
- Possibly an empty line, if the body is not empty
- Possibly the body of the answer (the content)

The answer to the query above.

```
HTTP/1.1 200 OK
Cache-Control: private, max-age=0
Content-Encodage: gzip
Content-Type: text/html; charset=UTF-8
Date: Tue, 23 Apr 2013 08:31:56 GMT
Expires: -1
Server: gws
```

Let's look at the elements one by one.

The HTTP methods are defined in RFC 2616 (http://www.w3.org/Protocols/rfc2616/rfc2616.html):

Method	Description
GET	Obtain a resource.
POST	Submit data to a resource for processing (ex: HTML form).
HEAD	Retrieve information from a resource
OPTIONS	Obtain the communication options of a resource.
PUT	Add or replace a resource on a server.
DELETE	Delete a resource from the server.
TRACE	Ask the server what it has received.
CONNECT	Use a proxy as a communication tunnel (ex: SSL connection).

Figure 7.2: RFC 2616 HTTP methods

There are several versions of the protocol:

- HTTP/0.9
- HTTP/1.0
- HTTP/1.1
- HTTP/2.0 (supported by JMeter through a third-party plugin)

Compared to HTTP/1.0, the HTTP/1.1 version provides better cache management and persistent connections by default.

The request/response headers allow us to add information to transmitted messages.

For example, we can define:

- Accepted languages (`Accept-Language`)
- The type of compression of the messages (`Accept-Encoding`)

Many headers exist, such as `Accept-Charset`, `Cache-Control`, `Content-Length`, `Content-Type`, `Hosts`, `Date`, `If-Modified-Since`, and so on.

The HTTP status codes (https://en.wikipedia.org/wiki/List_of_HTTP_status_codes) are grouped into five parts:

Code	Example
1XX: Information	100: waiting for further action
2XX: Success	200: request processed successfully
	202: request processed, but without the guarantee of result
3XX: Redirection	301: resource moved permanently
	304: resource not modified since the last request.
4XX: Client Errors	400: Query syntax is wrong .
	401: Authentication needed .
	403: Resource forbidden
	404: resource not found
5XX: Server Errors	500: Internal Server Error
	503: Service temporarily unavailable

Figure 7.3: HTTP status codes

Let's go back to the list of headers and status codes to learn how an HTTP cache works in a simplified way.

An HTTP cache avoids downloading a resource if it is still valid in a cache (for example, the cache of a web browser can store images from a visited website in order to avoid downloading them upon each visit).

This cache management relies on a number of headers (`Cache-Control`, `Expires`, `Last-Modified`, `If-Match` / `If-None-Match`, `If-Modified-Since` / `If-Unmodified-Since`, `If-Range`, `Age`, and `ETag`) and response codes (**200** and **304**).

The simplified algorithm for cache management is as follows:

1. The client requests a resource.
2. The browser looks in its local cache to see whether it has the resource and to see whether it is valid if it does (this is done through the headers of the query that was used to fetch this resource before and may lead to sending a query).
3. If so, it uses the response in the cache. Otherwise, the browser sends a request to the server to get the resource.

To determine whether the requested resource is still valid, the cache has two options:

- The resource itself declares its validity period using HTTP headers
- The cache tries to guess it heuristically

With these explanations, we understand the importance of the headers.

For example, the `GET` method is always cachable by default, unless a cache header forbids it. Indeed, `GET` methods are usually used for read-only data, which is usually cacheable. So, whether the data needs to be refreshed after some time or needs to always be fresh, the server will add cache headers to control caching and refreshing. In contrast, the `POST` method is non-cacheable by default, unless a cache header specifies otherwise.

If you have looked at the list of headers, you should have noticed two specific ones used for cookies (`Cookie` and `Set-Cookie`).

A cookie is a piece of information exchanged between the server and the client, allowing the HTTP protocol to have a state – in the sense of a browsing session (*stateful*).

This makes it possible to link several HTTP requests together (recording the journey on the user's site, storing the identifier of a customer, and so on).

Setup with JMeter

Let's see how JMeter implements it.

The main element is **HTTP Request**:

Figure 7.4: HTTP Request

We can easily find all that we previously saw.

Similarly, all HTTP methods are accessible:

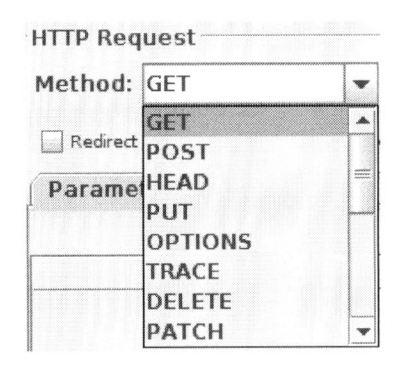

Figure 7.5: HTTP Request – HTTP methods

JMeter can use multiple implementations (**Java** or **HTTPClient4**) to handle HTTP requests.

It is recommended to use **HTTPClient4** (the default implementation) for performance, functionality, and compatibility reasons:

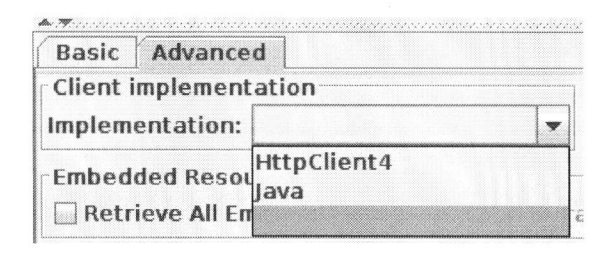

Figure 7.6: HTTP Request – HTTP implementations

Here are some features of **HTTPClient4** that are not available with a **Java** implementation:

- Better control of how connections are reused within Keep-Alive
- Virtual Host or IP spoofing
- Client certificate-based authentication
- Kerberos authentication
- Wider support for HTTP methods
- The ability to use the **DNS Cache Manager** element to have better control of DNS configuration
- Fine control of the retry mechanism

If we need to use a proxy to connect to the tested application, we can just configure it on the **Advanced** tab:

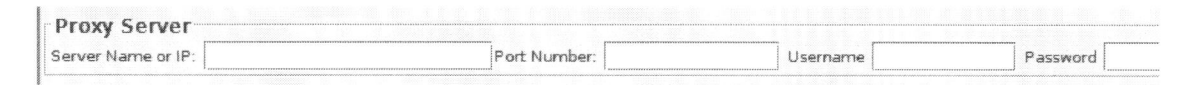

Figure 7.7: HTTP Request – using a proxy

Finally, if we want to simulate the loading of resources (images, CSS files, JavaScript files, and so on) in parallel, as on a real web browser, it is also possible (but beware – JMeter is not a web browser and will not execute URL calls triggered in JavaScript):

Figure 7.8: HTTP Request – loading resources

For example, an **HTTP Request** element that sends a **GET** request to www.qwant.fr:

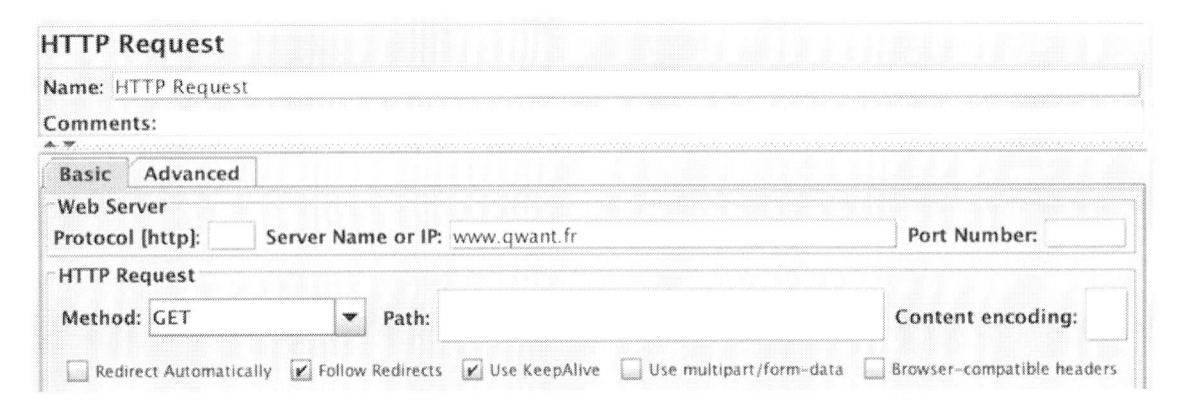

Figure 7.9: GET www.qwant.fr

As you can see, sending HTTP requests with JMeter is quite simple, but it can become counterproductive if you have to fill in all the fields for all HTTP requests or modify your script (for example, to modify the URL test target), and this despite the use of a proxy for recording our scripts.

To solve this problem, we will use a **Config Element**.

Let's start with **HTTP Header Manager**, which allows you to define HTTP headers for one or more HTTP requests:

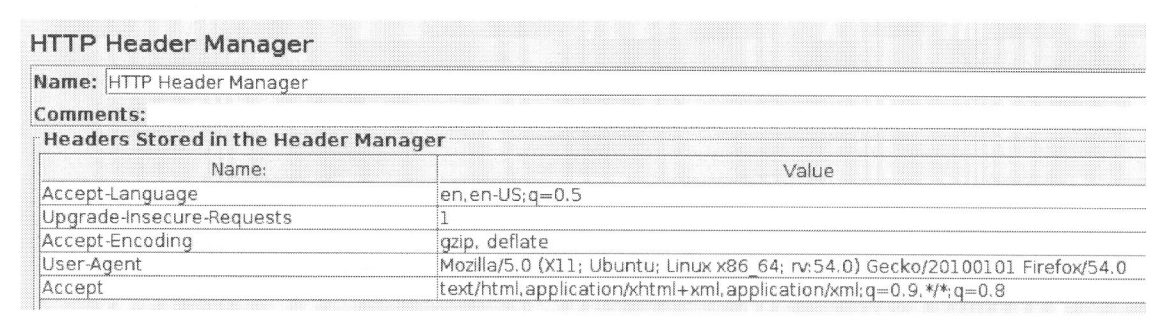

Name:	Value
Accept-Language	en,en-US;q=0.5
Upgrade-Insecure-Requests	1
Accept-Encoding	gzip, deflate
User-Agent	Mozilla/5.0 (X11; Ubuntu; Linux x86_64; rv:54.0) Gecko/20100101 Firefox/54.0
Accept	text/html,application/xhtml+xml,application/xml;q=0.9,*/*;q=0.8

Figure 7.10: HTTP Header Manager

In our test plan, you only need to modify the **User-Agent** header to simulate a different web browser (for example, a mobile web browser) for all requests:

Figure 7.11: Test Plan

Another interesting element is **HTTP Request Defaults**. As its name suggests, it allows us to set some HTTP parameters for one or more HTTP requests:

Figure 7.12: Default HTTP settings

Imagine that we scripted our scenario in the development environment, and now we have to run our scenario in another environment, which is ISO production.

There's nothing simpler – just set **Server Name or IP** in the **Web Server** part to the correct hostname (do not forget to delete this value in all HTTP requests for the test plan):

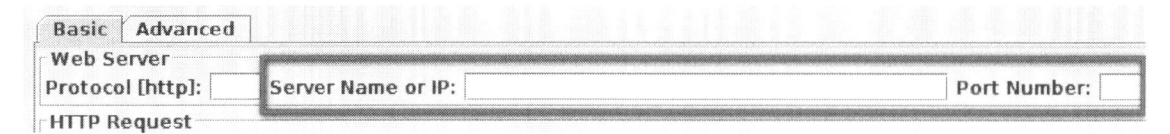

Figure 7.13: Default HTTP settings

Now let's look at how to make our virtual users as close as possible to a real web browser.

To do that, we will simulate a browser cache with **HTTP Cache Manager**:

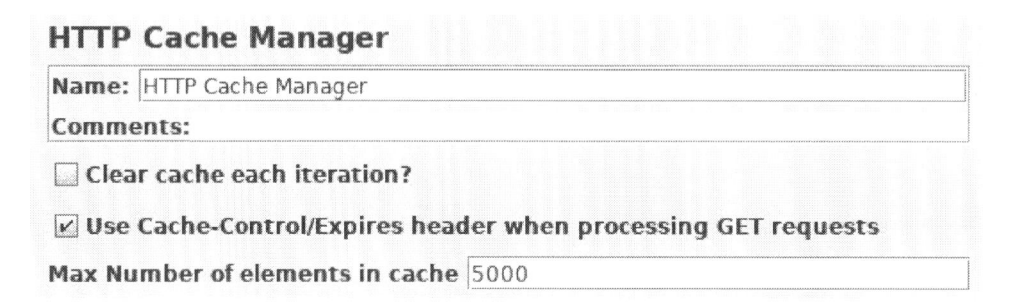

Figure 7.14: HTTP Cache Manager

The parameters of this element will be checked or unchecked according to the goals of your tests.

Now that cache management is ready, let's move on to cookie management with **HTTP Cookie Manager**:

Figure 7.15: HTTP Cookie Manager

HTTP Cookie Manager will take care of storing and sending our cookies as a web browser would.

The last element of the **Config Element** group specific to the HTTP protocol is **HTTP Authorization Manager**. It allows us to handle different authentication schemes (*basic-auth*, *digest-auth*, or *Kerberos auth*) for the parts of the tested website that need them:

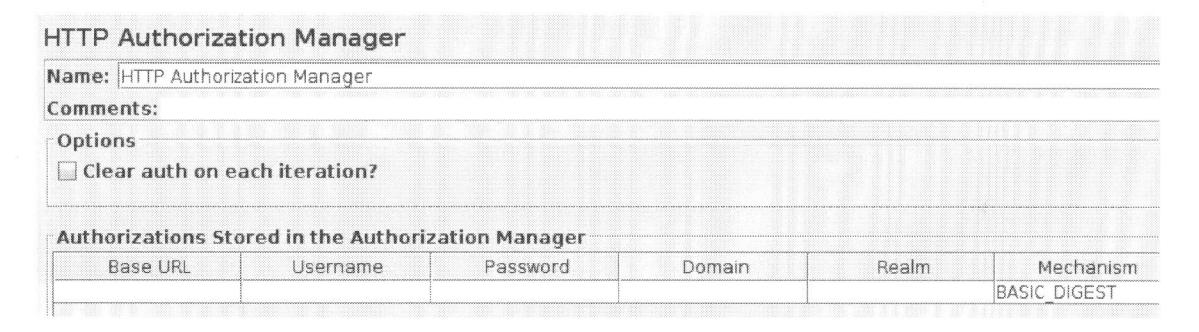

Figure 7.16: HTTP Authorization Manager

Methodology

Let's look at some best practices that will allow us to achieve successful load test campaigns.

The first step is to define our test plan to limit the scope and goals of the test campaign. Depending on the desired goals, you need to make different choices.

Some will impact scripting (datasets, and so on); others will impact the type of test (soak tests, stress tests, and so on) to be performed. The number of tests will also be impacted (the addition of technical tests and so on).

Studying and understanding the architecture of the system will have a big impact on the scripts.

For example, if the static resources (images, CSS files, and so on) are hosted outside the tested system (for example, on a *Content Delivery Network* (CDN)), there is no need to include them in our scripts.

We can exclude them when we record our scripts using the **Request Filtering** tab of **HTTP(S) Test Script Recorder**:

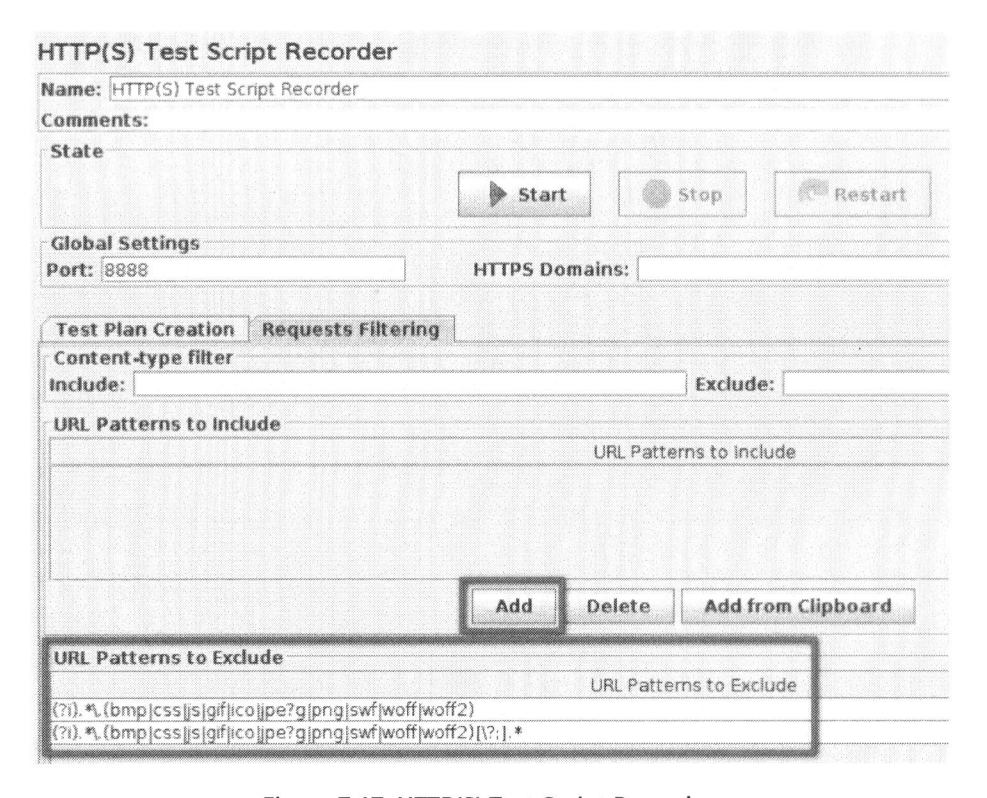

Figure 7.17: HTTP(S) Test Script Recorder

> **Note**
> This is done by default if you use **Template Recording**, shipped with JMeter.

Another example: if we test the availability of the architecture, it will be necessary to carry out technical tests (the impact of the crashing of certain components (node and so on) on the users and so on).

Let's move on to creating our JMeter scripts.

As with all other tests, one of the goals is to do it with a realistic load and behavior.

It is therefore recommended to use *think times* and the correct flow control strategy (number of fixed users, number of fixed requests, and so on).

For *think times*, you can record them when using **HTTP(S) Test Script Recorder**.

To do this, use the **Recording with Think Time** template, packaged with JMeter, but ensure when doing so that you reproduce the pauses made by a real user:

Figure 7.18: Recording with Think Time

An alternative is to add them through the pop-up menu – right-click on **Thread Group** or controller and click on **Add Think Times to children**:

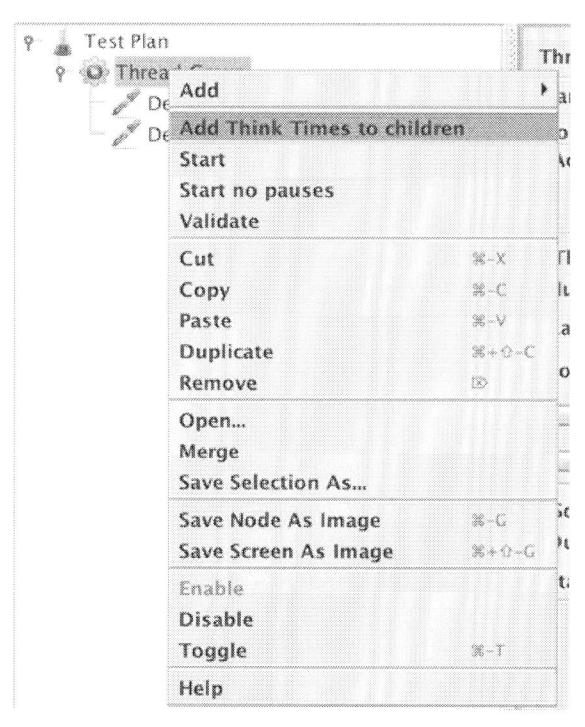

Figure 7.19: Menu Add Think Time to children

160 | Load Testing a Website

Then, adjust think times in the timer element called **Pause**, located under the flow control action element called **Think Time**, as by default it is created with a 1 second pause:

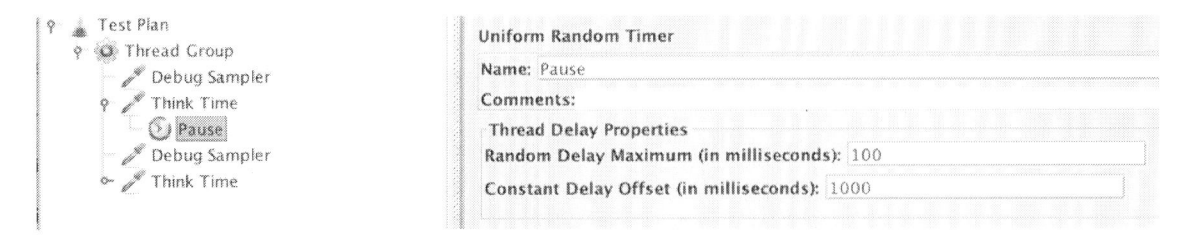

Figure 7.20: Adjust Pause in Think Time

To continue with the recording of our script, we can and should record the requests and responses so that we can use them during the correlation phase. This is also useful when you add **Assertions** and test correlation expressions with testers in **View Results Tree**.

Simply add **View Results Tree** to **HTTP(S) Test Script Recorder**:

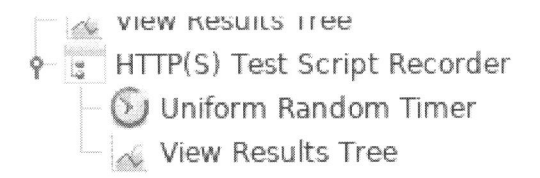

Figure 7.21: View Results Tree to receive record requests/responses

Set the filename, click on the **Configure** button, and select all of the fields that are related to XML output:

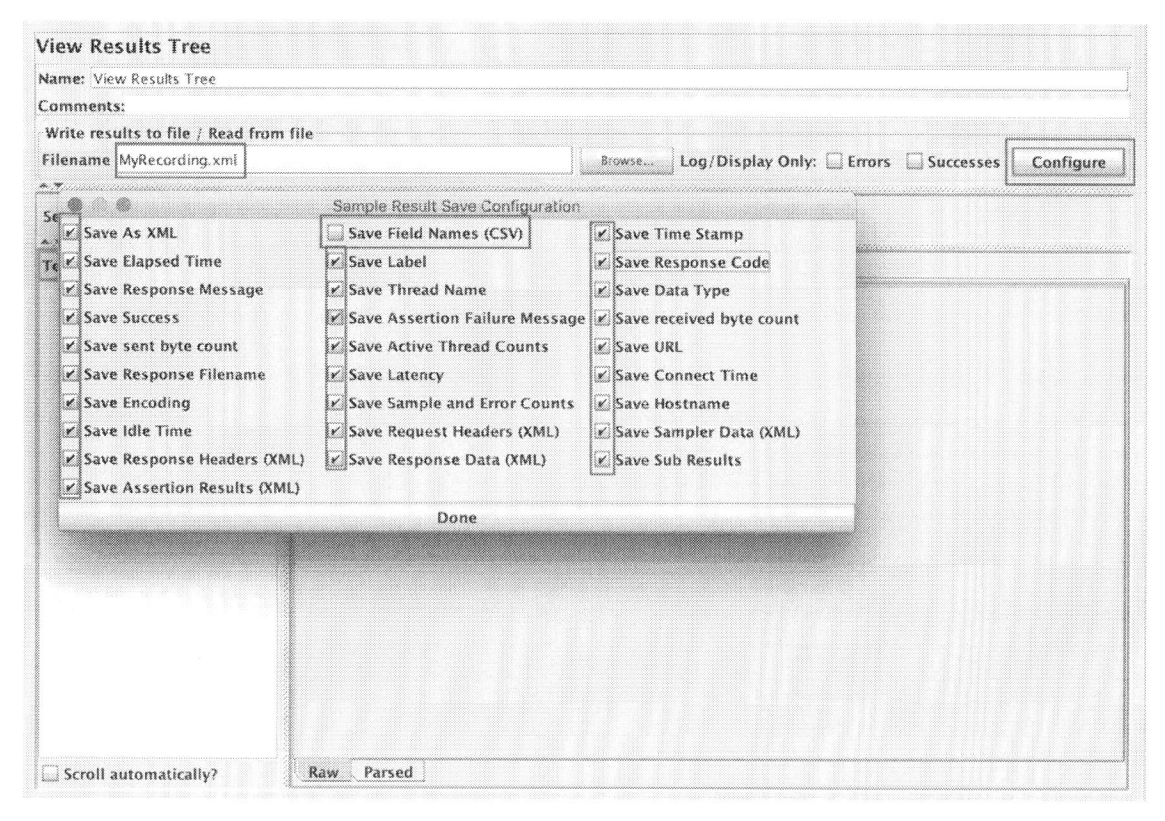

Figure 7.22: Configure XML format

> **Note**
> This is done by default if you use **Template Recording**, shipped with JMeter. Just modify the path of the output file.

Regarding the script, I also recommend testing each response with **Assertion** to verify that it is the expected one. This ensures that the response is really the expected one and not an error page or default redirection.

So, now we have a realistic test plan, we must ensure that the tested environment is realistic. Read *Chapter 5, Preparing the Test Environment (Injectors and Tested Systems)* for more details.

Finally, a load test campaign is an iterative process. Indeed, when you fix a contention or performance issue, a new one that was hidden by the previous one will surface. We must therefore be careful not to underestimate the duration of the campaign.

Put into Practice with JMeter

It's time to practice.

Example 1: Simulate Realistic Load

For this first example, we will use the Java EE 6 Pet Catalog application (https://netbeans.org/kb/samples/pet-catalog.html):

> **Note**
> This application is distributed with NetBeans; installation and configuration instructions are included.

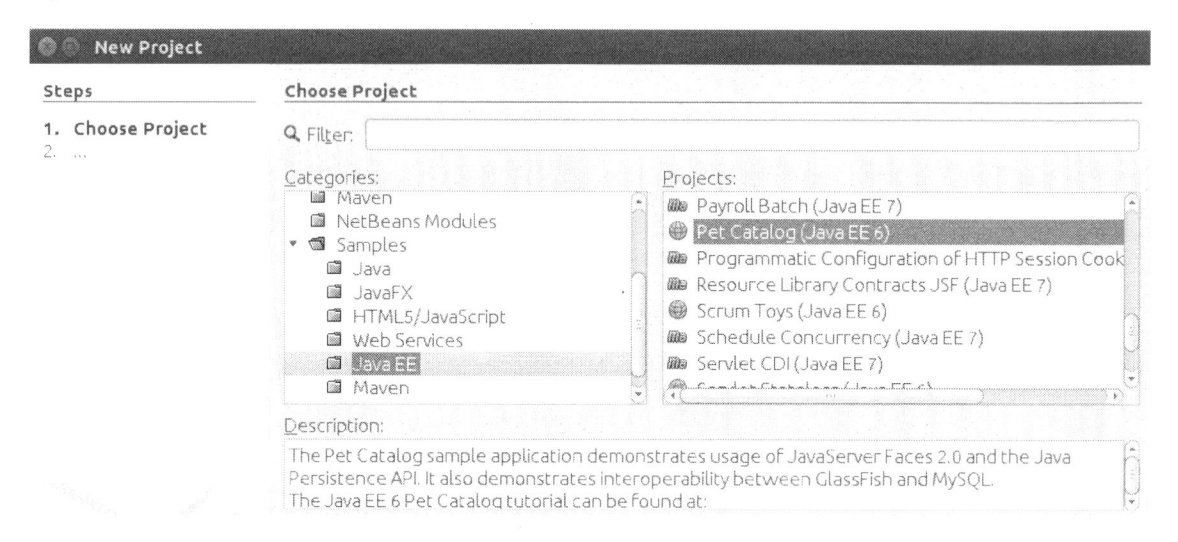

Figure 7.23: Java EE 6 Pet Catalog

In our scenario, we will be looking at the details of the animals available on the site.

The steps of our scenario will be:

1. Log in to the site:

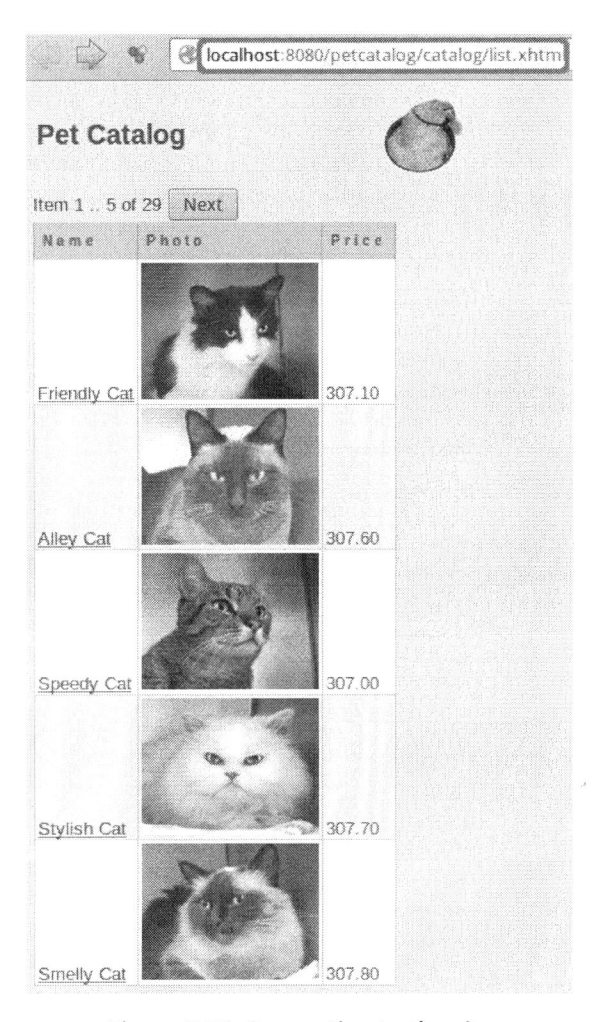

Figure 7.24: Connection to the site

2. Select and display the details of a cat:

Figure 7.25: Selection of a cat

Figure 7.26: Viewing the details

3. Go back to the list:

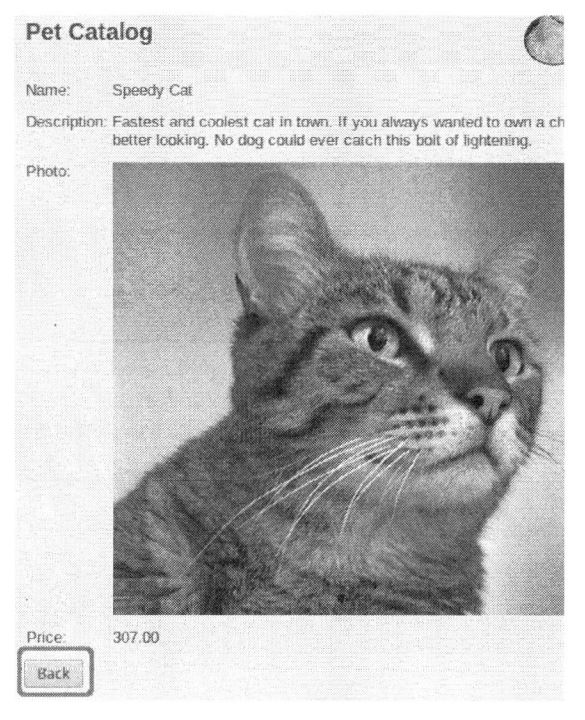

Figure 7.27: Back to the list

4. Show the next page:

Figure 7.28: Display next page

5. Select the details of a cat:

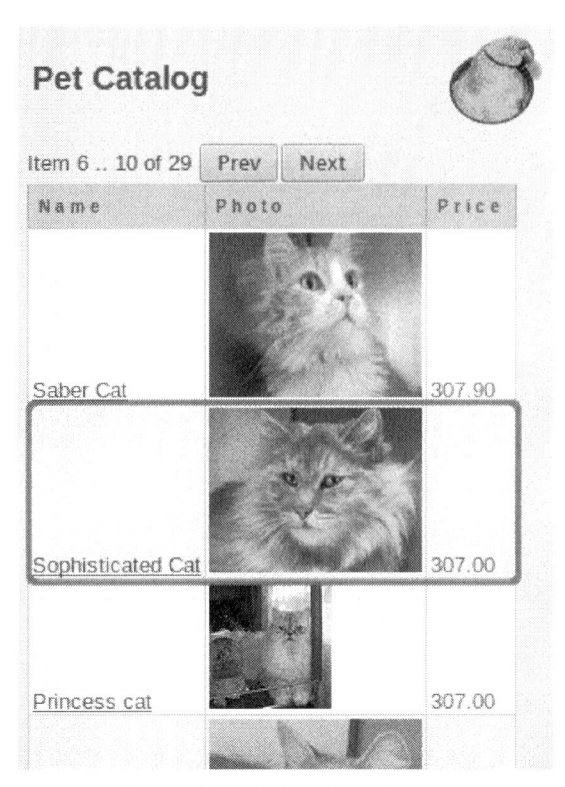

Figure 7.29: Selection of a cat

6. Let's use the **Template Recording with Think Time** wizard seen above and save our script (see *Chapter 1, Quick Start with JMeter*, for more details):

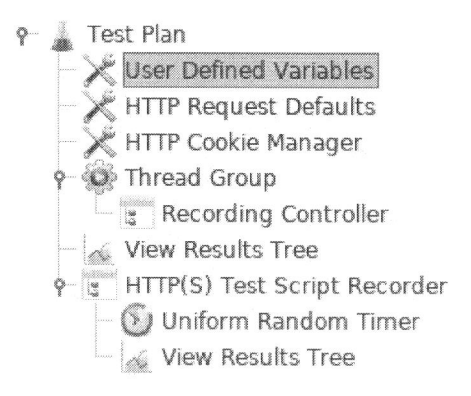

Figure 7.30: Recording preparation

> **Note**
> In **HTTP(S) Test Script Recorder**, check **Add Assertions** option to save time later.

Figure 7.31: Add assertions automatically when recording

> **Note**
> Similarly, let's define a prefix for the name of our HTTP requests.

Figure 7.32: Automatically add a prefix to the name of HTTP requests when recording

Once the recording is finished, we end up with this script:

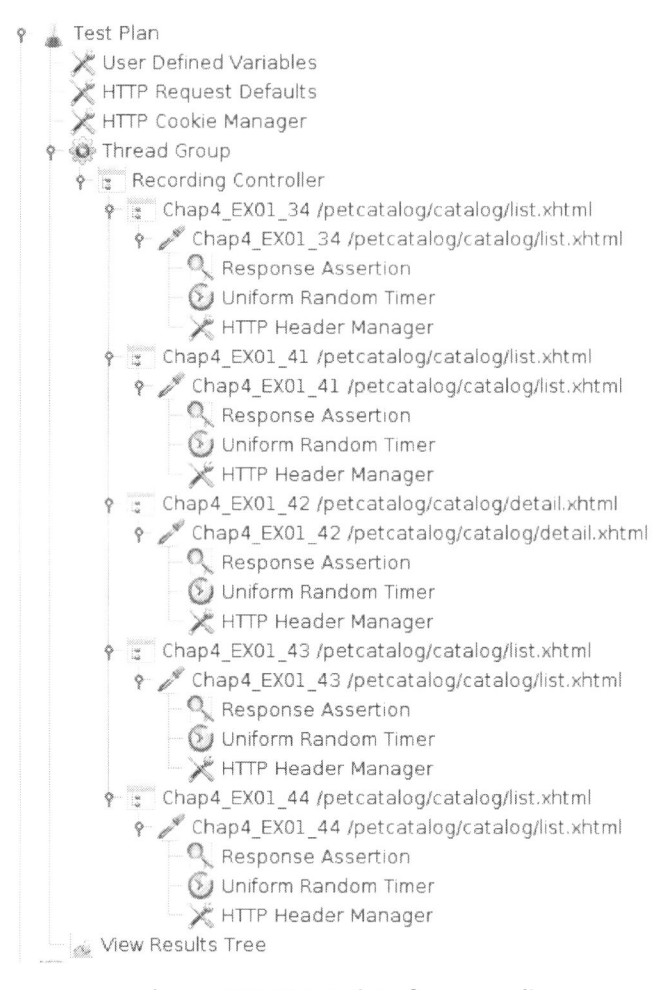

```
Test Plan
    User Defined Variables
    HTTP Request Defaults
    HTTP Cookie Manager
    Thread Group
        Recording Controller
            Chap4_EX01_34 /petcatalog/catalog/list.xhtml
                Chap4_EX01_34 /petcatalog/catalog/list.xhtml
                    Response Assertion
                    Uniform Random Timer
                    HTTP Header Manager
            Chap4_EX01_41 /petcatalog/catalog/list.xhtml
                Chap4_EX01_41 /petcatalog/catalog/list.xhtml
                    Response Assertion
                    Uniform Random Timer
                    HTTP Header Manager
            Chap4_EX01_42 /petcatalog/catalog/detail.xhtml
                Chap4_EX01_42 /petcatalog/catalog/detail.xhtml
                    Response Assertion
                    Uniform Random Timer
                    HTTP Header Manager
            Chap4_EX01_43 /petcatalog/catalog/list.xhtml
                Chap4_EX01_43 /petcatalog/catalog/list.xhtml
                    Response Assertion
                    Uniform Random Timer
                    HTTP Header Manager
            Chap4_EX01_44 /petcatalog/catalog/list.xhtml
                Chap4_EX01_44 /petcatalog/catalog/list.xhtml
                    Response Assertion
                    Uniform Random Timer
                    HTTP Header Manager
    View Results Tree
```

Figure 7.33: Our script after recording

The result of the recording may be different for you depending on the delay between two actions and the configuration of your browser.

7. This delay can be changed with the *proxy.pause* property or during recording using **HTTP(S) Test Script Recorder** with the **Create new transaction after request (ms)** option:

> **Note**
> Add this property to the **user.properties** file instead of editing the *jmeter.properties* file. This will ease the upgrading of the JMeter version and make it clear for others what differs from the default configuration.

Figure 7.34: Delay between two actions during recording

8. Let's now work on the recorded script (rename it, split into transactions, and so on) to have a more readable script and a meaningful report:

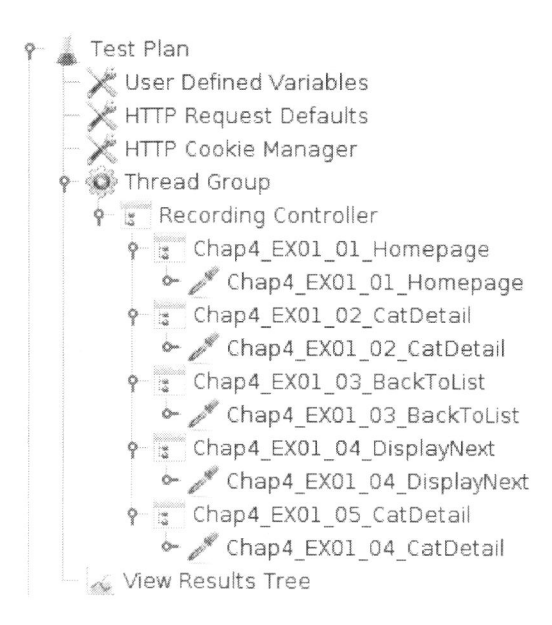

Figure 7.35: Our script once modified

9. Configure/add configuration items to better simulate a user (**HTTP Cache Manager**, **HTTP Cookie Manager**, and **HTTP Header Manager**) and make our work easier (**HTTP Request Defaults**).

   In our case, we will simulate a user who:

   Uses Firefox under Linux, using an English locale:

HTTP Header Manager

Name: HTTP Header Manager
Comments:

Headers Stored in the Header Manager

Name:	Value
Accept-Language	en,en-US;q=0.5
Accept-Encoding	gzip, deflate
User-Agent	Mozilla/5.0 (X11; Ubuntu; Linux x86_64; rv:55.0) Gecko/20100101 Firefox/55.0
Accept	text/html,application/xhtml+xml,application/xml;q=0.9,*/*;q=0.8

Figure 7.36: Firefox under English Linux

Logs in for the first time (**Clear cookies each iteration?**) and does not block cookies:

Figure 7.37: With cookies

Logs in for the first time (**Clear cache each iteration?**) and has a web browser with the cache enabled:

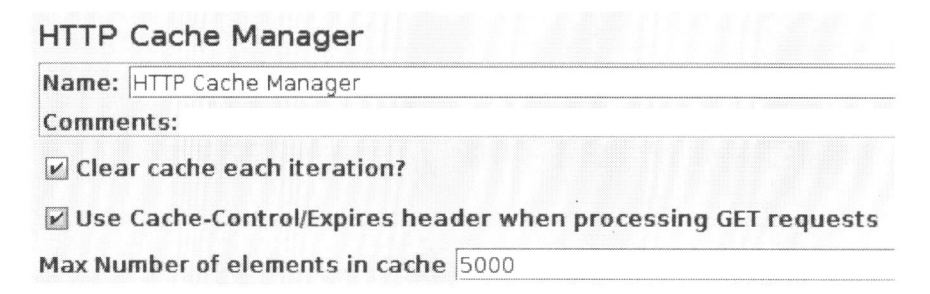

Figure 7.38: Cache enabled

10. Configure **Response Assertion** items to control each response:

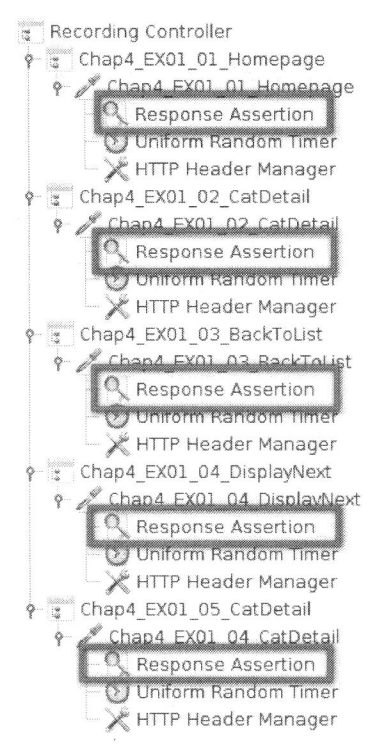

Figure 7.39: Response control

> **Note**
> Use **View Results Tree** under **HTTP(S) Test Script Recorder** to see the contents of each HTTP response.

For example, when displaying the detailed records of the first cat (Speedy Cat), a possible assertion is the following one:

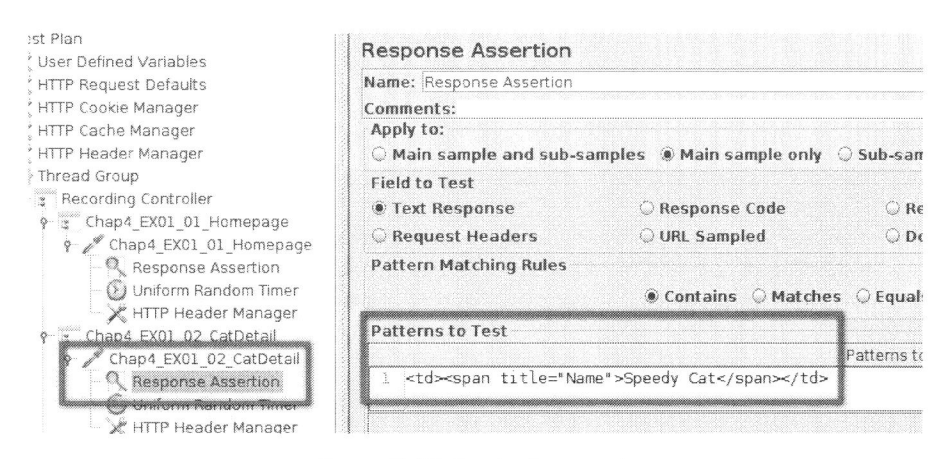

Figure 7.40: Control example

Let's now replay our script.

11. Looking at **View Results Tree**, we can see that our script is not working:

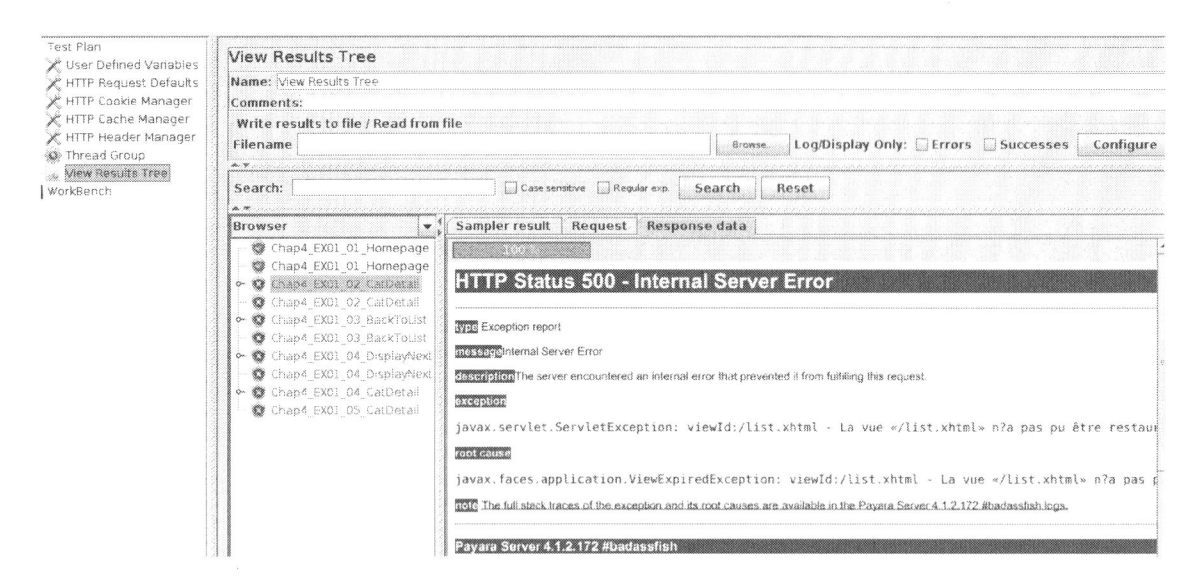

Figure 7.41: Failed to execute

> **Caution**
> In your case, it may work, depending on the settings of your application server and the time between the recording of your script and its replay.
>
> In any case, as we will see later, the script is not yet finalized and is incorrect for now.

Let's take a closer look at HTTP requests to find the source of the problem.

12. Note that the **javax.faces.ViewState** variable is used in many HTTP requests. **javax.faces.ViewState** is a hidden field used to store information in applications developed with *JavaServer Faces (JSF) technology*:

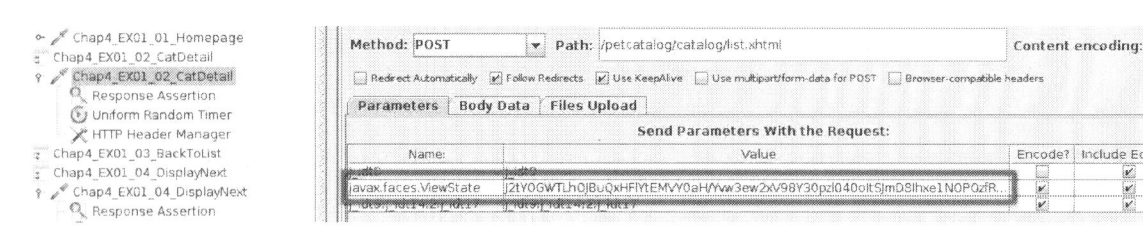

Figure 7.42: javax.faces.ViewState

13. In order to replay the requests successfully, we need to handle this dynamic parameter; this is called the correlation process. For this, we will retrieve the value of **javax.faces.ViewState** in the HTTP request where it first appears and inject it into the HTTP request that needs it. To do that, we can use a **CSS Selector Extractor** element, a **Regular Expression Extractor** element, or a **Boundary Extractor** element. The extraction technology chosen will depend on the format of the response that contains the value you need to extract:

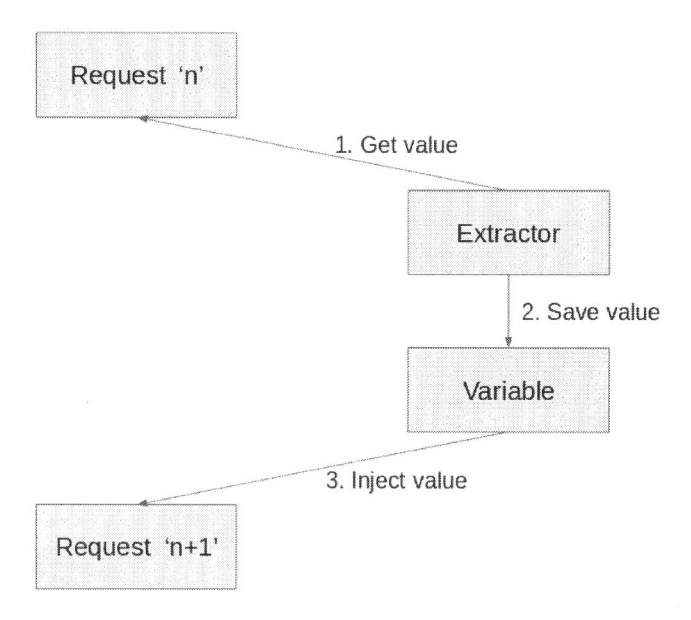

Figure 7.43: Correlation

14. For example, for the **/petcatalog/catalog/list.xhtml** (*Chap4_EX01_02_CatDetail*) HTTP request, you need to retrieve the value of **javax.faces.ViewState** in the HTTP request **/petcatalog/catalog/list.xhtml** (*Chap4_EX01_01_Homepage*):

> **Note**
> You can use the **Search** function of **View Results Tree** to find where **javax.faces.ViewState** is used.

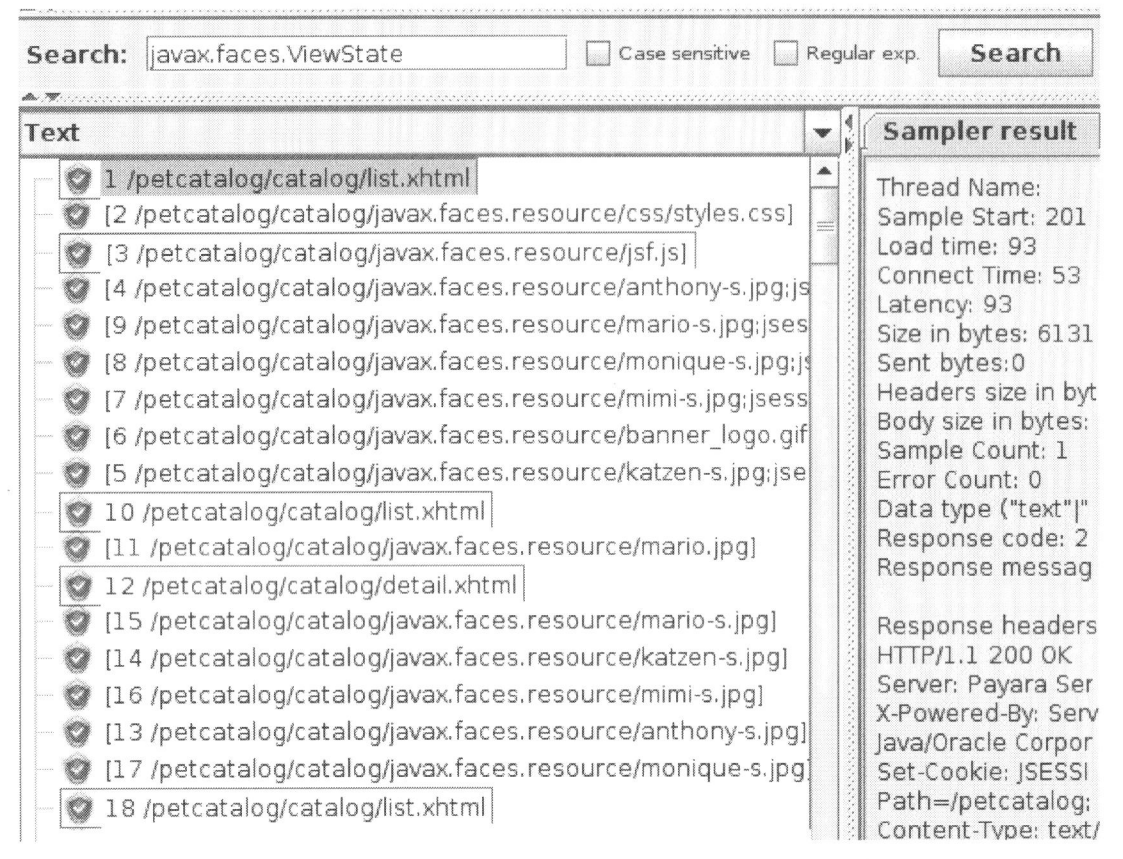

Figure 7.44: Localization of javax.faces.ViewState in View Results Tree

15. Before adding our extractor, let's look at the source code of the home page to determine which CSS selector or regular expression to use.

    The part of the source code we are interested in is the following:

    ```
    <input type="hidden" name="javax.faces.ViewState" id="j_id1:javax.
    faces.ViewState:0" value="74xRq/jpmh66f1Q=" autocomplete="off" />
    ```

    > **Caution**
    > The value of the **javax.faces.ViewState** variable should be different. In addition, to simplify its reading, we have shortened it.

Our regular expression will be:

```
<input type="hidden" name="javax.faces.ViewState" id="j_id1:javax.
faces.ViewState:0" value="(.+?)" autocomplete="off" />
```

16. Let's add and configure our **Regular Expression Extractor**:

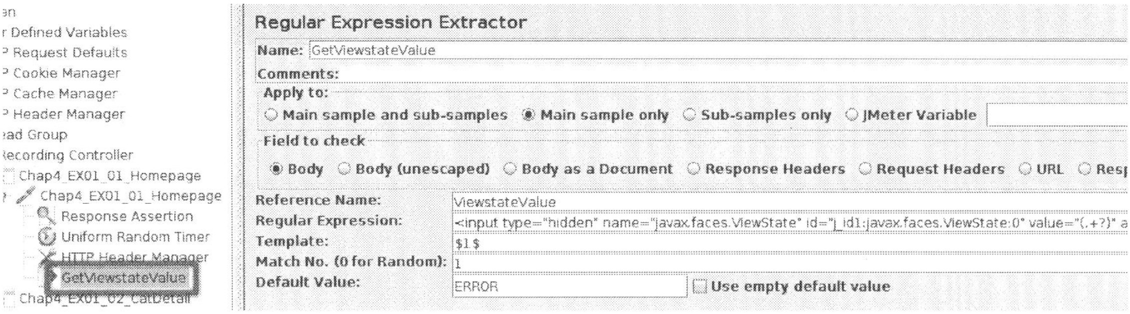

Figure 7.45: Regular Expression Extractor

Another easier and more maintainable way to extract data from an HTML page is to use **CSS/Jquery Selector Extractor** or **Boundary Extractor**:

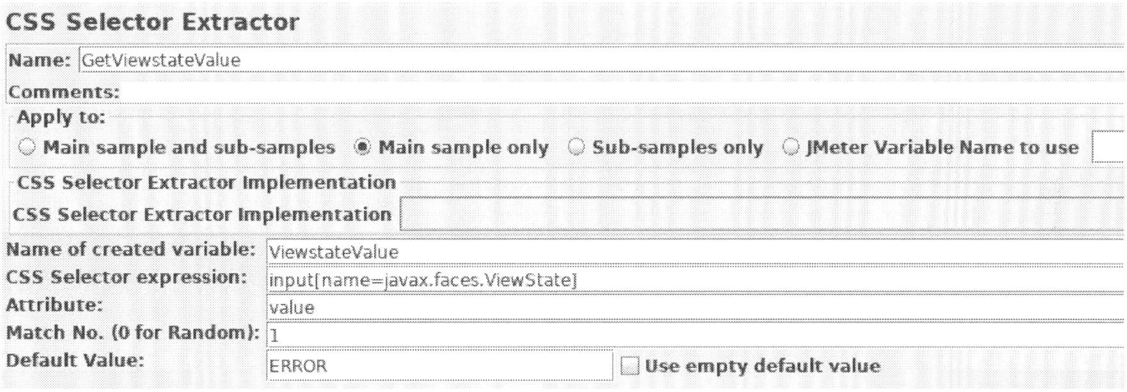

Figure 7.46: CSS Selector Extractor

As you can see, this extractor allows us to use CSS selectors. Here, the expression indicates to extract an input whose name is **javax.faces.ViewState**. The syntax is much simpler than that for regular expressions and much more powerful.

The element proposes two implementations (*JSoup* is the default):

JSoup (http://jsoup.org/cookbook/extracting-data/selector-syntax) is the default implementation used.

Jodd Lagarto (https://jodd.org/csselly/).

The syntax is very similar.

17. Now, let's use the value of **javax.faces.ViewState** that we retrieved:

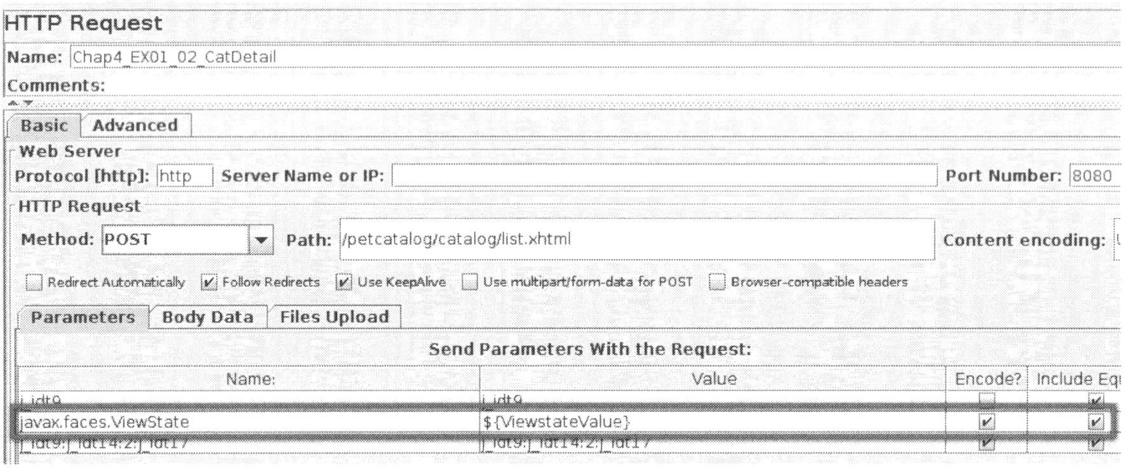

Figure 7.47: Use of the result

18. Let's do the same for the other requests. We can use the *Search/Replace* feature of JMeter and use **Replace All** or **Next / Replace&Find** to do this. This feature of JMeter is made to speed up the correlation process as it allows safe replacement in the values of the following elements:

HTTP Header Manager

HTTP Request

```
Chap4_EX01_01_Homepage
    Chap4_EX01_01_Homepage
        Response Assertion
        Uniform Random Timer
        GetViewstateValue
Chap4_EX01_02_CatDetail
    Chap4_EX01_02_CatDetail
        Response Assertion
        Uniform Random Timer
        HTTP Header Manager
        GetViewstateValue
Chap4_EX01_03_BackToList
    Chap4_EX01_03_BackToList
        Response Assertion
        Uniform Random Timer
        HTTP Header Manager
        GetViewstateValue
Chap4_EX01_04_DisplayNext
    Chap4_EX01_04_DisplayNext
        Response Assertion
        Uniform Random Timer
        HTTP Header Manager
        GetViewstateValue
Chap4_EX01_05_CatDetail
```

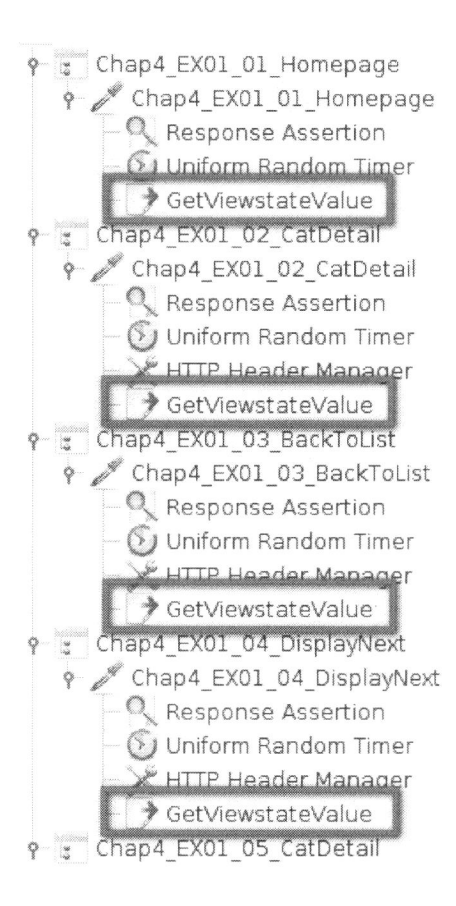

Figure 7.48: The generalization of regular expressions

19. Let's run our script (use the **Validate** feature for that, which runs the selected thread group with one thread and no pauses):

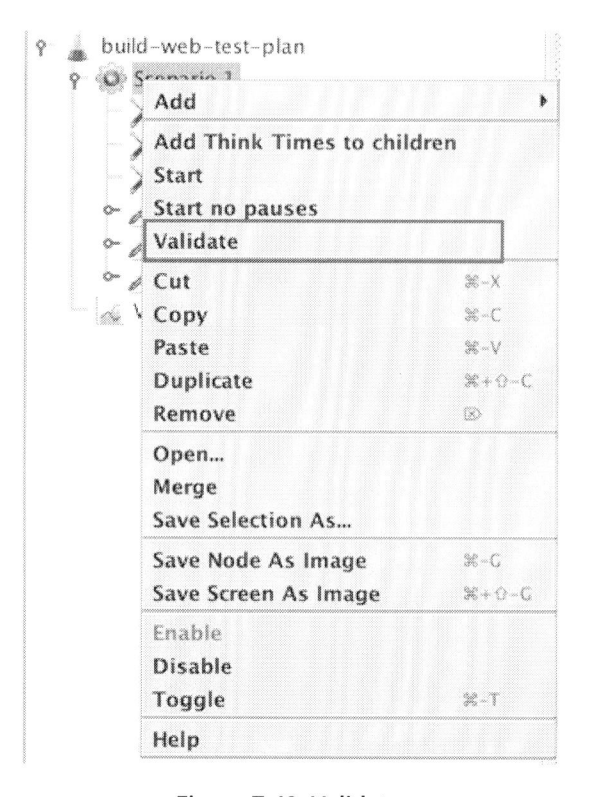

Figure 7.49: Validate

There is still an error:

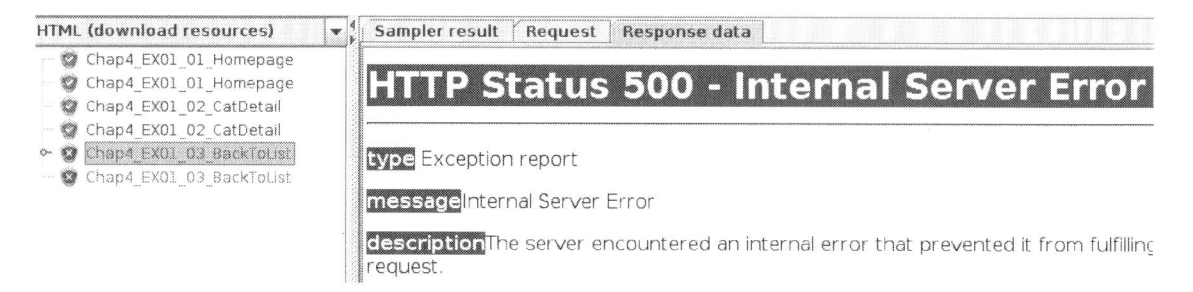

Figure 7.50: Result of execution

Looking a little closer, we notice that the value of **javax.faces.ViewState** is not encoded:

Figure 7.51: Unencoded value of javax.faces.ViewState

20. Let's check the box and verify that the script passes successfully:

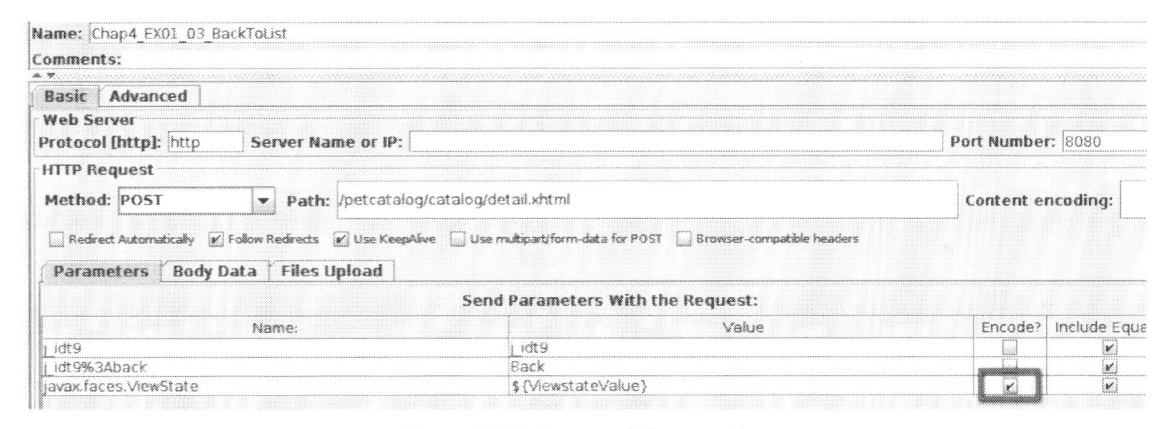

Figure 7.52: Successful execution

Unfortunately, the current script is still not realistic for a load test (there's no flow control, the same queries are always executed, and so on).

Let's fix these simulation realism problems.

21. Let's start by adding some randomness in our script to vary the HTTP requests.

For this, we will choose a random cat instead of always choosing the same two cats.

22. Let's look at the HTML code for the page (**Chap4_EX01_01_Homepage** in our case) and make the link with our HTTP request:

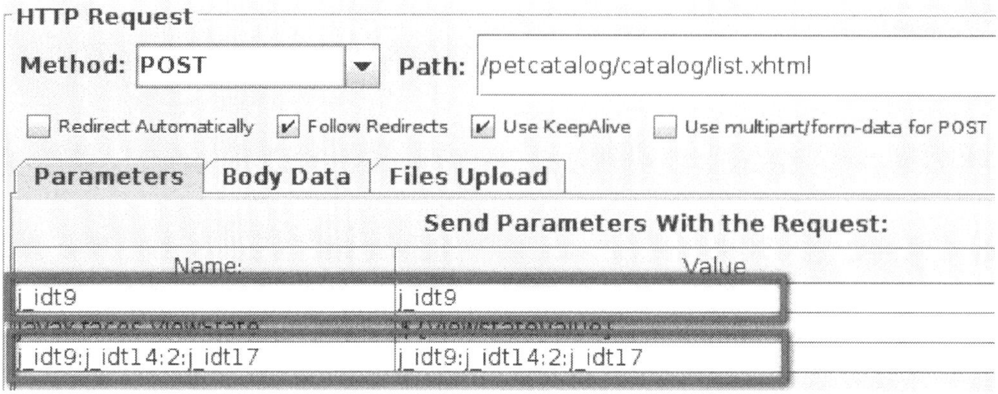

Figure 7.53: HTTP Request

> **Note**
> Some development knowledge and/or a discussion with the developer can save a lot of time.

After further thinking, we understand that there are several values to recover:

The value of the form:

    <input type="hidden" name="j_idt9" value="j_idt9" />

The associated regular expression:

    <input type="hidden" name="j_idt9" value="(.+?)" />

The four values defining the details of the selected cat:

    document.getElementById('j_idt9'),{'j_idt9:j_idt14:1:j_idt17':'j_idt9:j_idt14:1:j_idt17'},'');return false">Alley Cat</a></td>

The associated regular expression:

```
document\.getElementById\('(.+?)'\),\{'(.+?)':'(.+?)'\},''\);return false">(.+?)</a></td>
```

> **Note**
> In order to test our regular expressions, we can use the **RegExp Tester** function of **View Results Tree**.

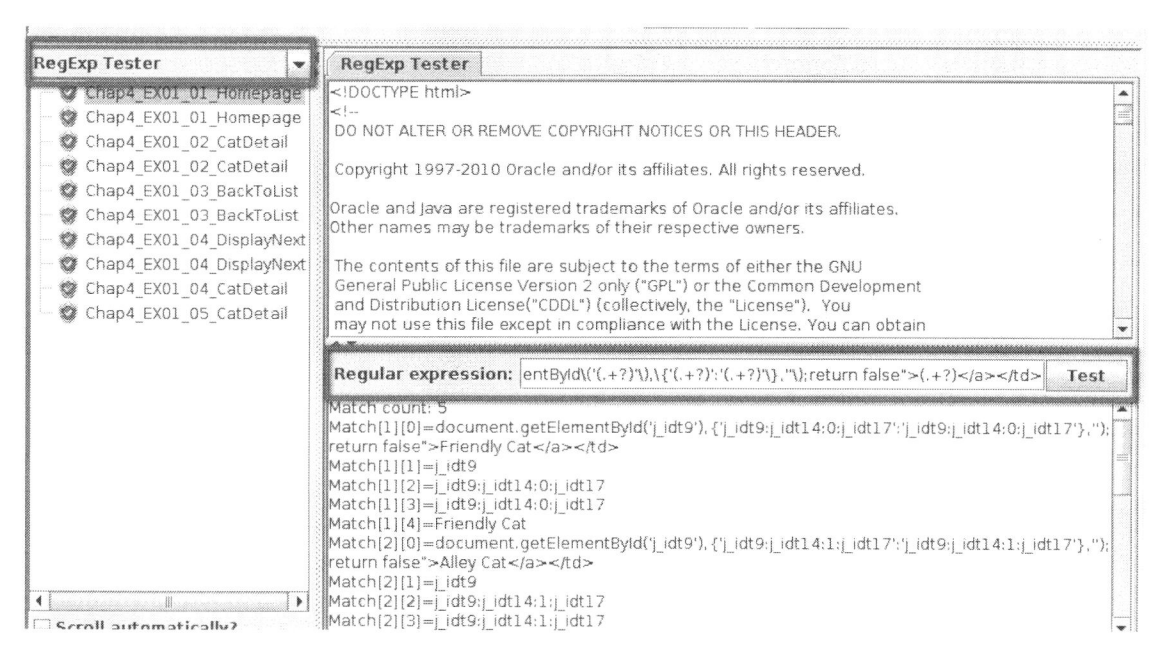

Figure 7.54: RegExp Tester

23. Let's add two **Regular Expression Extractor** to extract these values:

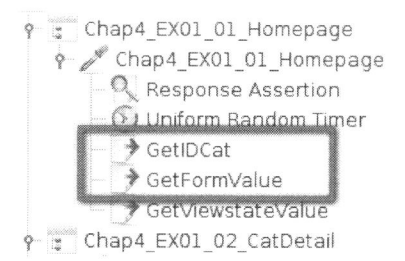

Figure 7.55: Regular Expression Extractor

24. Parameterize them:

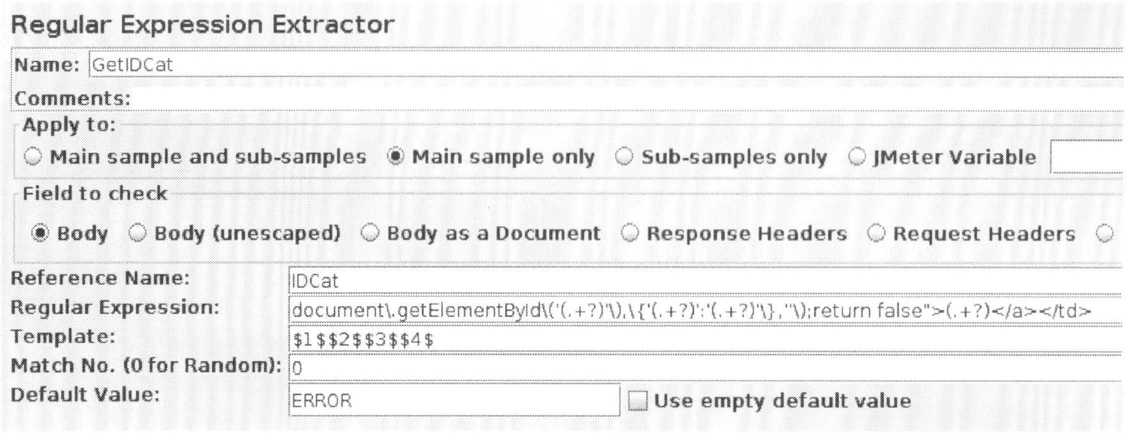

Figure 7.56: Retrieving the values defining the cat

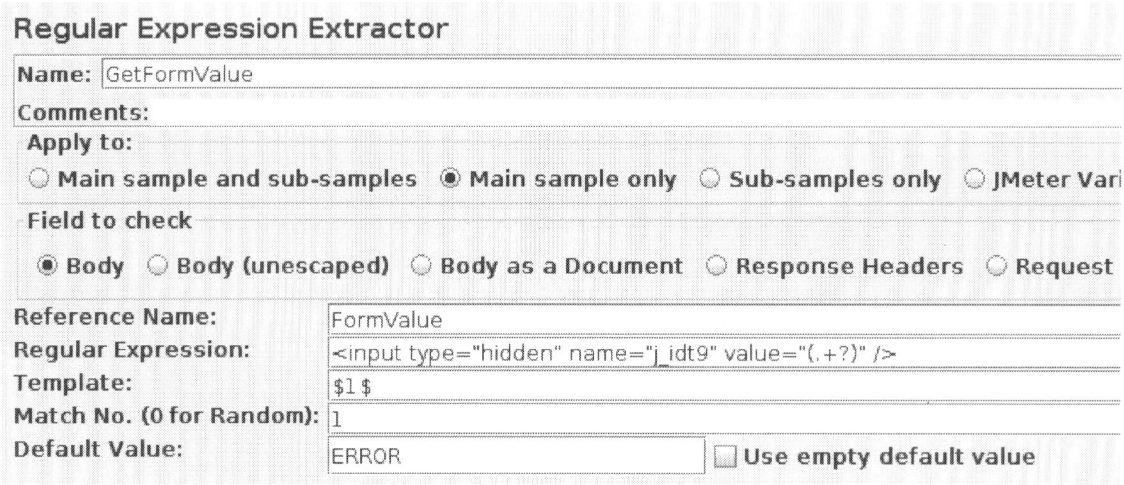

Figure 7.57: Retrieving the form value

About regular expression for IDCat. "default value"=="ERROR"

I tend to prefer having "IDCat_not_found" as a default value for the regexp extractor.

When extractor fails, and it is somehow used at subsequent steps, the use of detailed "default" makes it way easier to tell which regexp failed.

– Vladimir Sitnikov's quote (JMeter team member)

25. Now we can use the retrieved values in our script:

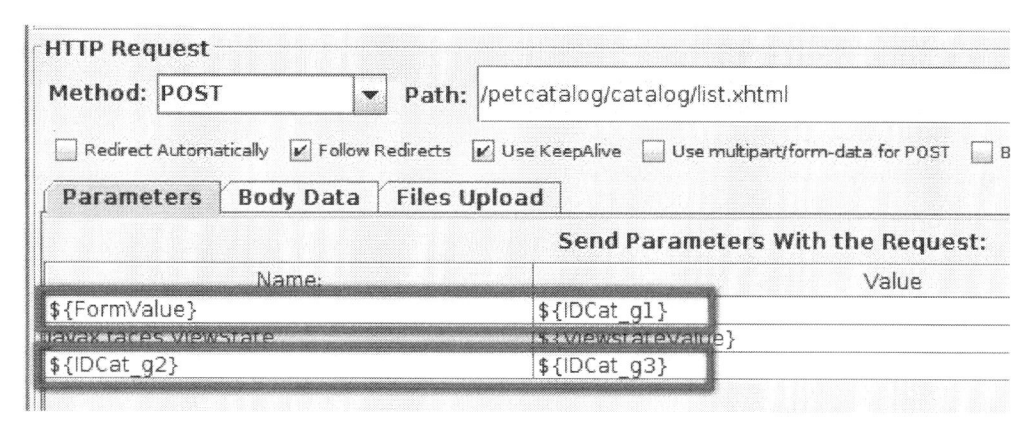

Figure 7.58: Using values

26. Do not forget to change the assertions, too:

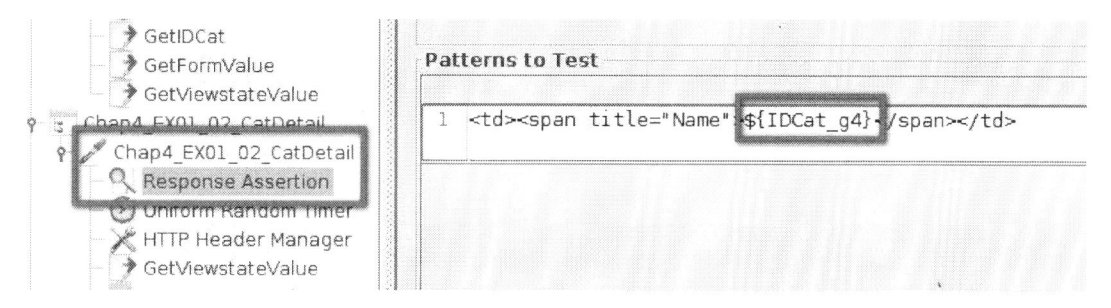

Figure 7.59: Our modified assertion

27. Let's do the same for our second selection:

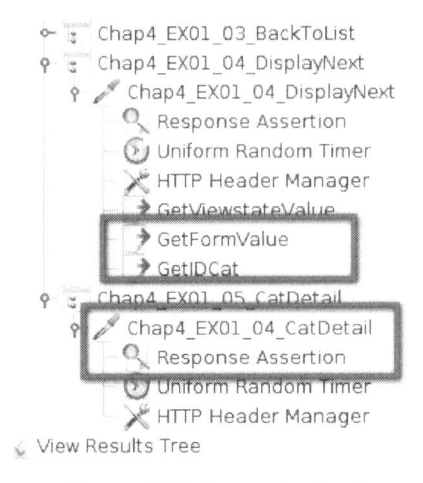

Figure 7.60: Second selection

28. Validate our test:

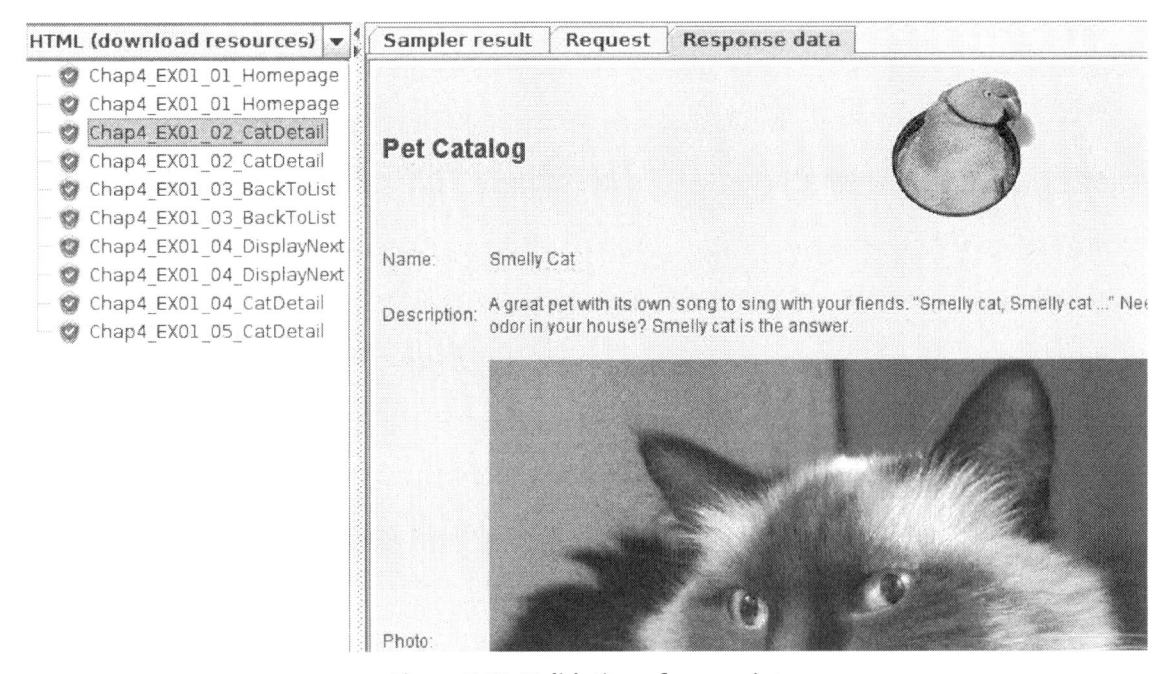

Figure 7.61: Validation of our script

Let's now improve the readability and maintainability of the test plan.

For the moment, we only have the *think time* (**Uniform Random Timer**) of the users that we have recorded.

29. Let's start by checking the number of iterations per minute of our script (called *pacing*) using **Constant Throughput Timer**:

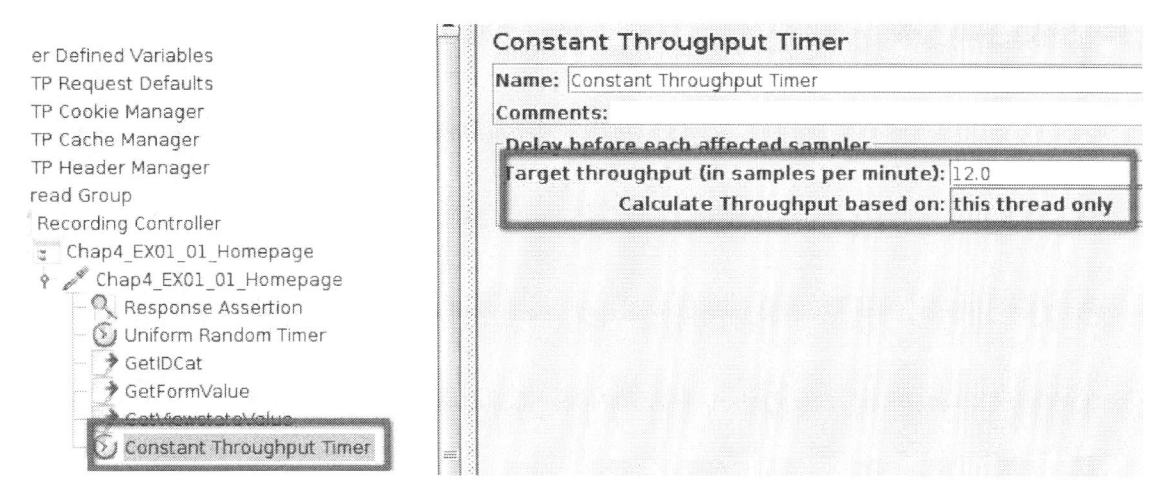

Figure 7.62: Constant Throughput Timer

> **Note**
> It is also possible to use **Precise Throughput Timer**, which is more accurate and powerful.

Here, we want each virtual user to execute a script iteration every 5 seconds (equivalent to 12 iterations per minute).

Now, we want to be sure that there is concurrency (at least two virtual users in our example) during the transaction displaying the detailed records of a cat (in our case, the first transaction, *Chap4_EX01_02_CatDetail*).

30. For this, we will use the concept of *Rendez-vous* using **Synchronizing Timer**.

This element allows you to set how much threads need to trigger at the same time the call of a Sampler. The thread will pause on the timer until the value for **Number of Simulated users to group by** is reached. When this number is reached, they will all stop waiting and trigger the call of the sampler that is to be run after the pause:

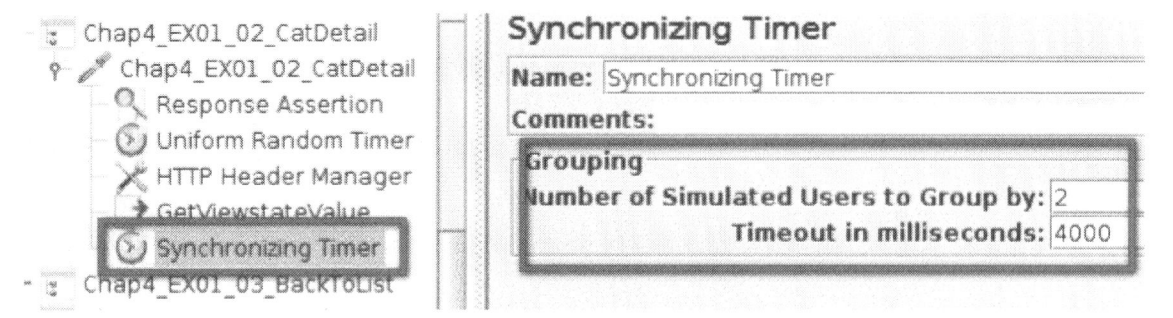

Figure 7.63: Synchronizing Timer

Sample #	Start Time	Thread Name	Label
1	23:35:44.756	Thread Group...	Chap4_EX01_01_Homepage
2	23:35:44.734	Thread Group...	Chap4_EX01_01_Homepage
3	23:35:48.823	Thread Group...	Chap4_EX01_01_Homepage
4	23:35:48.739	Thread Group...	Chap4_EX01_01_Homepage
5	23:35:52.206	Thread Group...	Chap4_EX01_02_CatDetail
6	23:35:44.770	Thread Group...	Chap4_EX01_02_CatDetail
7	23:35:52.747	Thread Group...	Chap4_EX01_01_Homepage
8	23:35:52.736	Thread Group...	Chap4_EX01_01_Homepage
9	23:35:56.209	Thread Group...	Chap4_EX01_02_CatDetail
10	23:35:52.765	Thread Group...	Chap4_EX01_02_CatDetail
11	23:35:56.242	Thread Group...	Chap4_EX01_02_CatDetail
12	23:35:48.842	Thread Group...	Chap4_EX01_02_CatDetail
13	23:35:56.831	Thread Group...	Chap4_EX01_01_Homepage
14	23:35:56.736	Thread Group...	Chap4_EX01_01_Homepage
15	23:35:56.858	Thread Group...	Chap4_EX01_03_BackToList
16	23:35:52.228	Thread Group...	Chap4_EX01_03_BackToList
17	23:36:00.503	Thread Group...	Chap4_EX01_04_DisplayNext
18	23:35:56.866	Thread Group...	Chap4_EX01_04_DisplayNext

Figure 7.64: The result of our Synchronizing Timer

Looking at the requests and responses on different runs in more detail, we notice that the content of our *Chap4_EX01_03_BackToList* and *Chap4_EX01_04_DisplayNext* transactions can vary in terms of the names of attributes:

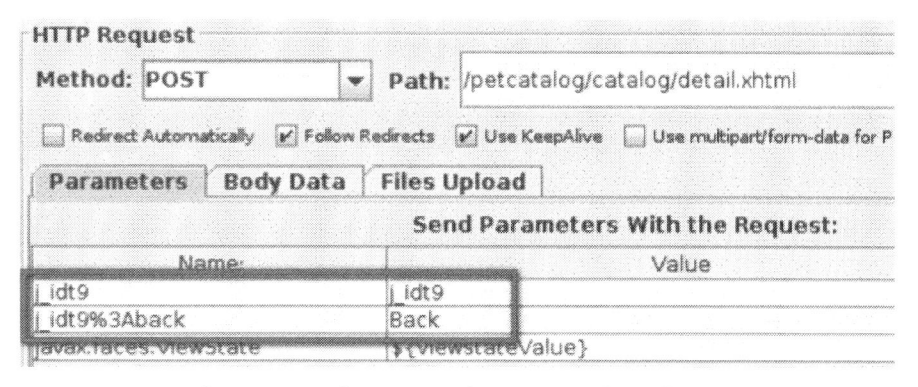

Figure 7.65: Changes to the names of attributes

Looking a little closer, we understand that we need to make the names and values of the **j_idt9**, **j_idt9%3Aback**, and **j_idt9:j_idt13** parameters more dynamic.

31. Hopefully, we can solve this using a regular expression and **Regular Expression Extractor**:

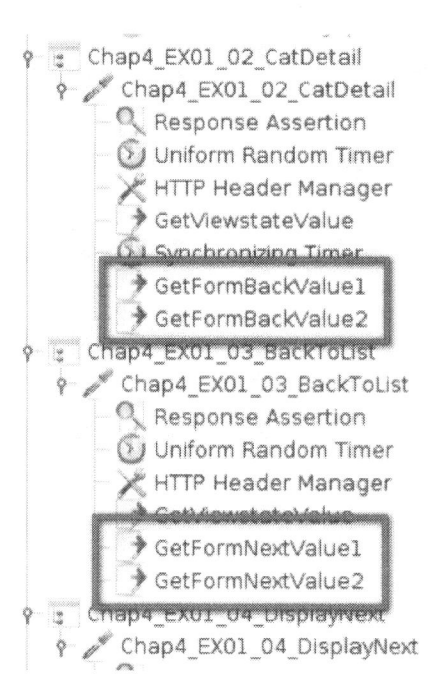

Figure 7.66: Regular Expression Extractor

> **Note**
> Notice the use of **(?s)** in our regular expression to switch to single-line mode and escape line breaks.

Figure 7.67: Using (?s)

32. Our script is now ready. We have to define the load that we want to inject. In our case, only 20 percent of users go to the second results page. In order to respect this constraint, we'll use **Throughput Controller**:

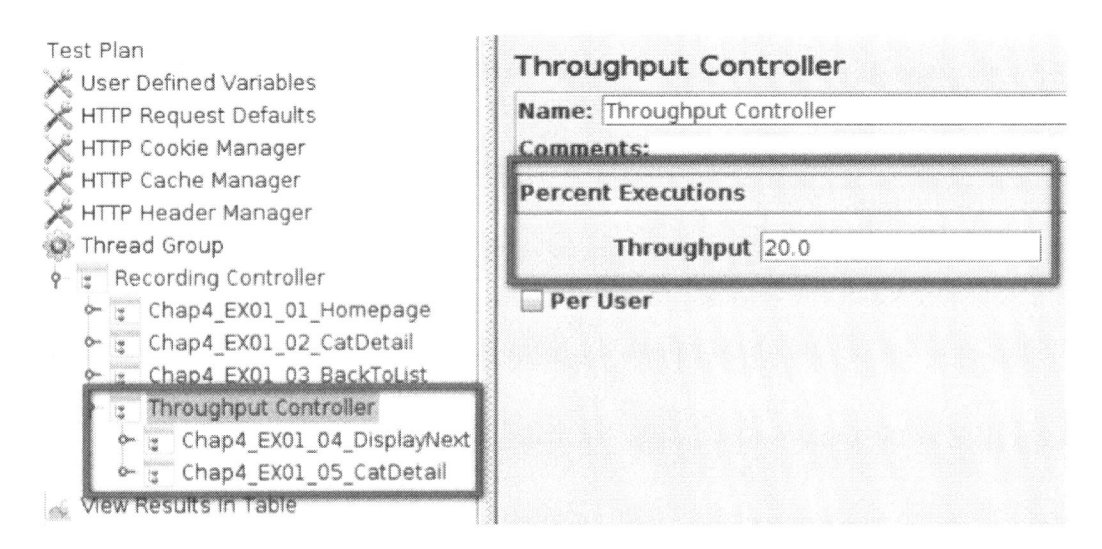

Figure 7.68: Throughput Controller

33. We run our scenario to check that only 20 percent of transactions go on the second results page:

Label	# Samples
Chap4_EX01_01_Homepage	100
Chap4_EX01_02_CatDetail	100
Chap4_EX01_03_BackToList	100
Chap4_EX01_04_DisplayNext	20
Chap4_EX01_05_CatDetail	20
TOTAL	340

Figure 7.69: The result of the execution

We finally have a realistic and operational JMeter script.

Example 2: Technical Tests with Byteman

For this example, we need some notion of how Java works.

A Java application is a set of source files (1) compiled into bytecode (2) by the Java compiler. This bytecode is executed by the JVM (3):

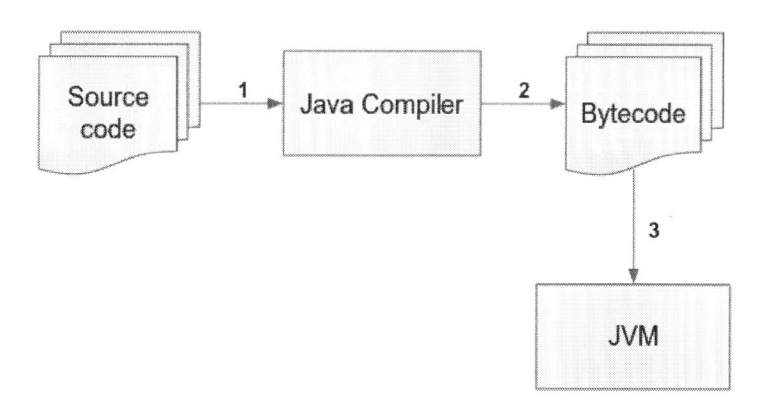

Figure 7.70: Java bytecode

There are many Java agents (programs that interface with the JVM) that can manipulate this bytecode. This allows us, in our case, to modify the behavior of our application without having to modify its source code.

Let's go back to our example.

A new application is developed: Spring PetClinic (https://github.com/SpringSource/spring-petclinic).

We have to load test it.

Tests are done using this JMeter script:

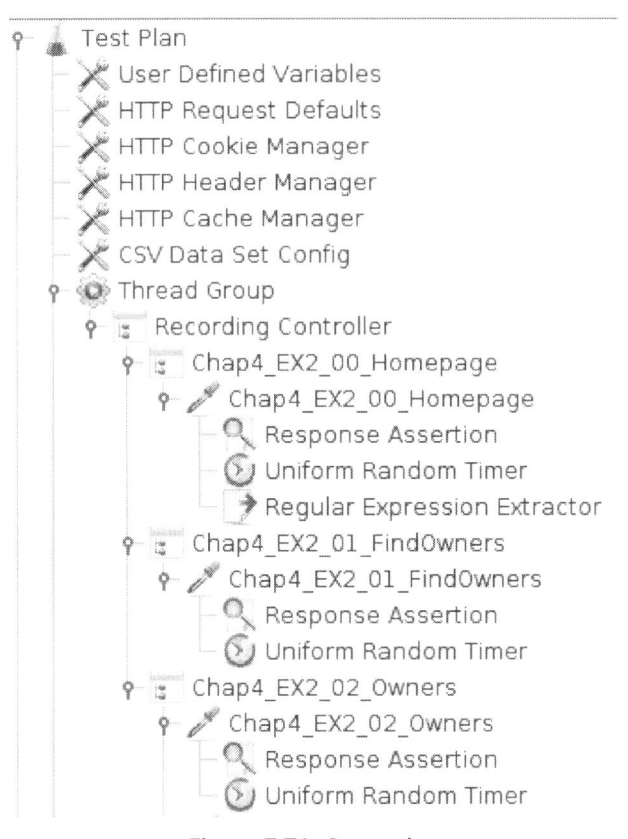

```
Test Plan
    User Defined Variables
    HTTP Request Defaults
    HTTP Cookie Manager
    HTTP Header Manager
    HTTP Cache Manager
    CSV Data Set Config
    Thread Group
        Recording Controller
            Chap4_EX2_00_Homepage
                Chap4_EX2_00_Homepage
                    Response Assertion
                    Uniform Random Timer
                    Regular Expression Extractor
            Chap4_EX2_01_FindOwners
                Chap4_EX2_01_FindOwners
                    Response Assertion
                    Uniform Random Timer
            Chap4_EX2_02_Owners
                Chap4_EX2_02_Owners
                    Response Assertion
                    Uniform Random Timer
```

Figure 7.71: Our script

This script consists of the following steps:

1. Go to the home page:

   Figure 7.72: Home

2. Do a search on the owner of a pet:

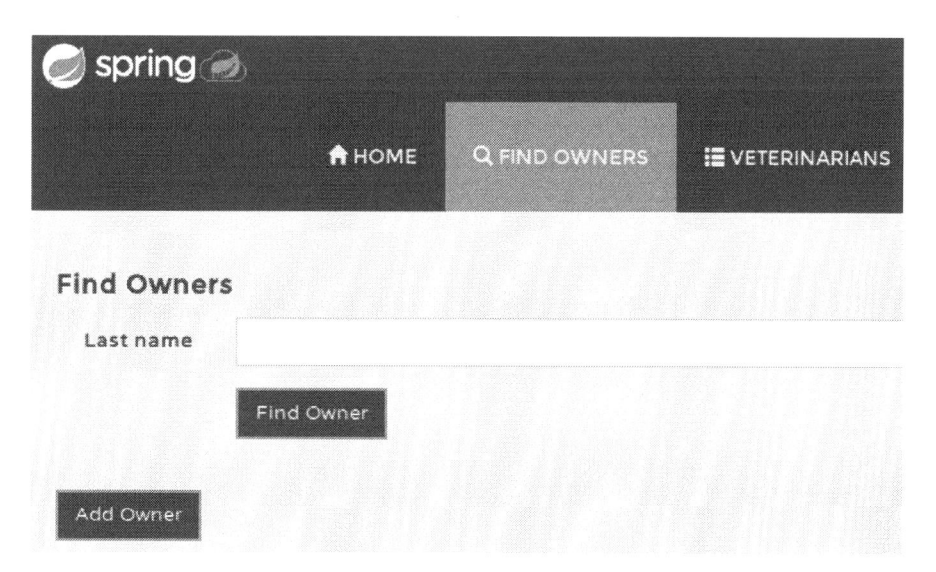

   Figure 7.73: Search

3. View the details:

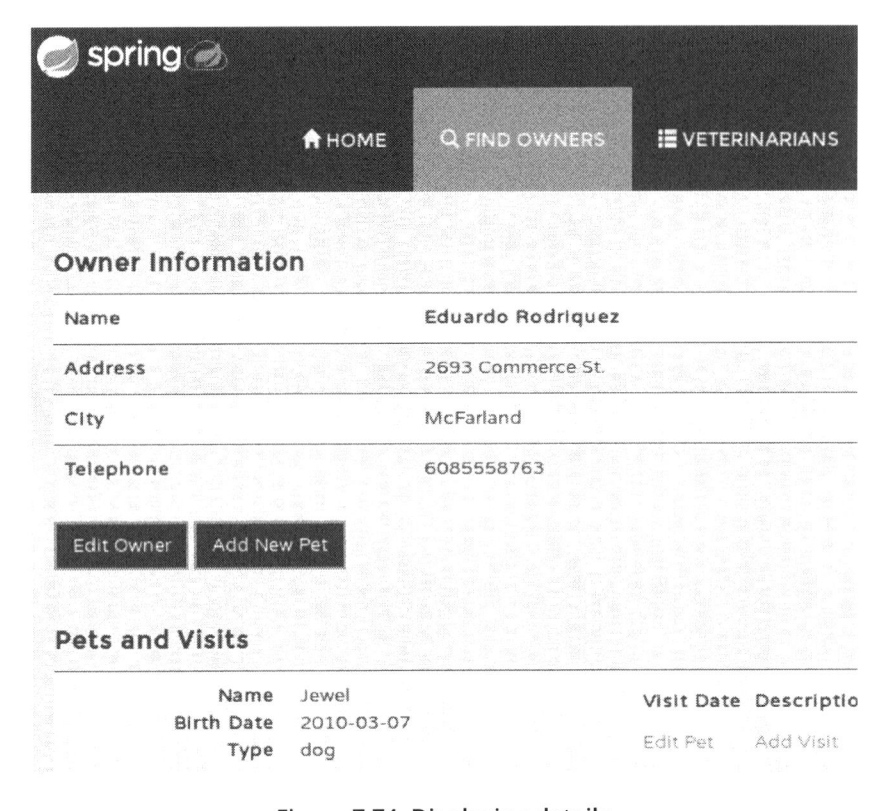

Figure 7.74: Displaying details

The contents of a CSV file are used with **CSV Data Set Config** for the input of the search function:

Figure 7.75: CSV Data Source

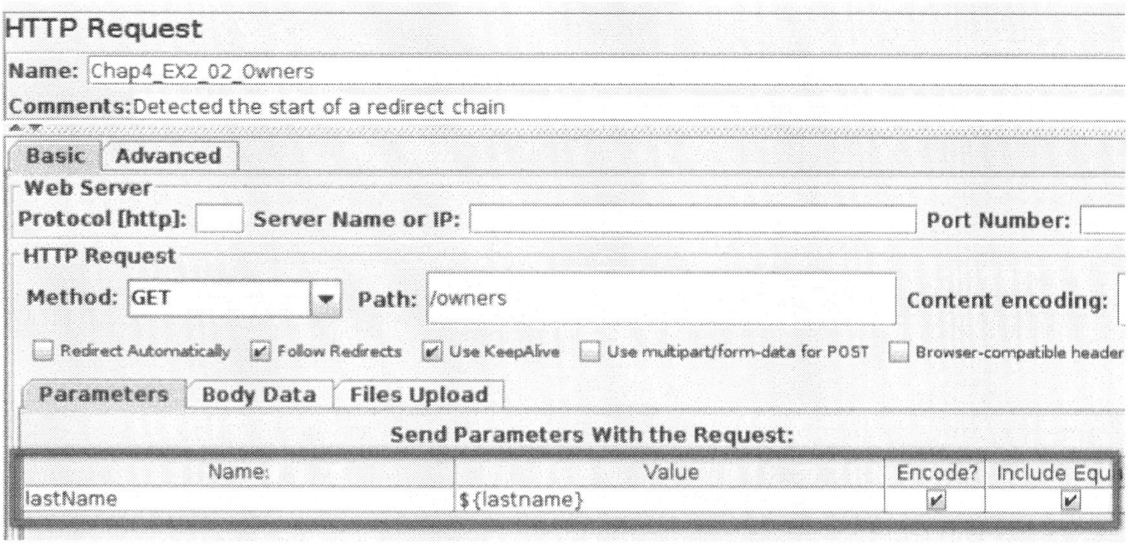

Figure 7.76: Using data from a CSV file

Everything works fine, but we have some doubts about some features of the application. We would like to see how the system (the application and its environment) will behave in degraded mode.

In particular, two questions often come up:

What happens if the response time of the search function is greater than X seconds?

What happens if the database server stops responding?

To dispel our doubts and answer these two questions, we decide to do some technical tests.

4. After some thought, we decide to use JBoss Byteman (http://byteman.jboss.org/). This tool will allow us to modify the bytecode of our application on the fly in order to force it to have the expected behavior.

5. Its use is quite simple, and that's how we will use it in our case: First, we have to attach the agent of *JBoss Byteman* to our running application using the **bminstall.sh "PID of our application"** command (it is, of course, possible to do this when launching our application by modifying its startup command line)

6. Start our load test.

7. Then, we will send Byteman our code modification rules using the **bmsubmit.sh -l "our rule file"** command 10 minutes after the start (you can change this depending on your test).

8. Then, 10 minutes after the previous action, we will disable rules using the `bmsubmit.sh -u "our rule file"` command:

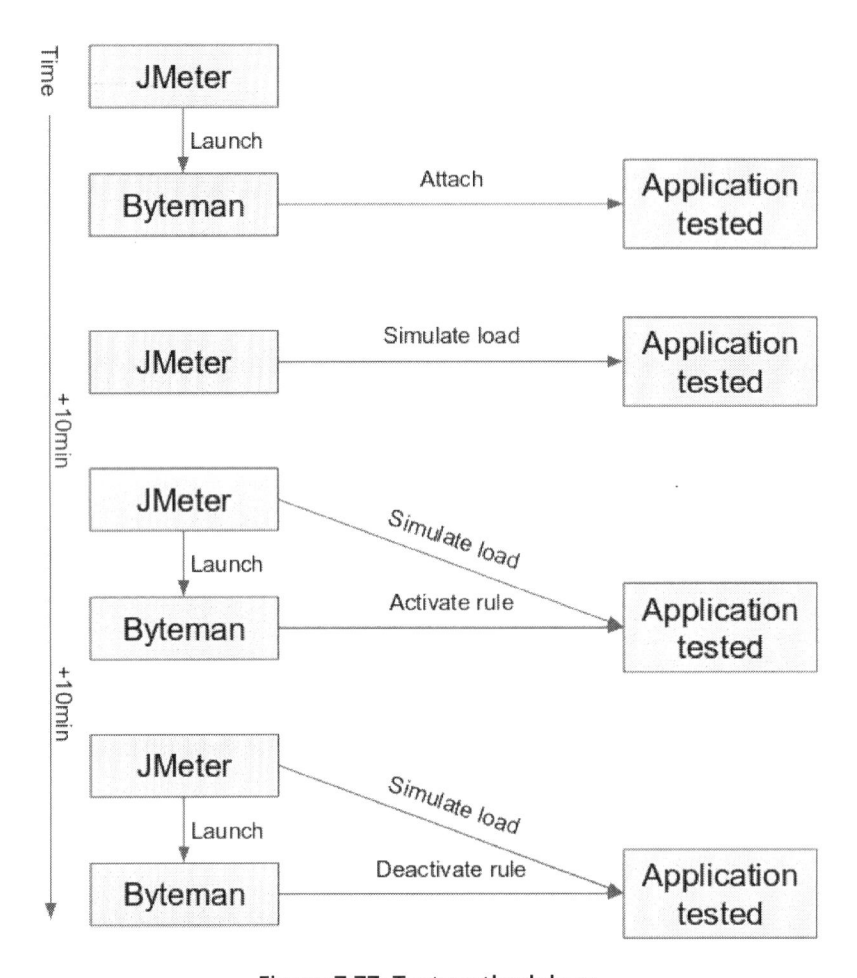

Figure 7.77: Test methodology

> **Note**
> Of course, during the load test, we'll be monitoring our application and servers.

To perform these tasks, we will use **OS Process Sampler**.

Let's move on to practice.

We'll now answer the question, "What happens if the response time of the search function is greater than 8 seconds?"

9. The first step is to extract the PID (https://en.wikipedia.org/wiki/Process_identifier) from our application using **OS Process Sampler** and **Regular Expression Extractor** in our **setUp Thread Group**:

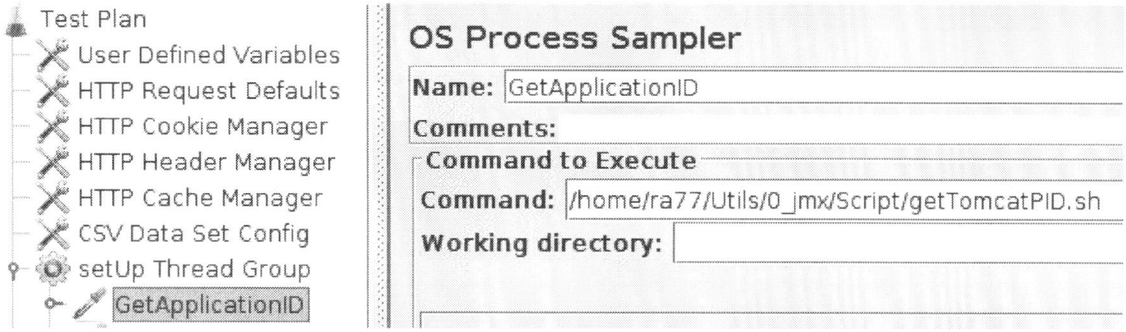

Figure 7.78: Running the PID recovery script

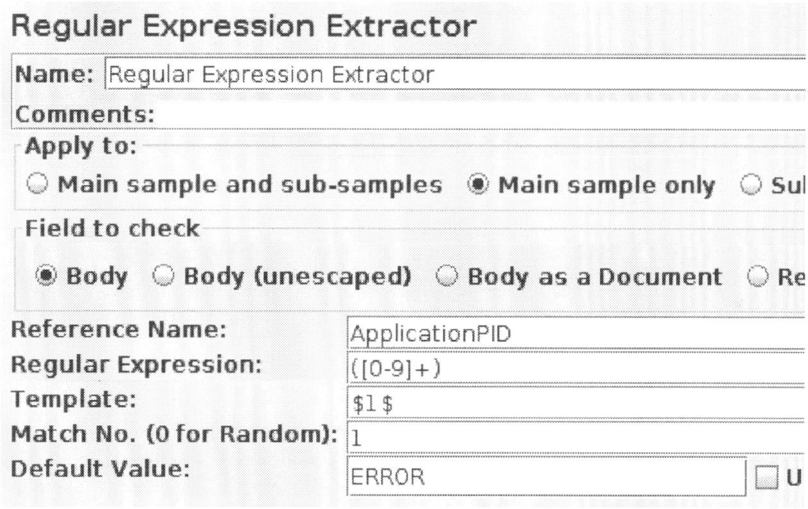

Figure 7.79: PID recovery

10. Then, attach *JBoss Byteman* agent to our application:

Figure 7.80: AttachAgent

11. Let's add a **Thread Group** that will send our *byteman* rule 10 minutes after launching our test.

12. Our rule will be the following and will consist of a pause of 9 seconds when the application does a search (the `processFindForm` function of the `OwnerController` class):

```
RULE Wait in OwnerController.processFindForm entry
CLASS OwnerController
METHOD processFindForm
AT ENTRY
IF true
DO Thread.sleep(9000)
ENDRULE
```

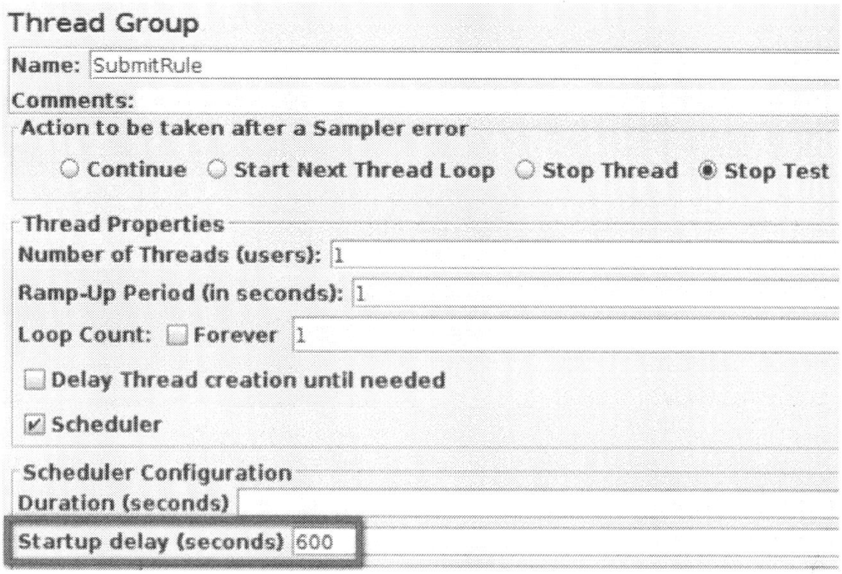

Figure 7.81: Activate the rule 10 minutes after the start

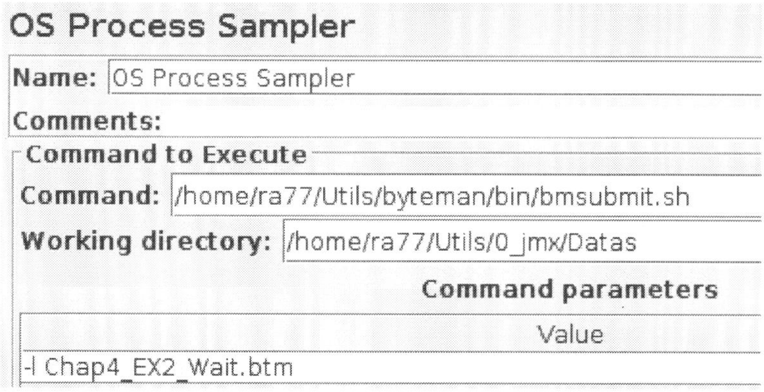

Figure 7.82: Activate the rule by JBoss Byteman

13. Then, do the same to disable this rule:

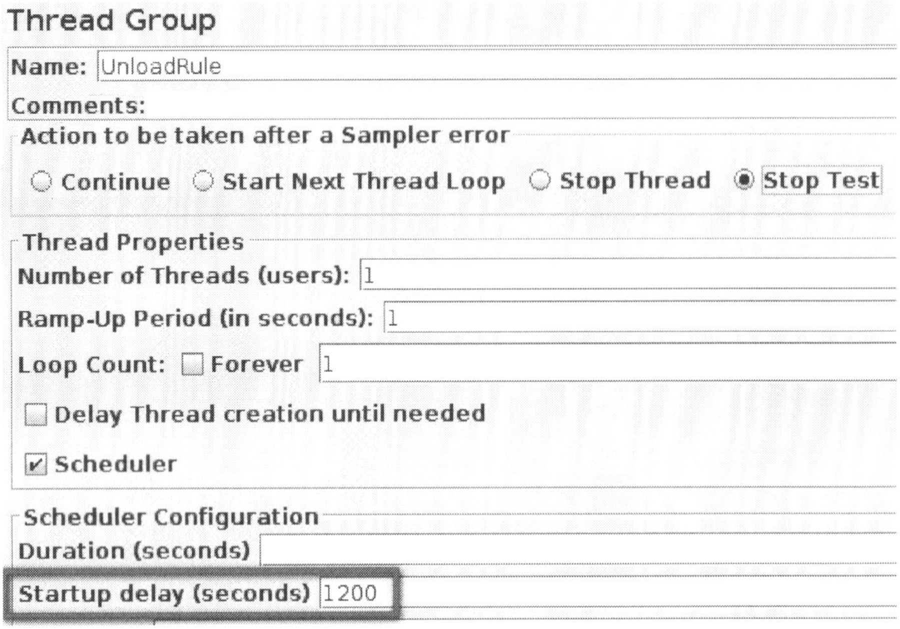

Figure 7.83: Disabling the rule 20 minutes after the start

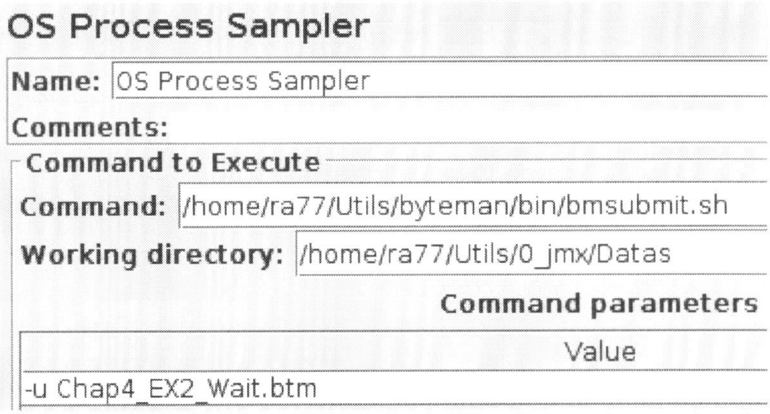

Figure 7.84: Disabling the rule by JBoss Byteman

Our script:

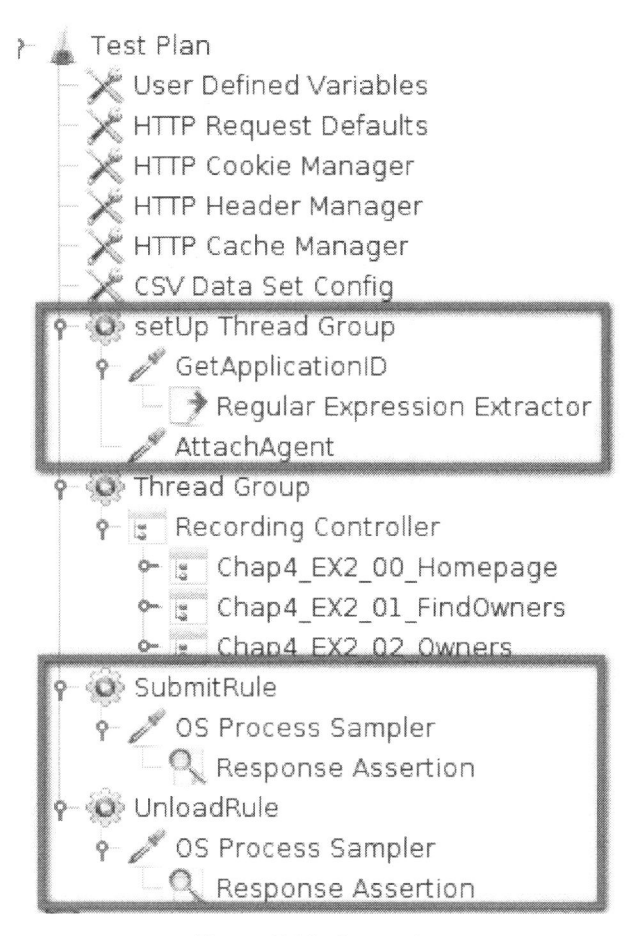

```
Test Plan
    User Defined Variables
    HTTP Request Defaults
    HTTP Cookie Manager
    HTTP Header Manager
    HTTP Cache Manager
    CSV Data Set Config
    setUp Thread Group
        GetApplicationID
            Regular Expression Extractor
        AttachAgent
    Thread Group
        Recording Controller
            Chap4_EX2_00_Homepage
            Chap4_EX2_01_FindOwners
            Chap4_EX2_02_Owners
    SubmitRule
        OS Process Sampler
            Response Assertion
    UnloadRule
        OS Process Sampler
            Response Assertion
```

Figure 7.85: Our script

14. Once executed, we can clearly see the impact on JMeter's results:

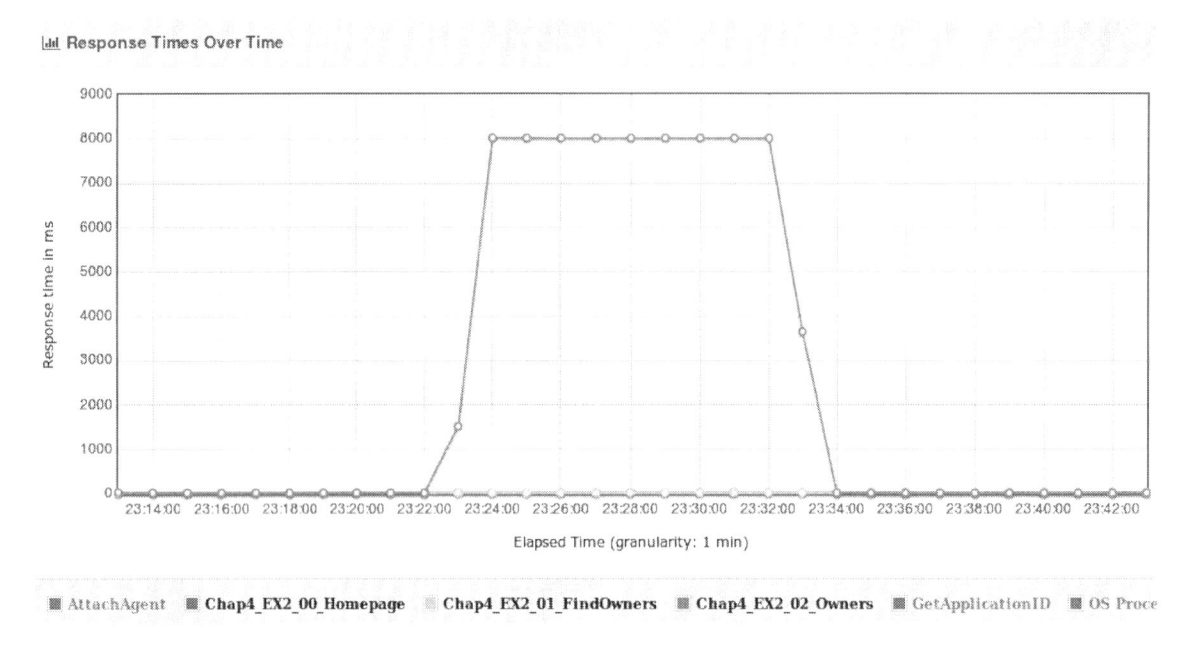

Figure 7.86: Impact on the results

> **Note**
> Do not forget to look at the results of monitoring tools to check the behavior of the tested system.
>
> This allows us to validate that there is no snowball effect that would degrade the entire system if the search function took longer than expected.

Let's now answer the question, "What happens if the database server stops responding?"

15. Our test will be exactly the same as before, but with the following *Byteman* script:

```
RULE OwnerController.processFindForm throw an exception
CLASS OwnerController
METHOD processFindForm
AT ENTRY
IF true
DO throw new org.springframework.dao.DataRetrievalFailureException("Db connection problem")
ENDRULE
```

Our *Byteman* rule is applied successfully during a manual test:

Figure 7.87: Manual test of our rule

We can also see how our application reacts during the load test with JMeter by looking at the error curve:

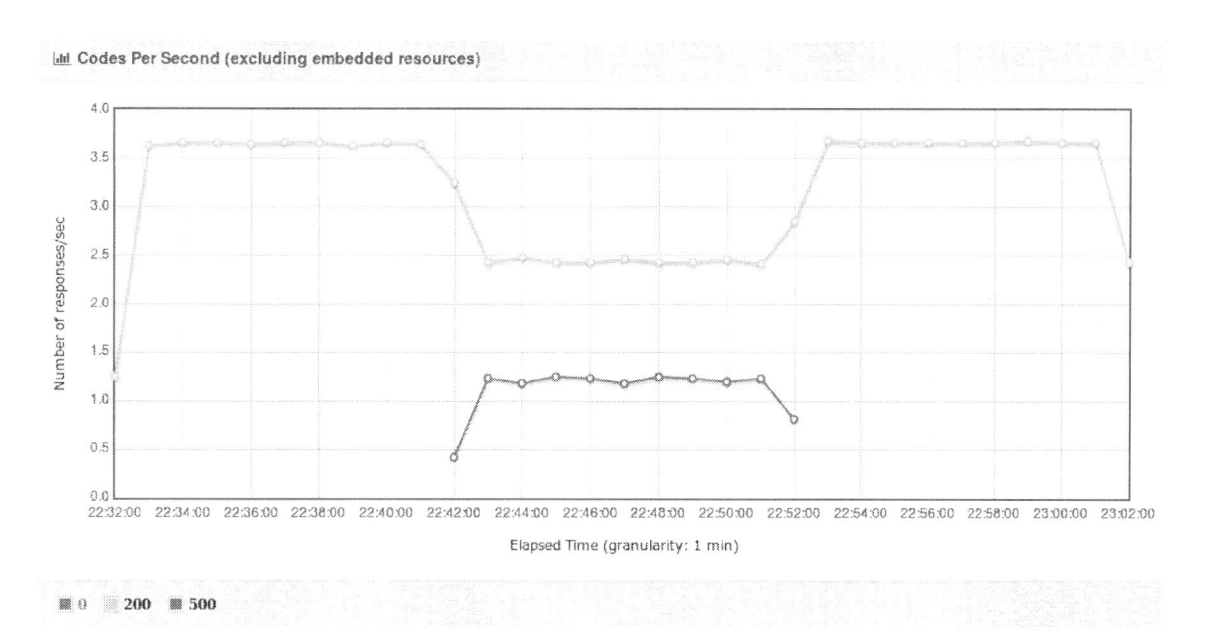

Figure 7.88: Result in JMeter

From these results, a number of actions can be implemented:

Implement a circuit-breaker pattern (https://en.wikipedia.org/wiki/Circuit_breaker_design_pattern)

Add caches between the application and the database

Add high availability at the database level

Improve recovery from errors at the user level

Our two scripts being the same except for the *Byteman* script, we decide to variabilize the name of the script in order to be able to change it without modifying our JMeter script.

16. To do that, we will use the **User Defined Variables** element combined with the __P() function in order to be able to pass the *Byteman* script when executing our test:

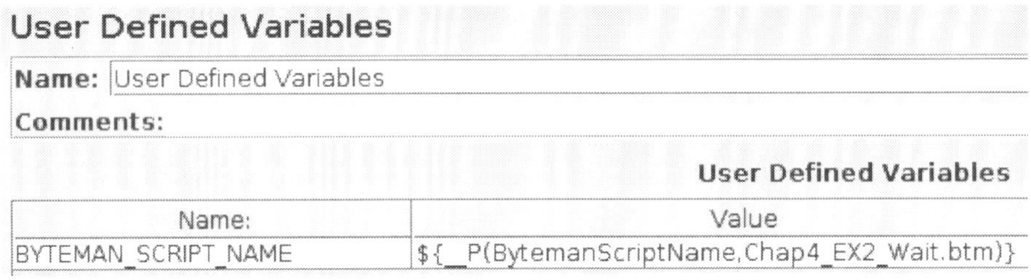

User Defined Variables	
Name:	Value
BYTEMAN_SCRIPT_NAME	${__P(BytemanScriptName,Chap4_EX2_Wait.btm)}

Figure 7.89: Using predefined variables associated with __P()

We just have to use our new variable.

Example 3: Technical Tests with JProfiler

Strange things happen (the application slows down) when our application (still *Spring PetClinic*) consumes more than 80 percent of the memory of our JVM.

We are being asked to develop a test that:

- Will do a memory dump to find out what is in memory
- Will do a thread dump to find out what takes time

After a few discussions, several constraints arise:

- The problem only appears with a load.
- Access to the server that hosts our application is not possible in graphical mode, and only command-line access is possible.
- Monitoring of the remote JVM is not possible.
- It is not possible to restart the JVM for now.

Despite our misfortune, we are lucky since we can use EJ JProfiler (https://www.ej-technologies.com/products/jprofiler/overview.html).

Among all the features of *JProfiler*, we are interested in the *Offline Profiling* mode associated with *Triggers*.

Offline Profiling will allow us to profile our application locally and without a GUI.

Triggers will allow us to trigger dumps under certain conditions.

The **jpenable** command will allow us to attach *JProfiler* to our application without restarting it:

1. Let's start by creating a *JProfiler* session using *JProfiler* (this session has the information needed to run profiling):

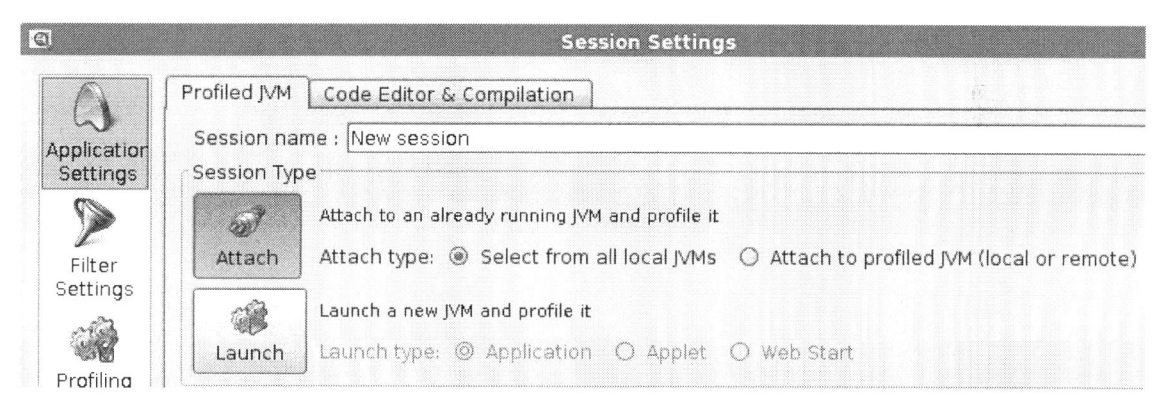

Figure 7.90: Session JProfiler

2. Let's create our first *Trigger*:

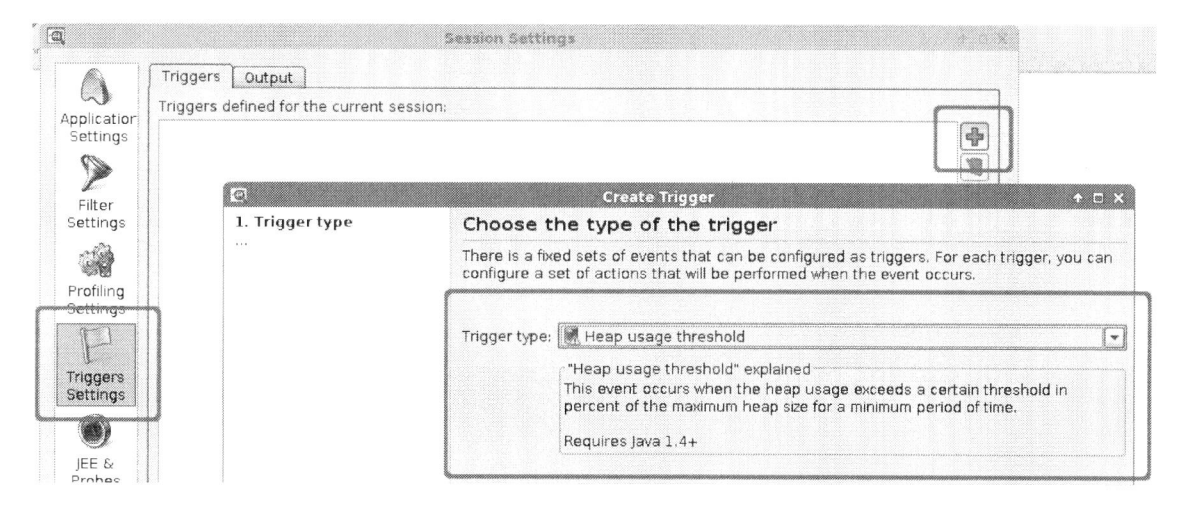

Figure 7.91: Trigger

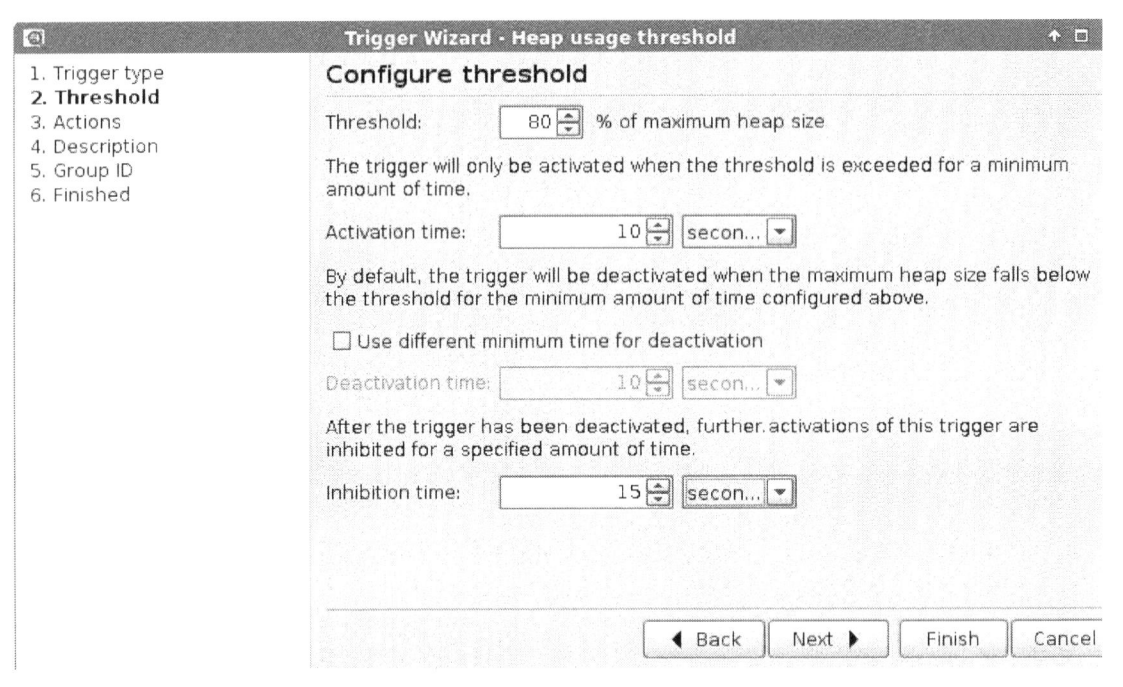

Figure 7.92: Trigger

3. The people who will analyze the dump have access to *JProfiler*, so we decide to replace the two dumps with a *JProfiler* dump that contains more information:

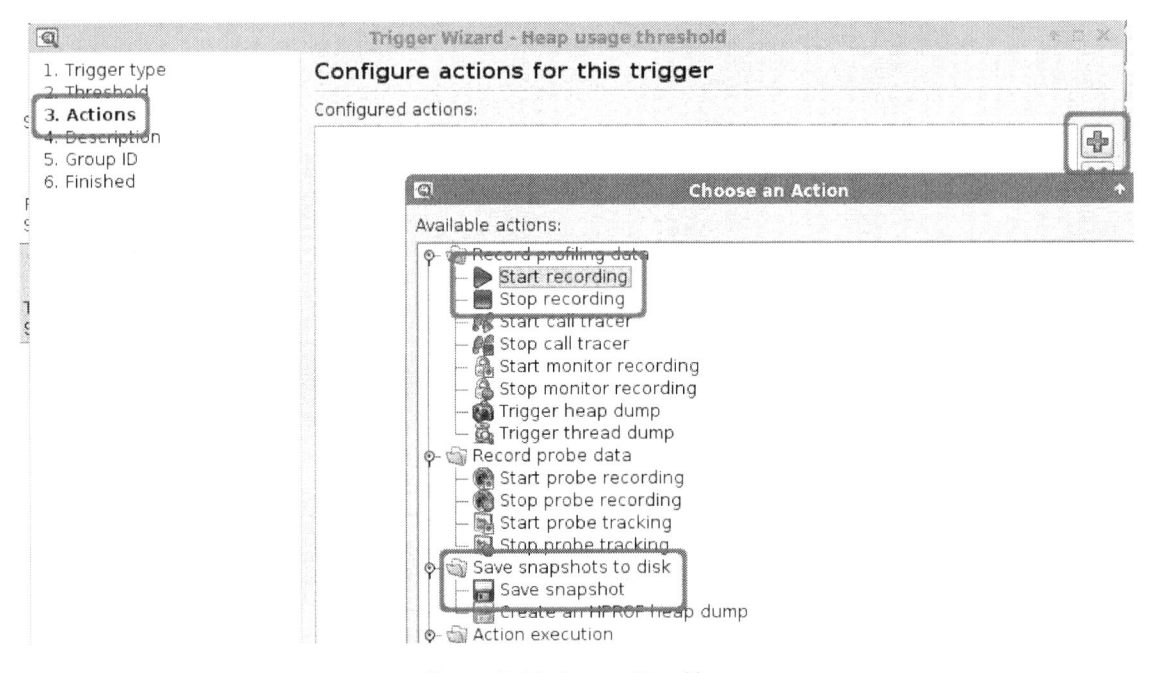

Figure 7.93: Dump JProfiler

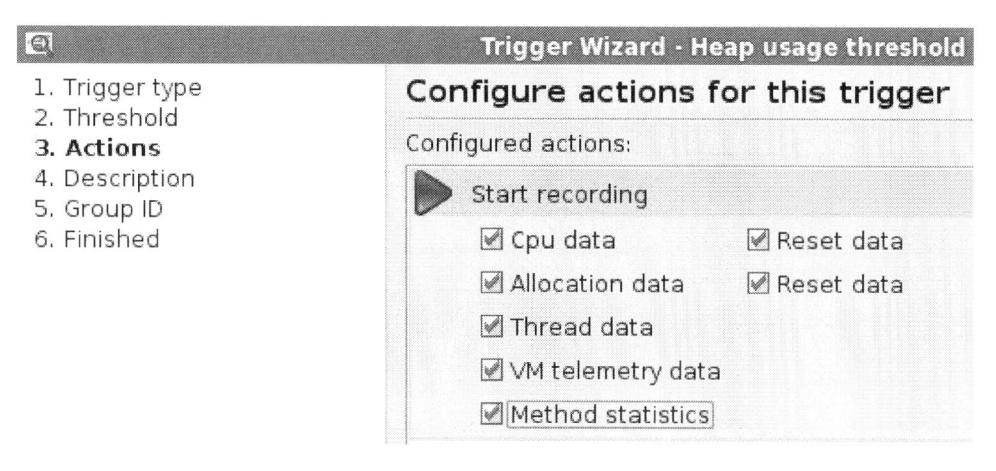

Figure 7.94: Dump JProfiler

Figure 7.95: Dump JProfiler

Our *JProfiler* session is ready:

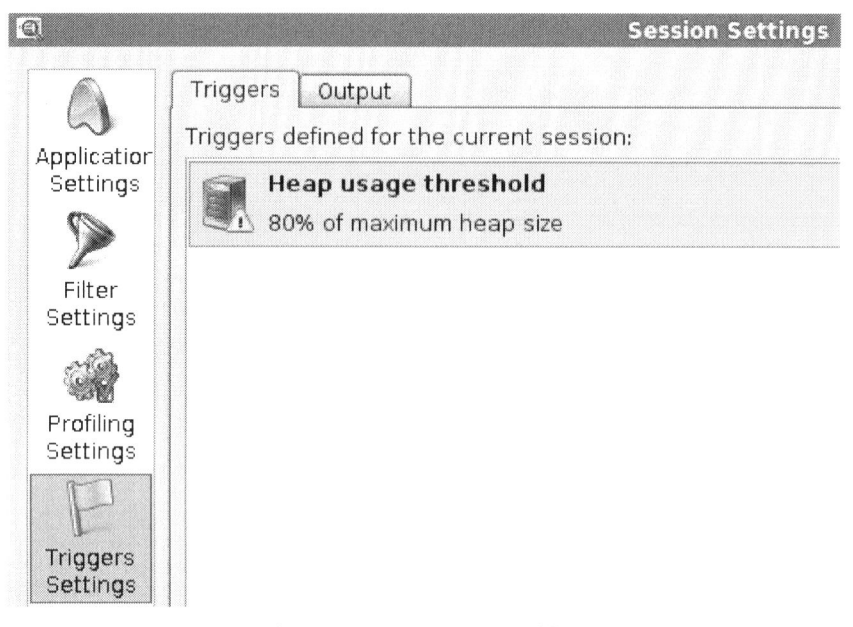

Figure 7.96: Session JProfiler

Let's move on to our JMeter script.

4. To attach *JProfiler* to our application, use **jpenable**. To do this, we will use **OS Process Sampler**:

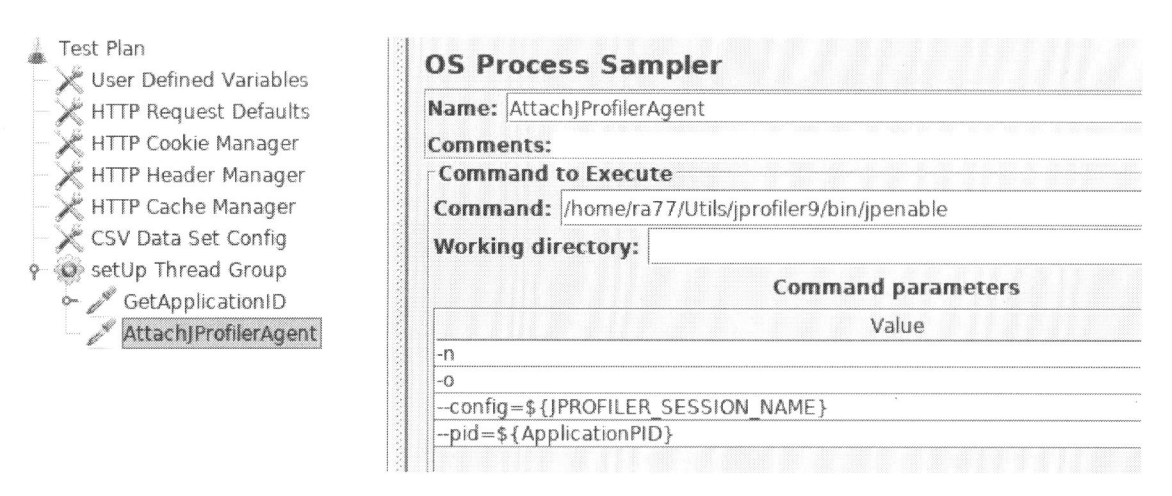

Figure 7.97: Attach JProfiler to our application

5. All we have to do is to execute our JMeter script and wait for the activation of the *trigger* programmed with *JProfiler*.

    At the end of our test, we end up with dump files that we can open with *JProfiler*.

    For example, for the memory:

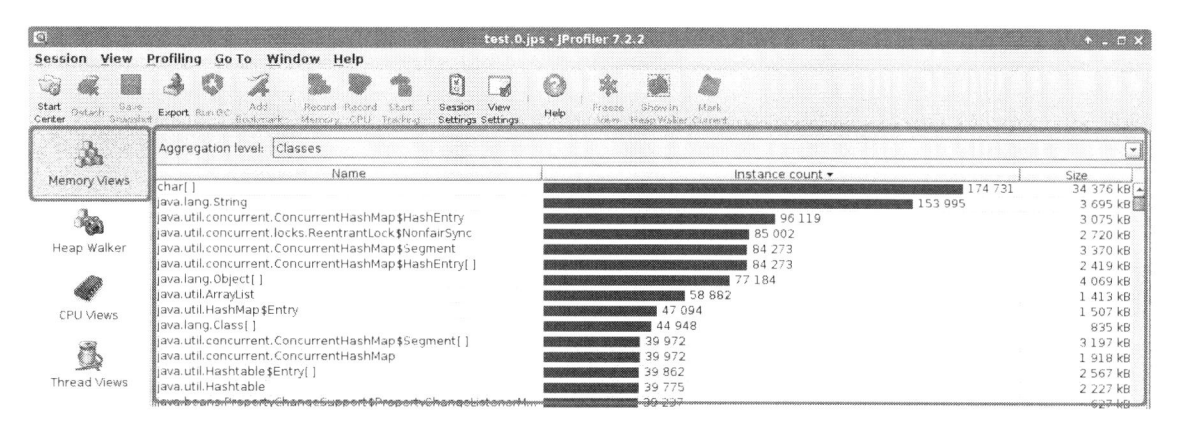

Figure 7.98: Memory dump

Of course, it is possible to do the same thing with all other *triggers*:

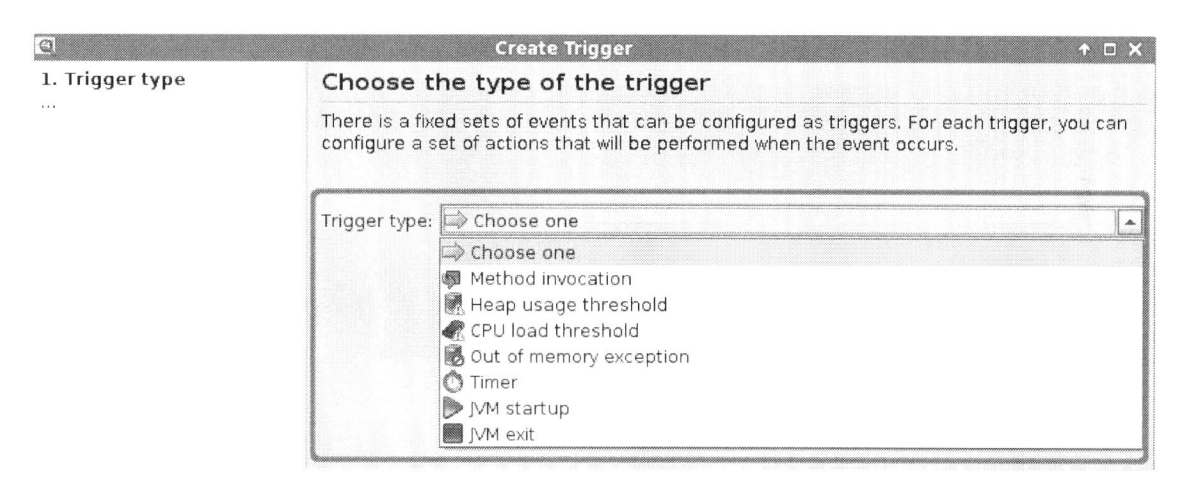

Figure 7.99: Other triggers

Similar things could have been achieved with Java Mission Control and Java Flight Recorder (which is included in Oracle JDK 8 – commercially usable only – and in OpenJDK 11 – universally usable).

Example 4: Tricking CAPTCHAs with a Java Request

This time, we are asked to test the robustness of the CAPTCHA system (protection that filters bots when accessing our site) that's set up on the site. To do this, we will use optical character recognition (OCR) software to translate the CAPTCHA into text so that we can use it later. While technically interesting, the real solution is of course to short-circuit the mechanism for load tests.

Several solutions are possible (including *Groovy* and **OS Process Sampler**). We select the **Java Request** sampler in order to implement our "CAPTCHA breaker":

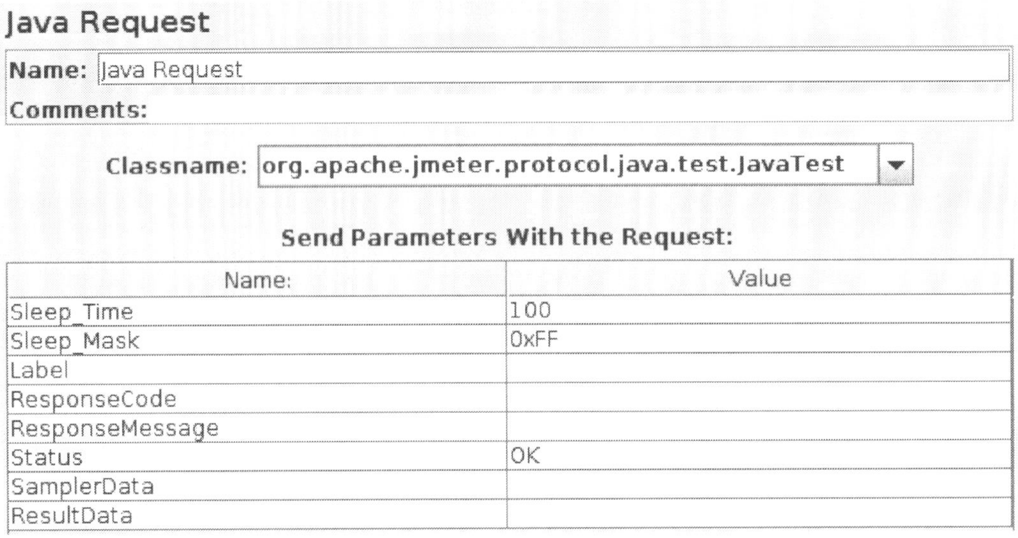

Java Request

Name:	Java Request
Comments:	

Classname: org.apache.jmeter.protocol.java.test.JavaTest

Send Parameters With the Request:

Name:	Value
Sleep_Time	100
Sleep_Mask	0xFF
Label	
ResponseCode	
ResponseMessage	
Status	OK
SamplerData	
ResultData	

Figure 7.100: Java Request

Our choice of OCR software is Tesseract (https://github.com/tesseract-ocr/tesseract).

A **Java Request** is simply the addition of a `jar` file implementing our action (here, breaking a CAPTCHA using *Tesseract*) in the `lib/ext` directory of JMeter.

To create this **jar** file, we need to create a Java project in our preferred IDE with the following constraints:

1. Include the **ApacheJMeter_core.jar** and **ApacheJMeter_java.jar** libraries.
2. Implement the **AbstractJavaSamplerClient** abstract class:

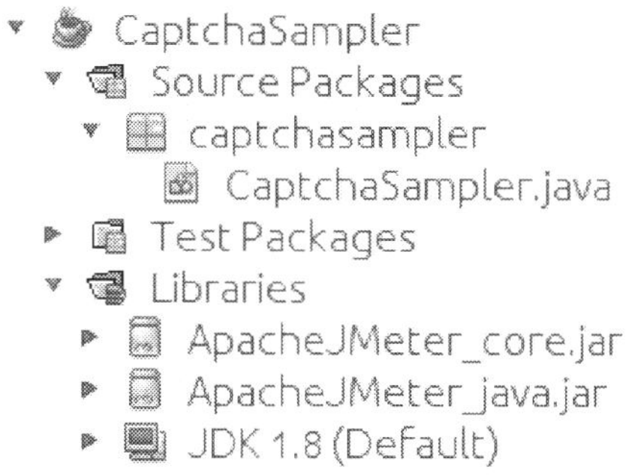

```
▼ ☕ CaptchaSampler
    ▼ 📦 Source Packages
        ▼ 📁 captchasampler
            📄 CaptchaSampler.java
    ▶ 📦 Test Packages
    ▼ 📦 Libraries
        ▶ 📦 ApacheJMeter_core.jar
        ▶ 📦 ApacheJMeter_java.jar
        ▶ 📦 JDK 1.8 (Default)
```

Figure 7.101: Project in our IDE

Our implementation will look like this:

```java
package captchasampler;

import java.io.BufferedReader;
import java.io.FileInputStream;
import java.io.InputStreamReader;
import org.apache.jmeter.config.Arguments;
import org.apache.jmeter.protocol.java.sampler.AbstractJavaSamplerClient;
import org.apache.jmeter.protocol.java.sampler.JavaSamplerContext;
import org.apache.jmeter.samplers.SampleResult;

public class CaptchaSampler extends AbstractJavaSamplerClient {

    private String FileToProcess;
    private String TesseractPath;
    private static final String DEFAULT_FILE_NAME = "/path to folder that contain images/image_captcha_example4.png";
    private static final String DEFAULT_TESSERACT = "/usr/bin/tesseract";
```

```java
    @Override
    public Arguments getDefaultParameters() {
        Arguments params = new Arguments();
        params.addArgument("FileToProcess", DEFAULT_FILE_NAME);
        params.addArgument("TesseractPath", DEFAULT_TESSERACT);
        return params;
    }

    @Override
    public SampleResult runTest(JavaSamplerContext context) {
        SampleResult sr = new SampleResult();
        sr.sampleStart();
        String str = TesseractPath + " " + FileToProcess + " /tmp/ocr -psm 7";
        StringBuilder request = new StringBuilder();
        StringBuilder sb = new StringBuilder();
        try {
            sr.setResponseCode("200");
            sr.setResponseMessage("OK");
            sr.setSuccessful(true);
            Process process = Runtime.getRuntime().exec(str);
            process = Runtime.getRuntime().exec(str);
            process.waitFor();
            request.append(str);
            try (FileInputStream fis = new FileInputStream("/tmp/ocr.txt");
                InputStreamReader isr = new InputStreamReader(fis);
                BufferedReader br = new BufferedReader(isr)) {
                String line;
                while ((line = br.readLine()) != null) {
                    sb.append(line).append("\n");
                }
            }
            sr.setSamplerData(request.toString());
            String resp = "Response=" + sb.toString();
            sr.setResponseData(resp, null);
            sr.setDataType(SampleResult.TEXT);
        } catch (Exception e) {
            sr.setResponseCode("500");
            sr.setResponseMessage("Error");
            sr.setSuccessful(false);
        } finally {
            sr.sampleEnd();
```

```
        }
        return sr;
    }

    @Override
    public void setupTest(JavaSamplerContext context) {
        FileToProcess = context.getParameter("FileToProcess", DEFAULT_
FILE_NAME);
        TesseractPath = context.getParameter("TesseractPath", DEFAULT_
TESSERACT);
    }

    @Override
    public void teardownTest(JavaSamplerContext arg0) {
    }
}
```

Our business code will be in the **runTest** function.

The **getDefaultParameters** and **setupTest** functions allow you to add parameters to your **Java Request**.

3. Let's add our **jar** file to the **lib/ext** directory and start JMeter to see our class appear in **Java Request**:

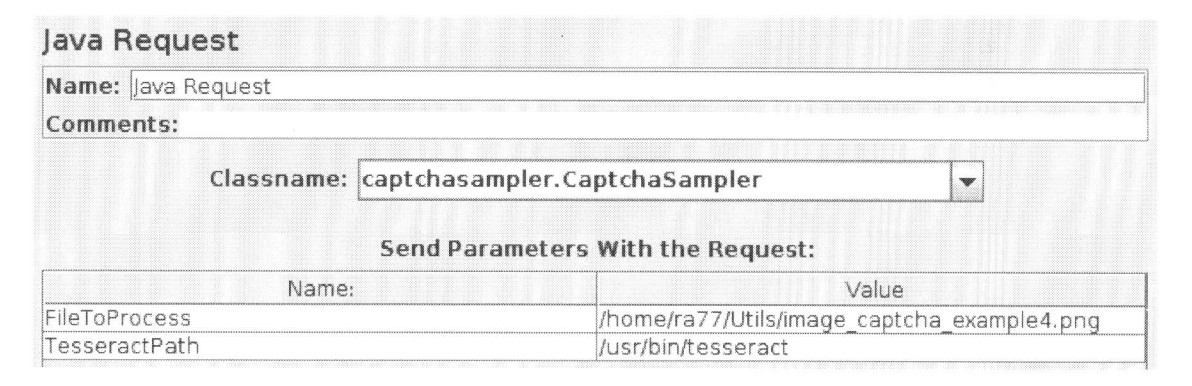

Java Request	
Name:	Java Request
Comments:	
Classname:	captchasampler.CaptchaSampler

Send Parameters With the Request:

Name:	Value
FileToProcess	/home/ra77/Utils/image_captcha_example4.png
TesseractPath	/usr/bin/tesseract

Figure 7.102: Java Request

Our script will look like this:

```
Test Plan
 Thread Group
  HTTP Request
   GetImagePath
  HTTP Request
   Save Responses to a file
  Java Request
```

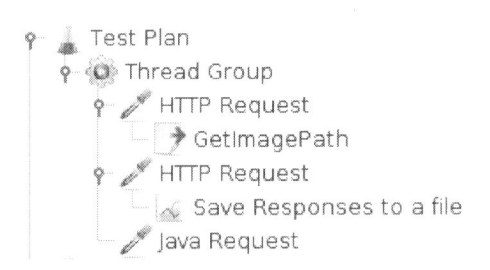

Figure 7.103: Our script

4. First, we will retrieve the link to the CAPTCHA image using **CSS Selector Extractor** (**GetImagePath**).

5. Then, we will save this image on disk using **Save Responses to a file**.

6. We'll pass this image path to our **Java Request**:

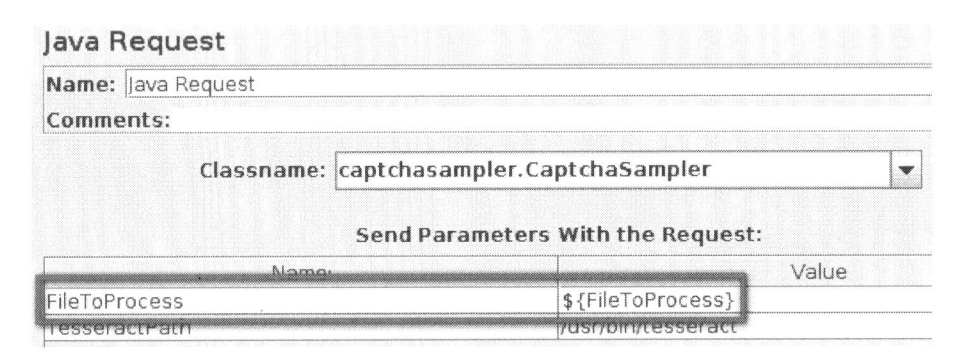

Figure 7.104: Filename

7. Let's do a test with this CAPTCHA (notice that the CAPTCHA image has been reworked to increase the contrast in order to facilitate the work of *Tesseract*). I advise you to do this (in the **Java Request** or another part) to increase the success rate of the script:

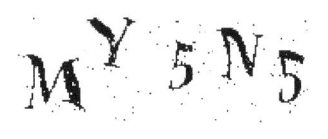

Figure 7.105: Our CAPTCHA

As you can see, the result is correct:

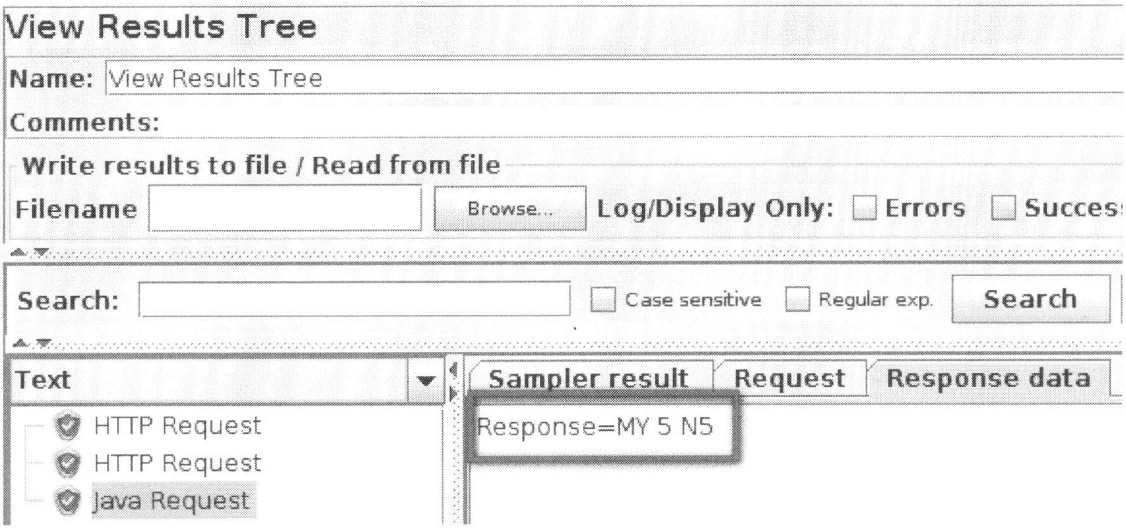

Figure 7.106: Result of execution

Conclusion

As we have just seen, JMeter is suitable for the load testing of a web application. All this can be done in a rather simple way thanks to JMeter's powerful features and, in particular, the use of HTTP(S) Test Script Recorder acting as a proxy to record our scripts.

In addition, JMeter can be used and extended to perform technical and security testing. Note that these examples are not specific to the HTTP protocol and may be used for other protocols, as we will see in the next chapters.

8
Load Testing Web Services

A Few Concepts

Nowadays, more and more applications use web services (https://en.wikipedia.org/wiki/Web_service) for several reasons:

- To adapt to new constraints
- To interface mobile applications
- To interface heterogeneous systems in distributed environments
- To provide services to partners
- To avoid tying interfaces to a particular library in a specific language, and so on

This service is frequently used, particularly with the success of microservice architectures (https://en.wikipedia.org/wiki/Microservices). Under the term "web services," several technologies exist, such as WS-* web services and REST web services. Let's look in more detail at these two technologies.

REST (REpresentational State Transfer) Web Services

To meet certain needs (such as a lower complexity of implementation, reducing the volume of data exchanged and reducing the parsing cost, particularly for mobile applications, and more), REST web services appeared. REST web services are based on the fundamentals of the HTTP protocol.

The following concepts come into play:

- Four main methods (**GET**, **POST**, **PUT**, and **DELETE**) that tend to be enriched by other existing HTTP methods (**PATCH** to modify a resource)
- Resource (anything that can be referenced by a link: a picture, an article, a service, or more) and its URI (*Uniform Resource Identifier*)
- Message (in XML or JSON format) with its HTTP header
- The HTTP communication protocol

For example, to retrieve article 40, the HTTP request could be **GET /articles/40**.

Similarly, to delete article 40, you could use **DELETE /articles/40**.

WS-* Web Services

The principle is to make remote method calls. For this, several specifications have been created. Its architecture is composed of:

- *Simple Object Access Protocol* (SOAP) Web Service
- *Web Service Description Language* (WSDL)
- *Universal Description Discovery and Integration* (UDDI)
- A consumer
- A producer

The producer is the service that hosts the remote method called.

The consumer is the one that will call it.

UDDI is a kind of phone book which informs the clients about the available services. This standard didn't meet the expected success, and it is rarely implemented nowadays.

WSDL is the language in which we describe the services interfaces (such as input data, return, and more). That's the main benefit of SOAP because it can accurately describe the grammar of XML messages and generate *stubs* (clients) in various languages. SOAP is the format of the request transmitted to the service; it is an XML grammar, so requests must respect the contract described in the WSDL.

Its usage workflow can be summarized in this diagram:

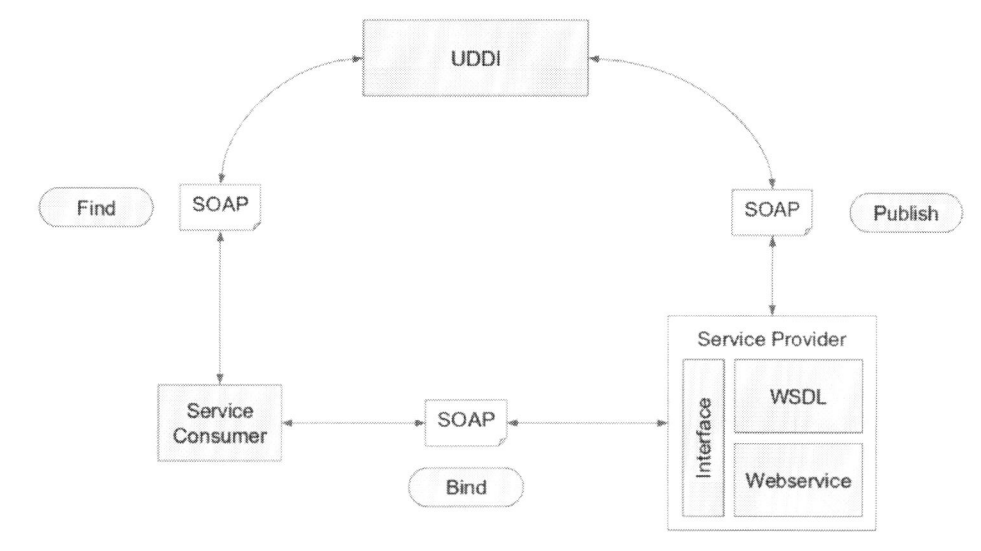

Figure 8.1: WS -* web services

- **Publish**: The producer publishes/registers its services in UDDI. This stack can be ignored or replaced by alternatives.

- **Find**: The consumer searches for the desired services in UDDI. This stack can be ignored or replaced by alternatives.

- **Bind**: Communication between the consumer and the producer.

At the end, the content of the exchanged messages includes the exchange format in order to have a personalized contract between the service provider and the consumer.

Setup with JMeter

Again, JMeter allows us to easily test web services. We can do it using **HTTP Request**:

Figure 8.2: HTTP Request

Do not forget to add an **HTTP Header Manager** with the correct parameters (here, **Content-Type** is equal to **text/xml; charset=utf-8**):

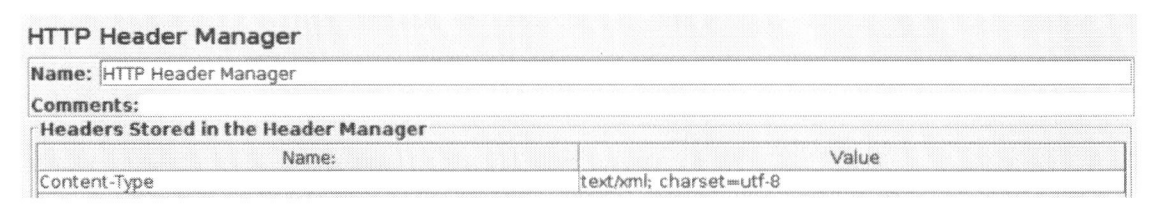

Figure 8.3: HTTP Header

> **Note**
> Note that JMeter provides the **Building a SOAP WebService Test Plan** template to speed up the configuration.

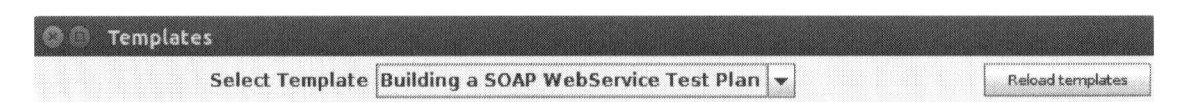

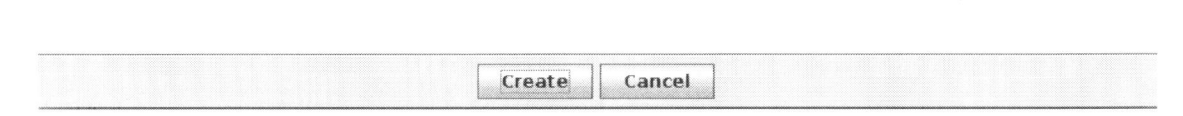

Figure 8.4: Building a SOAP WebService Test Plan template

To help us, we can use the excellent SoapUI (https://www.soapui.org/), which generates the message content of our call to the web service from the WSDL.

It even makes it possible to create Mock servers of the web service, allowing us to test it while its implementation is not yet available.

If your teams have already run tests with SoapUI, Postman (https://www.getpostman.com/), Swagger (https://swagger.io/), or any other similar tool, you can save a lot of time by setting JMeter as a proxy in these tools. JMeter will generate the test plan from the requests it receives.

Methodology

As we have just seen, there is much in common between testing a web service and a web server. This is why the recommendations in *Chapter 7, Load Testing a Website* apply here. Note that it is important to monitor the volume of data sent by web services. Indeed, messages can be quite verbose, so they can be the cause of performance problems.

Practice with JMeter

Let's move on to practice.

SOAP/XML-RPC Web Services

Our test application will be a web service named *Calculator* (an example provided with *Netbeans* 8.2):

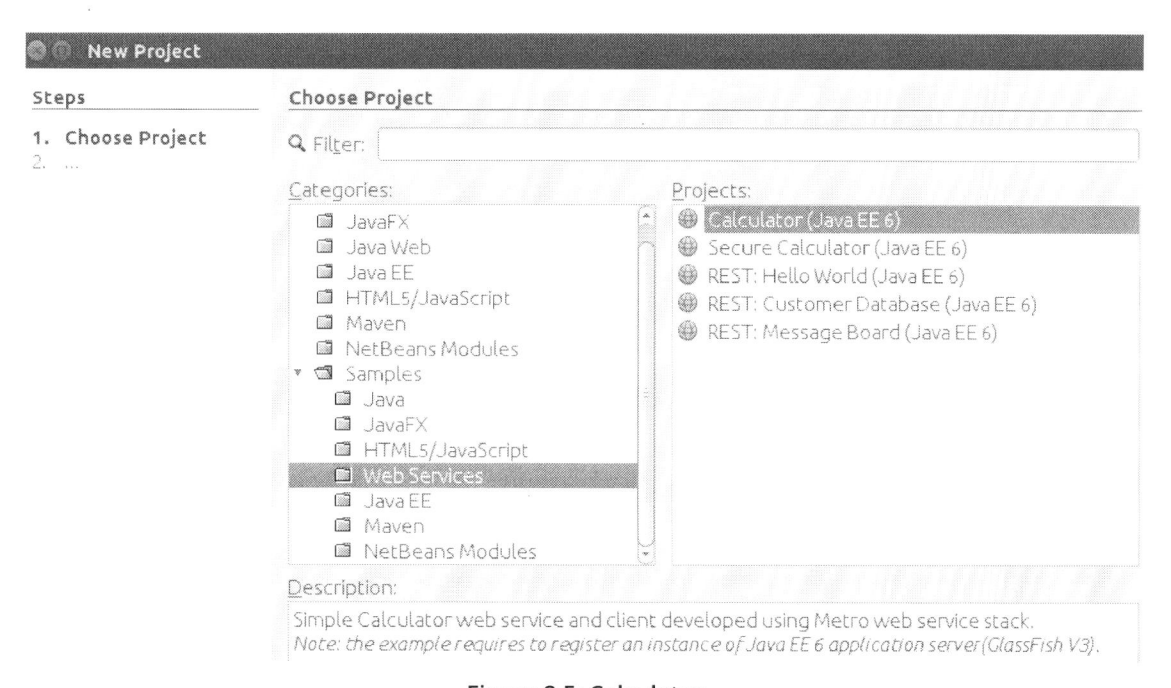

Figure 8.5: Calculator

Let's use **HTTP Request** and add in the *Path* and *Body Data* our call to the *CalculatorWSService* web service:

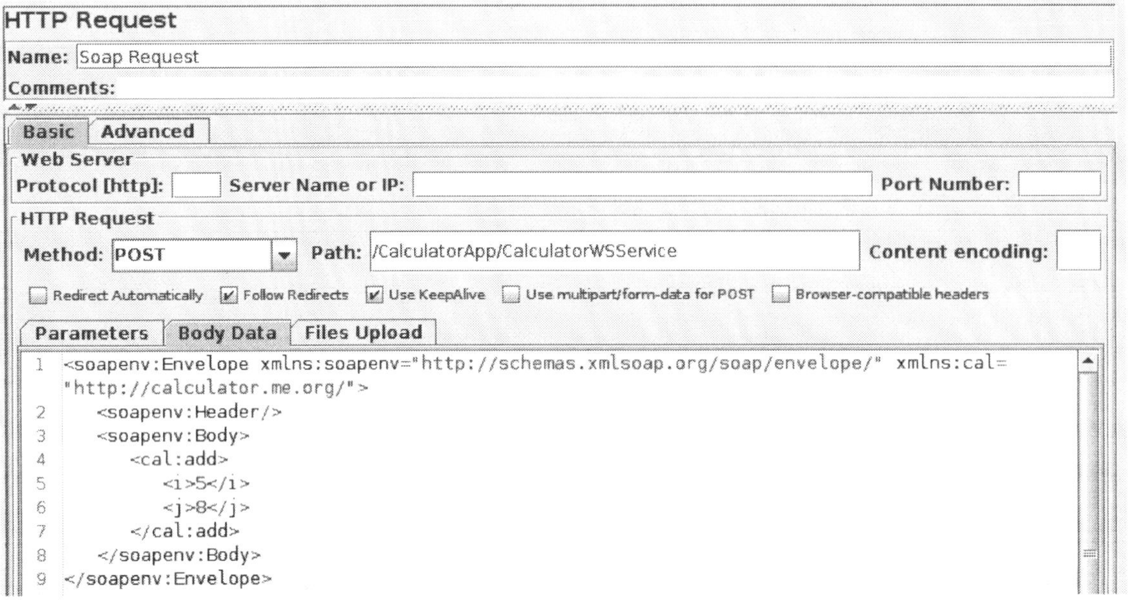

Figure 8.6: Web Service Call

Do not forget to add an assertion to control our response:

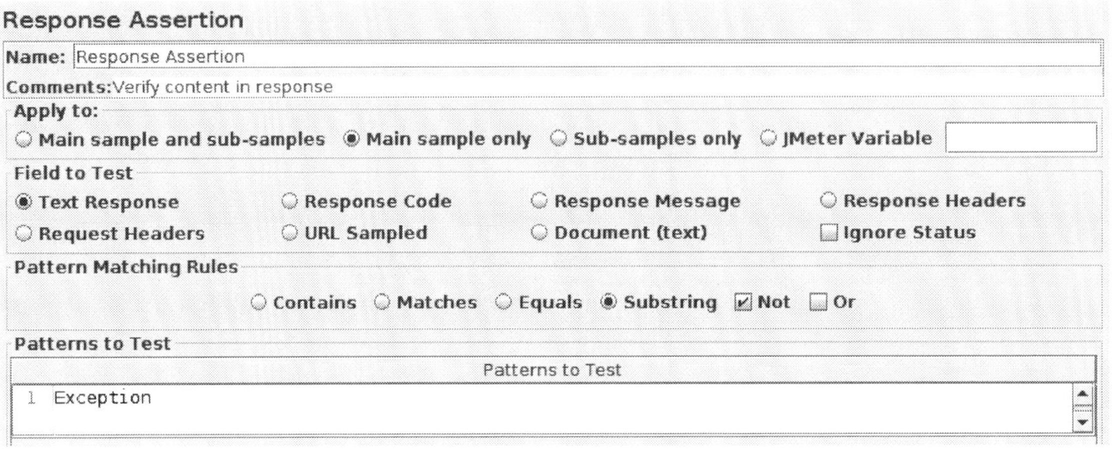

Figure 8.7: Result control

Here, we check that there is no exception returned by the web service.

Our test plan will look like this:

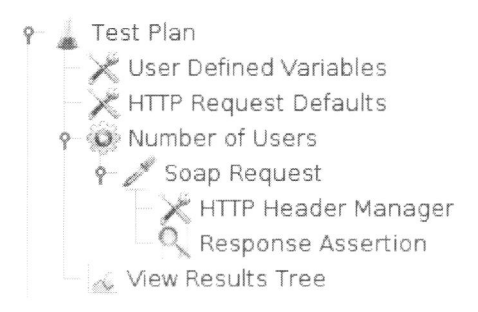

Figure 8.8: Test Plan

And, the result of the execution is:

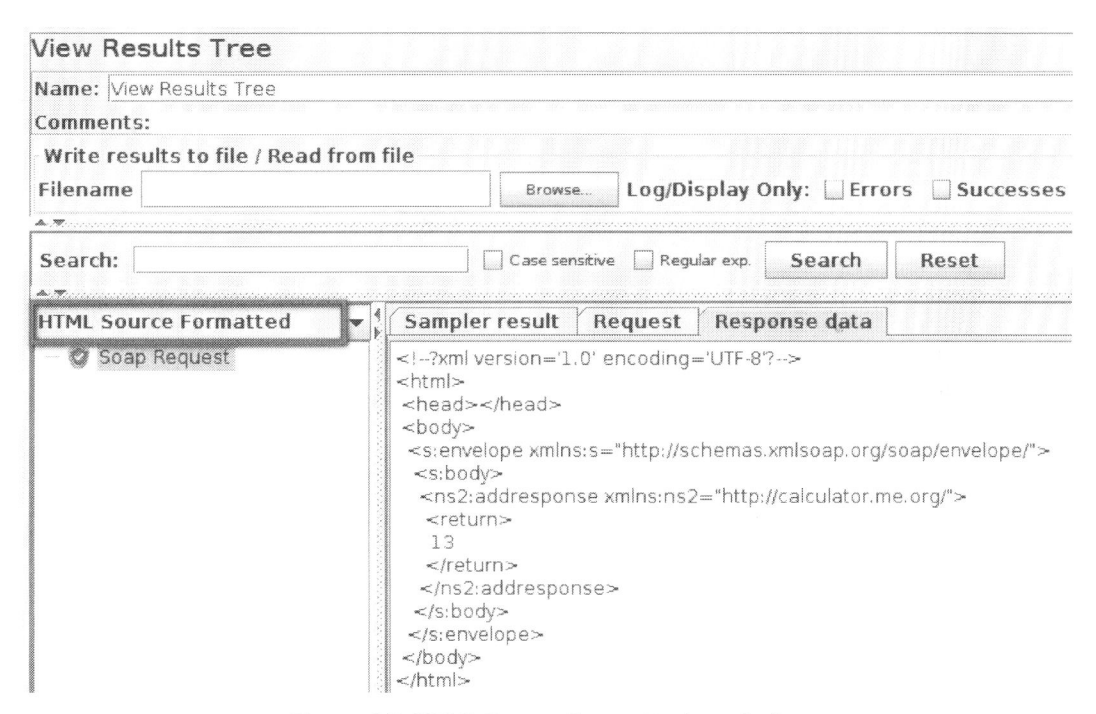

Figure 8.9: HTML Source Formatted rendering

> **Note**
> Here, we used **HTML Source Formatted** rendering for a better presentation of the answer. **XML** rendering is also possible.

222 | Load Testing Web Services

You can see the result of a call to the web service, *CalculatorWSService*, which makes an addition of 5 and 8.

To make the dataset as large as possible, we'll use the **__Random** function to generate a random number (between 0 and 999,999) for our addition.

Let's modify the **HTTP Request**:

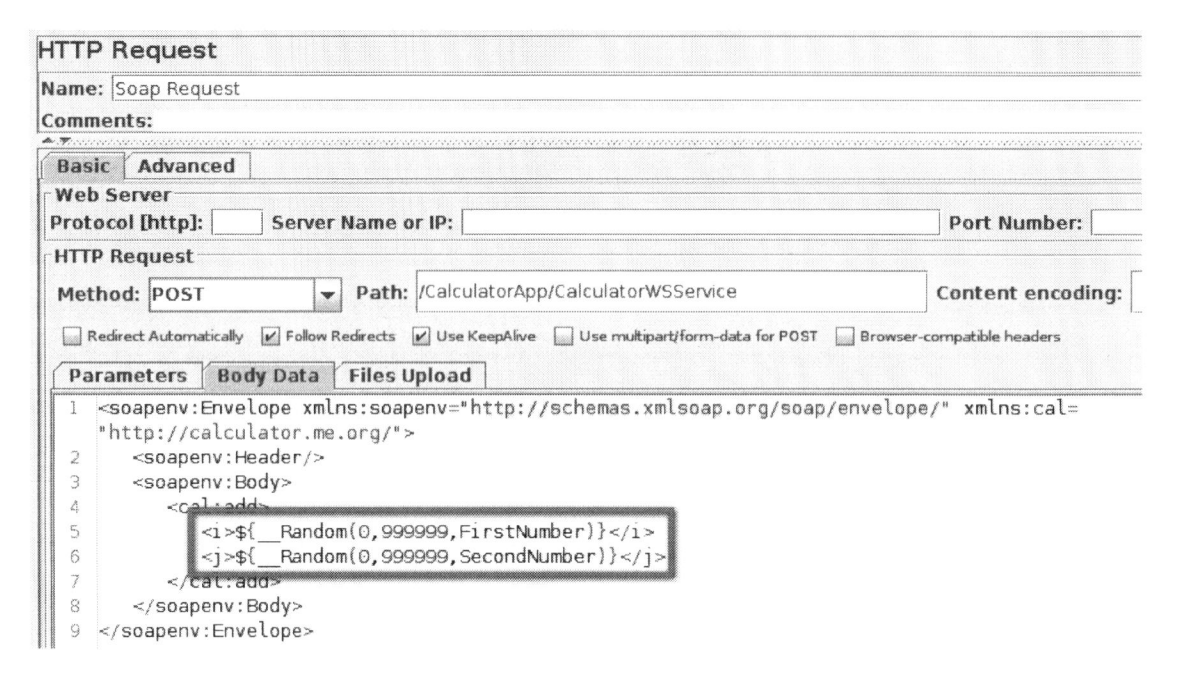

Figure 8.10: Using the __Random function

> **Note**
> We use the third parameter of the **__Random** function to store the result in a variable for later use in our assertion.

Likewise, for **Response Assertion**:

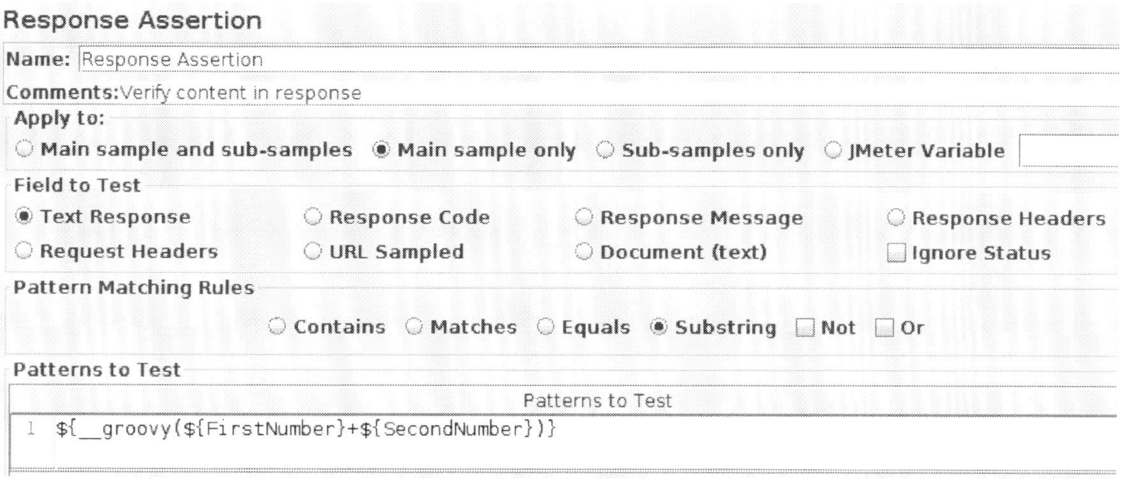

Response Assertion

Name: Response Assertion
Comments: Verify content in response

Apply to: ○ Main sample and sub-samples ● Main sample only ○ Sub-samples only ○ JMeter Variable

Field to Test:
● Text Response   ○ Response Code   ○ Response Message   ○ Response Headers
○ Request Headers ○ URL Sampled   ○ Document (text)   ☐ Ignore Status

Pattern Matching Rules:
○ Contains ○ Matches ○ Equals ● Substring ☐ Not ☐ Or

Patterns to Test:
1 ${__groovy(${FirstNumber}+${SecondNumber})}

Figure 8.11: Editing our assertion

We use the **__groovy** function to add the two digits and check the presence of the result in the response.

We could also use **__longSum**, but our tests show that the **__groovy** version performs twice better in terms of throughput:

```
${__longSum(${firstNumber},${secondNumber},)}
```

REST Web Service: Discussion Forum

Let's now test a REST web service.

This time, we will test a web service that manages a discussion forum (for example, *Message Board*, provided with *Netbeans* 8.2):

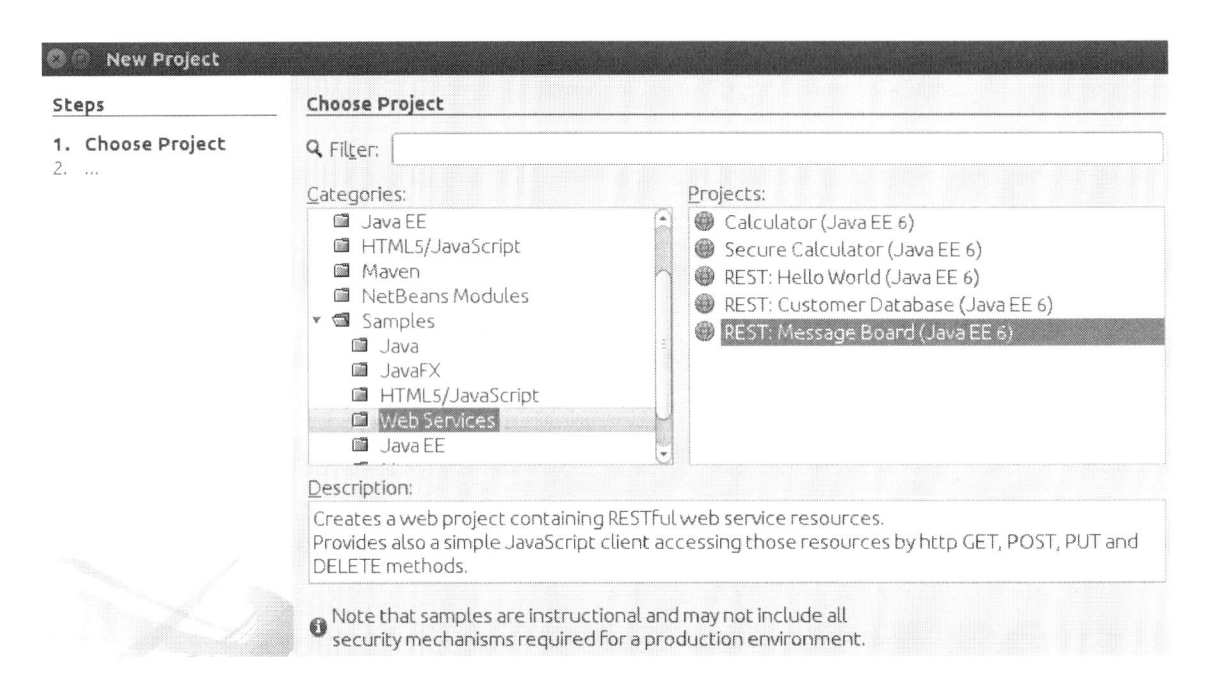

Figure 8.12: Discussion forum

The tests to be performed are:

- See all forum posts
- Retrieve a message
- Delete a message
- Create a message

MessageBoard sample

[LIST ALL MESSAGES]

Message id#: [   ] [GET MESSAGE]

Message id#: [   ] [DELETE MESSAGE]

Message: [   ] [ADD MESSAGE]

MessageBoard

query:

GET app/messages

result

1970-01-01T01:00:02+01:00msg221970-01-01T01:00:01+01:00msg111970-01-01T01:00:00+01:00msg00

Figure 8.13: Discussion forum

As with the previous application, we use **HTTP Request** associated with **HTTP Header Manager**.

Let's start by displaying all the forum posts:

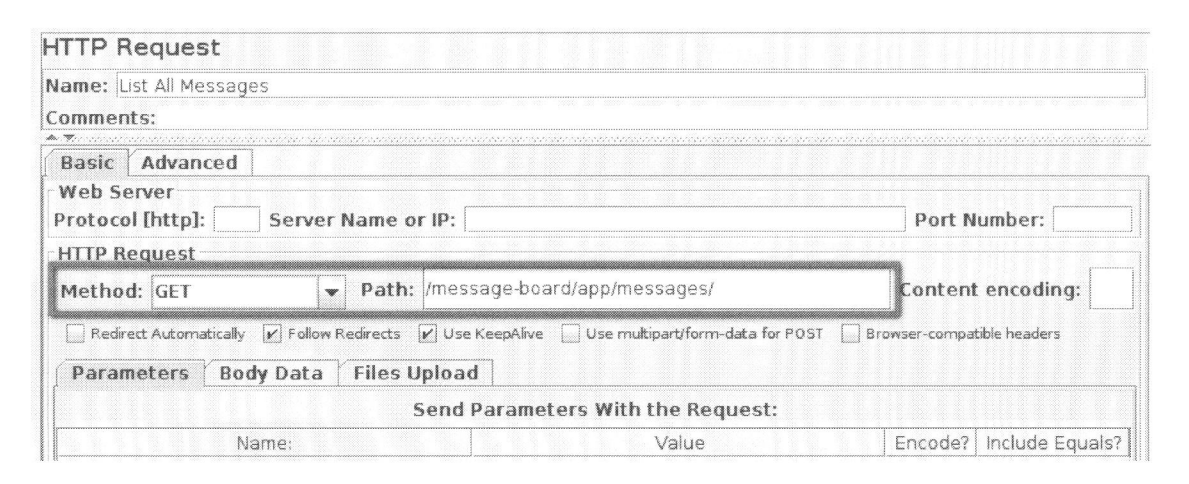

Figure 8.14: Viewing the forum posts

Depending on the expected response format, we will change the *Accept* value of **HTTP Header Manager**.

For an answer in XML format:

Figure 8.15: Configuration for an XML response

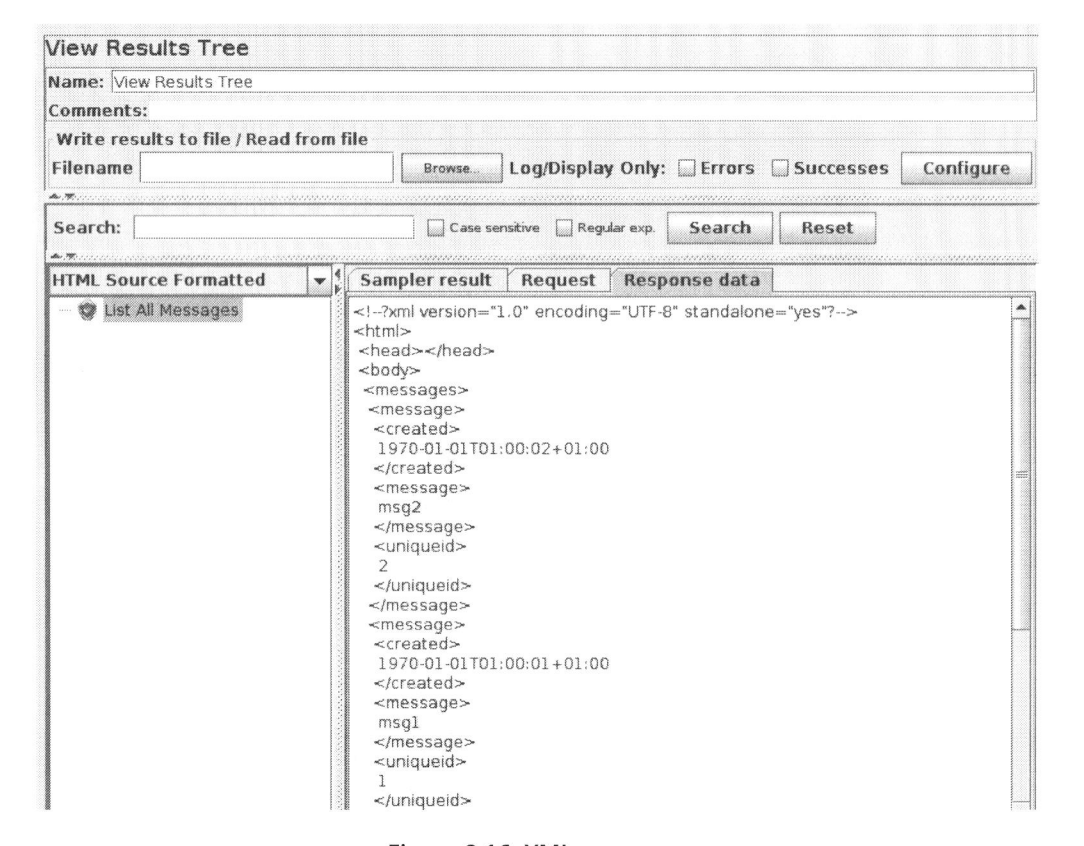

Figure 8.16: XML response

For an answer in HTML format:

Figure 8.17: Configuration for an answer in HTML format

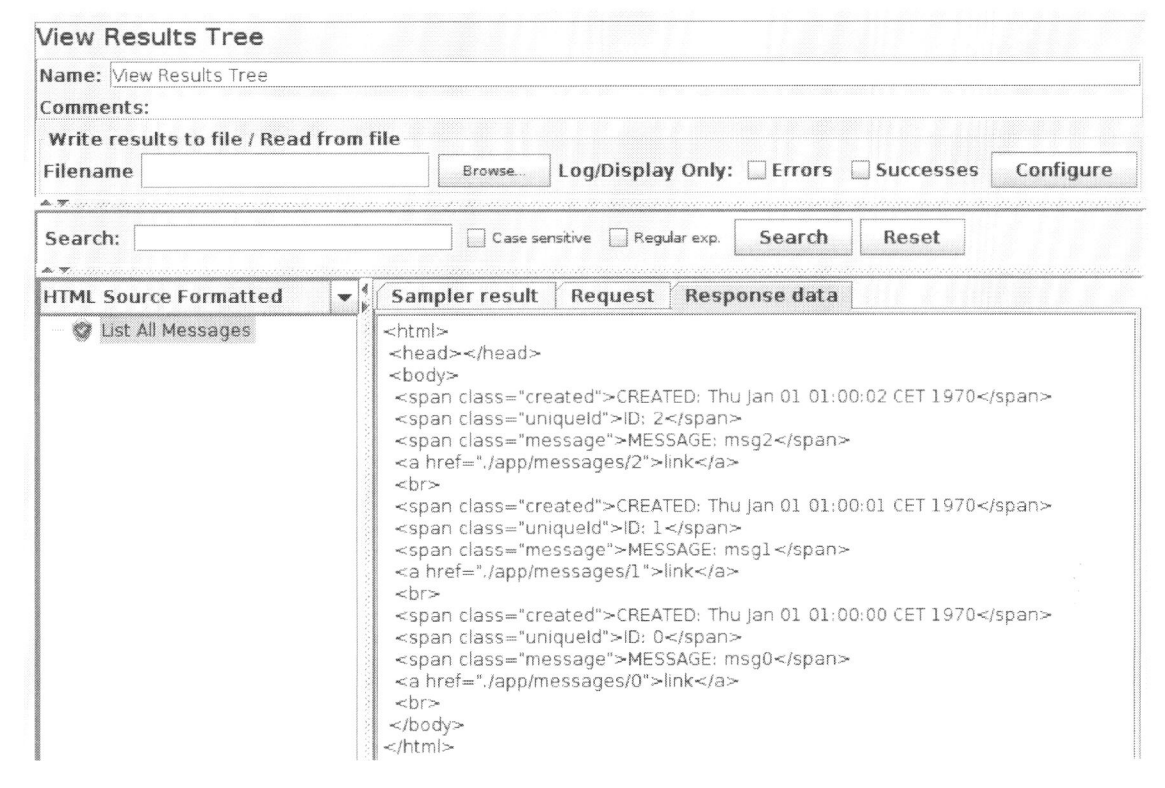

```
View Results Tree
Name: View Results Tree
Comments:
 Write results to file / Read from file
Filename                              Browse..  Log/Display Only:  ☐ Errors  ☐ Successes  Configure

Search:                        ☐ Case sensitive  ☐ Regular exp.  Search   Reset

HTML Source Formatted  ▼   Sampler result | Request | Response data
  ⊘ List All Messages        <html>
                              <head></head>
                              <body>
                               <span class="created">CREATED: Thu Jan 01 01:00:02 CET 1970</span>
                               <span class="uniqueId">ID: 2</span>
                               <span class="message">MESSAGE: msg2</span>
                               <a href="./app/messages/2">link</a>
                               <br>
                               <span class="created">CREATED: Thu Jan 01 01:00:01 CET 1970</span>
                               <span class="uniqueId">ID: 1</span>
                               <span class="message">MESSAGE: msg1</span>
                               <a href="./app/messages/1">link</a>
                               <br>
                               <span class="created">CREATED: Thu Jan 01 01:00:00 CET 1970</span>
                               <span class="uniqueId">ID: 0</span>
                               <span class="message">MESSAGE: msg0</span>
                               <a href="./app/messages/0">link</a>
                               <br>
                              </body>
                              </html>
```

Figure 8.18: HTML response

Retrieving a message is slightly more complicated.

First, we retrieve the identifier of the message using a **Regular Expression Extractor**:

```
Regular Expression Extractor
Name: Regular Expression Extractor
Comments:
Apply to:
 ○ Main sample and sub-samples  ● Main sample only  ○ Sub-samples only  ○ JMeter Variable
Field to check
 ● Body  ○ Body (unescaped)  ○ Body as a Document  ○ Response Headers  ○ Request Headers  ○ URL  ○ Response Code  ○ Response Message
Reference Name:          IDMessage
Regular Expression:      <uniqueId>([0-9]+)</uniqueId>
Template:                $1$
Match No. (0 for Random): 0
Default Value:           ERROR                    ☐ Use empty default value
```

Figure 8.19: Regular Expression Extractor

Note that it would be better to use **CSS Selector Extractor** here since the body is HTML. We could also use **Boundary Extractor** if it's a large scale test where performance is critical.

Then, we use the result of the regular expression in the HTTP message display request:

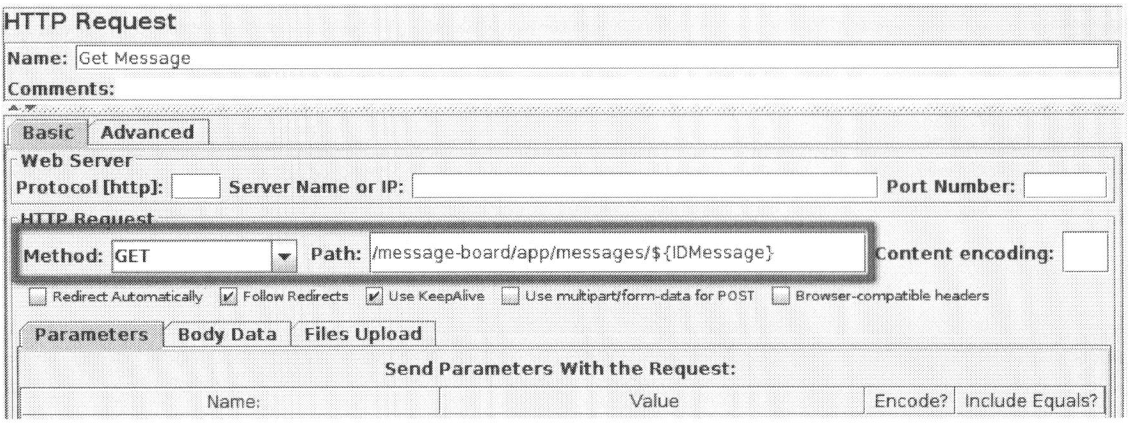

Figure 8.20: Message display

Deleting a message is almost identical:

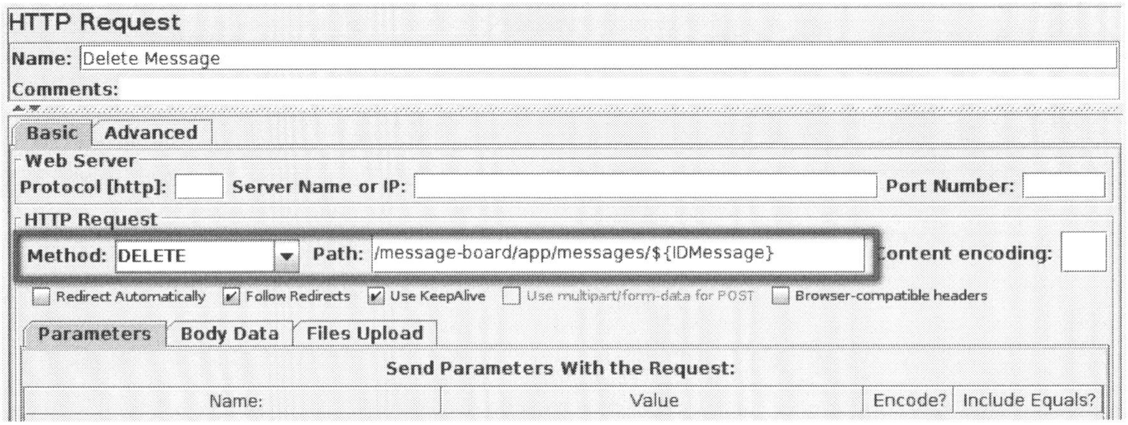

Figure 8.21: Deleting a message

And, finally, adding a message:

Figure 8.22: Adding a message

Note the use of the `__RandomString` function to generate a random string.

The addition of the assertions will finalize our script.

REST Web Service: Customer Database

This time, we need to test web services called *Customer Database*, which allow *Create*, *Read*, *Update*, and *Delete* (CRUD) actions to be performed on a database.

This example is also provided with *Netbeans* 8.2:

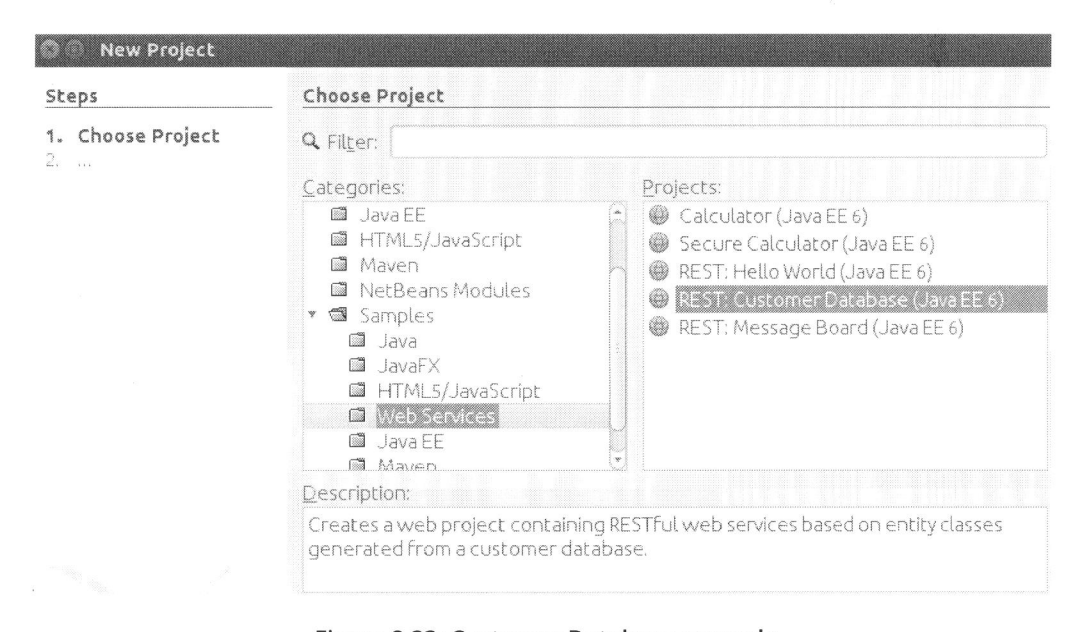

Figure 8.23: Customer Database example

After a discussion with the developers and/or recording using the JMeter proxy and/or looking at the source code of the web services, we get the following information:

- It's a REST architecture
- The exchange format can be JSON or XM
- The list of methods/calls from the web service.

Our first test will be to visualize customer records in a random way. Our first action is to retrieve the complete list of customer records in JSON format. For this, we execute the **HTTP GET /CustomerDB/webresources/entities.customer** request:

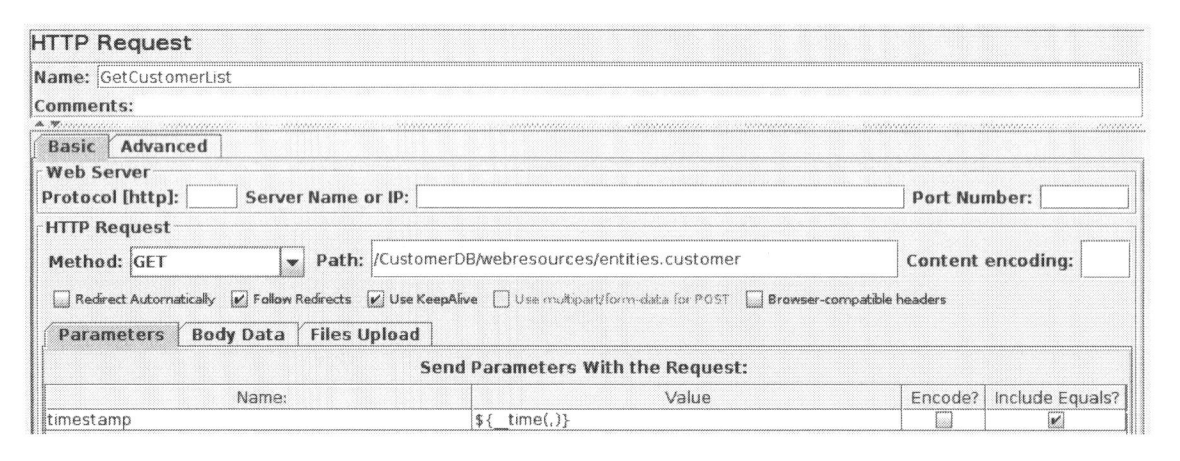

Figure 8.24: GET /CustomerDB/webresources/entities.customer

Note that some applications may require you to set the Content-Type. they are able to understand with **Accept** header. So, you may need to add **HTTP Header Manager** with **Accept** header equal to *application/json*.

For the JSON format:

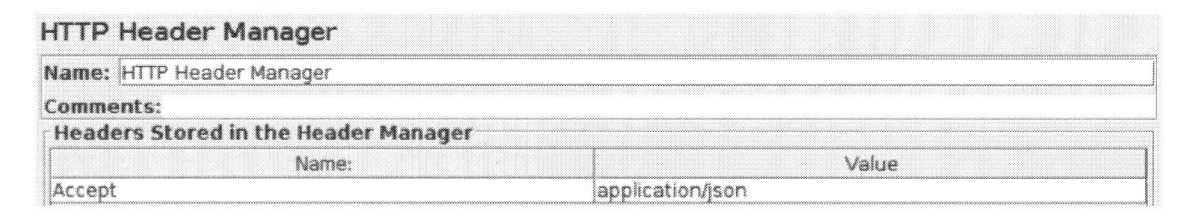

Figure 8.25: Changing the format

Let's add a **JSON Extractor** to randomly retrieve the identifier of a customer record:

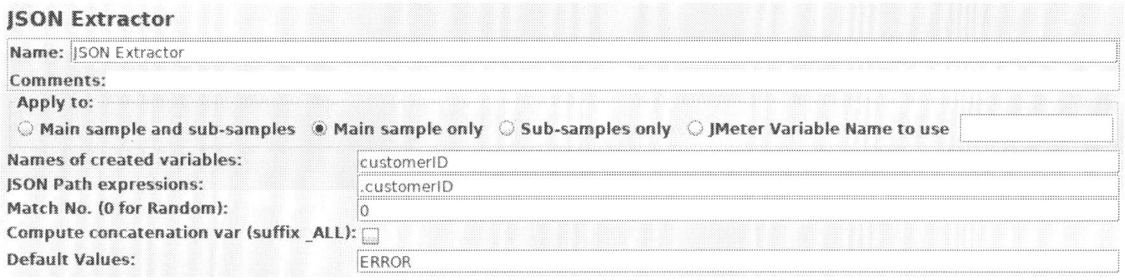

Figure 8.26: Retrieving the identifier with JSON Extractor

> **Note**
> The syntax used by the extractor is the JSON-PATH syntax (https://goessner.net/articles/JsonPath/).

If you prefer to use **Regular Expression Extractor**, it's possible, but its neither powerful nor stable in time:

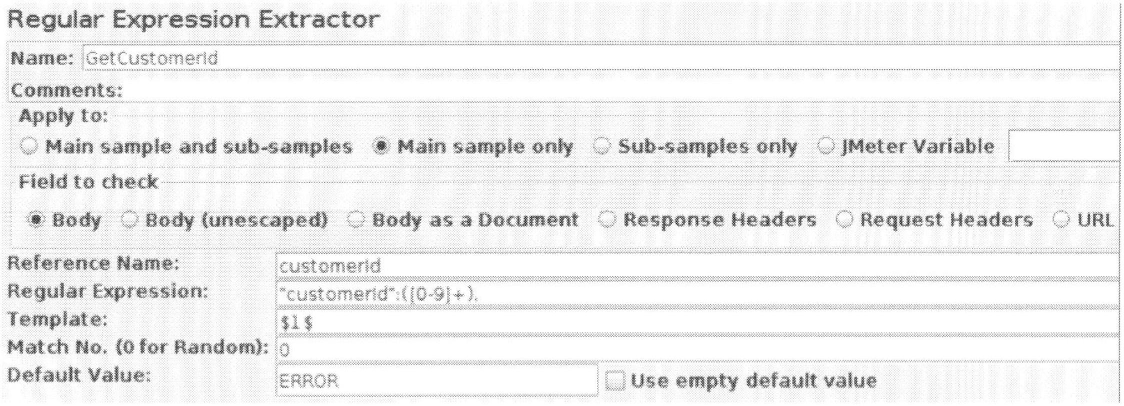

Figure 8.27: Retrieving the identifier with Regular Expression Extractor

Then, retrieve the record:

Figure 8.28: Retrieve the record

We obtain the following record list:

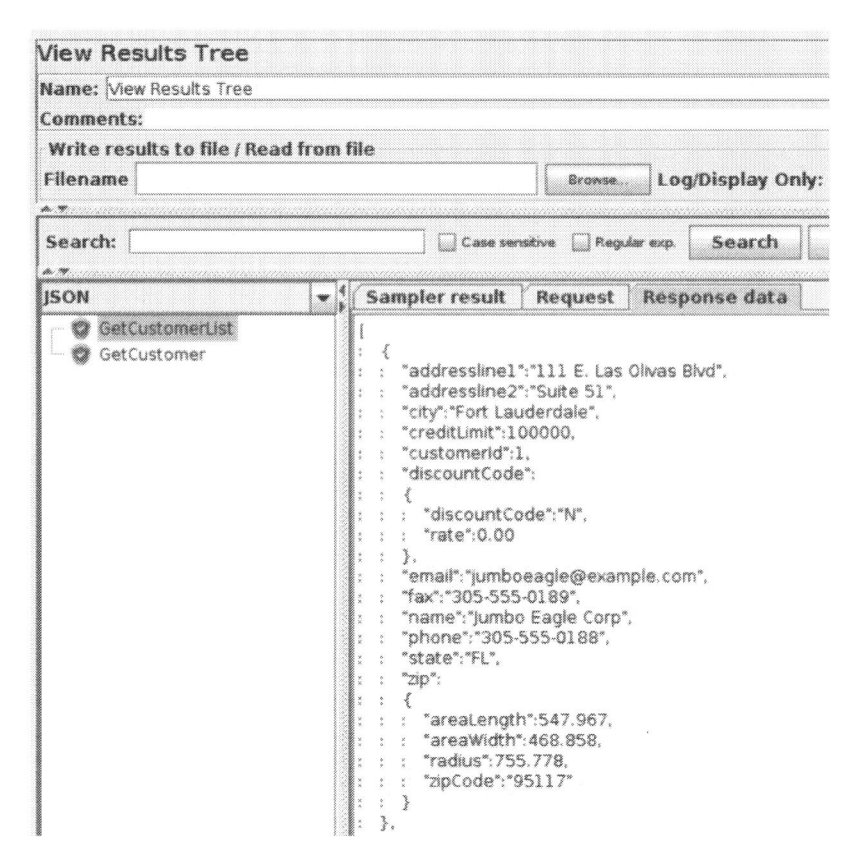

Figure 8.29: Result of retrieving the record list

And, the following record is retrieved:

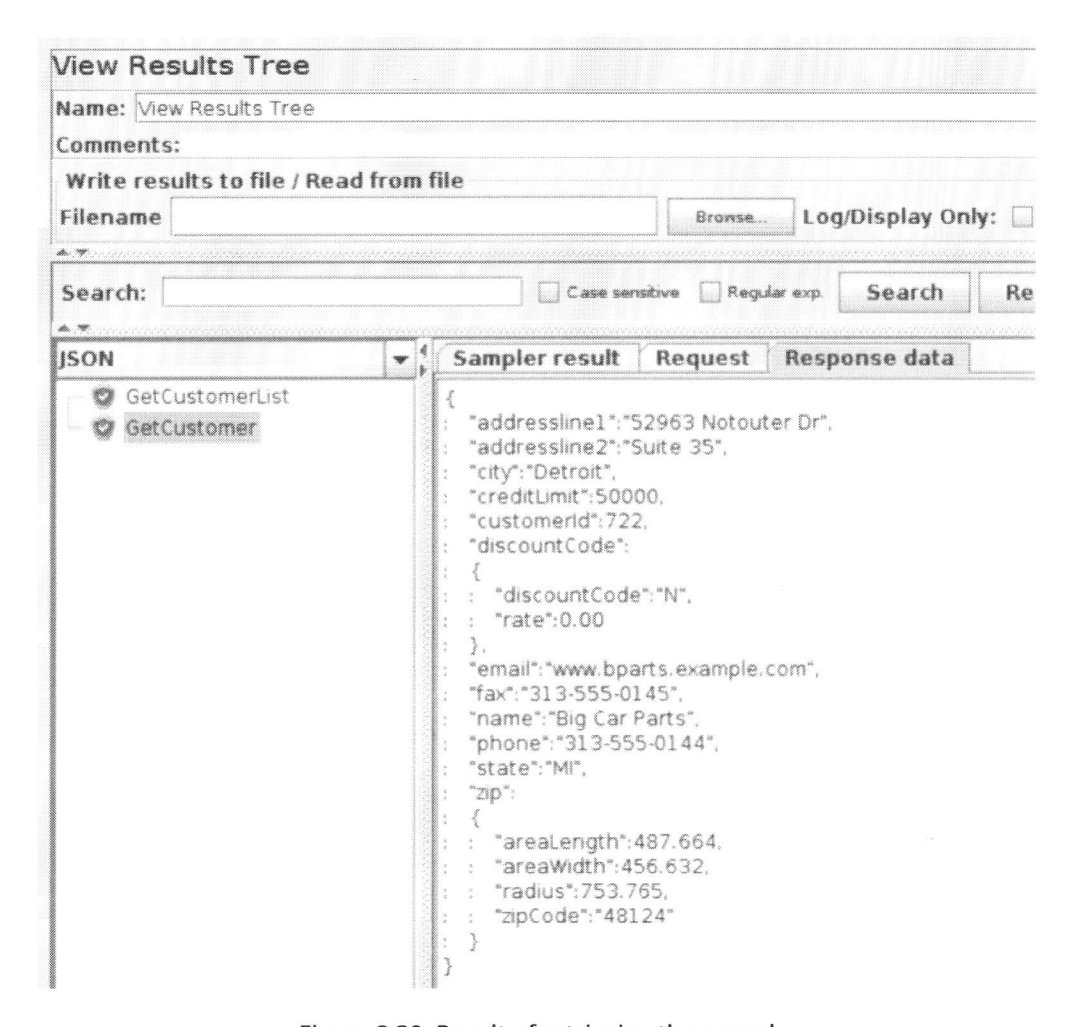

```
{
    "addressline1":"52963 Notouter Dr",
    "addressline2":"Suite 35",
    "city":"Detroit",
    "creditLimit":50000,
    "customerId":722,
    "discountCode":
    {
        "discountCode":"N",
        "rate":0.00
    },
    "email":"www.bparts.example.com",
    "fax":"313-555-0145",
    "name":"Big Car Parts",
    "phone":"313-555-0144",
    "state":"MI",
    "zip":
    {
        "areaLength":487.664,
        "areaWidth":456.632,
        "radius":753.765,
        "zipCode":"48124"
    }
}
```

Figure 8.30: Result of retrieving the record

All we have to do is set up and launch our test.

The results are encouraging. Now that everyone is confident, we continue with two additional requests:

- Compare the performance of the JSON and XML responses.
- Find the optimal size for pagination results from a performance point of view.

234 | Load Testing Web Services

Let's start with the performance comparison between JSON and XML.

Two modifications must be made:

- The value of the *Accept* field in our **HTTP Header Manager**
- Our **Regular Expression Extractor**, which randomly retrieves the identifier of a customer record.

There we go:

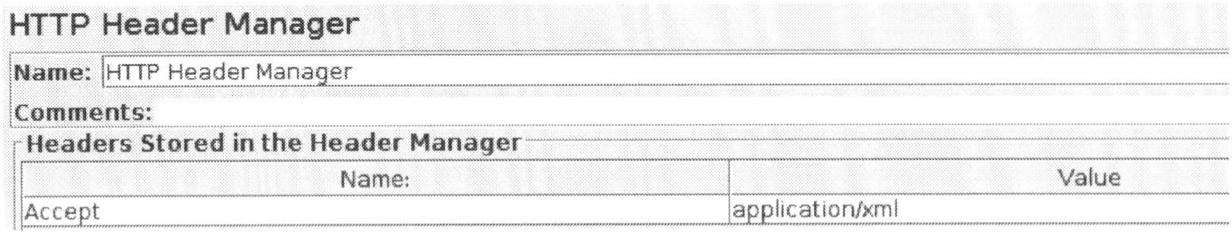

Figure 8.31: Changing the format

And, for the extraction, since it's XML, we modify **Regular Expression Extractor** in this way:

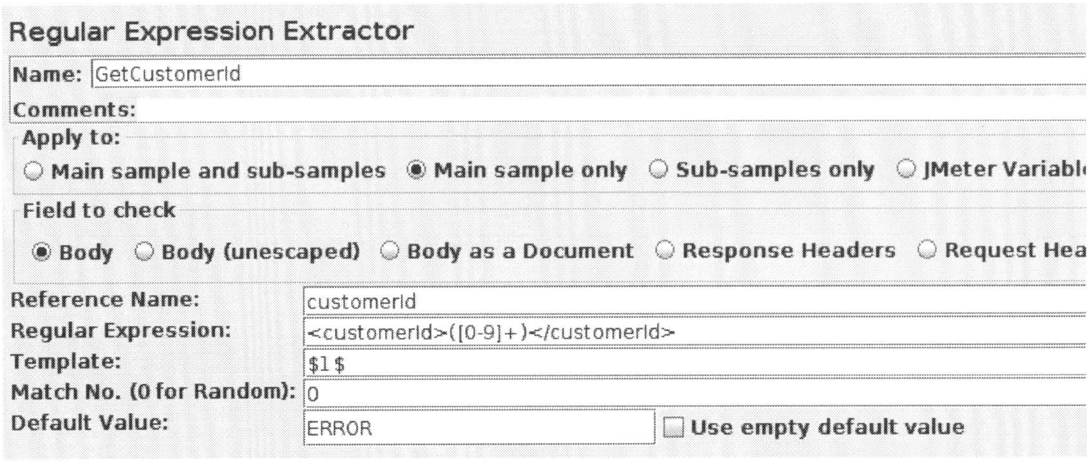

Figure 8.32: Regular Expression Extractor

> **Note**
> Note, in this case, it would be much better to use **XPath 2 Extractor** since it's particularly suited to XML data.

We end up with the following result:

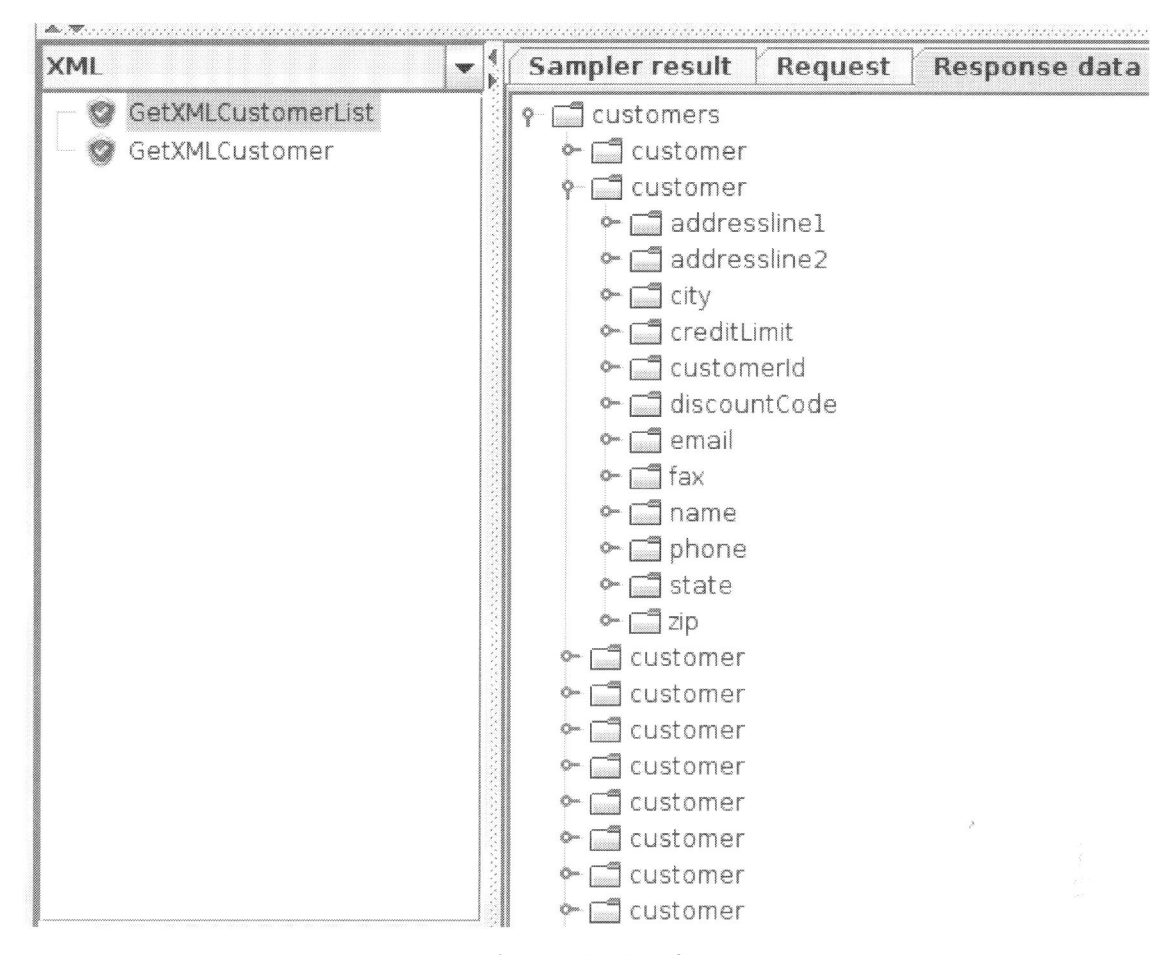

Figure 8.33: Result

We can even create two **Thread Groups** to compare the performance of both communication formats at the same time. But it is better to do it in two different tests as the performance issues of one format might impact the other format.

Don't forget to monitor the web service to check whether everything is running smoothly:

```
Test Plan
    HTTP Request Defaults
    JSON
        GetCustomerList
            HTTP Header Manager
            JSON Extractor
        GetCustomer
            HTTP Header Manager
    XML
        GetXMLCustomerList
            HTTP Header Manager
            GetCustomerId
        GetXMLCustomer
            HTTP Header Manager
```

Figure 8.34: Our script

Let's tackle the second request on the optimal size for pagination.

Our request to display the list of customers now has this format:

GET /CustomerDB/webresources/entities.customer/{from}/{to}

After a discussion with the UX team, the value of **{to}** should vary between 5 and 10. In our test, **{from}** will always be one. Several solutions are possible to implement this test case. We decide to use the **Counter** element of JMeter:

```
Counter
Name: Counter
Comments:
Starting value 5
Increment 1
Maximum value 10
Number format
Reference Name to
☐ Track counter independently for each user
☐ Reset counter on each Thread Group Iteration
```

Figure 8.35: Counter from 5 to 10

This will allow us, for each iteration and thread, to generate a number between 5 and 10 that will be stored in the *to* variable. Let's use this variable in our HTTP request:

Figure 8.36: Using the counter

> **Note**
> We name our HTTP request **GetCustomerList_${to}** in order to be able to differentiate our queries during the analysis.

We get this response in the **View Results Tree**:

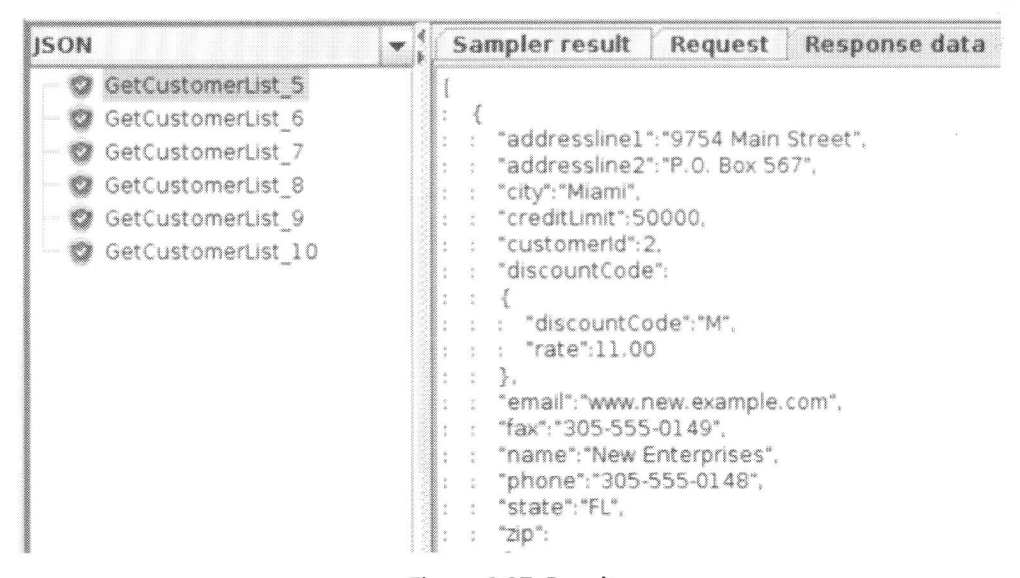

Figure 8.37: Result

Our script is ready (of course, don't forget to add an assertion)

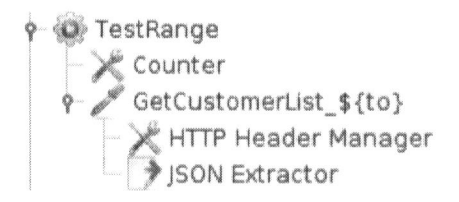

Figure 8.38: Our script

The application is increasingly successful; the features of editing, creating, and deleting the customer record are increasingly used. The creation of new scripts to cover these new needs is decided.

Let's start by deleting a customer record.

The request to delete a customer record is very similar to the one that displays a customer record. The only difference is the HTTP method used. We'll use the **DELETE** method instead of the **GET** method:

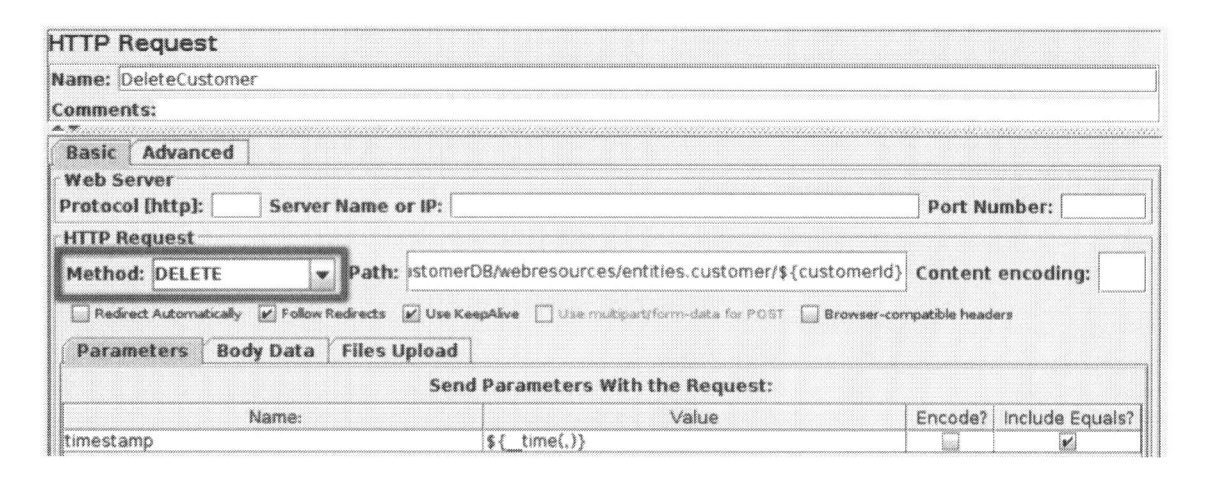

Figure 8.39: Deleting a customer record

Now, let's move on to creating a customer record.

Let's start by filling a CSV file with the necessary data:

NAME	ADDRESSLINE1	ADDRESSLINE2	CITY	STATE	PHONE	FAX	EMAIL	CREDIT_LIMIT
User1	MyAddresse100	MyAddresse200	PA	France	676213210	176213250	MyEmail1@mail.com	4000
User2	MyAddresse101	MyAddresse201	PA	France	676213211	176213251	MyEmail2@mail.com	4001
User3	MyAddresse102	MyAddresse202	PA	France	676213212	176213252	MyEmail3@mail.com	4002
User4	MyAddresse103	MyAddresse203	PA	France	676213213	176213253	MyEmail4@mail.com	4003
User5	MyAddresse104	MyAddresse204	PA	France	676213214	176213254	MyEmail5@mail.com	4004
User6	MyAddresse105	MyAddresse205	PA	France	676213215	176213255	MyEmail6@mail.com	4005
User7	MyAddresse106	MyAddresse206	PA	France	676213216	176213256	MyEmail7@mail.com	4006
User8	MyAddresse107	MyAddresse207	PA	France	676213217	176213257	MyEmail8@mail.com	4007
User9	MyAddresse108	MyAddresse208	PA	France	676213218	176213258	MyEmail9@mail.com	4008
User10	MyAddresse109	MyAddresse209	PA	France	676213219	176213259	MyEmail10@mail.com	4009
User11	MyAddresse110	MyAddresse210	PA	France	676213220	176213260	MyEmail11@mail.com	4010
User12	MyAddresse111	MyAddresse211	PA	France	676213221	176213261	MyEmail12@mail.com	4011
User13	MyAddresse112	MyAddresse212	PA	France	676213222	176213262	MyEmail13@mail.com	4012
User14	MyAddresse113	MyAddresse213	PA	France	676213223	176213263	MyEmail14@mail.com	4013
User15	MyAddresse114	MyAddresse214	PA	France	676213224	176213264	MyEmail15@mail.com	4014
User16	MyAddresse115	MyAddresse215	PA	France	676213225	176213265	MyEmail16@mail.com	4015
User17	MyAddresse116	MyAddresse216	PA	France	676213226	176213266	MyEmail17@mail.com	4016
User18	MyAddresse117	MyAddresse217	PA	France	676213227	176213267	MyEmail18@mail.com	4017
User19	MyAddresse118	MyAddresse218	PA	France	676213228	176213268	MyEmail19@mail.com	4018
User20	MyAddresse119	MyAddresse219	PA	France	676213229	176213269	MyEmail20@mail.com	4019
User21	MyAddresse120	MyAddresse220	PA	France	676213230	176213270	MyEmail21@mail.com	4020

Figure 8.40: CSV file

Then, let's integrate it with JMeter using **CSV Data Set Config**. Let's use these values in our HTTP request:

```
HTTP Request
Name: AddCustomer
Comments:

Basic | Advanced
Web Server
Protocol [http]:        Server Name or IP:                                               Port Number:
HTTP Request
Method: POST       ▼  Path: /CustomerDB/webresources/entities.customer             Content encoding:

  ☐ Redirect Automatically  ☑ Follow Redirects  ☑ Use KeepAlive  ☐ Use multipart/form-data for POST  ☐ Browser-compatible headers

Parameters | Body Data | Files Upload
1  {"addressline1":"${ADDRESSLINE1}","addressline2":"${ADDRESSLINE1}","city":"${CITY}","creditLimit":
   "${CREDIT_LIMIT}","customerId":"${__Random(50,999999999,)}","discountCode":{"discountCode":"H","rate":16},
   "email":"${EMAIL}","fax":"${FAX}","name":"${NAME}","phone":"${PHONE}","state":"PA","zip":{"areaLength":
   285.848,"areaWidth":173.794,"radius":368.386,"zipCode":"94401"}}
```

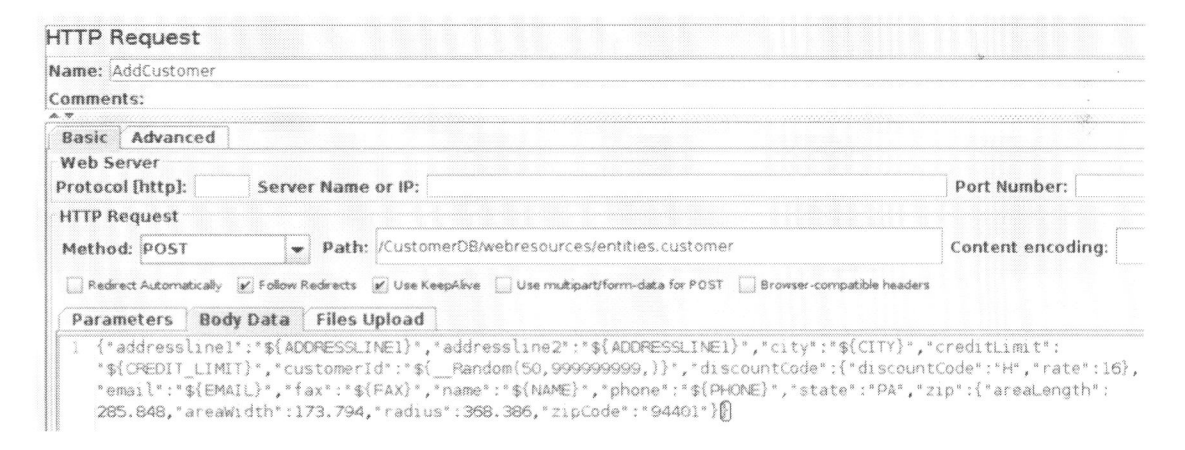

Figure 8.41: Our HTTP request

Do not forget the headers of our HTTP request:

HTTP Header Manager

Name:	Value
Accept	application/json, text/javascript, */*; q=0.01
Content-Type	application/json
X-Requested-With	XMLHttpRequest

Figure 8.42: The headers of our HTTP request

The information is sent by the HTTP **POST** method.

Our client record creation script is complete:

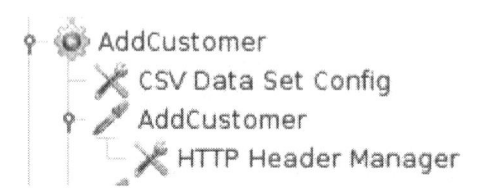

Figure 8.43: Our script

Conclusion

As you can see, the web services test looks a lot like a web application test, because both are based on the HTTP protocol. Everything you learned in *Chapter 7, Load Testing a Website* is also valid for this chapter.

9
Load Testing a Database Server

Microservices architectures are increasingly being used, which involves more and more databases being used as well.

244 | Load Testing a Database Server

Usually, databases are accessed through an API, and therefore, for a load test to be as realistic as possible, it is necessary to test the API, and not the database directly:

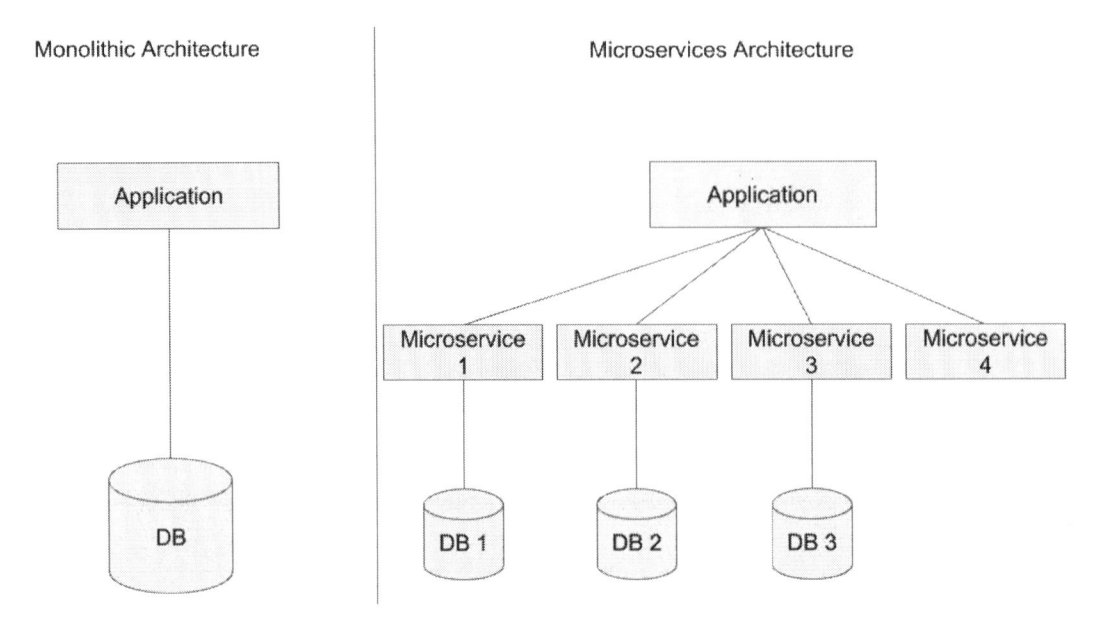

Figure 9.1: Microservices architecture versus monolithic architecture

However, it may be useful to test the database directly when:

- The API is not yet ready
- To compare JDBC drivers easily
- To tune database parameters
- To compare different databases
- To compare AWS RDS engine implementations (such as Aurora, Oracle, and SQL Server)
- To check the database configuration
- To check whether the cluster (as in, the VIP and load balancing strategy) is behaving well
- To test the database production server before going live without having an API server production-ready
- To do load testing on a database when a batch is running, or during replication/failover
- When, within a regular HTTP/JMS load test, we want to access the database to check/load/save some data in the database

A Bit of Theory

The architecture of a basic engine has become very complex, as shown in the following diagram (note that this is only a simplified overview of the Oracle architecture).

The complexity is such that user expertise in one version of Oracle is partly outdated as soon as the next version is released:

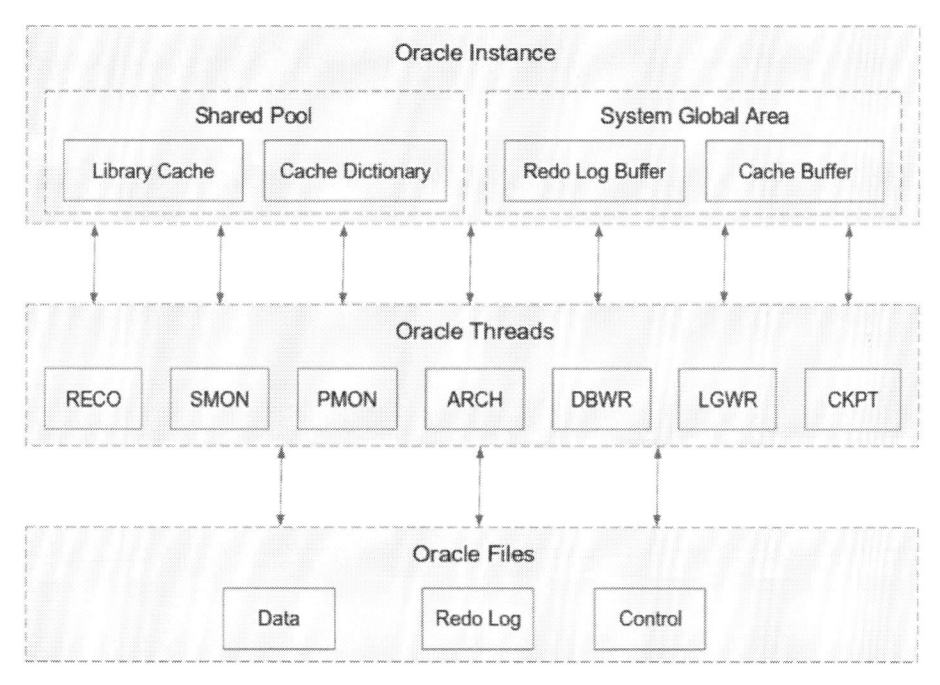

Figure 9.2: A simplified description of Oracle architecture

Each part of this architecture can be tuned based on the expected usage of the database.

Add to this the fact that misconfigured databases or unoptimized SQL queries are the cause of most common performance problems, and you can understand the importance of performing load tests on the database server.

For those who are not yet convinced of the importance of tuning the database engine architecture, the following graph shows an example of the response time of a SQL query on Oracle without tuning (where SGA, one of the Oracle database caches, is not correctly configured) versus an optimized Oracle (where the size of SGA has been increased to be consistent with the amount of the data stored in the database):

SQL Query response time

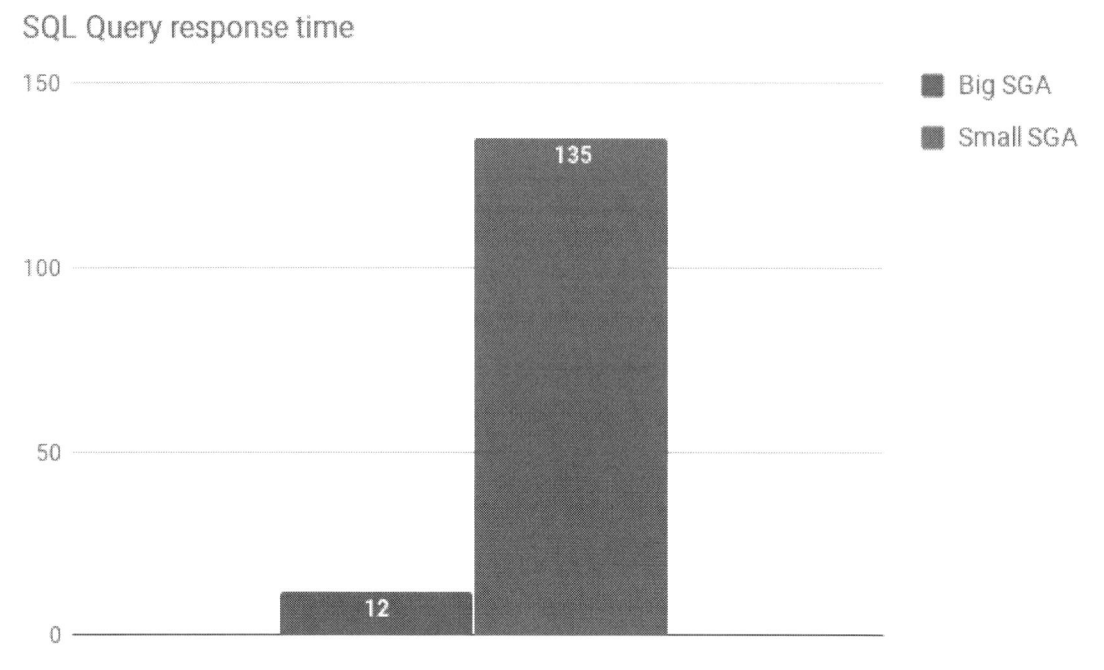

- Big SGA: 12
- Small SGA: 135

Figure 9.3: The importance of SGA

As you can see, it is worth spending some time optimizing Oracle with a load test.

Methodology

Before moving on to concrete examples, it is important to follow a methodology by which to perform the relevant tests. A critical thing when testing a database is to make sure that it is equivalent to production. Otherwise, make sure that:

- The difference between environments is acceptable
- The difference between environments is clearly identified
- The test remains meaningful and usable

By "equivalent to production," we mean two things:

- The configuration of the database engine must be identical to the production engine (if it exists).

- The volume of data in the database must also be as close as possible to that for the production database (the simplest way to do this is to have a backup of what is in production, or, if you start from scratch, to have an idea of the future volume).

For skeptics or those who are curious, we can see in the following graph the response time of the same SQL query executed on different volumes of data:

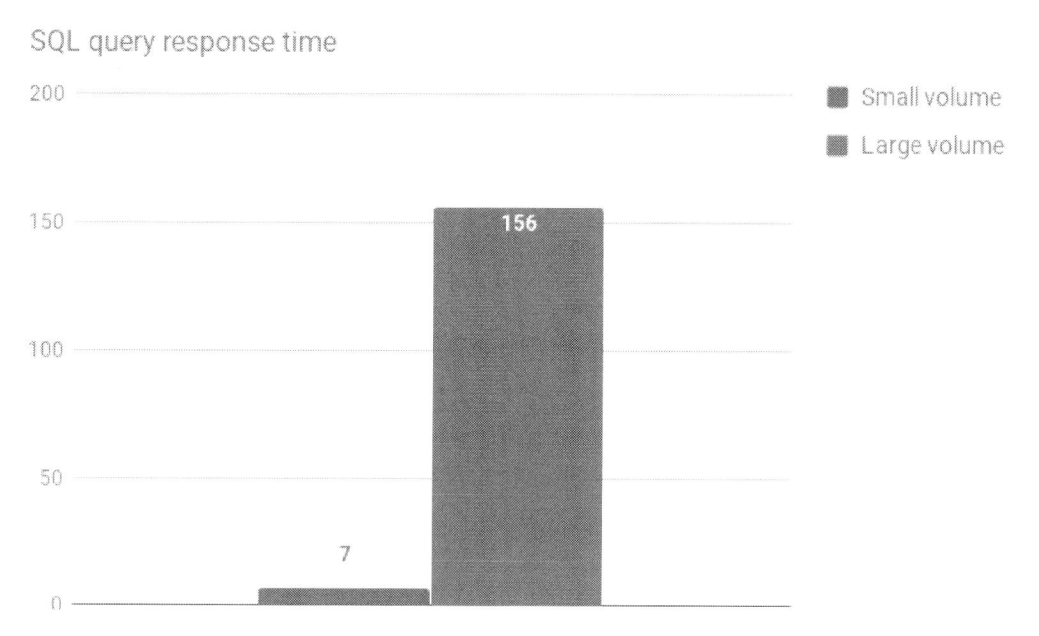

Figure 9.4: The importance of data volume

Now that we have an iso production database, let's see how to architect the test.

In our test plan, we must consider the duration of the tests, the diversity of the input SQL queries, and our input data.

Nowadays, there are necessarily caches in the architecture that we are going to test (whether at the database-engine level or at the level of other components of the technical architecture).

Caches are designed to prevent the same heavy processing (such as SQL queries) with the same parameters (such as parameter values) from being executed each time. For this purpose, a cache stores the results of heavy processing.

This means that the cache will be useless if the test time is too short, as it will not have enough time to fill up to be useful, and the cache will be overused if the requests (and, therefore, their types and parameters) that are sent are not diverse enough. Conversely, the cache will be useless if the dataset is too wide.

Let's now look at how JMeter allows you to test a database server.

Setup with JMeter

> **Note**
> Since JMeter is a Java program, access to a database is done using the JDBC protocol.

The first thing to do is put the JDBC driver in the JMeter classpath if that has not already been done.

The two simplest solutions to this are:

- Dropping the `.jar` driver file in `JMETER_HOME/lib/`
- Using the `user.classpath` property to reference the driver JAR

Once this is done, you must configure the connection to the database with the **JDBC Connection Configuration** element.

This will allow us to configure the connection string for our database (including the URL, port, connection ID, password, and so on):

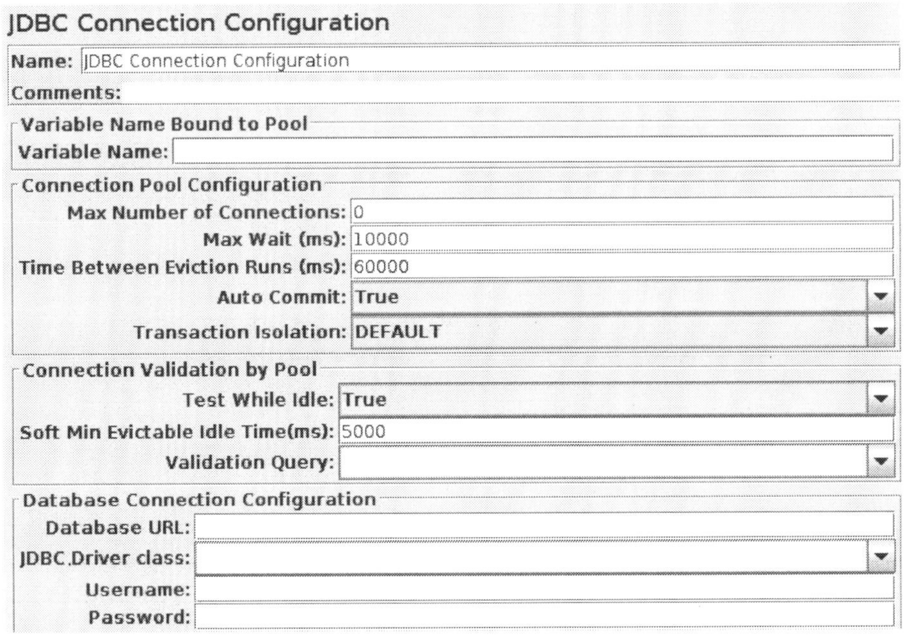

Figure 9.5: JDBC connection configuration

This element is composed of four parts, named as follows:

- **Variable Name Bound to Pool:** This name will further be used in **JDBC Requests**.
- **Connection Pool Configuration.**
- **Connection Validation by Pool.**
- **Database Connection Configuration.**

The property names are very self-explanatory, so we will not dwell any further. However, it is important to pay attention to:

- **Connection Pool Configuration**
- **Connection Validation by Pool**

This is necessary in order to avoid overloading both JMeter (by exceeding the maximum number of connections) and the database (transaction isolation level, auto commit, and validation request).

> **Note**
> It is, of course, possible to have several **JDBC Connection Configuration** elements that point to several databases.

250 | Load Testing a Database Server

Now, you can switch to the SQL queries themselves using the **JDBC Request** element:

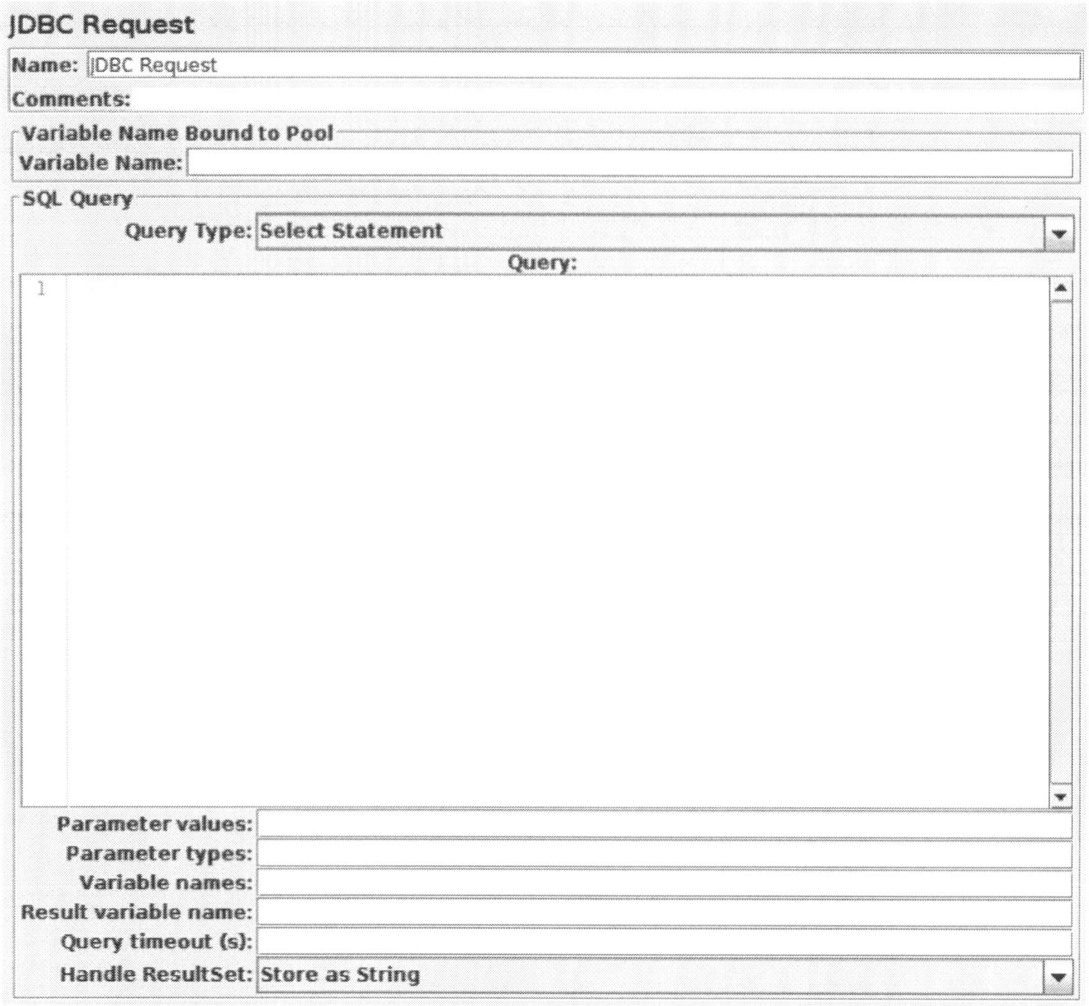

Figure 9.6: The JDBC Request element

First, we choose on which database the requests will be launched using the **Variable Name** field (the name defined in the **JDBC Connection Configuration** element).

Then, choose the **Query Type**. The list of available types includes UPDATE, SELECT, DELETE, INSERT, and stored procedure call, among others.

Using these two elements, you can test any type of database with any SQL query. The only requirement is the presence of a JDBC driver for the target database.

Putting Theory into Practice with JMeter

Let's move on to practice.

Example 1: Load Test of a Database

Let's start with a simple example (which we will enrich as we go along) that consists of testing a database under MySQL using a SQL query.

In this example, we will use the *Employees* database available at https://github.com/datacharmer/test_db.

Let's first deal with SQL queries of the **SELECT** type:

1. Let's start by configuring our connection to MySQL using the **JDBC Connection Configuration** item.

    For MySQL, the database URL must be in the form of `jdbc:mysql://host:port/dbname` and the JDBC driver class must be **com.mysql.jdbc.Driver**.

    In our case, the MySQL database is installed locally on the same machine as JMeter (**avoid this absolutely during real tests**). Its URL will be **jdbc:mysql://localhost:3306/employees**:

    > **Note**
    > If not already the case, set the maximum number of connections (**Max Number of Connections**) to zero so that each thread has its own connection.

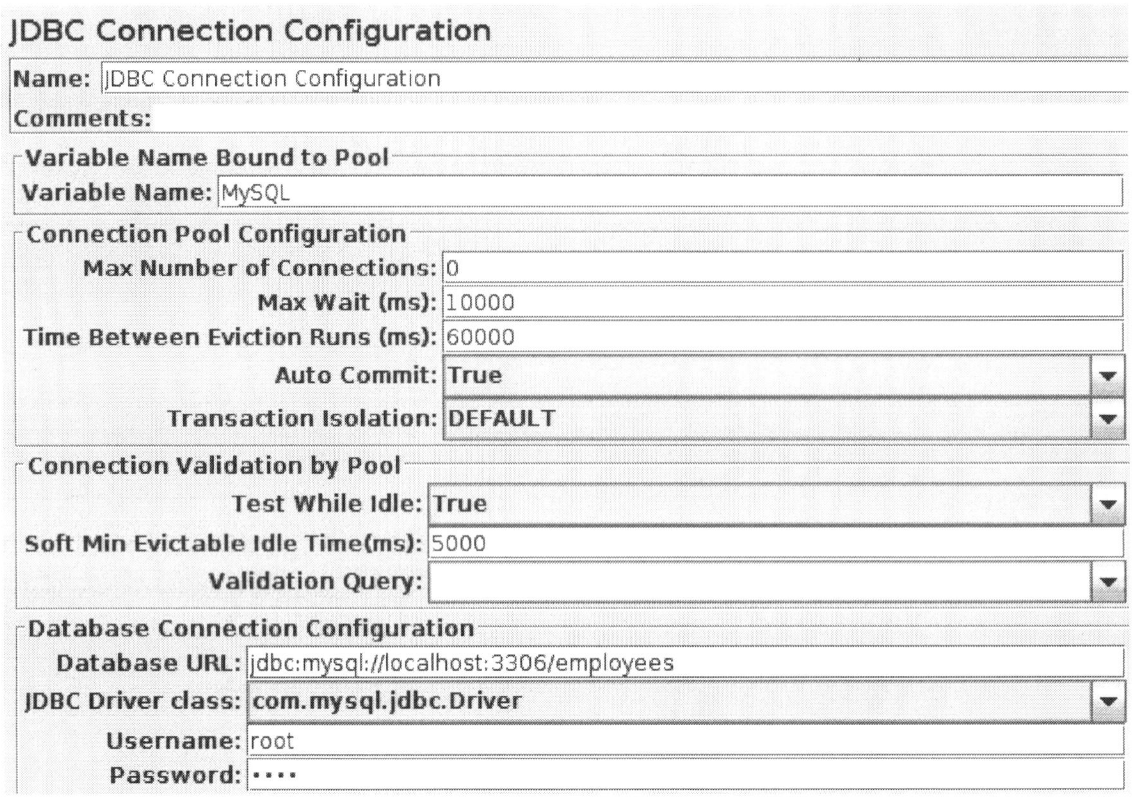

252 | Load Testing a Database Server

Figure 9.7: JDBC connection configuration

2. Now let's add a **JDBC Request** to execute our **SELECT** query.

3. Enter the name of the connection that we defined earlier.

4. Choose **Select Statement** as the type of SQL query.

5. Fill in the **Query** field with the SELECT query, using the syntax of SELECT first_name, last_name FROM employees WHERE last_name LIKE 'D%':

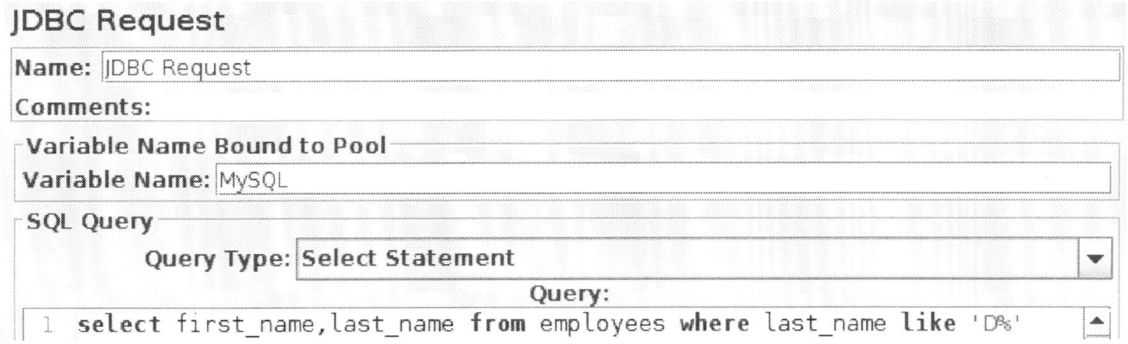

Figure 9.8: JDBC Request

6. Add an assertion to check for the proper execution of our request.

   In our case, when there is an execution error, the response will contain the expression **exceptions**:

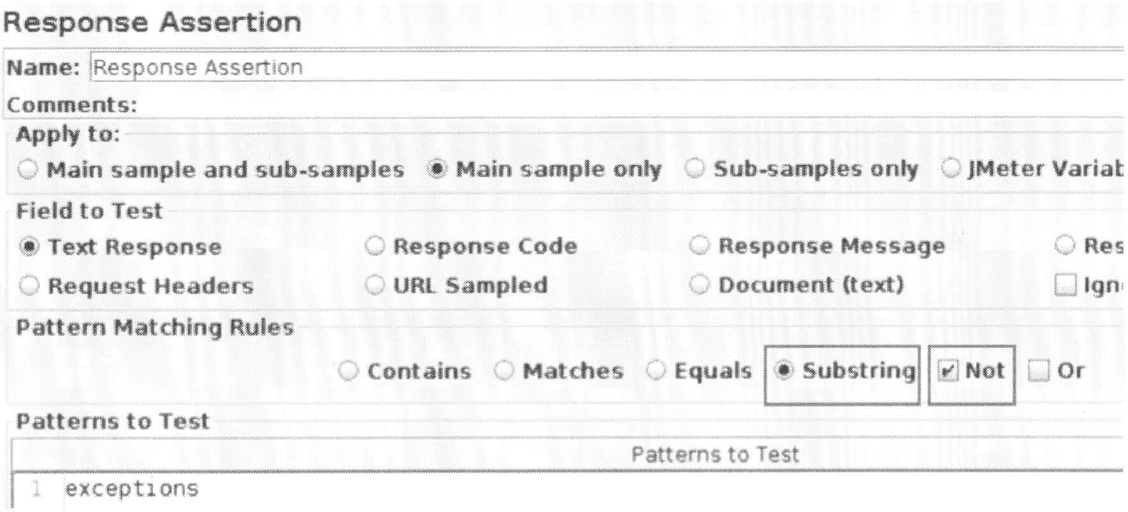

Figure 9.9: Our Response Assertion settings

7. Let's execute it:

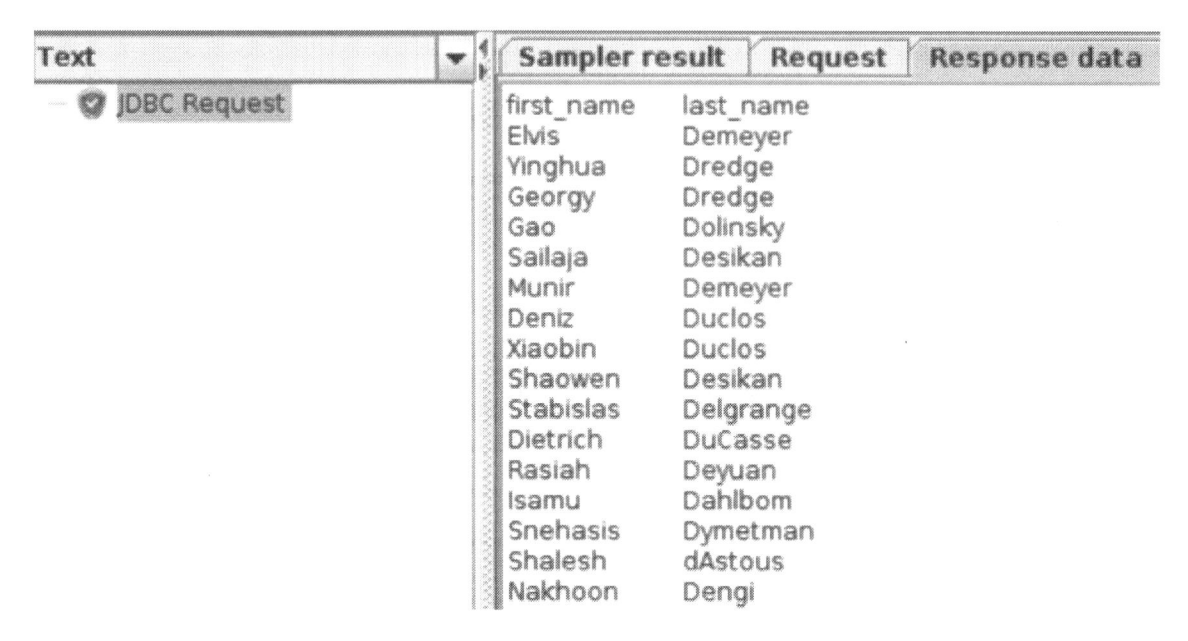

first_name	last_name
Elvis	Demeyer
Yinghua	Dredge
Georgy	Dredge
Gao	Dolinsky
Sailaja	Desikan
Munir	Demeyer
Deniz	Duclos
Xiaobin	Duclos
Shaowen	Desikan
Stabislas	Delgrange
Dietrich	DuCasse
Rasiah	Deyuan
Isamu	Dahlbom
Snehasis	Dymetman
Shalesh	dAstous
Nakhoon	Dengi

Figure 9.10: The results of our SQL query

For now, the script only covers a tiny part of a good test plan, as with a single SQL query, we will mainly test the caches.

Fortunately, we have a list of the main **SELECT** SQL queries executed.

A simple way to integrate these new requests into our script is to use a **CSV Data Set Config** element.

To do this, we will put all the requests into a CSV file.

8. *Extract from the CSV file*:

   ```
   SQL_QUERY
   select first_name,last_name from employees where last_name like 'D%'
   select last_name from employees
   select first_name,last_name from employees where gender ='M'
   select first_name,last_name from employees where last_name like 'T%'
   select first_name,last_name from employees where gender ='F'
   ```

9. We will enter the name of our CSV file in the **Filename** field of the **CSV Data Set Config** element.

10. Don't forget to change the value of the comma delimiter to a semicolon so that there is no problem with the commata that can be present in our SQL queries:

> **Note**
> Here, we do not need to define the name of the variable where the request will be stored in order to be used later, because it already exists in our CSV file as the first row.

Figure 9.11: The CSV data source

11. All we have to do now is to replace the query in the **Query** field of the **JDBC Request** element with our **${SQL_QUERY}** variable:

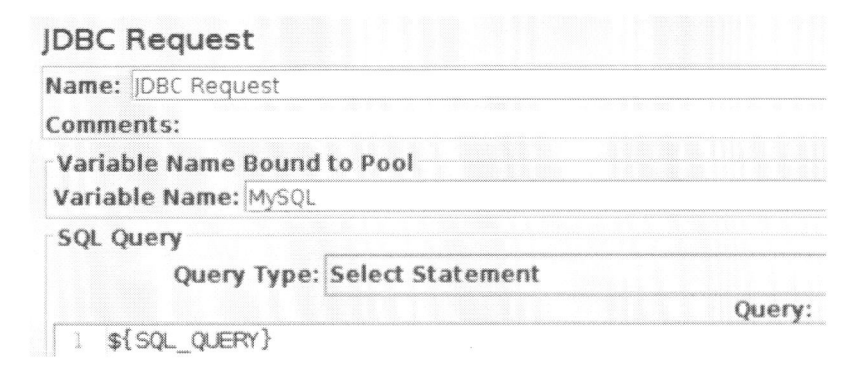

Figure 9.12: Using our ${SQL_QUERY} variable in JDBC Query

12. In order to verify that this works, we add a **View Results Tree** element to our test plan (don't forget to disable it when you run the load test):

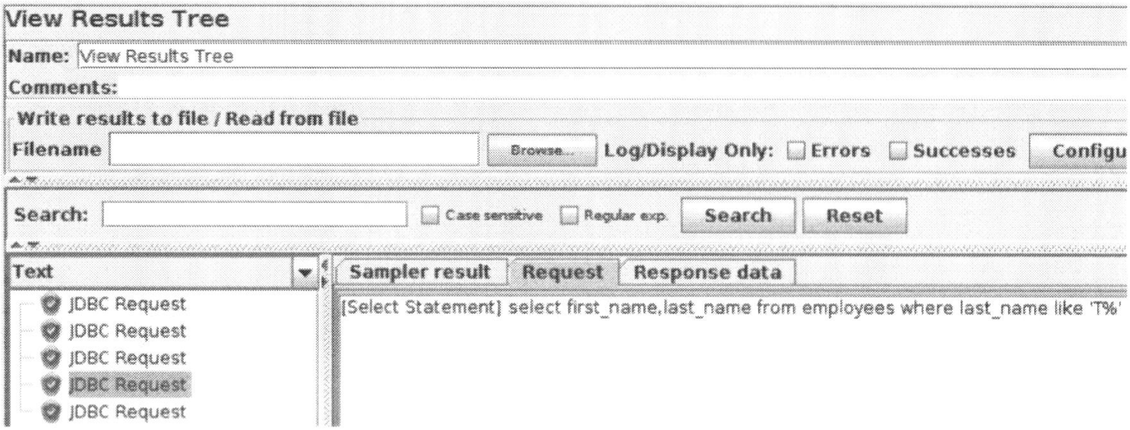

Figure 9.13: The View Results Tree window

This is much better, but the queries remain static, and after a while (which could be shorter or longer depending on the number of SQL queries in the CSV file), they will all end up in the cache.

In order to avoid this problem and make our test more realistic, we will make our SQL queries dynamic.

13. First, we will group our requests by family with the same syntactic form.

    In our case, we have two families:

    ```
    SELECT XXXXXXX FROM XXXXX WHERE XXXXX

    SELECT XXXXXXXXX FROM XXXXX
    ```

    We will, therefore, need two JDBC requests.

    Now, for each group of queries, we will note what can be variabilized.

    For example, consider the following query:

    ```
    SELECT first_name,last_name FROM employees WHERE last_name LIKE 'D%'
    ```

    This will become the following:

    ```
    SELECT {selection list} FROM {table} WHERE {where clause}
    ```

    All of these variables will be in a CSV file.

14. *Excerpt from the CSV file*:

    ```
    select_grp1;table_grp1;where_grp1
    first_name,last_name;employees;last_name like 'D%'
    first_name,last_name;employees;gender = 'M'
    first_name,last_name;employees;last_name like 'T%'
    first_name,last_name;employees;gender = 'F'
    ```

15. We modify our **CSV Data Set Config** element so that it points to our new CSV file.

16. Finally, we modify our **Query** field to become the following:

    ```
    SELECT ${select_grp1} FROM ${table_grp1} WHERE ${where_grp1}
    ```

    JDBC Request

    Name: JDBC Request
    Comments:
    Variable Name Bound to Pool
    Variable Name: MySQL
    SQL Query
       Query Type: Select Statement
                   Query:
    1 select ${select_grp1} from ${table_grp1} where ${where_grp1}

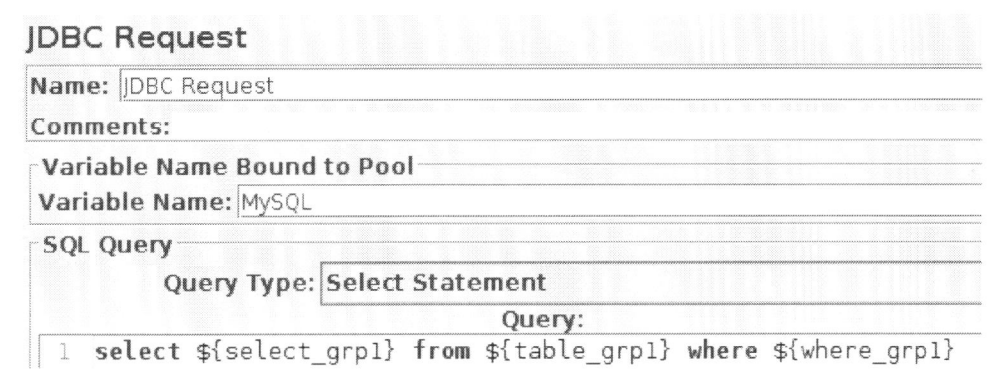

    Figure 9.14: Our SQL query

    The same is done for the second group of SQL queries.

17. *Excerpt from the CSV file*:

    ```
    select_grp2;table_grp2
    first_name,last_name;employees
    last_name;employees
    ```

18. Let's add the **Random Order Controller** element to add a little more realism by simulating users with different behaviors.

This element executes its children in a random order:

```
Thread Group
    Random Order Controller
        JDBC Request grp1
        JDBC Request grp2
```

Figure 9.15: Our Random Order Controller element

With a little more effort, we can make the **WHERE** clauses of our SQL queries even more realistic.

Note that the **WHERE** clause has been divided into several parts:

{where clause} = {left where clause} {condition where clause} {right where clause}

With the same methodology as before, we can refine our CSV file and our **JDBC Request** element to multiply the possible requests with a reduced dataset (it will be enough to use a script that generates our CSV file by combining the possible values).

19. *Excerpt from the CSV file:*

    ```
    select_grp1;table_grp1;where_grp1
    first_name,last_name;employees;last_name like 'D%'
    first_name,last_name;employees;gender = 'M'
    ```

20. This becomes the following:

    ```
    select_grp1;table_grp1;left_where_clause_grp1;condition_where_clause_grp1;right_where_clause_grp1
    first_name,last_name;employees;last_name;like;'D%'
    first_name,last_name;employees;gender;=;'M'
    ```

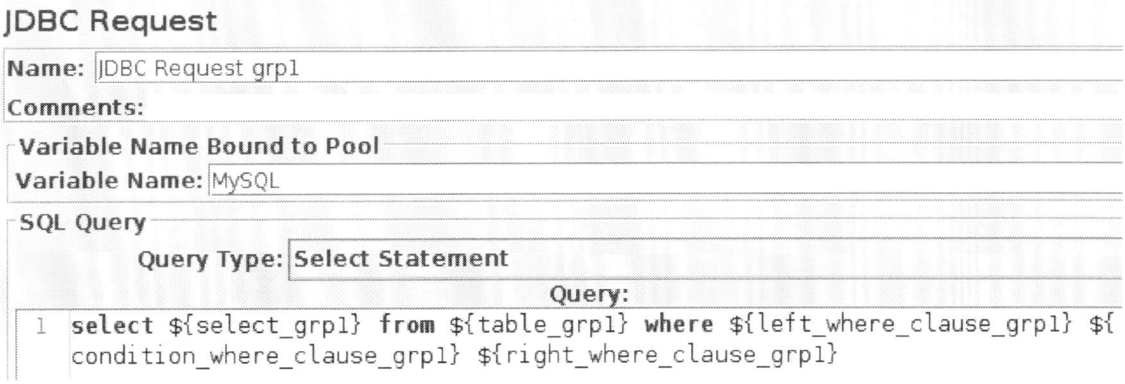

JDBC Request

Name: JDBC Request grp1
Comments:

Variable Name Bound to Pool
Variable Name: MySQL

SQL Query
Query Type: Select Statement

Query:
```
1  select ${select_grp1} from ${table_grp1} where ${left_where_clause_grp1} ${condition_where_clause_grp1} ${right_where_clause_grp1}
```

Figure 9.16: The JDBC request using our CSV file

In most cases, there are different users with modification rights (let's call them administrators) that will have to be simulated. Nothing is easier with JMeter.

21. In order to separate the two types of users, we will create another **Thread Group** element. This will allow each group to be fine-tuned.

    For example, if we know that 24% of our users have modification rights, then it will be easy to find the value of the *Number of Threads (users)* for each group.

    In order to avoid making an **UPDATE** that doesn't update anything, the conditions of our **UPDATE** queries will be the results of SQL queries executed just before **UPDATE**.

> **Note**
> A SQL query with a join would have been easier, but for practice, we will split it into two SQL queries.

Imagine that these users can increase the salary of all employees whose name begins with the letter G (via the **salary** field in the *salaries* table).

First, we need to retrieve the identification of the employees whose salary will be increased.

22. Let's use a **JDBC Request** element to execute this SQL query. We can take `select emp_no from employees where last_name like 'G%'` as a SQL query (I will let you apply what we just learned to make this SQL query more dynamic).

Load Testing a Database Server

23. Do not forget to retrieve the results of the SQL query:

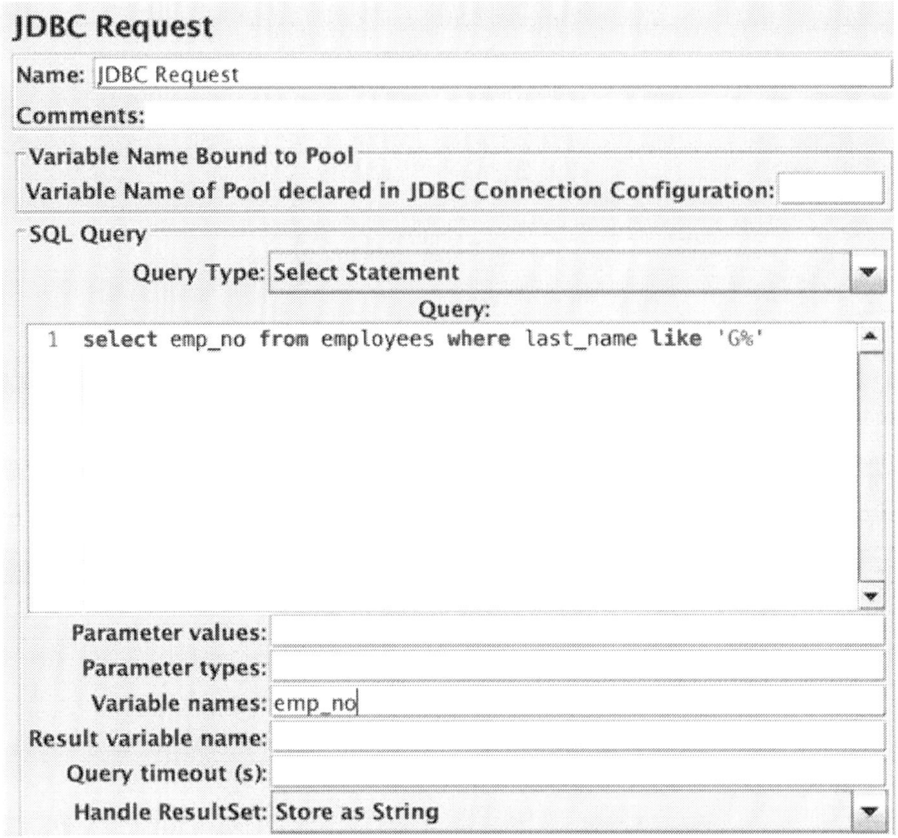

JDBC Request

Name: JDBC Request
Comments:

Variable Name Bound to Pool
Variable Name of Pool declared in JDBC Connection Configuration:

SQL Query
Query Type: Select Statement
Query:
```
1  select emp_no from employees where last_name like 'G%'
```

Parameter values:
Parameter types:
Variable names: emp_no
Result variable name:
Query timeout (s):
Handle ResultSet: Store as String

Figure 9.17: Our JDBC Request configuration

As we can see, the request retrieves several identifiers:

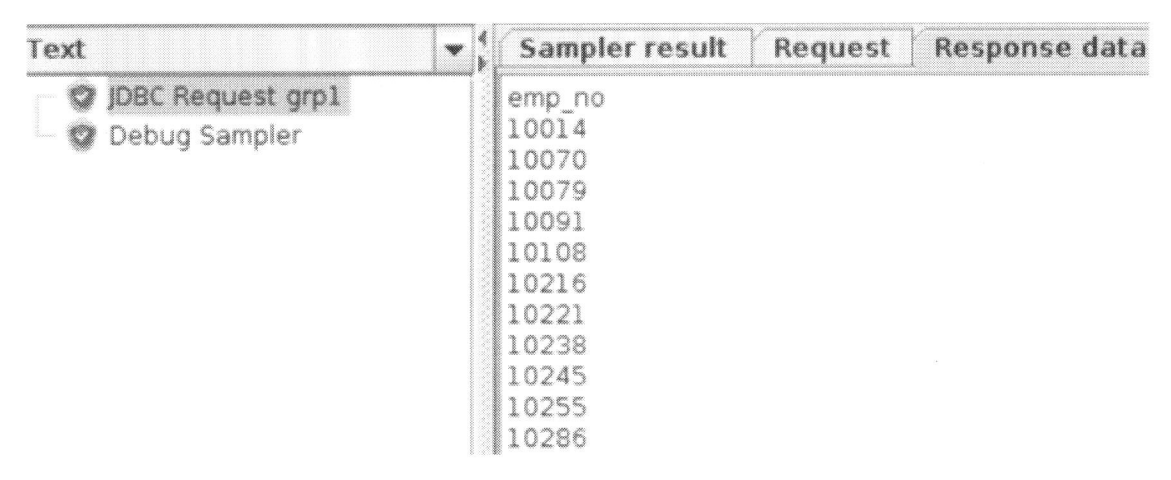

```
Text                          Sampler result  Request  Response data
  JDBC Request grp1           emp_no
  Debug Sampler               10014
                              10070
                              10079
                              10091
                              10108
                              10216
                              10221
                              10238
                              10245
                              10255
                              10286
```

Figure 9.18: The results of our SQL query

> **Note**
> To find the number of responses, we can use the **emp_no_#** variable exposed by the **JDBC Request** sampler.

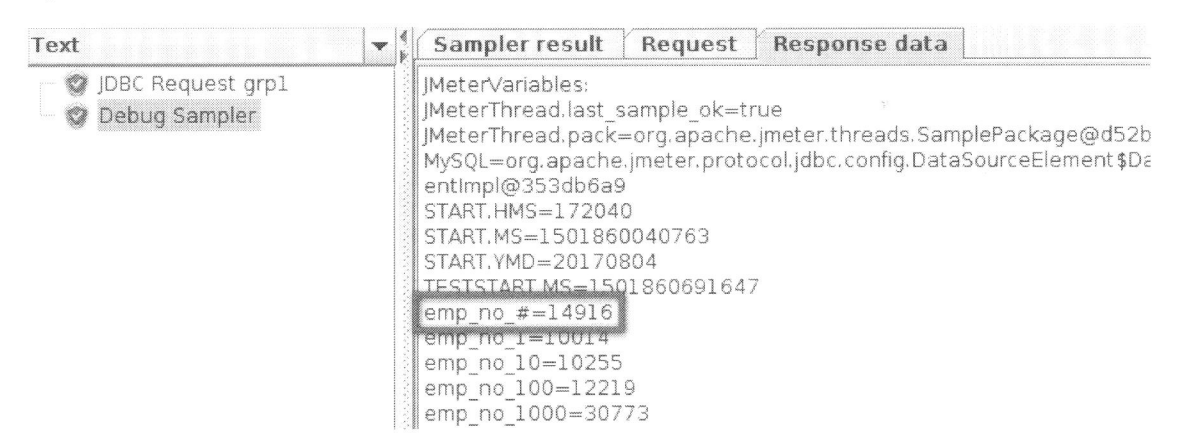

```
Text                          Sampler result  Request  Response data
  JDBC Request grp1           JMeterVariables:
  Debug Sampler               JMeterThread.last_sample_ok=true
                              JMeterThread.pack=org.apache.jmeter.threads.SamplePackage@d52b
                              MySQL=org.apache.jmeter.protocol.jdbc.config.DataSourceElement$Da
                              entImpl@353db6a9
                              START.HMS=172040
                              START.MS=1501860040763
                              START.YMD=20170804
                              TESTSTART.MS=1501860691647
                              emp_no_#=14916
                              emp_no_1=10014
                              emp_no_10=10255
                              emp_no_100=12219
                              emp_no_1000=30773
```

Figure 9.19: Number of responses

262 | Load Testing a Database Server

24. All we have to do now is use the **ForEach Controller** element to browse all the results in order to make our **UPDATE** query:

ForEach Controller
Name: ForEach Controller
Comments:
Input variable prefix emp_no
Start index for loop (exclusive)
End index for loop (inclusive)
Output variable name
☑ Add "_" before number ?

Figure 9.20: Results with a ForEach Controller element

25. For each employee, we need a new percentage increase.

    Let's use the **__Random** function.

26. We want increases of between 1% and 10%, which gives us **${__Random(1,10,increase)}**:

Function Helper

Choose a function: __Random

Function Parameters

Name:	Value
The minimum value allowed for a range of values	1
The maximum value allowed for a range of values	10
Name of variable in which to store the result (optional)	increase

Copy and paste function string: ${__Random(1,10,increase)}

The result of the function is: 1 9

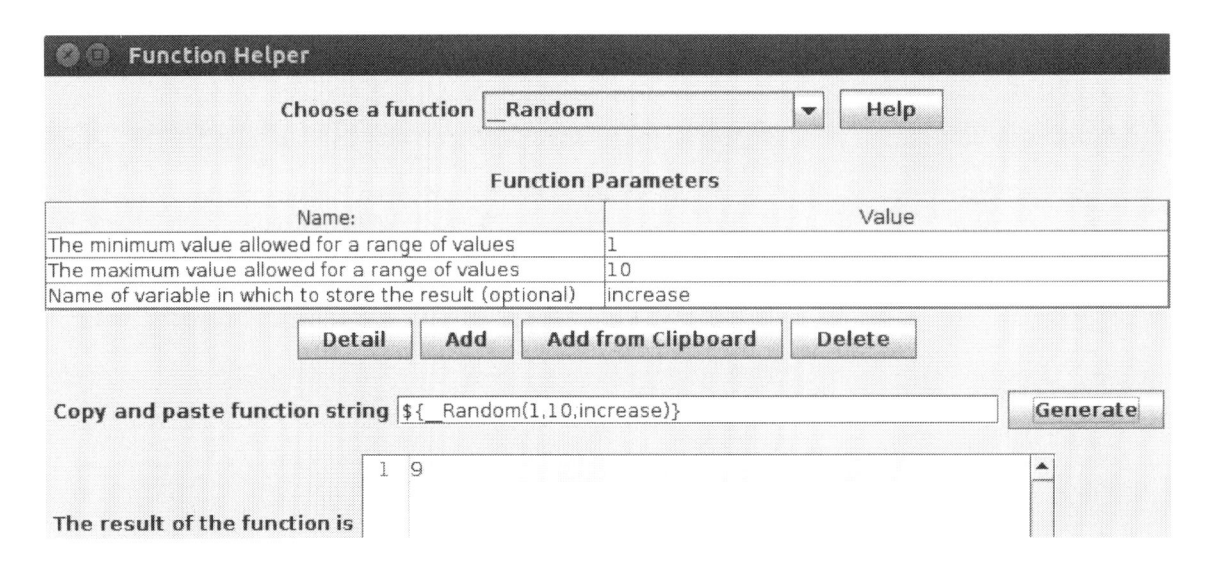

Figure 9.21: Percentage of random increase

27. All we have to do now is implement our salary increase with the percentage increase using another **JDBC Request** element.

    Our **UPDATE** query will look as follows:

    ```
    update salaries set salary = FLOOR(salary*(1 + ${__Random(1,10,increase)} / 100)) where emp_no = ${current_emp_no}
    ```

Figure 9.22: The JDBC request and salary increase code

Administrators also make **SELECT**-type SQL queries and the proportion of **SELECT** and **UPDATE** is known.

28. In order to implement this proportion, we will use the **Throughput Controller** element of JMeter.

    For example, here, we define that **UPDATE** requests represent 30% of total requests:

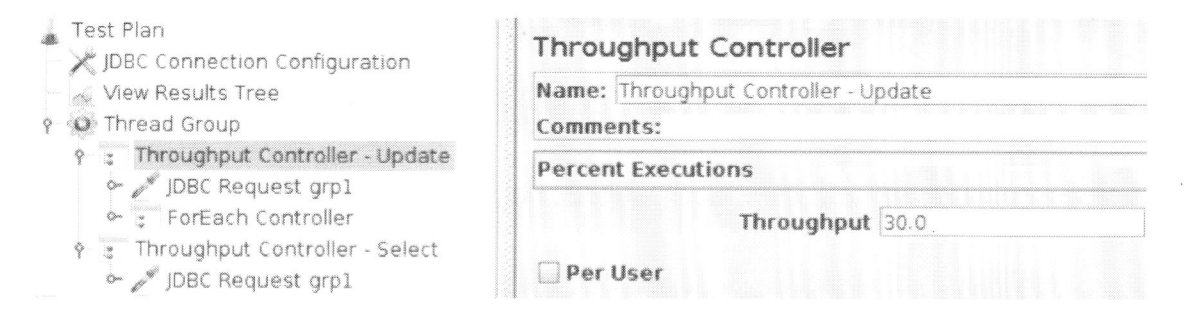

Figure 9.23: The Throughput Controller element

A good practice in software development is the *Don't Repeat Yourself* (DRY) philosophy.

Unfortunately, if we look at our last modification of the script, we can see that there are duplications in the part of the script that executes **SELECT** requests:

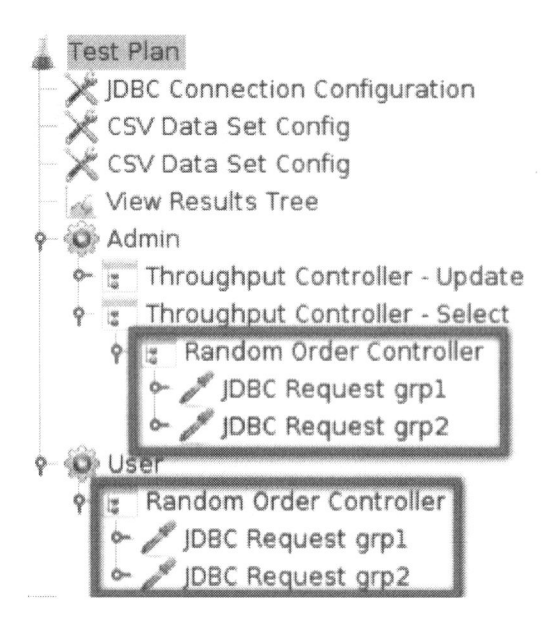

Figure 9.24: Duplications in the script

Avoiding Duplication using Include Controller

29. To avoid this duplication, we will use the **Include Controller** element, which allows us to include a script inside another script.

30. The first thing to do is to save the duplicated part of the script in a JMeter file:

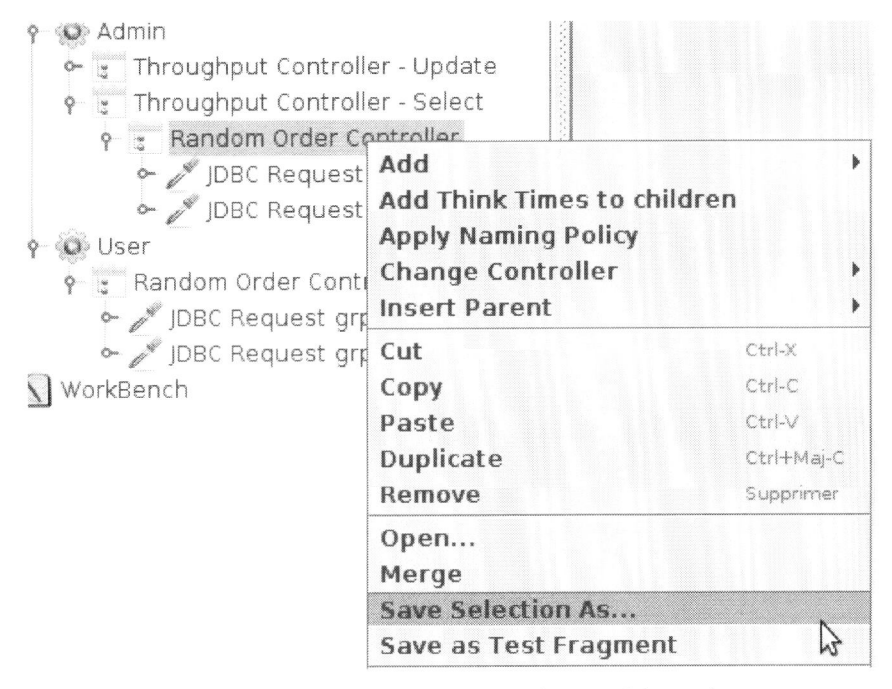

Figure 9.25: Saving the duplicated part of the script

31. Now, it is enough to replace the duplicated parts in the script with an **Include Controller** element, highlighted in the following screenshot:

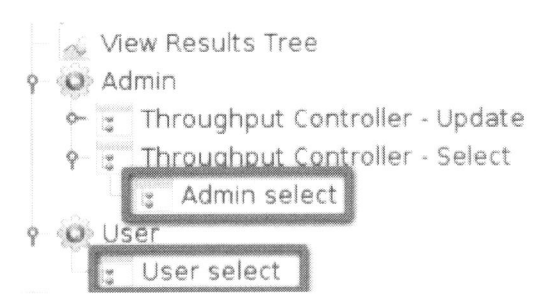

Figure 9.26: Include Controller

32. Then, we point them to our previously saved script:

Figure 9.27: Include Controller

Avoiding duplication using Module Controller

When you want to reuse test parts within the same test plan, it might be easier to use **Module Controller**.

33. To do so, add a **Test Fragment** and put in it the reusable code.

34. Use **Module Controller** and select **Module To Run** for the **Test Fragment** child you want to include:

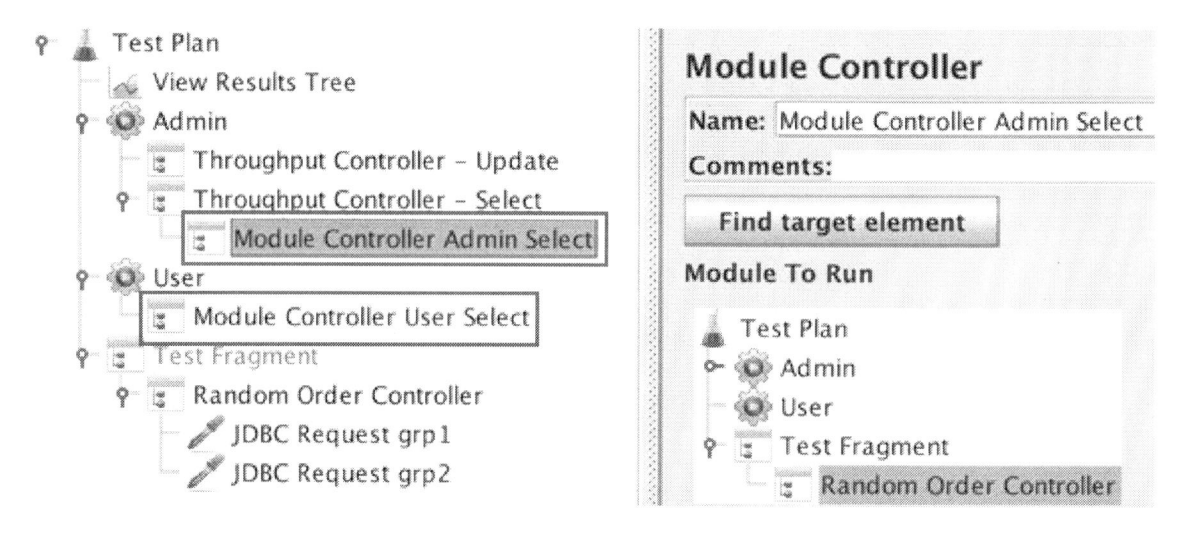

Figure 9.28: Module Controller

> **Note**
> **Module To Run** can only reference **Controller** elements, not other elements.

We could have stopped there while meeting the needs for a load test of our database server, but since the industrialization of tests is important, we will make some further changes.

This will make it easier to integrate our script into a software factory.

35. To achieve this with ease, we'll be using the **${__P(xxx,yyy)}** function, where **xxx** is the name of the property and **yyy** is its default value.

For example, we have the following configuration for the **Admin** thread group:

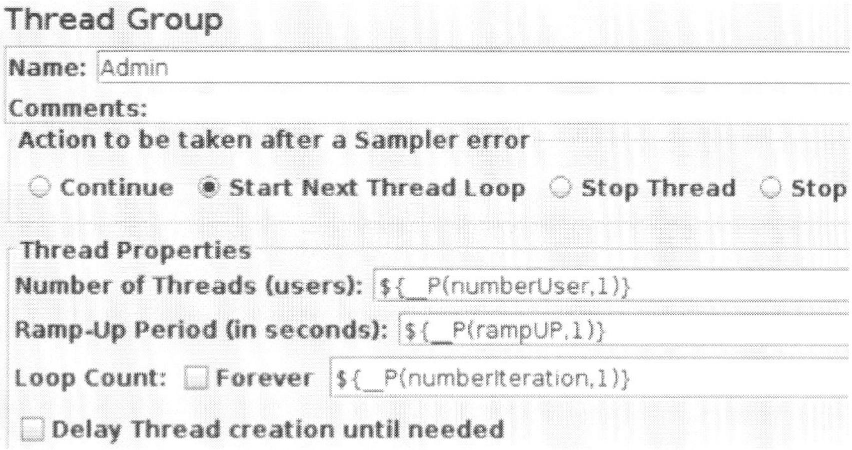

Figure 9.29: The Admin Thread Group

Here, we define that, by default, there is a unit that performs an iteration and that the ramp-up time is one second.

36. When running JMeter from the command line, we will, of course, change the values of these parameters. This is done by adding `-J{property name}={property value}`, as in the following example:

```
jmeter -n -l resultats.csv -t scenario.jmx -JnumberUser=10 -JrampUP=20 -JnumberIteration=100
```

Our test plan is now complete:

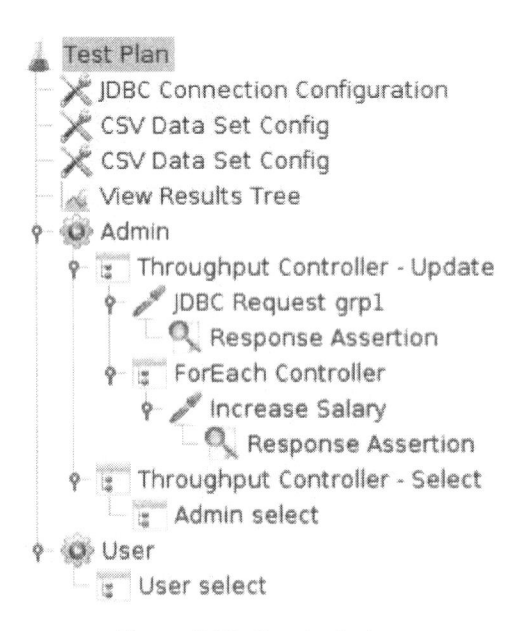

```
Test Plan
├── JDBC Connection Configuration
├── CSV Data Set Config
├── CSV Data Set Config
├── View Results Tree
├── Admin
│   ├── Throughput Controller - Update
│   │   └── JDBC Request grp1
│   │       └── Response Assertion
│   ├── ForEach Controller
│   │   └── Increase Salary
│   │       └── Response Assertion
│   └── Throughput Controller - Select
│       └── Admin select
└── User
    └── User select
```

Figure 9.30: Our test plan

Example 2: Studying the Impact of Indexes on Performance

In the SQL tuning field, indexes play a major role, but they come at a cost. To demonstrate this cost, a *Proof of Concept* (POC) will be performed using JMeter.

This time, our test will be performed on *Oracle 11g Express Edition* (don't forget to add Oracle's JDBC drivers in JMeter's *Classpath*).

Our final test plan will look like this:

```
Test Plan
├── JDBC Connection Configuration
├── setUp Thread Group
│   ├── OS Process Sampler
│   │   └── Response Assertion
│   └── JDBC Request
│       └── Response Assertion
└── Thread Group
    ├── CSV Data Set Config
    ├── 10 Select
    │   └── JDBC Request
    │       └── Response Assertion
    ├── 10 Update
    │   ├── Random Variable
    │   └── JDBC Request
    │       └── Response Assertion
    ├── Create Index
    │   └── Response Assertion
    └── Update stat
        └── Response Assertion
```

Figure 9.31: Our final test plan

1. Let's start by defining the connection to Oracle using the **JDBC Connection Configuration** element:

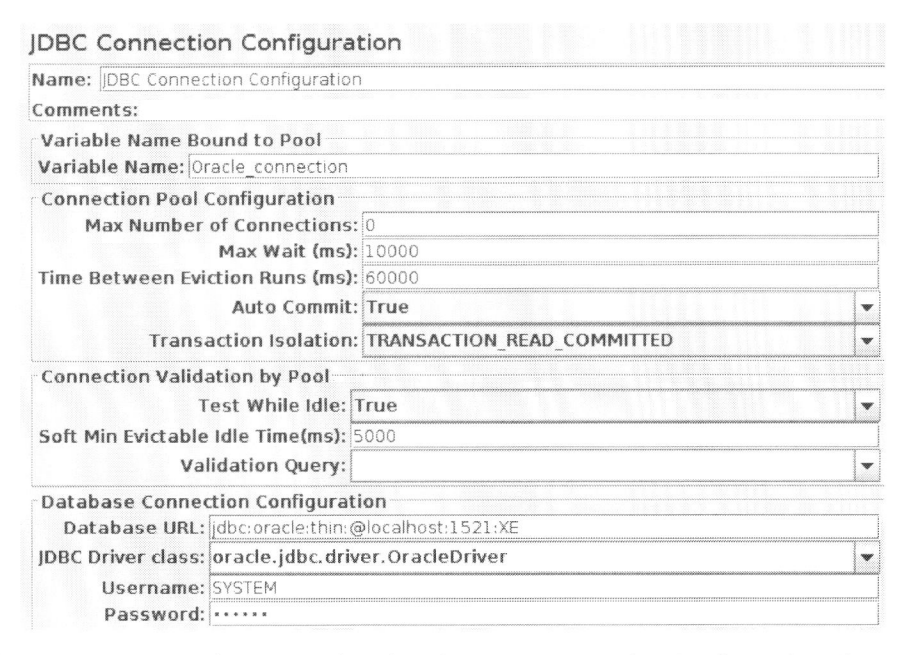

```
JDBC Connection Configuration
Name: JDBC Connection Configuration
Comments:
┌─ Variable Name Bound to Pool ──────────────────────┐
│ Variable Name: Oracle_connection                   │
└────────────────────────────────────────────────────┘
┌─ Connection Pool Configuration ────────────────────┐
│      Max Number of Connections: 0                  │
│                 Max Wait (ms): 10000               │
│  Time Between Eviction Runs (ms): 60000            │
│                    Auto Commit: True               │
│           Transaction Isolation: TRANSACTION_READ_COMMITTED │
└────────────────────────────────────────────────────┘
┌─ Connection Validation by Pool ────────────────────┐
│               Test While Idle: True                │
│  Soft Min Evictable Idle Time(ms): 5000            │
│              Validation Query:                     │
└────────────────────────────────────────────────────┘
┌─ Database Connection Configuration ────────────────┐
│         Database URL: jdbc:oracle:thin:@localhost:1521:XE │
│     JDBC Driver class: oracle.jdbc.driver.OracleDriver    │
│              Username: SYSTEM                      │
│              Password: ······                      │
└────────────────────────────────────────────────────┘
```

Figure 9.32: Connecting to Oracle using the JDBC Connection Configuration element

From now on, we can connect to our database, but unfortunately, it is empty.

2. Let's solve this problem with the **setUp Thread Group** element, which will allow us to execute commands at the beginning of the test.

   setUp Thread Group is always executed before any other **Thread Group**, even if located after them in JMeter.

   It's the equivalent of the *setUp method/@Before* JUnit annotation.

3. Let's add an **OS Process Sampler** element to it in order to fill this database (by loading a backup, or by creating data using SQL tools or commands, among other methods).

4. In order to ensure that the statistics in our database are up to date, we will ask Oracle to check this through the SQL procedure:

   ```
   dbms_stats.gather_table_stats('SYSTEM','Clients', cascade => TRUE).
   ```

   As in the previous example, we will use the **JDBC Request** element.

5. Calling an Oracle SQL procedure is done in the following way.

   The SQL query type must be *Callable Statement*.

   The **Query** field must use the following syntax:

   ```
   begin
   {call procedure SQL}
   end;
   ```

   So, we have the following code for our request:

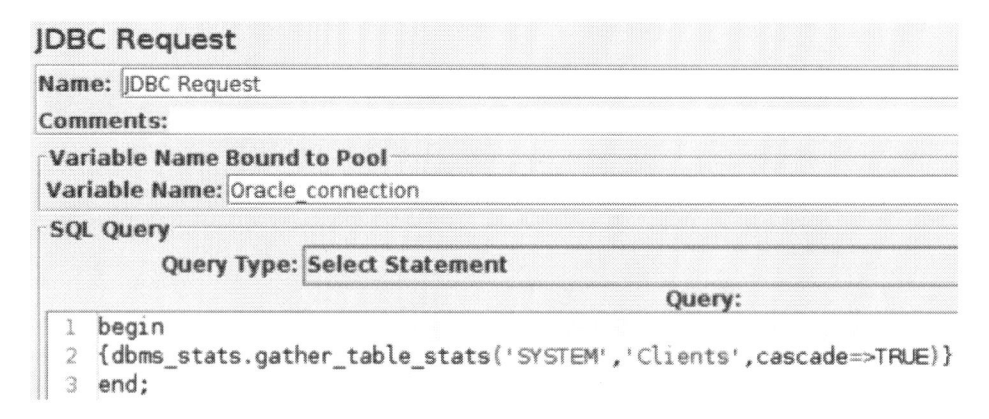

Figure 9.33: JDBC Request

6. Don't forget to check the response with a **Response Assertion** element.

   In the case of an error, Oracle returns an error code starting with `ORA-`:

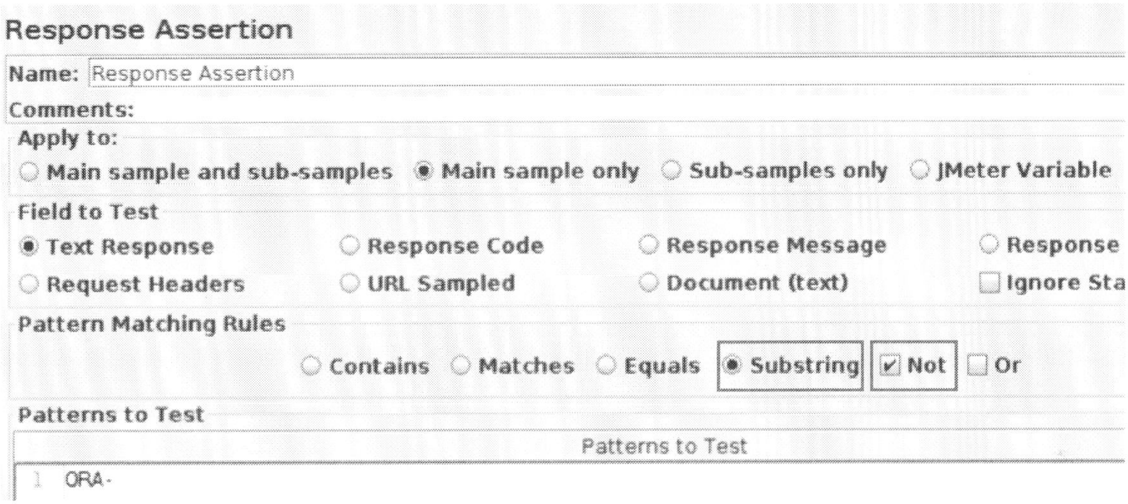

   Figure 9.34: Response Assertion

   Our database is ready.

   We want our test to run as long as there are indexes to create. Let's do this now.

7. We will use a **Thread Group** element whose number of iterations will be equal to infinity, and the number of threads will be equal to one:

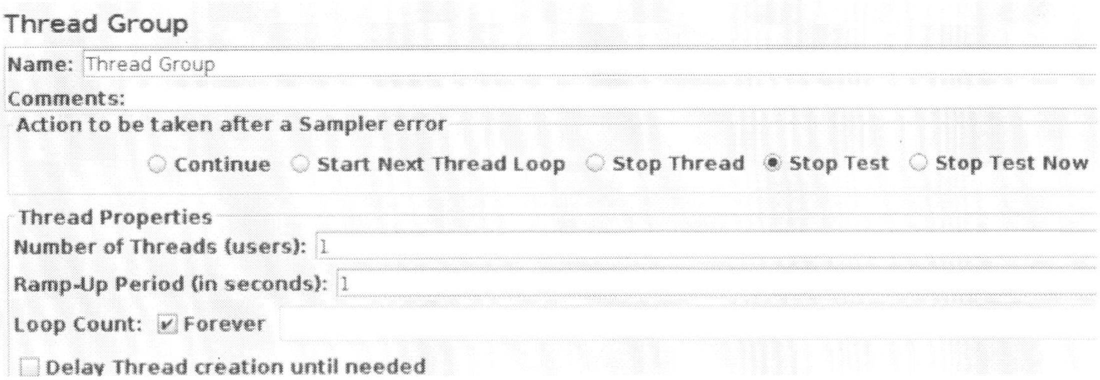

   Figure 9.35: The Thread Group element

8. Index creation requests will be in a CSV file. To stop our test at the end of the CSV file (and therefore on the creation of the last index), we will specify this in the **CSV Data Set Config** element, using the **Recycle on EOF?** option set to **False** and **Stop thread on EOF?** set to **True**:

Figure 9.36: Our CSV data source

Now let's move on to the execution of our **SELECT** requests. Using the **Loop Controller** element, we will perform 10 queries in order to have more accurate response times:

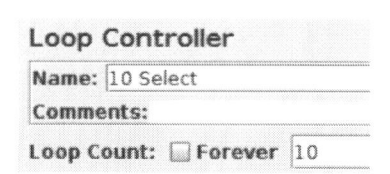

Figure 9.37: The Loop Controller element

9. Add our **SELECT** request:

Figure 9.38: Our SELECT request

10. Let's do the same for the **UPDATE** query. But this time, we will use **Prepared Update Statement** as the query type:

> **Note**
> Java applications usually use this type of statement to query the database.

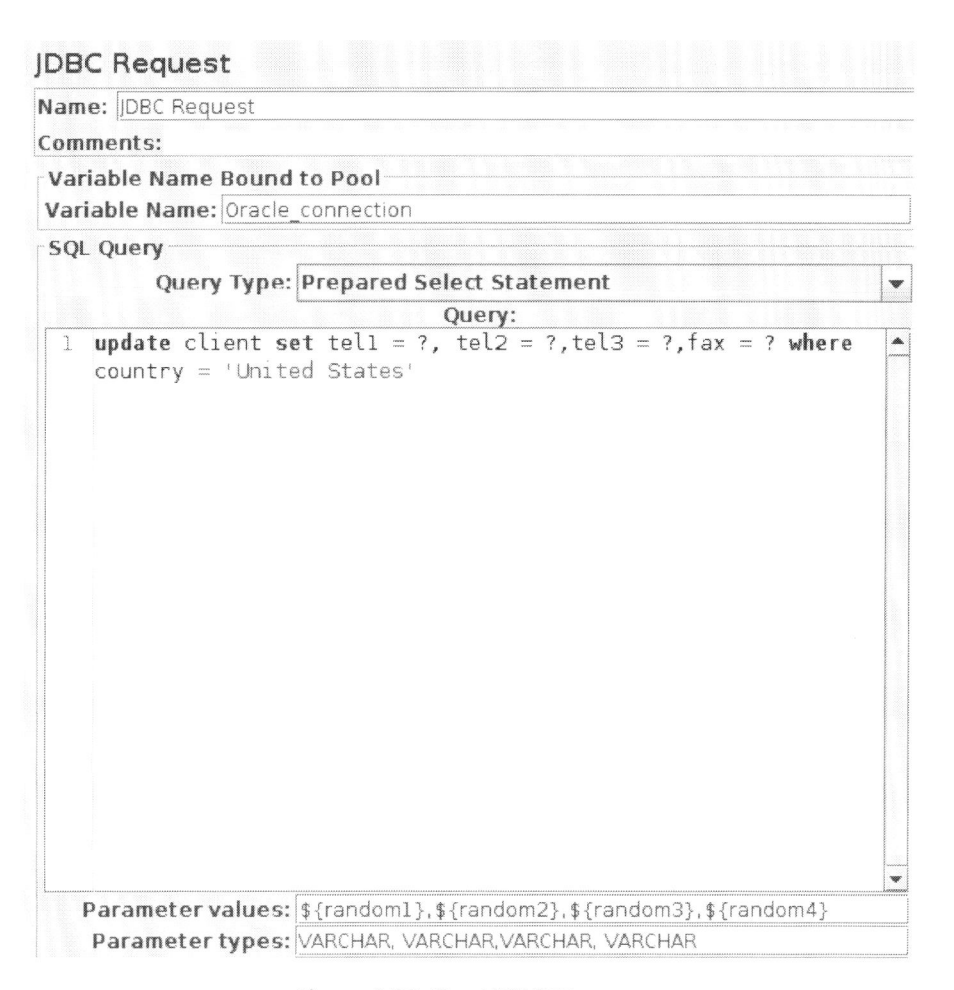

```
JDBC Request
Name: JDBC Request
Comments:
┌Variable Name Bound to Pool─────────────────────
 Variable Name: Oracle_connection
┌SQL Query───────────────────────────────────────
    Query Type: Prepared Select Statement     ▼
                    Query:
 1  update client set tel1 = ?, tel2 = ?,tel3 = ?,fax = ? where
    country = 'United States'




  Parameter values: ${random1},${random2},${random3},${random4}
  Parameter types: VARCHAR, VARCHAR,VARCHAR, VARCHAR
```

Figure 9.39: Our UPDATE query

It's time to create our first index automatically.

Again, we will use the **JDBC Request** element.

11. The SQL query for creating indexes will be directly retrieved using the `${Create_Index_SQL}` variable from the previously defined CSV file:

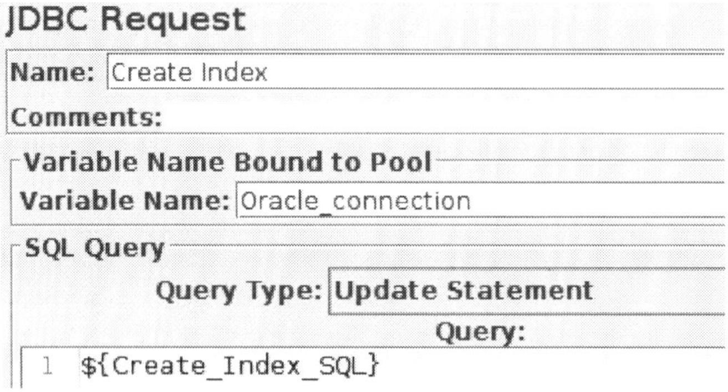

```
JDBC Request
Name: Create Index
Comments:
Variable Name Bound to Pool
Variable Name: Oracle_connection
SQL Query
       Query Type: Update Statement
                            Query:
1 ${Create_Index_SQL}
```

Figure 9.40: Index creation

12. Don't forget to update the statistics after the index is created.

    For the moment, it is impossible to analyze the result of the script in detail, because we are missing two pieces of information in the JMeter result file.

    The first piece of information is the number of indexes currently in place. In our case, it's the current iteration of Thread Group +1.

    Since JMeter 4.0, JMeter exposes this information in a variable named __jm__<Name of Thread Group>__idx, so in our case, it would be __jm__Thread Group__idx.

    The second piece of information is the SQL query used to create the index. It is already in the `${Create_Index_SQL}` variable.

13. So, to add these two pieces of information to the results file, we'll use the **sample_variables** property of the `user.properties` file of JMeter as follows:

    ```
    # Optional list of JMeter variable names whose values are to be saved in the result data files.
    # Use commas to separate the names. For example:    sample_variables=__jm__Thread Group__idx,Create_Index_SQL
    ```

    This concludes our test script.

Putting Theory into Practice with JMeter | 275

Example 3: ETL

In this last example, we will use JMeter as an *Extract-Transform-Load* (ETL) to allow us to transfer data from one database to another while applying transformations.

We will anonymize the *name* and *telephone_mobile* column data of a Clients table.

1. First, let's define our connections to both databases using the **JDBC Connection Configuration** element:

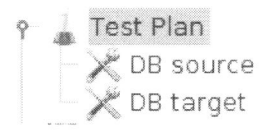

   Figure 9.41: Connections to both databases

2. In order to generate a new phone number, use the **Random Variable** element:

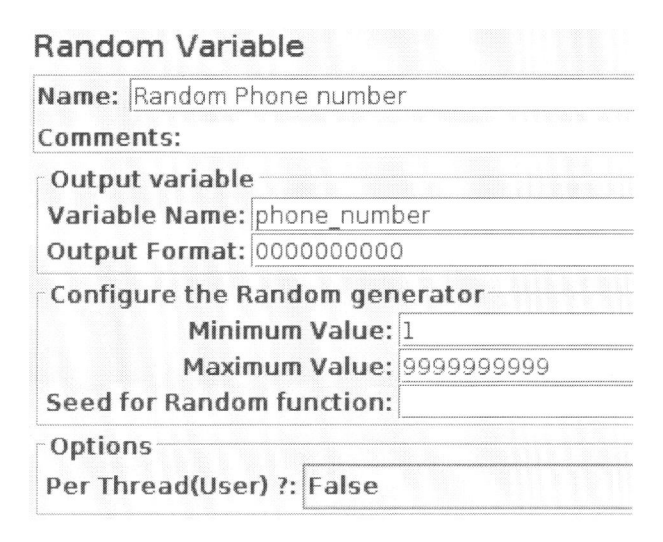

   Figure 9.42: Our Random Variable element

3. To create a new name, we use the following function:

   ${__RandomString(20,ABCDEFGHIJIJKLMNOPQRSTUVWXTZabcdefghiklmnopqrstuvwxyz,new_name)}

   A new 20-character name will then be available as **${new_name}**.

4. Let's start by retrieving the values from the source database (in our case, we will only retrieve some of the columns from the table) using a **JDBC Request** element:

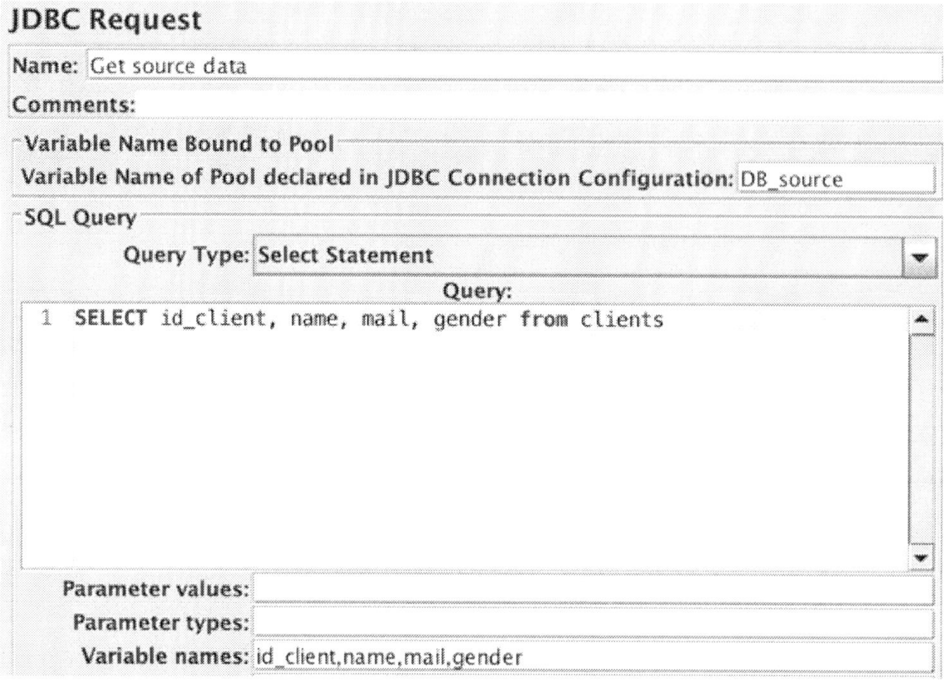

JDBC Request

Name: Get source data
Comments:

Variable Name Bound to Pool
Variable Name of Pool declared in JDBC Connection Configuration: DB_source

SQL Query
Query Type: Select Statement
Query:
```
1  SELECT id_client, name, mail, gender from clients
```

Parameter values:
Parameter types:
Variable names: id_client,name,mail,gender

Figure 9.43: Retrieving values from the source database

Several lines will be retrieved:

```
id_client_1=1
id_client_2=2
id_client_3=3
id_client_4=4

...

mail_1=john@hotmail.com
mail_2=jim@yahoo.com
mail_3=kumar@gmail.com

...
```

5. Now you must browse through each recovered line with the **ForEach Controller** element:

ForEach Controller

Name: ForEach Controller
Comments:
Input variable prefix id_client
Start index for loop (exclusive)
End index for loop (inclusive)
Output variable name id
☑ Add "_" before number ?

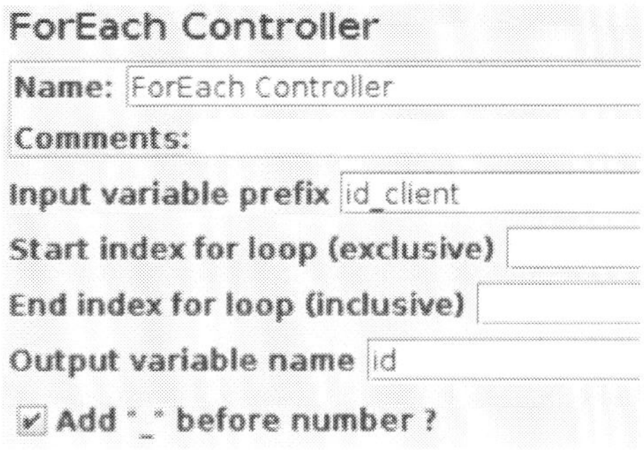

Figure 9.44: Our ForEach Controller element

As we can see, we can only loop on one variable (here, we have chosen `id_client`), so we lose the link with the other values of the same line (*name*, *mail*, and *gender*).

For example, *id_client_1* is associated with *name_1*, *mail_1* and *gender_1*.

Fortunately, it is easy to recreate the link between variables in the same line with the **Counter** element and the `${__V(xxx_${yyyyy})}` function.

The counter will allow us to generate an integer incremented by 1 at each iteration of the loop (so we will have 1, then 2, then 3, and so on):

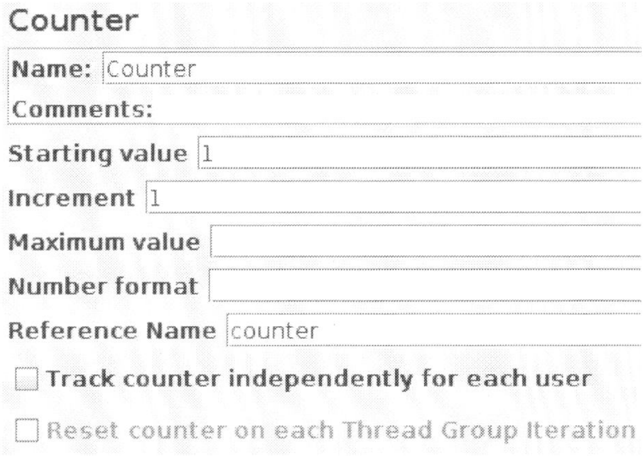

Counter

Name: Counter
Comments:
Starting value 1
Increment 1
Maximum value
Number format
Reference Name counter
☐ Track counter independently for each user
☐ Reset counter on each Thread Group Iteration

Figure 9.45: Our Counter element

Then, the **${__V(xxx_${yyy})}** function will concatenate the *xxx_* string with the value of the *yyyy* variable.

For example, **${__V(name_${counter})}** will return *name_1* if the counter is equal to one.

This function will be used in our SQL query to insert in the target database:

```
JDBC Request
Name: Write target data
Comments:
Variable Name Bound to Pool
Variable Name: DB_target
SQL Query
    Query Type: Update Statement
                                                  Query:
1 Insert into Clients(id_client,name,mail,gender)
2 values
3 {
4 ${id},'${__V(name_${counter})}','${__V(mail_${counter})}','${__V(gender_${counter})}'
5 }
```

Figure 9.46: Our SQL insertion query

Finally, our **Test Plan** will look like this:

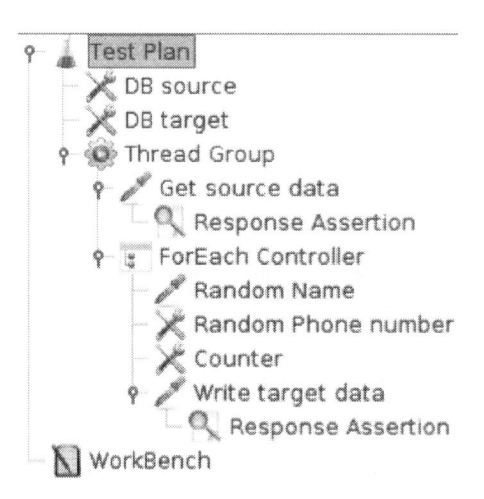

```
Test Plan
    DB source
    DB target
    Thread Group
        Get source data
            Response Assertion
        ForEach Controller
            Random Name
            Random Phone number
            Counter
            Write target data
                Response Assertion
    WorkBench
```

Figure 9.47: Our Test Plan

Conclusion

As we have seen, performing a load test on a database using JMeter is possible without any great difficulty. JMeter's capabilities also make it possible to design a realistic load test with which you can do just about anything that comes to mind, but don't forget to test the API/application that accesses the database. If you do forget, your tests may not be realistic.

10
Load Testing Message-Oriented Middleware (MOM) via JMS

A Bit of Theory

As architectures become more and more distributed (via microservices, the cloud, and so on), it is common to use a **Message-Oriented Middleware (MOM)** service to allow the exchange of messages/events.

Such architectures have numerous advantages. We'll look at some of them in this lesson.

Asynchronous Messages

The first advantage of an MOM service is the ability to use asynchronous messages.

In a synchronous system, the sender (that is, the producer) of the message must wait for the response before continuing:

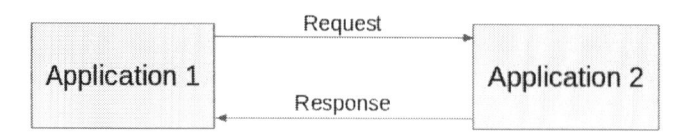

Figure 10.1: Synchronous architecture

In an asynchronous system, however, the producer of the message can continue their processing after sending the message without waiting for a response from the receiver:

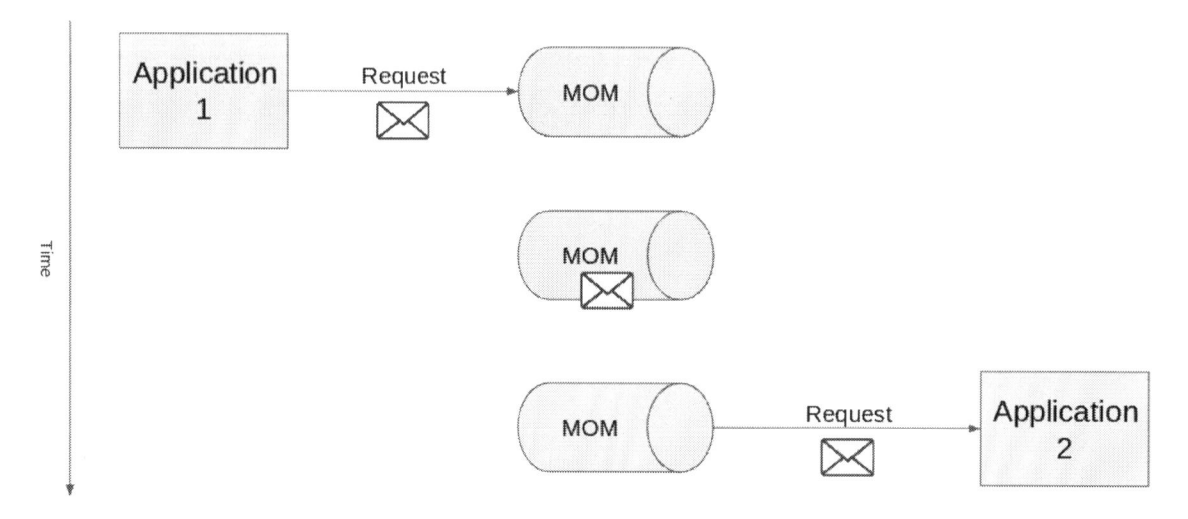

Figure 10.2: Asynchronous architecture

In asynchronous mode, the MOM will act as an intermediary and store the message until it is delivered to **Application 2**.

Decoupling

This proxy role allows for weak coupling between the different entities of the application.

Technology Decoupling

For example, we can have a producer in Java and a consumer in C++:

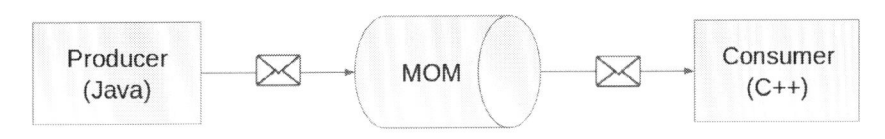

Figure 10.3: Technology decoupling

Geographical Decoupling (Location transparency)

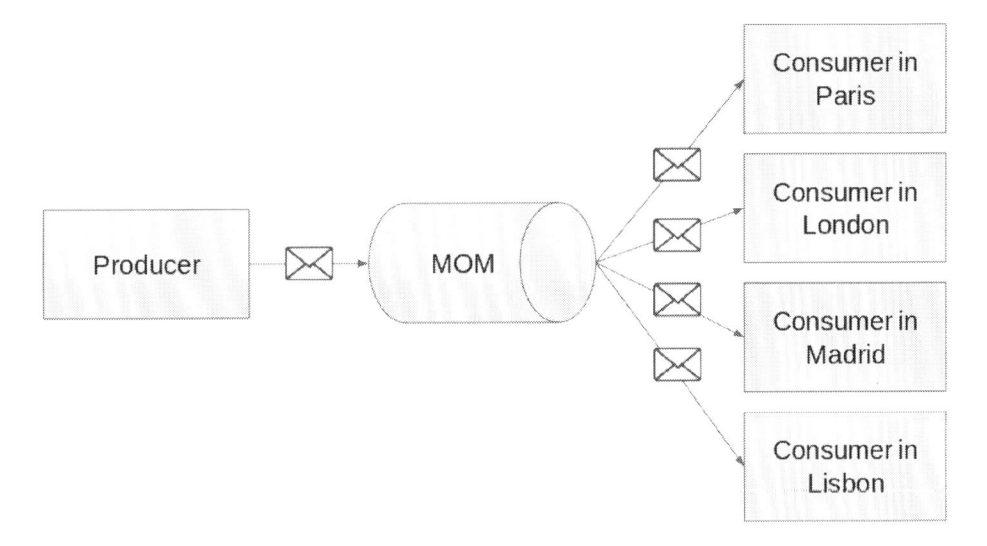

Figure 10.4: The producer doesn't know about the consumers' locations

Time Decoupling

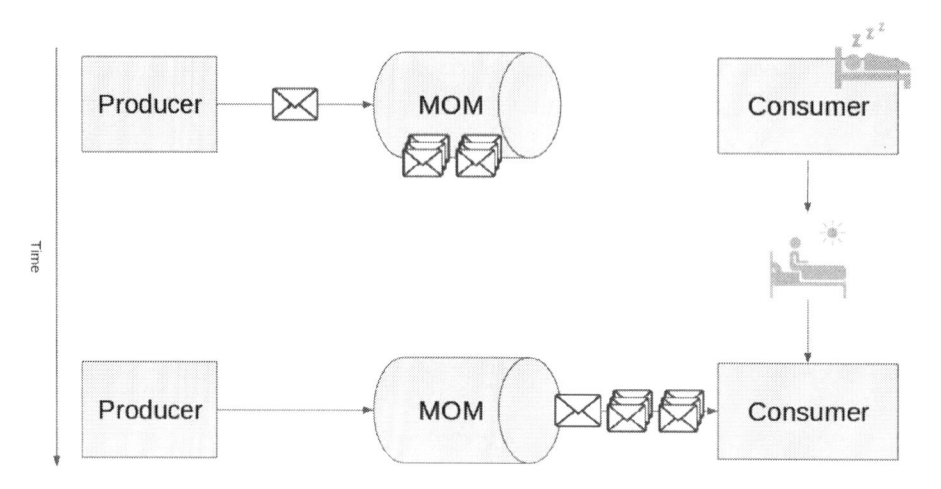

Figure 10.5: The producer can send data while the consumer is unavailable

Back Pressure

The **Producer Flow Control** feature allows us to implement the *back pressure* pattern.

This pattern slows down the producer when the consumers fail to follow the rate of message delivery in the MOM.

To do this, the MOM will use a locking mechanism to block the producer.

When a message is sent to the MOM by the producer, it waits (this is configurable) for an *Acknowledgement of Receipt* (ACK) from the MOM before proceeding to the next step (by removing the lock):

Figure 10.6: Producer Flow Control lock installation

Usually, this lock disappears quickly.

When a threshold on the MOM (such as the number of messages sent, or a certain amount of memory usage) is reached, the MOM keeps the lock to block the producer:

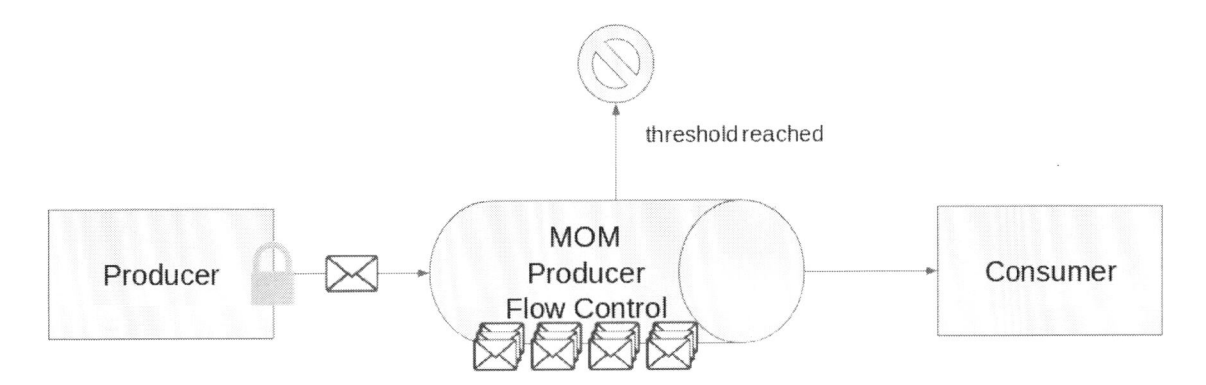

Figure 10.7: Producer Flow Control's triggering mechanism

This will give consumers time to consume messages in the MOM, which can then send the ACK to the producer to remove the lock.

Communication Models

There are three main models of communication:

- Point-to-point communication (*direct exchange*)

    Here, the producer sends the dedicated message in a queue. The consumer (who is unique) of this message consumes it in the First In, First Out (FIFO) order:

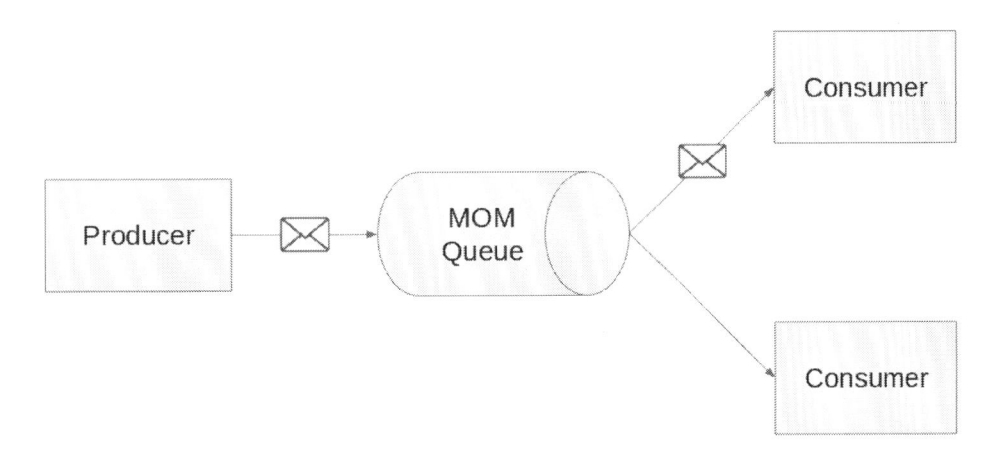

Figure 10.8: Point-to-point communication

- Publication/subscription communication (*Publish/subscribe* or *Topic exchange*)

    As the name suggests, the producer sends the messages about a subject in a topic, which are then retrieved by the subscribers to this subject (the message disappears from the topic once all consumers have retrieved it). Several consumers can subscribe to the same topic:

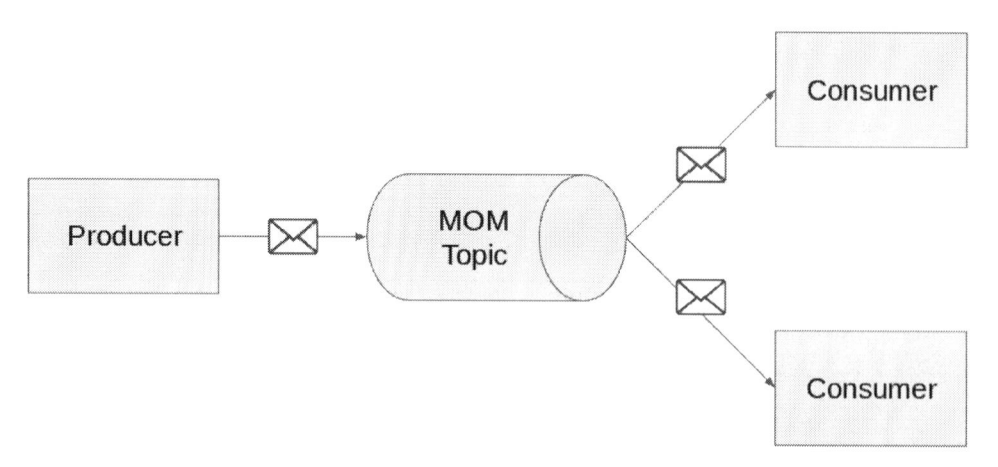

    Figure 10.9: Publish/subscribe communication

- *Broadcast* or *Fanout Exchange*

    In this mode, several MOMs follow each other, with the first being in charge of distributing the message to all others:

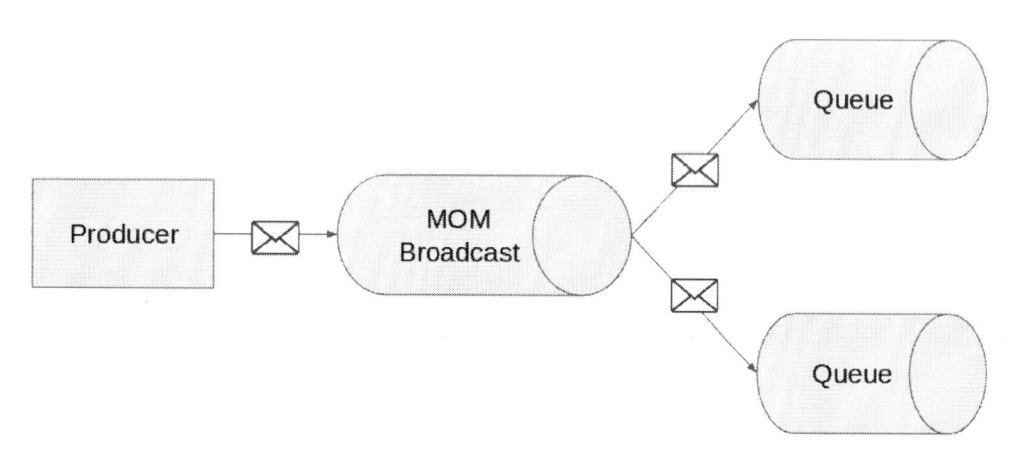

    Figure 10.10: Broadcast communication

What is a Message Composed of?

In order to make the best use of JMeter's extractors and assertions, let's look at the structure of a message.

A message is divided into three parts:

- The **Header** contains metadata about the message. The keys of the headers are part of the Java Message Service (JMS) standard. The main fields in the header are **JMSMessageID** (a unique identifier of the message), **JMSDestination** (the identifier of the queue/topic of the message), and **JMSCorrelationID** (which links the current message to other messages).
- **Properties** also contain metadata about the message, but properties can be specific to either the MOM provider or the application.
- The **Body** (text, binary, and so on) is contained in the last part:

JMS Message

Headers
JMSMessageId
JMSDestination
JMSCorrelationID
Etc.
Properties
Custom
Body

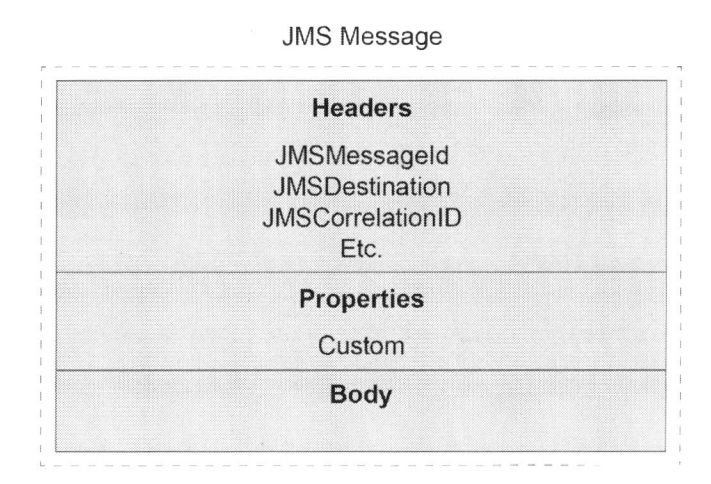

Figure 10.11: Composition of a message

Now that you understand how MOMs work, let's study how to load test them using JMeter.

Setup with JMeter

JMeter is a Java program, and as such, it accesses MOM through the JMS API.

Installing the MOM libraries

The first thing to do is to install the JMS client implementation of the MOM provider (usually a `.jar` file) in the `JMETER_HOME/lib` directory.

For example, for Apache ActiveMQ, take the *activemq-all-X.X.X.jar* file (where X.X.X depends on the version that you're using).

The JMS Point-to-Point Element

To simulate point-to-point communication, JMeter offers the **JMS Point-to-Point** element:

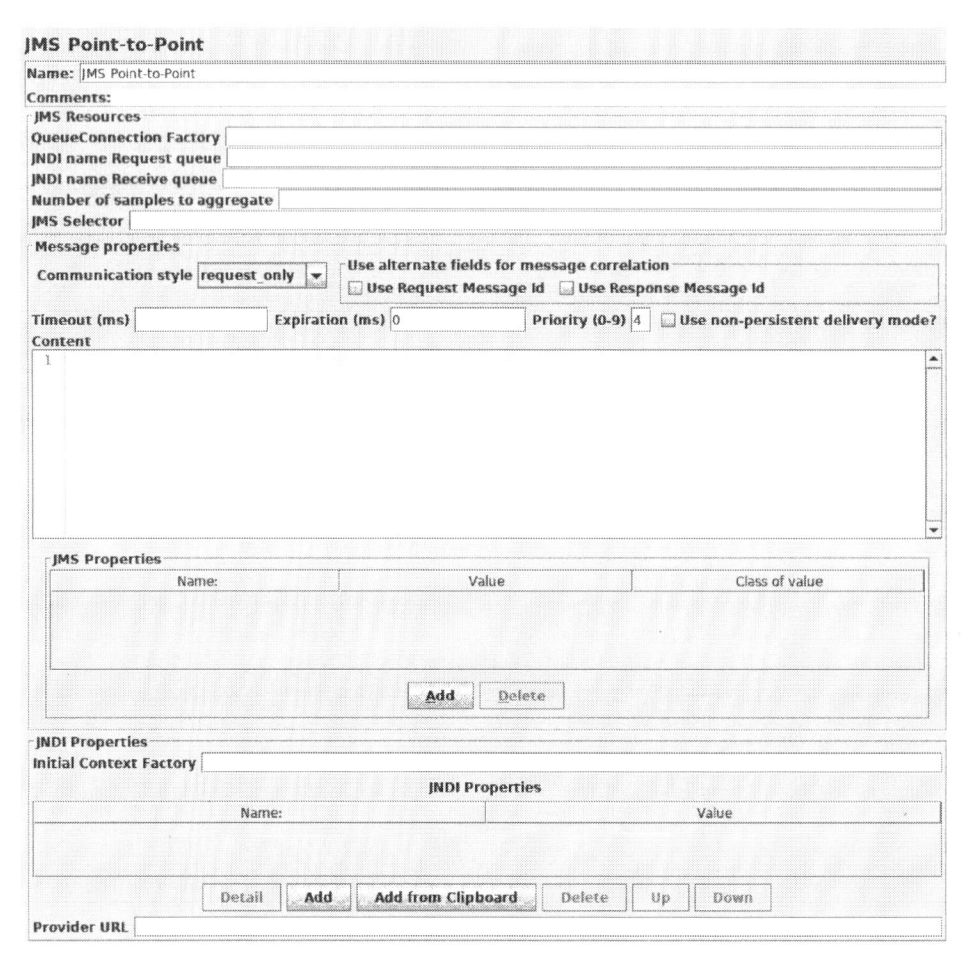

Figure 10.12: A JMS Point-to-Point request

Let's look in more detail at some of the parameters.

JMS Resources and JNDI Properties

Let's start with the **JMS Resources** and **JNDI Properties** settings.

Java Naming and Directory Interface (JNDI) is a Java programming interface (API) for Java object naming inside the Java virtual machine; so, in short, it is a directory.

In the case of JMS, JNDI is used to retrieve the instances of the destination objects (*Topic* or *Queue*) and **Connection Factory** (which allows you to create a connection to the JMS provider).

In order to fill the fields of these two features, it will be necessary to look at the configuration of the MOM and/or to ask the architect or the developers.

If we want to use automatically created temporary queues, we will have to follow a naming convention for the values of **JMS Properties** and **JNDI Properties**.

For example, if the value of the **JNDI name Request queue** field is **Q.SEND**, then a field named **queue.Q.SEND** will be required in **JNDI Properties**:

Figure 10.13: The JNDI name of the Request queue

For (http://activemq.apache.org/):

- **QueueConnection Factory** will be **ConnectionFactory**.
- **Initial Context Factory** (the class used to create a connection) will be **org.apache.activemq.jndi.ActiveMQInitialContextFactory**.
- **Provider URL** (the address and access port for ActiveMQ) will be **tcp://MyServer:61616** under the default configuration.

For (https://activemq.apache.org/artemis/index.html):

- **QueueConnection Factory** will be **ConnectionFactory**.
- **Initial Context Factory** (the class used to create a connection) will be **org.apache.activemq.artemis.jndi.ActiveMQInitialContextFactory**.
- **Provider URL** (the address and access port for Artemis ActiveMQ) will be **tcp://MyServer:61616** under the default configuration.

Communication Style

Another important field is **Communication style** in the **Message properties** section. It can have several values, but let's look at the most useful ones. **request_only**, as its name indicates, corresponds to the sending of a request:

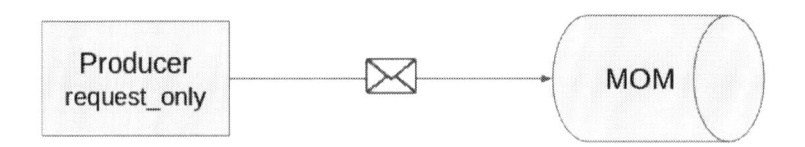

Figure 10.14: Communication type: request_only

Be aware that in this configuration, messages present in the *Queue* are not consumed, so remember to purge and/or consume them.

The second possible value is **request_reply**.

Here we send (*request*) and wait for the answer (*reply*) synchronously.

If the values of the **JNDI Name Request Queue** and **JNDI Name Receive Queue** fields are the same, JMeter will take care of the two steps (sending and retrieving the response):

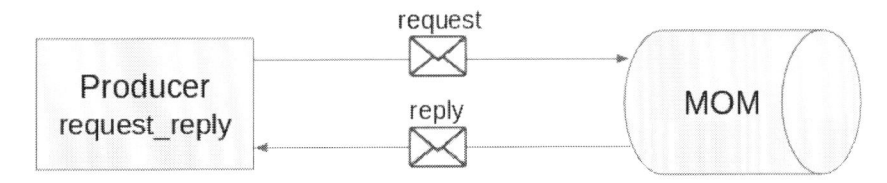

Figure 10.15: Communication type: request_reply

However, if the two queues have different values, the message sent must be consumed to receive the ACK.

If the message is not consumed, we will have an error after the delay defined in *Timeout (ms)*:

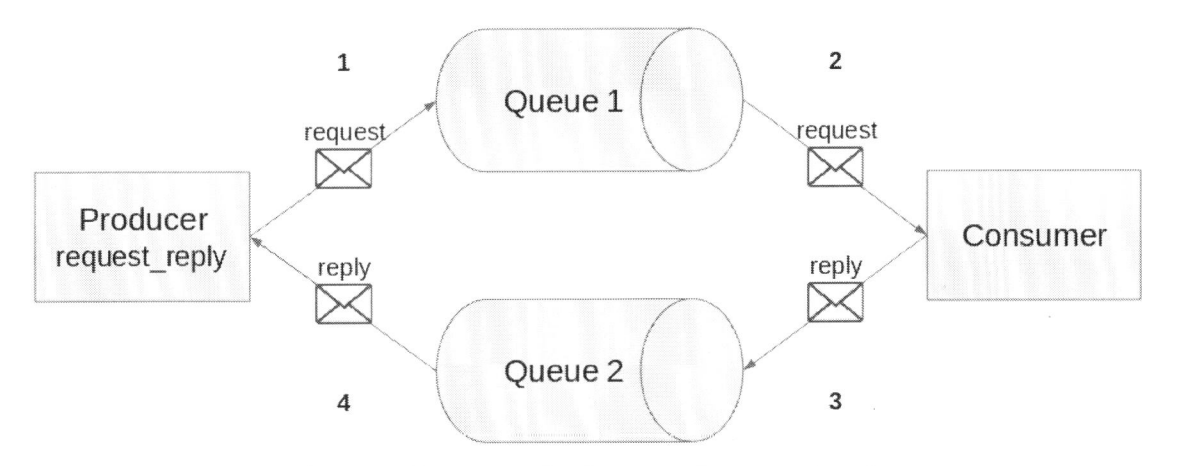

Figure 10.16: Communication steps for request_reply

1. JMeter is the producer of the message in **Queue 1**.
2. The consumer listening on **Queue 1** receives it.
3. The consumer sends the answer to **Queue 2**.
4. JMeter, which is listening for the answer in **Queue 2**, receives it.

Priority

We can manage the priority of a message using the **Priority** parameter:

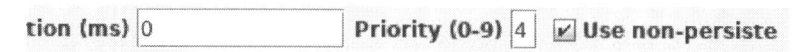

Figure 10.17: Choosing the priority of a message

Without a priority level set, the behavior will be as follows:

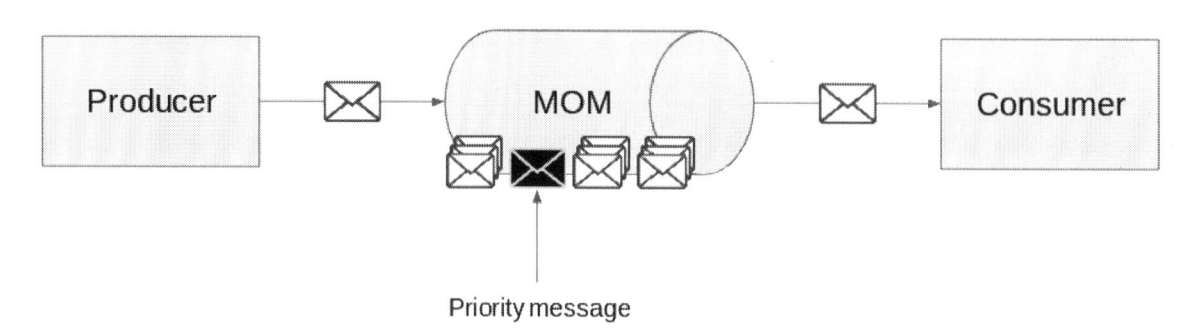

Figure 10.18: All messages are sent with the same priority

If we give a higher priority to our message, it will be processed before others:

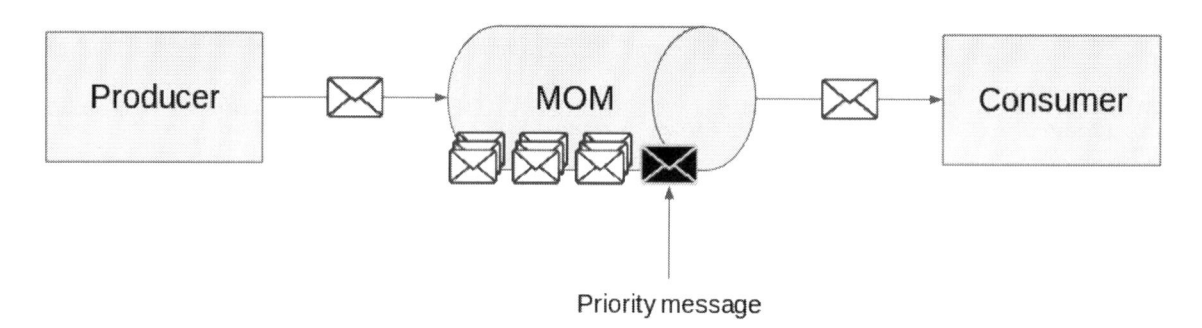

Figure 10.19: All messages are sent with different priorities

Using Non-Persistent Delivery Mode

The **Use non-persistent delivery mode** parameter allows us to avoid persisting the message on disk or on the database. Persisting a message ensures that the MOM will not lose the message if the MOM crashes.

The persistence mechanism is as follows. The MOM is configured to persist messages on disk:

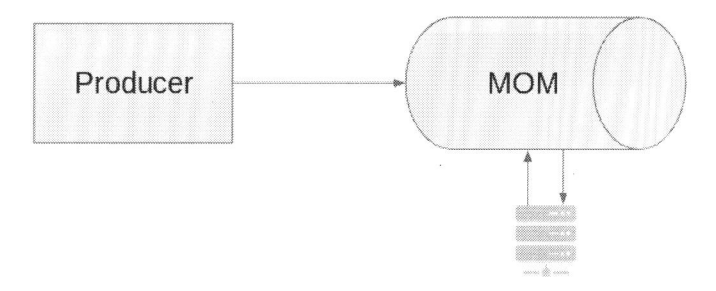

Figure 10.20: Persistence of messages: how things start

When sending a message, a lock is put on the producer side:

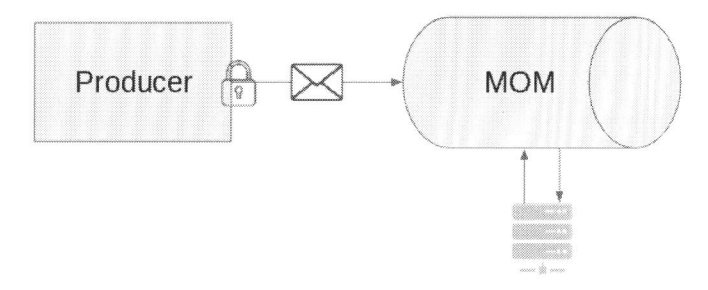

Figure 10.21: Persistence of messages: setting the lock when sending

The MOM receives the message and prepares to persist it:

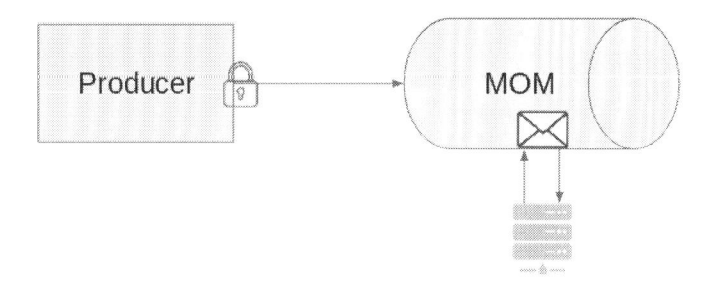

Figure 10.22: Persistence of messages: receipt of the message

The MOM writes the file to disk in a safe way (it waits for an acknowledgment):

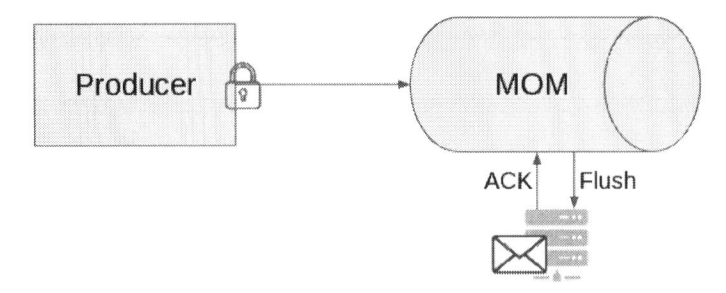

Figure 10.23: Persistence of messages: writing the message to disk

The MOM sends an acknowledgment to the producer:

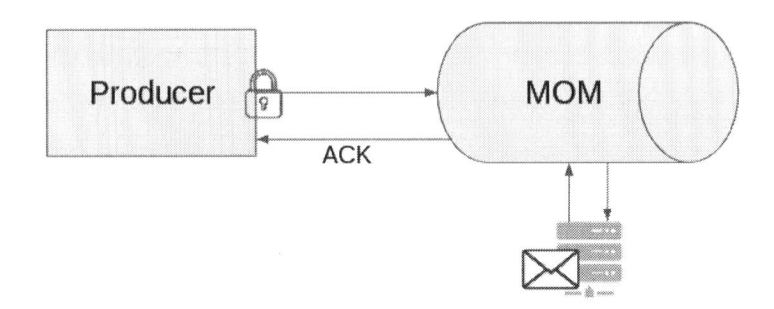

Figure 10.24: Persistence of messages: acknowledgment of receipt

The lock on the producer is removed:

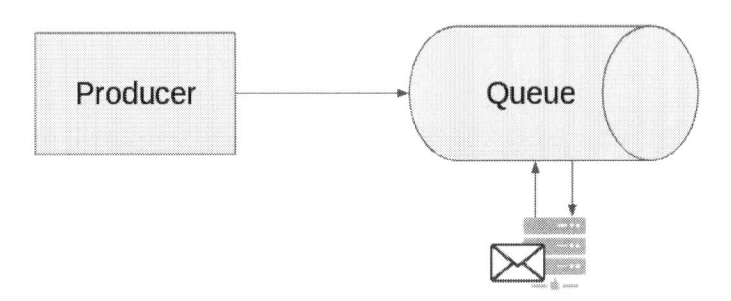

Figure 10.25: Persistence of messages: final state

JMS Selector

Another parameter is **JMS Selector**, which allows a consumer to read only a certain type of message.

The consumer will only process messages that match the selector expression and ignore others:

```
JNDI name Receive queue  Q.RECEIVE
Number of samples to aggregate
JMS Selector  SUM > 500
Message properties
  Communication style  request_reply
                                        Use alternate fields for message correlation
                                          ✔ Use Request Message Id   ✔ Use Response Message Id
  Timeout (ms) 1000    Expiration (ms) 0    Priority (0-9) 4   ✔ Use non-persist
  Content
    1  GO

JMS Properties
  Name:              Value                       Class of
  SUM                ${ Random(100,5000,)}       java.lang.Integer
```

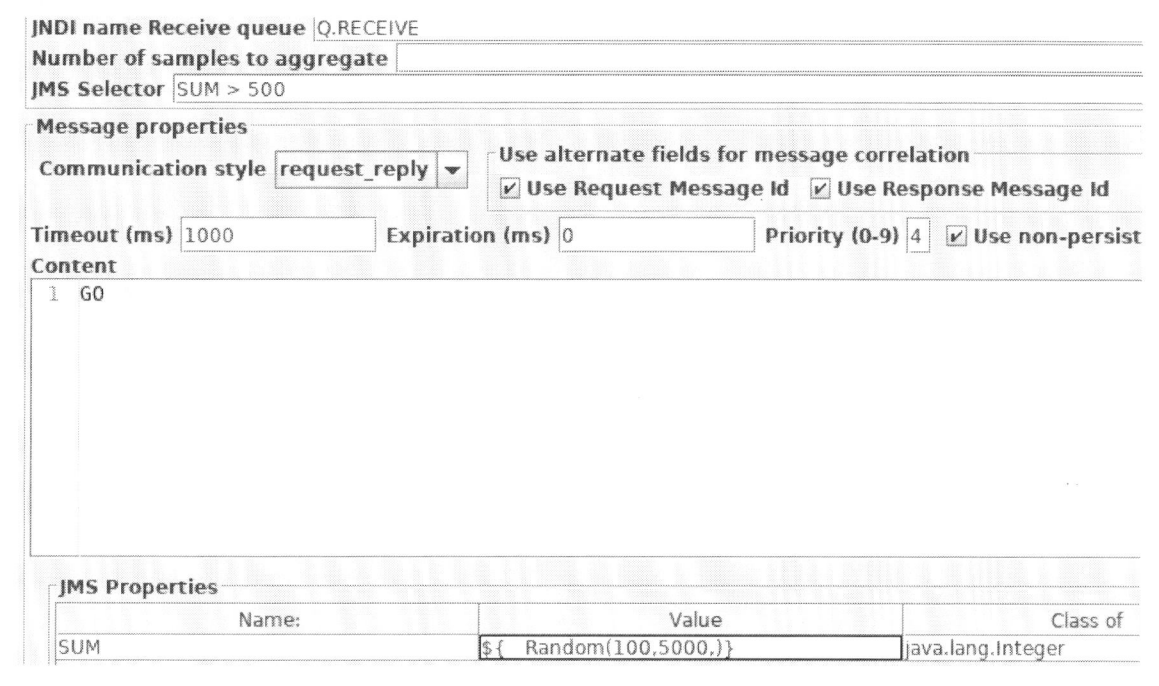

Figure 10.26: The JMS Selector parameter

This will give us the following architecture with a **SUM** property:

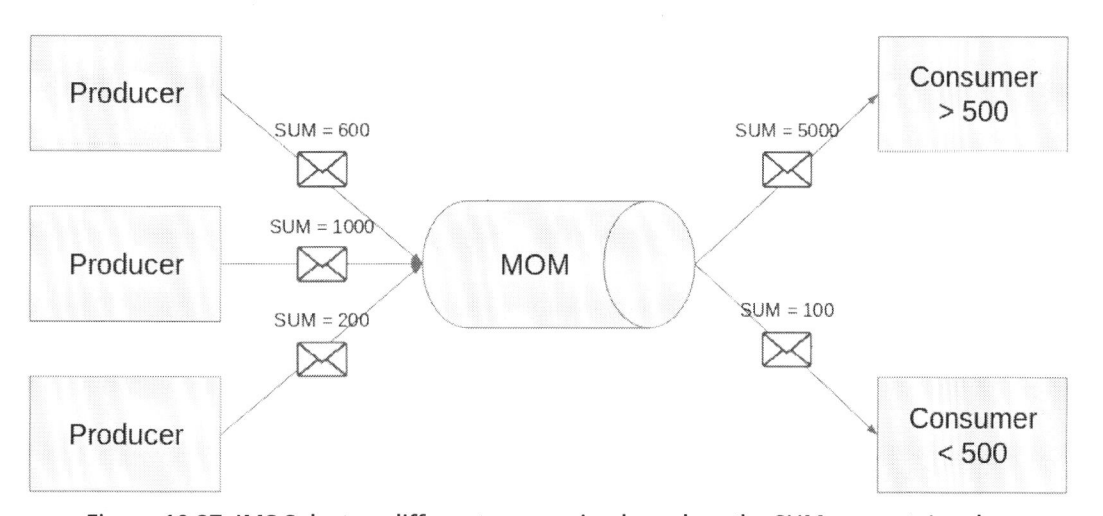

Figure 10.27: JMS Selector: different processing based on the SUM property's value

Example with Apache ActiveMQ

With a default installation of Apache ActiveMQ, we end up with the following:

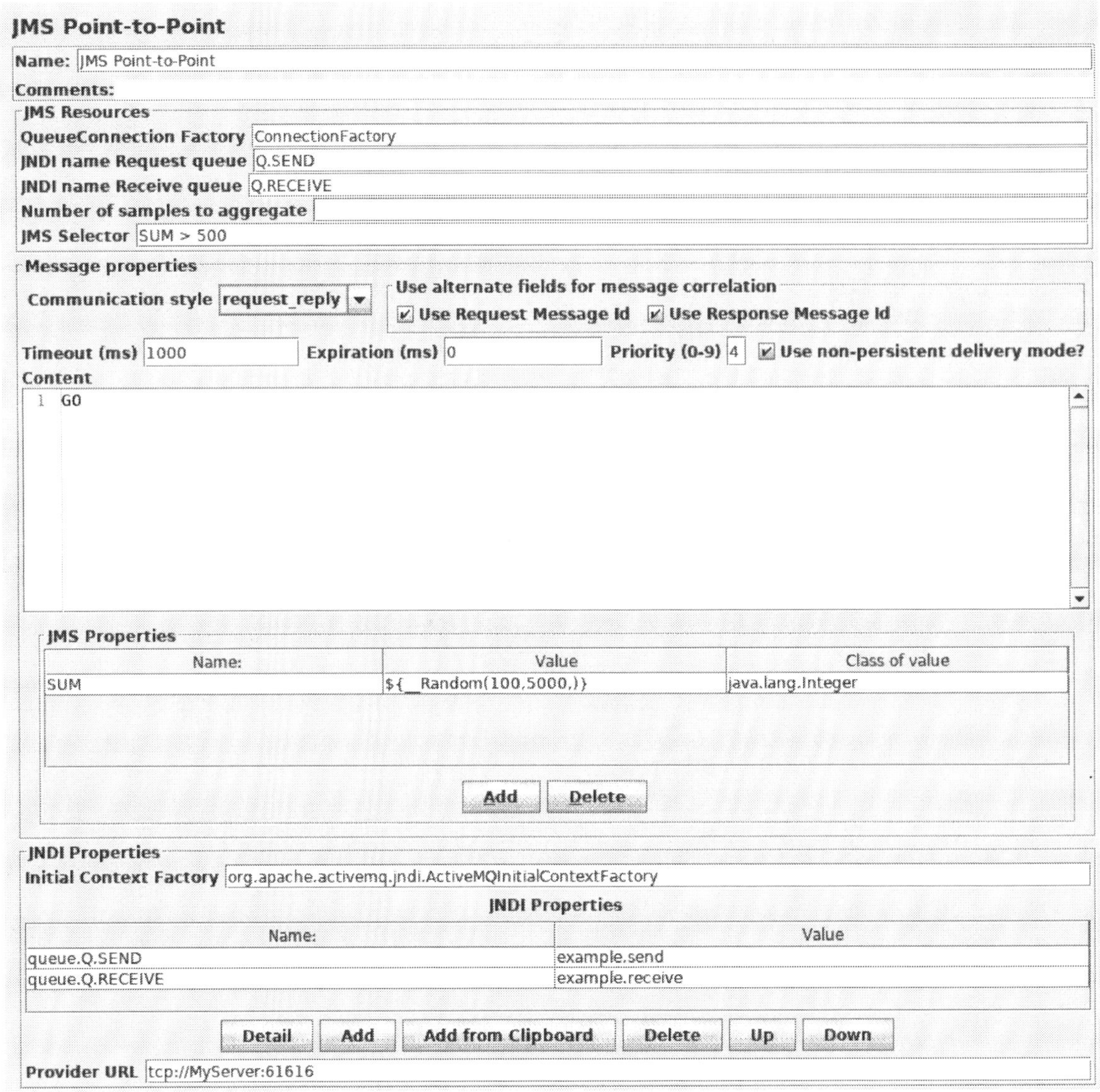

Figure 10.28: Point-to-Point JMS Request for ActiveMQ

Publish/Subscribe

Finally, *publish/subscribe* communication is implemented with **JMS Publisher** and **JMS Subscriber**.

JMS Publisher

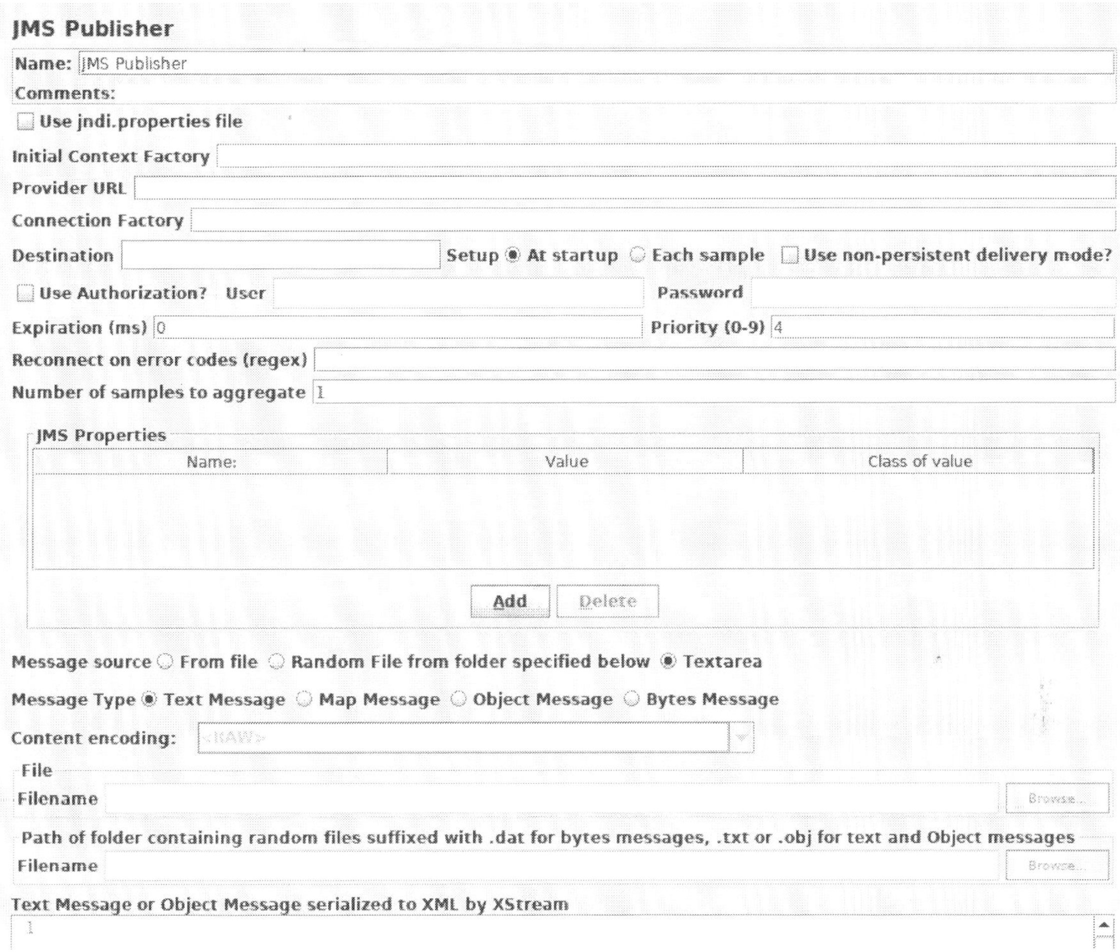

Figure 10.29: A JMS Publication Request

As we can see, most parameters are the same as before.

JMS Subscriber

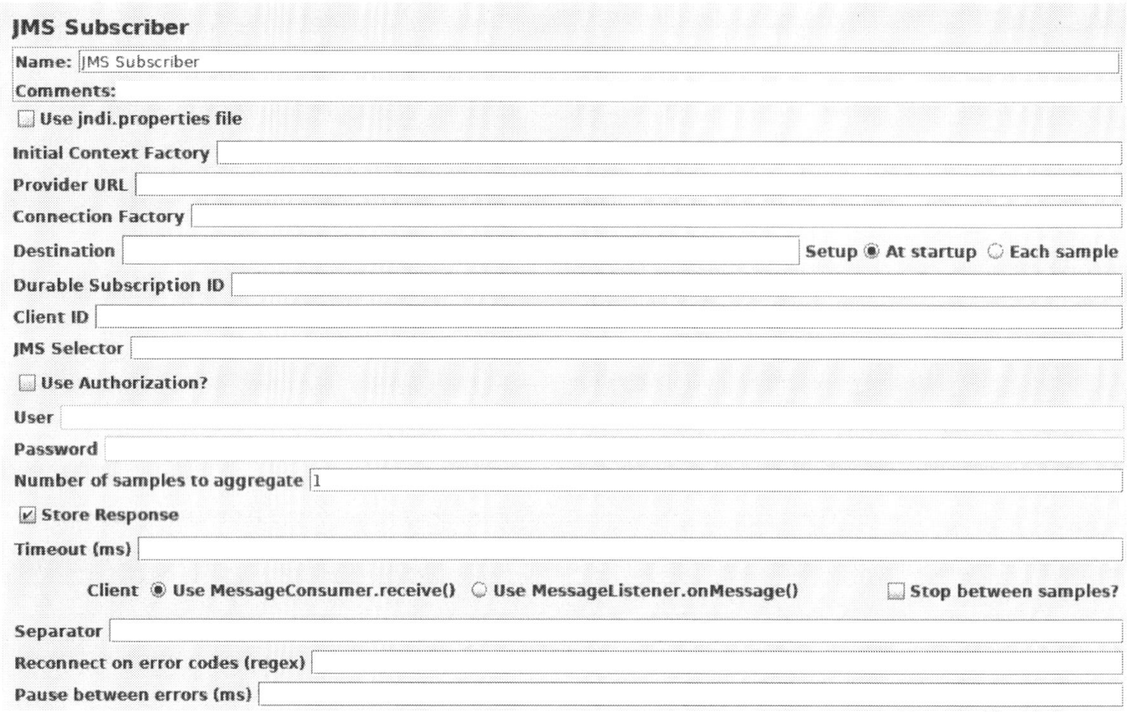

Figure 10.30: A JMS Subscription request

Two new parameters appear:

- **Durable Subscription ID**
- **Client ID**

These parameters allow the use of a *Durable Subscriber*.

A *Durable Subscriber* is a subscriber that has established a durable subscription. In such a configuration, messages published while the subscriber is not connected will be redistributed whenever it reconnects.

Let's see what a Durable Subscriber is.

Without a *Durable Subscriber*, both consumers are active and read message 1:

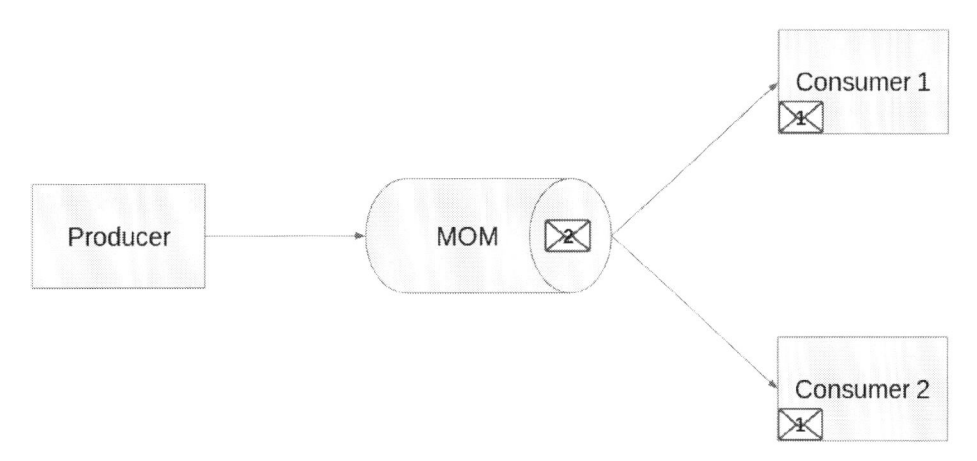

Figure 10.31: Without a Durable Subscriber: two active consumers

Consumer 2 becomes inactive before reading message 2:

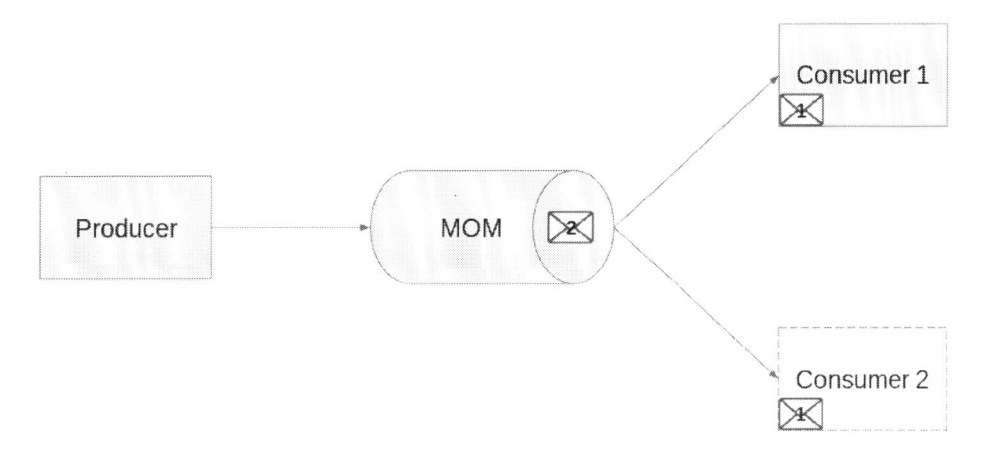

Figure 10.32: Without a Durable Subscriber: Consumer 2 is inactive

Consumer 1 reads message 2:

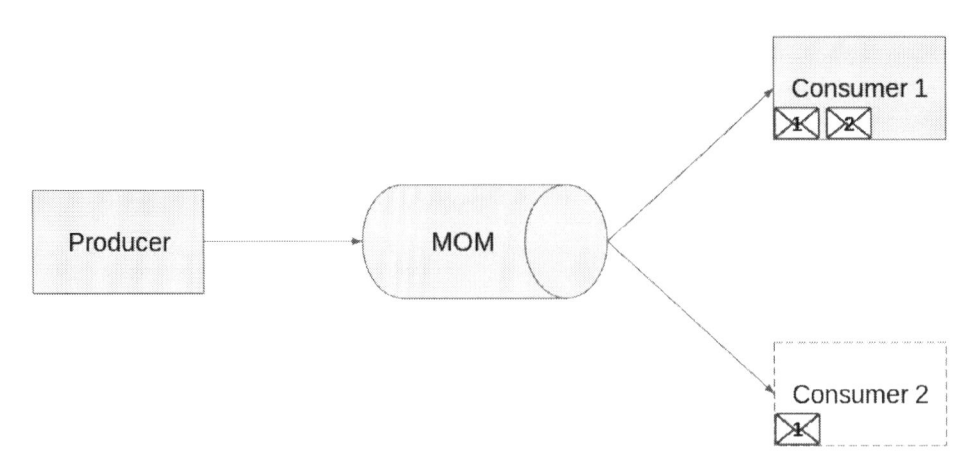

Figure 10.33: Without a Durable Subscriber: message 2 consumed by Consumer 1

Consumer 2 is active again, but unfortunately, message 2 is no longer present in the MOM.

Message 2 will never be processed by **Consumer 2** since it is a nondurable receiver, so it can only retrieve messages published after its subscription and must remain active to receive them:

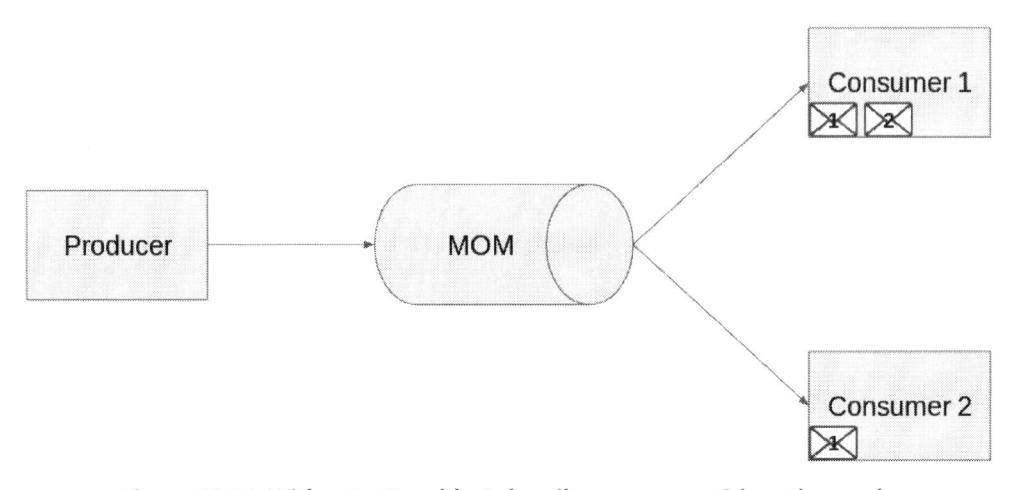

Figure 10.34: Without a Durable Subscriber: message 2 is active again

With a *Durable Subscriber*, message 2 would have been processed by **Consumer 2**. Indeed, in this case, the receiver receives all the messages sent while it was down. This happens as soon as it reconnects.

The MOM will take care of storing message 2 until all *Durable Subscribers* have processed it:

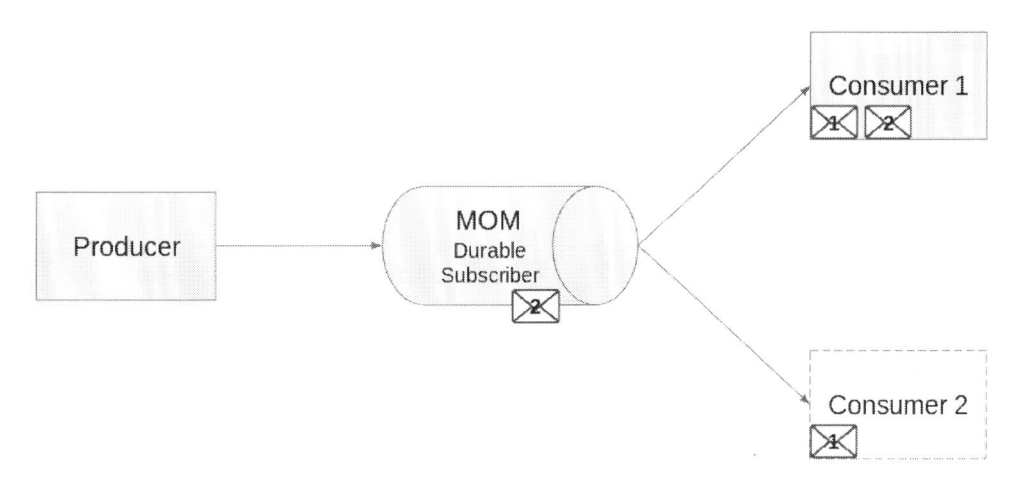

Figure 10.35: With a Durable Subscriber: message 2 is stored

When **Consumer 2** is active again, it processes message 2, which is removed from the MOM:

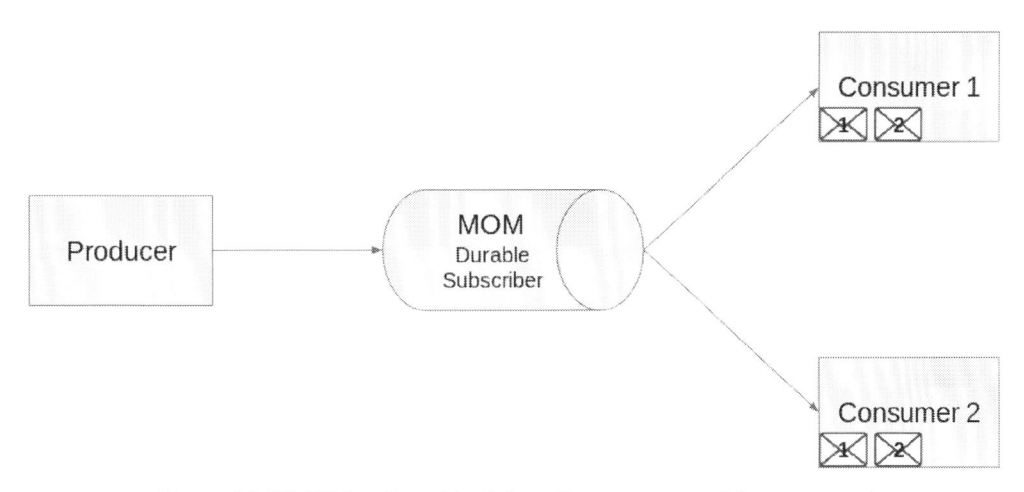

Figure 10.36: With a Durable Subscriber: message 2 is processed

302 | Load Testing Message-Oriented Middleware (MOM) via JMS

Note that we can choose from the following options to set how the message will be consumed:

Client ● Use **MessageConsumer.receive()** ○ Use **MessageListener.onMessage()**

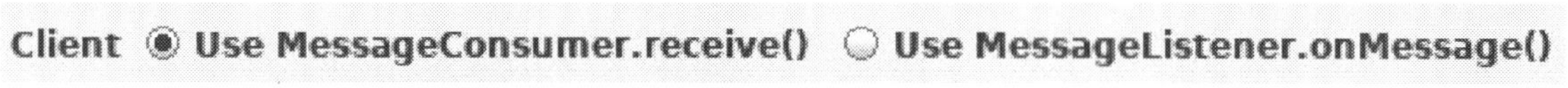

Figure 10.37: Settings for how the message will be consumed by a JMS Subscription Request

The choice is between **MessageConsumer.receive()** and **MessageListener.onMessage()**:

- With the first choice (**MessageConsumer.receive()**), the message is consumed synchronously by the application (the `receive()` method blocks until a message is consumed or the waiting time is exceeded (which is defined by the *Timeout(ms)* parameter).

- With the second choice, the consumption of the message by the application is asynchronous (an object of type *MessageListener* is registered and its `onMessage()` method will be called on each message reception).

Let's go back to our default installation of Apache ActiveMQ.

We will use the Apache ActiveMQ feature, which allows us to dynamically create topics. This will consist of naming our destination with the *dynamicTopic/* prefix:

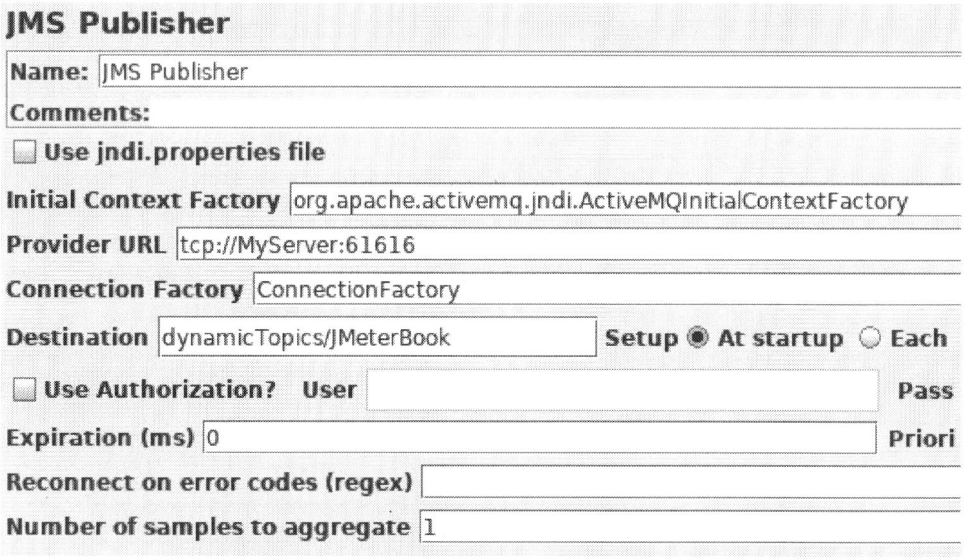

Figure 10.38: JMS query posting and the dynamic creation of topics

Methodology

As with all tests, testing an MOM and/or server should be as realistic as possible.

For example, if the messages exchanged are persistent, the same thing must be done with JMeter. Likewise, the same applies to the other parameters (such as delay, authentication, and so on).

> **Note**
> My advice is to speak with the developers and/or architects about allowing the test to be configured so that it is as representative of reality as possible.

Let's look at what we need to test.

JMeter can test the following (note that this is a non-exhaustive list):

- The configuration of the MOM – for this, JMeter must play the roles of producer and consumer:

Figure 10.39: Testing the configuration of the MOM

- The performances of our consumer – here, we will only use JMeter as a producer:

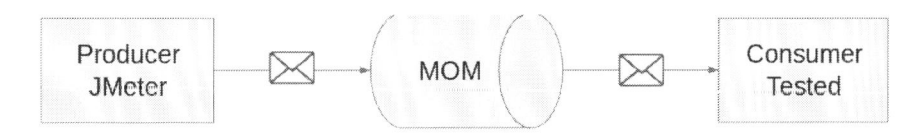

Figure 10.40: Testing the performance of the consumer

- The resilience of our MOM configuration – in this case, JMeter plays the roles of producer and consumer, and injects errors (*Failure injection*).

Let's move on to practice.

Putting It into Practice with JMeter

To simplify the examples, we will not implement all the good practices outlined in the *Chapter 5, Prepare Test Environments (Injectors and Tested System)* and *Chapter 3, Design a Test Case*.

In particular, note that the tests will be performed locally (on JMeter and MOM) – avoid this in real life!

Example 1: Testing the Configuration of an MOM server with Point-to-Point Messaging

Our first test will be on an MOM server with point-to-point messaging.

We will use ActiveMQ as our MOM:

1. Before starting with our JMeter test plan, let's create a queue named *JMeterBook*.
2. At first, we will send a message in a queue.
3. In JMeter, we will configure **JMS Point-to-Point** as follows:

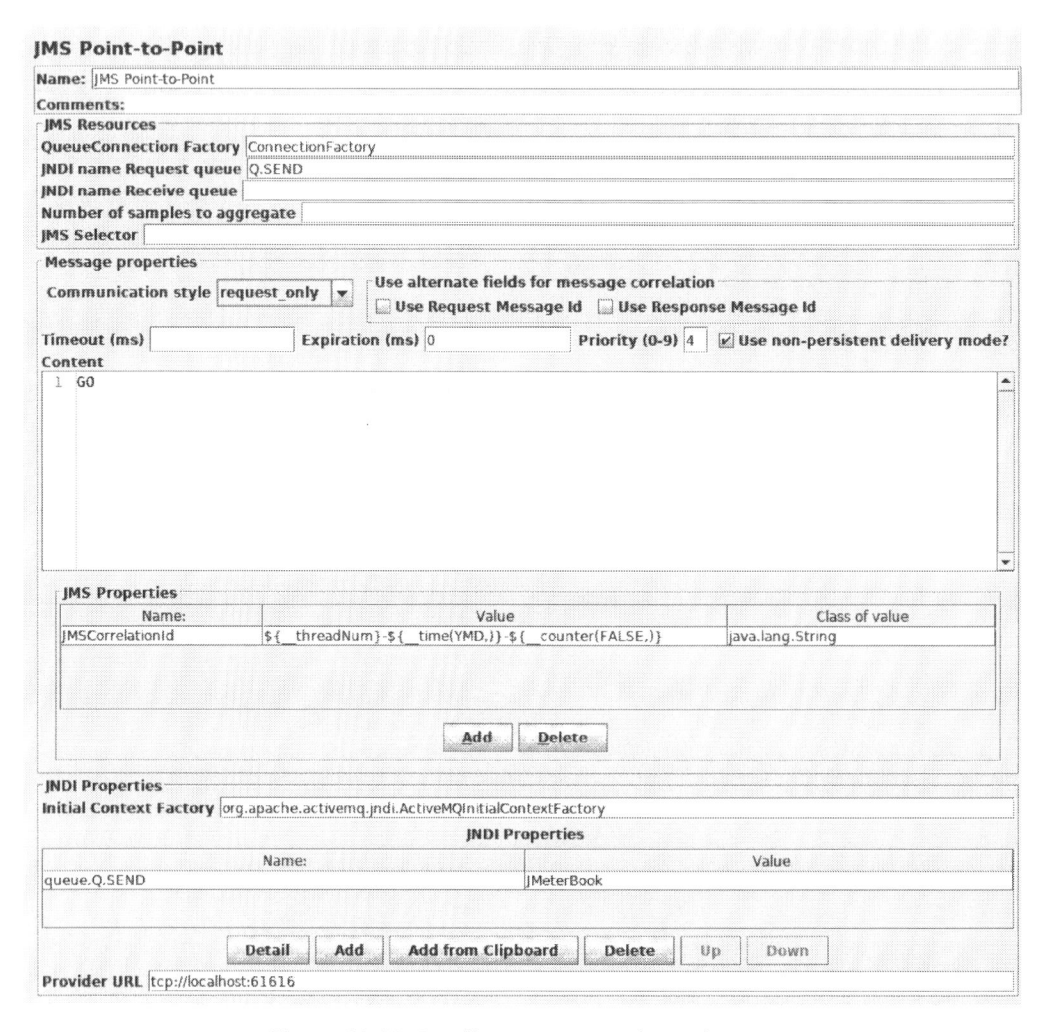

Figure 10.41: Sending a message in ActiveMQ

In this example, we generate a unique **JMSCorrelationId** identifier using the following JMeter functions:

- `${__time(YMD,)}`: Returns the current date
- `${__threadNum}`: Returns the number of the current thread
- `${__counter(FALSE,)}`: Returns a unique number for each call

Validate our script by sending a message.

In JMeter, we can see our message using **View Results Tree**:

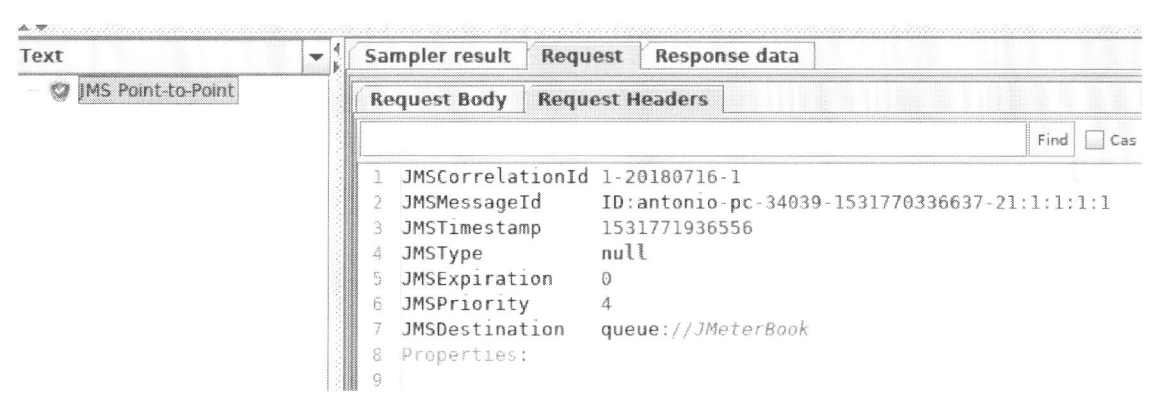

Figure 10.42: The result of sending the message in JMeter

In the ActiveMQ administration console, we can see that the message has arrived, but has not yet been consumed:

Figure 10.43: The result of sending the message in ActiveMQ

Now we want to consume the messages sent.

To do this, we will configure **JMS Point-to-Point** to read the message.

Let's change the values of these parameters as follows:

- **Communication style** in **request_reply**.
- Make the **JNDI name Receive queue** value equal to the value for **JNDI name Request queue**:

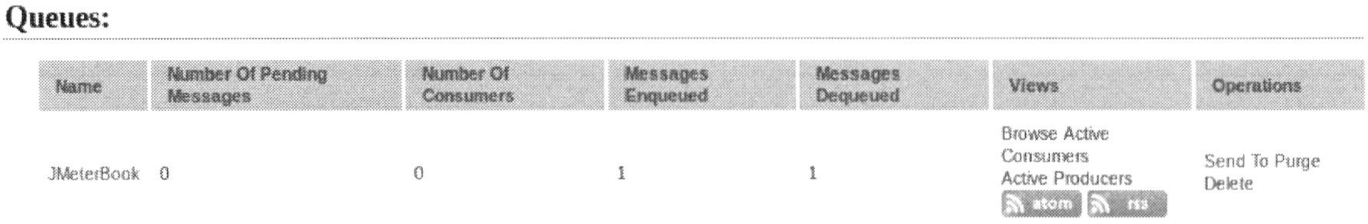

Queues:

Name	Number Of Pending Messages	Number Of Consumers	Messages Enqueued	Messages Dequeued	Views	Operations
JMeterBook	0	0	1	1	Browse Active Consumers Active Producers atom rss	Send To Purge Delete

Figure 10.44: The result of sending/receiving the message in ActiveMQ

Now that our script is ready, we only have to test all the parameters and their combinations in order to find the most appropriate ones for our project.

At this point, the configurations of the server (that is, the memory, the processor, and so on) and ActiveMQ (that is, the size of the JMS queues, among other things) are validated.

We are now required to test the following scenario: "What happens if the queue is purged while serving the application?"

Our test protocol will be the following:

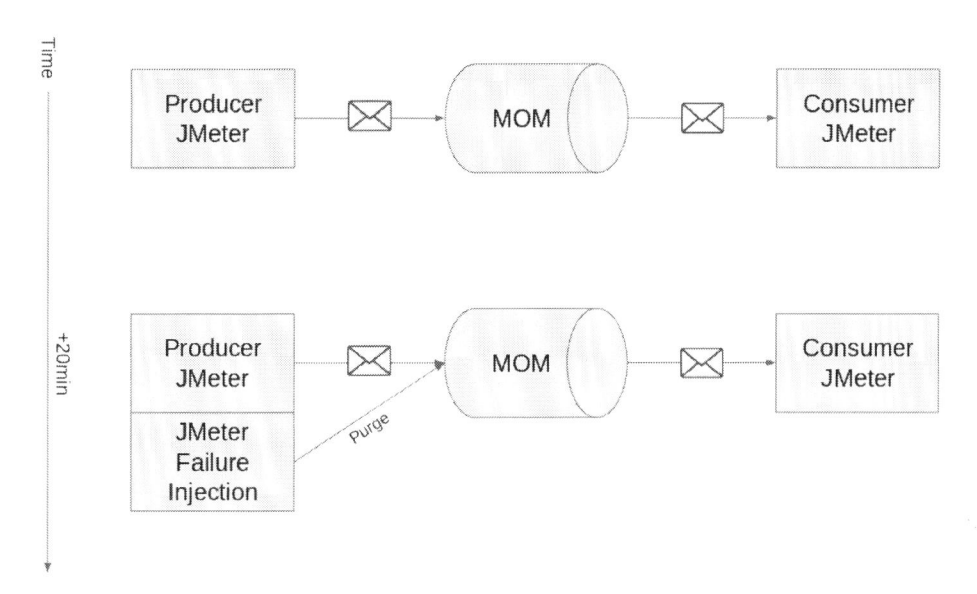

Figure 10.45: Our test protocol

We can purge a queue in many ways:

- Using the REST API
- Using Java Management Extensions (JMX)
- Using the CLI

In our example, we will use the first solution: the REST API.

Our call will be as follows:

```
http://127.0.0.1:8161/api/jolokia/exec/org.apache.
activemq:type=Broker,brokerName=localhost,destinationType=Queue,
destinationName=JMeterBook/purge
```

And in JMeter, we'll use the following settings:

Figure 10.46: Purging a queue with JMeter

A new, real-life scenario we need to check: "With our current configuration, can we lose messages if the MOM crashes?"

To do this, we will continue to use the ActiveMQ REST API.

The call to kill the JVM that runs ActiveMQ will be as follows:

`http://127.0.0.1:8161/api/jolokia/exec/org.apache.activemq:type=Broker,brokerName=localhost/terminateJVM/0`

In JMeter, we'll use the following settings:

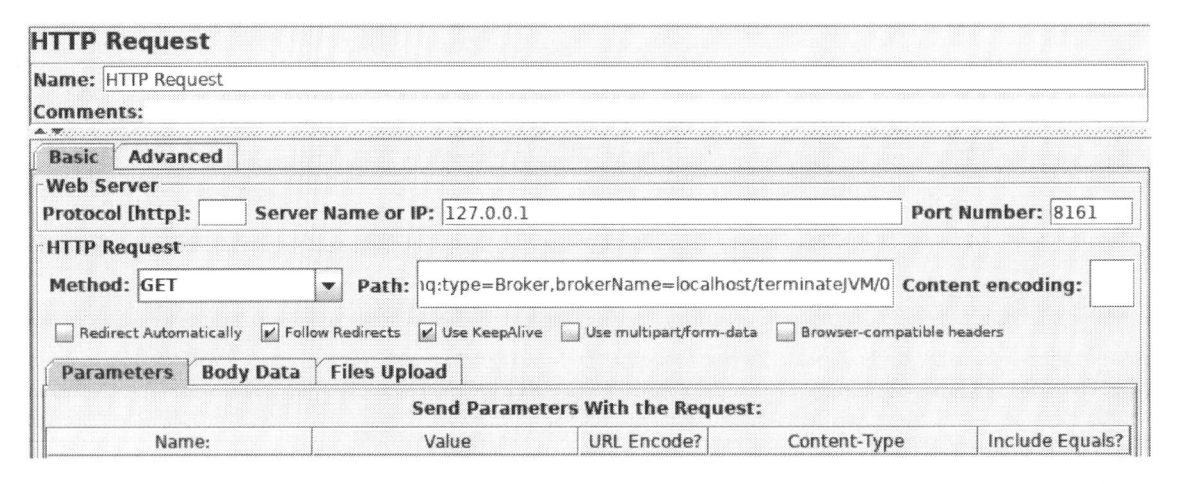

Figure 10.47: Crash the MOM using JMeter

The tests were successful.

Example 2: Testing the Performance of Our Consumer with JMS Publish/Subscribe

In this example, we will use Apache ActiveMQ Artemis.

To do this, install the **artemis-jms-client-all-X.X.X.jar** file from ActiveMQ Artemis into the **lib** directory of JMeter.

To reproduce this example, perform the following steps:

1. To create the necessary, run the following command:

    ```
    artemis create JMeterBookBrokerExamples --name JMeterBookBroker --user user --password password --allow-anonymous*
    ```

2. We will add our topic, JMeterBookTopic. In the configuration file of the MOM, **<broker-instance>/etc/broker.xml**, add the following lines in the *addresses* section:

    ```xml
    <address name="JMeterBookTopic">
        <multicast>
            <queue name="JMeterBookTopic" />
        </multicast>
    </address>
    ```

3. Let's run our MOM with this command:

    ```
    artemis run
    ```

    You can also use the following command:

    ```
    artemis-service start
    ```

    Let's make sure everything works by using the Artemis ActiveMQ console available at **http://localhost:8161/console/**:

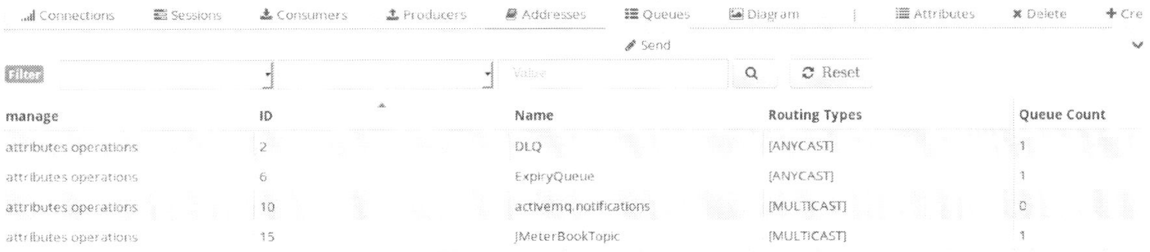

Figure 10.48: Checking that the addresses have been created

manage	ID	Name	Address	Routing Type	Filter	Durable
attributes op...	4	DLQ	DLQ	ANYCAST		true
attributes op...	8	ExpiryQueue	ExpiryQueue	ANYCAST		true
attributes op...	17	JMeterBookTopic	JMeterBookTopic	MULTICAST		true

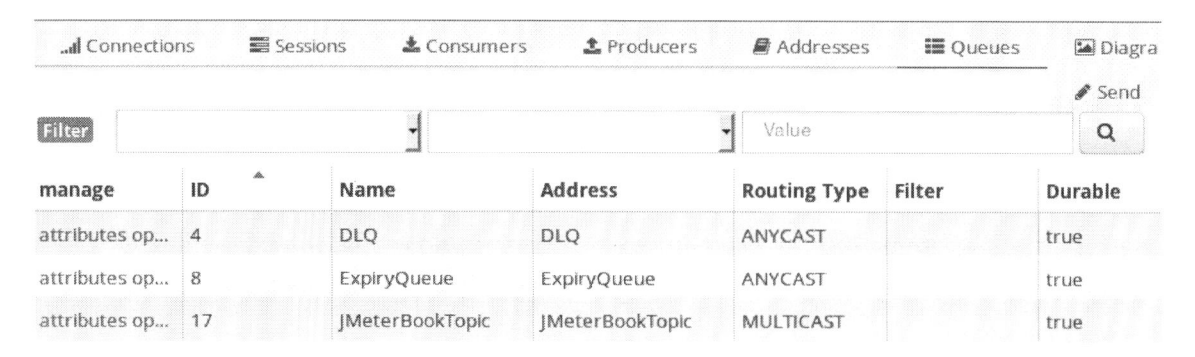

Figure 10.49: Checking that our topic has been created

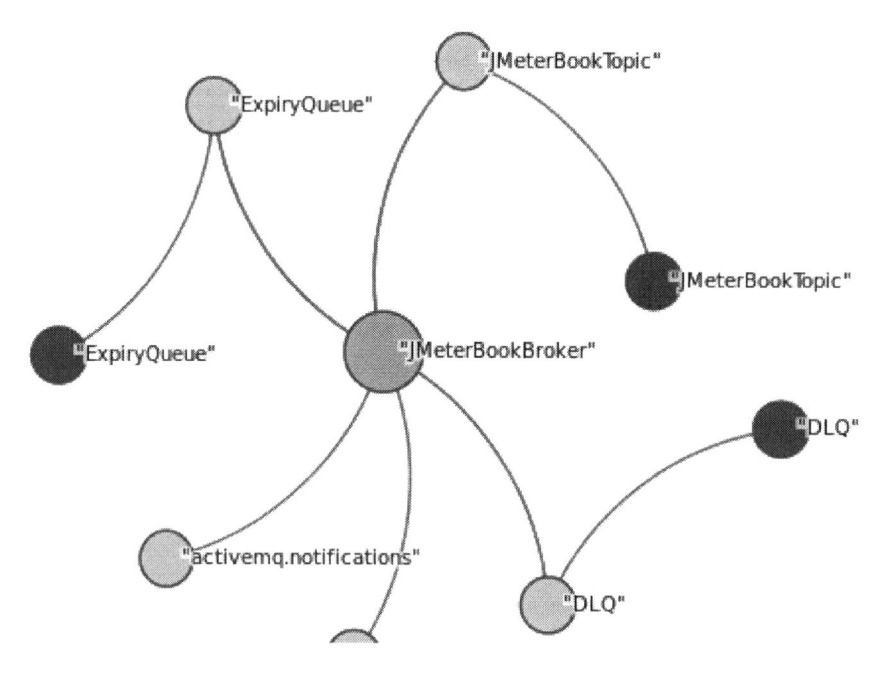

Figure 10.50: Our ActiveMQ Artemis configuration

4. Let's create a **jndi.properties** file:

   ```
   java.naming.factory.initial=org.apache.activemq.artemis.jndi.
   ActiveMQInitialContextFactory
   connectionFactory.ConnectionFactory=tcp://localhost:61616
   topic.topic/JMeterBookTopic=JMeterBookTopic
   ```

> **Note**
> With the default configuration, ActiveMQ Artemis blocks the producer if the disk is more than 90% full. You can modify this setting if necessary.

5. The first thing to do is to add our `jndi.properties` file to the *classpath* of JMeter.
6. The solution we've chosen is to use the **Add directory or jar to classpath** option in **Test Plan**:

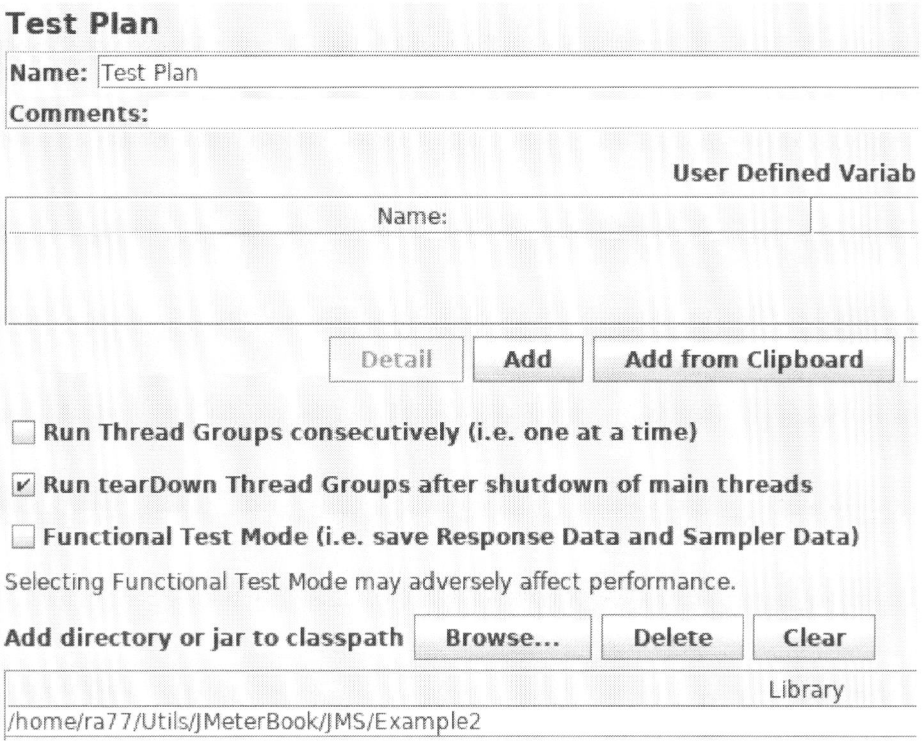

Figure 10.51: Adding the jndi.properties file to the JMeter classpath

7. Let's add a **JMS Publisher** element to our script and configure it as follows:

   Make sure that the **Use jndi.properties file** option is checked.

Connection Factory = **ConnectionFactory**.

Destination = **topic/JMeterBookTopic**:

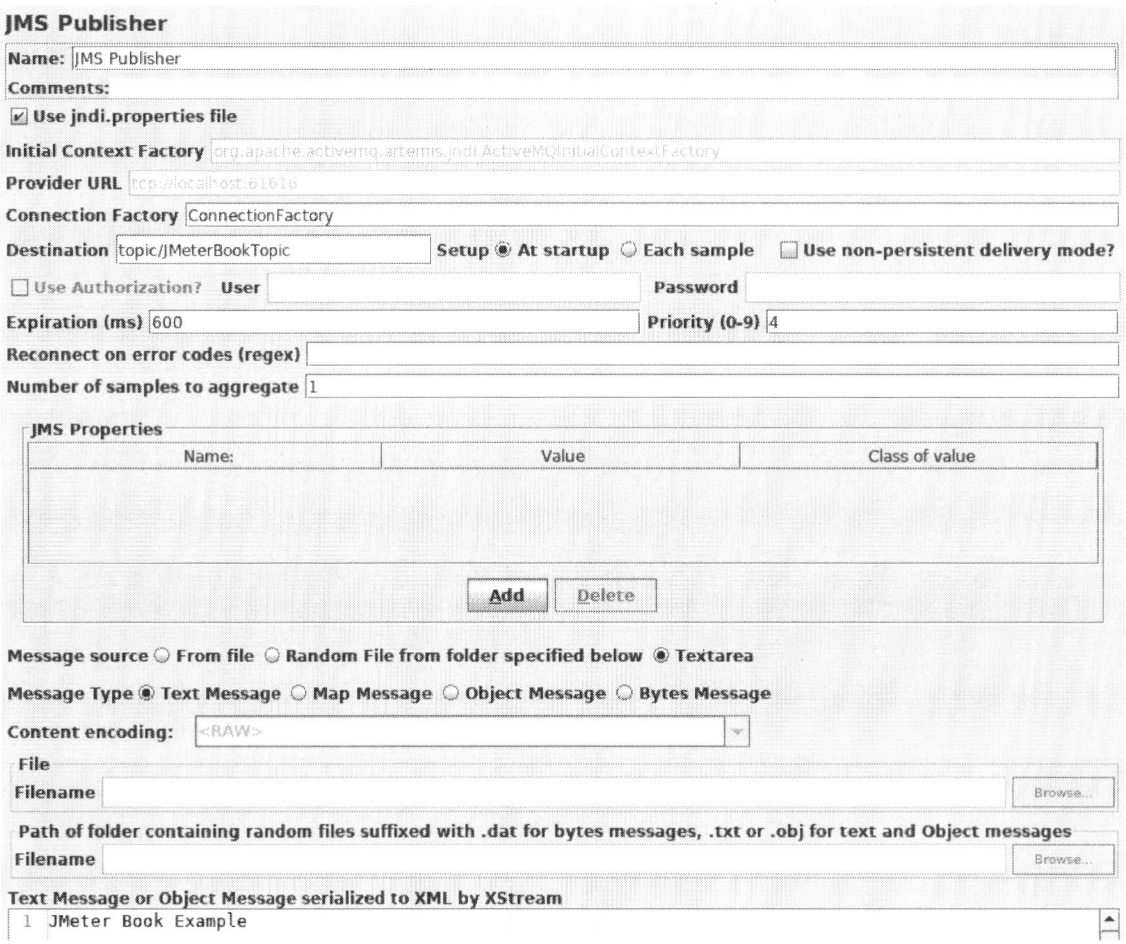

Figure 10.52: JMS Publisher

Finally, we execute our script to produce the messages and validate the correct behavior of our consumer.

Example 3: Testing the Configuration of an MOM Server with Publish/Subscribe

For **JMS Publisher**, we will take the example outlined in the preceding section and complete it:

1. In a new **Thread Group**, add a **JMS Subscriber** element with the following options:

    Make sure that the **Use jndi.properties file** option is checked.

    Connection Factory = **ConnectionFactory**.

    Destination = **topic/JMeterBookTopic**:

Figure 10.53: JMS Subscriber

Our script looks like this:

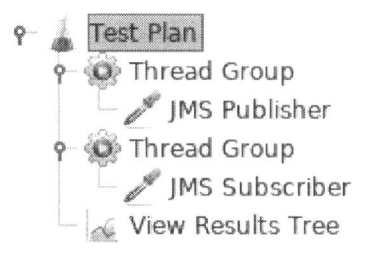

Figure 10.54: JMS Pub/Sub Script

2. Let's execute it. During the validation phase of the script, we can use **View Results Tree** for this purpose:

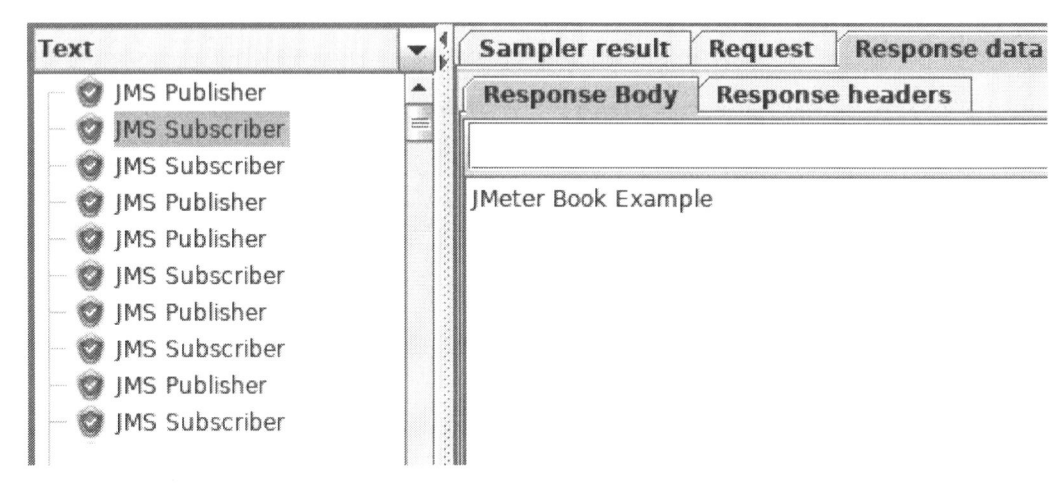

Figure 10.55: Validation of the receipt of the message with View Results Tree

During the load test, the ActiveMQ administration console Artemis will come to the rescue.

Validation that the consumer is present looks as follows:

Figure 10.56: Consumer validation

Validation that the producer is present looks as follows:

Figure 10.57: Validation of the producer

Validation that the topic works looks as follows:

Figure 10.58: Topic validation

Now, our customer asks, "What happens if consumers take more time to consume the messages?"

3. To handle this, we only need to add a **Constant Timer** element to our **Thread Group** containing **JMS Subscriber**:

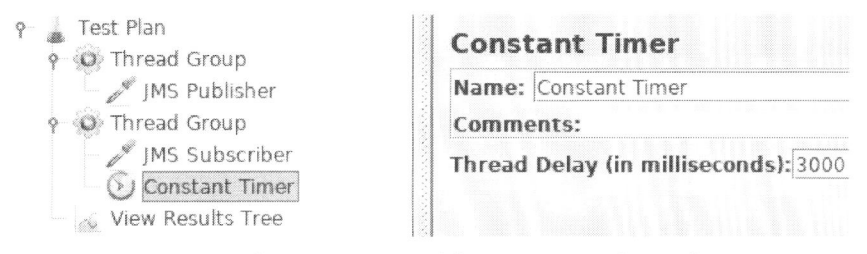

Figure 10.59: Slow consumer with a Constant Timer element

Our customer asks, "What happens if the Topic is paused for 5 minutes?"

4. To simulate this, we will use the ActiveMQ Artemis management capabilities with its API (https://activemq.apache.org/artemis/docs/latest/management.html) to pause the topic.

The script to pause the topic is as follows:

```
import javax.jms.Message;
import javax.jms.Queue;
import javax.jms.QueueConnection;
import javax.jms.QueueConnectionFactory;
import javax.jms.QueueRequestor;
import javax.jms.QueueSession;
import javax.jms.Session;
import javax.naming.InitialContext;

import org.apache.activemq.artemis.api.core.management.ResourceNames;
import org.apache.activemq.artemis.api.jms.ActiveMQJMSClient;
import org.apache.activemq.artemis.api.jms.management.JMSManagementHelper;

QueueConnection connection = null;
InitialContext initialContext = null;

try {
    initialContext = new InitialContext();
    QueueConnectionFactory cf = (QueueConnectionFactory) initialContext.lookup("ConnectionFactory");
    connection = cf.createQueueConnection();
    QueueSession session = connection.createQueueSession(false, Session.AUTO_ACKNOWLEDGE);

    Queue managementQueue = ActiveMQJMSClient.createQueue("activemq.management");
    QueueRequestor requestor = new QueueRequestor(session, managementQueue);
    connection.start();
    Message m = session.createMessage();
    JMSManagementHelper.putOperationInvocation(m, ResourceNames.QUEUE + "JMeterBookTopic", "pause");
    Message reply = requestor.request(m);

    return "OK";

} finally {
```

```
            if (initialContext != null) {
                initialContext.close();
            }
            if (connection != null) {
                connection.close();
            }
        }
```

5. Let's add this script in a **JSR223 Sampler** element:

JSR223 Sampler

Name: JSR223 Sampler
Comments:
Script language (e.g. Groovy, beanshell, javascript, jexl ...)
Language: groovy   (Groovy 2.4.15 / Groovy Scripting Engine 2.0)
Parameters to be passed to script (=> String Parameters and String []args)
Parameters:
Script file (overrides script)
File Name: Browse...
Script compilation caching
Cache compiled script if available: ☑
Script (variables: ctx vars props SampleResult sampler log Label Filename Parameters args[] OUT)
Script:

```
 1  import javax.jms.Message;
 2  import javax.jms.Queue;
 3  import javax.jms.QueueConnection;
 4  import javax.jms.QueueConnectionFactory;
 5  import javax.jms.QueueRequestor;
 6  import javax.jms.QueueSession;
 7  import javax.jms.Session;
 8  import javax.naming.InitialContext;
 9
10  import org.apache.activemq.artemis.api.core.management.ResourceNames;
11  import org.apache.activemq.artemis.api.jms.ActiveMQJMSClient;
12  import org.apache.activemq.artemis.api.jms.management.JMSManagementHelper;
13
14  QueueConnection connection = null;
15  InitialContext initialContext = null;
16
17  try {
18      initialContext = new InitialContext();
19      QueueConnectionFactory cf = (QueueConnectionFactory) initialContext.lookup("ConnectionFactory");
20      connection = cf.createQueueConnection();
21      QueueSession session = connection.createQueueSession(false, Session.AUTO_ACKNOWLEDGE);
22
23      Queue managementQueue = ActiveMQJMSClient.createQueue("activemq.management");
24      QueueRequestor requestor = new QueueRequestor(session, managementQueue);
25      connection.start();
26      Message m = session.createMessage();
27      JMSManagementHelper.putOperationInvocation(m, ResourceNames.QUEUE + "JMeterBookTopic", "pause");
28      Message reply = requestor.request(m);
29
```

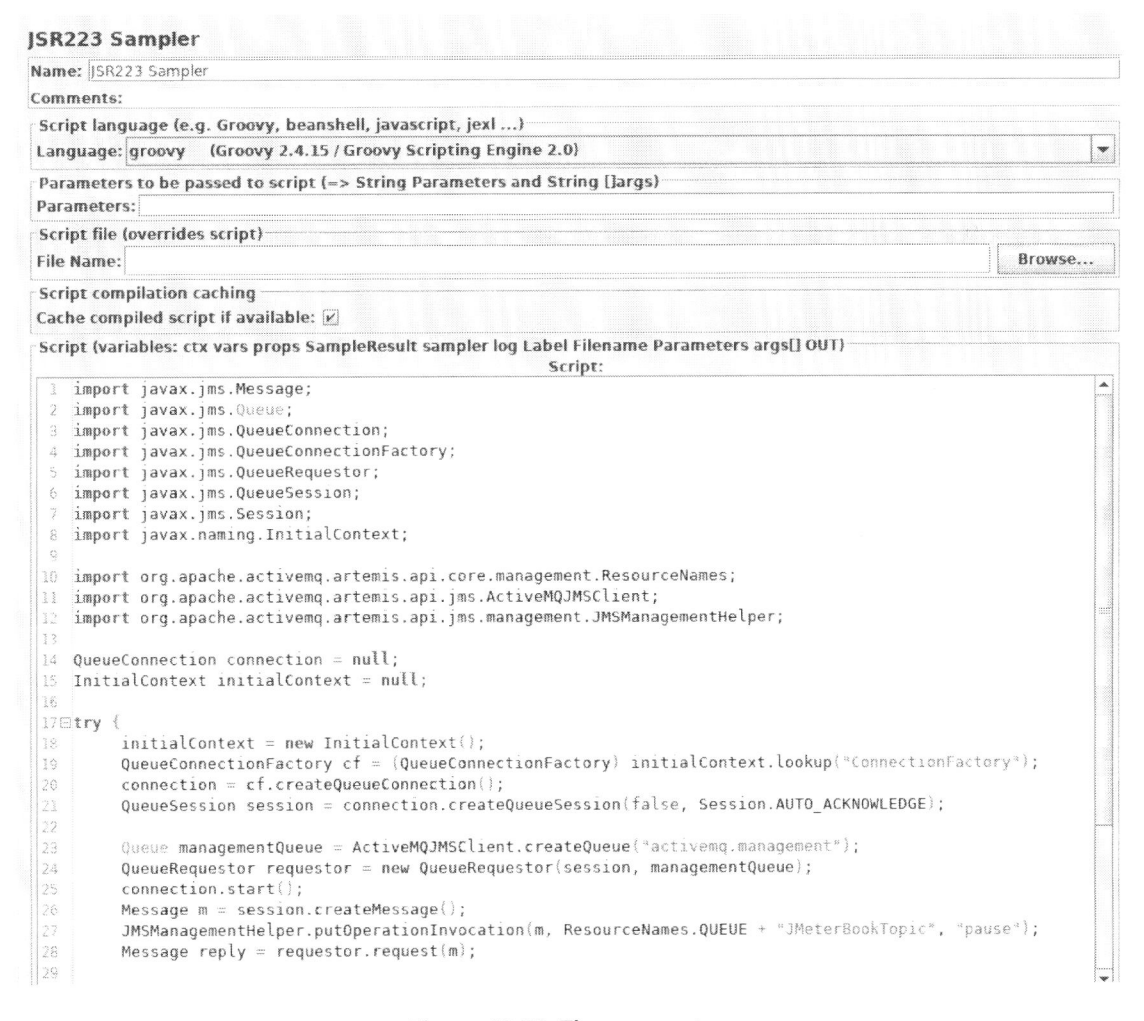

Figure 10.60: The pause step

318 | Load Testing Message-Oriented Middleware (MOM) via JMS

6. Validate that it works well using the Artemis ActiveMQ management interface:

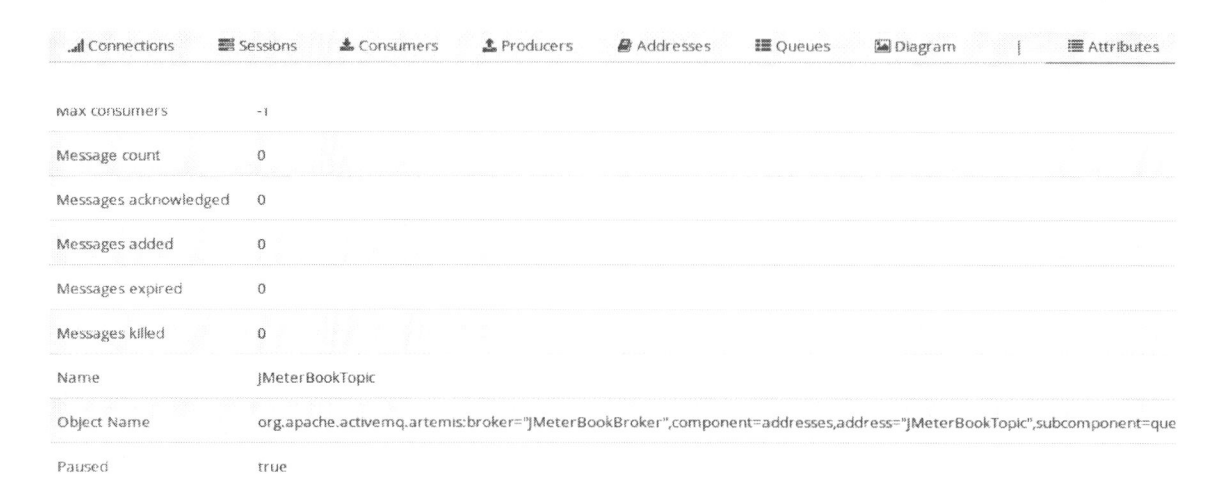

Max consumers	-1
Message count	0
Messages acknowledged	0
Messages added	0
Messages expired	0
Messages killed	0
Name	JMeterBookTopic
Object Name	org.apache.activemq.artemis:broker="JMeterBookBroker",component=addresses,address="JMeterBookTopic",subcomponent=que
Paused	true

Figure 10.61: Confirming that the topic has been paused

7. Now let's add the resume step. The script is almost the same, we just call *resume* instead of *pause*:

```
import javax.jms.Message;
import javax.jms.Queue;
import javax.jms.QueueConnection;
import javax.jms.QueueConnectionFactory;
import javax.jms.QueueRequestor;
import javax.jms.QueueSession;
import javax.jms.Session;
import javax.naming.InitialContext;

import org.apache.activemq.artemis.api.core.management.ResourceNames;
import org.apache.activemq.artemis.api.jms.ActiveMQJMSClient;
import org.apache.activemq.artemis.api.jms.management.JMSManagementHelper;

QueueConnection connection = null;
InitialContext initialContext = null;

try {
```

```
        initialContext = new InitialContext();
        QueueConnectionFactory cf = (QueueConnectionFactory) initialContext.
lookup("ConnectionFactory");
        connection = cf.createQueueConnection();
        QueueSession session = connection.createQueueSession(false, Session.
AUTO_ACKNOWLEDGE);

        Queue managementQueue = ActiveMQJMSClient.createQueue("activemq.
management");
        QueueRequestor requestor = new QueueRequestor(session,
managementQueue);
        connection.start();
        Message m = session.createMessage();
        JMSManagementHelper.putOperationInvocation(m, ResourceNames.QUEUE +
"JMeterBookTopic", "resume");
        Message reply = requestor.request(m);

        return "OK";

} finally {
    if (initialContext != null) {
        initialContext.close();
    }
    if (connection != null) {
        connection.close();
    }
}
```

320 | Load Testing Message-Oriented Middleware (MOM) via JMS

Let's add this script in a **JSR223 Sampler** element:

```
import javax.jms.Message;
import javax.jms.Queue;
import javax.jms.QueueConnection;
import javax.jms.QueueConnectionFactory;
import javax.jms.QueueRequestor;
import javax.jms.QueueSession;
import javax.jms.Session;
import javax.naming.InitialContext;

import org.apache.activemq.artemis.api.core.management.ResourceNames;
import org.apache.activemq.artemis.api.jms.ActiveMQJMSClient;
import org.apache.activemq.artemis.api.jms.management.JMSManagementHelper;

QueueConnection connection = null;
InitialContext initialContext = null;

try {
    initialContext = new InitialContext();
    QueueConnectionFactory cf = (QueueConnectionFactory) initialContext.lookup("ConnectionFactory");
    connection = cf.createQueueConnection();
    QueueSession session = connection.createQueueSession(false, Session.AUTO_ACKNOWLEDGE);

    Queue managementQueue = ActiveMQJMSClient.createQueue("activemq.management");
    QueueRequestor requestor = new QueueRequestor(session, managementQueue);
    connection.start();
    Message m = session.createMessage();
    JMSManagementHelper.putOperationInvocation(m, ResourceNames.QUEUE + "JMeterBookTopic", "resume");
    Message reply = requestor.request(m);
```

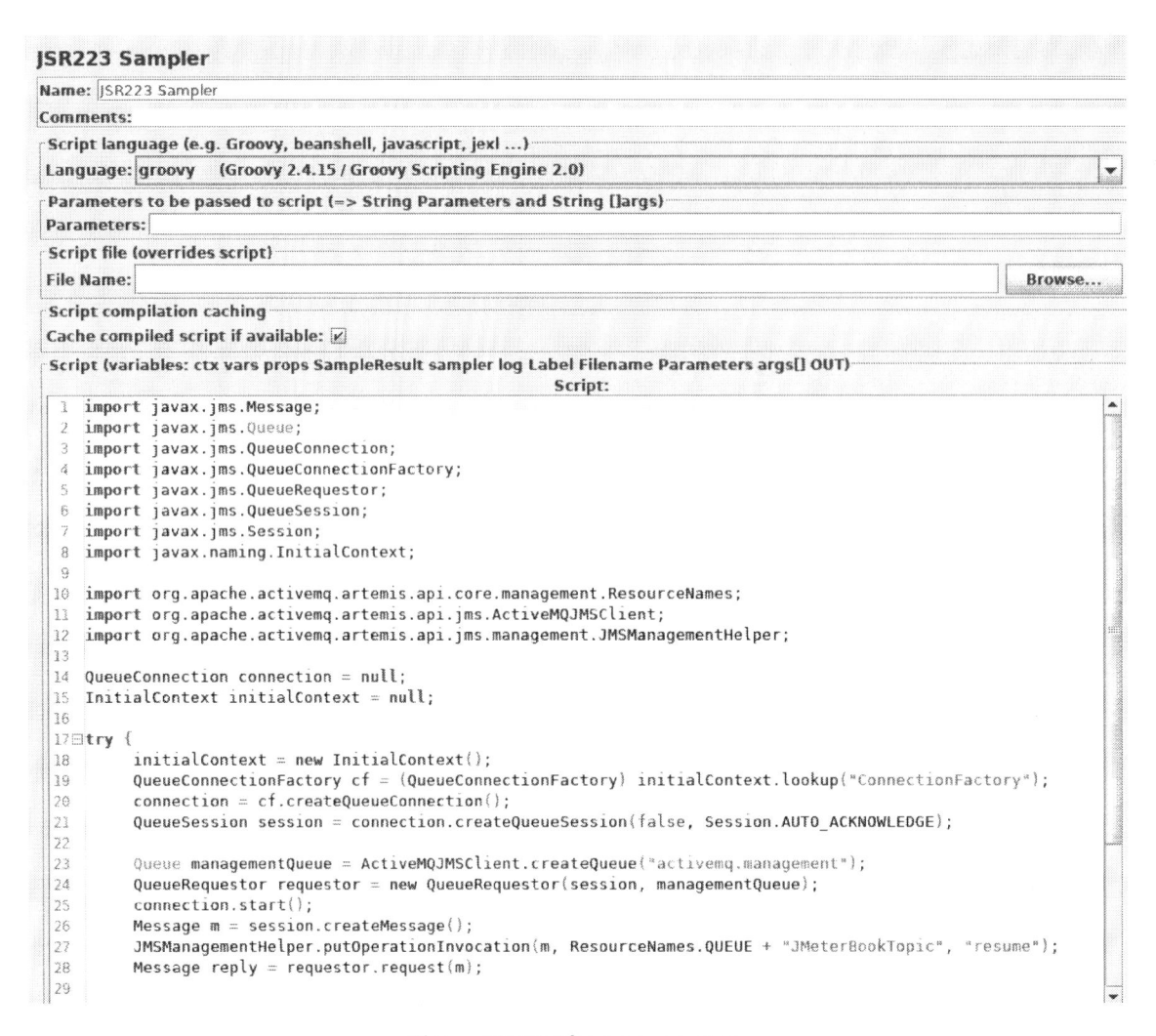

Figure 10.62: The resume step

8. Validate that it works well using the Artemis ActiveMQ management interface:

∨ 📁 JMeterBookTopic	Messages expired	0
∨ 📁 queues	Messages killed	0
∨ 📁 "multicast"	Name	JMeterBookTopic
⚙ JMeterBookTopic	Object Name	org.apache.activem
	Paused	false

Figure 10.63: Check the status of the Topic

9. Let's put these two **JSR223 Sampler** elements in a **Thread Group** element.
10. Then add a **Flow Control Action** element to pause for 5 minutes (300,000 ms) between the two elements.
11. Let's add a **Response Assertion** element to check that the script returns the word OK.

    Do not forget to configure our **Thread Groups** to stop the test whether an error occurs during the manipulation (the *pause* and *resume* operations) of our topic:

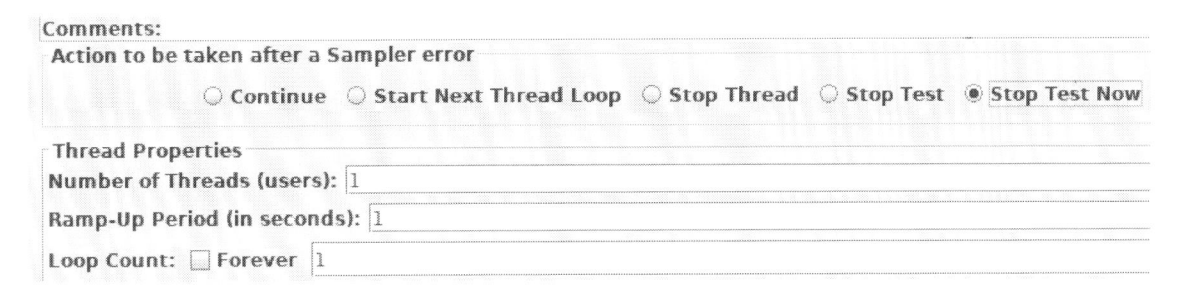

```
Comments:
─ Action to be taken after a Sampler error ─
         ○ Continue  ○ Start Next Thread Loop  ○ Stop Thread  ○ Stop Test  ● Stop Test Now
─ Thread Properties ─
Number of Threads (users): 1
Ramp-Up Period (in seconds): 1
Loop Count: ☐ Forever  1
```

Figure 10.64: Configuration of our thread groups

> **Note**
> Another thing to remember, run this **Thread Groups** at the right time depending on the test case (at the beginning of the test, or waiting for peak load, and so on).

Our final test plan looks like this:

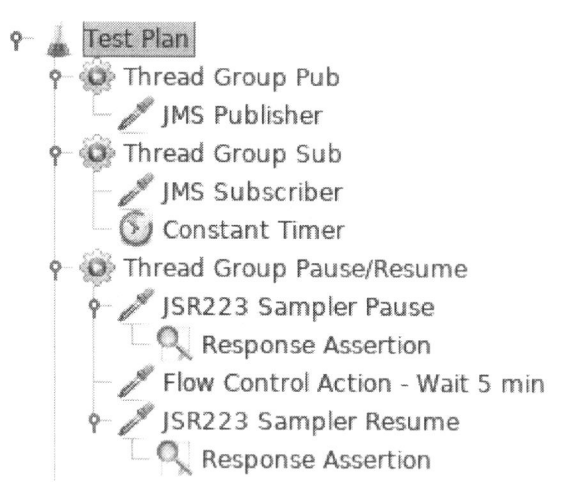

```
○─ ▲ Test Plan
   ○─ ⚙ Thread Group Pub
   │   └─ ✎ JMS Publisher
   ○─ ⚙ Thread Group Sub
   │   ├─ ✎ JMS Subscriber
   │   └─ ⏱ Constant Timer
   ○─ ⚙ Thread Group Pause/Resume
       ○─ ✎ JSR223 Sampler Pause
       │   └─ 🔍 Response Assertion
       ├─ ✎ Flow Control Action - Wait 5 min
       ○─ ✎ JSR223 Sampler Resume
           └─ 🔍 Response Assertion
```

Figure 10.65: Our final test plan

Example 4: Testing Any MOM

It may happen that testing our MOM with JMeter's standard JMS elements is impossible. For example, consider the following cases:

- An in-house framework that encapsulates JMS calls.
- A given MOM's functionality isn't supported by JMS.

We will be able to work around this problem thanks to **JSR223 Sampler**.

The Java development of the consumer and the producer JMS is finished – let's go to the tests.

The producer and the consumer are distributed as a JAR file:

1. To test them, let's add this JAR file to JMeter's classpath so that we can use these new JMS consumers and producers.

   > **Note**
   > Do not forget to restart JMeter to take into account the new JAR files.

2. All we need to do is change the JMS elements with **JSR223 Sampler** elements and use a Groovy script.

   A simple import of the package into the Groovy script will be enough (here, it will be **import jmeter.book.example_p2p.JMeterTestJMS**):

```
JSR223 Sampler
Name: JSR223 Sampler - Send message
Comments:
Script language (e.g. Groovy, beanshell, javascript, jexl ...)
Language: groovy    (Groovy 2.4.15 / Groovy Scripting Engine 2.0)
Parameters to be passed to script (=> String Parameters and String []args)
Parameters:
Script file (overrides script)
File Name:
Script compilation caching
Cache compiled script if available: ☑
Script (variables: ctx vars props SampleResult sampler log Label Filename
                                       Script:
1  import Jmeter.book.example_p2p.JMeterTestJMS
2
3  JMeterTestJMS JMSExample = new JMeterTestJMS();
4  JMSExample.getInitialContext();
5  JMSExample.connectAndCreateSession();
6  JMSExample.produceMessage("Example sent by JMeter");
7
8  return "OK";
```

Figure 10.66: Using the JMS transmitter with Groovy

And now, to have a more realistic script, it's possible to change the message sent using **CSV Data Set Config** or from a table in the database.

Conclusion

In this chapter, we have seen the following main features of MOMs:

- Asynchronicity
- Decoupling
- Back pressure
- Point-to-point communication
- The publish/subscribe communication model
- Broadcast
- Priority of messages
- Persistence of messages
- JMS Selector
- Durable Subscribers

We have tested these features in our JMeter scripts using Apache ActiveMQ and Apache ActiveMQ Artemis.

Then, we saw how to take advantage of the management features of MOMs using JMeter (specifically, the **JSR223 Sampler** element and a REST API).

When the core JMS elements of JMeter are not sufficient, it is still possible to do our tests using the integration between JMeter and Groovy via a **JSR223 Sampler** element.

Once again, you can see the endless possibilities that JMeter offers.

11

Performing a Load Test

Introduction

In the previous chapters, we learned how to create our load test scripts. It is now time to execute these scripts.

We will take this opportunity to bust some myths about JMeter not being suitable for "big load tests."

To do this, we will look at the different ways to perform a test and the best practices to follow in order to succeed.

Methodology

The method we recommend to execute your test campaign is the following:

1. Create your scripts with the GUI.
2. Maintain your scripts with the GUI.
3. Run `mini-tests` with the GUI to validate your scripts, the datasets used, and the platform (both the injection platform and the target platform).
4. Run the proper load test from the command line.
5. If you need to test multiple (**Internet Protocol**) **IP** sources or go very high in terms of the number of virtual users, run the test in distributed mode or with a cloud injection platform.

Testing Your Script with the Graphical User Interface

As mentioned in the previous chapters, we will use the JMeter GUI to create, maintain, and validate our scripts:

> **Note**
> Refer to the previous chapters for more information.

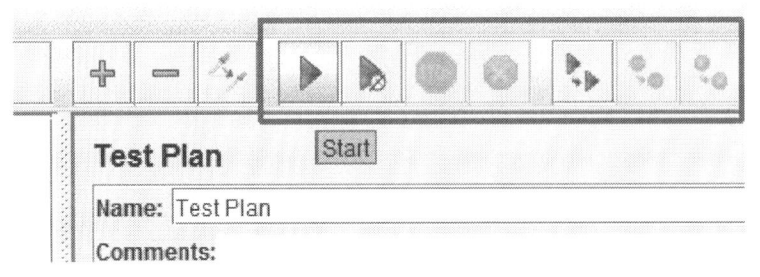

Figure 11.1: Testing your script with the GUI

Running Your Test from the Command Line

Once everything has been validated, it is time to start our load test. Best practices recommend using the JMeter command line.

The benefit that the command line has over the GUI is that it consumes fewer resources and gives more reliable results:

- The GUI management thread no longer disrupts injection.
- Many memory-intensive components in GUI mode are not active in CLI mode (such as **View Results Tree**).
- The listeners will no longer interrupt or interfere with the injection to refresh themselves (no more interruptions from graph updates and counters, for instance).

Here is the command line to execute JMeter:

```
<JMETER_HOME>/bin/jmeter -n -t <Path + JMeter scripts file> -l <Results file path>/results.csv
```

- **n**: CLI mode (also called non-GUI mode in JMeter)
- **l**: Result file
- **t**: JMeter scripts file

Another interesting option is `-J{name of the variable}={value of the variable}`, which allows you to define a key-value pair corresponding to a property used in our script (using `${__P(host,www.example.com)}`, for example).

For example:

```
jmeter -n -l results.csv -t MyScript.jmx -JNumberOfUnits=100 -Jrampup=50 -JNumberOfIterations=1000
```

If you need to use a proxy, use the following two settings:

- H: The proxy address
- P: The proxy port

Our previous command line becomes:

```
jmeter -n -l results.csv -t MyScript.jmx -JNumberOfUnits=100 -Jrampup=50
-JNumberOfIterations=1000 -H myProxy.xom -P 9999
```

> **Note**
> Avoid load testing behind a proxy as seen in *Chapter 5, Preparing Test Environments* (injectors and tested system).

Once the test is launched, we can track its progress using **Summarizer** (enabled by default since version 2.11):

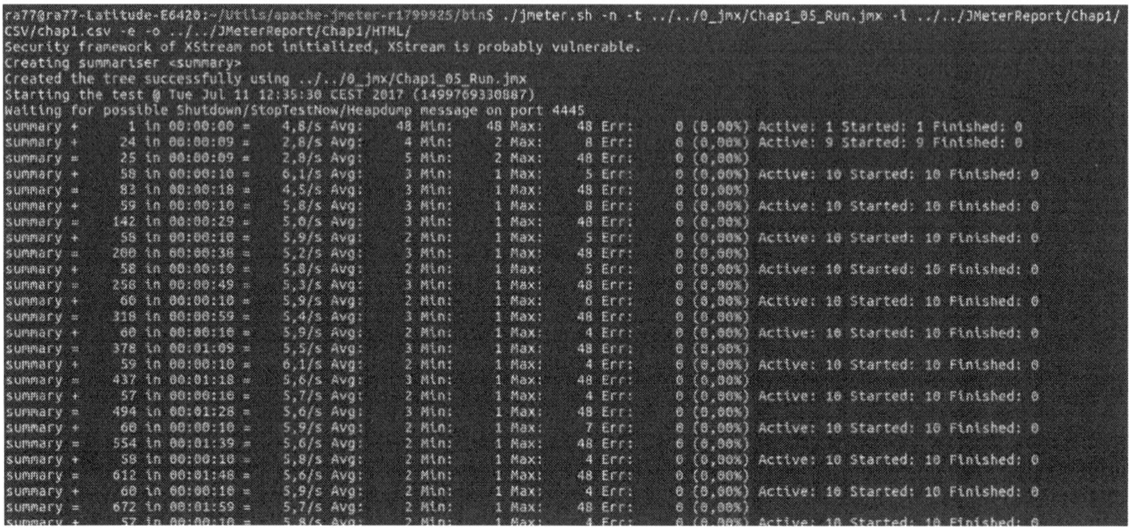

Figure 11.2: Following a test with Summarizer

This component displays, at regular intervals, two rows:

- A summary of the last interval (30 seconds by default). That's how you can detect a spike in response times or error rates
- A summary from the beginning of the test

We can also use **Backend Listener**, which allows you to send the results to *Graphite* and *InfluxDB* with core JMeter or to other backends with plugins:

Backend Listener	
Name:	Backend Listener
Comments:	
Backend Listener implementation	org.apache.jmeter.visualizers.backend.influxdb.InfluxdbBackendListenerClient
Async Queue size	5000

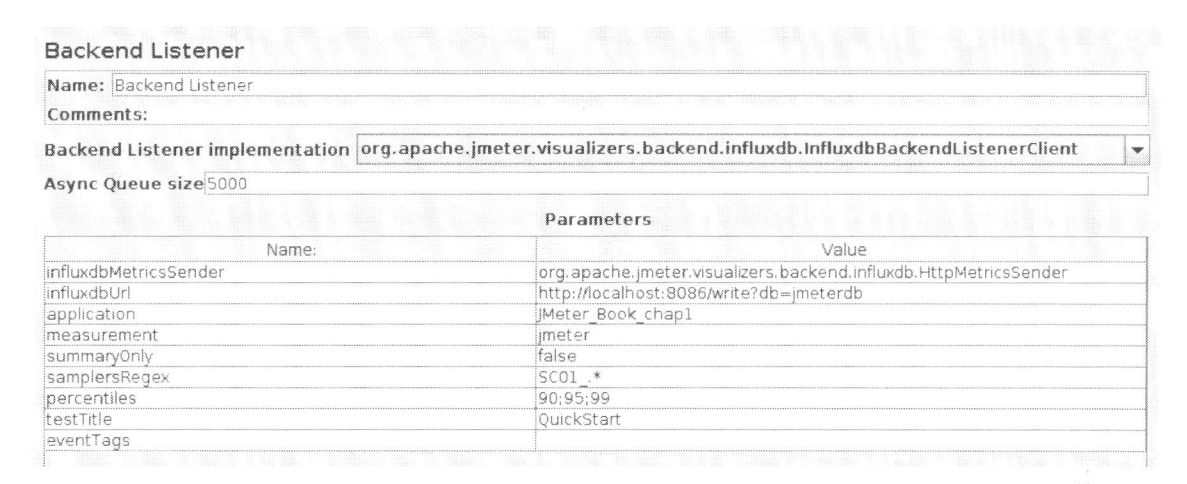

Parameters	
Name:	Value
influxdbMetricsSender	org.apache.jmeter.visualizers.backend.influxdb.HttpMetricsSender
influxdbUrl	http://localhost:8086/write?db=jmeterdb
application	JMeter_Book_chap1
measurement	jmeter
summaryOnly	false
samplersRegex	SC01_.*
percentiles	90;95;99
testTitle	QuickStart
eventTags	

Figure 11.3: The Backend Listener element

We advise you to use InfluxDB as it's a time-series database, which is the most suitable for load testing, as load testing depends on time.

> **Note**
> There is a plugin called JMeter ElasticSearch Backend Listener (https://github.com/delirius325/jmeter-elasticsearch-backend-listener) to send the results to *ElasticSearch*.

Running Your Test on the Command Line with Taurus

Taurus (https://gettaurus.org/) is a command-line tool for running load test scripts from various tools, including JMeter.

To perform a JMeter test, it's easy:

```
bzt myscript.jmx
```

332 | Performing a Load Test

The advantage over the classic JMeter command line is that this provides more information while running:

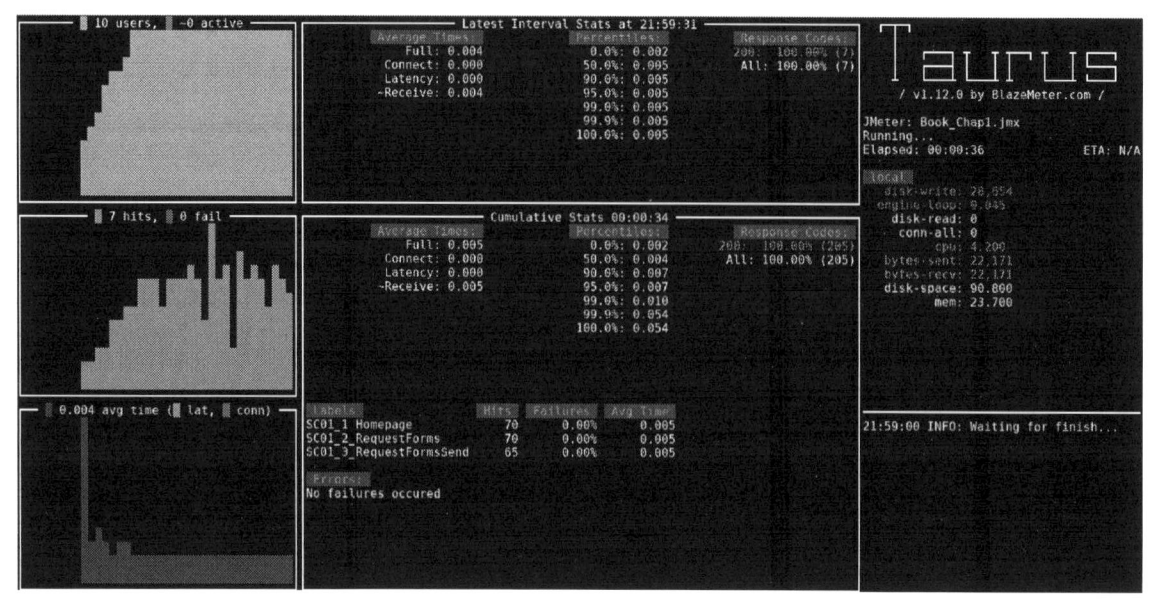

Figure 11.4: Taurus

If you want to use more advanced features of Taurus, you need to create a YAML file – let's call it **demo.yml**. Be careful: the YAML syntax is very sensitive to indentation.

In the following example, we will do three things:

1. Define how the load will be injected (ramp-up, plateau, and so on) by this syntax:

   ```
   execution:
   - scenario: existing
     competition: 10
     hold-for: 10s
     ramp-up: 30s

   scenarios:
    existing:
        script: demo.jmx
   ```

   We tell Taurus to run the **demo.jmx** script with 10 threads by setting a ramp from 0 to 10 virtual users in 30 seconds, then a virtual user level of 10 that will last 10 seconds.

2. Generate a JMeter HTML report to get a wealth of information to analyze your load test modules:

   ```
   jmeter:
       ...
       properties:
           jmeter.save.saveservice.subresults: true
           jmeter.reportgenerator.overall_granularity: 1000
           jmeter.reportgenerator.report_title: Mastering JMeter Book
           jmeter.reportgenerator.exporter.html.series_filter:
   ^(ClickNext|HP|scenario)(-success|-failure)?$
           output: ${TAURUS_ARTIFACTS_DIR}/output/

   services:
   - module: shellexec
     post-process:
     - ~/.bzt/jmeter-taurus/bin/jmeter -p ~/.bzt/jmeter-taurus/bin/jmeter.properties -q ${TAURUS_ARTIFACTS_DIR}/jmeter-bzt.properties -Jjmeter.save.saveservice.assertion_results_failure_message=false -g ${TAURUS_ARTIFACTS_DIR}/output/output.csv -o ${TAURUS_ARTIFACTS_DIR}/report
   ```

   In the example here, we use the **shellexec** module, which runs the report generation command.

   In the **properties** block, we have defined the specific properties of the report as the title, granularity, and transactions we want.

3. Generate the BlazeMeter dynamic report, which allows us to have a dynamic web graph during and after the shooting:

   ```
   reporting:
   - module: final-stats
   - module: console
   - module: blazemeter
   ```

   Here, we activate three reports:

   > **Note**
   > The BlazeMeter report is only available for a limited time unless you subscribe to an account.

334 | Performing a Load Test

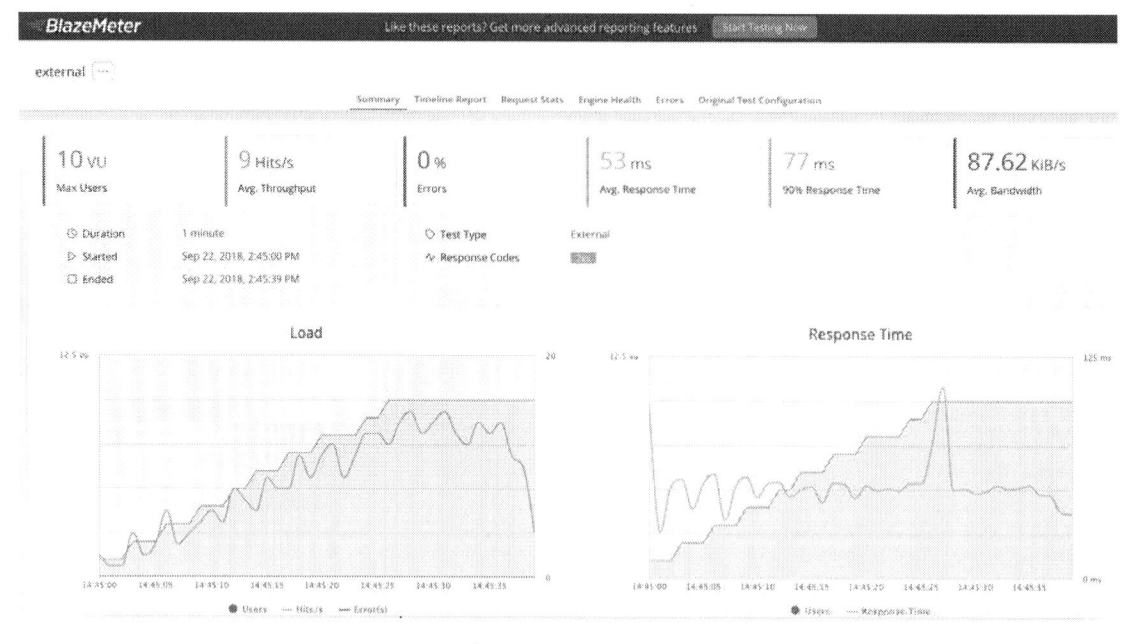

Figure 11.5: Taurus

This gives us:

```
execution:
- scenario: existing
  competition: 10
  hold-for: 10s
  ramp-up: 30s

scenarios:
 existing:
     script: demo.jmx

modules:
 jmeter:
     path: ~/.bzt/jmeter-taurus/bin/jmeter
     version: 5.0
     download-link: https://archive.apache.org/dist/jmeter/binaries/
apache-jmeter-{version}.zip
     detect-plugins: false
     properties:
       jmeter.save.saveservice.subresults: true
       jmeter.reportgenerator.overall_granularity: 1000
       jmeter.reportgenerator.report_title: Mastering JMeter Book
       jmeter.reportgenerator.exporter.html.series_filter:
```

```
        ^(ClickNext|HP|scenario)(-success|-failure)?$
            output: ${TAURUS_ARTIFACTS_DIR}/output/

    services:
    - module: shellexec
      post-process:
      - ~/.bzt/jmeter-taurus/bin/jmeter -p ~/.bzt/jmeter-taurus/bin/jmeter.
    properties -q ${TAURUS_ARTIFACTS_DIR}/jmeter-bzt.properties -Jjmeter.save.
    saveservice.assertion_results_failure_message=false -g ${TAURUS_ARTIFACTS_
    DIR}/output/output.csv -o ${TAURUS_ARTIFACTS_DIR}/report


    reporting:
    - module: final-stats
    - module: console
    - module: blazemeter
```

4. To launch the test:

    ```
    bzt demo.yml
    ```

Running Your Test from Apache Maven

If your project uses *Apache Maven*, there is a plugin named JMeter Maven Plugin (https://github.com/jmeter-maven-plugin/jmeter-maven-plugin).

For *Maven*, everything happens in the **pom.xml** file (POM stands for **Project Object Model**).

Add a **<build>** section to your **pom.xml** as follows:

```xml
<?xml version="1.0" encoding="UTF-8"?>

 <project xmlns="http://maven.apache.org/POM/4.0.0" xmlns:xsi="http://www.
w3.org/2001/XMLSchema-instance" xsi:schemaLocation="http://maven.apache.org/
POM/4.0.0 http://maven.apache.org/xsd/maven-4.0.0.xsd">

        <modelVersion>4.0.0.0</modelVersion>

        <groupId>org.awesomebooks</groupId>

        <artifactId>masterjmeter</artifactId>

        <version>1.0-SNAPSHOT</version>

        <name>maven-jmeter-demo</name>

        <packaging>pom</packaging>

        <properties>
```

```xml
        <project.build.sourceEncoding>UTF-8</project.build.sourceEncoding>
    </properties>
    <build>
<plugins>
    <plugin>
        <groupId>com.lazerycode.jmeter</groupId>
        <artifactId>jmeter-maven-plugin</artifactId>
        <version>2.8.5</version>
        <executions>
            <execution>
                <id>jmeter-tests</id>
                <phase>verify</phase>
                <goals>
                    <goal>jmeter</goal>
                </goals>
            </execution>
            <execution>
                <id>jmeter-check-results</id>
                <goals>
                    <goal>results</goal>
                </goals>
            </execution>
        </executions>
    </plugin>
</plugins>
    </build>
</project>
```

Then add your scripts to the `${project.base.base.directory}/src/test/jmeter` directory.

Finally, all we have to do now is to execute *Maven*:

```
mvn clean verify
```

> **Note**
> We run *goal verify* because the POM file refers to the *verify phase* (<phase>verify</phase>).

At the end of the load test, you get the HTML report from JMeter and the build will be marked *Failed* if errors are present:

Figure 11.6: Result of a Maven test

Of course, other features are available (for instance, for selecting what tests to run, for using plugins, for modifying properties, for running distributed tests, and more).

> **Note**
> To read about these features, refer to the plugin site (https://github.com/jmeter-maven-plugin/jmeter-maven-plugin/wiki).

Running Your Test from Jenkins

In the context of continuous integration/testing, it is possible, as we will see in *Chapter 13*, *Integration of JMeter in the DevOps Tool Chain*, to run tests from *Jenkins*.

Running Your Test from Apache Ant

It is also possible to run your test with *Apache Ant*.

This allows you to easily integrate JMeter into the development life cycle.

In the *extra* directory of JMeter, there is an example of a **build.xml** file to use JMeter and *Ant*.

To use it, simply run **ant** as follows:

```
ant -Dtest=myScript
```

myScript should be the name of the JMeter script file without its extension.

For example:

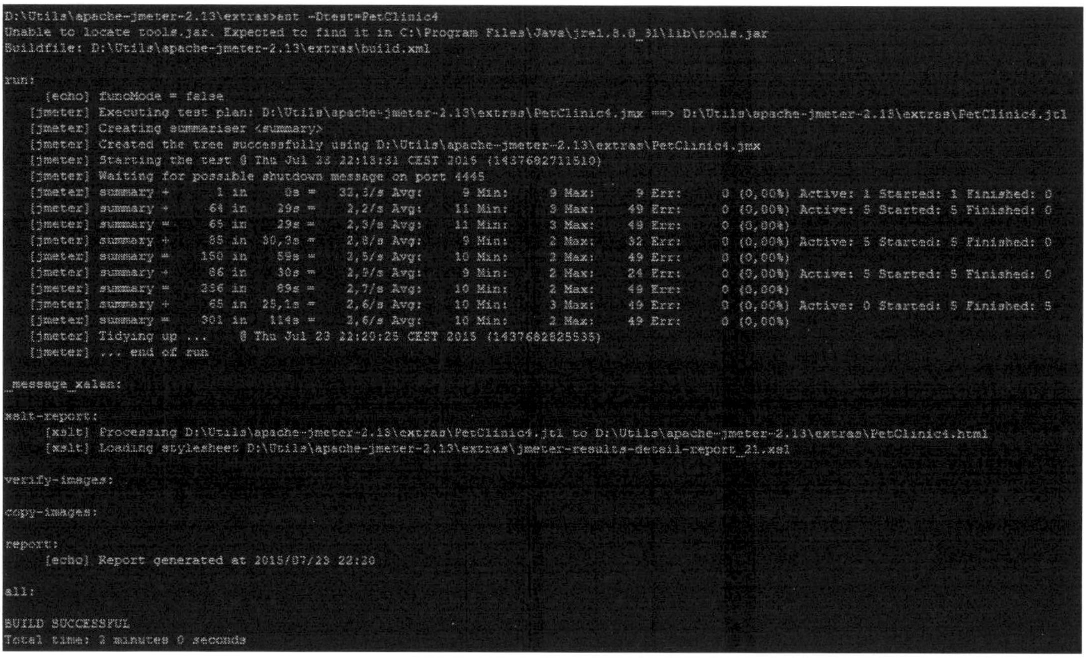

```
D:\Utils\apache-jmeter-2.13\extras>ant -Dtest=PetClinic4
Unable to locate tools.jar. Expected to find it in C:\Program Files\Java\jre1.8.0_31\lib\tools.jar
Buildfile: D:\Utils\apache-jmeter-2.13\extras\build.xml

run:
     [echo] funcMode = false
   [jmeter] Executing test plan: D:\Utils\apache-jmeter-2.13\extras\PetClinic4.jmx ==> D:\Utils\apache-jmeter-2.13\extras\PetClinic4.jtl
   [jmeter] Creating summariser <summary>
   [jmeter] Created the tree successfully using D:\Utils\apache-jmeter-2.13\extras\PetClinic4.jmx
   [jmeter] Starting the test @ Thu Jul 23 22:18:31 CEST 2015 (1437682711510)
   [jmeter] Waiting for possible shutdown message on port 4445
   [jmeter] summary +      1 in     0s =   33,3/s Avg:     9 Min:     9 Max:     9 Err:     0 (0,00%) Active: 1 Started: 1 Finished: 0
   [jmeter] summary +     64 in    29s =    2,2/s Avg:    11 Min:     3 Max:    49 Err:     0 (0,00%) Active: 5 Started: 5 Finished: 0
   [jmeter] summary =     65 in    29s =    2,3/s Avg:    11 Min:     3 Max:    49 Err:     0 (0,00%)
   [jmeter] summary +     85 in  30,3s =    2,8/s Avg:     9 Min:     2 Max:    32 Err:     0 (0,00%) Active: 5 Started: 5 Finished: 0
   [jmeter] summary =    150 in    59s =    2,5/s Avg:    10 Min:     2 Max:    49 Err:     0 (0,00%)
   [jmeter] summary +     86 in    30s =    2,9/s Avg:     9 Min:     2 Max:    24 Err:     0 (0,00%) Active: 5 Started: 5 Finished: 0
   [jmeter] summary =    236 in    89s =    2,7/s Avg:    10 Min:     2 Max:    49 Err:     0 (0,00%)
   [jmeter] summary +     65 in  25,1s =    2,6/s Avg:    10 Min:     3 Max:    49 Err:     0 (0,00%) Active: 0 Started: 5 Finished: 5
   [jmeter] summary =    301 in   114s =    2,6/s Avg:    10 Min:     2 Max:    49 Err:     0 (0,00%)
   [jmeter] Tidying up ...    @ Thu Jul 23 22:20:25 CEST 2015 (1437682825535)
   [jmeter] ... end of run

_message_xalan:

xslt-report:
     [xslt] Processing D:\Utils\apache-jmeter-2.13\extras\PetClinic4.jtl to D:\Utils\apache-jmeter-2.13\extras\PetClinic4.html
     [xslt] Loading stylesheet D:\Utils\apache-jmeter-2.13\extras\jmeter-results-detail-report_21.xsl

verify-images:

copy-images:

report:
     [echo] Report generated at 2015/07/23 22:20

all:

BUILD SUCCESSFUL
Total time: 2 minutes 0 seconds
```

Figure 11.7: Result of a test run with Ant

At the end of the execution, you get a report in HTML format:

Load Test Results

Date report: 2015/07/23 22:20   Designed for use with JMeter and Ant.

Summary

# Samples	Failures	Success Rate	Average Time	Min Time	Max Time
301	0	100.00%	10 ms	2 ms	49 ms

Pages

URL	# Samples	Failures	Success Rate	Average Time	Min Time	Max Time	
Echantillon BeanShell	1	0	100.00%	9 ms	9 ms	9 ms	+
Clients_00_HomePage	100	0	100.00%	6 ms	2 ms	49 ms	+
Clients_01_Find_Owners_Page	100	0	100.00%	6 ms	2 ms	11 ms	+
Clients_02_Owner_Information_Page	100	0	100.00%	18 ms	6 ms	49 ms	+

Figure 11.8: Ant HTML report

Summary

# Samples	Failures	Success Rate	Average Time	Min Time	Max Time
301	0	100.00%	10 ms	2 ms	49 ms

Pages

URL	# Samples	Failures	Success Rate	Average Time	Min Time	Max Time	
Echantillon BeanShell	1	0	100.00%	9 ms	9 ms	9 ms	+
Clients_00_HomePage	100	0	100.00%	6 ms	2 ms	49 ms	+
Clients_01_Find_Owners_Page	100	0	100.00%	6 ms	2 ms	11 ms	+
Clients_02_Owner_Information_Page	100	0	100.00%	18 ms	6 ms	49 ms	−

Details for Page "Clients_02_Owner_Information_Page"

Thread	Iteration	Time (milliseconds)	Bytes	Success
Clients 1-1	1	31	3325	true
Clients 1-2	2	21	4497	true
Clients 1-3	3	17	3326	true
Clients 1-1	4	25	4976	true
Clients 1-4	5	21	3320	true
Clients 1-2	6	20	3330	true
Clients 1-5	7	24	3337	true
Clients 1-3	8	24	4508	true
Clients 1-1	9	10	3326	true

Figure 11.9: Ant HTML report – details

> **Note**
> I'll let you take a closer look at the **build.xml** file to understand how it works.

Best Practices

Now that we know how to run a test, we will discuss some best practices to get the most out of JMeter.

These best practices come from:

- The author's experience
- The JMeter wiki
- Ubik-Ingenierie's blog (http://www.ubik-ingenierie.com/blog/ – with the kind permission of its authors)

Have Well-Prepared Injectors

As we have seen in *Chapter 5, Preparing the Test Environment* (Injectors and Tested Systems), it is important to prepare and calibrate our injectors.

Generating Reports at the End of the Test

The generation of reports during a load test can be very expensive and can introduce problems.

It is therefore strongly recommended to generate them only at the end of a test.

To monitor your test, the best solution is to set up the **Backend Listener** element to give real-time feedback on the test through third-party components such as Grafana and InfluxDB.

Remove all other listeners from your script before running the load test.

If you still want to use one or more listeners, here is a list of those you should absolutely avoid unless you configure them as finely as possible:

Element	Causes
View Results in Table	OutOfMemory Risk
View Results Tree	Risk of OutOfMemory in GUI mode, disk access in CLI mode
Assertion Results	OutOfMemory Risk
Graph Results	Performance Problem

Figure 11.10: List of listeners

> **Note**
> A better way to configure the **View Results Tree** item is to save only errors.

This reduces the consumption of the elements and allows for analysis of the errors that occurred during the test:

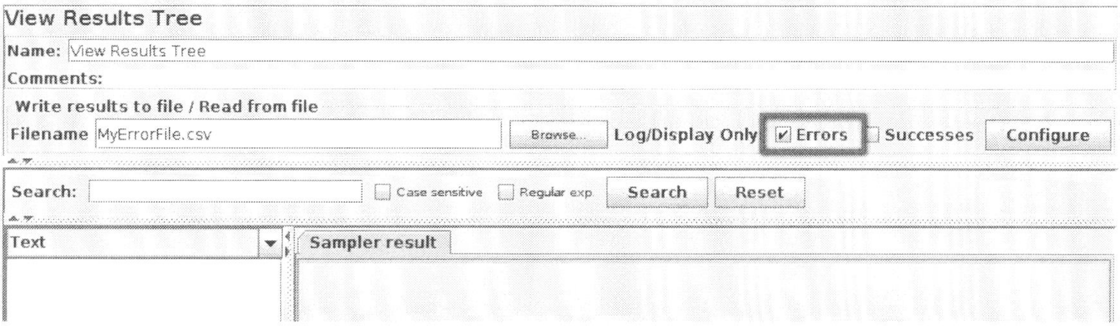

Figure 11.11: Results tree configured to keep errors

Good Use of Extractors

Regular Expression Extractor

The **Regular Expression Extractor** element is very useful, as we have seen in previous chapters. In order to make the best use of it, it is important that it works with the smallest possible amount of data.

To do this, configure the **Apply to** and **Field to check** parts correctly.

For the **Field to check** part, do not use **Body (unescaped)** as it's a performance killer.

Be aware that a wrongly built regular expression can lead to big performance issues in the program that uses it (JMeter here). The blog *Catastrophic Backtracking*, (http://www.regular-expressions.info/catastrophic.html) describes the worst manifestation of the problem in depth. So, be sure to write the most restrictive regular expression when using this extractor:

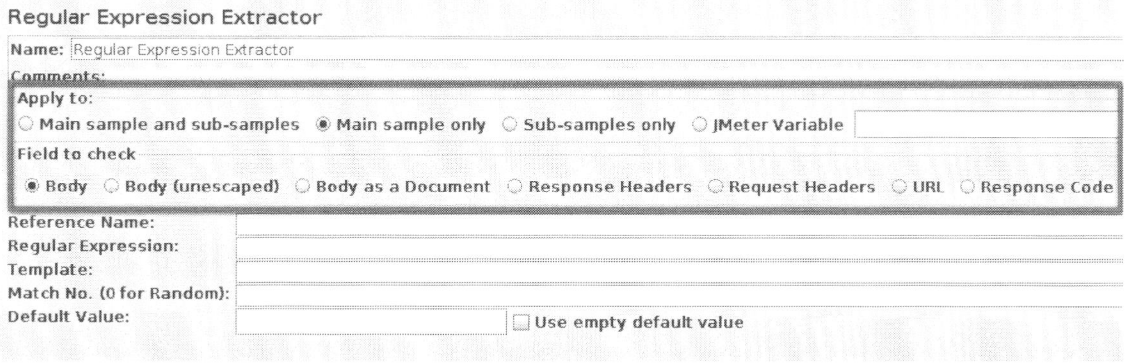

Figure 11.12: Important part of Regular Expression Extractor

XPath Extractor

Don't use **XPath Extractor**, because it is memory- and CPU-intensive (for reasons to do with loading the response into a DOM tree and DOM parsing, respectively). Never use it to parse HTML, as you may have seen in some old blogs. For HTML, you should favor **CSS Selector Extractor** as it's much more powerful and performs better.

Since JMeter 5.0, you should favor **XPath2 Extractor** for XML content, as it performs better and is much more powerful than **XPath Extractor**. It enables the easy use of namespaces in XPath queries and supports the XPath 2.0 syntax.

Extractor Performance

In terms of performance, we sort the extractors here from the best-performing extractor (at the start of the list) to the worst-performing extractor (at the bottom):

- **Boundary Extractor**
- **Regular Expression Extractor**
- **JSON Extractor**
- **CSS Selector Extractor**
- **XPath2 Extractor**
- **XPath Extractor**

Use Assertions with Care

Our advice is to use an **Assertion** after each transaction/request. But ensure you use **Response Assertion** (prefer *substring* instead of *contains*) and **Size Assertion**, which should cover the majority of your needs. When your assertion check text contains a variable that can vary a lot, you should fill in **Custom failure message** to avoid having so many rows in the HTML error report that it is unreadable.

Avoid the most expensive assertions:

- **XML Assertion**
- **XML Schema Assertion**
- **XPath Assertion**

Good Use of Custom Scripting

There are many ways to extend JMeter:

- BeanShell, using all BeanShell elements
- JavaScript, using the `__javaScript` function and JSR223 test elements with JavaScript as the language
- Any JSR223 language

BeanShell was the first language available to extend JMeter, but it is now old, doesn't understand Java syntax higher than 5.0, and performs slowly compared to alternatives, so our advice is to move to JSR223 test elements with Groovy.

You'll get all the power of the Groovy language, better error messages, better performance, and the ability to use the latest Java features.

JavaScript is also a way to extend JMeter; it is a very popular language, but you should be aware when using it in JMeter that it reduces Jmeter's scalability due to its bad performance under high thread contention compared to Groovy.

In summary, use JSR223 test elements combined with Groovy to get the most out of JMeter:

> **Note**
> Don't forget to check *Cache compiled script if available*.

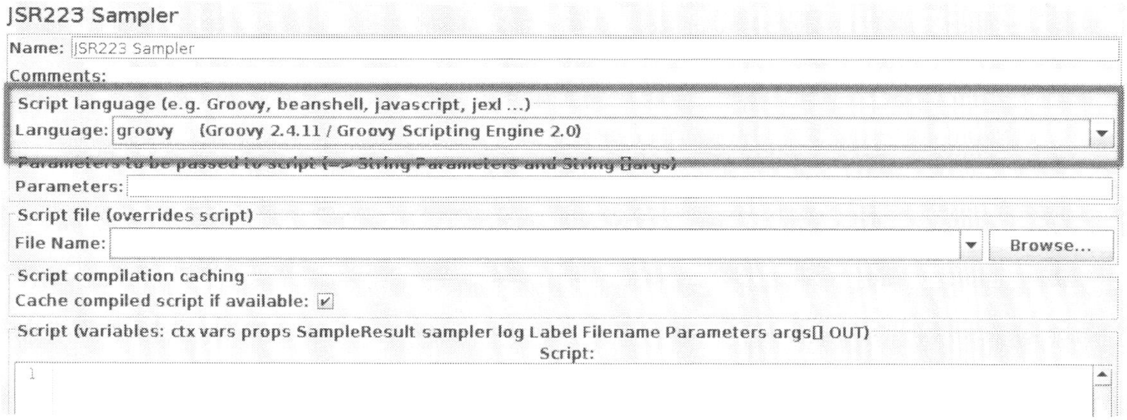

Figure 11.13: Using Groovy in JSR223 Sampler

Conclusion

As we have seen, JMeter can be adapted to many use cases. Whether by the command line, by its GUI, or with a preferred integration tool (*Ant*, *Maven*, or *Jenkins*, for example), by following some good practices, it is easily possible to perform a load test.

Before moving on to the integration of JMeter in a DevOps environment, let's look at how to use the results of a test.

12

Visualizing and Analyzing the Load Testing Results

Introduction

Visualizing and analyzing the results of a load test is an important step.

It allows us to:

- Validate that our scripting is realistic (by checking that the number of executions of business transactions during the test run matches the expected number).
- Debug the script.
- Know how the targeted platform handles the load.
- See how the response times evolve over time.
- See what errors and issues occur.

Viewing results from JMeter is based on **Listener** elements.

JMeter allows the recording of results in different formats:

- CSV files are the default format. The data comes in as one line per sample at a particular time, and the fields are separated by a configurable separator (by default, the comma).

- An XML file that stores the different fields as tags or XML attributes. It allows us to fully record the sent and received data, thus providing an exhaustive view of the requests and responses, allowing us to analyze the errors.

- As data in databases like InfluxDB, Elasticsearch, Graphite, and so on.

Visualizing the Results with Listeners

JMeter provides a lot of listeners (and even more through JMeter plugins). That is why we will focus on the most important ones.

View Results Tree

View Results Tree provides the most detailed view of the test sample, **Transaction Controller**, or **Response Assertion**.

It indicates the response times and various information concerning the result (size in bytes, latency, state, and so on), the response headers, and the response data, but also the request headers and any data transmitted with all of its parameters.

This receiver is particularly useful during the development of a test scenario, notably thanks to the testers (Regexp, CSS Selector, XPath2, and Boundary).

> **Note**
> In graphical mode (GUI mode), since this component stores a lot of data, it will impact injection, so make sure to only use GUI mode for debugging.
>
> To reduce the risk of OutOfMemory errors, the last few versions of JMeter keep only 500 sample results (adjustable through the `view.results.tree.max_results` property) by default and refreshes the screen at regular intervals.

Sampler result Tab

The **Sampler result** tab displays a summary of the sampler result:

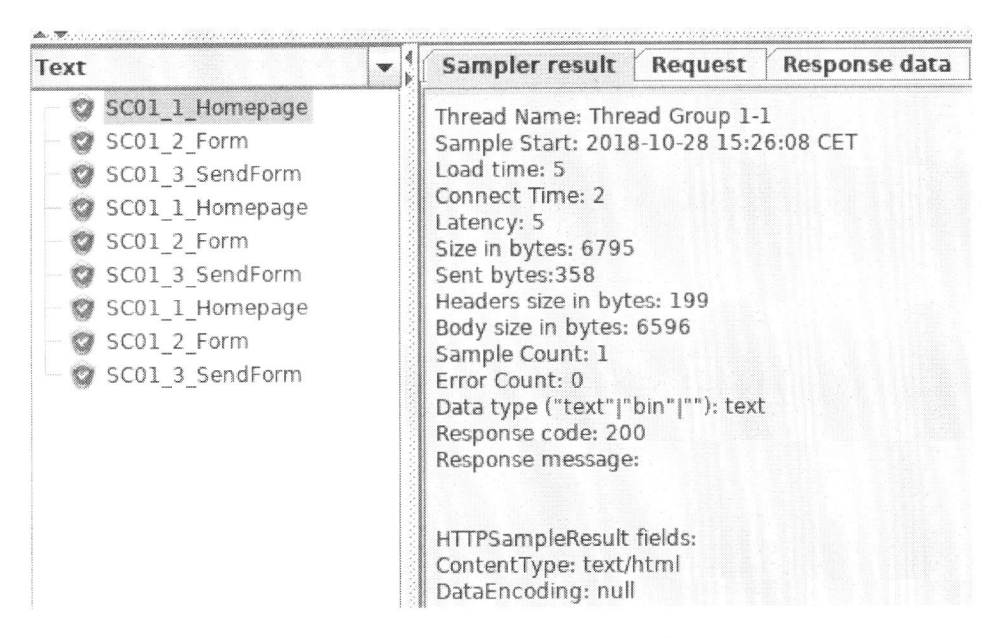

```
Sampler result | Request | Response data

Thread Name: Thread Group 1-1
Sample Start: 2018-10-28 15:26:08 CET
Load time: 5
Connect Time: 2
Latency: 5
Size in bytes: 6795
Sent bytes:358
Headers size in bytes: 199
Body size in bytes: 6596
Sample Count: 1
Error Count: 0
Data type ("text"|"bin"|""): text
Response code: 200
Response message:


HTTPSampleResult fields:
ContentType: text/html
DataEncoding: null
```

Figure 12.1: Sampler result tab

The fields for the first tab, **Sampler result**, relate to the response times and different performance indicators for the query.

It also provides additional information for the sent request, such as the data encoding and content type used.

Request Tab

The **Request** tab displays the data transmitted in the request to the server.

It's composed of two tabs.

350 | Visualizing and Analyzing the Load Testing Results

The **Request Body** tab contains the following:

- The URL generated by JMeter with, if necessary, the parameters sent in the HTTP method
- Any data in the HTTP method, if it's a method that allows a body
- Cookie data (if any)

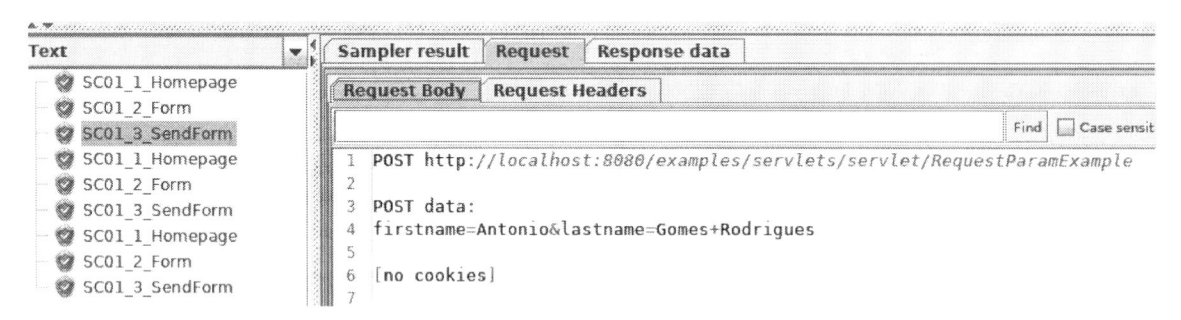

Figure 12.2: Request Body tab

The **Request Headers** tab shows the following information:

Sent HTTP headers (often through the **HTTP Header Manager**)

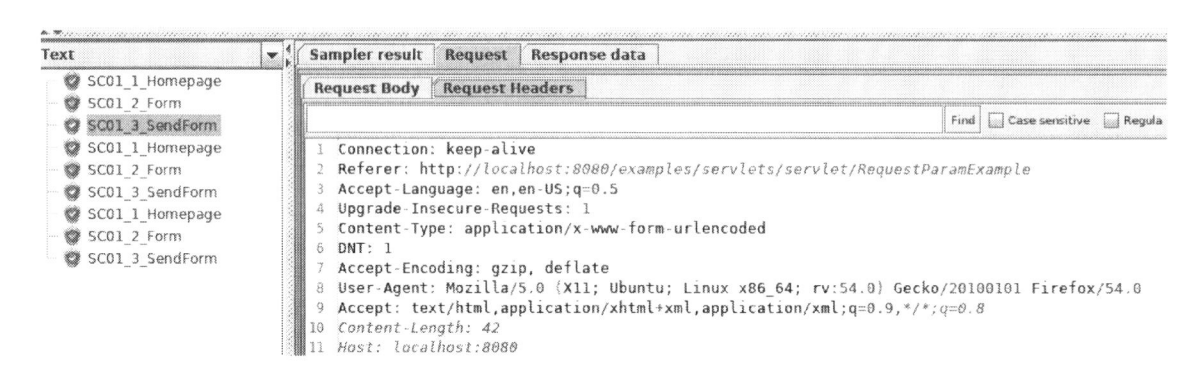

Figure 12.3: Request Headers tab

Response Data Tab

The **Response data** tab is also composed of two tabs.

The **Response Body** tab is used to do the following:

- Change the display format of the response data.
- You will usually select the **Tester** that is the most suitable for the response format and validate that your extractors work as expected.

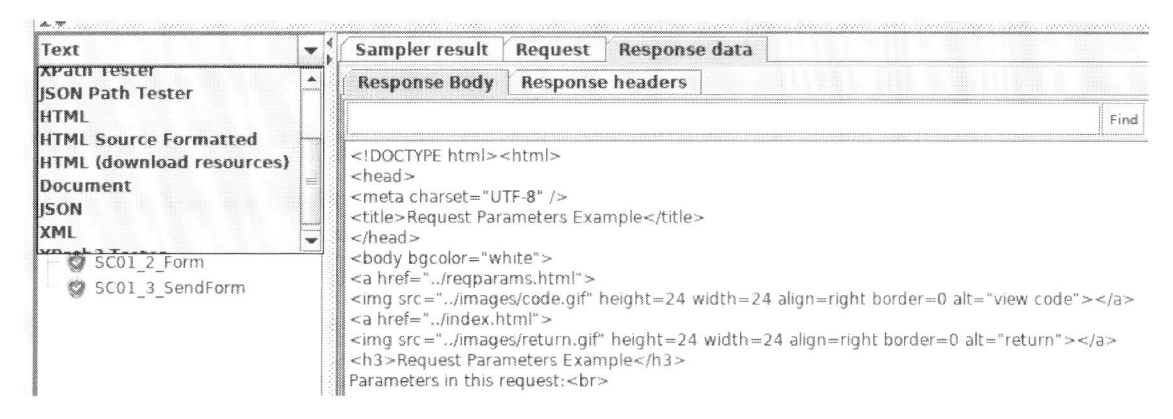

Figure 12.4: Response Body tab

Response headers Tab

Response headers

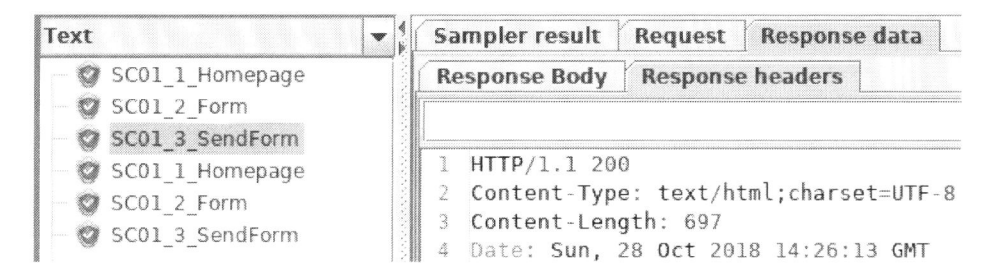

Figure 12.5: Response headers tab

Summary Report

Summary Report gives statistics of response times and results based on the label of the samples or transaction controller:

Figure 12.6: Summary Report

Aggregate Report

Aggregate Report is the same as **Summary Report**, but with percentiles:

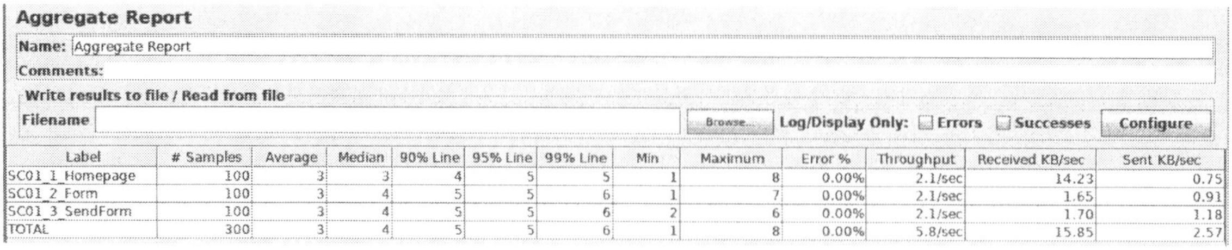

Label	# Samples	Average	Median	90% Line	95% Line	99% Line	Min	Maximum	Error %	Throughput	Received KB/sec	Sent KB/sec
SC01_1_Homepage	100	3	3	4	5	5	1	8	0.00%	2.1/sec	14.23	0.75
SC01_2_Form	100	3	4	5	5	6	1	7	0.00%	2.1/sec	1.65	0.91
SC01_3_SendForm	100	3	4	5	5	6	2	6	0.00%	2.1/sec	1.70	1.18
TOTAL	300	3	4	5	5	6	1	8	0.00%	5.8/sec	15.85	2.57

Figure 12.7: Aggregate Report

Note that it is possible to modify the desired percentile values using these properties:

- `aggregate_rpt_pct1=90`
- `aggregate_rpt_pct2=95`
- `aggregate_rpt_pct3=99`

> **Note**
> **Summary Report** performs better than **Aggregate Report** in graphical mode, but percentiles are the correct values to report.

Backend Listener

Since version 2.13 of JMeter, the **Backend Listener** has been added.

This receiver allows us to send measures to a third-party system such as Graphite (http://graphite.wikidot.com/), InfluxDB (https://influxdb.com/), or Elasticsearch (https://www.elastic.co).

The benefits are the following:

- Have real-time results during the load test.
- Store the results of tests in a durable way for future comparison.
- Be able to compare test results over time.
- Be able to create whatever graph we want from the data using libraries such as Grafana (https://grafana.com/) or Kibana (https://www.elastic.co/products/kibana).

- Centralize the measures of JMeter with our other monitoring metrics (including system measurements from CollectD (https://collectd.org/) or Telegraf (https://www.influxdata.com/time-series-platform/telegraf/), JMX measurements from JMXTrans (http://www.jmxtrans.org/), measures from AWS CloudWatch (https://aws.amazon.com/cloudwatch/), and so on).

- Be able to use the advanced capabilities (such as alerts, automatic report generation, and so on) of the third-party system.

- Share web dashboards with other teams and management and so on

For using the **Backend Listener**, nothing could be simpler – just add a **Backend Listener** to your test plan:

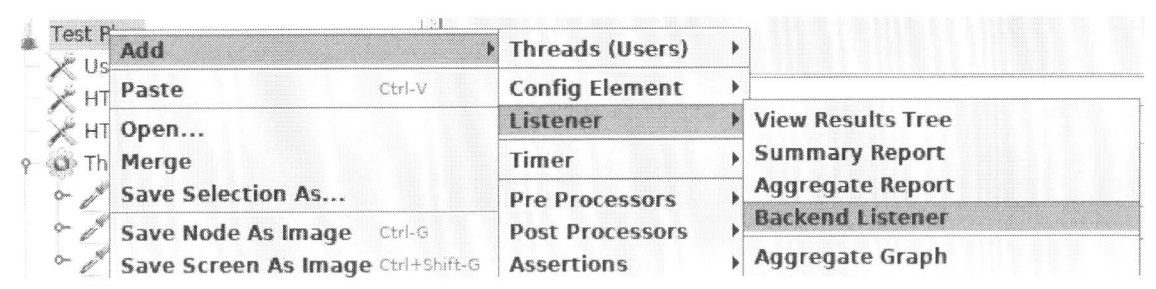

Figure 12.8: Adding a Backend Listener

> **Note**
> Ensure that your third-party system scales well to avoid impacting the test results.

Let's take a closer look at this configuration:

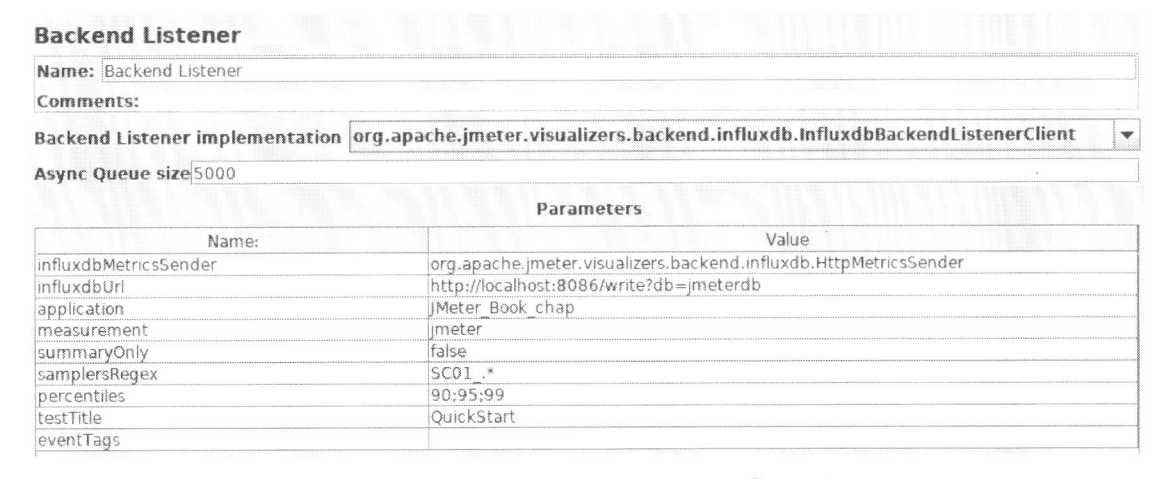

Figure 12.9: Our Backend Listener configuration

354 | Visualizing and Analyzing the Load Testing Results

Let's focus on two parameters in particular.

The **summaryOnly** parameter, when set to *true*, tells JMeter to send only overall information, not specific samples. This makes it possible to limit the number of measures while retaining the ability to see the evolution of the response times.

When we want to have the details of response times per transaction/sample, we set the **summaryOnly** field to **false**.

The other interesting parameter is **samplersRegex**. This is the list of samples for which we want JMeter to create measurements.

This allows us to:

- Reduce the load on JMeter, since it will be computing measurements for a reduced number of Samplers
- Reduce the load on our third-party system
- Make analysis easier

For example, in our test plan, we do not want to compute any metric for the sample SetPathCSV.

Once our **Backend Listener** is set up, as well as our third-party system (we will use InfluxDB), all we have to do is run our test.

Let's look at the same data in Grafana, which makes the display of our data more pleasant to look at:

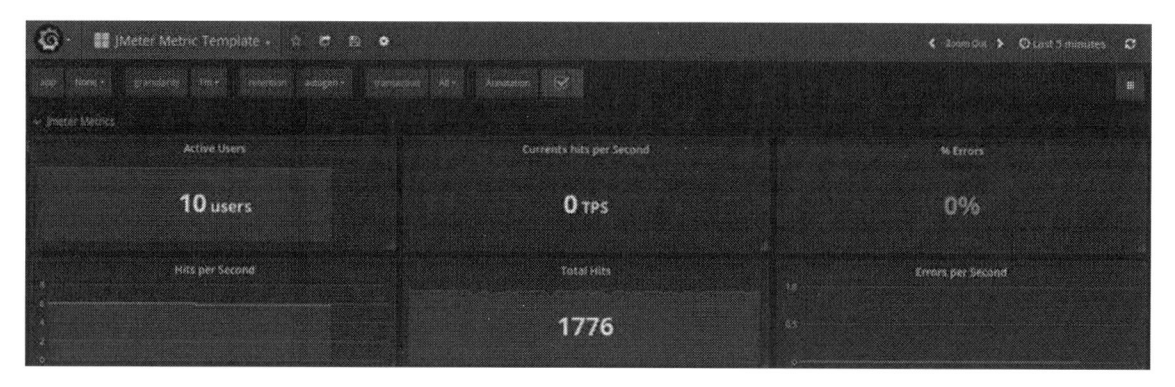

Figure 12.10: Grafana

The **Backend Listener** makes it easy to add other implementations, so you could imagine writing in:

- A database
- A JMS bus
- Datadog (https://www.datadoghq.com/)
- AWS CloudWatch (https://aws.amazon.com/cloudwatch/)
- Elasticsearch (note that there is an implementation by delirius325 (https://github.com/delirius325/jmeter-elasticsearch-backend-listener))

Report Dashboard

Since version 3 of JMeter, it is possible to generate an HTML report at the end of our test.

To do this, we will use the following command line:

```
<JMETER_HOME>/bin/jmeter -n -t [jmx file] -l [results file] -e -o [Path to output folder]
```

It is also possible to generate an HTML report from a result file of a test run at any time by command line or GUI.

In JMeter, go to **Tools** -> `Generate HTML report`:

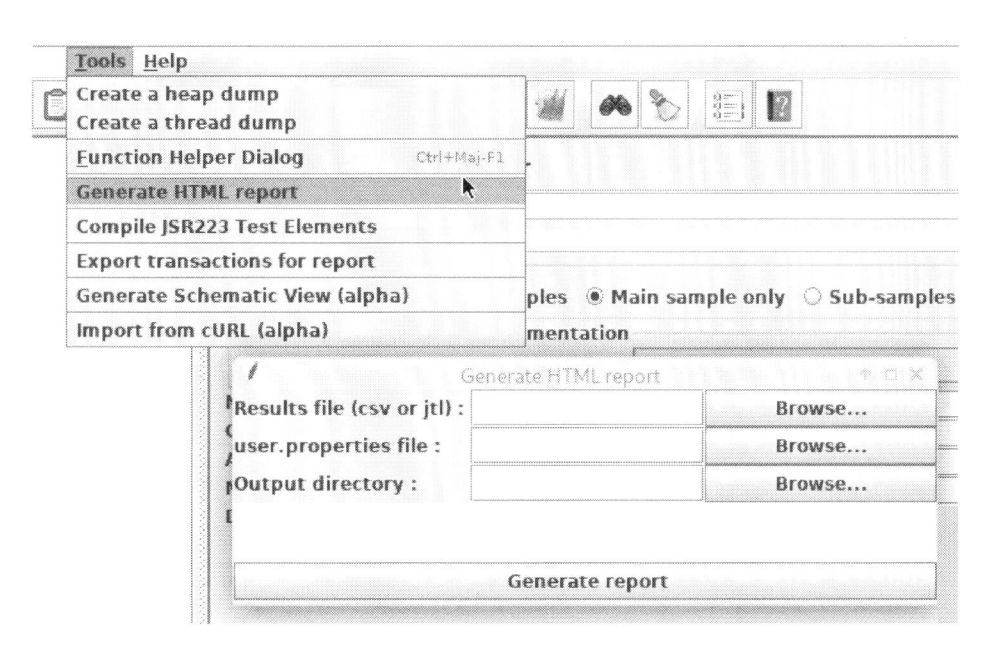

Figure 12.11: HTML report generation from GUI

The report is very rich in data – we've left it for you to look at in the reference documentation (http://jmeter.apache.org/usermanual/generating-dashboard.html).

> **Note**
> When using the Report Dashboard, it is important to **apply naming convention** on the *Transaction Controller* that corresponds to the reported business transactions.
>
> It is also very important to uncheck, in the *Transaction Controller*, the **Generate Parent Sample** property, otherwise, some graphs and tables (errors) will be empty.

Particularities of the Visualization of Results a Distributed Load Test before JMeter 5.0

When using this component in distributed fire mode, be sure to prefix your **Thread Group** with an injector ID. You can use the `__machineName` function, as follows:

```
${__machineName()}_ThreadGroup
```

If you are hosting multiple injectors on the same machine, you can pass a property to each injector and use it in the name to ensure uniqueness:

```
${__machineName()}_${__P(JVM_ID)}_ThreadGroup
```

> **Note**
> Since JMeter 5.0, this is **not** needed anymore since JMeter alone will add the necessary information.

Visualizing the Results with Third Party Visualizing Tools

If listeners are not sufficient, you can use third-party software.

Here is a (non-exhaustive) list of possible software to use:

- Data analysis software, such as Apache Zeppelin, QlikView, Jupyter, R, and so on
- Big data solutions (such as ElasticSearch + Kibana, InfluxDB + Grafana, and so on)
- A spreadsheet such as Microsoft Excel, Apache OpenOffice Calc, LibreOffice Calc, and so on
- Database management software such as Microsoft Access, Apache OpenOffice Base, LibreOffice Base, MySQL, PostgreSQL, SQLite, and so on

- Graphing software such as gnuplot and so on
- A custom program

Visualizing the Results with PaaS Load Testing tools

Another solution to avoid the management of the visualization part (InfluxDB...) is to use PaaS load testing tools.

Redline13

For example, with Redline13 (https://www.redline13.com/) we can plot the following graphs:

Figure 12.12: Redline13's summary report

Figure 12.13: Redline13 Request Metrics

BlazeMeter

As we saw when using Taurus in *Chapter 11, Performing a Load Test*, you can also use BlazeMeter PaaS:

Figure 12.14: BlazeMeter's Summary report

> **Note**
> With a free account, this graph would remain visible for a limited amount of time.

Some Tips to Read the Results

If we don't know how to read the results, our analysis will be false. To prevent this, let's look at some tips.

Prefer Percentiles over Average

Average is used a lot because it's easy to understand and calculate.

But mean and median values do not correctly reflect the user experience:

- They tend to hide outliers.
- They distort reality.
- They hide the distribution of the data.

Different datasets can give you the same average as we can see in Anscombe's quartet (https://en.wikipedia.org/wiki/Anscombe's_quartet) or in this publication (https://www.autodeskresearch.com/publications/samestats).

In these two graphs, the averages are the same and equal to 5.578947368:

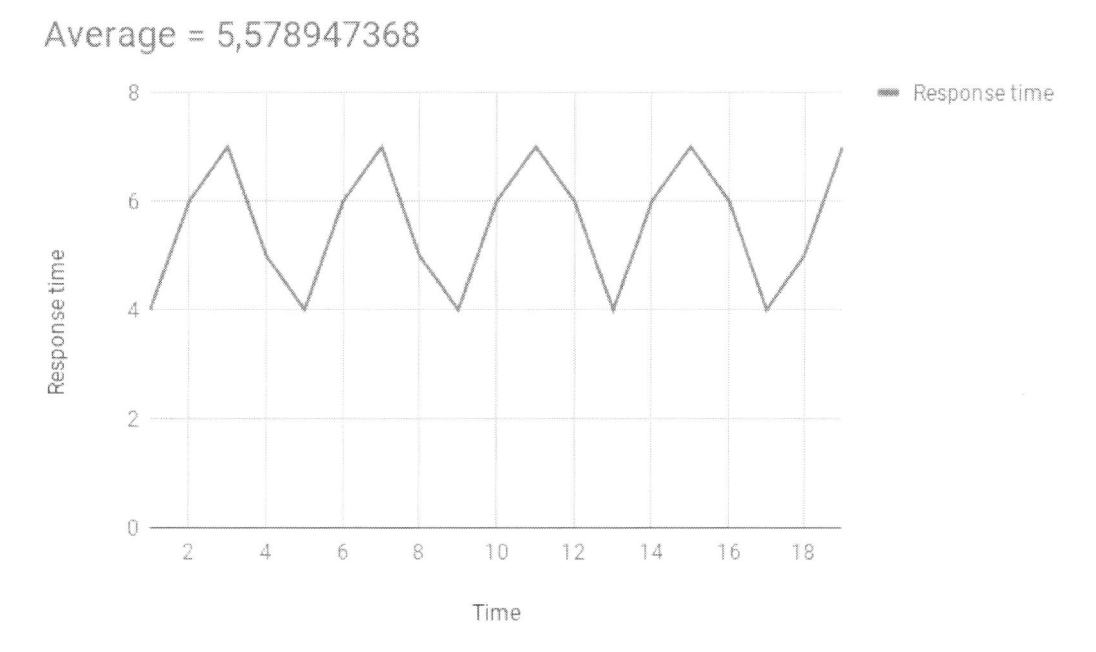

Figure 12.15: Average = 5.578947368

Average = 5,578947368

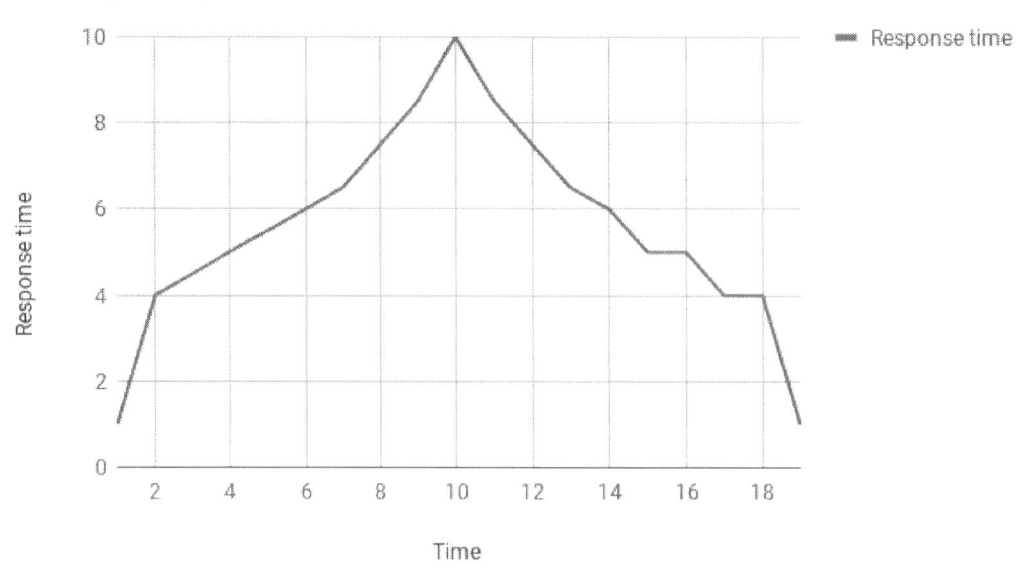

Figure 12.16: The same average as the previous graph (5.578947368)

One solution to solve these problems is to use percentiles (https://en.wikipedia.org/wiki/Percentile).

The XXth percentile (pXX) is the value below which XX% of the values may be found.

But we must be careful with percentiles for the following reasons:

- Just because our 99th percentile is good, it doesn't mean that the response time will be good in real life.

    In real life, we will have the following:

    ```
    % of page views attempts experiencing 99%'ile >= (1 - (0.99^N)) * 100%
    ```

    Where N is the number of [resource requests/objects/HTTP GETs] per page

    For more information, see Gil Tene's blog post called "MOST *page loads will experience the 99%'ile server response*" (http://latencytipoftheday.blogspot.com/2014/06/latencytipoftheday-most-page-loads.html).

- Sometimes, series databases store percentiles as aggregated metrics, collected over a given time frame.

  This means that if we want to have another percentile, we will no longer have the complete distribution of the metric values originally collected. This makes it impossible to calculate this new percentile.

- There are different algorithms for calculating percentiles, and therefore, we can have different results from one tool to the next.

Be Careful with Downsampling and Data Retention

Downsampling is the process of reducing the number of samples in data.

Some time-series databases will only store high-precision data for a limited time and will store the rest of the data with lower accuracy. This means that if we need to make an analysis after downsampling, we will lose accuracy. This is why we should not wait too long to do the analysis in this case.

Here, we have a point every 30 seconds:

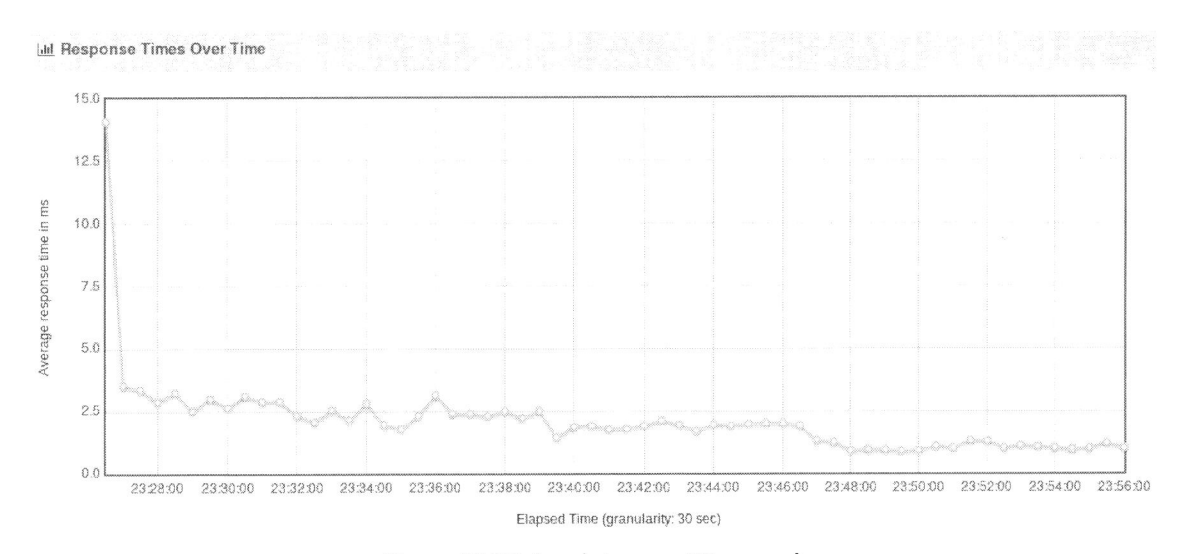

Figure 12.17: A point every 30 seconds

Now let's look at the same data, but with a point every 5 minutes:

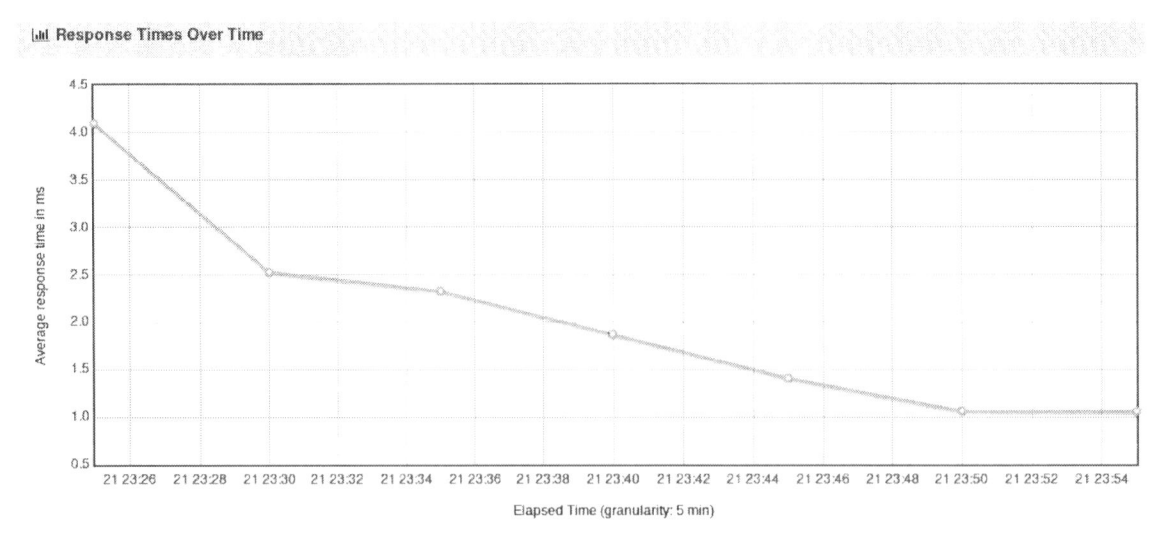

Figure 12.18: A point every 5 minutes

As we can see, with the same data, the results look quite different (the maximum average time is not the same and so on).

If you use a time-series database such as InfluxDB, or monitoring tools such as Dynatrace, you should be aware that data is modified based on:

- Retention policies: data is deleted if it's older than a certain number of days.
- Data aggregation policies: to reduce the volume of data, it is aggregated, increasing the resolution from a few seconds to a few minutes.

So, ensure that you either configure those policies correctly or analyze your results early enough.

Be Careful with Metric Definition

It is also critical to understand the meaning of the metric you are studying. If you don't understand the metric, your interpretation will be false.

For example, average response time in JMeter is:

    network time taken by the request to go from JMeter to the application under test

                            +

    time for the application under test to process the response (backend)

                            +

    network time taken by the response to go from the application under test to JMeter

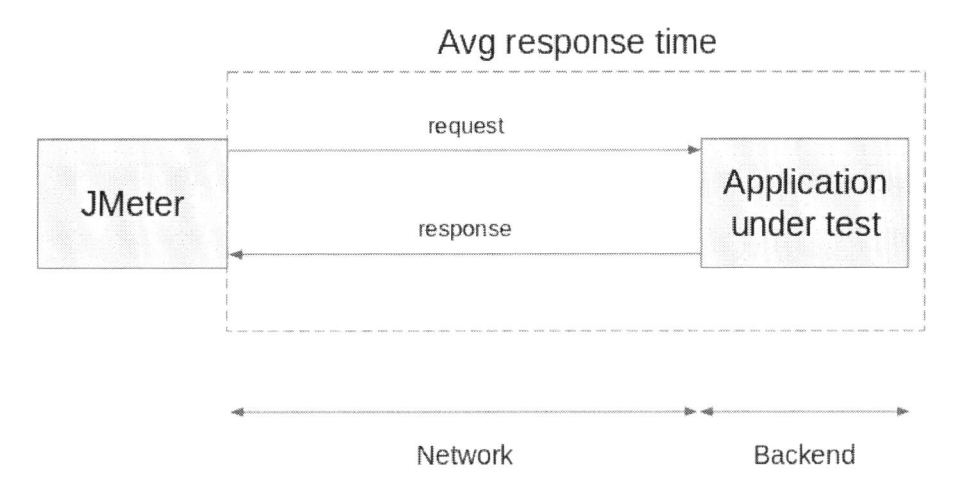

Figure 12.19: Average response time in JMeter

Whereas in a browser, average response time would be:

    network time taken by the request to go from the browser to the application under test

                              +

    time for the application under test to process the response

                            +

    network time taken by the response to go from the application under test to the browser

                            +

    time for the browser to render the response (This is partly defined by WebPerf strategy)

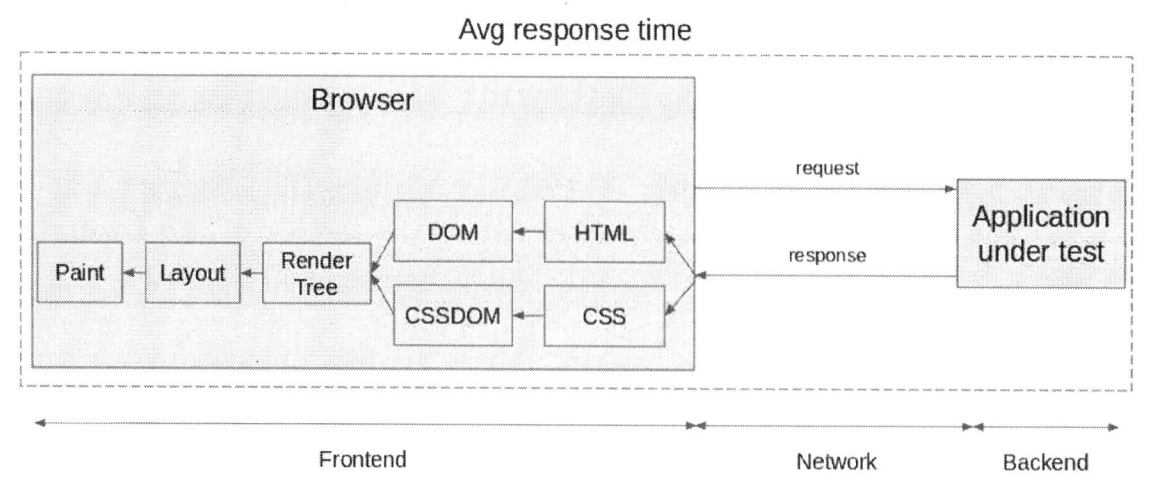

Figure 12.20: Average response time in a browser

Be Careful with Response Time at the Beginning of the Load Test

As we have seen in a previous chapter, at the beginning of the load test, heavy processing on the tested platform side will probably happen as follows:

- Create/initiate resources (database connections, brokers queues, and so on)
- Fill the caches
- Initiate the *auto scaling* mechanism
- Distribute the load uniformly (load balancer and so on)
- The pool size increases
- Warm up the JIT of the JVM/CLR of the tested application

This means that response times during this period will differ from the response times of the rest of the load test. They might be poorer due to application warm-up events, but they might be better due to application degrading under load.

For example, in the next screenshot, we can see that the response times for the few first minutes are higher than the rest, but in this particular case, they are not representative, because we know that the application is warming up after a restart:

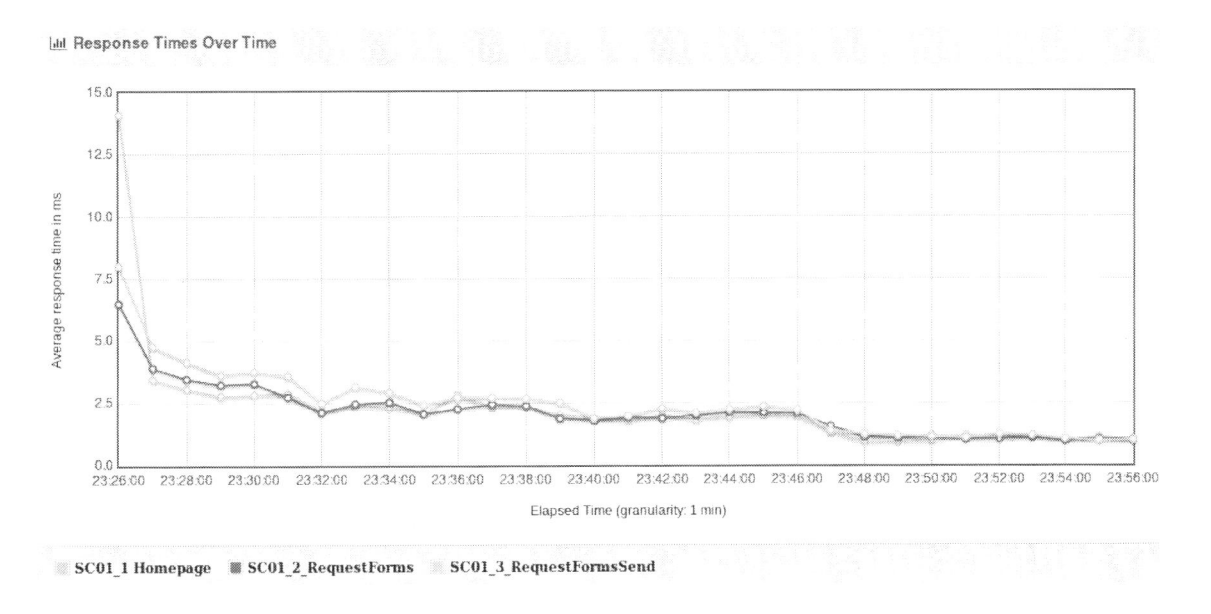

Figure 12.21: The first few minutes after an application restart are not representative

> **Note**
> You should always warm up an application after a restart unless it is the goal of your test to see how the application behaves after a restart.

> **Note**
> Whether to include or exclude the ramp-up from the presented results depends on the use case.
>
> For an e-commerce Black Friday event, for example, extreme ramp-up occurs quite frequently, and you would include the results in your metrics measurements.

Don't Rely on the Metrics of a Short Load Test

Basing the average or percentiles on a few measurements is meaningless and will mislead you.

For example, the 90th percentile for: 15, 35, 56, 32, 21, 12, 33, 300 will be 300.

As you can see, the value 300 has a high impact on the few results we have.

Also, keep in mind that a short load test duration introduces a lot of risks, as discussed in *Chapter 3, Designing a Test Case*.

Check Response Time Distribution

Whatever the metric you choose (percentile, average...), it is important to look at the distribution of response times.

The distribution of response times will allow us to validate the correct behavior of the application.

For example, a response-time graph pattern for a well-performing application will look like a half-normal distribution (https://en.wikipedia.org/wiki/Half-normal_distribution):

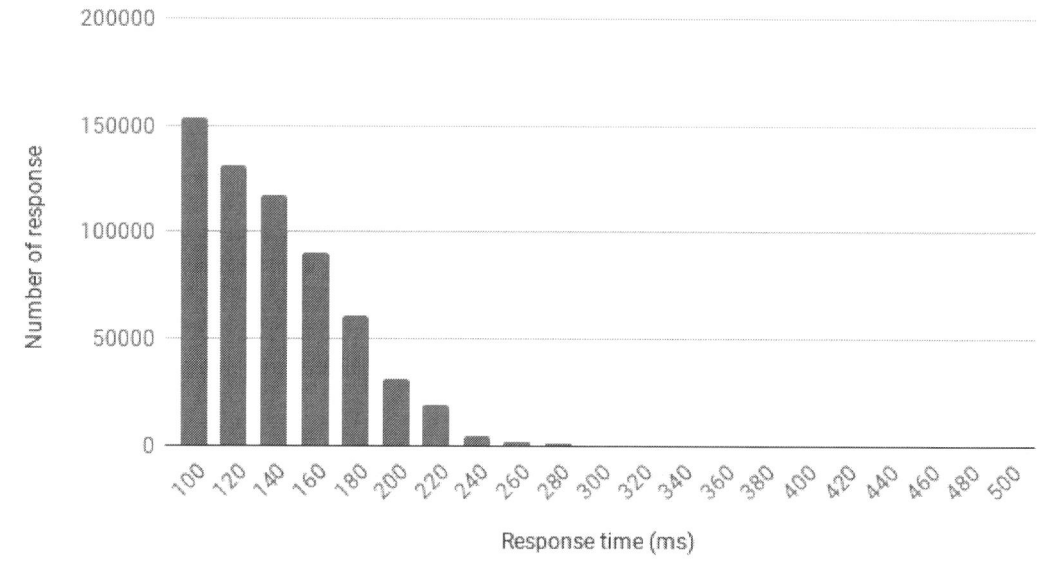

Figure 12.22: Good response time distribution

By contrast, the response-time graph pattern for a poorly performing application will more likely look like:

- Two or more half-normal distributions
- No half-normal distribution at all:

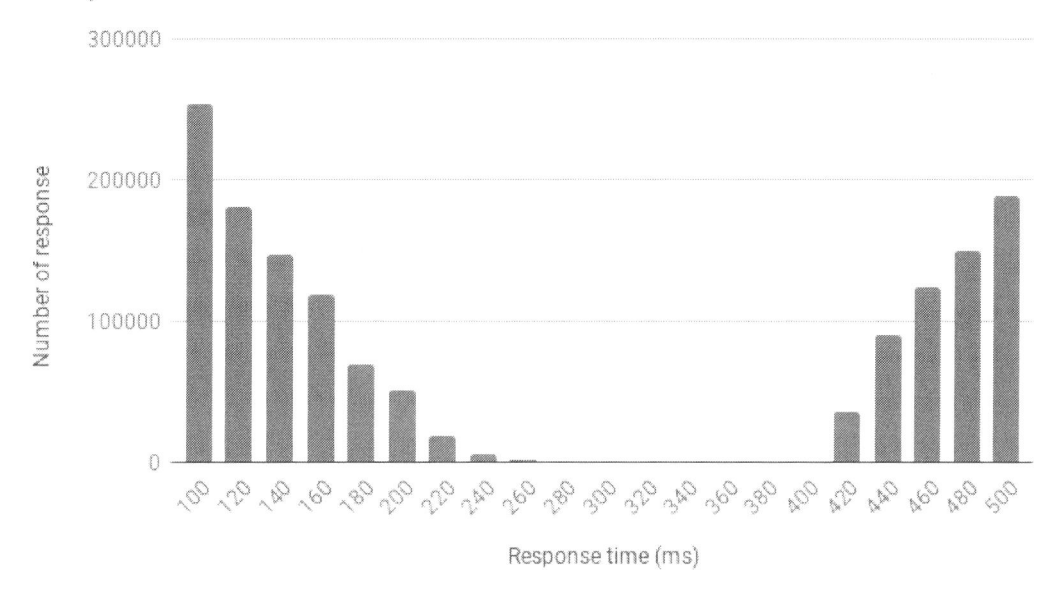

Figure 12.23: Bad response-time distribution

Two bell curves could mean that we have two patterns for the requests, such as, for example:

- Quick requests
- Slow requests that wait for a token in a synchronized part of the system of a slower database

Some Tips to Present the Results

After a load test, we will have found a lot of things. It's then time to present them to:

- Give an idea of response times and stability before going into production
- Allow Ops to fix configuration problems
- Allow developers to fix problems
- Ask for budget increases for hardware/licenses
- Inform the CTO and so on

But presenting numbers through a graph is not as easy as it seems.

To help us, let's look at some tips.

Don't Average Percentiles

Computing the average of percentiles is mathematically incorrect.

Be careful with the tool used to display results:

- Check whether it can compute the new percentile (see the *Prefer Percentiles over Averages* section for more details)
- Check how the tool proceeds with metrics if the screen resolution is too small to display all points

For more details, see Gil Tene's blog post called "*You can't average percentiles. Period.*" (http://latencytipoftheday.blogspot.com/2014/06/latencytipoftheday-you-cant-average.html).

Define the Number of Metrics to Display in a Time Series Line Graph

Line graphs lose their usefulness when too many time series are displayed in one graph:

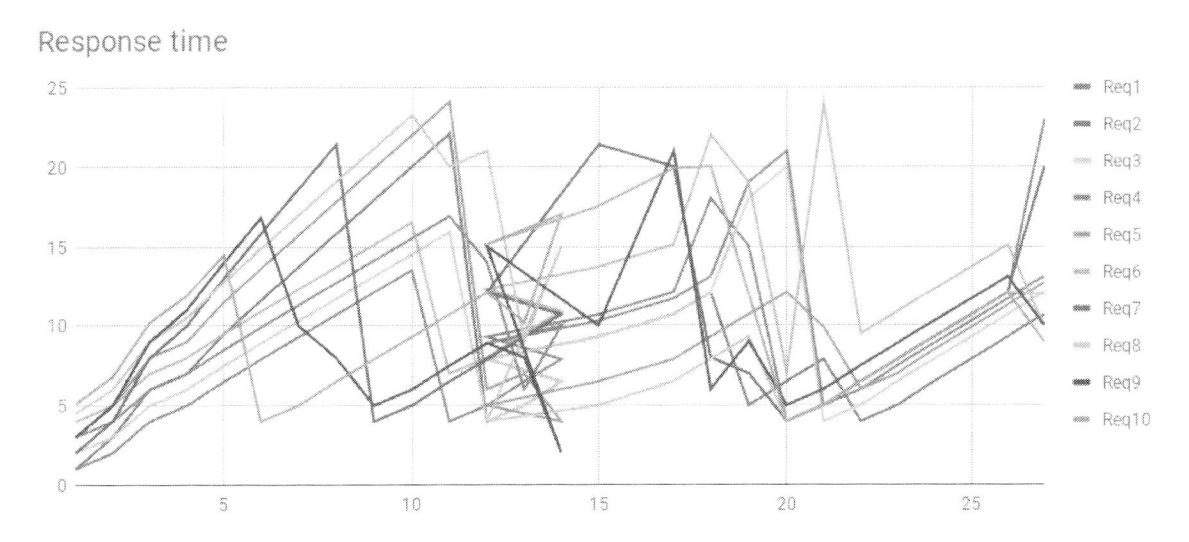

Figure 12.24: Too much metrics

To solve this problem, we need to:

- Ask ourselves what we want to show with every graph.
- Select appropriate metrics.

For example, we have seen a problem during a load test and we want to highlight it. The problem is that:

- Up to 17 VUs, we have a stable response time of around 5s.
- After 18 VUs, the response time becomes unstable.

To do it, we need:
- Active VUs
- Query response time

Response time vs active VU

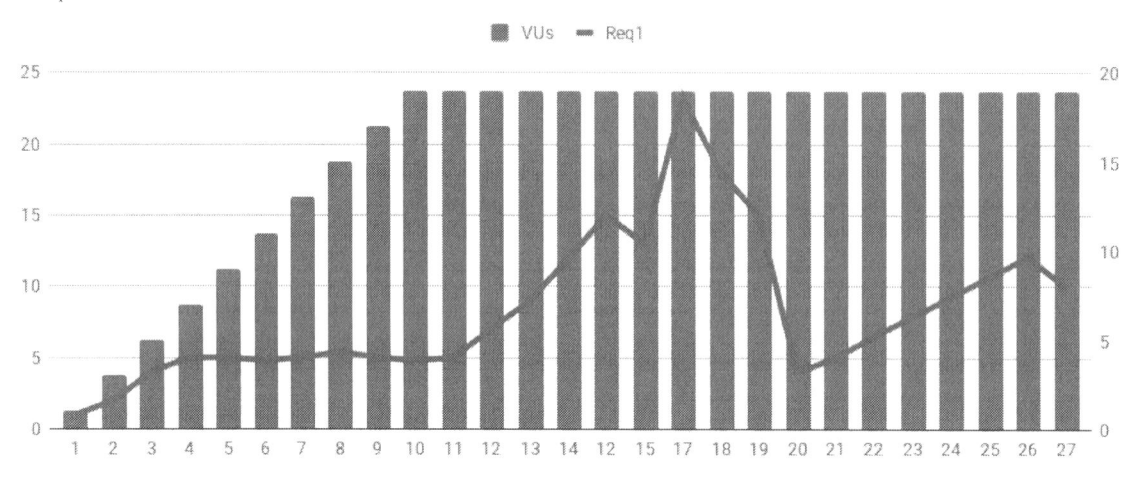

Figure 12.25: Only one goal by graph

Define the Resolution/Granularity of the Measures

As with downsampling, modifying the granularity of the measures can:
- Modify the shape of the graph
- Hide some measures (max and so on)
- Make a graph unreadable
- Make a graph readable

For example, this graph with 1 minute granularity is readable:

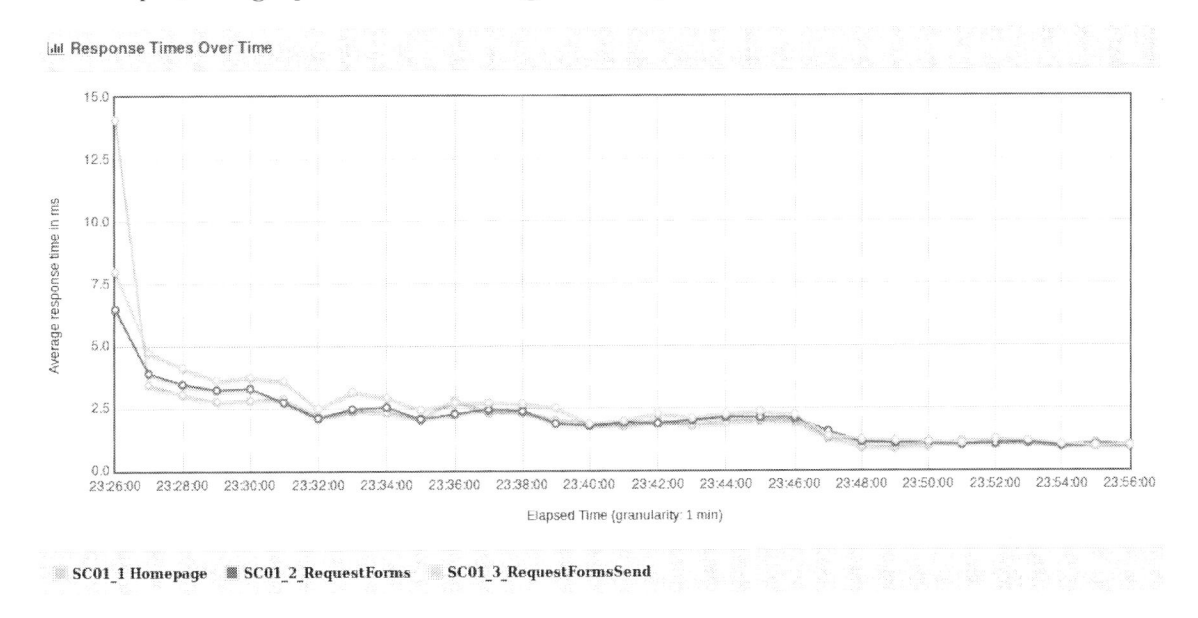

Figure 12.26: Granularity equal to 1 minute

However, the same input but with a 3-second granularity is unreadable:

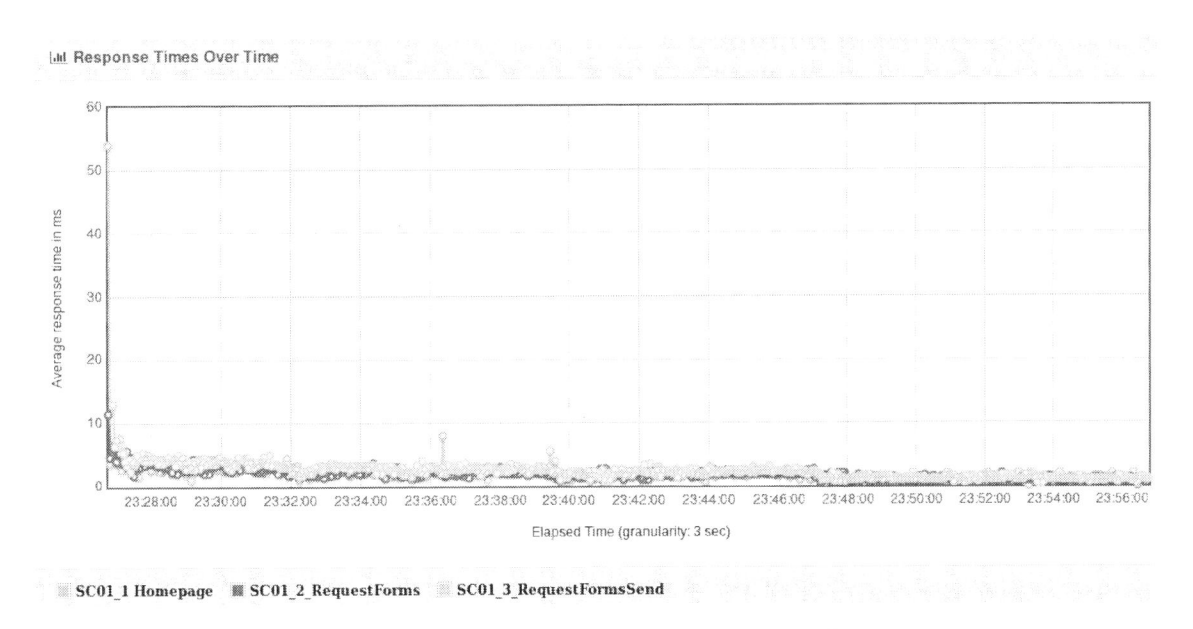

Figure 12.27: Granularity equal to 3 seconds

Don't Forget to Add Labels, Legends, and Units in Graphs

A graph without information (labels, legends, unity, and so on) is useless.

For example, in this graph, we can't guess if the result is fine:

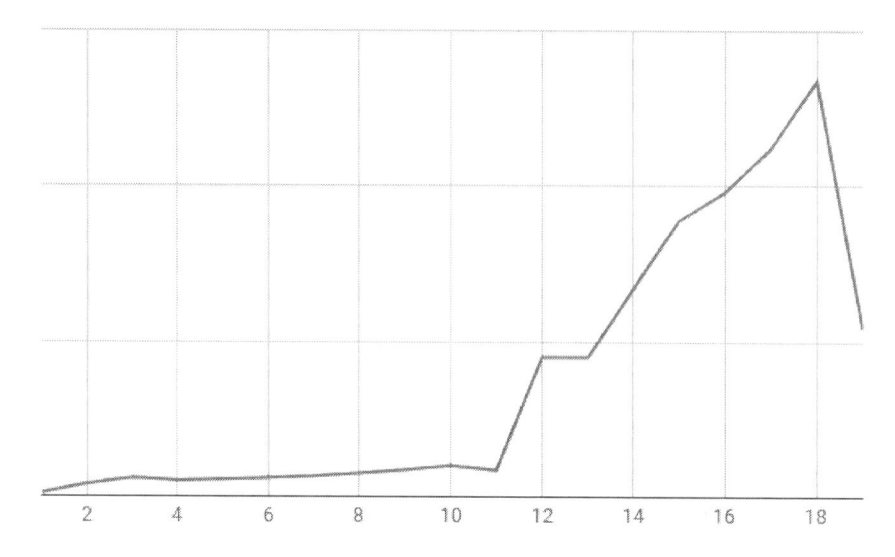

Figure 12.28: Unusable graph

Always add the correct level of details to the chosen graph.

Axis Forced 0

The first impression that emerges from this graph is that the throughput with option 2 is twice as good as the others:

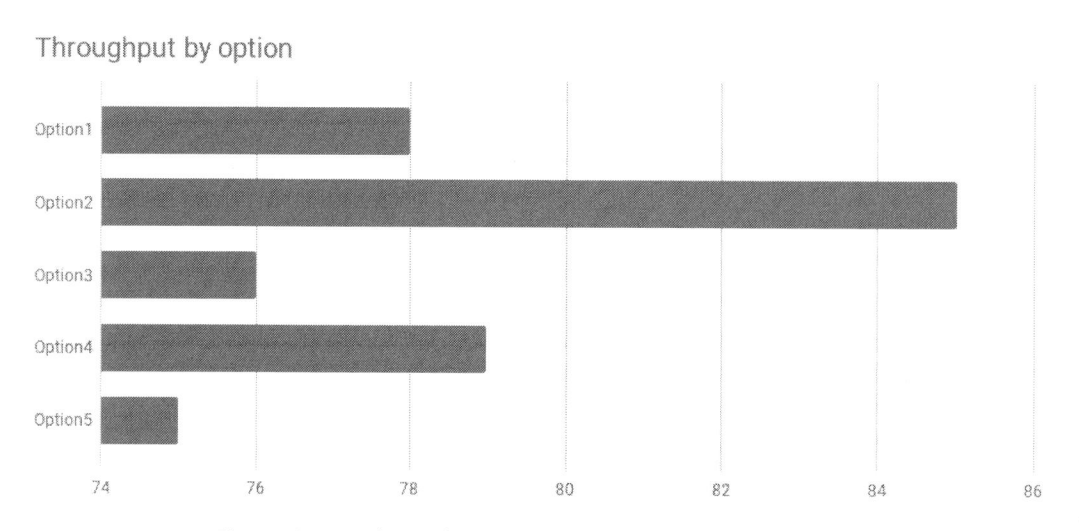

Figure 12.29: Throughput with option 2 is twice as better?

But if we check the starting value on the *x* axis, we can see that it is **74**:

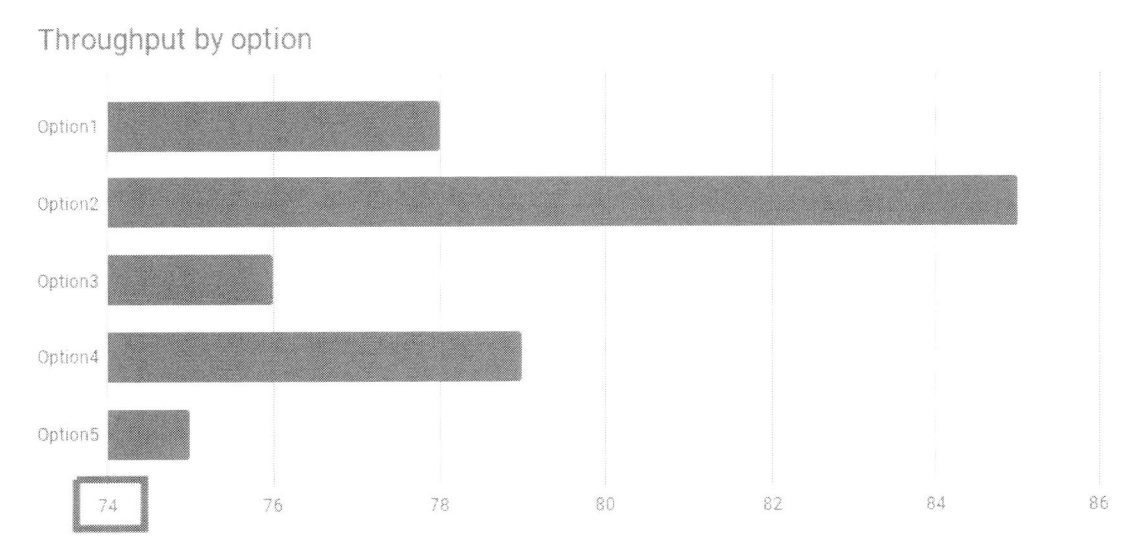

Figure 12.30: Starting value in the x-axis

If we set the *x*-axis to 0, we can see the real difference between the options:

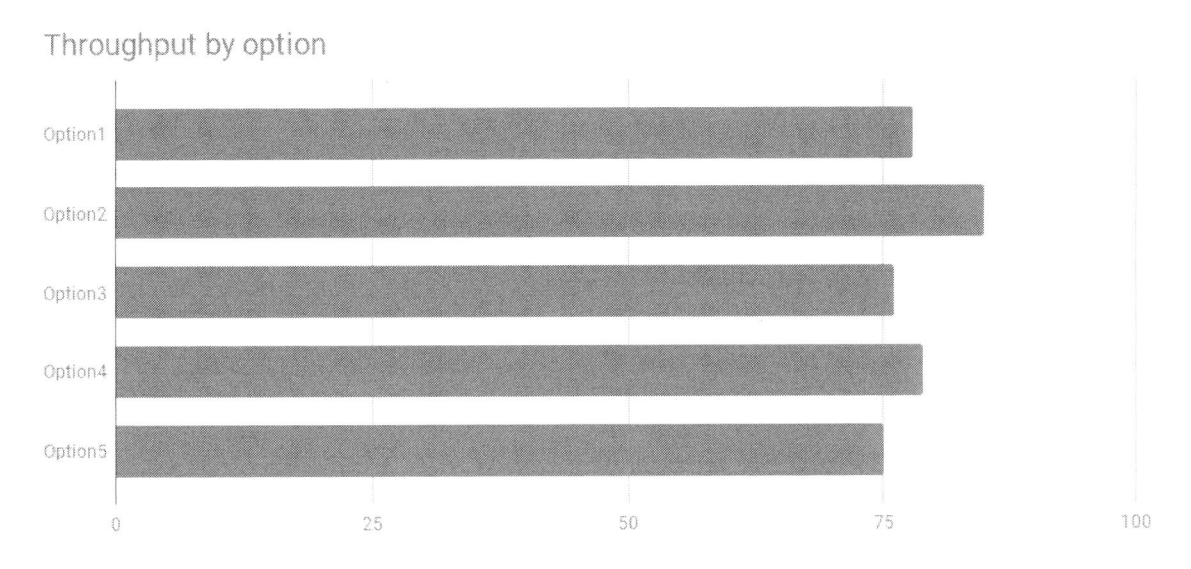

Figure 12.31: x-axis forced to 0

Depending on what you want to show, decide whether or not to force the axis to 0.

Don't Use Pie Charts

As my teacher said: "Don't use pie charts."

There are numerous problems with pie charts:

- It's almost impossible to compare the relative size of the slices:

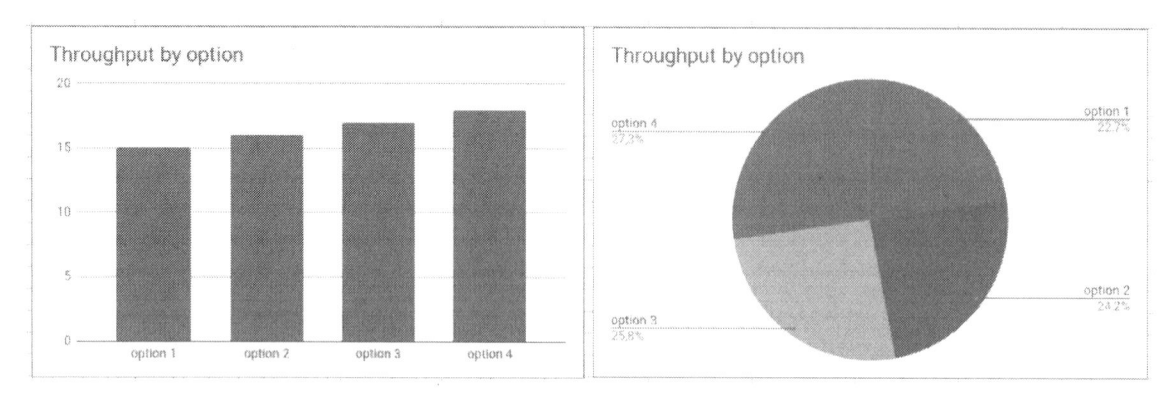

Figure 12.32: A bar chart versus a pie chart

As you can see, the bar chart is a far better solution to compare four options.

- Unreadable when there are lots of slices or some of the slices are ridiculously small:

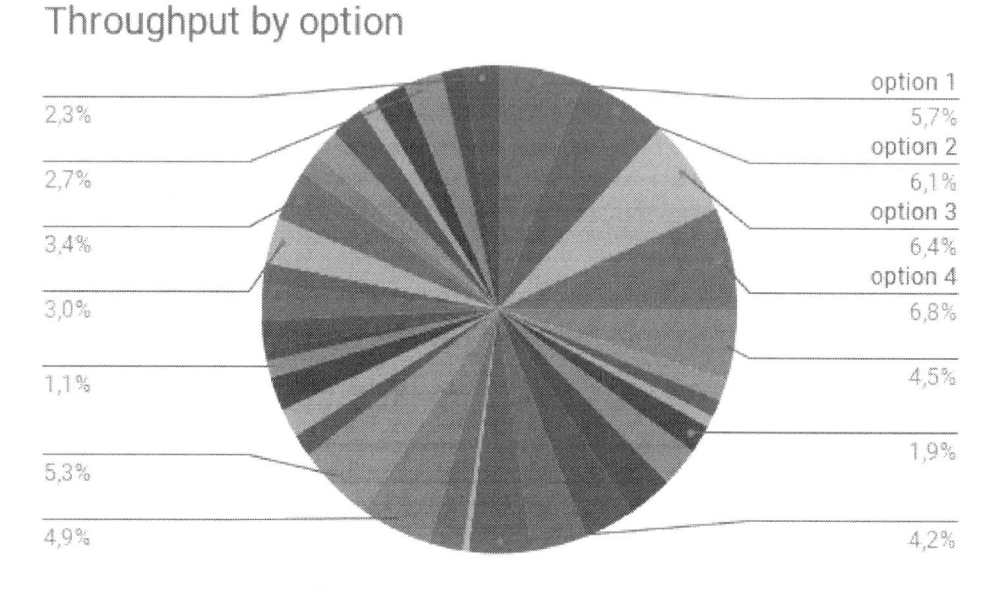

Figure 12.33: Unreadable pie chart

Prefer Bar Graphs When We Have Sparse Metrics

Time series line graphs are a poor choice for sparse metrics because the graphing tool will try to interpolate between points.

The result is spiky graphs that make it harder to see peaks and troughs:

Figure 12.34: Spiky graphs

Bar graphs are better for sparse metrics because they are rendered without interpolation:

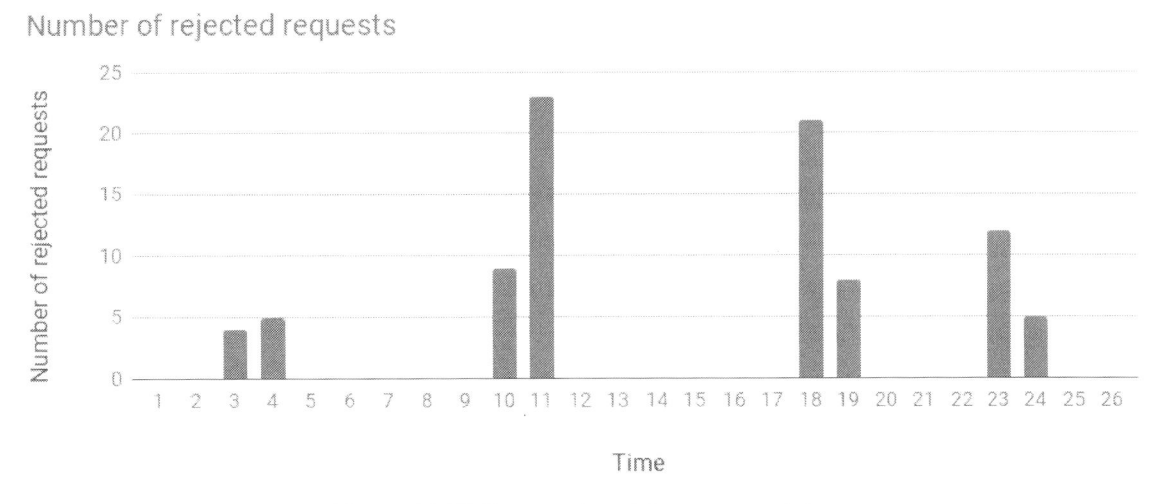

Figure 12.35: Bar graphs with sparse metrics

Present Errors with Toplist

Having a graph with errors is great (that's why we have included it in the **HTML Report Dashboard**).

It will allow us to:

- See when errors occur.
- See which types of errors occur.

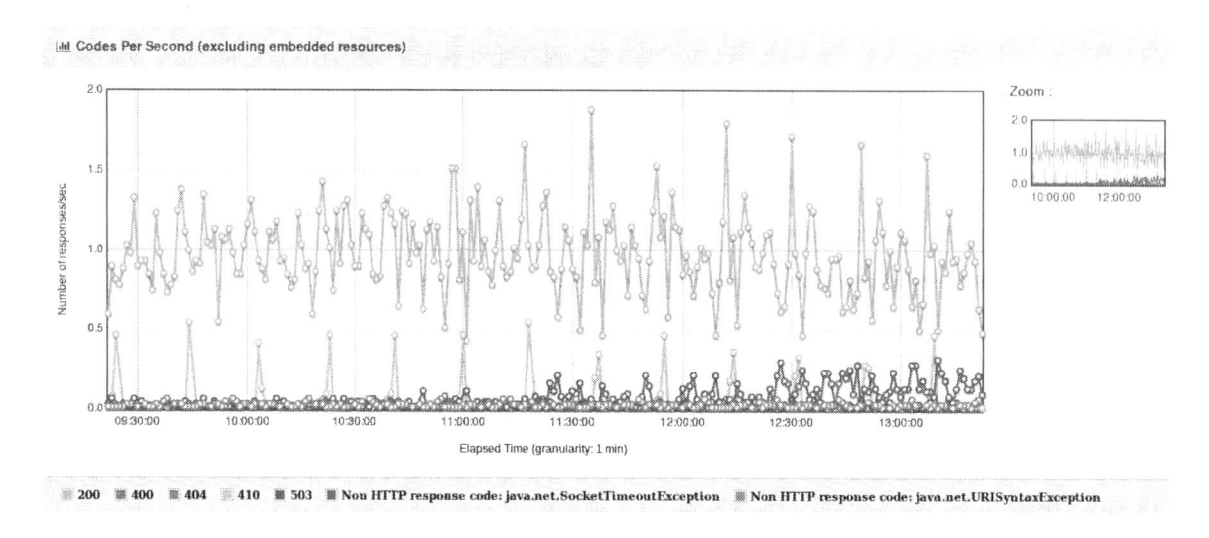

Figure 12.36: Codes per second graph

But this graph has limitations:

- We don't have the number of errors.
- We don't have the percentage of errors.
- We don't have the distribution of the types of errors.
- We don't have labels for the errors.

Fortunately, the **HTML Report Dashboard** provides a top list of errors out of the box. If you don't use it, don't forget to add a top list of errors to your report in a different way:

Errors

Type of error	Number of errors	% in errors	% in all samples
Non HTTP response code: java.net.SocketTimeoutException/Non HTTP response message: Read timed out	942	39.07%	5.73%
410/Gone	507	21.03%	3.08%
503/Service Unavailable	306	12.69%	1.86%
404/Not Found	155	6.43%	0.94%
Assertion failed	140	5.81%	0.85%

Figure 12.37: Toplist of errors

Time Series Graphs and Single-Value Summaries

Single-value summaries are aggregates computed from all query values over a given time window (be it a complete load test or only a partial one).

This visualization is easy to understand but can hide some interesting information.

For example, in this example from **HTML Report Dashboard**:

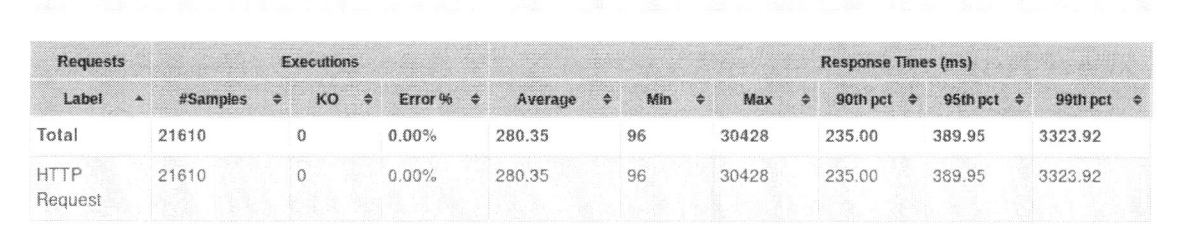

Statistics

Requests		Executions			Response Times (ms)					
Label	#Samples	KO	Error %	Average	Min	Max	90th pct	95th pct	99th pct
Total	21610	0	0.00%	280.35	96	30428	235.00	389.95	3323.92
HTTP Request	21610	0	0.00%	280.35	96	30428	235.00	389.95	3323.92

Figure 12.38: Single-value summaries

If we check the values of percentiles (**90th pct**, **95th pct** and **99th pct**), we can conclude than the response time is not stable. But that's all we can say.

To have more information, we need to check the *Over Time* graph provided by the **HTML Report Dashboard**.

In this case, the most useful graph will be *Response Times Over Time*:

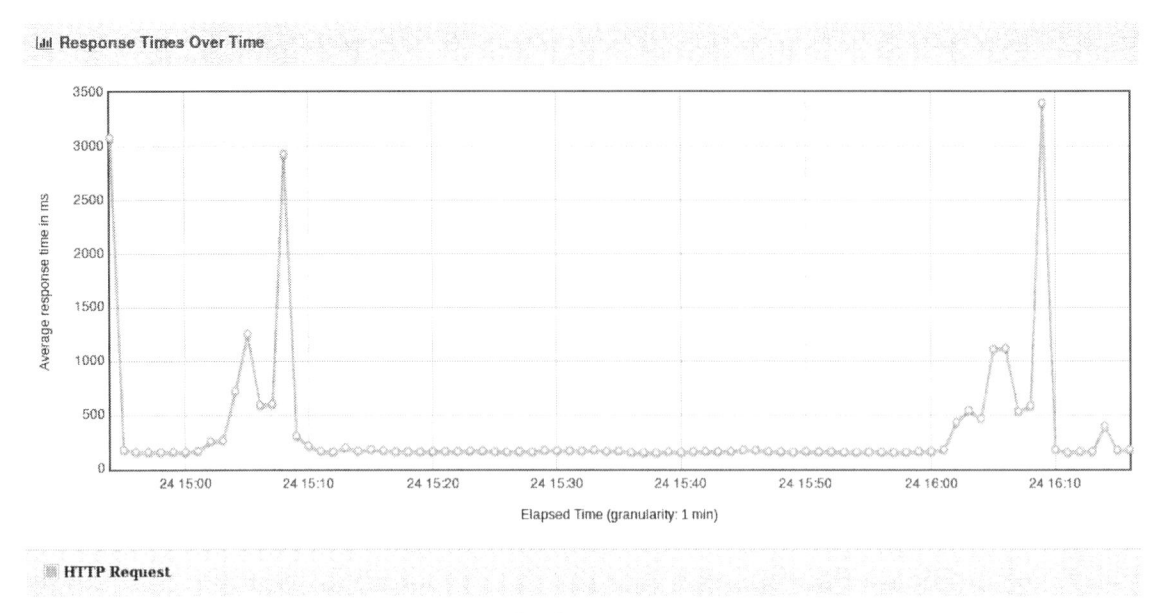

Figure 12.39: Graph of response times over time

We can see two peaks in response times at exactly 1-hour intervals. These peaks correspond to the execution of a batch.

This example shows that the two graphs are interesting and required.

Conclusion

As we have seen, analyzing the results of your load test is a step that can be done in several ways using JMeter or another tool.

We recommend using these three features of JMeter:

- **View Results Tree** during script design and only for error recording during testing.
- **Backend Listener** for real-time response times and storage.
- **HTML Report Dashboard** at the end of the test.

If that's not enough, any tool that can handle CSV files will do the trick.

When it's time to present the results, one piece of advice is not to use one representation (for example, time series line graphs) for everything. For each objective you want to present, use the appropriate graphic representation.

13

Integration of JMeter in the DevOps Tool Chain

Introduction

Nowadays, time to market is critical, and we have several solutions to reduce it:

- Agile methods
- Minimum Viable Product (MVP)
- DevOps, etc

Load testing must support these changes. As a consequence, we need to test earlier and often.

The first point to consider is that the earlier the tests are performed, the better it is.

Indeed, a bug discovered early in a project life cycle:

- Is easier to fix since it is ideally fixed within the development phase. Fixing a bug during the integration phase means digging into more layers to find the root cause, which leads to higher costs.
- Costs less than a production bug, as it does not impact customers. Think of a bug on pricing as an illustration.

The second point to consider is that tests must be performed at all stages of the application's life cycle: from development to integration, to production.

This approach of testing earlier is called *Shift-Left*, and it can naturally be applied to load testing.

To reach these goals, we will discuss:

- Organization/team topology
- The *Shift-Left* strategy
- Integration of JMeter in the software factory
- Automation

Organization/Team Topology

There is no magic team topology that suits each organization, and we will see different topologies in no order of preference.

Load Testing Team in Its Ivory Tower

For years, we had a load testing team that could decide whether an application could be put into production after testing it.

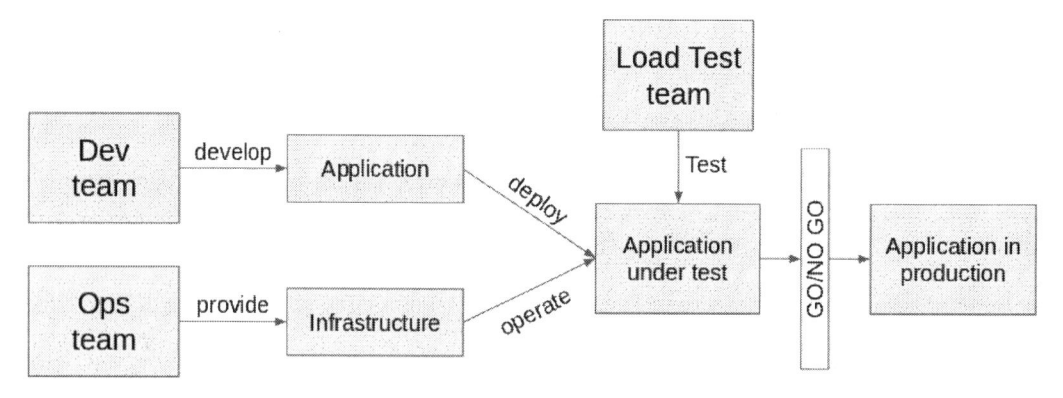

Figure 13.1: Load test team in its ivory tower

There are pros, such as:
- More time to test the application
- Full-time test teams
- Experienced team

But with the multiplication of deliveries (Agile method) and the multiplication of applications/services (microservices), this topology must be adapted.

DevOps and Load Test Team Collaboration

The main difference with *load testing team is in its ivory tower*, is that the performance tester is integrated into the DevOps team (standup meeting, demo, task in sprints, and so on):

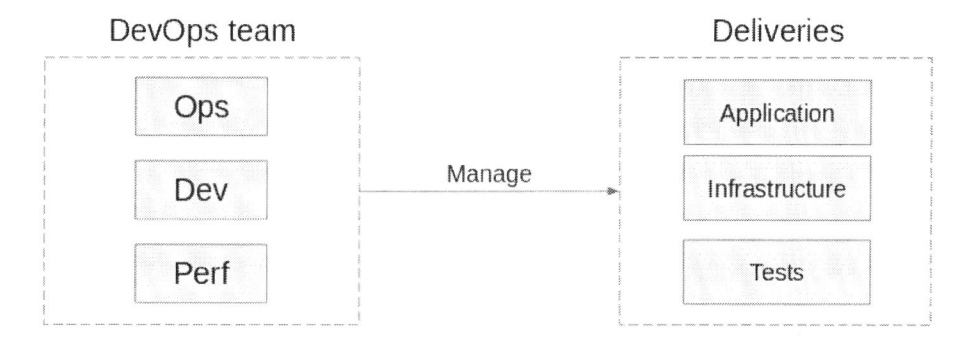

Figure 13.2: DevOps and load test team collaboration

It may be difficult for the performance tester to deliver if they need to support the DevOps teams too much.

One Performance Tester Integrated on DevOps Team

Having a performance tester in each DevOps team has the following benefits:
- Good knowledge of the application (functional and technical)
- Team empowerment
- Full-time performance tester in the team

- A load testing expert in the team

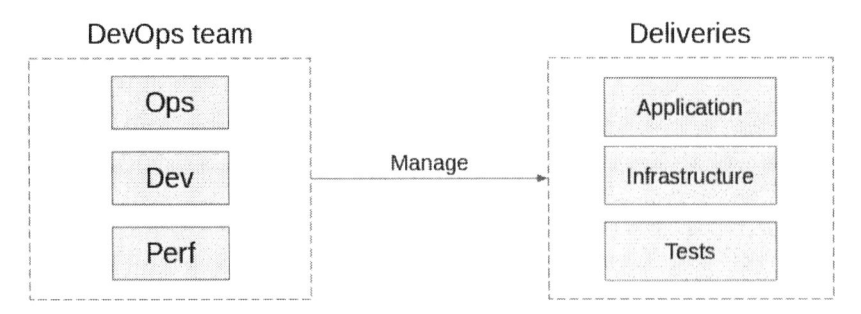

Figure 13.3: One performance tester integrated in DevOps team

The main problem is that it's difficult to have one performance tester and potentially a backup per team due to:

- Budget impact
- Recruitment challenges
- The need for the team to provide enough tasks to justify a full-time tester

No Performance Tester

In this topology, the development and/or operations teams manage load tests:

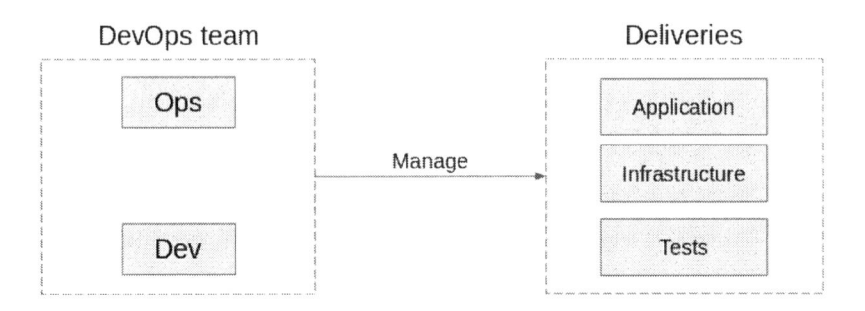

Figure 13.4: No performance tester

Although it may look like a good idea and is trending at the time of this writing, a good development or operations team member does not always make a good performance tester. The reciprocal is also true.

Moreover, it's very difficult to master these skills at the same time.

As you can guess, we think that the concept of *full stack developer* is a legend and more of a hype nowadays.

Other problems are that:
- It's difficult to acquire and maintain all these skills
- Load tests can be set aside if the team is late on its sprint

Team of Evangelists Performance Testers

In this configuration, the team of performance testers does not perform load tests 100% of the time.

Instead, it helps with training, supporting the DevOps team to do so, and improving the tooling and methods.

However, we believe it is essential that the members of this team continue to conduct performance tests to keep their feet on the ground.

Such a team would help spread a culture of performance testing in the company.

If the company cannot afford to have such a team, it may use consultancy services.

Figure 13.5: Team of evangelists performance testers

It allows to performance tester team to be up to date on performance domain and to empower the DevOps team while giving the resources to achieve it.

Setting Up Shift-Left Strategy

In load testing, *Shift-Left* would result in:
- Early load tests across project phases, particularly in the development and testing phases
- The automation of load tests and integration in the build pipeline

Still, *Shift-Left* is not that easy for many reasons:

- The ability to load test depends, at minimum, on the environment and the availability of test data. As we have seen in previous chapters, data has a huge impact on load test quality.
- The ability to automate load tests depends, at minimum, on the availability of environments, the automation cost (which depends on the application architecture), and the ability to mock third parties.
- Return of investment (ROI) of tested features. You may hold that 100 percent of the application should be tested, but that's probably impossible for the majority of applications.

Here are a few examples of how much testing technologies can cost a company (the more "'+'" signs there are, the more expensive the solution is):

Type of technology	Load Testing Cost
HTTP REST/SOAP Micro Service	+
JMS Micro Service	++
Simple HTML UI	++ / +++
Ajax Based UI	+++ / ++++
GWTRPC UI	++++++
SAP BI Web UI	+++++++
SAP GUI	++++++++++
Citrix Exposed Application	++++++++++

Figure 13.6: Costs depending on the type of technology used for a solution

Here are a few examples of cost depending on the application type:

Type of application	Cost	Causes
Search Engine	+	Data can be reused and is simple to create
E-Commerce Application	+++	The complexity lies in the data of the order tunnel and the number of virtual users to be simulated
ERP	+++++	Non Idempotent scenario, each step consumes data of previous step. Data preparation is complex
CMS Application	+++++	Dynamic data structures make data creation complex, and scripting hard

Figure 13.7: Costs depending on the type of application

A realistic approach would be this one:

Type of Load Test	Objective	Cost
Automate load testing of software building blocks early in the process, in modern architectures, these are usually Micro-Services exposed as HTTP REST Webservices	Detect performance issues within development phase with low cost load tests	+
Detect performance issue very soon in coding without spending too much time on developing the load test	Detect performance issues in partially integrated software or validate the new architecture of a product	++
Manually load test the fully integrated application. This might be automated for every campaign.	Detect a performance issues and validate future scalability before Go Live	+++

Figure 13.8: Realistic approach

Modification in JMeter Script to Implement Shift-Left Strategy

With the Shift-Left strategy, we need to test the application in different environments.

It's important to have the same end-to-end script to:

- Avoid having a script for each environment
- Avoid having a script for each type of load test (such as stress tests, endurance tests, and others)
- Test the same scope in each environment

The script will be promoted from one environment to another.

In a dev environment, we will use the script and development associated properties (`dev.properties`):

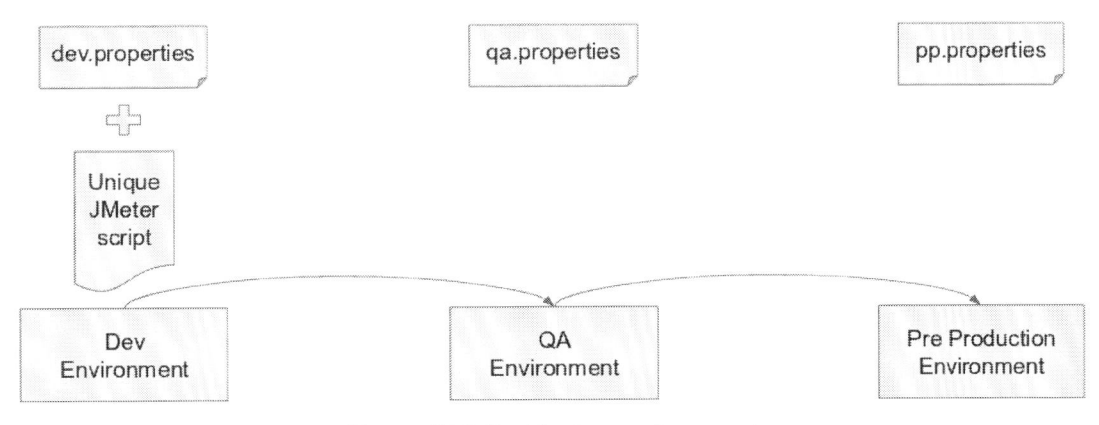

Figure 13.9: Test in dev environment

388 | Integration of JMeter in the DevOps Tool Chain

If the test succeeds, the script will be promoted to the QA environment. A test with the script and QA-associated properties (`qa.properties`) will be executed.

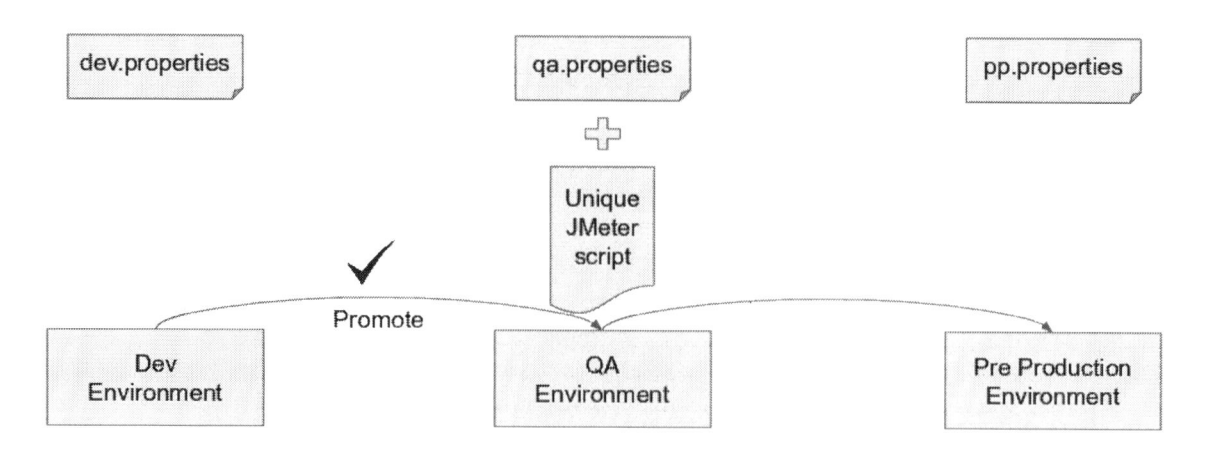

Figure 13.10: Script promoted to test in the QA environment

If the test succeeds, the script will be promoted to the pre-production environment. A test with the script and pre-production associated properties (`pp.properties`) will be executed:

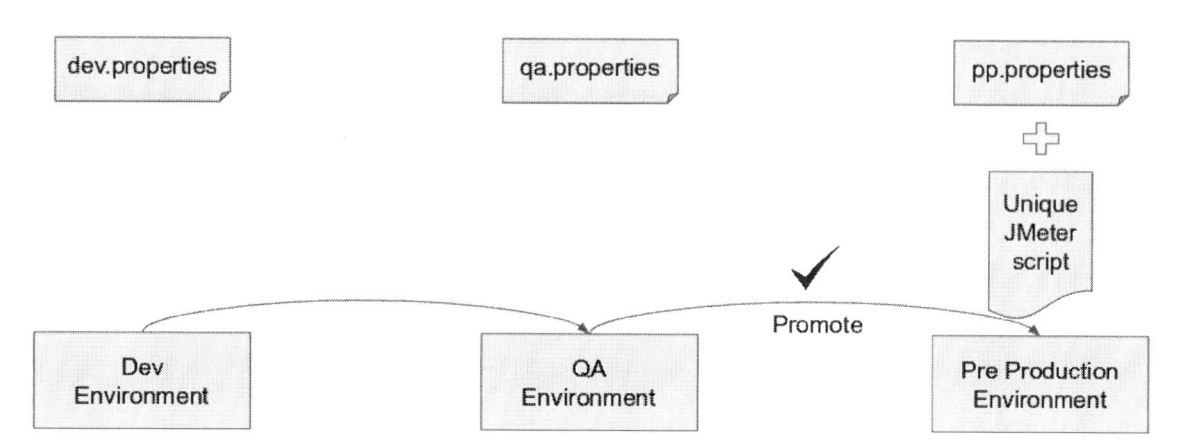

Figure 13.11: Script promoted to test in the pre-production environment

To reach this goal, we will use JMeter properties and the `${__P(,)}` function.

Our advice is to configure at least:

- *Number of Threads (users)* in **Thread Group**
- *Ramp-up Period (in seconds)* in **Thread Group**
- *Loop Count* or *Duration* in **Thread Group**
- Throughput in **Precise Throughput Timer** or **Constant Throughput Timer**

- *Protocol* in **HTTP Request** or, even better, in **HTTP Request Defaults**
- *Server Name or IP* in **HTTP Request** or, even better, in **HTTP Request Defaults**
- *Port Number* in **HTTP Request** or, even better, in **HTTP Request Defaults**

For example, we can configure our **Thread Group** as follows:

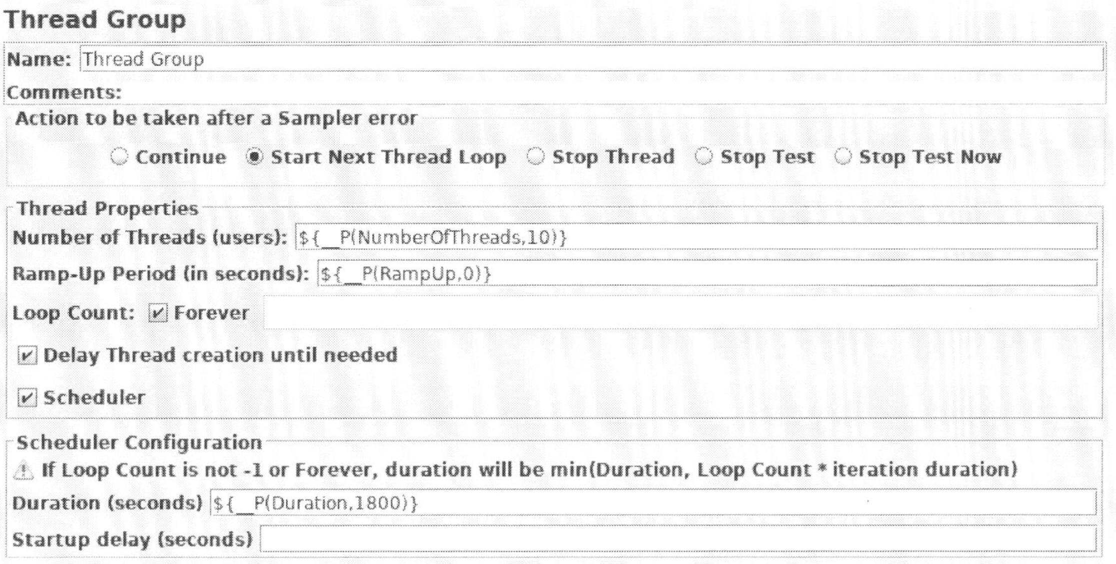

Figure 13.12: Configure Thread Group with properties

To execute our load test without modifying the script, we have two options:

- Use the **-J** command-line parameter of JMeter:

    ```
    jmeter -t MyScript.jmx -JNumberOfThreads=100 -JRampUp=50 -JDuration=3600
    ```

- Use a properties file and the **-p** command-line parameter of JMeter

For example, the `PreProductionProperties.properties` file will have our properties for the pre-production environment:

```
NumberOfThreads=100
RampUp=50
Duration=3600
    jmeter -p PreProductionProperties.properties -t MyScript.jmx
```

For PaaS load testing tools, we can use properties, too.

For example, in RedLine13:

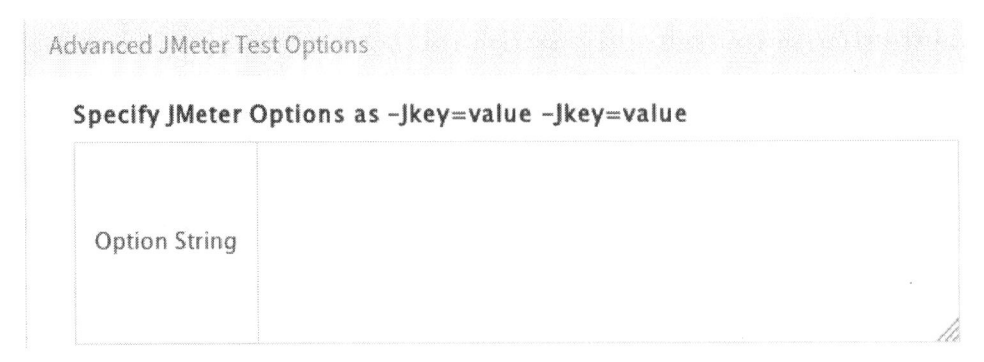

Figure 13.13: Configure properties in RedLine13

Integrating JMeter in Our Software Factory

Adding JMeter in our software factory is mandatory for *Shift-Left* strategy.

A software factory looks like this:

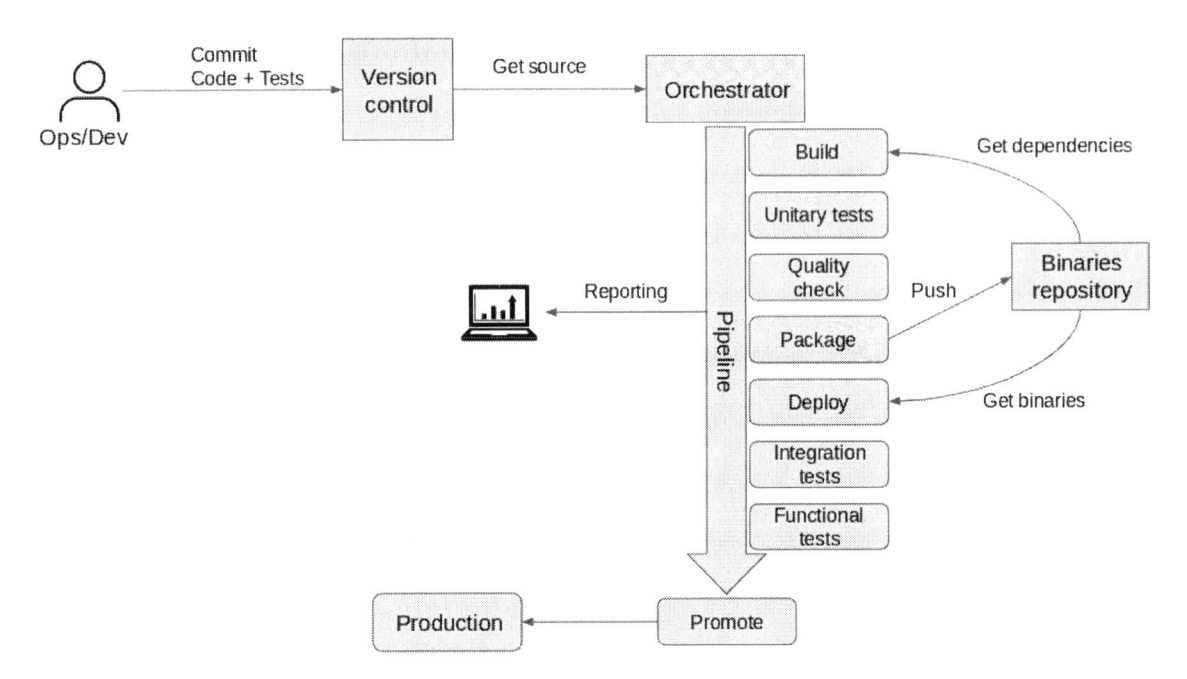

Figure 13.14: Software factory without a performance load test

The goal is to add JMeter in this way:

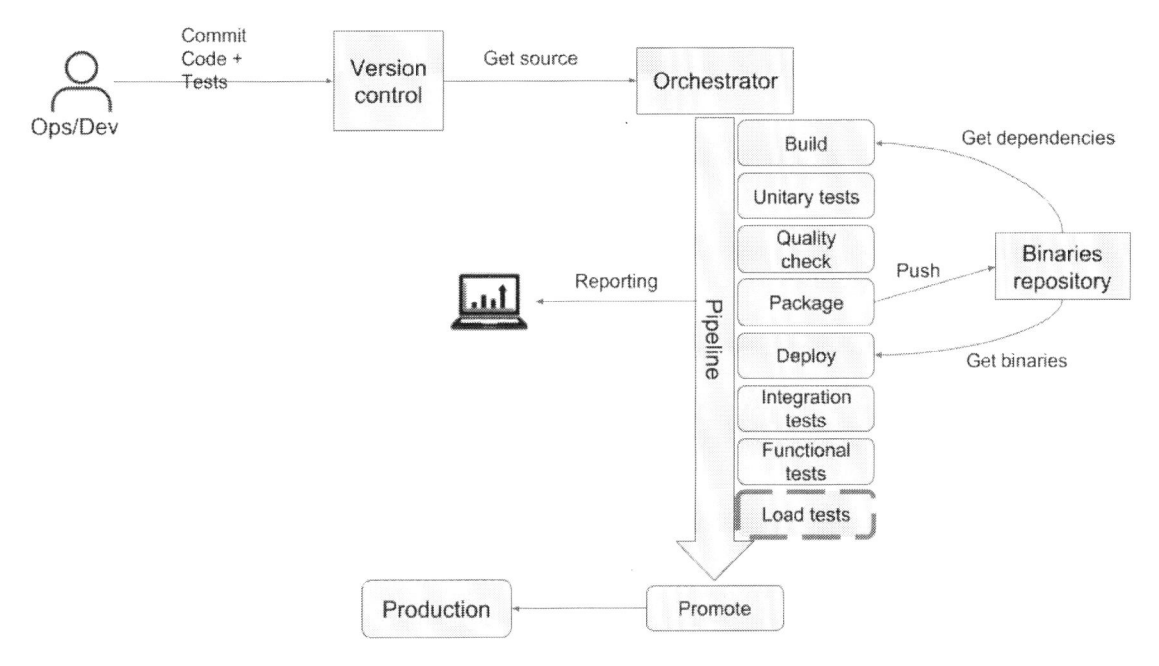

Figure 13.15: Software factory with performance load tests

Example 1: Integrating with Jenkins Using Maven

After a few load testing campaigns, you'll find that one of the main critiques of load testing is that the load tests come too late in the application's life cycle.

On the other hand, application changes can break test scripts, so it often happens that at the last minute, scripts need to be modified instead of spending time on tests.

To solve these two problems, we decide to use the project's continuous integration infrastructure.

The continuous integration tool used is Jenkins (http://jenkins-ci.org/).

Jenkins interfaces quite easily with JMeter using Maven.

392 | Integration of JMeter in the DevOps Tool Chain

Next step: Let's configure our project.

We're going to use the same project that we used in *Chapter 8, Running Your Test from Apache Maven*.

1. First, we create a **New Item**, give it a name, and select **Maven project** as the type of item:

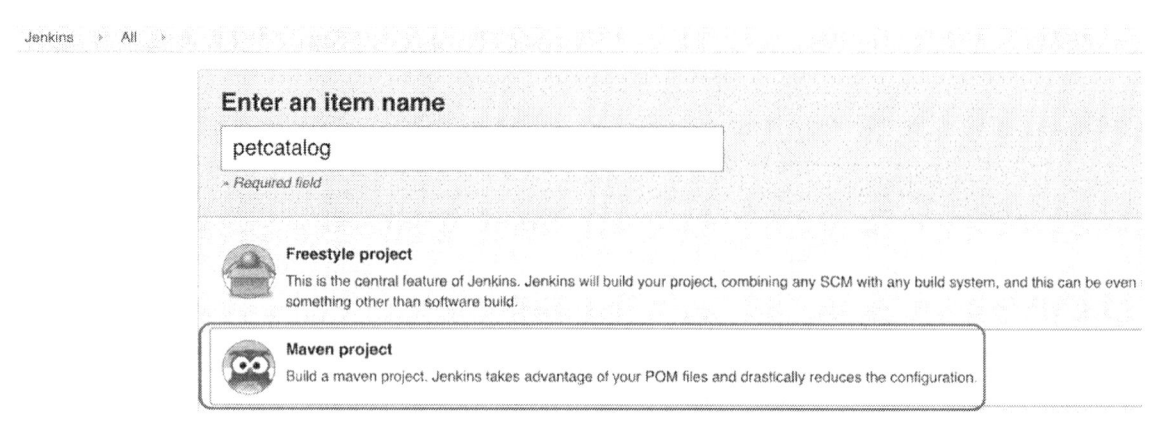

Figure 13.16: Jenkins – JMeter configuration

2. We then configure the source code location; in our case, the project is on a Git server and is hosted on GitHub:

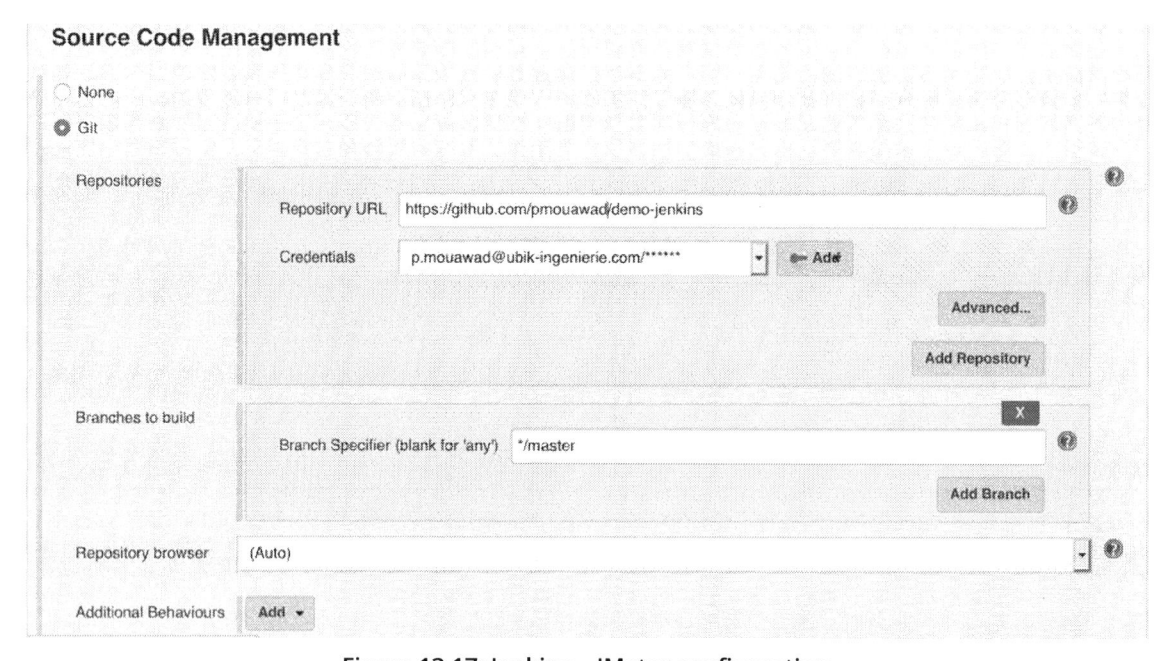

Figure 13.17: Jenkins – JMeter configuration

3. We then configure under what conditions the load test will be triggered. In our case, we decide:

   To trigger it on each SNAPSHOT dependency build, but this choice is up to you:

   Build Triggers
   - ☑ Build whenever a SNAPSHOT dependency is built
   - ☐ Schedule build when some upstream has no successful builds
   - ☐ Trigger builds remotely (e.g., from scripts)
   - ☐ Build after other projects are built
   - ☐ Build periodically
   - ☐ GitHub hook trigger for GITScm polling
   - ☐ Poll SCM

   Figure 13.18: Jenkins – JMeter configuration

   To run a load test only if the build is successful:

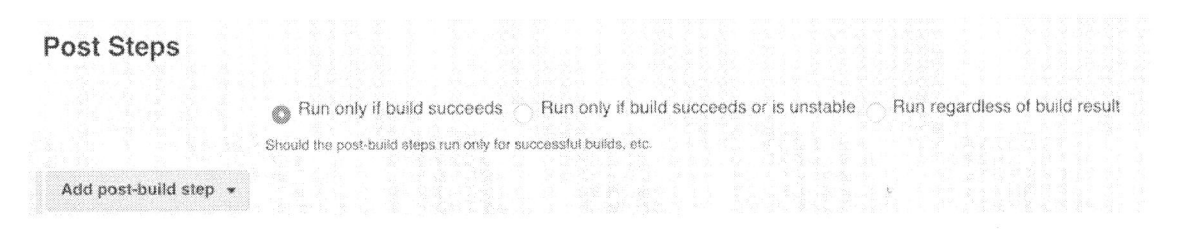

   Post Steps
   - ◉ Run only if build succeeds ○ Run only if build succeeds or is unstable ○ Run regardless of build result
   - Should the post-build steps run only for successful builds, etc.

   Add post-build step ▼

   Figure 13.19: Jenkins – JMeter configuration

Ensuring the Load Tests are Run on Correct Nodes

1. The next thing we need to do is restrict the running of load test on slaves that match certain criteria.

   Indeed, as we have seen previously, running a load test requires that the machine running it is correctly configured to deliver the best performance.

2. To ensure that, we will configure slaves dedicated to load testing and label them LOAD_TEST.

   Doing this also ensures that the load test runs on a machine that is correctly configured for such type of task and not on a master, which would be parasitized by a lot of other tasks.

3. To configure a node, we go to **Manage Jenkins** and select **Manage Nodes**:

Figure 13.20: Jenkins – Manage Nodes

4. Then select **New Node** and configure the node as follows; note the **Labels** field:

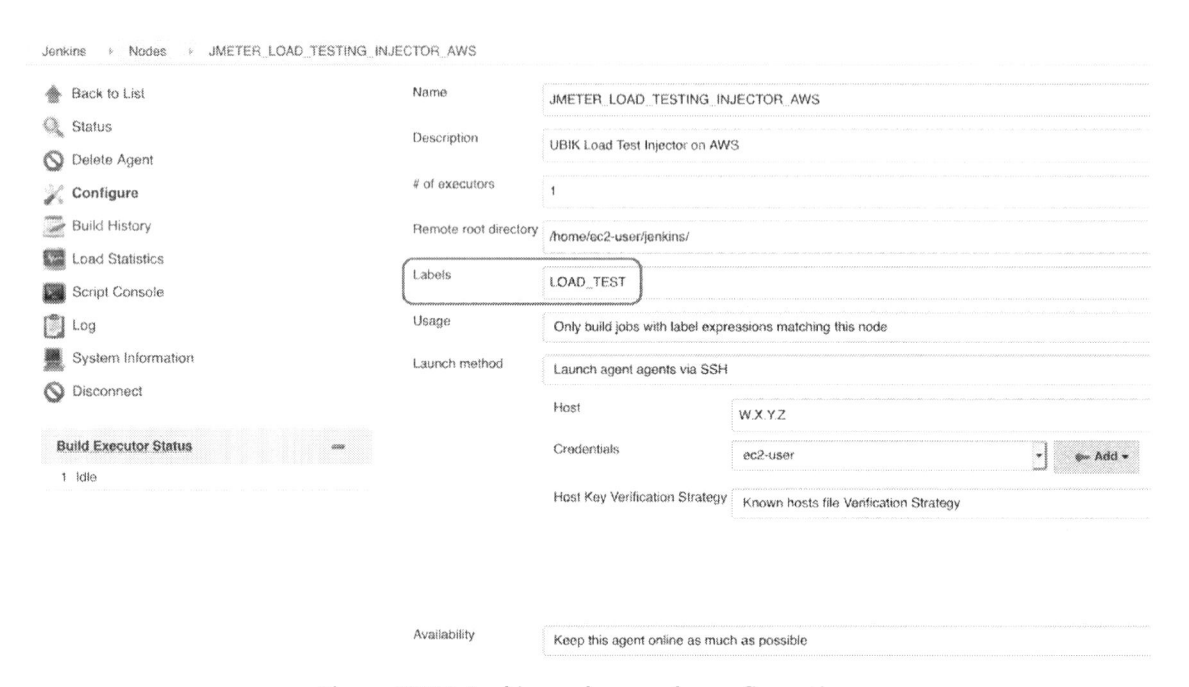

Figure 13.21: Jenkins – slave node configuration

5. Click the **Advanced** button and check **Tool Locations**:

Figure 13.22: Jenkins – slave node configuration

We now have finished the slave configuration and can do the configuration at the project level:

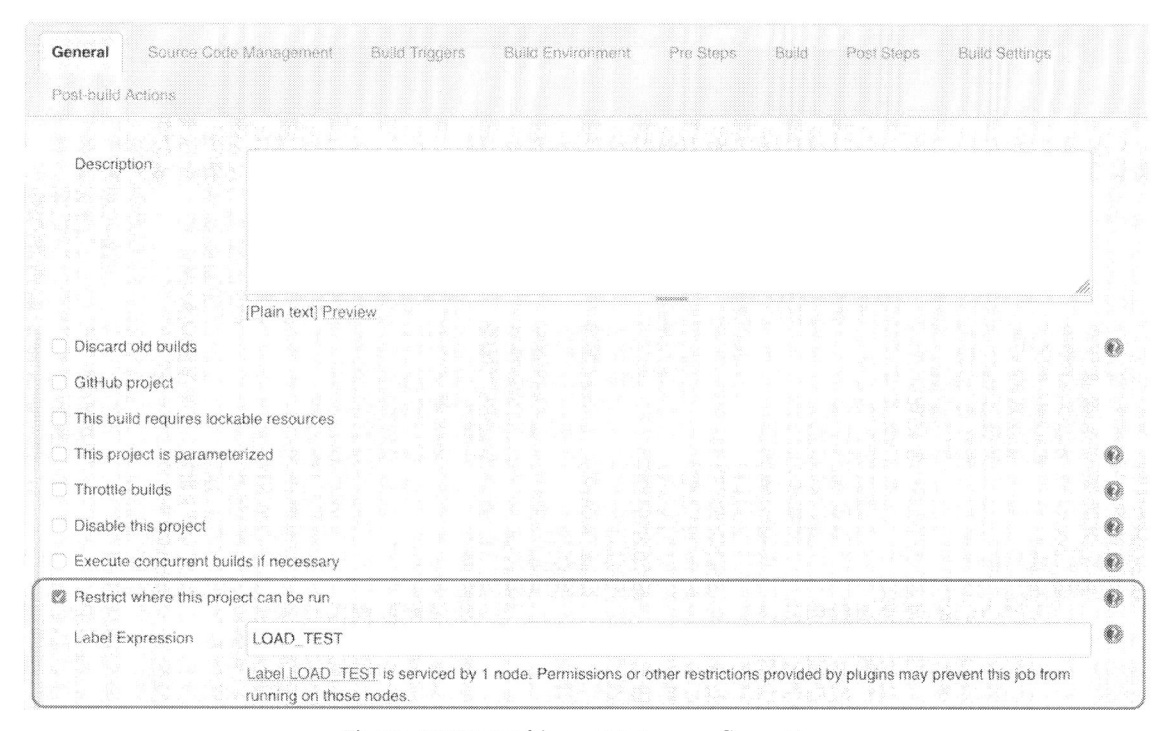

Figure 13.23: Jenkins – JMeter configuration

Configuring the Load Test Using jmeter-maven-plugin

1. We then configure how the test is run.

   The launch of our tests will be done using *Maven* and *JMeter-Maven-Plugin*:

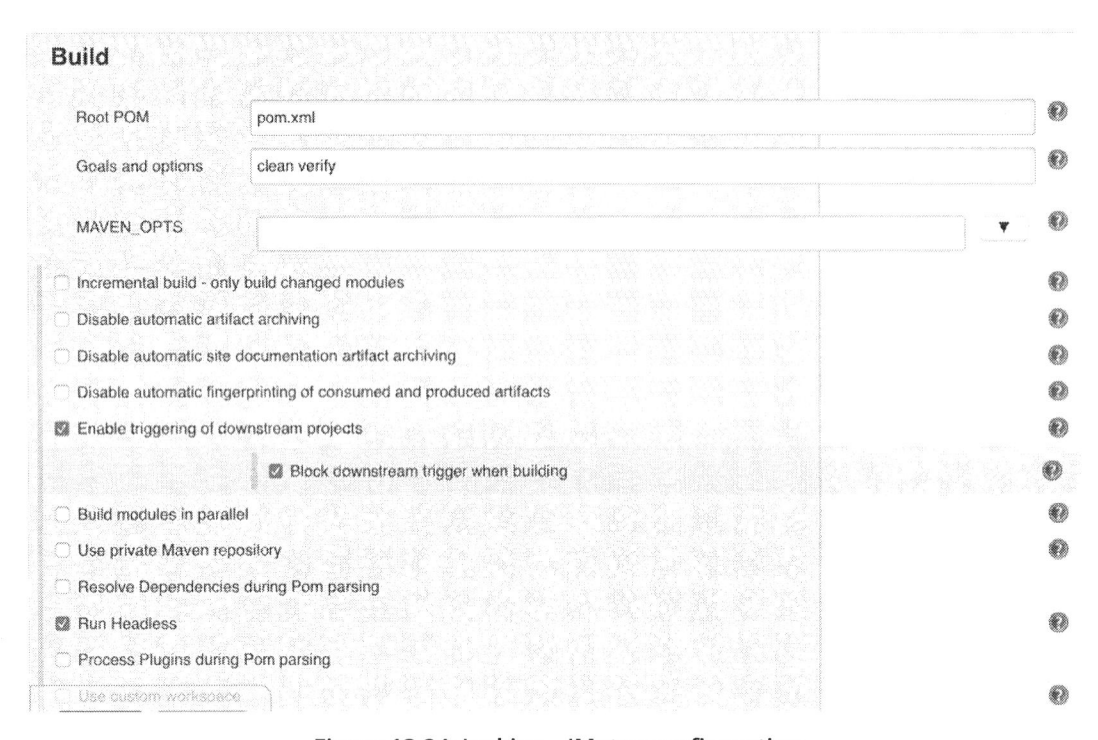

   Figure 13.24: Jenkins – JMeter configuration

Failing the Build if the Error Rate of the Load Test is over a Threshold

1. We'll use the **errorRateThresholdInPercent** element inside the **configuration** element:

   ```
   <configuration>
       <errorRateThresholdInPercent>1</errorRateThresholdInPercent>
   </configuration>
   ```

2. In the preceding configuration, we fail the build if the error rate exceeds 1 percent.

Configuring the HTML Report

1. In order to have the HTML report correctly generated at the end of the load test, we'll amend the **pom.xml** file to:

   Set the report title

Change the overall granularity to 1 second instead of 1 minute

Filter the transactions that we want in our report

2. We'll use the **propertiesJMeter** element inside the **configuration** element:

   ```
   <configuration>
     <propertiesJMeter>
       <jmeter.reportgenerator.report_title>Master JMeter Book</jmeter.reportgenerator.report_title>
       <jmeter.reportgenerator.overall_granularity>1000</jmeter.reportgenerator.overall_granularity>
       <jmeter.reportgenerator.exporter.html.series_filter>^(HP|Scenario|Search)(-success|-failure)?$</jmeter.reportgenerator.exporter.html.series_filter>
     </propertiesJMeter>
     ...
   </configuration>
   ```

> **Note**
> Notice that to set a JMeter property, we use its key as the element name and the element content as the property value.

Configuring the Memory Used by JMeter

1. We'll use the **jMeterProcessJVMSettings** element inside the **configuration** element:

   ```
   <configuration>
     <jMeterProcessJVMSettings>
       <arguments>
         <argument>-Xms128m</argument>
         <argument>-Xmx128m</argument>
         <argument>-XX:MaxMetaspaceSize=256m</argument>
       </arguments>
     </jMeterProcessJVMSettings>
     ...
   </configuration>
   ```

> **Note**
> Note that the preceding values may vary depending on your test.

2. We end up with this configuration:

```xml
<plugin>
  <groupId>com.lazerycode.jmeter</groupId>
  <artifactId>jmeter-maven-plugin</artifactId>
  <version>2.8.5</version>
  <configuration>
    <errorRateThresholdInPercent>1</errorRateThresholdInPercent>
    <testResultsTimestamp>false</testResultsTimestamp>
    <propertiesJMeter>
      <jmeter.reportgenerator.report_title>Master JMeter Book</jmeter.reportgenerator.report_title>
      <jmeter.reportgenerator.overall_granularity>1000</jmeter.reportgenerator.overall_granularity>
      <jmeter.reportgenerator.exporter.html.series_filter>^(HP|Scenario|Search)(-success|-failure)?$</jmeter.reportgenerator.exporter.html.series_filter>
    </propertiesJMeter>
    <jMeterProcessJVMSettings>
      <arguments>
        <argument>-Xms128m</argument>
        <argument>-Xmx128m</argument>
        <argument>-XX:MaxMetaspaceSize=256m</argument>
      </arguments>
    </jMeterProcessJVMSettings>
  </configuration>
  <executions>
    <execution>
      <id>jmeter-tests</id>
      <phase>verify</phase>
      <goals>
        <goal>jmeter</goal>
      </goals>
    </execution>
    <execution>
      <id>check-results</id>
      <phase>verify</phase>
      <goals>
```

```
            <goal>results</goal>
          </goals>
      </execution>
   </executions>
</plugin>
```

In order to publish the report in Jenkins, we'll use **HTML Publisher Plugin** (https://wiki.jenkins.io/display/JENKINS/HTML+Publisher+Plugin).

Let's start with the installation of *HTML Publisher Plugin*.

3. In Jenkins, we click on "**Manage Jenkins**":

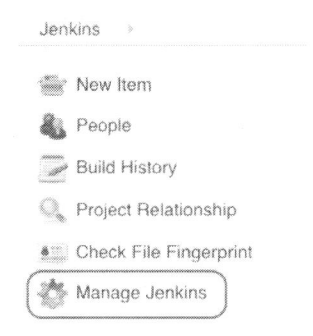

Figure 13.25: Jenkins – Manage Jenkins

4. Then click on **Manage Plugins**:

Figure 13.26: Jenkins – Manage Plugins

5. Let's install **HTML Publisher Plugin**:

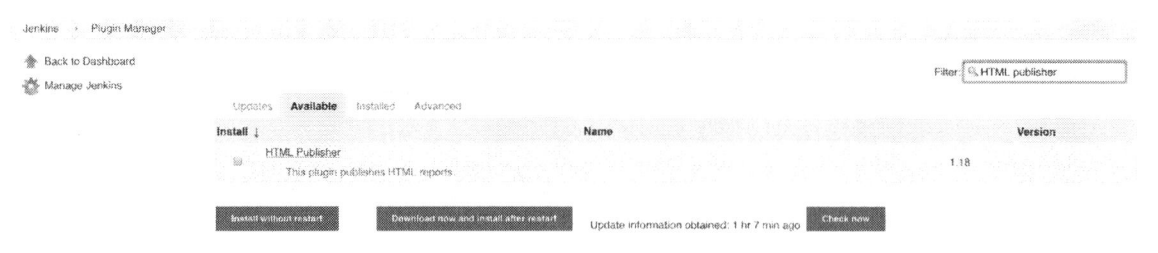

Figure 13.27: Jenkins – HTML Publisher Plugin

Now let's configure the project. We first go to **Post Build Action** and select **Publish HTML reports**:

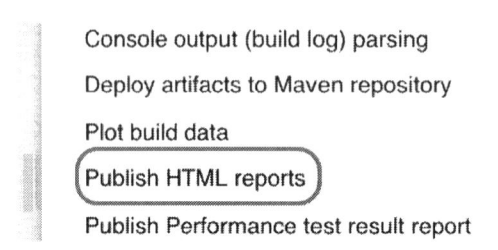

Figure 13.28: Jenkins – Post Build Action

6. Then we configure it as follows, giving it the path to the HTML report generated by **JMeter Maven Plugin**:

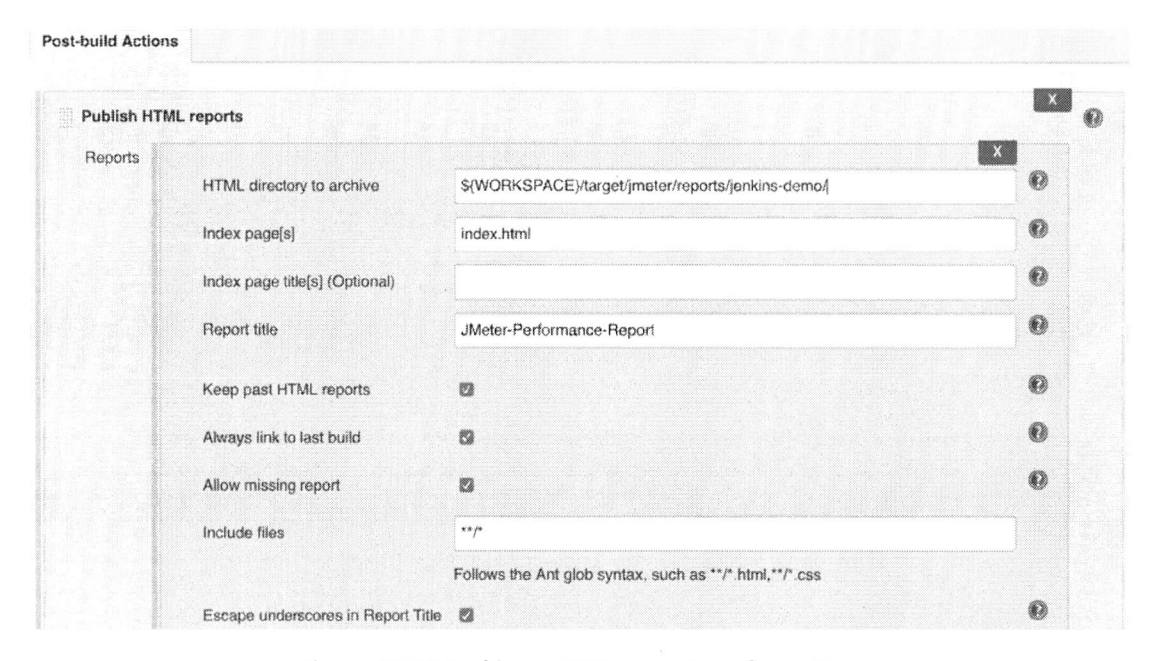

Figure 13.29: Jenkins – HTML report configuration

If you build the job, you'll notice that the report is not displayed correctly. This is due to the content security policy (https://wiki.jenkins.io/display/JENKINS/Configuring+Content+Security+Policy#ConfiguringContentSecurityPolicy-Implementation) in Jenkins.

To allow the correct display of the report, you need to configure Java System property **hudson.model.DirectoryBrowserSupport.CSP**.

7. You can set this property by creating a Groovy script file, **$JENKINS_HOME/init.groovy**, or any **.groovy** file in the **$JENKINS_HOME/init.groovy.d/** directory containing:

    ```
    System.setProperty("hudson.model.DirectoryBrowserSupport.CSP", "default-src 'self'; style-src 'self' 'unsafe-inline'; script-src * 'unsafe-inline'; font-src *;img-src 'self' data: *;frame-ancestors 'self'")
    ```

8. If we run the job, we get the HTML-Report link:

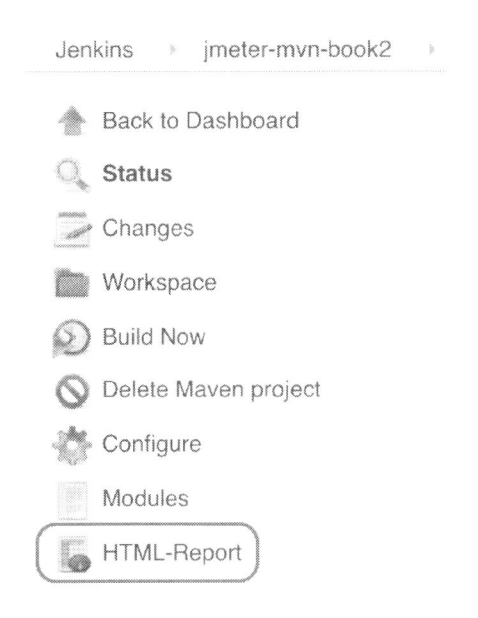

Figure 13.30: Jenkins – HTML-Report link

9. If we click on it, we get the HTML report:

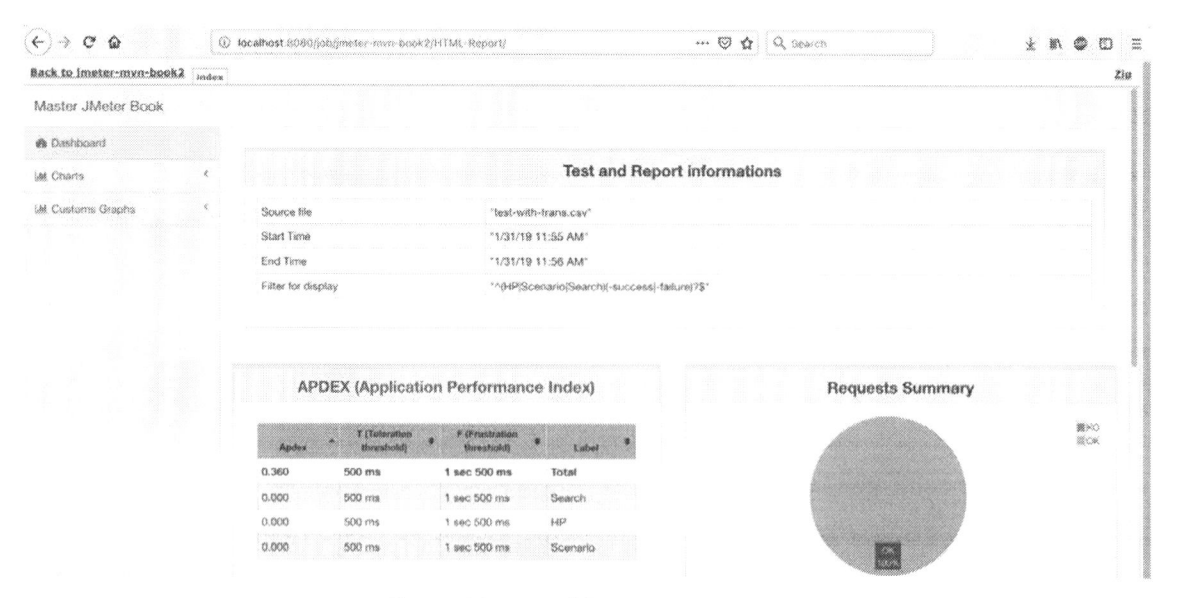

Figure 13.31: Jenkins – HTML report

Now we have:

- Automated our load test triggering in Jenkins
- Automated report generation

This is nice, but what we'd like now is to be able to compare the performance of build over time.

Example 2: Enhancing Integration with Jenkins Using Performance Plugin

To be able to compare the performance of builds over time, we'll use Performance Plugin (https://wiki.jenkins-ci.org/display/JENKINS/Performance+Plugin) to:

- Generate reports showing the changes in response times, error rates, and throughput across builds
- Fail the build if degradation occurs between builds

Let's start with the installation of *Performance Plugin*.

1. In Jenkins, we click on **Administer Jenkins**.:

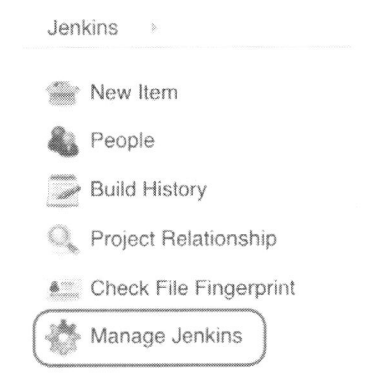

Figure 13.32: Jenkins – Manage Jenkins

2. Then click on **Manage Plugins**:

Figure 13.33: Jenkins – Manage Plugins

3. Let's install **Performance Plugin**:

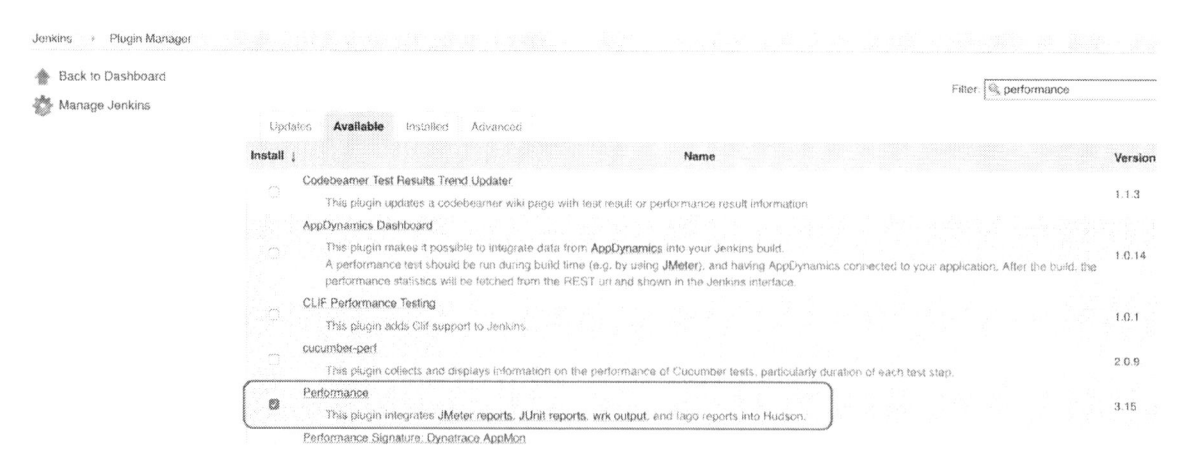

Figure 13.34: Jenkins – Performance Plugin

Last modification: The configuration of the publication/aggregation of the test results using "**Performance Plugin**".

4. We click "**Add post-build action**", and select "**Publish Performance test result report**":

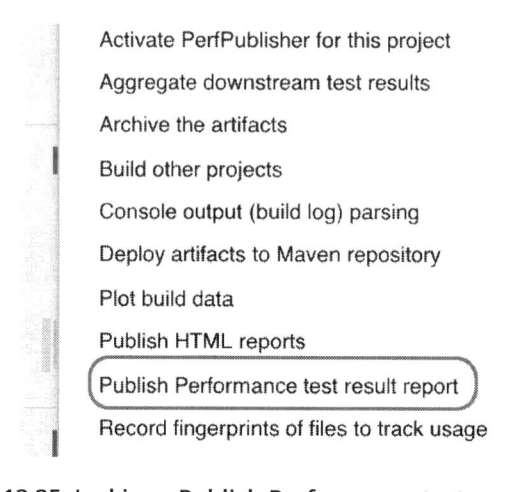

Figure 13.35: Jenkins – Publish Performance test result report

5. We then configure **Source data files (autodetects format):** and **Regex for included samplers**:

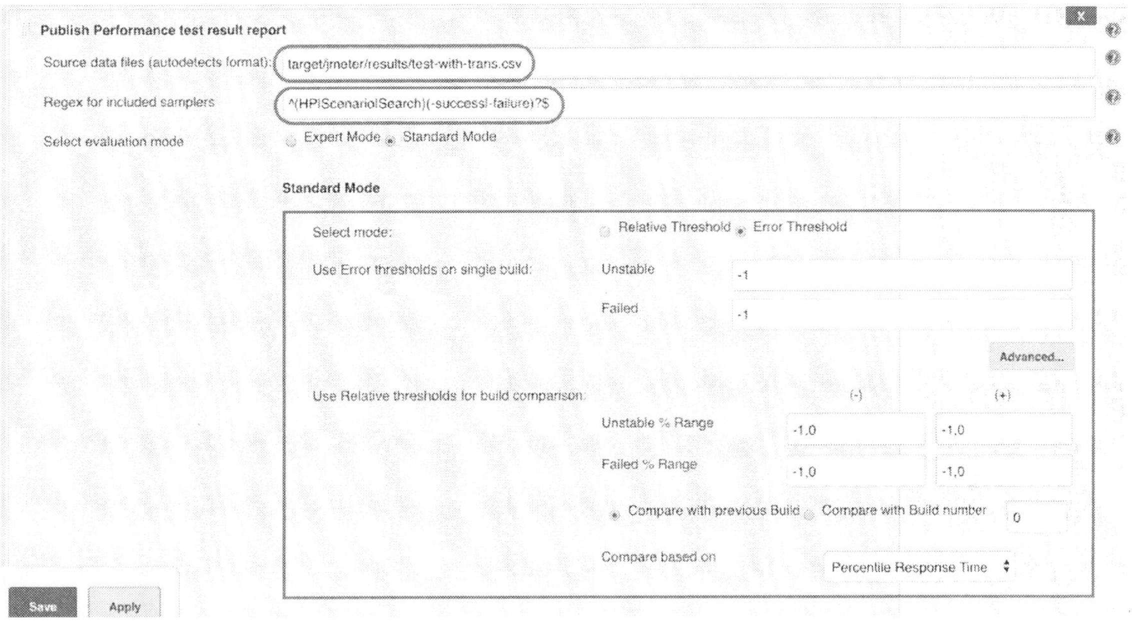

Figure 13.36: Jenkins – Publish Performance test result report configuration

Notice the **Regex for included samplers** field. This field appeared in version 3.16 (not released yet at the time of writing) and is a contribution of one of this book's writers.

It allows the plugin to compute metrics only for the transactions we want to track.

The regular expression should match the `jmeter.reportgenerator.exporter.html.series_filter` JMeter property.

6. We can then configure **Relative Threshold** to:

   Compare builds based on percentile response time

   Make it **Unstable** if response times increase by more than 2 percent

Make it **Failed** if response times increase by more than 5 percent:

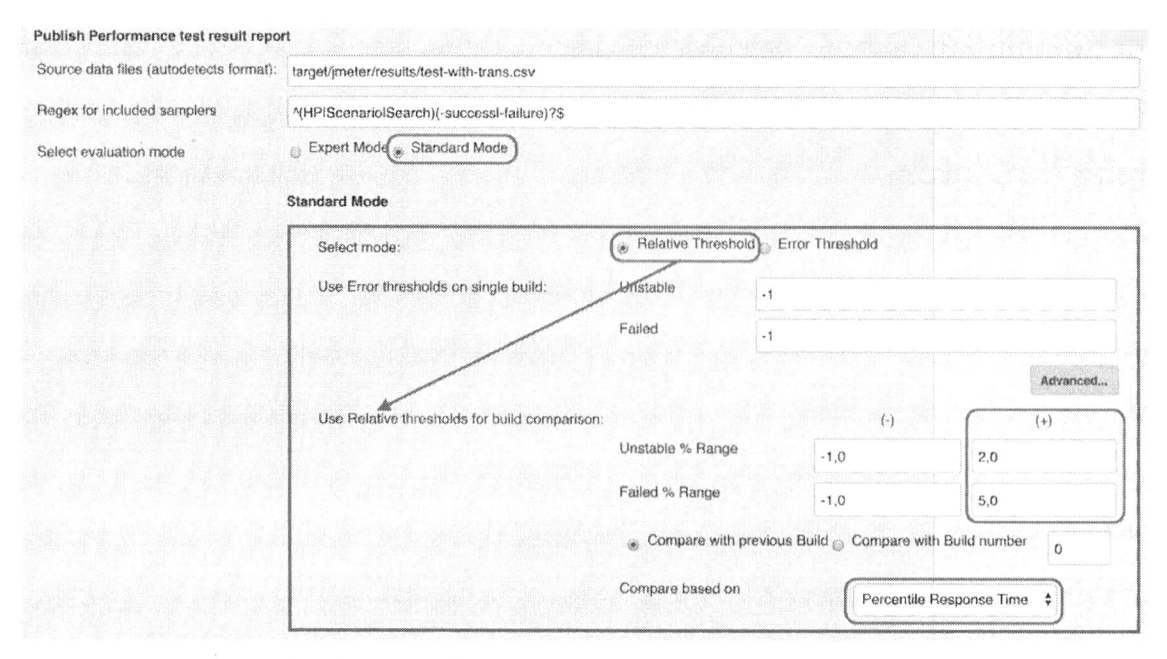

Figure 13.37: Jenkins – relative thresholds configuration

7. Now, when response times improve, you get logs such as these and a successful build:

```
Comparison build no. - 12 and 14 using 90 Percentile response time

URI         PrevBuildURI90%   CurrentBuildURI90%   RelativeDiff   RelativeDiff(%)
Performance: Parsing report file '/Users/Shared/Jenkins/Home/jobs/jmeter-mvn-book2/builds/12/performance-reports/JMeterCSV/test-with-trans.csv' with filterRegex '^(HP|Scenario|Search){-success|-failure}?$'
HP              3755              827             -2928           -77.98%
Scenario        6999              2164            -4835           -69.08%
Search          4434              1477            -2957           -66.69%
Finished: SUCCESS
```

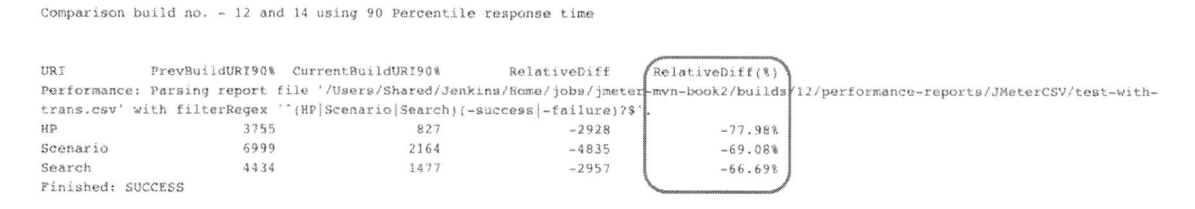

Figure 13.38: Jenkins – Relative thresholds configuration

8. And when response times decrease, you get logs such as these and a successful build:

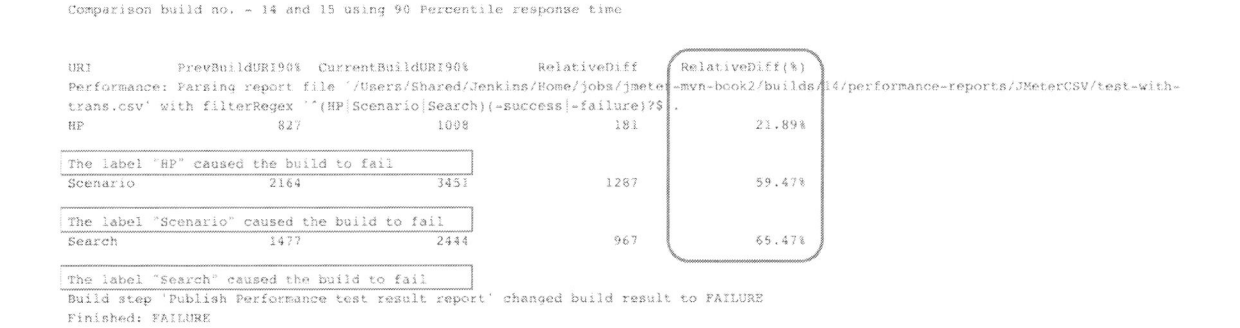

```
Comparison build no. - 14 and 15 using 90 Percentile response time

URI           PrevBuildURI90%   CurrentBuildURI90%   RelativeDiff   RelativeDiff(%)
Performance: Parsing report file '/Users/Shared/Jenkins/Home/jobs/jmeter-mvn-book2/builds/14/performance-reports/JMeterCSV/test-with-
trans.csv' with filterRegex '^(HP|Scenario|Search)(-success|-failure)?$'.
HP                  827              1008              181            21.89%

The label "HP" caused the build to fail
Scenario           2164              3451             1287            59.47%

The label "Scenario" caused the build to fail
Search             1477              2444              967            65.47%

The label "Search" caused the build to fail
Build step 'Publish Performance test result report' changed build result to FAILURE
Finished: FAILURE
```

Figure 13.39: Jenkins – Relative thresholds configuration

9. After a build, the JMeter tests are started and the results are aggregated by the plugin.

10. In the menu, "**Performance Trend**" appears, which allows you to look at the performance trend:

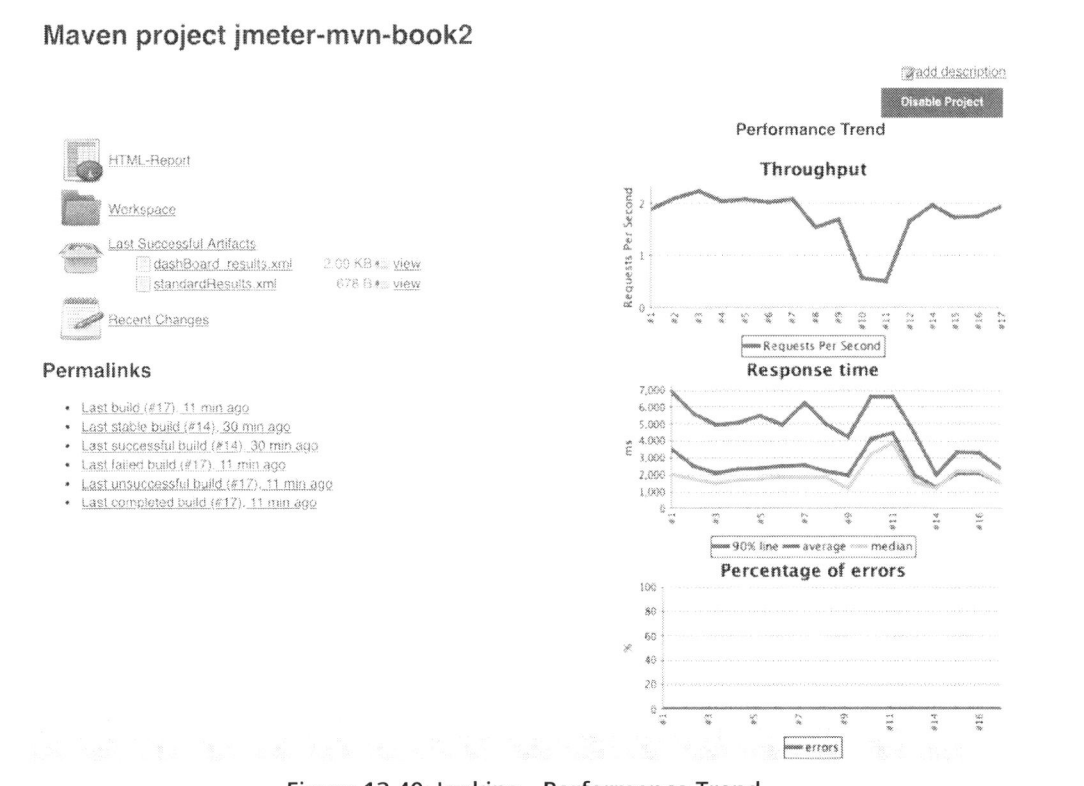

Figure 13.40: Jenkins – Performance Trend

Performance Trend

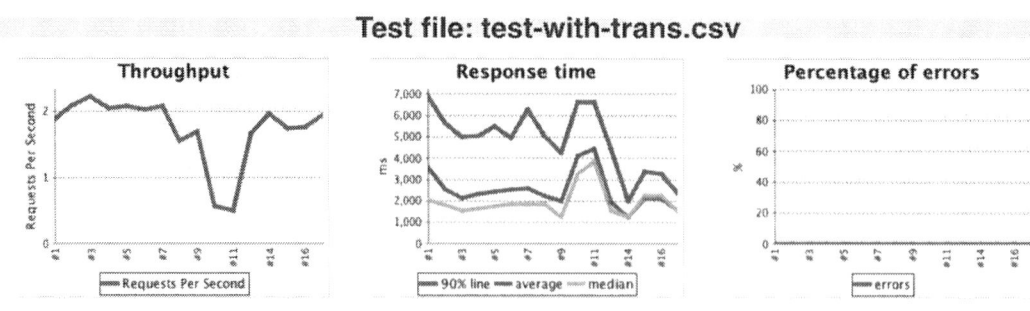

Last Report
Filter trend data

Figure 13.41: Jenkins – Performance Trend results

11. The reports for each build remain available:

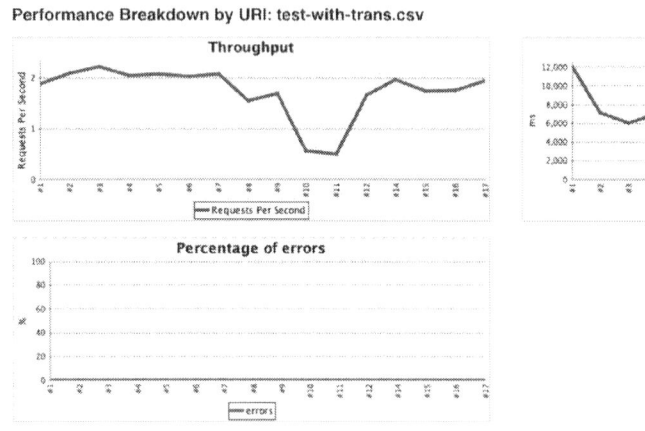

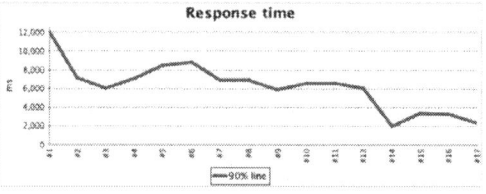

Figure 13.42: Jenkins – reports of each test

12. There are details for each transaction of the test:

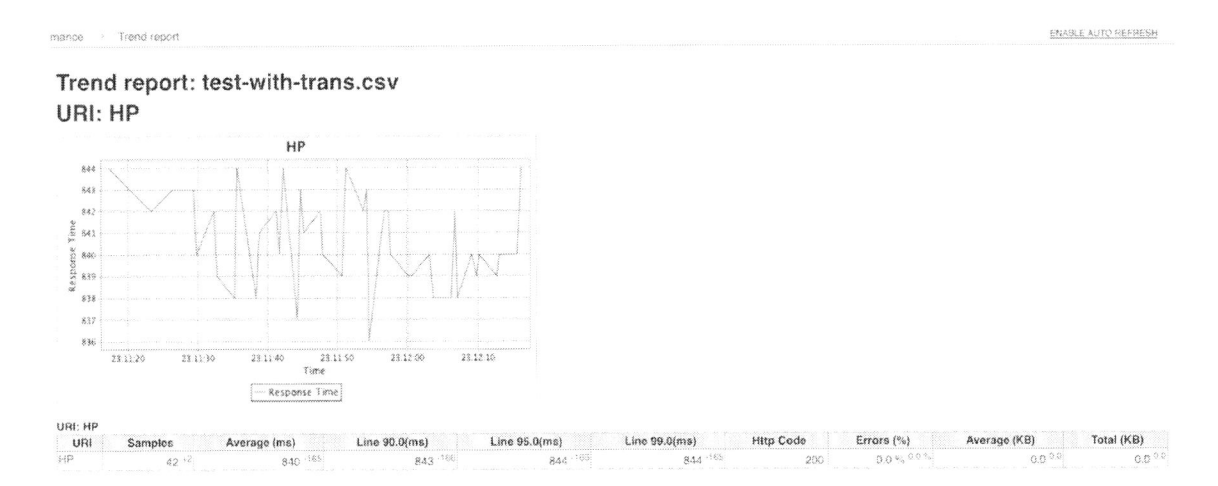

Figure 13.43: Jenkins – reports of each test

Figure 13.44: Jenkins – reports of each test

As we can see, the results meet our expectations well.

Automation

We can automate a lot of things and integrate JMeter with other tools.

We will see some examples of automation in this section.

> **Note**
> The source code given in the examples has been deliberately simplified to make reading it more enjoyable.
>
> Furthermore, we do not follow best practices (for instance, injectors and tested applications are running on the same server). In the real world, you should replace in **OS Process Sampler** simple commands by remote ssh calls.

Example 3: Non-Regression Testing of Memory Consumption with EJ JProfiler

In *Chapter 7, Load Testing a Website*, we saw how to use JProfiler during our technical tests. We will continue to use it in other technical tests, all in an automated way.

We want to create memory dumps of our application at the start of our test and at the end.

This will allow us to ensure that the new version of the tested application does not consume too much memory compared to the old version.

1. To check this, we will compare the dumps of the two versions.

2. Let's go back to our script that tests the PetClinic application:

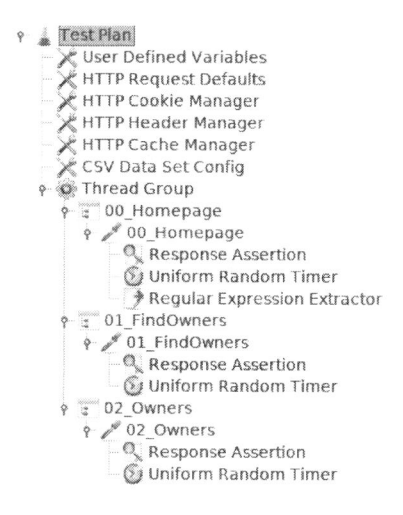

Figure 13.45: PetClinic script

We will modify this script to have this process:

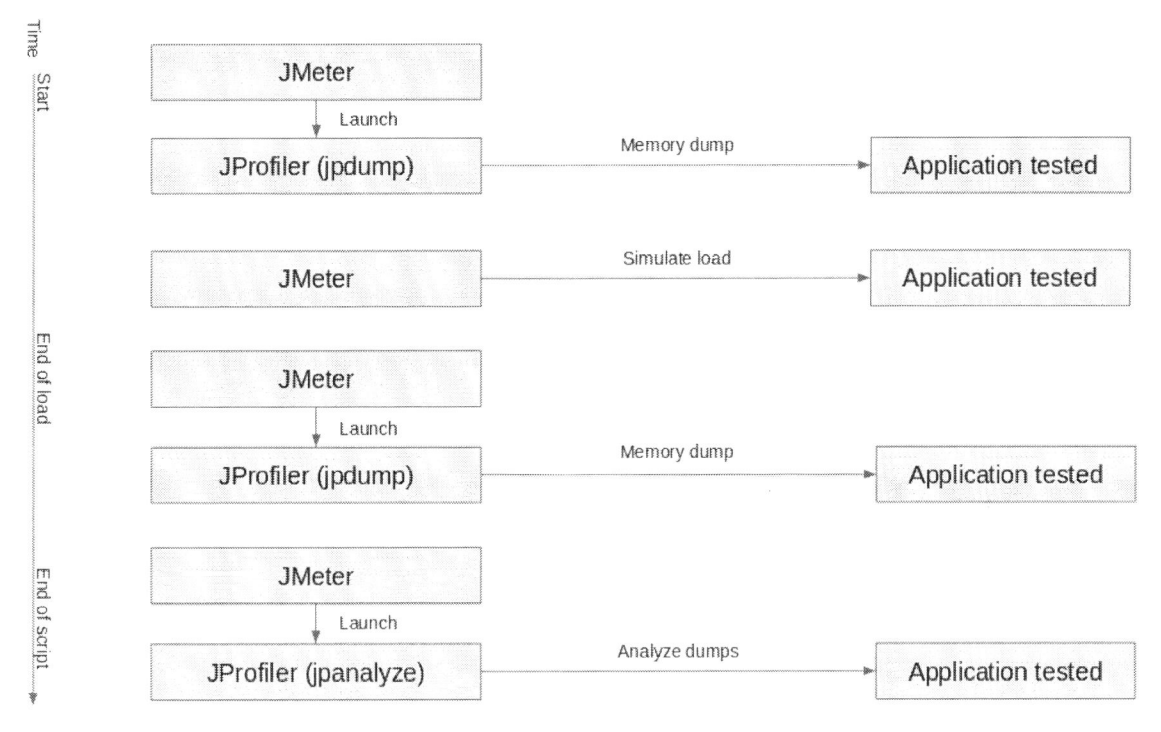

Figure 13.46: Non-regression test of the memory consumption process

3. Let's use the jpdump tool delivered with JProfiler to make our memory dumps. To do this, we must execute the following command:

   ```
   jpdump -p PID
   ```

4. First, let's get the process ID (PID) of our application (more precisely, the PID of the Tomcat running PetClinic) as in *Chapter 7, Load Testing a Website*:

Figure 13.47: PID retrieval

5. In order to use this PID when dumping at the end of our test (and therefore in a different **Thread Group**), we will have to save it in a property using the **JSR223 PostProcessor** element to share it with our **tearDown Thread Group**:

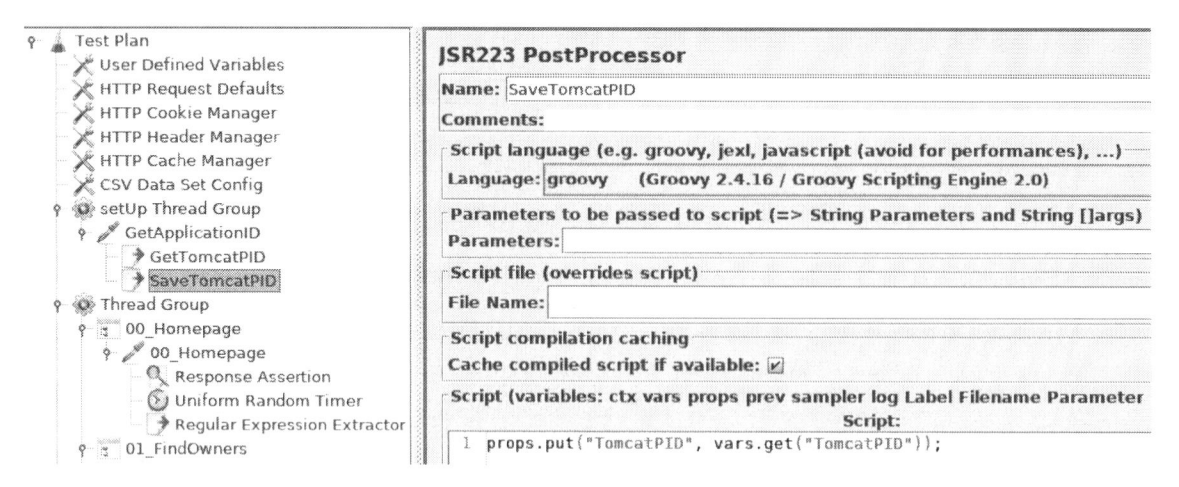

Figure 13.48: Save PID

6. Let's run our first dump using the **OS Process Sampler** element:

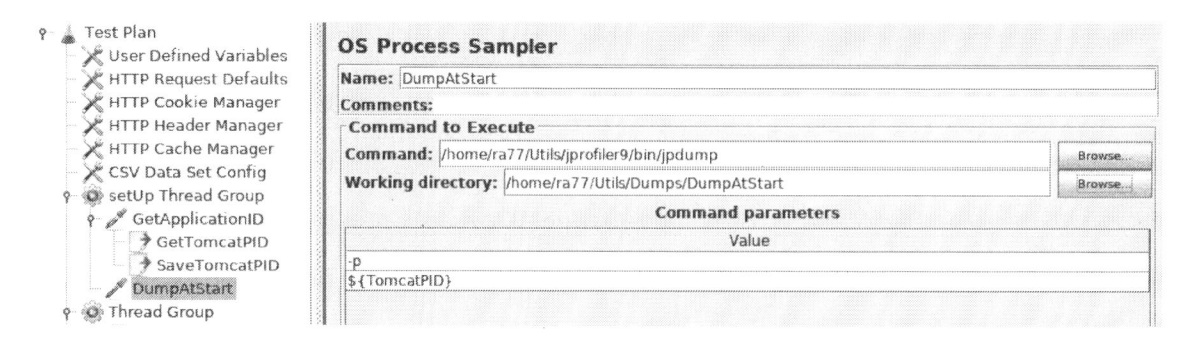

Figure 13.49: Dump

> **Note**
> All dumps will be saved in the same directory. You can modify the script to create a directory by iteration/execution.

7. Let's verify the successful creation of the dump with an assertion:

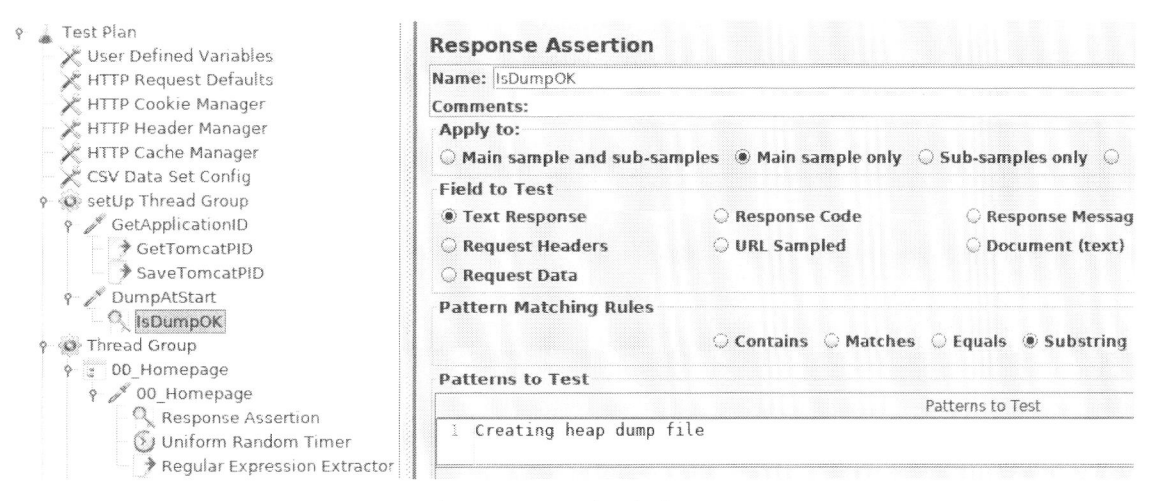

Figure 13.50: Check dump

8. Now let's go to the dump at the end of our test.

   In our **tearDown Thread Group** element, let's add the same **OS Process Sampler** element with: A different backup directory

   Using the **${__property(PIDTomcat)}** function to recover the previously saved PID:

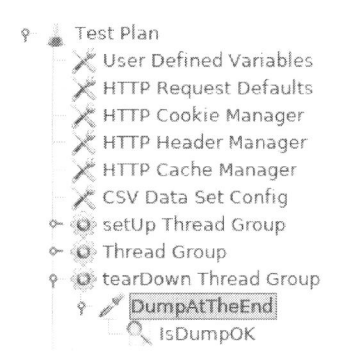

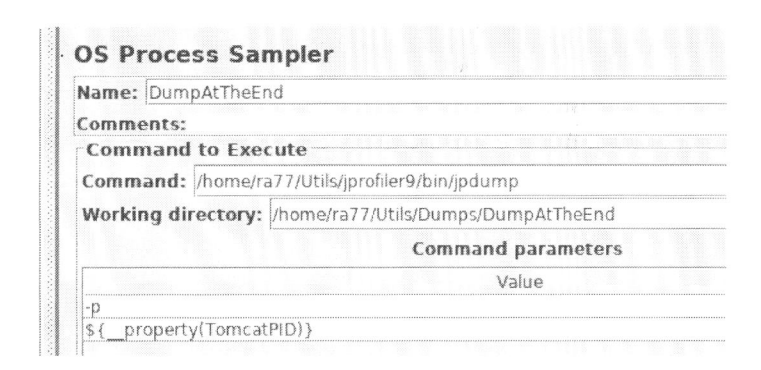

Figure 13.51: Second dump

9. As the last step, we will use the jpanalyze tool delivered with JProfiler to analyze the dump so that the opening is fast in JProfiler:

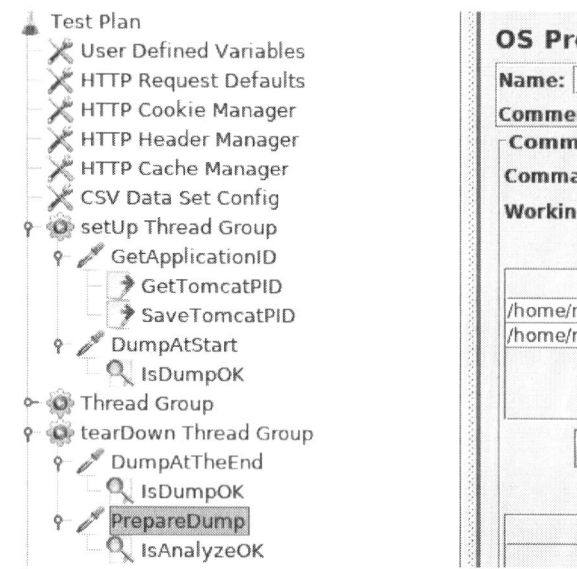

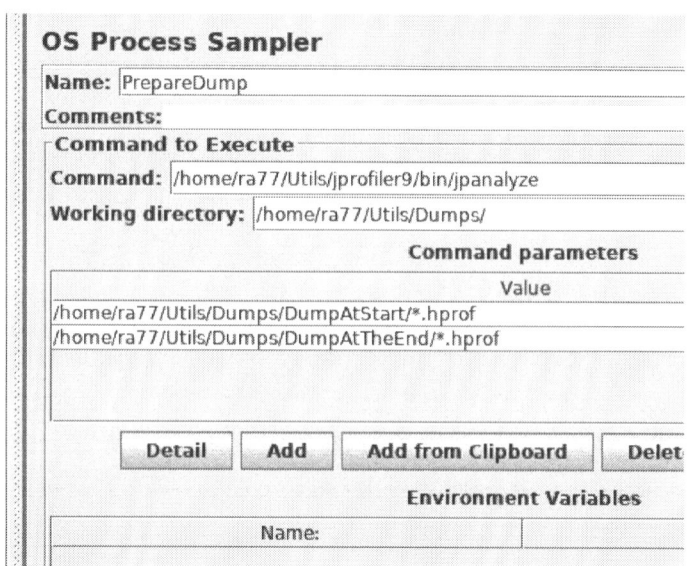

Figure 13.52: Dump analysis

> **Note**
> The paths are hardcoded in the preceding example; you can use properties to avoid this.

10. This will result in the creation of a directory with the data analyzed by dump:

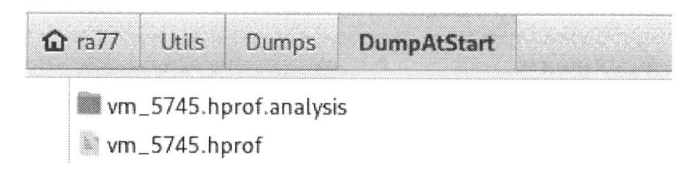

Figure 13.53: Dump analysis – results

11. As usual, do not forget to test the response:

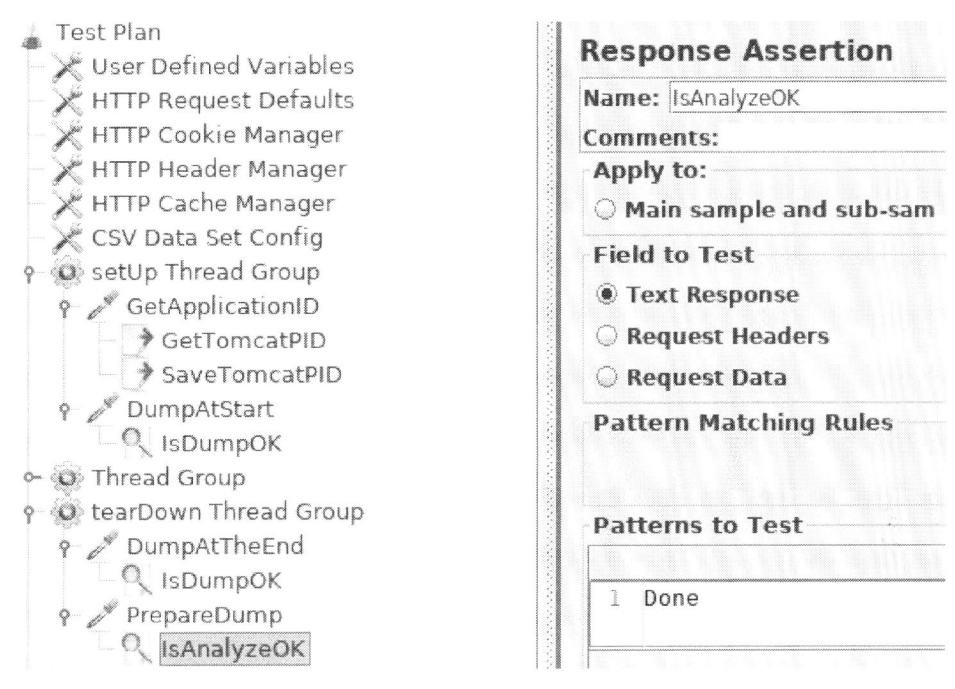

Figure 13.54: Checking the dump analysis

12. Let's run JProfiler:

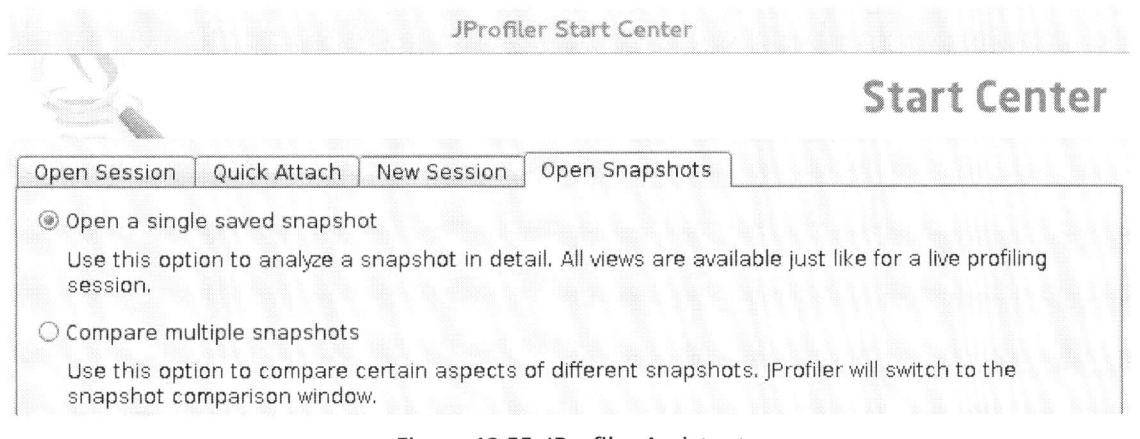

Figure 13.55: JProfiler Assistant

13. Let's open our dump:

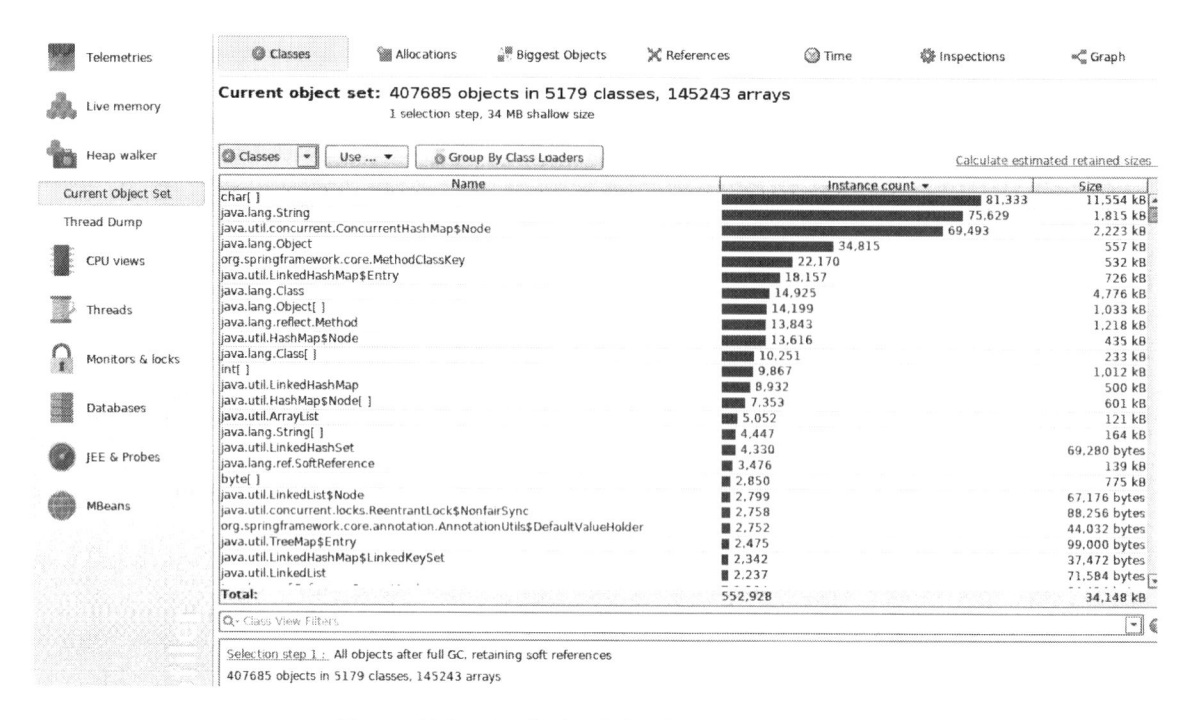

Figure 13.56: Analysis of the dump in JProfiler

To deepen the analysis, we'll need to understand the differences in terms of memory usage between the two versions of the application.

We either know the application well enough to do this ourselves, or we have to work with a developer.

The comparison of two dumps can also be made on the command line, which we will see in the next example.

Example 4: Detecting a Memory Leak during an Endurance Test with EJ JProfiler

Let's continue our use of JProfiler and the exploration of the memory of our application. This time, we suspect that there's a slow memory leak in production.

As a workaround to avoid the crashing of the application, it is restarted every 24 hours in the production environment.

This complicates our analysis; indeed, since the leak is small, the short lifetime of the application does not allow us to diagnose it.

We therefore decide to run an endurance test over several days in the pre-production environment and perform memory dumps with JProfiler in order to study the dumps after the test.

In order to do this, we will:

1. Reuse the script from example 3
2. Add a **Thread Group** element to execute the dump (always using jdump) once every 6 hours (to be refined according to the duration of the test)
3. Generate an analysis of the comparison of the dumps with the jpcompare tool delivered with JProfiler

> **Note**
> I let you do step 2 to focus on step 3.

4. In order to compare our memory dumps, we will execute the following command:

    ```
    jpcompare dump1.hprof,dump2.hprof,dumpX.hprof -outputdir=/home/ra77/Utils/
    Dumps/ Objects -format=html -aggregation=class DumpCompare.html
    ```

5. All this is done using an **OS Process Sampler** element:

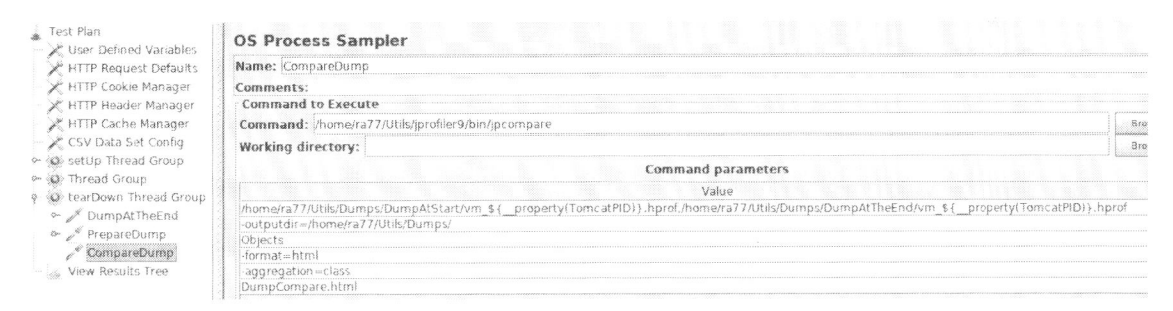

Figure 13.57: Comparison of dumps in JMeter

The result will be as follows:

Objects comparison

Snapshots: 1. vm_5745.hprof [2019-02-03 17:49:17]
2. vm_5745.hprof [2019-02-03 18:19:18]
Time of export: Sunday, February 3, 2019 8:13:48 PM CET

Objects: Heap snapshot objects
Aggregation: Classes

Name	Instance count	Size
java.lang.ref.SoftReference	+2,806 (+419 %)	+112 kB
java.util.jar.JarEntry	+267 (+Inf %)	+23,496 bytes
org.apache.tomcat.util.buf.ByteChunk	+109 (+76 %)	+5,232 bytes
org.apache.tomcat.util.buf.CharChunk	+98 (+75 %)	+4,704 bytes
org.apache.tomcat.util.buf.MessageBytes	+92 (+76 %)	+4,416 bytes
java.util.concurrent.ConcurrentLinkedQueue$Node	+88 (+93 %)	+2,112 bytes
java.lang.Object	+52 (+0 %)	+832 bytes
java.nio.HeapByteBuffer	+33 (+62 %)	+1,584 bytes
byte[ ]	+22 (+1 %)	+123 kB

Figure 13.58: HTML dumps comparison report

Same thing in JProfiler:

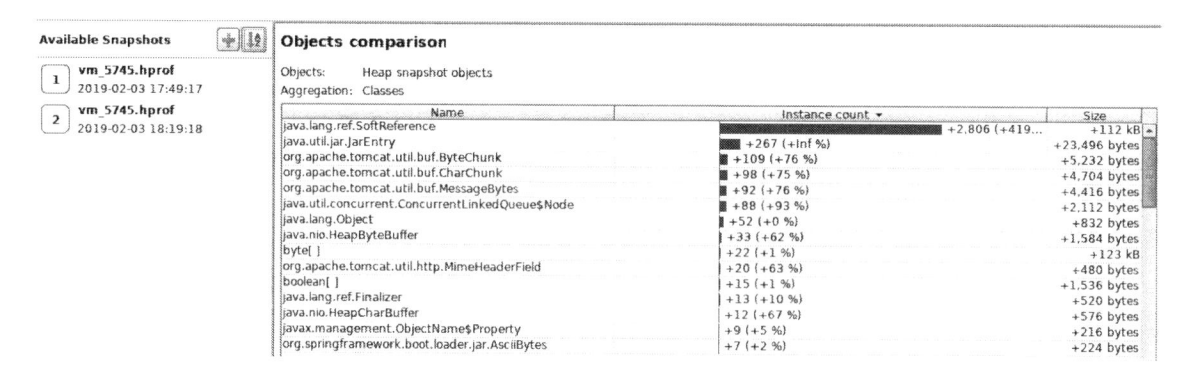

Figure 13.59: Dump comparison report in JProfiler

Or aggregated by packages:

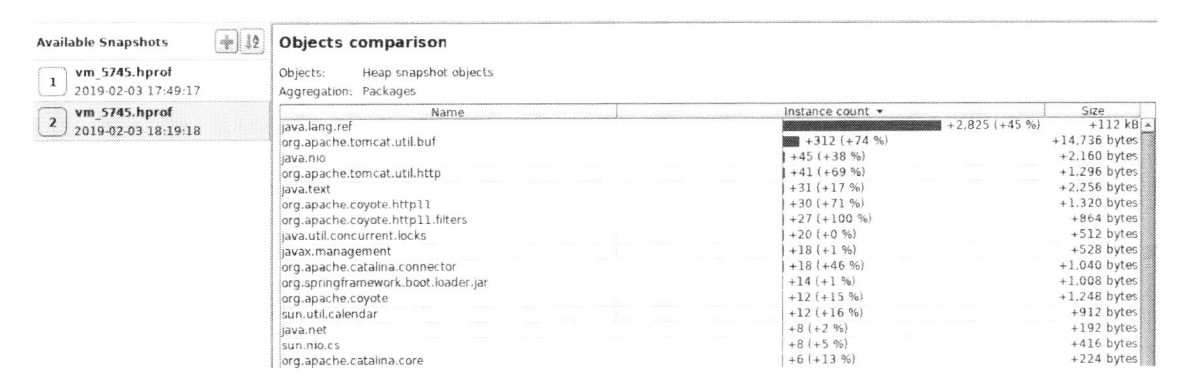

Figure 13.60: Dump comparison report in JProfiler aggregated by packages

6. The benefit of seeing the comparison of memory dumps in JProfiler is that it is possible to drill down in the analysis by right-clicking:

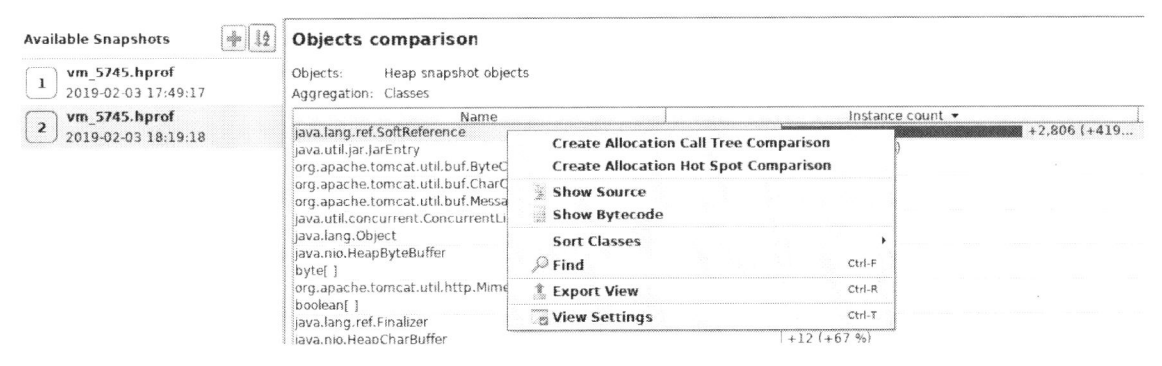

Figure 13.61: Dump analysis

> **Note**
> We have only seen some of the possibilities of the jcompare tool, so don't hesitate to take a closer look at it.

Example 5: Retrieving SQL Queries Executed during a Load Test with YourKit Java Profiler

YourKit Java Profiler (https://www.yourkit.com/), or yjp for short, is another widely used Java profiler.

Instead of using command-line tools, as in the previous examples, we will use yjp's API to retrieve all SQL queries executed during our load test.

For that, we will:

1. Attach the yjp agent to the tested application
2. Run our load test
3. Save a dump in yjp format
4. Export the information we are interested in (SQL queries) into CSV format
5. Send an email with a copy of the CSV file

Now, let's see the above steps in detail.

Our script will have the following form:

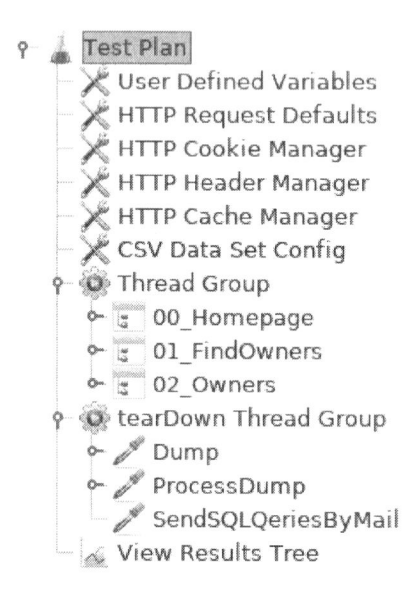

```
Test Plan
    User Defined Variables
    HTTP Request Defaults
    HTTP Cookie Manager
    HTTP Header Manager
    HTTP Cache Manager
    CSV Data Set Config
    Thread Group
        00_Homepage
        01_FindOwners
        02_Owners
    tearDown Thread Group
        Dump
        ProcessDump
        SendSQLQeriesByMail
    View Results Tree
```

Figure 13.62: Our JMeter script

1. Our first task is to attach the yjp agent to our application during its startup.

    A yjp wizard allows you to do this automatically; we get a new start file for Tomcat.

    As you can see, when editing the file, yjp uses the **-agentpath** parameter to attach its agent to the Tomcat JVM.

2. To simplify the example, we will ask the yjp agent to activate SQL probes directly at startup using the **probe_on=.Databases** parameter:

    ```
    -agentpath:/home/ra77/Utils/yjp-9.5.6/bin/linux-x86-64/libyjpagent.
    so=disablestacktelemetry,disableexceptiontelemetry,delay=10000,
    sessionname=Tomcat,probe_on=.Databases,probetablelengthlimit=2000000
    ```

Our test application is now started with the yjp agent, which collects SQL queries.

3. To perform the dump at the end of our load test, we use the API delivered with yjp.
4. Let's add this API (JAR files) to our script:

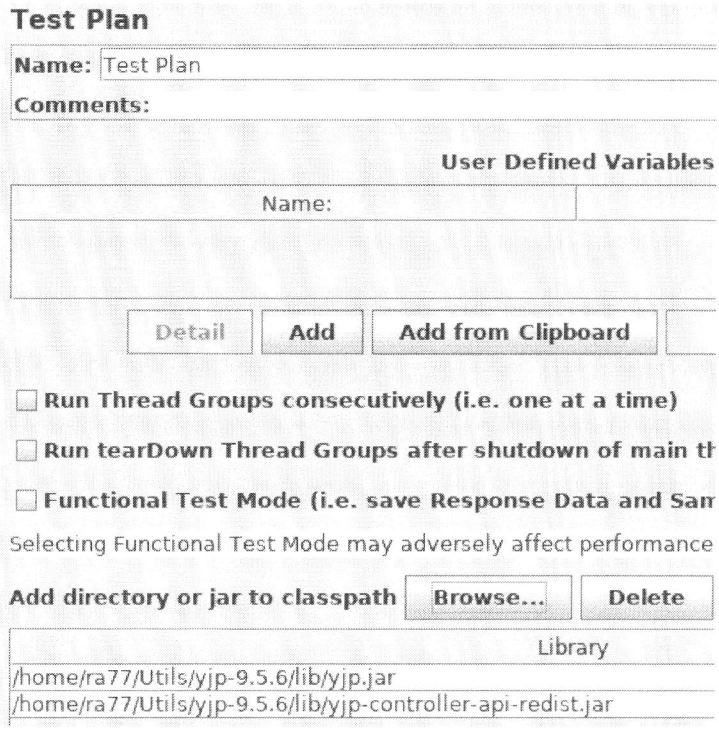

Figure 13.63: Added yjp API

> **Note**
> A better way to add those JARs would be to use the user.classpath JMeter property (https://jmeter.apache.org/usermanual/properties_reference.html#classpath).

5. Now, we will use a **tearDown Thread Group** to perform our actions after our load test.

6. The dump is done in a **JSR223 Sampler** using the Groovy language:

```groovy
import com.yourkit.api.Controller;
import com.yourkit.api.MemorySnapshot;
// Connection to the monitored application
final Controller controller = new Controller("localhost",10001);

//Creation of the dump
final String snapshotFileName = controller.captureMemorySnapshot();
//save dump name backup
props.setProperty("FileName", snapshotFileName);
```

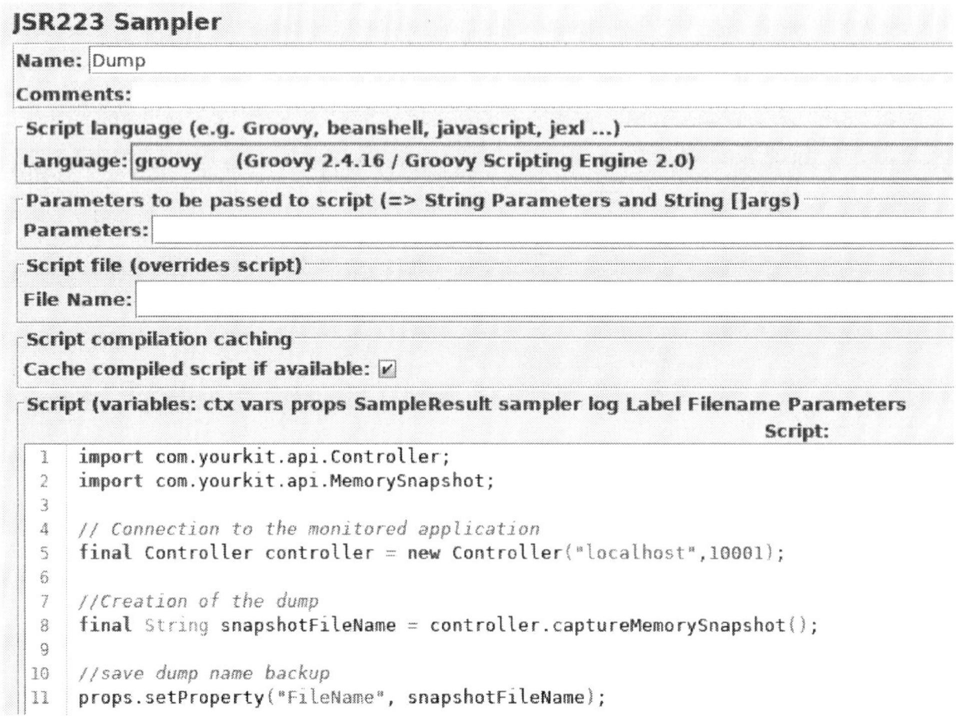

Figure 13.64: Making a dump with the yjp API

7. The processing of the dump to extract SQL queries in CSV format is done using an **OS Process Sampler** and the tool delivered with yjp:

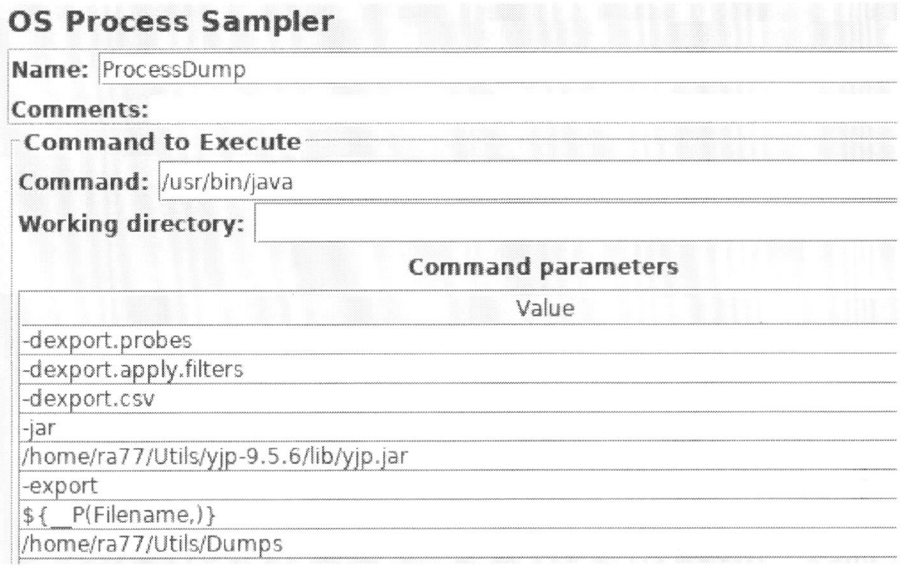
OS Process Sampler
Name: ProcessDump
Comments:
Command to Execute
Command: /usr/bin/java
Working directory:
Command parameters
Value
-dexport.probes
-dexport.apply.filters
-dexport.csv
-jar
/home/ra77/Utils/yjp-9.5.6/lib/yjp.jar
-export
${__P(Filename,)}
/home/ra77/Utils/Dumps

Figure 13.65: Dump processing

ID	uptime_ns	Database_id	SQL	Class	resource_object_id
9525	232968965432	9485	SELECT id, first_name, last_name, address, city, telephone FROM owners WHERE last_name like ?	org.apache.commons.dbcp.DelegatingPreparedStatement	733
9529	232972143317	5144	SELECT id, first_name, last_name, address, city, telephone FROM owners WHERE last_name like ?	org.apache.commons.dbcp.DelegatingPreparedStatement	732
9531	232972225393	5126	SELECT id, first_name, last_name, address, city, telephone FROM owners WHERE last_name like ?	org.hsqldb.jdbc.JDBCPreparedStatement	731
9559	233014134743	9485	SELECT id, name, birth_date, type_id, owner_id FROM pets WHERE owner_id=?	org.apache.commons.dbcp.DelegatingPreparedStatement	737
9561	233014181414	5144	SELECT id, name, birth_date, type_id, owner_id FROM pets WHERE owner_id=?	org.apache.commons.dbcp.DelegatingPreparedStatement	736
9563	233014216587	5126	SELECT id, name, birth_date, type_id, owner_id FROM pets WHERE owner_id=?	org.hsqldb.jdbc.JDBCPreparedStatement	735
9659	233102993727	9485	SELECT id, name FROM types ORDER BY name	org.apache.commons.dbcp.DelegatingPreparedStatement	740
9661	233103073605	5144	SELECT id, name FROM types ORDER BY name	org.apache.commons.dbcp.DelegatingPreparedStatement	739
9663	233103108964	5126	SELECT id, name FROM types ORDER BY name	org.hsqldb.jdbc.JDBCPreparedStatement	738
9675	233108996698	9485	SELECT id, visit_date, description FROM visits WHERE pet_id=?	org.apache.commons.dbcp.DelegatingPreparedStatement	745
9677	233109057222	5144	SELECT id, visit_date, description FROM visits WHERE pet_id=?	org.apache.commons.dbcp.DelegatingPreparedStatement	744
9679	233109098554	5126	SELECT id, visit_date, description FROM visits WHERE pet_id=?	org.hsqldb.jdbc.JDBCPreparedStatement	743
9214	233125080922	9216	SELECT id, first_name, last_name, address, city, telephone FROM owners WHERE id= ?	org.apache.commons.dbcp.DelegatingPreparedStatement	750
9218	233125203983	5144	SELECT id, first_name, last_name, address, city, telephone FROM owners WHERE id= ?	org.apache.commons.dbcp.DelegatingPreparedStatement	749
9220	233125247165	5126	SELECT id, first_name, last_name, address, city, telephone FROM owners WHERE id= ?	org.hsqldb.jdbc.JDBCPreparedStatement	748
9229	233129244969	9216	SELECT id, name, birth_date, type_id, owner_id FROM pets WHERE owner_id=?	org.apache.commons.dbcp.DelegatingPreparedStatement	753
9231	233129296828	5144	SELECT id, name, birth_date, type_id, owner_id FROM pets WHERE owner_id=?	org.apache.commons.dbcp.DelegatingPreparedStatement	752
9233	233129335379	5126	SELECT id, name, birth_date, type_id, owner_id FROM pets WHERE owner_id=?	org.hsqldb.jdbc.JDBCPreparedStatement	751
9241	233130758340	9216	SELECT id, name FROM types ORDER BY name	org.apache.commons.dbcp.DelegatingPreparedStatement	756
9243	233130808368	5144	SELECT id, name FROM types ORDER BY name	org.apache.commons.dbcp.DelegatingPreparedStatement	755

Figure 13.66: CSV file with our SQL queries

8. We also send an email with a CSV file attached to the database administrator using an **SMTP Sampler**:

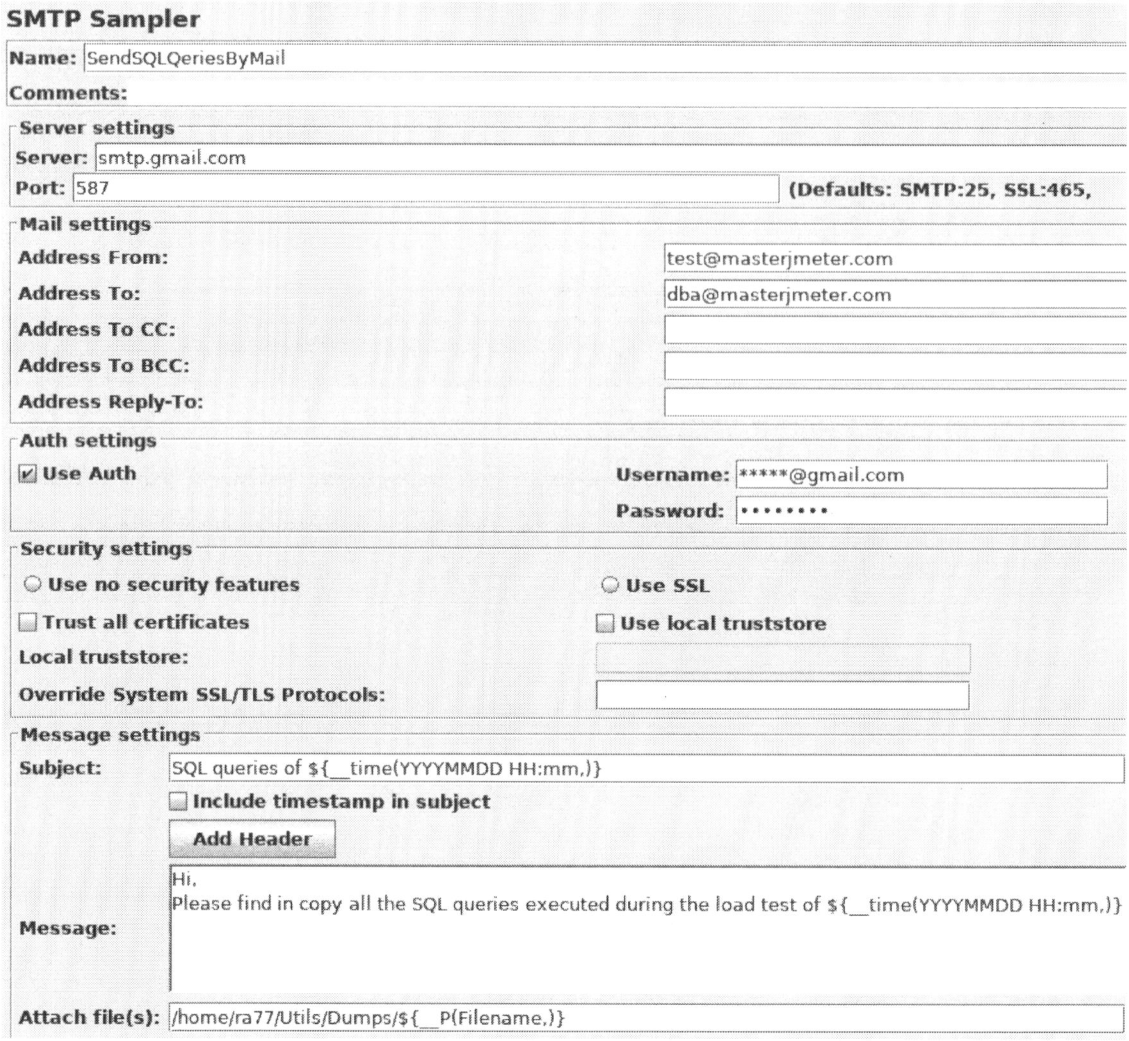

SMTP Sampler

Name:	SendSQLQeriesByMail
Comments:	

Server settings
- Server: smtp.gmail.com
- Port: 587   (Defaults: SMTP:25, SSL:465,

Mail settings
- Address From: test@masterjmeter.com
- Address To: dba@masterjmeter.com
- Address To CC:
- Address To BCC:
- Address Reply-To:

Auth settings
- ☑ Use Auth
- Username: *****@gmail.com
- Password: ••••••••

Security settings
- ○ Use no security features   ○ Use SSL
- ☐ Trust all certificates   ☐ Use local truststore
- Local truststore:
- Override System SSL/TLS Protocols:

Message settings
- Subject: SQL queries of ${__time(YYYYMMDD HH:mm,)}
- ☐ Include timestamp in subject
- [Add Header]
- Message: Hi,
Please find in copy all the SQL queries executed during the load test of ${__time(YYYYMMDD HH:mm,)}
- Attach file(s): /home/ra77/Utils/Dumps/${__P(Filename,)}

Figure 13.67: Sending the email

9. We use the `${__time(YYYYMMDD HH:mm,)}` function to have in the email title the exact date of the test, in order to differentiate them.

Of course, yjp allows you to retrieve other measurements (on threads, for instance) that we can process in the same way.

Example 6: Analysis of the Garbage Collector (GC) Log File with GCViewer

The activation of the GC logs allows you to collect valuable information on the behavior of the JVM.

Collecting this information has a very low impact on the performance of the application, so it is advisable to do so even in production (check the disk space beforehand and enable the rotation of those files).

To process these log files, many tools are available. We will focus here on GCViewer (https://github.com/chewiebug/GCViewer).

GCViewer has many advantages over other tools, such as the following:

- Support for many JVMs (such as IBM and Oracle)
- Support for many GC strategies (such as G1 and CMS)
- It's free of charge
- It's open source
- It can be used from the command line

We will see how to:

- Enable GC verbose logs using JMX
- Run a load test on our application
- Disable GC verbose logs using JMX
- Process the GC log file to obtain metrics
- Retrieve the metric named Throughput (time spent in the application and not in GC processing)
- Send emails depending on the value of Throughput

Our final test plan will be as follows:

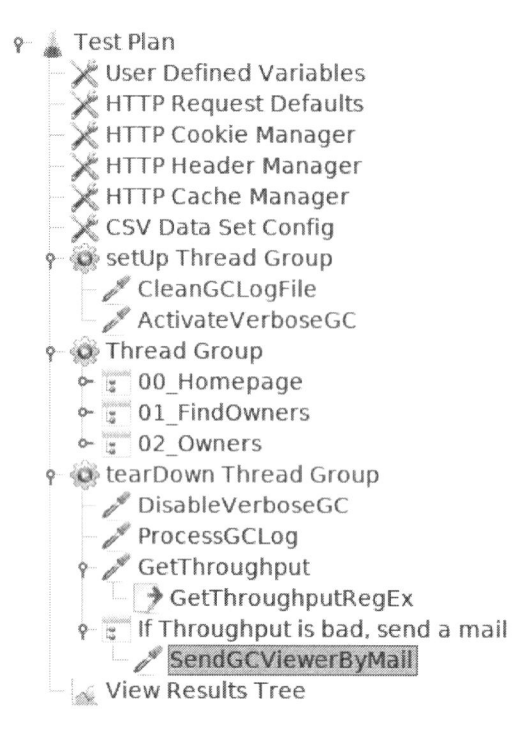

```
Test Plan
    User Defined Variables
    HTTP Request Defaults
    HTTP Cookie Manager
    HTTP Header Manager
    HTTP Cache Manager
    CSV Data Set Config
    setUp Thread Group
        CleanGCLogFile
        ActivateVerboseGC
    Thread Group
        00_Homepage
        01_FindOwners
        02_Owners
    tearDown Thread Group
        DisableVerboseGC
        ProcessGCLog
        GetThroughput
            GetThroughputRegEx
        If Throughput is bad, send a mail
            SendGCViewerByMail
    View Results Tree
```

Figure 13.68: Our test plan

But before starting our JMeter script, we configure the **-Xloggc** parameter and any additional parameters in our application startup script to:

- Be able to find our GC log file later
- Have all the information necessary for deeper analysis:

    ```
    -verbose:gc -Xloggc:gc_%p.log -XX:+PrintGCDetails -XX:+PrintGCCause
    -XX:+PrintTenuringDistribution -XX:+PrintHeapAtGC
    -XX:+PrintGCApplicationConcurrentTime -XX:+PrintAdaptiveSizePolicy
    -XX:+PrintGCApplicationStoppedTime -XX:+PrintGCDateStamps
    ```

Similarly, we add the following parameters to enable JMX on port 1105:

- `Dcom.sun.management.jmxremote`
- `Dcom.sun.management.jmxremote.port=1105`
- `Dcom.sun.management.jmxremote.authenticate=false`
- `Dcom.sun.management.jmxremote.ssl=false`

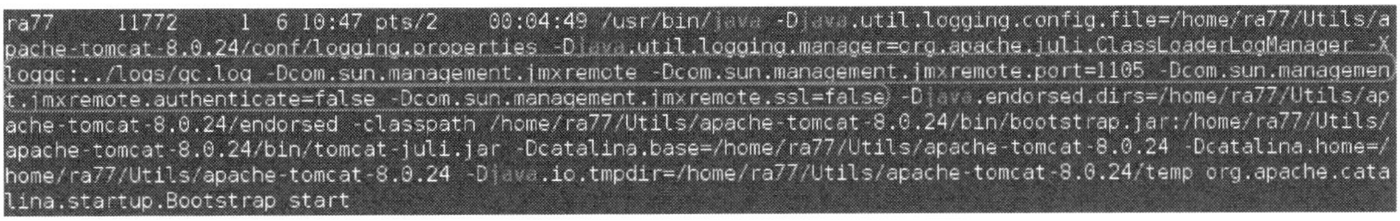

Figure 13.69: Parameters of our JVM

1. Let's start with the activation of verbose GC logs in **setUp Thread Group**.
2. First, we will empty the log file to make sure we only have the information from our load test.
3. To do this, we will use this script with the **OS Process Sampler** element:

   `/usr/bin/echo -n > /home/ra77/Utils/apache-tomcat-8.0.24/logs/gc.log`

4. Then let's activate our verbose GC logs using a Groovy program executed by the **JSR223 Sampler** element:

   ```
   import java.lang.management.*
    import javax.management.ObjectName
    import javax.management.remote. JMXConnectorFactory as JmxFactory
    import javax.management.remote. JMXServiceURL as JmxUrl
    def serverUrl = "service:jmx:rmi:////jndi/rmi://localhost:1105/jmxrmi
    def String beanName = "com.sun.management:type=HotSpotDiagnostic"
    def server = JmxFactory.connect(new JmxUrl(serverUrl)).
   MBeanServerConnection
    def MBean = new GroovyMBean(server, beanName)
    MBean.setVMOption('HeapDumpOnOutOfOfMemoryError','true')
    MBean.setVMOption('PrintGC','true')
    MBean.setVMOption('PrintGCDetails','true')
    MBean.setVMOption('PrintGCDateStamps','true')
   ```

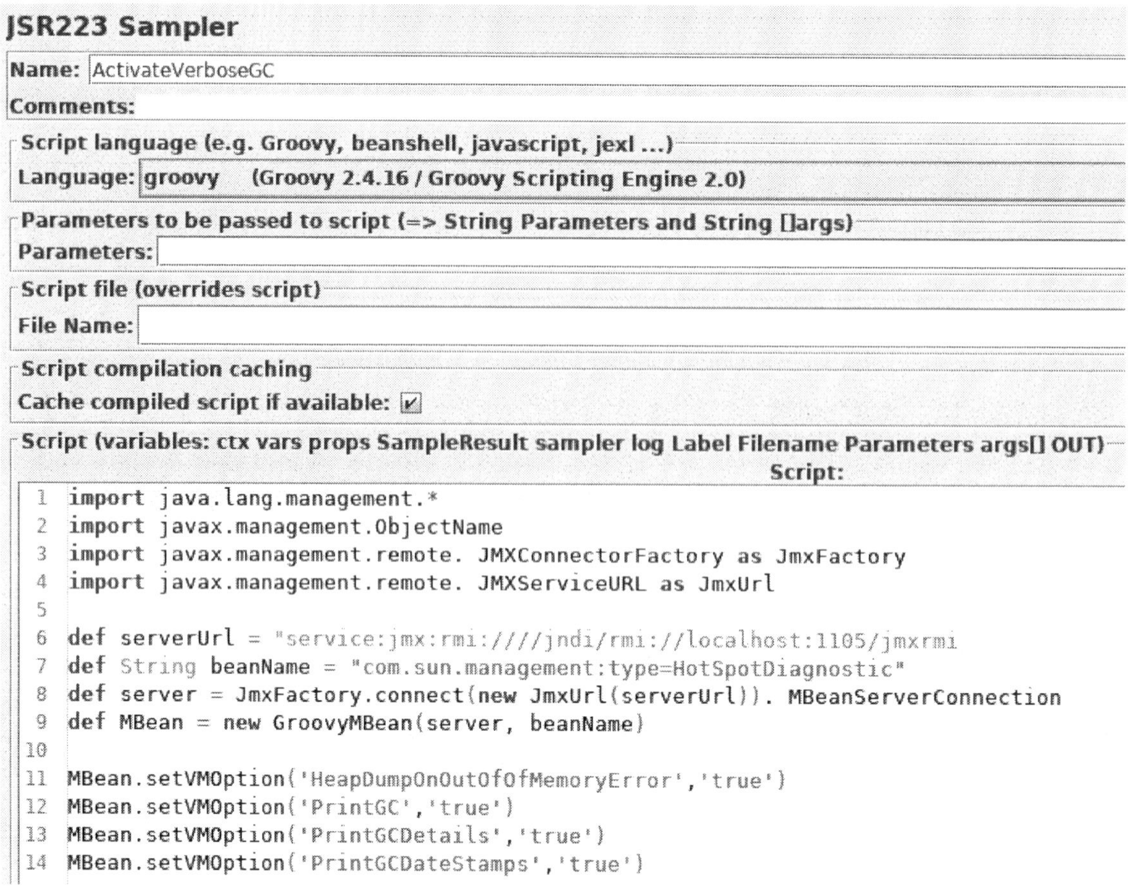

JSR223 Sampler

Name: ActivateVerboseGC
Comments:

Script language (e.g. Groovy, beanshell, javascript, jexl ...)
Language: groovy   (Groovy 2.4.16 / Groovy Scripting Engine 2.0)

Parameters to be passed to script (=> String Parameters and String []args)
Parameters:

Script file (overrides script)
File Name:

Script compilation caching
Cache compiled script if available: ☑

Script (variables: ctx vars props SampleResult sampler log Label Filename Parameters args[] OUT)
Script:

```groovy
import java.lang.management.*
import javax.management.ObjectName
import javax.management.remote.JMXConnectorFactory as JmxFactory
import javax.management.remote.JMXServiceURL as JmxUrl

def serverUrl = "service:jmx:rmi:////jndi/rmi://localhost:1105/jmxrmi"
def String beanName = "com.sun.management:type=HotSpotDiagnostic"
def server = JmxFactory.connect(new JmxUrl(serverUrl)). MBeanServerConnection
def MBean = new GroovyMBean(server, beanName)

MBean.setVMOption('HeapDumpOnOutOfOfMemoryError','true')
MBean.setVMOption('PrintGC','true')
MBean.setVMOption('PrintGCDetails','true')
MBean.setVMOption('PrintGCDateStamps','true')
```

Figure 13.70: Verbose GC logs activation

At the end of our test, we will process this log file using a **tearDown Thread Group**.

5. Let's start by restoring our GC logs to their original state:

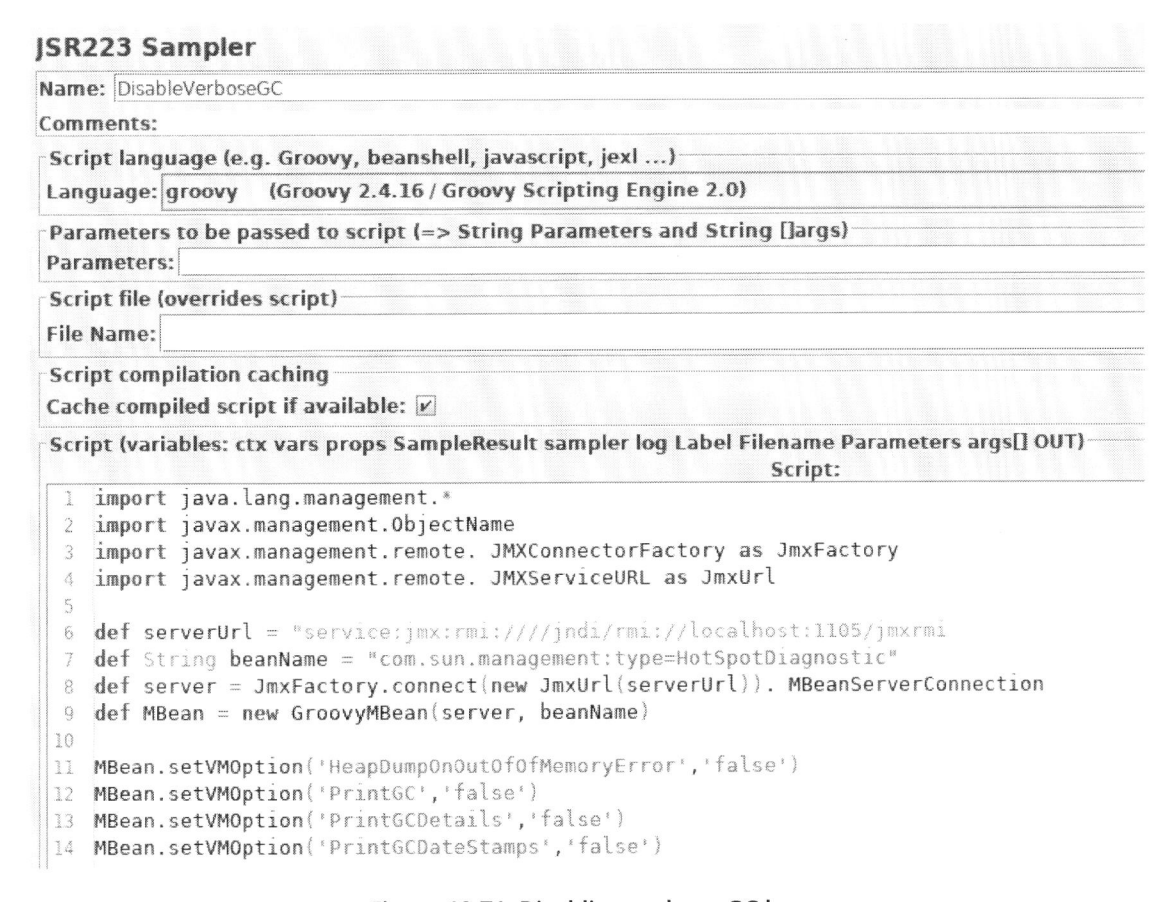

```
JSR223 Sampler
Name: DisableVerboseGC
Comments:
Script language (e.g. Groovy, beanshell, javascript, jexl ...)
Language: groovy    (Groovy 2.4.16 / Groovy Scripting Engine 2.0)
Parameters to be passed to script (=> String Parameters and String []args)
Parameters:
Script file (overrides script)
File Name:
Script compilation caching
Cache compiled script if available: ☑
Script (variables: ctx vars props SampleResult sampler log Label Filename Parameters args[] OUT)
Script:
 1  import java.lang.management.*
 2  import javax.management.ObjectName
 3  import javax.management.remote.JMXConnectorFactory as JmxFactory
 4  import javax.management.remote.JMXServiceURL as JmxUrl
 5
 6  def serverUrl = "service:jmx:rmi:////jndi/rmi://localhost:1105/jmxrmi"
 7  def String beanName = "com.sun.management:type=HotSpotDiagnostic"
 8  def server = JmxFactory.connect(new JmxUrl(serverUrl)).MBeanServerConnection
 9  def MBean = new GroovyMBean(server, beanName)
10
11  MBean.setVMOption('HeapDumpOnOutOfOfMemoryError','false')
12  MBean.setVMOption('PrintGC','false')
13  MBean.setVMOption('PrintGCDetails','false')
14  MBean.setVMOption('PrintGCDateStamps','false')
```

Figure 13.71: Disabling verbose GC logs

6. Then let's run GCViewer to process the log file:

```
OS Process Sampler
Name: ProcessGCLog
Comments:
Command to Execute
Command: /usr/bin/java
Working directory:
                                                    Command parameters
                                                              Value
-jar
/home/ra77/Utils/gcviewer-1.35.jar
/home/ra77/Utils/apache-tomcat-8.0.24/logs/gc.log
/home/ra77/Utils/GCLogs/summary.csv
```

Figure 13.72: Processing of the log file by GCViewer

430 | Integration of JMeter in the DevOps Tool Chain

7. Let's get the throughput from the GCViewer output file using a script:

```
grep throughput /home/ra77/Utils/GCLogs/summary.csv| cut -d";" -f2 | tr -d ' ' | cut -d"," -f1
```

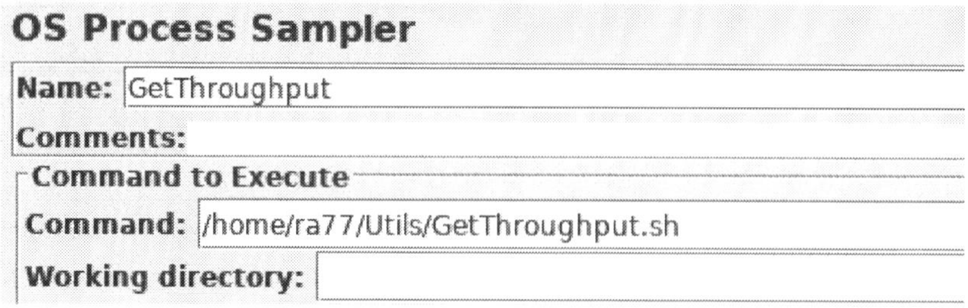

Figure 13.73: Retrieving the throughput – Script

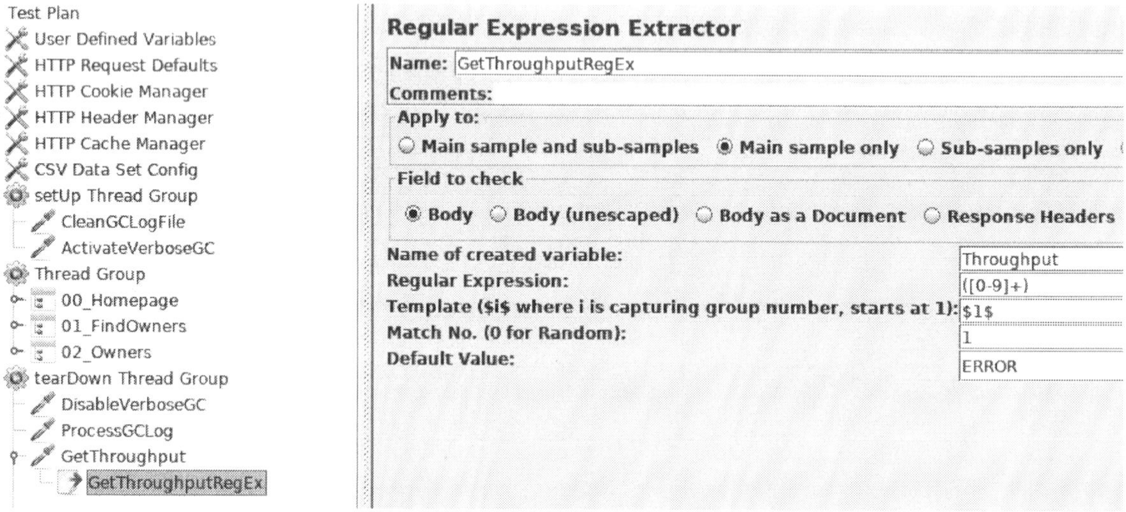

Figure 13.74: Retrieving the throughput – regular expression

8. If the value of the throughput is greater than or equal to 97 percent, we send an email with the GCViewer output file to allow more analysis:

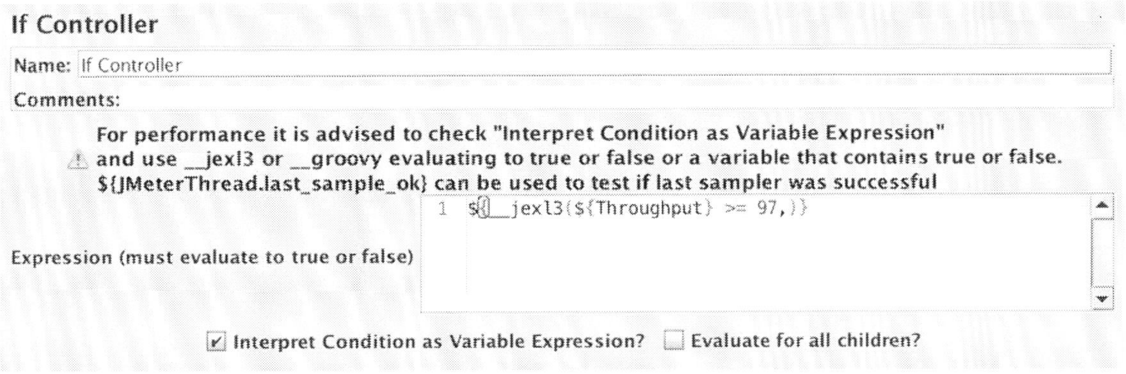

Figure 13.75: Is the throughput greater than or equal to 97%?

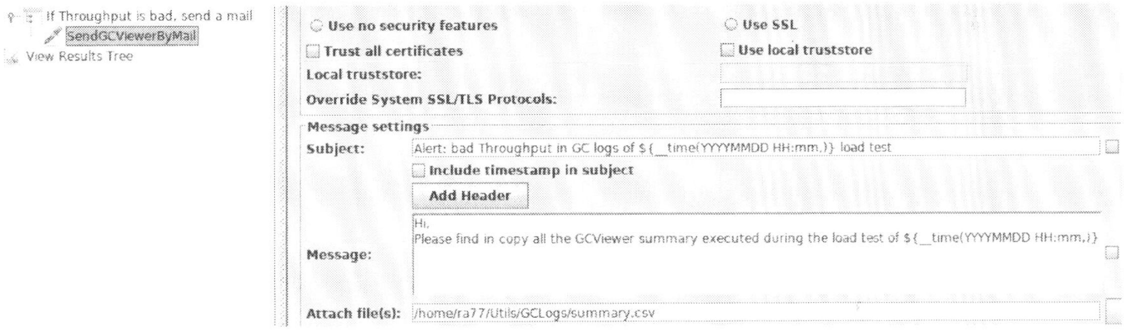

Figure 13.76: Sending our alerting email

9. The next step is to look in GCViewer for more information:

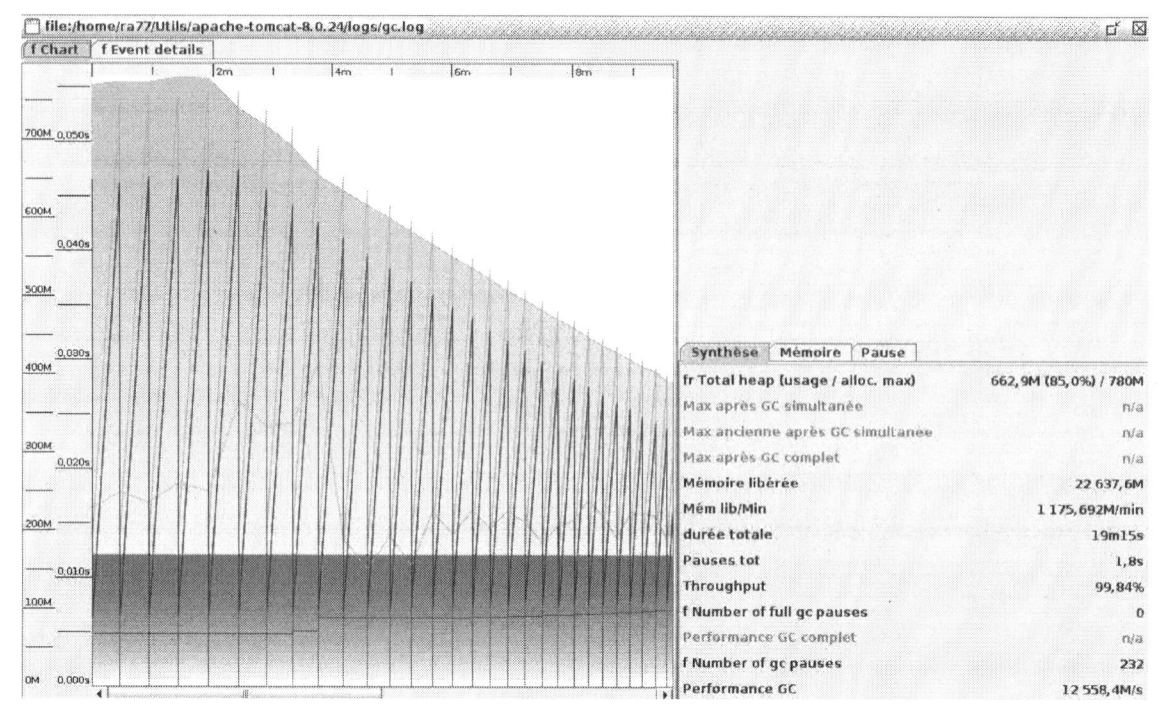

Figure 13.77: GCViewer

This saves us time by allowing us to only look at the GC logs if necessary. Of course, it is quite possible to use other indicators in the same way.

Example 7: Non-Regression Testing of Web APIs with Dynatrace AppMon

Running load tests every night is a best practice, but it can quickly become very time-consuming as there is often a lot of data (including false positives) to analyze every morning.

An intermediate solution can be to test at the API level and look only at certain metrics (such as the number of database queries and the number of method executions).

In this particular case, Dynatrace AppMon can be very useful to us, thanks to its *Web API tests* (https://www.dynatrace.com/support/doc/appmon/continuous-delivery-test-automation/capture-performance-data-from-tests/web-api-tests/) feature.

The REST API reference is https://www.dynatrace.com/support/doc/appmon/continuous-delivery-test-automation/automation-and-integration/rest-interfaces-for-test-automation/.

To illustrate its use, we will create a JMeter script at the API level that will run at each commit/every night.

For these scripts to be considered *Web API tests*, we will modify the HTTP request headers so that Dynatrace AppMon can identify them.

Let's look at what our JMeter script will look like:

```
Test Plan
    setUp Thread Group
        HTTP Authorization Manager
        RegisterTestRunToDynatrace
            HTTP Header Manager
            GetTestId
            ExportVarAsProperty
    customers
        Test_000_ShowVets
            /petclinic/vets.html
                HTTP Header Manager
                Response Assertion
```

Figure 13.78: Non-regression testing of Web APIs – our final script

This script is composed of the following steps:

1. Register our test at the Dynatrace AppMon level using its REST API
2. Retrieve the test execution ID returned by Dynatrace AppMon
3. Export this variable as a property to be available for all threads
4. Modify the **x-dynatrace** header of our HTTP request
5. Execute our test
6. Visualize the results in Dynatrace AppMon

Registering to Dynatrace using a setup Thread Group

We first use a **setup Thread Group**, which is run before any other **Thread Group**.

1. Let's start by using the **HTTP Authorization Manager** element to add basic authentication to our Dynatrace AppMon call:

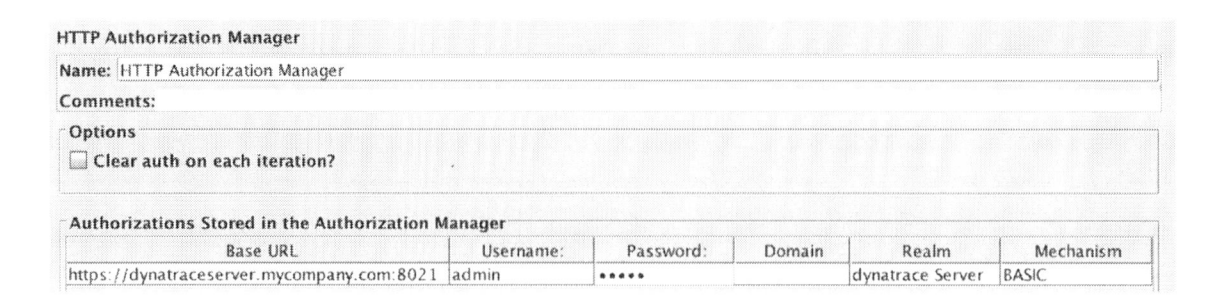

Figure 13.79: HTTP Authorization Manager

2. Next, we register our test at the Dynatrace AppMon level using an **HTTP Request** element and **HTTP Header Manager** with the Content-Type=application/json header:

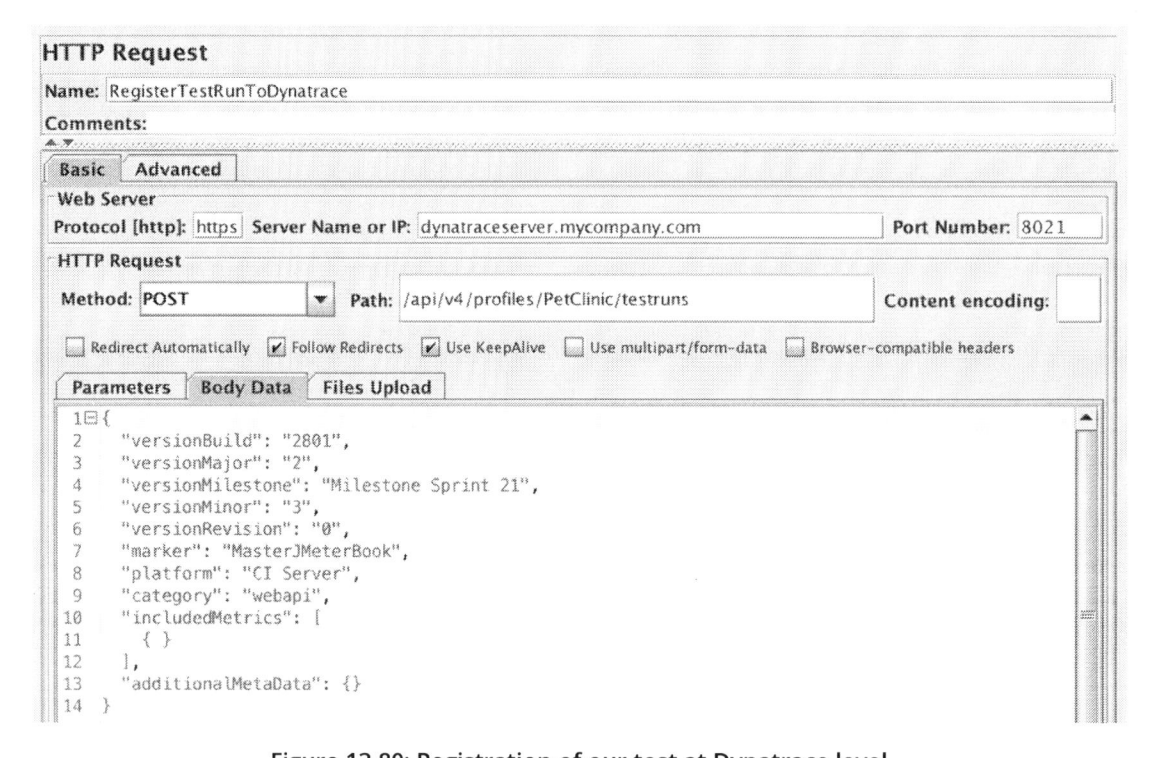

Figure 13.80: Registration of our test at Dynatrace level

3. Now we extract the **id** from the response that looks like this:

```
{
  "id": "7a0520fc-eda9-4f78-a8fa-4cb7d04ac8b8",
  "category": "webapi",
  "versionBuild": "2801",
  "versionMajor": "2",
  "versionMilestone": "Milestone Sprint 21",
  "versionMinor": "3",
  "versionRevision": "0",
  "platform": "CI Server Linux",
  "startTime": "2019-02-09T14:34:39.070+01:00",
  "systemProfile": "PetClinic",
  "marker": "MasterJMeterBook",
  "href": "https://localhost:8021/api/v4/profiles/sampleProfile/testruns/7a0520fc-eda9-4f78-a8fa-4cb7d04ac8b8",
  "creationMode": "MANUAL",
  "numDegraded": 0,
  "numFailed": 0,
  "numImproved": 0,
  "numInvalidated": 0,
  "numPassed": 0,
  "numVolatile": 0,
  "finished": false,
  "includedMetrics": []
}
```

4. We use a **JSON Extractor** element using **id JSON Path expression**:

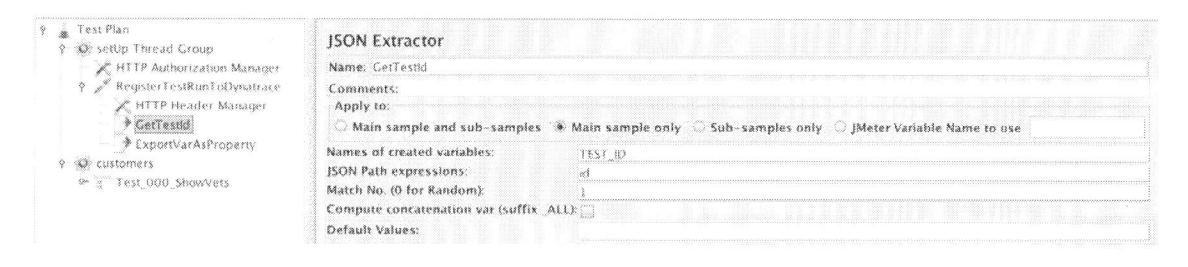

Figure 13.81: Retrieving the test execution identifier returned by Dynatrace

5. Now, since **TEST_ID** must be used by other **Thread Groups**, and since the **setup Thread Group**'s threads end before the start of the other **Thread Group**'s threads, we must export the **TEST_ID** variable into the **testId** property:

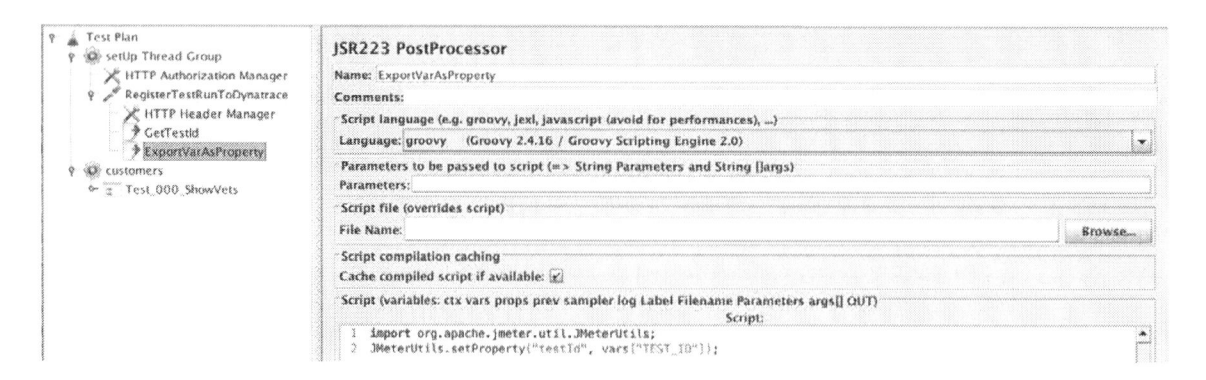

Figure 13.82: Saving the test execution identifier returned by Dynatrace AppMon

Using testId in Other Thread Groups

1. Finally, in our test's **Thread Group**, we use a **HTTP Header Manager** that will contain the **X-dynaTrace** header of our HTTP request:

Figure 13.83: Modification of the HTTP header

2. Let's now look at our results in Dynatrace AppMon.

    In the following screenshot, we can see:

    Our test (here, **Test_000_ShowVets**)

    A number of metrics that have been automatically computed (Count, DB Count, and PurePath Duration)

A graph of the metrics with thresholds (in pink) that automatically adjust themselves:

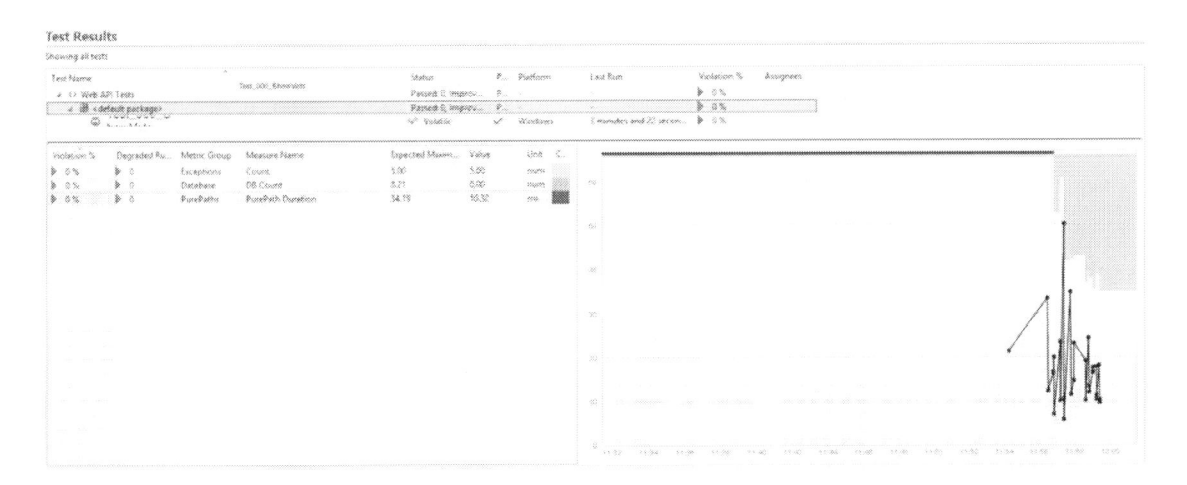

Figure 13.84: The Web API tests functionality of Dynatrace APM

This feature allows us to have fewer data to analyze compared to a conventional load test while being accurate enough to detect performance regression's problems.

Of course, it is possible to add our own custom metrics.

For a more complete and easier integration of JMeter with Dynatrace, you can use this commercial plugin – https://www.youtube.com/watch?v=26-1FhJB-1E – provided by *UbikLoadPack*, which allows you to:

- Record Dynatrace sessions, allowing you to keep metrics precision across time
- Automatically tag requests and transactions in the APM

Conclusion

As we can see, the use of JMeter in a continuous integration process is easy due to the richness of its ecosystem and its flexibility. But be careful: as with performance, DevOps is much more than just the use of tools to achieve continuous integration.

Index

About

All major keywords used in this book are captured alphabetically in this section. Each one is accompanied by the page number of where it appears.

A

activemq: 288, 290, 296, 302, 304-310, 314, 316, 318-319, 321, 324
address: 6, 84, 87, 90, 290, 309, 329
administer: 403
anscombe: 359
anti-bot: 84
apache: 8, 23-24, 29, 78, 87, 106, 114, 127, 129, 131, 135, 144-145, 209, 288, 290, 296, 302, 307-310, 316, 318, 324, 334-335, 338, 356, 392, 421
append: 210
appmon: 432-434, 436
argument: 78, 397-398
artemis: 290, 309-310, 314, 316, 318, 321, 324
artifactid: 335-336, 398
assertion: 12-13, 46, 66-67, 72-76, 106, 115-116, 131, 161, 170-171, 183, 220, 222-223, 238, 253, 271, 321, 333, 335, 342, 348, 413
aurora: 244
average: 59, 359-360, 362-364, 366, 368

B

backend: 17, 29, 101, 331, 340, 352-355, 363, 378
backtolist: 186
backup: 247, 270, 384, 413, 422
balancer: 50, 82, 84-86, 91, 364

bandwidth: 36, 60, 84
basic-auth: 157
beanname: 427
beanshell: 343
binaries: 334
binary: 287
blazemeter: 25, 96-97, 102, 119, 333, 335, 358
blocked: 86, 91
blogspot: 360, 368
bminstall: 193
bmsubmit: 193-194
broadcast: 286, 324
browser: 1, 5, 8, 58, 101, 103, 108, 112, 147, 150-151, 154-157, 168, 170, 363-364
button: 6-7, 11, 13, 160, 395
bypass: 84
bytecode: 189, 193
byteman: 189, 193, 196-198, 200-202

C

cacheable: 151
caches: 50, 59, 202, 246-247, 254, 364
caching: 151
cannot: 36, 129, 139, 385
captcha: 91, 208-209, 212
cascade: 270
catalog: 162, 173
catdetail: 173, 185
charset: 149, 218
charts: 374
chewiebug: 425
chrome: 96-97, 103
circuit: 201
classname: 114

classpath: 248, 268, 311, 322, 421
clause: 256, 258
clicknext: 333, 335
client: 46, 147, 151, 153, 240, 276-277, 288, 298
cloudwatch: 353, 355
cluster: 89, 244
collectd: 353
command: 17-18, 24, 77, 99, 109, 193-194, 203, 268, 309, 328-333, 344, 355, 411, 416-417, 425
commata: 255
competitor: 36
compiler: 50, 189
components: 83-84, 109, 158, 247, 329, 340
computing: 354, 368
config: 60, 67, 78, 87, 114, 118, 121, 125, 128-129, 154, 157, 192, 209, 239, 254, 257, 272, 323
console: 120, 305, 309, 314, 333, 335
constant: 43, 56, 185, 315, 388
cookie: 61, 143-145, 151, 156-157, 169, 350
crashing: 36, 45, 158, 416
csselly: 176

D

darcula: 24
database: 17, 28-29, 50, 57, 90-92, 106, 136, 138, 193, 200, 202, 229, 243-251, 267, 270-271, 273, 275-276, 278-279, 292, 323, 331, 355-356, 362, 364, 367, 424, 432

datadog: 355
datadoghq: 355
dbname: 251
debugging: 95, 109, 145, 348
devops: 127, 338, 344, 381, 383-385, 437
directory: 28, 208, 211, 288-289, 309, 311, 337-338, 401, 412-414
download: 112
driver: 248, 250-251
dumping: 412
dynatrace: 362, 432-437

E

emails: 92, 425
errors: 19, 59, 90, 106, 112, 118, 202, 303, 337, 340-341, 347-348, 356, 376-377
extensions: 307

F

fields: 3, 10, 55, 154, 160, 287, 289, 291, 348-349
firefox: 5-6, 148, 169
firewall: 84, 91
font-src: 401

G

gclogs: 430
gcviewer: 425, 429-432
gnuplot: 357
grafana: 17-19, 26, 29, 340, 352, 354, 356
graphs: 19, 356-357, 359, 369, 372, 375, 377-378

groovy: 25, 128, 130-131, 135, 143, 208, 223, 323-324, 343, 401, 422, 427
groupid: 335-336, 398

I

identifier: 151, 195, 216, 227, 231, 234, 287, 305, 435-436
if-match: 151
if-range: 151
img-src: 401
indexof: 138
influxdata: 17, 353
influxdb: 17, 26, 29, 331, 340, 348, 352, 354, 356-357, 362
in-house: 322
intellij: 119

J

javafx: 112
javascript: 25, 103, 135, 154, 343
javase: 128
javaserver: 172
javatest: 114
jcompare: 419
jenkins: 29, 338, 344, 391-396, 399-409
jenkins-ci: 391, 402
jeopardize: 88
jmeterbook: 304, 307
jmeter-bzt: 333, 335
jmxfactory: 427
jmxremote: 427
jmxrmi: 427
jmxtrans: 353

jmxurl: 427
jolokia: 307-308
jpanalyze: 414
jpcompare: 417
jpdump: 411
jpenable: 203, 206
jprofiler: 202-207, 410-411, 414-419
jquery: 175
json-path: 231
jupyter: 29, 356
jython: 25

K

kerberos: 153, 157
kotlin: 25

L

lazerycode: 336, 398
linux-x: 420
lookup: 316, 319

M

machine: 50, 84, 91, 251, 289, 356, 393
maven-: 335
memory: 35, 55, 59, 88, 202, 207, 285, 306, 397, 410-411, 416-417, 419
metadata: 287
method: 148, 151, 196, 200, 216, 238, 240, 270, 302, 328, 350, 383, 432
metrics: 19, 26, 32, 353, 357, 361, 365-366, 368-369, 375, 405, 425, 432, 436-437

microsoft: 24, 29, 356
middleware: 28, 281
mycookie: 144
mycounter: 138-139
myheader: 135
myproxy: 330
myscript: 132-133, 329-331, 338, 389
myserver: 290

N

navigation: 4-5, 7, 9, 46, 60
netbeans: 119, 162, 219, 224, 229
network: 5, 19, 27-28, 36, 55, 82-84, 86, 101, 120, 158, 363
non-gui: 17, 55, 329
numfailed: 435
numpassed: 435

O

octoperf: 25
openjdk: 207
openoffice: 356

P

password: 57, 69, 125, 248, 309
percentile: 33, 352, 360-361, 366, 368, 405
perfmon: 16
postgresql: 356
profiler: 419

Q

qlikview: 29, 356

R

randomdate: 121
regexp: 111, 181-182, 348
regression: 88, 437
rendezvous: 61

S

sampler: 19, 69-70, 72-75, 104, 113-115, 117, 120, 122, 124, 131, 135, 138, 140-141, 144-145, 186, 194-195, 206, 208-209, 261, 270, 317, 320-324, 343, 349, 410, 412-413, 417, 422-424, 427
script: 1, 3, 7, 11, 13-15, 17, 26-27, 46, 54-55, 69-71, 82-83, 87-88, 90, 96, 98, 101-104, 107-109, 114, 119, 121-122, 125, 130-136, 138-139, 141, 145, 147, 154, 158-161, 166-169, 171-172, 178-179, 183-185, 188-191, 195, 199-200, 202, 206-207, 212-213, 229, 236, 238, 240, 254, 258, 264-267, 274, 305-306, 311-312, 314, 316-318, 320-321, 323, 328-329, 332, 334, 338, 340, 343, 347, 378, 387-389, 401, 410-412, 417, 420-421, 426-427, 430, 433

script-src: 401
server: 3, 5-8, 10-11, 28, 36, 50-51, 58-59, 82, 84, 90, 92, 101, 108, 143, 147, 149, 151, 156, 172, 193, 200, 202, 219, 243-245, 247, 267, 303-304, 306, 313, 349, 360, 389, 392, 410, 427, 435
serverurl: 427
servlet: 8
servlets: 8
set-cookie: 151
setuptest: 211
setupvars: 132-133
shellexec: 333, 335
showvets: 436
software: 23, 26, 89, 208, 264, 267, 356-357, 382, 390-391
spoofing: 84-87, 153
sqlite: 356
stickiness: 85-86
syntactic: 256
syntax: 78, 176, 231, 253, 270, 332, 342-343

T

telegraf: 353
telerik: 120
terminal: 18
tesseract: 208-212
tester: 110-111, 181, 350, 383-385
timers: 69-73
tointeger: 138
tomcat: 8, 411, 420
tomlinson: 34
trigger: 120, 186, 203-204, 207, 393

U

ubuntu: 148

V

version: 77, 87, 90, 148-150, 168, 223, 245, 288, 330, 334-336, 352, 355, 398, 405, 410

W

webapi: 435
webperf: 103, 363
webservice: 218
website: 8, 18, 29, 36, 45-46, 57, 108, 147, 150, 157, 219, 240, 410-411
wikidot: 352
window: 6-7, 120, 256, 377

X

x-axis: : 373
x-jmeter: 135
xmeter: 25
xml-rpc: 219

Y

yourkit: 419, 422
youtube: 437

Z

zeppelin: 29, 356

Printed in Great Britain
by Amazon

Cloud Networking

Cloud Networking
Understanding Cloud-based
Data Center Networks

Gary Lee

AMSTERDAM • BOSTON • HEIDELBERG • LONDON
NEW YORK • OXFORD • PARIS • SAN DIEGO
SAN FRANCISCO • SINGAPORE • SYDNEY • TOKYO

Morgan Kaufmann is an imprint of Elsevier

Acquiring Editor: Todd Green
Editorial Project Manager: Lindsay Lawrence
Project Manager: Punithavathy Govindaradjane
Designer: Russell Purdy

Morgan Kaufmann is an imprint of Elsevier
225 Wyman Street, Waltham, MA 02451 USA

Copyright © 2014 Gary Lee. Published by Elsevier Inc. All rights reserved.

No part of this publication may be reproduced or transmitted in any form or by any means, electronic or mechanical, including photocopying, recording, or any information storage and retrieval system, without permission in writing from the publisher. Details on how to seek permission, further information about the Publisher's permissions policies and our arrangements with organizations such as the Copyright Clearance Center and the Copyright Licensing Agency, can be found at our website: www.elsevier.com/permissions.

This book and the individual contributions contained in it are protected under copyright by the Publisher (other than as may be noted herein).

Notices

Knowledge and best practice in this field are constantly changing. As new research and experience broaden our understanding, changes in research methods or professional practices, may become necessary. Practitioners and researchers must always rely on their own experience and knowledge in evaluating and using any information or methods described herein. In using such information or methods they should be mindful of their own safety and the safety of others, including parties for whom they have a professional responsibility.

To the fullest extent of the law, neither the Publisher nor the authors, contributors, or editors, assume any liability for any injury and/or damage to persons or property as a matter of products liability, negligence or otherwise, or from any use or operation of any methods, products, instructions, or ideas contained in the material herein.

Library of Congress Cataloging-in-Publication Data
Lee, Gary, 1958
 Cloud networking : developing cloud-based data center networks / Gary Lee.
   pages cm
 ISBN 978-0-12-800728-0
 1. Cloud computing. I. Title.
 QA76.585.L434 2014
 004.67'82–dc23

2014006135

British Library Cataloguing-in-Publication Data
A catalogue record for this book is available from the British Library.

ISBN: 978-0-12-800728-0

Printed and bound in the United States of America
14 15 16 17 18   10 9 8 7 6 5 4 3 2 1

For information on all MK publications
visit our website at www.mkp.com

Working together
to grow libraries in
developing countries

www.elsevier.com • www.bookaid.org

Contents

About the Author xiii
Preface xv

CHAPTER 1 Welcome to Cloud Networking 1
    Introduction 1
    Networking Basics 2
        The network stack 2
        Packets and frames 3
        Network equipment 4
        Interconnect 4
    What Is a Cloud Data Center? 4
    What Is Cloud Networking? 5
    Characteristics of Cloud Networking 5
        Ethernet usage 6
        Virtualization 6
        Convergence 7
        Scalability 7
        Software 8
    Summary of This Book 8

CHAPTER 2 Data Center Evolution—Mainframes to the Cloud ... 11
    The Data Center Evolution 11
        Early mainframes 12
        Minicomputers 12
        Servers 13
        Enterprise data centers 14
        Cloud data centers 14
        Virtualized data centers 15
    Computer Networks 16
        Dedicated lines 17
        ARPANET 17
        TCP/IP 18
        Multi-Protocol Label Switching 19
        SONET/SDH 20
        Asynchronous Transfer Mode 21
        Token Ring/Token Bus 22
        Ethernet 23

Fibre Channel 23
InfiniBand 23
Ethernet 24
Ethernet history 24
Ethernet overview 25
Carrier Ethernet 27
Enterprise Versus Cloud Data Centers 28
Enterprise data center networks 29
Cloud data center networks 30
Movement to the Cloud 31
Driving forces 31
Cloud types 32
Public cloud services 33
Review 35

CHAPTER 3 Switch Fabric Technology 37

Switch Fabric Architecture Overview 37
Shared bus architecture 38
Shared bus performance limitations 39
Shared memory architecture 39
Shared memory performance limitations 40
Crossbar switch 40
Crossbar switch performance limitations 41
Synchronous serial switching 42
Synchronous serial performance limitations 43
Switch Fabric Topologies 43
Ring topology 43
Mesh topology 44
Star topology 45
Fat-tree topology 46
Congestion Management 47
Causes of congestion 47
Load balancing algorithms 48
Traffic buffering 49
Flow Control 50
Link-level flow control 51
Virtual output queuing 53
Multistage switch fabric flow control 54
Traffic Management 55
Frame classification engine 55
Multilevel scheduler 55
Traffic shaping 57

Switch Chip Architecture Examples 58
    Cell-based designs 58
    Input-output-queued designs 60
    Output-queued shared memory designs 62
Review 64

CHAPTER 4   Cloud Data Center Networking Topologies 65

Traditional Multitiered Enterprise Networks 65
    Cost factors 65
    Performance factors 67
Data Center Network Switch Types 68
    Virtual switch 69
    ToR switch 70
    EoR switch 71
    Fabric extenders 72
    Aggregation and core switches 73
Flat Data Center Networks 74
    Data center traffic patterns 74
    ToR switch features 76
    Core switch features 77
Rack Scale Architectures 79
    Disaggregation of resources 81
    Microservers 82
Network Function Virtualization 83
Review 85

CHAPTER 5   Data Center Networking Standards 87

Ethernet Data Rate Standards 87
    10GbE 88
    40GbE and 100GbE 88
Virtual Local Area Networks 89
Data Center Bridging 90
    Priority-based flow control 91
    Enhanced transmission selection 93
    Quantized congestion notification 94
    DCB exchange protocol 95
Improving Network Bandwidth 96
    Spanning tree 96
    Equal cost multipath routing 97
    Shortest path bridging 98
    Transparent interconnection of lots of links 98

	Remote Direct Memory Access	100
	Data center requirements	100
	Internet Wide-Area RDMA Protocol	101
	RDMA over Converged Ethernet	102
	Review	102
CHAPTER 6	**Server Virtualization and Networking**	**103**
	VM Overview	103
	Hypervisors	104
	VMware	105
	Microsoft	105
	Virtual Switching	106
	vSphere Distributed Switch	106
	Hyper-V virtual switch	107
	Open vSwitch	108
	Virtual machine device queues	108
	PCI Express	110
	Background	110
	Single-root IO virtualization	112
	Multiroot IO virtualization	113
	Edge Virtual Bridging	114
	VEPA	114
	VN-Tag	115
	Industry adoption	116
	VM Migration	117
	Memory migration	117
	Network migration	118
	Vendor solutions	119
	Review	120
CHAPTER 7	**Network Virtualization**	**121**
	Multi-tenant Environments	121
	Network requirements	122
	MAC address learning	123
	Traditional Network Tunneling Protocols	123
	Q-in-Q	124
	MPLS	124
	VN-Tags	126
	VXLAN	126
	Frame format	127

VTEP encapsulation	128
VTEP de-encapsulation	129
NVGRE	130
Generic routing encapsulation	130
Frame format	131
NVE encapsulation	131
NVE de-encapsulation	132
Tunnel Locations	133
vSwitch	134
Network interface card	134
Top of rack switch	135
Load Balancing	135
Hash-based algorithms	135
Equal cost multipath routing	136
Review	137

CHAPTER 8 Storage Networks 139

Storage Background	139
Storage hierarchy	140
Hard disk drives	141
Flash storage	142
Direct attached storage	143
Storage area networks	143
Network attached storage	144
Advanced Storage Technologies	145
Object storage and metadata	145
Data protection and recovery	145
Tiered storage	147
Data deduplication	149
Storage Communication Protocols	149
SCSI	149
SATA	150
SAS	151
Fibre Channel	152
Network Convergence	153
Requirements	153
Network File System and Server Message Block	154
iSCSI	154
FCoE	155
Industry adoption	157

Software-Defined Storage 157
    Storage abstraction 158
    Storage virtualization.. 158
    Open interface 158
Storage in Cloud Data Centers 158
    Distributed storage 159
    Data center PODs 159
    Rack scale architecture 160
Review 161

CHAPTER 9 Software-Defined Networking 163

Data Center Software Background 163
    Traditional data center network software 164
    Evolving data center requirements 164
    Application programming interface 165
    Software-defined data center 165
OpenStack 167
    Networking components 167
OpenFlow 168
    Open API 169
    Forwarding table implementation 170
    Industry adoption 171
Network Function Virtualization 171
    Background 172
    Network security 173
    Load balancing 174
    Network monitoring 175
    Implementation 175
    Open daylight foundation 176
SDN Deployment 176
    Controller locations 176
    SDN at the network edge 177
Review 178

CHAPTER 10 High-Performance Computing Networks 179

HPC System Architectures 179
    Large compute nodes 180
    Arrays of compute nodes 180
Multisocket CPU Boards 180
    HyperTransport 181
    Intel® QuickPath Interconnect 182

RapidIO 182
PCIe NTB 183
HPC Networking Standards 184
Fabric configurations 184
Myrinet™ 185
Infiniband 185
Ethernet 186
HPC Network Performance Factors 186
Fabric interface 186
Switch 187
Fabric architecture 188
HPC Networking Software 188
Message Passing Interface 188
Verbs 189
Review 189

CHAPTER 11 Future Trends 191

Rack Scale Architectures 191
Resource disaggregation 192
CPU modules 193
Memory and storage modules 193
Distributed fabric 194
Memory Technology 195
Non-volatile memory and storage 195
Memory interface 196
Switch Fabric Technology 197
Frame overhead 197
Port bandwidth 197
Modular design 198
Cabling Technology 199
Copper cabling 199
Optical cabling 200
Wireless interconnect 201
Software-Defined Infrastructure 201
Data center automation 201
Network function virtualization 202
Big data analytics 202
Review 203

CHAPTER 12 Conclusions 205

Technology Evolution 205
Industry Standards 206

Networking 206
Storage and HPC 207
Data Center Virtualization 208
Software-Defined Infrastructure 208
Concluding Remarks 208

Index 211

About the Author

Gary Lee has been working in the semiconductor industry since 1981. He began his career as a transistor-level chip designer specializing in the development of high-performance gallium arsenide chips for the communication and computing markets. Starting in 1996 while working for Vitesse® Semiconductor, he led the development of the world's first switch fabric chip set that employed synchronous high-speed serial interconnections between devices, which were used in a variety of communication system designs and spawned several new high performance switch fabric product families. As a switch fabric architect, he also became involved with switch chip designs utilizing the PCI Express interface standard while working at Vitesse and at Xyratex®, a leading storage system OEM. In 2007, he joined a startup company called Fulcrum Microsystems who was pioneering low latency 10GbE switch silicon for the data center market. Fulcrum was acquired by Intel Corporation in 2011 and he is currently part of Intel's Networking Division. For the past 7 years he has been involved in technical marketing for data center networking solutions and has written over 40 white papers and application notes related to this market segment. He received his BS and MS degrees in Electrical Engineering from the University of Minnesota and holds 7 patents in several areas including transistor level semiconductor design and switch fabric architecture. His hobbies include travel, playing guitar, designing advanced guitar tube amps and effects, and racket sports. He lives with his wife in California and has three children.

Preface

Over the last 30 years I have seen many advances in both the semiconductor industry and in the networking industry, and in many ways these advances are intertwined as network systems are dependent upon the constant evolution of semiconductor technology. For those of you who are interested, I thought I would start by providing you with some background regarding my involvement in the semiconductor and networking industry as it will give you a feel of from where my perspective originates.

When I joined the semiconductor industry as a new college graduate, research labs were still trying to determine the best technology to use for high performance logic devices. I started as a silicon bipolar chip designer and then quickly moved to Gallium Arsenide (GaAs), but by the 1990s I witnessed CMOS becoming the dominant semiconductor technology in the industry. About the same time I graduated from college, Ethernet was just one of many proposed networking protocols, but by the 1990s it had evolved to the point where it began to dominate various networking applications. Today it is hard to find other networking technologies that even compete with Ethernet in local area networks, data center networks, carrier networks, and modular system backplanes.

In 1996 I was working at Vitesse Semiconductor and after designing GaAs chips for about 12 years I started to explore ideas of utilizing GaAs technology in new switch fabric architectures. At the time, silicon technology was still lagging behind GaAs in maximum bandwidth capability and the switch fabric chip architectures that we know today did not exist. I was lucky enough to team up with John Mullaney, a network engineering consultant, and together we developed a new high-speed serial switch architecture for which we received two patents. During this time, one name continued to come up as we studied research papers on switch fabric architecture. Nick McKeown and his students conducted much of the basic research leading to today's switch fabric designs while he was a PhD candidate at the University of California at Berkeley. Many ideas from this research were employed in the emerging switch fabric architectures being developed at that time. By the late 1990s CMOS technology had quickly surpassed the performance levels of GaAs, so our team at Vitesse changed course and started to develop large CMOS switch fabric chip sets for a wide variety of communications markets. But we were not alone.

From around 1996 until the end of the telecom bubble in the early 2000s, 20 to 30 new and unique switch fabric chip set designs were proposed, mainly for the booming telecommunications industry. These designs came from established companies like IBM® and from startup companies formed by design engineers who spun out of companies like Cisco® and Nortel. They also came from several institutions like Stanford University and the University of Washington. But the bubble eventually burst and funding dried up, killing off most of these development efforts. Today there are only a few remnants of these companies left. Two examples are Sandburst and Dune Networks which were acquired by Broadcom®.

At the end of this telecom boom cycle, several companies remaining in the switch fabric chip business banded together to form the Advanced Switching Interconnect Special Interest Group (ASI-SIG) which was led by Intel®. It's goal was to create a standard switch fabric architecture for communication systems built around the PCI Express interface specification. I joined the ASI-SIG as the Vitesse representative on the ASI Board of Director's midway through the specification development and it quickly became clear that the spec was over-ambitious. This eventually caused Intel and other companies slowly pulled back until ASI faded into the sunset. But for me this was an excellent learning experience on how standards bodies work and also gave me some technical insights into the PCI Express standard which is widely used in the computer industry today.

Before ASI completely faded away, I started working for Xyratex, a storage company looking to expand their market by developing shared IO systems for servers based on the ASI standard. Their shared IO program was eventually put on hold so I switched gears and started looking into SAS switches for storage applications. Although I only spent 2 years at Xyratex, I did learn quite a bit about Fibre Channel, SAS, and SATA storage array designs, along with the advantages and limitations of flash based storage from engineers and scientists who had spent years working on these technologies even before Xyratex spun out of IBM.

Throughout my time working on proprietary switch fabric architectures, my counterparts in the Ethernet division at Vitesse would poke at what we were doing and say "never bet against Ethernet." Back in the late 1990s I could provide a list of reasons why we couldn't use Ethernet in telecom switch fabric designs, but over the years the Ethernet standards kept evolving to the point where most modular communication systems use Ethernet in their backplanes today. One could argue that if the telecom bubble hadn't killed off so many switch fabric startup companies, Ethernet would have.

The next stop in my career was my third startup company called Fulcrum Microsystems, which at the time I joined had just launched its latest 24-port 10GbE switch chip designed for the data center. Although I had spent much of my career working on telecom style switch fabrics, over the last several years I have picked up a lot of knowledge related to data center networking and more recently on how large cloud data centers operate. I have also gained significant knowledge about the various Ethernet and layer 3 networking standards that we continue to support in our switch silicon products. Intel acquired Fulcrum Microsystems in September 2011, and as part of Intel, I have learned much more about server virtualization, rack scale architecture, microserver designs, and software-defined networking.

Life is a continuous learning process and I have always been interested in technology and technological evolution. Some of this may have been inherited from my grandfather who became an electrical engineer around 1920 and my father who became a mechanical engineer around 1950. Much of what I have learned comes from the large number of colleagues that I have worked with over the years. There are too many to list here, but each one has influenced and educated me in some way.

I would like to extend a special thank you to my colleagues at Intel, David Fair and Brian Johnson, for providing helpful reviews on some key chapters on this book. I would also like to thank my family and especially my wife Tracey who always was my biggest supporter even when I dragged her across the country from startup to startup.

CHAPTER 1

Welcome to Cloud Networking

Welcome to a book that focuses on cloud networking. Whether you realize it or not, the "Cloud" has a significant impact on your daily life. Every time you check someone's status on Facebook®, buy something on Amazon®, or get directions from Google® Maps, you are accessing computer resources within a large cloud data center. These computers are known as servers, and they must be interconnected to each other as well as to you through the carrier network in order for you to access this information. Behind the scenes, a single click on your part may spawn hundreds of transactions between servers within the data center. All of these transactions must occur over efficient, cost effective networks that help power these data centers.

This book will focus on networking within the data center and not the carrier networks that deliver the information to and from the data center and your device. The subject matter focuses on network equipment, software, and standards used to create networks within large cloud data centers. It is intended for individuals who would like to gain a better understanding of how these large data center networks operate. It is not intended as a textbook on networking and you will not find deep protocol details, equations, or performance analysis. Instead, we hope you find this an easy-to-read overview of how cloud data center networks are constructed and how they operate.

INTRODUCTION

Around the world, new cloud data centers have been deployed or are under construction that can contain tens of thousands and in some cases hundreds of thousands of servers. These are sometimes called hyper-scale data centers. You can think of a server as something similar to a desktop computer minus the graphics and keyboard but with a beefed up processor and network connection. Its purpose is to "serve" information to client devices such as your laptop, tablet, or smart phone. In many cases, a single web site click on a client device can initiate a significant amount of traffic between servers within the data center. Efficient communication between all of these servers, and associated storage within the cloud data center, relies on advanced data center networking technology.

In this chapter, we will set the stage for the rest of this book by providing some basic networking background for those of you who are new to the subject, along with providing an overview of cloud computing and cloud networking. This background information should help you better understand some of the topics that are covered later in this book. At the end of this chapter, we will describe some of the key characteristics of a cloud data center network that form the basis for many of the chapters in this book.

NETWORKING BASICS

This book is not meant to provide a deep understanding of network protocols and standards, but instead provides a thorough overview of the technology inside of cloud data center networks. In order to better understand some of the subject presented in this book, it is good to go over some basic networking principals. If you are familiar with networking basics, you may want to skip this section.

The network stack

Almost every textbook on networking includes information on the seven-layer Open Systems Interconnect (OSI) networking stack. This model was originally developed in the 1970s as part of the OSI project that had a goal of providing a common network standard with multivendor interoperability. OSI never gained acceptance and instead Transmission Control Protocol/Internet Protocol (TCP/IP) became the dominant internet communication standard but the OSI stack lives on in many technical papers and textbooks today.

Although the networking industry still refers to the OSI model, most of the protocols in use today use fewer than seven layers. In data center networks, we refer to Ethernet as a layer 2 protocol even though it contains layer 1 and layer 2 components. We also generally refer to TCP/IP as a layer 3 protocol even though it has layer 3 and layer 4 components. Layers 5-7 are generally referred to in the industry as application layers. In this book, we will refer to layer 2 as switching (i.e., Ethernet) and layer 3 as routing (i.e., TCP/IP). Anything above that, we will refer to as the application layer. Figure 1.1 shows an example of this simplified model including a simple data center transaction.

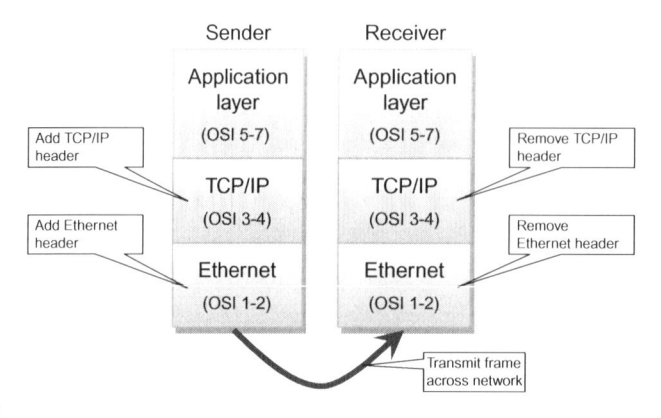

FIGURE 1.1

Example of a simple data center transaction.

In this simplified example, the sender application program presents data to the TCP/IP layer (sometimes simply referred to as layer 3). The data is segmented into frames (packets) and a TCP/IP header is added to each frame before presenting the frames to the Ethernet layer (sometimes simply referred to as layer 2). Next, an Ethernet header is added and the data frames are transmitted to the receiving device. On the receive side, the Ethernet layer removes the Ethernet header and then the TCP/IP layer removes the TCP/IP header before the received frames are reassembled into data that is presented to the application layer. This is a very simplified explanation, but it gives you some background when we provide more details about layer 2 and layer 3 protocols later in this book.

As an analogy, think about sending a package from your corporate mail room. You act as the application layer and tell your mail room that the gizmo you are holding in your hand must be shipped to a given mail station within your corporation that happens to be in another city. The mail room acts as layer 3 by placing the gizmo in a box, looking up and attaching an address based on the destination mail station number, and then presenting the package to the shipping company. Once the shipping company has the package, it may look up the destination address and then add its own special bar code label (layer 2) to get it to the destination distribution center. While in transit, the shipping company only looks at this layer 2 label. At the destination distribution center, the local address (layer 3) is inspected again to determine the final destination. This layered approach simplifies the task of the layer 2 shipping company.

Packets and frames

Almost all cloud data center networks transport data using variable length frames which are also referred to as packets. We will use both terms in this book. Large data files are segmented into frames before being sent through the network. An example frame format is shown in Figure 1.2.

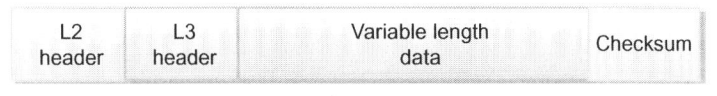

L2 header	L3 header	Variable length data	Checksum

FIGURE 1.2

Example frame format.

The data is first encapsulated using a layer 3 header such as TCP/IP and then encapsulated using a layer 2 header such as Ethernet as described as part of the example in the last section. The headers typically contain source and destination address information along with other information such as frame type, frame priority, etc. In many cases, checksums are used at the end of the frame to verify data integrity of the entire frame. The payload size of the data being transported and the frame size depend on the protocol. Standard Ethernet frames range in size from 64 to 1522 bytes. In some cases jumbo frames are also supported with frame sizes over 16K bytes.

Network equipment

Various types of network equipment can be used in cloud data centers. Servers contain network interface cards (NICs) which are used to provide the server CPU(s) with external Ethernet ports. These NICs are used to connect the servers to switches in the network through data cables. The term switch is generally used for equipment that forwards data using layer 2 header information. Sometimes, an Ethernet switch may also be referred to as an Ethernet bridge and the two terms can be used interchangeably. The term router is generally used for equipment that forwards data using layer 3 header information. Both switches and routers may be used within large cloud data center networks, and, in some cases, Ethernet switches can also support layer 3 routing.

Interconnect

In the data center, servers are connected to each other, connected to storage, and connected to the outside network through switches and routers. These connections are made using either copper or optical cabling. Historically, copper cabling has been a lower-cost solution, while optical cabling has been used when higher bandwidth and/or longer cabling distances are required. For example, shorter, copper cabling may be used as a connection between the servers and switches within a rack, and high bandwidth optical cabling may be used for uplinks out of the rack in order to span longer distances. We will provide more information on cable types later in this chapter.

WHAT IS A CLOUD DATA CENTER?

In the early days of the world wide web (remember that term?) data was most likely delivered to your home computer from a room full of servers in some sort of corporate data center. Then, the internet exploded. The number of people accessing the web grew exponentially as did the number of web sites available as well as the average data download sizes. Popular web service companies such as Google and Amazon needed to rapidly expand their data centers to keep up with demand. It quickly got to the point where they needed to erect large dedicated server warehouses that are today known as cloud data centers.

The term "cloud" started emerging around the same time wireless handheld devices started to become popular in the marketplace. When accessing the web via a wireless handheld device, it seems like you are pulling data out of the clouds. It is natural, then, that the data centers providing this information should be called cloud data centers. Today, it appears that everyone is jumping on the "cloud" bandwagon with all kinds of cloud companies, cloud products, and cloud services entering the market.

Cloud data centers are being rapidly deployed around the world. Since these installations must support up to hundreds of thousands of servers, data center efficiency and cost of operations have become critical. Because of this, some cloud data centers have been erected near cheap electrical power sources, such as hydroelectric dams, or in colder climates to help reduce cooling costs. Some companies, such as Microsoft®, are building modular data centers using pods, which are self-contained server storage and networking modules the size of a shipping container. These modules are trucked in, stacked up, and connected to power, cooling, and networking. Other data centers use server racks as the basic building block and contain rows and rows of these racks. No matter what the structure, networking is an important part of these large cloud data center networks.

A recent Cisco® white paper entitled *Cisco Global Cloud Index: Forecast and Methodology, 2012–2017* provides some interesting insights into cloud data centers. They predict that global IP data center traffic will grow by 25% each year at least through 2017. They also predict that by 2017 over two thirds of all data center traffic will be based in the cloud and 76% percent of this traffic will be between devices within the cloud data center as opposed to data traveling in and out of the data center. They also predict that server virtualization (multiple virtual servers running on a physical server) will have a large impact on cloud data center networks. They use the ratio of the total number of server workloads divided by the total number of physical servers and predict that, by 2017, this ratio will be above 16 versus about 2-3 for traditional data centers today. In other words, server virtualization (which will be discussed later in this book) will continue to be a dominant feature in cloud data centers. All of these factors have an impact on how large cloud data centers are designed and operated along with how cloud data center networking is implemented.

WHAT IS CLOUD NETWORKING?

With cloud data centers utilizing racks of servers or stacks of data center pods, networking all of these components together becomes a challenge. Cloud data center administrators want to minimize capital and operating expenses which include network adapter cards, switches, routers, and cabling. Ethernet has emerged as the low-cost layer 2 network for these large data centers, but these networks have special requirements that are different from traditional corporate Local Area Networks (LANs) or enterprise data center networks. We will call this type of network a "cloud data center network" throughout the rest of this book, and we will describe many of the key differences that set these networks apart from traditional enterprise networks.

CHARACTERISTICS OF CLOUD NETWORKING

Most cloud data centers have special requirements based on maximizing performance while minimizing cost. These requirements are reflected in their network designs which are typically built using Ethernet gear that takes advantage of Ethernet economies of scale while at the same time providing high bandwidth and features tailored for the data center. In this section, we will provide some background on these trends, including information on Ethernet cabling technology, along with an overview of network virtualization, network convergence, and scalability requirements.

Ethernet usage

When I started working on switch fabric chip designs in the mid-1990s, Ethernet was considered a LAN technology and, for critical telecom applications, an unreliable transport mechanism that would drop packets under heavy congestion. But it was always the lowest cost networking technology, mainly due to its wide deployment and use of high volume manufacturing. Ethernet has come a long way since then and many features and improvements have been added to the Ethernet specification over the last 10 years. Today, Ethernet is truly everywhere, from interconnecting the boards within network appliances to use in long distance carrier network links.

In the data center, Ethernet has become the standard network technology and this book will cover several of the advanced Ethernet features that are useful for large cloud data center networks. One of the advantages of Ethernet is the low-cost cabling technology that is available. You may be familiar with the classic Category 5 (Cat5) copper cabling that is used to make a wired Ethernet connection between a computer and a wall jack. This type of cabling has been used extensively in data centers for 1Gbit Ethernet (1GbE) connections due to its low cost and long reach. Now that data centers are adopting 10Gbit Ethernet (10GbE), a new interconnect standard called 10GBase-T has become available, which allows the use of low-cost Category 6 (Cat6) copper cables for distances up to 100 m. This is very similar to Cat5 and is much lower cost than optical cabling at these distances. One issue with 10GBase-T is the high latency it introduces compared to the low cut-through latencies available in new data center switches. It can also add power and cost to Ethernet switches compared to some alternative interface options. Because of this, many cloud data center server racks are interconnected using what is called direct attach copper cabling, which can support 10GbE and 40GbE connections for distances up to a few meters with reasonable cost. For longer distances or higher bandwidths, there are some interesting low-cost optical technologies coming into the market which will be discussed further in Chapter 11.

Virtualization

In cloud data centers, server virtualization can help improve resource utilization and, therefore, reduce operating costs. You can think of server virtualization as logically dividing up a physical server into multiple smaller virtual servers, each running its own operating system. This provides more granular utilization of server resources across the data center. For example, if a small company wants a cloud service provider to set up a web hosting service, instead of dedicating an underutilized physical server, the data center administrator can allocate a virtual machine allowing multiple web hosting virtual machines to be running on a single physical server. This saves money for both the hosting data center as well as the consumer. We will provide more information on server virtualization in Chapter 6.

Virtualization is also becoming important in the cloud data center network. New tunneling protocols can be used at the edge of the network that effectively provide separate logical networks for services such as public cloud hosting where multiple corporations may each have hundreds of servers or virtual machines that must communicate with each other across a shared physical network. For this type of application, these multitenant data centers must provide virtual networks that are separate, scalable, flexible, and secure. We will discuss virtual networking in Chapter 7.

Convergence

Cloud data centers cannot afford to provide separate networks for storage and data because this would require a large number of separate switches and cables. Instead, all data and storage traffic is transported through the Ethernet network. But storage traffic has some special requirements because it usually contains critical data and cannot be dropped during periods of high congestion in the network. Because of this, data center bridging standards have been developed for use within Ethernet switches that can provide lossless operation and minimum bandwidth guarantees for storage traffic. We will provide further information on data center bridging in Chapter 5.

Scalability

Data center networks must interconnect tens of thousands of servers including storage nodes and also provide connections to the outside carrier network. This becomes an architectural challenge when the basic network building blocks are integrated circuits with only up to 100 ports each. These building blocks must be used to create data center networks that can be easily scaled to support thousands of endpoints while at the same time providing low latency along with minimal congestion. There are many ways to interconnect these integrated circuits to form scale-out data center networks and these will be covered in Chapters 3 and 4.

One hardware initiative that is helping to improve server density and, therefore, increase data center scaling is the Open Compute Project that is being sponsored by Facebook along with several Original Equipment Manufacturers (OEMs) and Original Design Manufactures (ODMs). The mission statement from the opencompute.org web site is:

> *The Open Compute Project Foundation is a rapidly growing community of engineers around the world whose mission is to design and enable the delivery of the most efficient server, storage and data center hardware designs for scalable computing. We believe that openly sharing ideas, specifications and other intellectual property is the key to maximizing innovation and reducing operational complexity in the scalable computing space. The Open Compute Project Foundation provides a structure in which individuals and organizations can share their intellectual property with Open Compute Projects.*

One of their goals is to create rack scale architectures that provide higher density server shelves by utilizing 21″ wide racks instead of the traditional 19″ racks. This will require some higher density networking solutions as well as including rack scale architectures which we will discuss in Chapters 4 and 11.

Software

Large cloud data center networks are set up, configured, and monitored using software. Cloud data center server and storage resources may also be set up, configured, and monitored using different sets of software. In many cases, setting up a new tenant in a public cloud requires tight coordination between the network, server, and storage administrators and may take days to complete. In addition, the networking software may be tightly coupled to a given network equipment vendors hardware, making it very difficult to mix and match equipment from different vendors.

To get around some of these issues and to reduce cost, many cloud data centers are buying lower-cost networking equipment designed to their specifications and built by ODMs in Asia. Google was one of the first companies to do this, and others are following suit. They are also developing their own software which is targeted to their specific needs and doesn't carry the overhead associated with traditional networking equipment software. These industry changes are being facilitated by software defined networking (SDN) initiatives such as OpenFlow. The high-level goal is to provide a central orchestration layer that configures both the network and servers in a matter of minutes instead of days with little risk of human error. It also promises to simplify the networking equipment and make the network operating system hardware agnostic, allowing the use of multiple switch vendors and, therefore, further reducing cost for the data center administrator. We will discuss SDN in more detail in Chapter 9.

SUMMARY OF THIS BOOK

This book should give the reader a good overview of all of the different technologies involved in cloud data center networks. In Chapter 2, we will go through a history of the evolution of the data center from early mainframe computers to cloud data centers. In Chapter 3, we will describe switch fabric architectures at the chip level and how they have evolved based on data center requirements. In Chapter 4, we will move up one level and describe the various types of networking equipment that utilize these communication chips and how this equipment is interconnected to form large cloud data center networks. In Chapter 5, we will discuss several industry standards that are useful in cloud data center networks and how these standards are implemented. Chapter 6 goes into server virtualization, focusing on the networking aspects of this technology. Chapter 7 provides an overview of network virtualization including some new industry standards that are useful in multitenant data centers. Chapter 8 highlights some key aspects of storage networking that are useful in understanding cloud data center networks and Chapter 9 provides information on SDN and how it can be used to configure control and monitor cloud data centers. Chapter 10 is an overview of high performance computing networks. Although this is not generally relevant to cloud data centers today, many of these same technologies may be used in future data center networks. Finally, Chapter 11 provides a glimpse into the future of cloud data center networking.

CHAPTER 2

Data Center Evolution—Mainframes to the Cloud

The modern age of computing began in the 1950s when the first mainframe computers appeared from companies like IBM®, Univac, and Control Data. Communication with these computers was typically through a simple input/output (I/O) device. If you needed to compute something, you would walk to the computer room, submit your job as a stack of punch cards, and come back later to get a printout of the results. Mainframes later gave way to minicomputers like the PDP-11 from Digital Equipment Corporation (DEC), and new methods of computer networking started to evolve. Local area networks (LANs) became commonplace and allowed access to computing resources from other parts of the building or other parts of the campus. At the same time, small computers were transformed into servers, which "served up" certain types of information to client computers across corporate LANs. Eventually, servers moved into corporate data centers and they evolved from systems that looked like high-performance tower PCs into rack-mounted gear.

When the Advanced Research Projects Agency Network (ARPANET) gave birth to the internet, things started to get interesting. In order to provide web hosting services, dedicated data center facilities full of servers began to emerge. Initially, these data centers employed the same LAN networking gear used in the corporate data centers. By the end of the 1990s, Ethernet became the predominant networking technology in these large data centers, and the old LAN-based networking equipment was slowly replaced by purpose-built data center networking gear. Today, large cloud data center networks are common, and they require high-performance networks with special cloud networking features. This chapter will provide a brief history of the evolution of computer networking in order to give the reader a perspective that will be useful when reading the following chapters in this book.

THE DATA CENTER EVOLUTION

Over the past 50 years or so, access to computer resources has come full circle from dumb client terminals connected to large central mainframes in the 1960s, to distributed desktop computing starting in the 1980s, to handhelds connected to large centralized cloud data centers today. You can think of the handheld device as a terminal receiving data computed on a server farm in a remote cloud data center, much like the terminal connected to the mainframe. In fact, for many applications, data processing is moving out of the client device and into the cloud. This section will provide an overview of how computer networks have evolved from simple connections with large mainframe computers into today's hyper-scale cloud data center networks.

Early mainframes

Mainframes were the first electronic computing systems used widely by businesses, but due to their high capital and operating costs, even large business or universities could afford only one computer at a given site. Because of the cost, time sharing became the mode of operation for these large computers. Client communication involved walking over to the computer center with a stack of punch cards or a paper tape, waiting a few hours, and then picking up a printout of the results. Later, teletype terminals were added, allowing users to type in commands and see results on printed paper. Originally, teletypes printed program commands on paper tape, which was manually fed into the computer. Later, teletypes were connected directly to the computer using proprietary communication protocols as shown in Figure 2.1. In the late 1960s, CRT terminals were becoming available to replace the teletype.

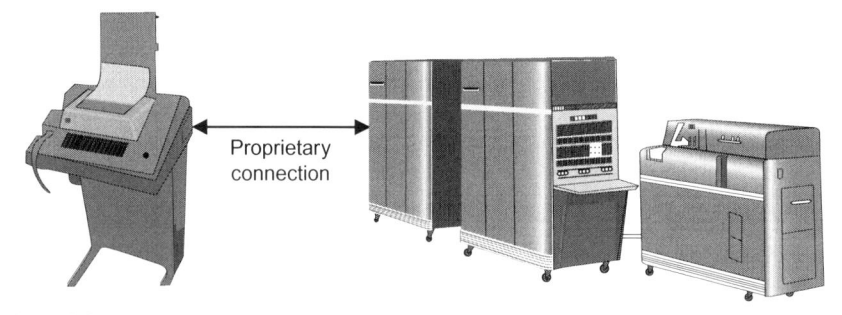

FIGURE 2.1

Mainframe client terminal connections.

Minicomputers

In the late 1970s, integrated circuits from companies like Intel® were dramatically reducing the cost and size of the business computer. Companies such as DEC took advantage of these new chips to develop a new class of computing system called the minicomputer. Starting with the PDP-8 and then more famously the PDP-11, businesses could now afford multiple computing systems per location. I can remember walking through Bell Labs in the early 1980s where they were proudly showing a room full of PDP-11 minicomputers used in their research work. These computer rooms are now typically called enterprise data centers.

Around this same time, more sophisticated computer terminals were developed, allowing access to computing resources from different locations in the building or campus. By now, businesses had multiple minicomputers and multiple terminals accessing these computers as shown in Figure 2.2. The only way to efficiently connect

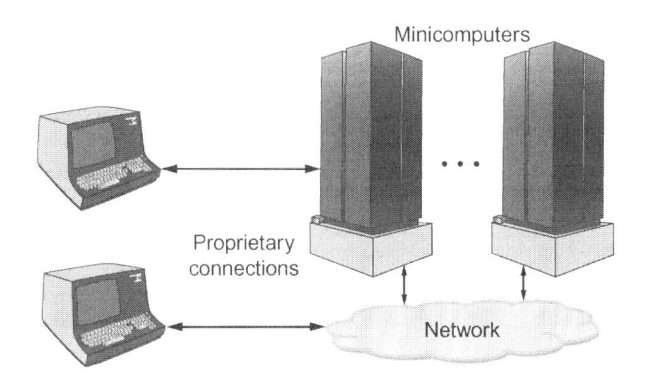

FIGURE 2.2

Minicomputer client terminal connections.

these was to build some sort of Local Area Network (LAN). This spawned a lot of innovation in computer network development which will be discussed in more detail in the next section.

Servers

Around the late 1980s, IT administrators realized that there were certain types of information such as corporate documents and employee records that did not need the computing power of mainframes or minicomputers, but simply needed to be accessed and presented to the client through a terminal or desktop computer. At around the same time, single board computers were becoming more powerful and evolved into a new class of computers called workstations. Soon corporations were dedicating these single board computers to serve up information across their LANs. The age of the compute server had begun as shown in Figure 2.3.

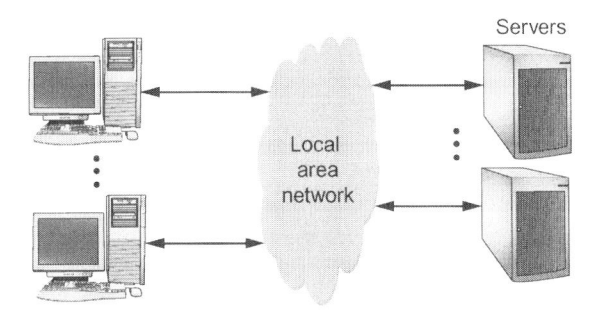

FIGURE 2.3

Early server network block diagram.

By the 1990s, almost all business employees had a PC or workstation at their desk connected to some type of LAN. Corporate data centers were becoming more complex with mixtures of minicomputers and servers which were also connected to the LAN. Because of this, LAN port count and bandwidth requirements were increasing rapidly, ushering in the need for more specialized data center networks. Several networking technologies emerged to address this need, including Ethernet and Token Ring which will be discussed in the next sections.

Enterprise data centers

Through the 1990s, servers rapidly evolved from stand-alone, single board computers to rack-mounted computers and blade server systems. Ethernet emerged as the chosen networking standard within the data center with Fibre Channel used for storage traffic. Within the data center, the Ethernet networks used were not much different from the enterprise LAN networks that connected client computers to the corporate data center. Network administrators and network equipment manufacturers soon realized that the data center networks had different requirements compared with the enterprise LAN, and around 2006, the first networking gear specifically designed for the data center was introduced. Around that same time, industry initiatives, such as Fibre Channel over Ethernet (FCoE), were launched with the goal of converging storage and data traffic onto a single Ethernet network in the data center. Later in this chapter, we will compare traditional enterprise data center networks to networks specifically designed for the data center. Figure 2.4 shows a LAN connecting client computers to an enterprise data center that employs enterprise networking equipment.

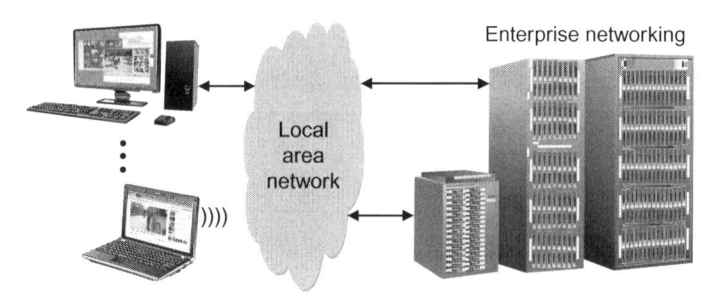

FIGURE 2.4

Enterprise data center networks.

Cloud data centers

When I was in high school, I remember listening to the *Utopia* album from Todd Rundgren. This album had one side dedicated to a song called "The Ikon," which impressed upon me the idea of a central "mind" from which anyone could access any information they needed anytime they needed it. Well, we are definitely headed in that direction with massive cloud data centers that can provide a wide variety of data and services to your handheld devices wherever and whenever you need it. Today, whether you are searching on Google, shopping on Amazon, or checking your status on Facebook, you are connecting to one of these large cloud data centers.

Cloud data centers can contain tens of thousands of servers that must be connected to each other, to storage, and to the outside world. This puts a tremendous strain on the data center network, which must be low cost, low power, and high bandwidth. To minimize the cost of these data centers, cloud service providers are acquiring specialized server boards and networking equipment which are built by Original Design Manufacturers (ODMs) and are tailored to their specific workloads. Facebook has even gone as far as spearheading a new server rack standard called the Open Compute Project that better optimizes server density by expanding to a 21-inch wide rack versus the old 19-inch standard. Also, some cloud data center service providers, such as Microsoft, are using modular Performance Optimized Data center modules (PODs) as basic building blocks. These are units about the size of a shipping container and include servers, storage, networking, power, and cooling. Simply stack the containers, connect external networking, power, and cooling, and you're ready to run. If a POD fails, they bring in a container truck to move it out and move a new one in. Later in this chapter, we will provide more information on the types of features and benefits enabled by these large cloud data centers. Figure 2.5 is a pictorial representation showing client devices connected through the Internet to a large cloud data center that utilizes specialized cloud networking features.

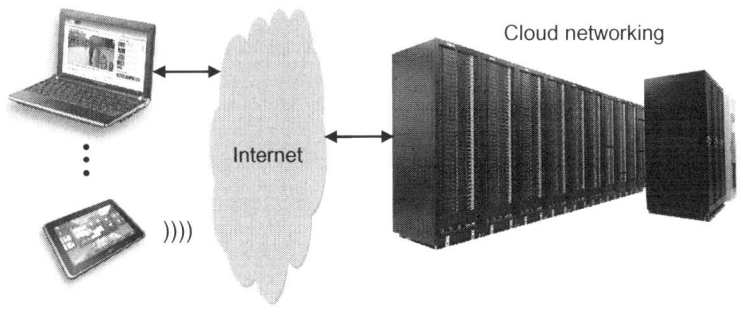

FIGURE 2.5

Cloud data center networks.

Virtualized data centers

Many corporations are seeing the advantage of moving their data center assets into the cloud in order to save both capital and operating expense. To support this, cloud data centers are developing ways to host multiple virtual data centers within their physical data centers. But the corporate users want these virtual data centers to appear to them as private data centers. This requires the cloud service provider to offer isolated, multitenant environments that include a large number of virtual machines and virtualized networks as shown in Figure 2.6. In this simplified view, we show three tenants that are hosted within a large cloud data center.

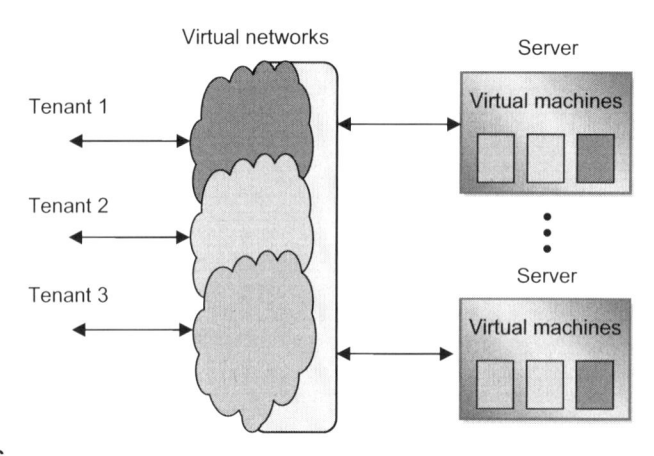

FIGURE 2.6

The virtualized data center.

Within the physical servers, multiple virtual machines (virtual servers) can be maintained which help maximize data center efficiency by optimizing processing resource utilization while also providing server resiliency. Within the network, tunneling protocols can be used to provide multiple virtual networks within one large physical network. Storage virtualization can also be used to optimize storage performance and utilization. In this book, we will not go very deep into storage virtualization and only describe virtual machines in the context of data center networking. But we will dive deeper into some of the network tunneling standards that are employed for these multitenant environments.

COMPUTER NETWORKS

In the last section, we went through a brief history of enterprise computing and the evolution toward cloud data centers. We also mentioned local area networking as a key technology development that eventually evolved into purpose-built data center networks. A variety of different network protocols were developed over the last 50 years for both LANs and wide area networks (WANs), with Ethernet emerging as the predominant protocol used in local area, data center, and carrier networks today. In this section, we will provide a brief history of these network protocols along with some information on how they work and how they are used. For completeness, we are including some protocols that are used outside the data center because they provide the reader with a broader view of networking technology. Ethernet will be covered separately in the following section.

Dedicated lines

As you may have guessed, the initial methods used to communicate with mainframe computers were through dedicated lines using proprietary protocols. Each manufacturer was free to develop its own communication protocols between computers and devices such as terminals and printers because the end customer purchased everything from the same manufacturer. These were not really networks per se, but are included in this chapter in order to understand the evolution to true networking technology. Soon, corporations had data centers with multiple computer systems from different manufacturers along with remote user terminals, so a means of networking these machines together using industry standard protocols became important. The rest of this section will outline some of these key protocols.

ARPANET

The ARPANET was one of the first computer networks and is considered to be the father of today's internet. It was initially developed to connect mainframe computers from different universities and national labs through leased telephone lines at the astounding rate of 50Kbit per second. To put it into today's terms, that's 0.00005Gbps. Data was passed between Interface Message Processors (IMPs), which today we would call a router. Keep in mind that there were only a handful of places you could route a message to back then, including universities and research labs.

ARPANET also pioneered the concept of packet routing. Before this time, both voice and data information was forwarded using circuit-switched lines. Figure 2.7 shows an example of the difference between the two. In a circuit-switched network, a connection path is first established, and data sent between point A and B will always take the same path through the network. An example is a phone call where a number is dialed, a path is set up, voice data is exchanged, the call ends, and then the path is taken down. A new call to the same number may take a different path through the network, but once established, data always takes the same path. In addition, data is broken up into fixed sized cells such as voice data chucks before it is sent through the network (see the section "SONET/SDH").

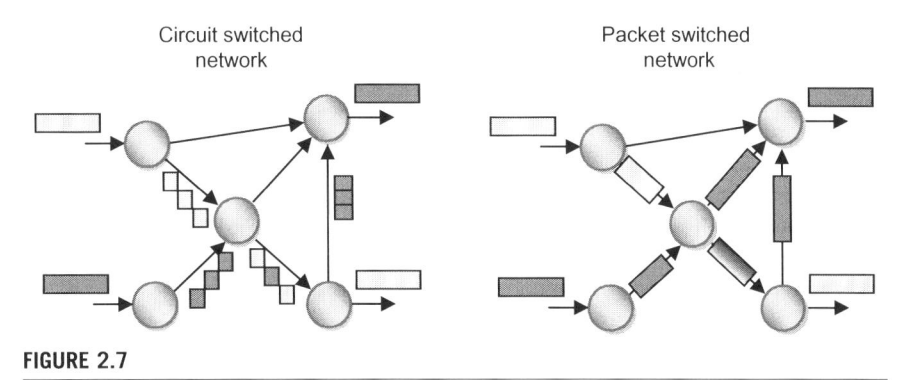

FIGURE 2.7

Circuit switched verse packet switched network.

ARPANET established the new concept of packet switching, in which variable sized packets are used that can take various paths through the network depending on factors such as congestion and available bandwidth, because no predefined paths are used. In fact, a given exchange of information may take multiple different paths. To do this, each packet was appended with a network control protocol (NCP) header containing information such as the destination address and the message type. Once a node received a packet, it examined the header to determine how to forward it. In the case of ARPANET, the IMP examined the header and decided if the packet was for the locally attached computer or whether it should have been passed through the network to another IMP. The NCP header was eventually replaced by the Transmission Control Protocol/Internet Protocol (TCP/IP), which will be described in more detail below.

TCP/IP

With the ARPANET in place, engineers and scientists started to investigate new protocols for transmitting data across packet based networks. Several types of Transmission Control Protocol (TCP) and Internet Protocol (IP) standards were studied by universities and corporate research labs. By the early 1980s, a new standard called TCP/IP was firmly established as the protocol of choice, and is what the internet is based on today. Of course, what started out as a simple standard has evolved into a set of more complex standards over the years; these standards are now administered by the Internet Engineering Task Force (IETF). Additional standards have also emerged for sending special types of data over IP networks; for example, iSCSI for storage and iWARP for remote direct memory access, both of which are useful in data center networks. Figure 2.8 shows a simplified view some of the high-level functions provided by the TCP/IP protocol.

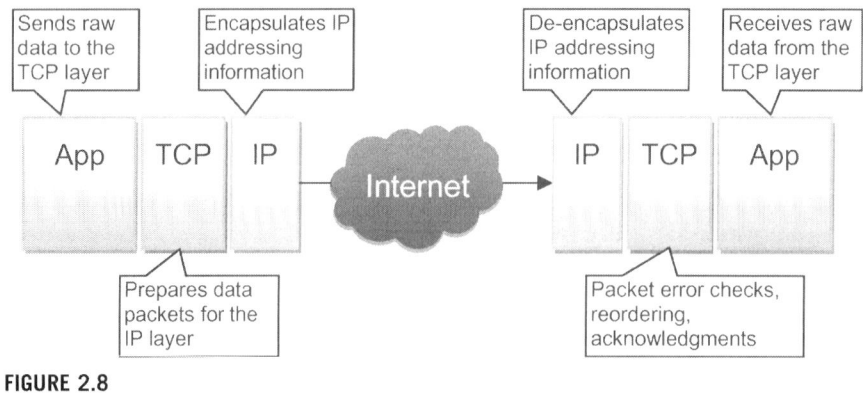

FIGURE 2.8

High-level TCP/IP functions.

The application hands over the data to be transmitted to the TCP layer. This is generally a pointer to a linked list memory location within the CPU subsystem.

The TCP layer then segments the data into packets (if the data is larger than the maximum packet size supported), and adds a TCP header to each packet. This header includes information such as the source and destination port that the application uses, a sequence number, an acknowledgment number, a checksum, and congestion management information. The IP layer deals with all of the addressing details and adds a source and destination IP address to the TCP packet. The Internet shown in the figure contains multiple routers that forward data based on this TCP/IP header information. These routers are interconnected using layer 2 protocols such as Ethernet that apply their own L2 headers.

On the receive side, the IP layer checks for some types of receive errors and then removes the IP address information. The TCP layer performs several transport functions including acknowledging received packets, looking for checksum errors, reordering received packets, and throttling data based on congestion management information. Finally, the raw data is presented to the specified application port number. For high-bandwidth data pipes, this TCP workload can bog down the CPU receiving the data, preventing it from providing satisfactory performance to other applications that are running. Because of this, several companies have developed TCP offload engines in order to remove the burden from the host CPU. But with today's high-performance multicore processors, special offload processors are losing favor.

As you may have gathered, TCP/IP is a deep subject and we have only provided the reader with a high-level overview in this section. Much more detail can be found online or in various books on networking technology.

Multi-Protocol Label Switching

When a router receives a TCP/IP packet, it must look at information in the header and compare this to data stored in local routing tables in order to determine a proper forwarding port. The classic case is the 5-tuple lookup that examines the source IP address, destination IP address, source port number, destination port number, and the protocol in use. When packets move into the core of the network and link speeds increase, it becomes more difficult to do this lookup across a large number of ports while maintaining full bandwidth, adding expense to the core routers.

In the mid-1990s, a group of engineers at Ipsilon Networks had the idea to add special labels to these packets (label switching), which the core routers can use to forward packets without the need to look into the header details. This is something like the postal zip code. When a letter is traveling through large postal centers, only the zip code is used to forward the letter. Not until the letter reaches the destination post office (identified by zip code) is the address information examined. This idea was the seed for Multi-Protocol Label Switching (MPLS) which is extensively used in TCP/IP networks today. This idea is also the basis for other tunneling protocols such as Q-in-Q, IP-over-IP, FCoE, VXLAN, and NVGRE. Several of these tunneling protocols will be discussed further in later chapters in this book.

Packets enter an MPLS network through a Label Edge Router (LER) as shown in Figure 2.9. LERs are usually at the edge of the network, where lower bandwidth

FIGURE 2.9

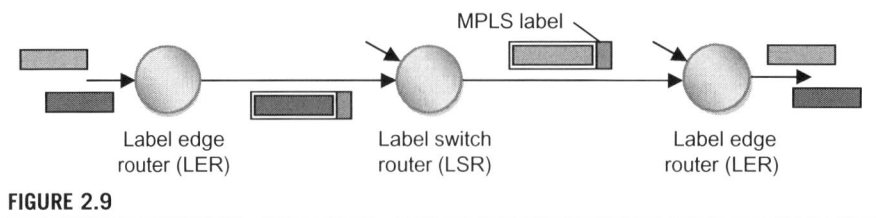

MPLS packet forwarding.

requirements make it easier to do full header lookups and then append an MPLS label in the packet header. Labels may be assigned using a 5-tuple TCP/IP header lookup, where a unique label is assigned per flow. In the core of the network, label switch routers use the MPLS label to forward packets through the network. This is a much easier lookup to perform in the high-bandwidth network core. In the egress LER, the labels are removed and the TCP/IP header information is used to forward the packet to its final destination. Packets may also work their way through a hierarchy of MPLS networks where a packet encapsulated with an MPLS header from one network may be encapsulated with another MPLS header in order to tunnel the packet through a second network.

SONET/SDH

Early telephone systems used manually connected patch panels to route phone calls. Soon, this evolved into mechanical relays and then into electronic switching systems. Eventually, voice calls became digitized, and, with increased bandwidth within the network, it made sense to look at ways to combine multiple calls over a single line. And why not also transmit other types of data right along with the digitized voice data? To meet these needs, Synchronous Optical Network (SONET) was created as a circuit-switched network originally designed to transport both digitized DS1 and DS3 voice and data traffic over optical networks. But to make sure all data falls within its dedicated time slot, all endpoints and transmitting stations are time synchronized to a master clock, thus the name Synchronous Optical Network. Although the differences in the standards are very small, SONET, developed by Telcordia and American National Standards Institute (ANSI), is used in North America, while Synchronous Digital Hierarchy (SDH), developed by the European Telecommunications Standards Institute, is used in the rest of the world.

At the conceptual level, SONET/SDH can be depicted as shown in Figure 2.10. SONET/SDH uses the concept of transport containers to move data throughout the network. On the left of the figure, we have lower speed access layers where packets are segmented into fixed length frames. As these frames move into the higher bandwidth aggregation networks, they are grouped together into containers and these containers are grouped further into larger containers as they enter the core network. An analogy would be transporting automobiles across the country. Multiple automobiles from different locations may be loaded on a car carrier truck. Then multiple car carrier trucks may be loaded onto a railroad flatcar. The SONET/SDH frame transport

FIGURE 2.10

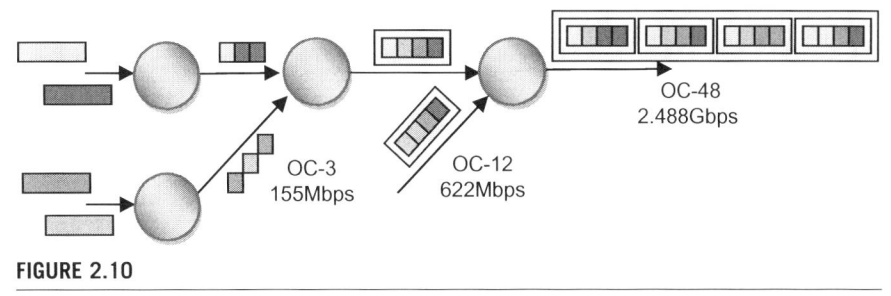

SONET/SDH transport.

time period is constant so the data rates are increased by a factor of four at each stage (OC-3, OC-12, OC-48...). Therefore, four times the data can be placed within each frame while maintaining the same frame clock period. Time slot interchange chips are used to shuffle frames between containers at various points in the network and are also used extensively in SONET/SDH add-drop multiplexers at the network edge.

SONET/SDH has been used extensively in telecommunication networks, whereas TCP/IP has been the choice for internet traffic. This led to the development of IP over SONET/SDH systems that allowed the transport of packet based IP traffic over SONET/SDH networks. Various SONET/SDH framer chips were developed to support this including Asynchronous Transfer Mode (ATM) over SONET, IP over SONET, and Ethernet over SONET devices. But several factors are reducing the deployment of SONET/SDH in transport networks. One factor, is that most of all traffic today is packet based (think Ethernet and IP phones). Another factor is that Carrier Ethernet is being deployed around the world to support packet based traffic. Because of these and other factors, SONET/SDH networks are being slowly replaced by carrier Ethernet networks.

Asynchronous Transfer Mode

In the late 1980s, ATM emerged as a promising new communication protocol. In the mid-1990s, I was working with a group that was developing ATM over SONET framer chips. At the time, proponents were claiming that ATM could be used to transfer voice, video, and data throughout the LAN and WAN, and soon every PC would have an ATM network interface card. Although ATM did gain some traction in the WAN with notable equipment from companies like Stratacom (acquired by Cisco) and FORE Systems (acquired by Marconi), it never replaced Ethernet in the LAN.

The ATM frame format is shown in Figure 2.11. This frame format shows some of the strong synergy that ATM has with SONET/SDH. Both use fixed size frames along with the concept of virtual paths and virtual channels. ATM is a circuit-switched technology in which virtual end-to-end paths are established before transmission begins. Data can be transferred using multiple virtual channels within a virtual path, and multiple ATM frames will fit within a SONET/SDH frame.

			Byte
Generic flow control	Virtual path identifier		1
Virtual path identifier	Virtual channel identifier		2
Virtual channel identifier			3
Virtual channel identifier	Payload type	CLP	4
Header error control			5
48-byte payload			6
			53

FIGURE 2.11

Asynchronous Transfer Mode frame format.

The advantage of using a fixed frame size is that independent streams of data can easily be intermixed providing low jitter, and fixed frames also work well within SONET/SDH frames. In packet based networks, a packet may need to wait to use a channel if a large packet is currently being transmitted, causing higher jitter. Because most IT networks use variable sized packets, as link bandwidths increase it becomes more difficult to segment and reassemble data into 53-byte frames, adding complexity and cost to the system. In addition, the ATM header overhead percentage can be larger than packet based protocols, requiring more link bandwidth for the same effective data rate. These are some of the reasons that ATM never found success in the enterprise or data center networks.

Token Ring/Token Bus

So far in this section, we have been describing several network protocols mainly used in telecommunication and wide area networks. We will now start to dig into some network protocols used within the enterprise to interconnect terminals, PCs, mainframes, servers, and storage equipment.

One of the earliest local area networking protocols was Token Ring, originally developed by IBM in the early 1980s. Token Bus is a variant of Token Ring where a virtual ring is emulated on a shared bus. In the mid-1980s, Token Ring ran at 4Mbps, which was increased to 16Mbps in 1989. Both speeds were eventually standardized by the IEEE 802.5 working group. Other companies developing Token Ring networks included Apollo Computer and Proteon. Unfortunately, IBM network equipment was not compatible with either of these companies' products, segmenting the market.

In a Token Ring network, empty information frames are continuously circulated around the ring as shown in Figure 2.12. In this figure, when one device wants to send data to another device, it grabs an empty frame and inserts both the packet data and destination address. The frame is then examined by each successive device, and if the frame address matches a given device, it takes a copy of the data and sets the token to 0. The frame is then sent back around the ring to the sending device as an

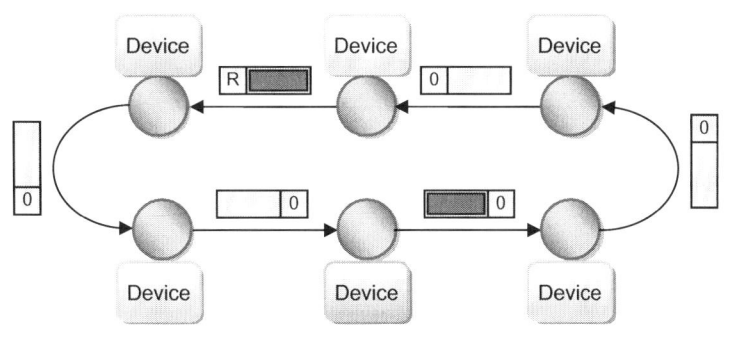

FIGURE 2.12

Token Ring network.

acknowledgment, which then clears the frame. Although this topology is fine for lightly loaded networks, if each node wants to continuously transmit data, it will get only $1/N$ of the link bandwidth, where N is the number of nodes in the ring. In addition, it can have higher latency than directly connected networks. Because of this and other factors, Token Ring was eventually replaced by Ethernet in most LAN applications.

Ethernet

Ethernet was introduced in 1980 and standardized in 1985. Since then, it has evolved to be the most widely used transport protocol for LANs, data center networks, and carrier networks. In the following section, we will provide an overview of Ethernet technology and how it is used in these markets.

Fibre Channel

Many data centers have separate networks for their data storage systems. Because this data can be critical to business operations, these networks have to be very resilient and secure. Network protocols such as Ethernet allow packets to be dropped under certain conditions, with the expectation that data will be retransmitted at a higher network layer such as TCP. Storage traffic cannot tolerate these retransmission delays and for security reasons, many IT managers want to keep storage on an isolated network. Because of this, special storage networking standards were developed. We will describe Fibre Channel networks in more detail in Chapter 8 which covers storage networking.

InfiniBand

In the early 1990s, several leading network equipment suppliers thought they could come up with a better networking standard that could replace Ethernet and Fibre Channel in the data center. Originally called Next Generation I/O and Future I/O, it soon became known as InfiniBand. But like many purported world beating technologies, it never lived up to its promise of replacing Ethernet and Fibre Channel in the data center and is now mainly used in high-performance computing (HPC) systems and some storage applications. What once was a broad ecosystem of suppliers has been reduced to Mellanox® and Intel (through an acquisition of the InfiniBand assets of QLogic®).

InfiniBand host channel adapters (HCAs) and switches are the fundamental components used in most HPC systems today. The HCAs sit on the compute blades which are interconnected through high-bandwidth, low-latency InfiniBand switches. The HCAs operate at the transport layer and use verbs as an interface between the client software and the transport functions of the HCA. The transport functions are responsible for in-order packet delivery, partitioning, channel multiplexing, transport services, and data segmentation and reassembly. The switch operates at the link layer providing forwarding, QoS, credit-based flow control and data integrity services. Due to the relative simplicity of the switch design, InfiniBand provides very high-bandwidth links and forward packets with very low latency, making it an ideal solution for HPC applications. We will provide more information on high performance computing in Chapter 10.

ETHERNET

In the last section, we described several popular communication protocols that have been used in both enterprise and carrier networks. Because Ethernet is such an important protocol, we will dedicate a complete section in this chapter to it. In this section, we will provide a history and background of Ethernet along with a high-level overview of Ethernet technology including example use cases in carrier and data center networks.

Ethernet history

You can make an argument that the Xerox® Palo Alto Research Center (PARC) spawned many of the ideas that are used in personal computing today. This is where Steve Jobs first saw the mouse, windows, desktop icons, and laser printers in action. Xerox PARC also developed what they called Ethernet in the early to mid-1970s.

The development of Ethernet was inspired by a wireless packet data network called ALOHAnet developed at the University of Hawaii, which used a random delay time interval to retransmit packets if an acknowledgment was not received within a given wait time. Instead of sharing the airwaves like ALOHAnet, Ethernet shared a common wire (channel). By the end of the 1970s, DEC, Intel, and Xerox started working together on the first Ethernet standard which was published in 1980. Initially, Ethernet competed with Token Ring and Token Bus to connect clients with mainframe and minicomputers. But once the IBM PC was released, hundreds of thousands of Ethernet adapter cards began flooding the market from companies such as 3Com and others. The Institute of Electrical and Electronic Engineers (IEEE) decided to standardize Ethernet into the IEEE 802.3 standard which was completed in 1985.

Initially Ethernet became the *de facto* standard for LANs within the enterprise. Over the next two decades, Ethernet port bandwidth increased by several orders of magnitude making it suitable for many other applications including carrier networks, data center networks, wireless networks, industrial automation, and automotive applications. To meet the requirements of these new markets, a wide variety of features were added to the IEEE standard, making Ethernet a deep and complex subject that can fill several books on its own. In this book, we will focus on how Ethernet is used in cloud data center networks.

Ethernet overview

Ethernet started as a shared media protocol where all hosts communicated over a single 10Mbps wire or channel. If a host wanted to communicate on the channel, it would first listen to make sure no other communications were taking place. It would then start transmitting and also listen for any collisions with other hosts that may have started transmitting at the same time. If a collision was detected, each host would back off for a random time period before attempting another transmission. This protocol became known as Carrier Sense Multiple Access with Collision Detection (CSMA/CD). As Ethernet speeds evolved from 10Mbps to 100Mbps to 1000Mbps (GbE), a shared channel was no longer practical. Today, Ethernet does not share a channel, but instead, each endpoint has a dedicated full duplex connection to a switch that forwards the data to the correct destination endpoint.

Ethernet is a layer 2 protocol compared to TCP/IP which is a layer 3 protocol. Let's use a railroad analogy to explain this. A shipping company has a container with a bar code identifier that it needs to move from the west coast to the east coast using two separate railway companies (call them Western Rail and Eastern Rail). Western Rail picks up the container, reads the bar code, loads it on a flatcar and sends it halfway across the country through several switching yards. The flat car has its own bar code, which is used at the switching yard to reroute the flat car to the destination. Half way across the country, Eastern Rail now reads the bar code on the container, loads it onto another flatcar, and sends it the rest of the way across the country through several more switching yards.

In this analogy, the bar code on the container is like the TCP/IP header. As the frame (container) enters the first Ethernet network (Western Rail), the TCP/IP header is read and an Ethernet header (flatcar bar code) is attached which is used to forward the packet through several Ethernet switches (railroad switching yards). The packet may then be stripped of the Ethernet header within a layer 3 TCP/IP router and forwarded to a final Ethernet network (Eastern Rail), where another Ethernet header is appended based on the TCP/IP header information and the packet is sent to its final destination. The railroad is like a layer 2 network and is only responsible for moving the container across its domain. The shipping company is like the layer 3 network and is responsible for the destination address (container bar code) and for making sure the container arrives at the destination. Let's look at the Ethernet frame format in Figure 2.13.

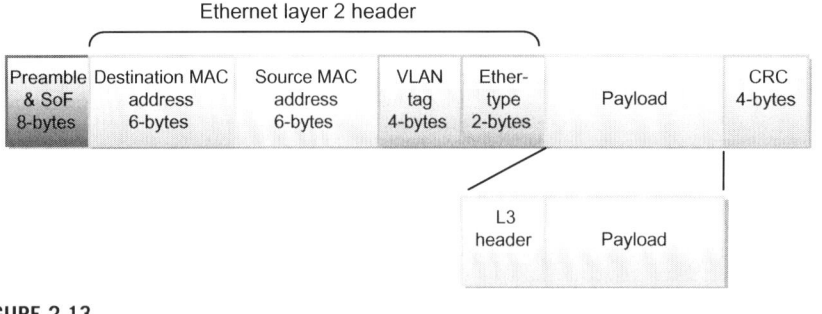

FIGURE 2.13

Ethernet frame format.

The following is a description of the header fields shown in the figure. An interframe gap of at least 12 bytes is used between frames. The minimum frame size including the header and cyclic redundancy check (CRC) is 64 bytes. Jumbo frames can take the maximum frame size up to around 16K bytes.

- *Preamble and start-of-frame (SoF)*: The preamble is used to get the receiving serializer/deserializer up to speed and locked onto the bit timing of the received frame. In most cases today, this can be done with just one byte leaving another six bytes available to transfer user proprietary information between switches. A SoF byte is used to signal the start of the frame.
- *Destination Media Access Control (MAC) address*: Each endpoint in the Ethernet network has an address called a MAC address. The destination MAC address is used by the Ethernet switches to determine how to forward packets through the network.
- *Source MAC address*: The source MAC address is also sent in each frame header which is used to support address learning in the switch. For example, when a new endpoint joins the network, it can inject a frame with an unknown designation MAC. Each switch will then broadcast this frame out all ports. By looking at the MAC source address, and the port number that the frame came in on, the switch can learn where to send future frames destined to this new MAC address.
- *Virtual local area network tag (optional)*: VLANs were initially developed to allow companies to create multiple virtual networks within one physical network in order to address issues such as security, network scalability, and network management. For example, the accounting department may want to have a different VLAN than the engineering department so packets will stay in their own VLAN domain within the larger physical network. The VLAN tag is 12-bits, providing up to 4096 different virtual LANs. It also contains frame priority information. We will provide more information on the VLAN tag in Chapter 5.
- *Ethertype*: This field can be used to either provide the size of the payload or the type of the payload.
- *Payload*: The payload is the data being transported from source to destination. In many cases, the payload is a layer 3 frame such as a TCP/IP frame.
- *CRC (frame check sequence)*: Each frame can be checked for corrupted data using a CRC.

Carrier Ethernet

With Ethernet emerging as the dominant networking technology within the enterprise, and telecom service providers being driven to provide more features and bandwidth without increasing costs to the end users, Ethernet has made significant inroads into carrier networks. This started with the metro networks that connect enterprise networks within a metropolitan area.

The Metro Ethernet Forum (MEF) was founded in 2001 to clarify and standardize several Carrier Ethernet services with the idea of extending enterprise LANs across the wide area network (WAN). These services include:

- *E-line*: This is a direct connection between two enterprise locations across the WAN.
- *E-LAN*: This can be used to extend a customer's enterprise LAN to multiple physical locations across the WAN.
- *E-tree*: This can connect multiple leaf locations to a single root location while preventing interleaf communication.

This movement of Ethernet out of the LAN has progressed further into the carrier space using several connection oriented transport technologies including Ethernet over SONET/SDH and Ethernet over MPLS. This allows a transition of Ethernet communication, first over legacy transport technologies, and, ultimately, to Ethernet over Carrier Ethernet Transport, which includes some of the following technologies.

Carrier Ethernet networks consist of Provider Bridge (PB) networks and a Provider Backbone Bridge (PBB) network as shown in Figure 2.14. Provider bridging utilizes an additional VLAN tag (Q-in-Q) to tunnel packets between customers using several types of interfaces. Customer Edge Ports (CEP) connect to customer equipment while Customer Network Ports (CNP) connect to customer networks. Provider

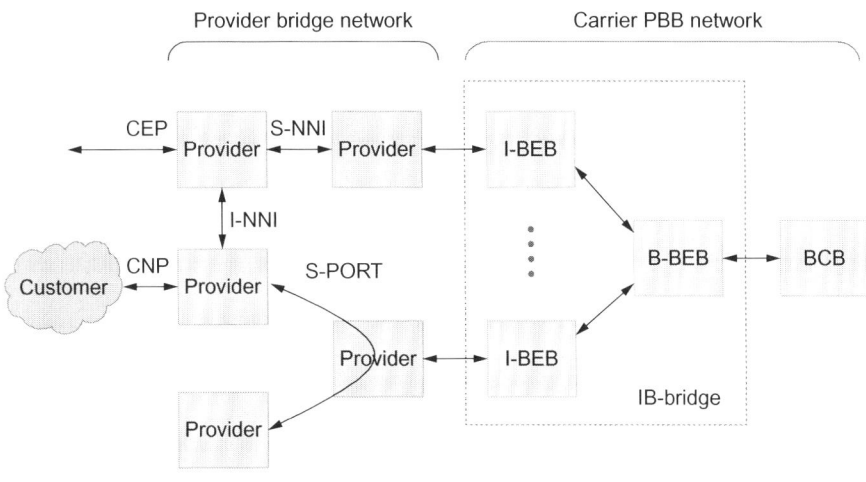

FIGURE 2.14

Carrier Ethernet block diagram.

equipment can be interconnected directly using an I-NNI interface, or tunneled through another provider network using an S-PORT CNP interface. Two service providers can be interconnected through an S-NNI interface. A fundamental limitation of Provider Bridging is that only 4096 special VLAN tags are available, limiting the scalability of the solution.

In the carrier PBB network, an additional 48-bit MAC address header is used (MAC-in-MAC) to tunnel packets between service providers, supporting a much larger address space. The I-component Backbone Edge Bridge (I-BEB) adds a service identifier tag and new MAC addresses based on information in the PB header. The B-component Backbone Edge Bridge (B-BEB) verifies the service ID and forwards the packet into the network core using a backbone VLAN tag. The Backbone Core Bridge (BCB) forwards packets through the network core.

As carrier networks migrate from circuit switching to packet switching technologies, they must provide Operation Administration and Maintenance (OAM) features that are required for robust operation and high availability. In addition, timing synchronization must be maintained across these networks. As Carrier Ethernet technology replaces legacy SONET/SDH networks, several new standards have been developed such as Ethernet OAM (EOAM) and Precision Time Protocol (PTP) for network time synchronization.

While Carrier Ethernet standards such as PB, PBB, and EOAM have been in development by the IEEE for some time, other groups have been developing a carrier class version of MPLS called MPLS-TE for Traffic Engineering or T-MPLS for Transport MPLS. The idea is that MPLS has many of the features needed for carrier class service already in place, so why develop a new Carrier Ethernet technology from scratch? The tradeoff is that Carrier Ethernet should use lower cost switches versus MPLS routers, but MPLS has been around much longer and should provide an easier adoption within carrier networks. In the end, it looks like Carrier networks will take a hybrid approach, using the best features of each depending on the application.

Data centers are connected to the outside world and to other data centers through technology such as Carrier Ethernet or MPLS-TE. But within the data center specialized data center networks are used. The rest of this book will focus on Ethernet technology used within the cloud data center networks.

ENTERPRISE VERSUS CLOUD DATA CENTERS

Originally, servers were connected to clients and to each other using the enterprise LAN. As businesses started to deploy larger data centers, they used similar enterprise LAN technology to create a data center network. Eventually, the changing needs of the data center required network system OEMs to start developing purpose-built data center networking equipment. This section will describe the major differences between enterprise networks and cloud data center networks.

Enterprise data center networks

If you examine the typical enterprise LAN, you will find wired Ethernet connections to workgroup switches using fast Ethernet (or 1Gb Ethernet) and wireless access points connected to the same workgroup switches. These switches are typically in a 1U pizza-box form factor and are connected to other workgroup switches either through 10Gb Ethernet stacking ports or through separate 10GbE aggregation switches. The various workgroup switches and aggregation switches typically sit in a local wiring closet. To connect multiple wiring closets together, network administrators may use high-bandwidth routers, which also have external connections to the WAN.

When enterprise system administrators started to develop their own high-density data centers, they had no choice but to use the same networking gear as used in the LAN. Figure 2.15 shows an example of how such an enterprise data center may be configured. In this figure, workgroup switches are repurposed as top of rack (ToR) switches with 1GbE links connecting to the rack servers and multiple 1GbE or 10GbE links connecting to the aggregation switches. The aggregation switches then feed a core router similar to the one used in the enterprise LAN through 10Gb Ethernet links.

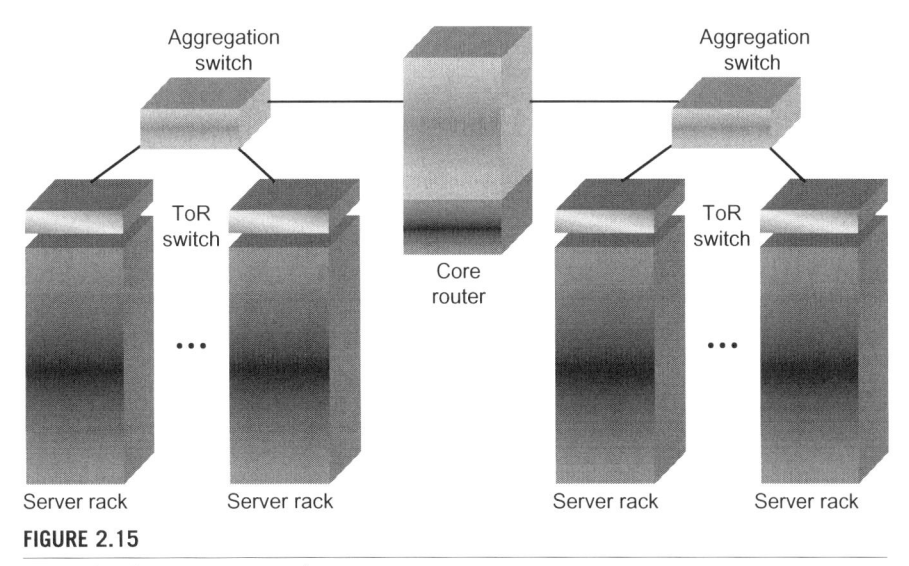

FIGURE 2.15

Enterprise data center network.

There are several issues with this configuration. First, packets need to take multiple hops when traveling between servers. This increases latency and latency variation between servers, especially when using enterprise networking gear that has relatively high latency, as latency is not a concern in the LAN. Second, enterprise networks will drop packets during periods of high congestion. Data center storage traffic needs lossless operation, so, in this case, a separate network such as Fibre Channel will be needed. Finally, core routers are very complex and expensive given that they need to process layer 3 frames at high-bandwidth levels. In addition, enterprise equipment typically comes with proprietary and complex software that is not compatible with other software used in the data center.

Cloud data center networks

Because of the issues listed above, and the cost of using more expensive enterprise hardware and software in large cloud data centers, network equipment suppliers have developed special networking gear targeted specifically for these data center applications. In some cases, the service providers operating these large cloud data centers have specified custom built networking gear from major ODMs and have written their own networking software to reduce cost even further.

Most data center networks have been designed for north-south traffic. This is mainly due to that fact that most data center traffic up until recently has been from clients on the web directly communicating with servers in the data center. In addition, enterprise switches that have been repurposed for the data center typically consist of north-south silos built around departmental boundaries. Now we are seeing much more data center traffic flowing in the east-west direction due to server virtualization and changing server workloads. Besides complexity, the problem with enterprise style networks is latency and latency variation. Not only is the latency very high for east-west traffic, it can change dramatically, depending on the path through the network. Because of this, data center network designers are moving toward a flat network topology as shown in Figure 2.16.

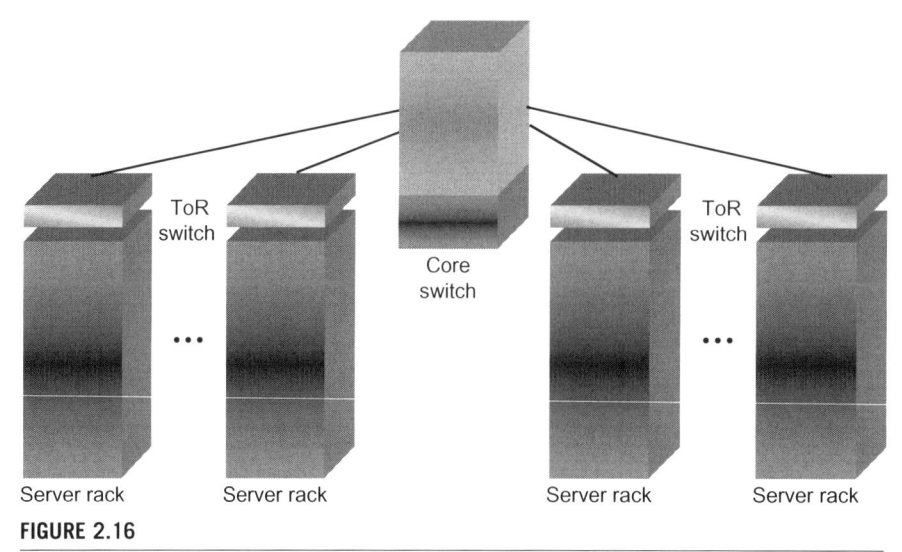

FIGURE 2.16

Cloud data center network.

By providing 10GbE links to the rack servers, the network can support the convergence of storage and data traffic into one network, reducing costs. As shown in the figure, ToR switches are used with high-bandwidth links to the core and the core routers have been replaced with simpler core switches with a larger number of ports allowing them to absorb the aggregation function, making this a "flatter" network. This type of network can better support all of the east-west traffic that is seen in large data centers today with lower latency and lower latency variation. In addition, by moving the tunneling and forwarding intelligence into the ToR switch, a simpler core switch can be developed using high-bandwidth tag forwarding much like an MPLS label switch router. More information on cloud data center network topologies will be presented in Chapter 4.

MOVEMENT TO THE CLOUD

Enterprise data centers have continued to add more equipment and services in order to keep pace with their growing needs. Offices once dominated by paperwork are now doing almost everything using web-based tools. Design and manufacturing companies rely heavily on arrays of computing resources in order to speed their time to market. But now, many corporations are seeing the value of outsourcing their computing needs to cloud service providers. This section will describe some of the driving forces behind this transition, along with security concerns. We will also describe several types of cloud data centers and the cloud services they provide.

Driving forces

Designing, building, and maintaining a large corporate data center is a costly affair. Expensive floor space, special cooling equipment, and high power demands are some of the challenges that data center administrators must face. Even with the advent of virtualized servers, low server utilization is a common problem as the system administrator must design for periods of peak demand. As an illustrative example, consider a small company doing large chip designs. Early in the design process, computing demands can be low. But as the chip design is being finalized, chip layout, simulation, and design verification tools create peak workloads that the data center must be designed to accommodate. Because of this, if a company is only developing one chip per year, the data center becomes underutilized most of the time.

Over the last 10 years or so, large data centers have become very common across the world. Some of this has been driven by the need to support consumers such as in the case of companies like Amazon, Google, and Facebook. And some of this has been driven by the need to support services such as web hosting. Building a large data center is not an easy task due to power cooling and networking requirements. Several internet service providers have become experts in this area and now deploy very efficient hyper-scale data centers across the world.

Starting in 2006, Amazon had the idea to offer web services to outside developers, who could take advantage of their large efficient data centers. This idea has taken root and several cloud service providers now offer corporations the ability to outsource some of their data center needs. By providing agile software and services, the cloud service provider can deliver on-demand virtual data centers to their customers. Using the example above, as the chip design is being finalized, external data center services could be leased during peak demand, reducing the company's internal data center equipment costs. But the largest obstacle keeping companies from moving more of their data center needs over to cloud service providers are concerns about security.

Security concerns
In most surveys of IT professionals, security is listed as the main reason as to why they are not moving all of their data center assets into the cloud. There are a variety of security concerns listed below.

- Data access, modification, or destruction by unauthorized personnel.
- Accidental transfer of data between customers.
- Improper security methods limiting access to authorized personnel.
- Accidental loss of data.
- Physical security of the data center facility.

Data access can be controlled through secure gateways such as firewalls and security appliances, but data center tenants also want to make sure that other companies cannot gain accidental access to their data. Customers can be isolated logically using network virtualization or physically with dedicated servers, storage, and networking gear. Today, configuring security appliances and setting up virtual networks are labor intensive tasks that take time. Software defined networking promises to automate many of these tasks at a higher orchestration level, eliminating any errors that could cause improper access or data loss. We will provide more information on software defined networking in Chapter 9. Physical security means protecting the data center facility from disruption in power, network connections, or equipment operation by fire, natural disaster, or acts of terrorism. Most data centers today are built with this type of physical security in mind.

Cloud types
Large cloud data centers can be dedicated to a given corporation or institution (private cloud) or can be shared among many different corporations or institutions (public cloud). In some cases, a hybrid cloud approach is used. This section will describe these cloud data center types in more detail and also list some of the reasons that a corporation may choose one over the other.

Private cloud
Large corporations may choose to build a private cloud, which can be administered either internally or through an outside service, and may be hosted internally or at an external location. What sets a private cloud apart from a corporate data center is the efficiency of operation. Unlike data centers that may be dedicated to certain groups within a corporation, a private cloud can be shared among all the groups within the corporation. Servers that may have stayed idle overnight in the United States can now be utilized at other corporate locations around the world. By having all the corporate IT needs sharing a physical infrastructure, economies of scale can provide lower capital expense and operating expense. With the use of virtualized services and software defined networking, agile service redeployments are possible, greatly improving resource utilization and efficiencies.

Public cloud
Smaller corporations that don't have the critical mass to justify a private cloud can choose to move to a public cloud. The public cloud has the same economies of scale and agility as the private cloud, but is hosted by an external company and data center resources are shared among multiple corporations. In addition, corporations can pay as they go, adding or removing compute resources on demand as their needs change.

The public cloud service providers need to develop data centers that meet the requirements of these corporate tenants. In some cases, they can provide physically isolated resources, effectively hosting a private cloud within the public cloud. In the public cloud domain, virtualization of compute and networking resources allows customers to lease only the services they need and expand or reduce services on the fly. In order to provide this type of agility while at the same time reducing operating expense, cloud service providers are turning to software defined networking as a means to orchestrate data center networking resources and quickly adjust to changing customer requirements. We will provide more details on software defined networking in Chapter 9 of this book.

Hybrid cloud
In some cases, corporations are unwilling to move their entire data center into the public cloud due to the potential security concerns described above. But in many cases, corporations can keep sensitive data in their local data center and exploit the public cloud without the need to invest in a large data center infrastructure and have the ability to quickly add or reduce resources as the business needs dictate. This approach is sometimes called a hybrid cloud.

Public cloud services
The public cloud service providers can host a wide variety of services from leasing hardware to providing complete software applications, and there are now several providers who specialize in these different types of services shown in Figure 2.17.

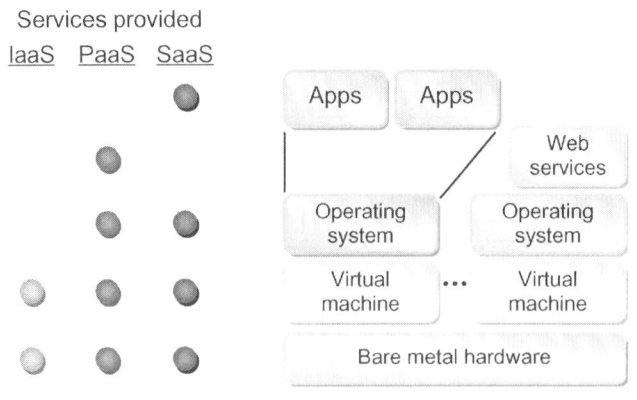

FIGURE 2.17

Services available from cloud service providers.

Infrastructure as a Service (IaaS) includes hardware resources such as servers, storage, and networking along with low-level software features such as hypervisors for virtual machines and load balancers. Platform as a Service (PaaS) includes higher layer functions such as operating systems and/or web server applications including databases and development tools. Software as a Service (SaaS) provides web-based software tools to both individuals and corporations. Figure 2.17 shows typical data center functional components along with the types of services provided by IaaS, PaaS, and SaaS. Some applications offered by large cloud service providers that we use every day are very similar to SaaS, but are not classified that way. For example Google Search, Facebook, and the App Store are applications that are run in large data centers, but are not necessarily considered SaaS.

Infrastructure as a Service

With IaaS, the service provider typically leases out the raw data center building blocks including servers, storage, and networking. This allows the client to build their own virtual data center within the service provider's facility. An example of this is hosting a public cloud. The service provider may provide low-level software functions such as virtual machine hypervisors, network virtualization services, and load balancing, but the client will install their own operating systems and applications. The service provider will maintain the hardware and virtual machines, while the client will maintain and update all the software layers above the virtual machines. Some example IaaS providers include Google Compute Engine, Rackspace®, and Amazon Elastic Compute Cloud.

Platform as a Service

This model provides the client with a computing platform including operating system and access to some software tools. An example of this is web hosting services, in which the service provider not only provides the operating system on which a web site will be hosted, but also access to database applications, web development tools, and tools to gather web statistics. The service provider will maintain the operating system and tools, while the client will maintain their own database and web pages. The service provider can provide a range of services and a variety of hosting options with added hardware performance depending on expected web traffic volume. Some example PaaS providers include Windows Azure Cloud Services, Google App Engine, and a variety of web hosting companies.

Software as a Service

Cloud service providers can also deliver software applications and databases to the end user through the SaaS business model. With this model, the end user pays a subscription fee or on a per-use basis for on-demand software services. The service provider maintains the data infrastructure, operating systems, and software, while the end user simply runs the applications remotely. This has the potential to reduce corporate IT operating costs by outsourcing the maintenance of hardware and software to the SaaS provider. Some example SaaS providers are Microsoft Office 360 and Google Apps. It's interesting how we have evolved from running time-sharing software on large mainframes to running applications on large cloud data centers. In both cases, clients use remote "terminals" to access centralized computer resources.

REVIEW

In this chapter, we provided a brief history of how corporate data center resources have evolved from mainframes to the cloud. We also provided some background on key networking technologies that have been used over the years with a focus on Ethernet. We described the differences between enterprise data centers and cloud data centers along with the reasons that many corporations are moving their data centers into the cloud. Finally, we described several cloud services that are some of the driving forces behind the movement to the cloud. In the next chapter, we will introduce switch fabric technologies which are the fundamental building blocks of cloud data center networking equipment.

CHAPTER 3

Switch Fabric Technology

To fully understand the performance and limitations of cloud networks, you must first understand the performance and limitations of the basic silicon building blocks that are used in the cloud network equipment. Even when using state-of-the-art silicon processing and package technology, there are limits in signal speed, signal count, on-chip memory, maximum power dissipation, and other parameters that can impact data center network performance.

Because of this, switch fabric designers have been required to come up with new architectures, both at the chip level and the system level, that adapt to these limitations. As silicon process technology has provided more capabilities over time, these architectures have also evolved. A key driving force in this evolution is switch fabric performance as network link bandwidth has increased from 100Mbps to over 10Gbps.

This chapter provides a brief history of how switch fabric architectures have evolved over time. In addition, it covers switch fabric topologies, congestion management, and provides several examples of current chip-level implementations. While this chapter examines switch fabrics at the chip level, it also provides a basis for the next chapter, which will examine switch networks at the system level.

SWITCH FABRIC ARCHITECTURE OVERVIEW

Transmitting data from point A to point B is a fundamental part of any electronic system, and performance of these systems, in most cases, depends on how fast the data can be moved. In switch fabrics, this communication is performed over high-bandwidth links between large ASICs utilizing high-performance input/output (I/O) circuits. In order to maximize bandwidth performance of these I/O circuits, multiple parallel links are sometimes employed, and, over time, there is a continued increase in the per link bandwidth.

Transmitting high-bandwidth data from point A to point B inside a chip is generally not a problem as hundreds of wires can be used in parallel at high clock rates. Once these high-bandwidth signals leave the chip, their signal strength must be boosted significantly using special output buffer circuits in order to drive the circuit board transmission lines and the receiving chip termination resistors. The number of these high-bandwidth output buffers is limited by the overall chip area and power. Because of this, high-bandwidth serializers/deserializers (SerDes) are now used in most switch fabric applications as they provide more bandwidth per unit power and area than traditional parallel connections. But this was not always the case.

This section will provide a historical overview of switch fabric architectures from the early shared bus designs to the latest high-bandwidth switch configurations. For each architecture shown, the hardware requirements and performance limitations will also be discussed.

Shared bus architecture

When more than a few devices need to pass data to each other, it becomes impractical and expensive to have a dedicated connection between every device. A more cost effective method is to use a shared bus architecture, also known as a bus network, like that shown in Figure 3.1. Typically, the bus consists of multiple signals in parallel in order to increase overall performance. This configuration was used in many early computing systems in which multiple processing boards were connected to each other across a bus. A device simply places data on the bus along with address information. All other devices listen to the bus and access data that is addressed to them.

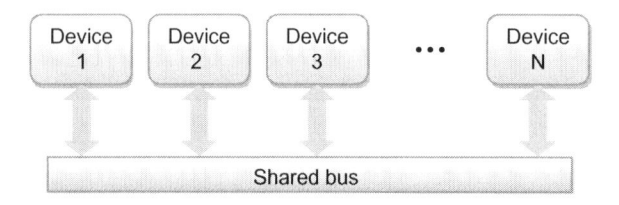

FIGURE 3.1

Shared bus architecture block diagram.

When a device wants to communicate over the bus, it must first listen to the bus to see if any other communication is in progress. If not, it will start transmitting on the bus and listen for any collisions that may occur due to simultaneous transmissions. If a collision does occur, the sender may retransmit after a random delay time, until successful. Other methods include the use of arbitration or dedicated time slots to gain bus access.

Think of early Ethernet as a single lane bus. Here are a few examples of shared bus protocols.

- *Early Ethernet IEEE 802.3*, implemented using CSMA/CD
- *I^2C 2-wire interface*, used as a management bus on many boards today
- *32-bit and 64-bit PCI bus*, used in older computing systems

The advantage of a shared bus is that it is very cost effective and it is easy to add more devices, but it also requires some sort of collision avoidance mechanism so that multiple devices don't try to transmit on the bus at the same time. In some implementations, arbitration methods are used in which a device will request access to the bus through a central arbiter which will grant access based on factors such as request arrival times and message priorities.

Shared bus performance limitations

While shared bus architectures are fairly straightforward to implement, they run into several fundamental limitations when high-bandwidth and/or low-latency communication is required. One key fundamental limit is that only one transaction can exist on the bus at one time. So, if there are N devices on the bus, each device can use only about $1/N$ of the total bus data capacity even though the device interface must be able to drive the full bus bandwidth during its given time slot.

To improve overall bus bandwidth, designers can increase the bandwidth of each wire on the bus and/or increase the width of the bus. As frequencies are increased past a certain point, a single wire on the bus needs to be treated like a transmission line. But, by its nature, a bus has multiple stubs along the transmission line, causing signal degradation due to difficult termination and reflection issues. Because of this, shared busses must be limited in either maximum frequency or the number of devices connected to the bus.

Increasing the width of the bus also provides design challenges. Increasing the bus width increases the pin count in both the device package and the board connectors and increases the board complexity, leading to higher system costs. As the bus frequency increases, faster edge rates require better isolation between signal pins along with carful board design to reduce crosstalk. In addition, signals must arrive within a certain skew window across all of the pins on the bus in order to be clocked into the receiving device properly. Because of these limitations, the industry has been moving toward high-speed serial interfaces such as those used with protocols such as PCI Express.

Shared memory architecture

In a shared memory architecture, devices exchange information by writing to and reading from a pool of shared memory as shown in Figure 3.2. Unlike a shared bus architecture, in a shared memory architecture, there are only point-to-point connections between the device and the shared memory, somewhat easing the board design and layout issues. Also, each interface can run at full bandwidth all the time, so the overall fabric bandwidth is much higher than in shared bus architectures.

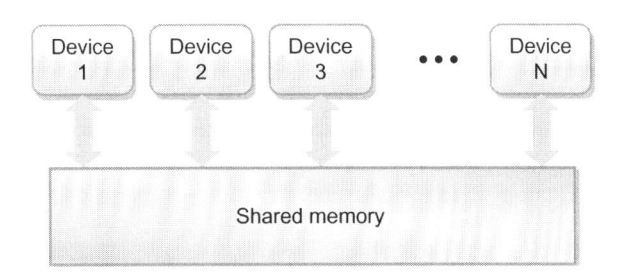

FIGURE 3.2

Shared memory architecture block diagram.

In theory, the shared memory architecture provides ideal switch fabric performance under the assumption that all ports can read and write simultaneously to the same memory structure. In practice, the devices may require an external arbiter in order to gain fair access to the memory with no collisions. This architecture also requires a high pin count memory structure when supporting a large number of devices.

Shared memory performance limitations

A shared memory switch fabric requires a very high-performance memory architecture, in which reads and writes occur at a rate much higher than the individual interface data rate. For example, if there are N devices connected to the shared memory block each with an interface operating at data rate D, the memory read and write data rate must be $N*D$ in order to maintain full performance. If this performance level cannot be maintained, an arbitration scheme may be required, limiting the read/write bandwidth of each device. This is not ideal but will still provide higher performance than a shared bus architecture. Another way around this memory performance limitation is to use an input/output-queued (IOQ) architecture which will be described later in this chapter.

A second limitation with a shared memory architecture is pin count. The number of pins required on the memory block is proportional to the number of devices connected to it. When using parallel interfaces to increase bandwidth, the total pin count can quickly exceed the number of pins available on a single memory device. This requires the use of multiple memory devices and the striping of data across these devices, which can cause interface timing issues requiring clock tuning and/or bandwidth reduction on each interface. The next step in the switch fabric evolution was to look at fully serial solutions in order to reduce pin count and avoid these issues.

Crossbar switch

The use of high-bandwidth serial interconnect is one way to provide a larger number of high-bandwidth ports in a switch fabric device, while at the same time, eliminating some of the timing issues described above. Around the mid-1990s, silicon vendors released the first 1Gbps SerDes circuits, which were first used in single port transceivers. At the same time, transceivers utilizing gallium arsenide (GaAs) technology were also emerging with SerDes operating above 2Gbps. For the first time, these allowed switch fabric implementations using individual transceivers connected to large, asynchronous crossbar switch chips. Figure 3.3 shows a switch fabric architecture based on an asynchronous crossbar switch that contains multiple high-bandwidth serial interfaces connected to transceivers.

Switch Fabric Architecture Overview

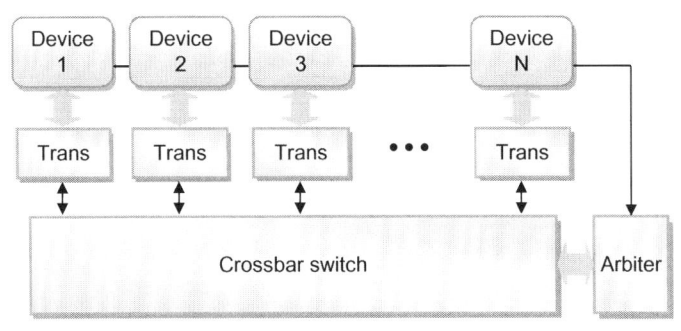

FIGURE 3.3

Crossbar architecture block diagram.

A crossbar switch can be programmed through an arbiter interface in order to connect any given input to any given output as long as not more than one input is connected to a given output. A single input can be connected to multiple outputs for broadcast or multicast traffic. With an asynchronous crossbar, data flows directly from input to output with no reclocking, much like data flowing through a set of logic gates.

In this architecture, the parallel data from each device must be serialized using a transceiver before transmission through the crossbar switch. Before transmission, the devices must request access through the arbitration units so that two devices don't attempt to transmit to the same output at the same time. The arbitration unit also configures the crossbar through a parallel interface. In most applications, the data being transferred is first divided up into uniform sized cells so that arbitration and data transfer can be aligned to a global cell clock. Because of this, special transceivers may be used that not only include SerDes blocks, but also buffer memory and logic to segment packets into cells and reassemble cells back into packets. This is known as a segmentation and reassembly (SAR) unit. The buffer memory may also serve to temporarily hold data if arbitration is not granted during a given cell period.

Crossbar switch performance limitations

To better understand the limitations of this design, we will start by providing a brief background on how serial data is transmitted from transceiver to transceiver. The sending transceiver uses a local clock to provide transmit bit timing and the receiving transceiver uses a phase lock loop (PLL) to recover this bit timing from the received serial stream. The receive clock output from the PLL should have low jitter in order to eliminate receive bit errors, which typically requires a PLL with a low loop bandwidth. Low loop bandwidth means that the receiving PLL reacts relatively slowly to changes in the received serial data stream bit timing.

When sending serial streams through asynchronous crossbar switches, a receiving transceiver can start receiving a new serial stream from different sending transceivers using different transmit clocks at any time after a new crossbar connection is made. Using a PLL with low loop bandwidth means that the receiving transceiver will take some time to reacquire the proper receive clock timing from the new sending transceiver. These gaps in data transfer while the PLL is recovering can dramatically reduce the overall system performance. To mitigate this, designers came up with fast phase acquisition transceivers that can recover the receive clock within several bit times. While this greatly improves performance, it's a very complex design and difficult to make robust across all corner cases with no bit errors.

If a cell-based design is used to improve the fabric efficiency, the receiving side must reassemble the incoming cells into packets. This is also a difficult design challenge when operating at high data rates. If a bit error occurs, a cell could be lost requiring segment numbering and packet drop after cell receiver timeout. Because of these limitations, only a few designs of this type found their way into production systems.

Synchronous serial switching

By the late 1990s, silicon vendors were starting to integrate multiple serial transceiver blocks on a single piece of silicon. One of the first silicon chip vendors to do this was LSI® Logic with their GigaBlaze® 1Gbps transceiver cores. At the same time, GaAs chip vendors such as Vitesse® Semiconductor were integrating multiple transceivers operating over 2Gbps onto a single chip. For the first time, switch fabric designers could develop switch chips that were continuously synchronized with the connected transceivers, eliminating the need for fast phase acquisition after each switch connection change as described above for large asynchronous crossbar designs. Vitesse was a pioneer in this area, creating the first merchant synchronous serial switch fabric chip set called CrossStream in 1997.

Figure 3.4 shows an example synchronous serial switch block diagram in which multiple devices send data through local transceivers which are connected across a backplane to a central switch chip. The central switch chip integrates multiple

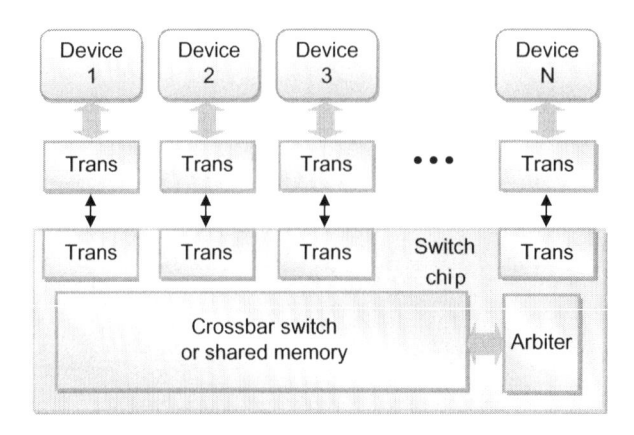

FIGURE 3.4

Synchronous serial architecture block diagram.

transceivers along with a crossbar switch and an arbitration unit. In some designs the crossbar may be replaced by a shared memory, or a combination of crossbar and memory. Arbitration is typically performed when each remote transceiver sends in-band request signals that may be granted by the central arbiter before data is transmitted.

Because there are N transceivers in the system and N local clocks, there must be at least N clock domain crossings in the fabric. This is typically done using first in, first out (FIFO) buffer memory structures that have separate write and read clocks. In the early days, in order to simplify the switch design, these FIFO were pushed out into the transceivers. These FIFOs are now typically integrated within the transceivers on the switch chip. Today, almost all merchant switch silicon follows this architectural model.

Synchronous serial performance limitations

Although synchronous serial switch fabrics are widely used today, they are limited by factors such as the maximum number of transceivers that will fit on a single chip and limitations in crossbar and memory architectures. These will be discussed in more detail in the last section in this chapter where we provide some examples of existing chip set architectures.

SWITCH FABRIC TOPOLOGIES

In the last section, we described several switch fabric architectures along with the limitations in implementing these architectures based on factors such as chip technology. For these basic network building blocks, a primary limitation is port count. Data center networks require tens of thousands of high-bandwidth endpoints while the best chip technology can provide around 100 high-bandwidth ports. To get around this limitation, multistage fabric technologies must be employed.

In the next chapter, we will discuss the configuration of data center networks using network equipment as the basic building block. In this section, we will describe some of the basic multistage fabric architectures used inside of this network equipment or used to create larger network topologies. In the last section, we called one of the chips at the edge of the fabric a transceiver. Over time, these chips have become more complex and the industry generally refers to them now as fabric interface chips (FICs). We will use this terminology moving forward.

Ring topology

One of the simplest topologies to implement is the ring topology shown in Figure 3.5. To transfer information, a device will place data on the ring using the FIC, and it will be passed from FIC to FIC until it reaches its destination based on embedded address information that is read by the FIC. At that point, the destination FIC will present the information to the receiving device.

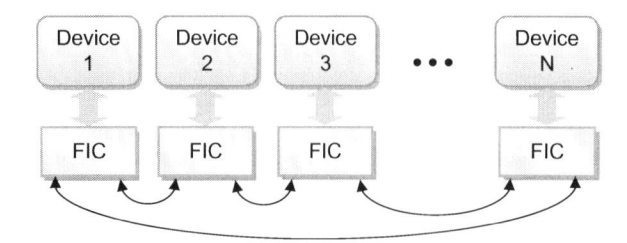

FIGURE 3.5

Ring topology block diagram.

Data can be passed clockwise or counterclockwise around the ring, providing resiliency in the case of a single link failure. In some cases, dual rings are used for added resiliency. An advantage of the ring topology is that the FIC is a relatively simple device that needs only a few ports and the ring can be easily scaled by simply adding more devices into the ring. A major disadvantage of this topology is that as the number of devices is increased, the traffic load through every FIC must also increase in order to maintain the same level of performance per device. Because of this, ring topologies are usually deployed where each device only requires a fraction of the link bandwidth. Another issue is that a failed device can break the ring communication. Example use cases are Token Ring networks in the LAN or SONET rings in the carrier network.

Mesh topology

In a mesh topology, bandwidth between devices is improved compared to a ring structure by providing a dedicated link between every device as shown in Figure 3.6. Although this improves fabric performance, it requires $N-1$ ports on every FIC when N devices are connected to the fabric, limiting the scale of the fabric. The FIC must also direct traffic to a given output port instead of simply placing all traffic on a single ring port. An example use case is in an ATCA backplane, which can use either a mesh or a star configuration.

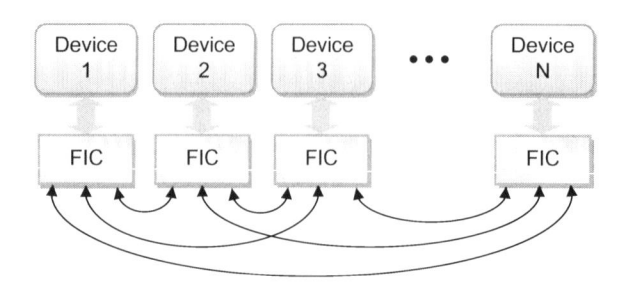

FIGURE 3.6

Mesh topology block diagram.

Fabric designers have also scaled mesh and ring designs in multiple dimensions, creating fabric configurations called two-dimensional rings or Torus structures. These are very complex topologies that are typically only deployed in applications such as high-performance computing, so we will not go into any detail in this book which is focusing on cloud data center networks.

Star topology

Many high port count switches and routers are designed as modular chassis. These systems utilize multiple line cards containing processing resources and/or externally facing ports along with FICs. The chassis will also contain several switch cards containing switch chips that connect to the line cards across a passive backplane. The fabric configuration in these chassis is known as a star topology as shown in Figure 3.7. Today, this is one of the most widely deployed topologies in modular switch, router, or network appliance systems.

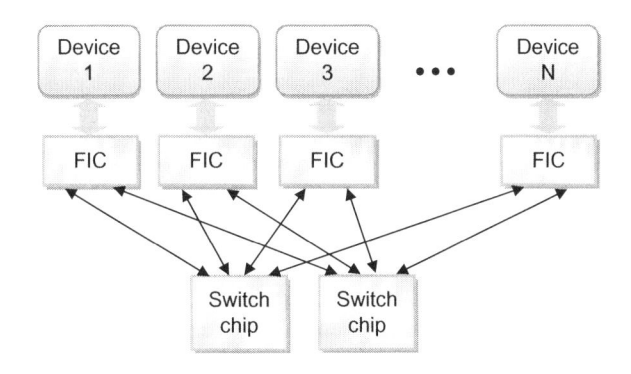

FIGURE 3.7

Star topology block diagram.

In this topology, the FIC needs as few as one connection to each switch chip in the system, reducing its port count and simplifying its design. Scalability in this topology is limited by the port count on the switch chip, and a given switch card can contain multiple switch chips in order to increase the backplane bandwidth. Multiple switch cards can be used for resiliency, so that if one switch card fails, traffic can continue across the remaining switch card(s). In many cases, the bandwidth from the FIC across the backplane is designed to be about twice as high as the bandwidth between the device and the FIC in order to provide over-speed which minimizes congestion and provides additional bandwidth in case of a switch card failure. Switch cards can be run in active-active mode, meaning traffic utilizes both switch cards, or in active-protective mode, meaning one switch card is an idle backup. In some cases, more than two switch cards are used to limit the backplane bandwidth reduction when any one switch card fails.

Fat-tree topology

The star topology can be scaled even further by adding higher port count FIC devices and increasing the number of switch chips in the system. One way to do this is to use the same switch device at both stages of the fabric. This can even be expanded to three or four stages although in many cases this is not practical. The first person to propose such an architecture was Charles Clos in 1953. Although he was thinking in terms of telephone switching systems instead of switch chips, the concept is used today and is sometimes known as a fat-tree architecture. Figure 3.8 is a two-stage fat-tree configuration. In this configuration, the leaf switches connect to the externally facing ports, and the spine switches form the second stage of the fabric.

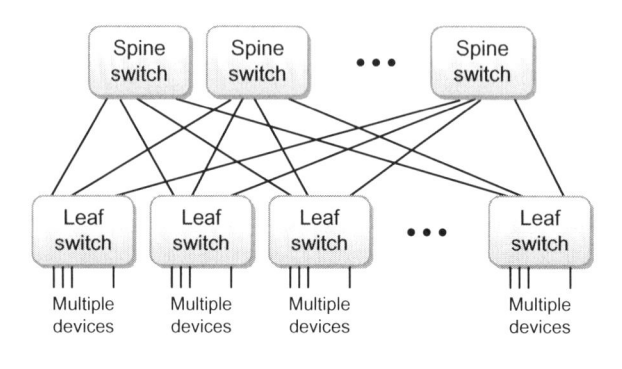

FIGURE 3.8

Two-stage fat-tree topology block diagram.

In order to maintain the bandwidth between the stages at the same level as the bandwidth of the external ports on the leaf switches, half of the leaf switch ports must be connected to the spine switches. Therefore, the maximum number of spine switches equals half of the number of ports on a leaf switch and the maximum number of leaf switches equals the total number of ports on a spine switch. For example:

- *Using 24-port switch chips*, the maximum number of ports is $24 \times 12 = 288$ using 36 devices.
- *Using 64-port switch chips*, the maximum number of ports is $64 \times 32 = 2048$ using 96 devices.

Although this topology can scale nicely as the switch chip port count increases, care must be taken in balancing the total incoming traffic load across the second stage of switch chips. If the load is not balanced properly, congestion can occur, reducing the overall system bandwidth. If more than two stages are used, load balancing and congestion management become even more problematic. In the next section, we will take a look at this in more detail.

CONGESTION MANAGEMENT

Congestion can slow down the local flow of traffic in a network and can quickly spread to other parts of the network if not mitigated in a timely fashion. The switch fabric architecture has a strong influence on potential congestion points, and most architectures include some sort of mechanism for congestion management. In this section, we will describe how congestion occurs and how it can be reduced or avoided with either careful architecture design or through mechanisms such as flow control. Throughout this section, we will use the analogy of freeway traffic in order to provide the reader a better understanding of congestion and congestion management concepts.

Causes of congestion

Congestion is generally caused by multiple traffic sources attempting to gain access to the same resource in the network (i.e., egress link or egress queue). One area where this occurs is at the communication links between chips. Inside of a chip, high-bandwidth data paths can be created using hundreds or thousands of wires in parallel. This is because on-chip wiring dimensions are relatively small and small transistors can drive these wires at high speeds. But once a signal must be transmitted from one chip to another, much larger transistors with elaborate signaling methods must be used to drive the relatively large PCB transmission lines between devices. This and other factors such as maximum chip power dissipation, limits the total number of high-speed output signals per chip. For example, some of the largest switch chips today have on the order of 128 10G SerDes, compared to tens of thousands of on-chip high-speed signals.

Think of the situation like a large city with a river cutting through the middle. On each side of the river there may be hundreds of surface streets, but maybe only 5-10 bridges crossing the river. At rush hour, there may be cars from many surface streets trying to access a single bridge causing congestion. This is why switch fabric chip architects spend a lot of time coming up with clever ways to avoid this type of congestion, which will be discussed later in this section. Let's start with describing some types of congestion these limited resources can cause.

Head-of-line blocking

Head-of-line (HoL) blocking occurs if there is a single queue of data packets waiting to be transmitted, and the packet at the head of the queue (line) cannot move forward due to congestion, even if other packets behind this one could. Using the bridge analogy, let's say that there is a single lane bridge crossing the river. The car at the far end of the bridge wants to exit on First Street, but First Street is congested so it has to wait, blocking all the other cars on the bridge. The cars behind this one that want to cross the bridge and exit on other noncongested roads have no choice but to wait.

Unbalanced traffic

In many switch fabric topologies like a fat-tree, attempts are made to uniformly distribute the traffic load across multiple second stage switches in order to ease congestion. Although this can help, as switch fabric topologies get more complex, congestion can still crop up due to factors such as unbalanced traffic patterns, or inefficient load distribution algorithms. Consider the two-stage fat-tree topology shown in Figure 3.8. Although this is a fairly simple configuration compared to the complexities found in a complete data center network, it serves to illustrate some of the key causes of congestion that may occur in more complex fabric topologies.

In Figure 3.8, traffic enters the fabric at the bottom of the leaf switches. Some traffic will simply exit the bottom of the same leaf switch, but other traffic must travel through one of the spine switches to reach its final destination. But which spine switch? This is an example of where load balancing comes into play. By efficiently distributing incoming packets across multiple spine switches, full fabric bandwidth can be maintained. But it's not that easy. In certain fabric technologies such as Ethernet, a given flow of data like a video stream must be transported in many thousands of packets and these packets must arrive in the order that they were transmitted. If these flows are distributed across multiple spine switches, they could arrive out of order due to factors such as temporary congestion in one of the spine switches. This means that flow-based load distribution must be employed, where all the packets for a given flow are transmitted through the same spine switch. If there are multiple flows like this, a spine switch can become congested, due to the nonuniform load distribution. One way around this is to provide a packet reordering unit at each egress leaf switch although this can add significant complexity to each leaf switch design.

Another source of congestion comes from large frames including jumbo frames, which can be as large as 16KB. Considering again the limited external port resources on a switch chip. If a low-priority jumbo frame starts to exit on a given egress port, and just after it starts transmission, a small high-priority frame wants to use that same egress port, it must wait for the jumbo frame to complete transmission. One way to get around this issue is to segment all packets into uniform size cells. In this way, a jumbo frame broken into small cells could be interspersed with the higher priority frames on the same link. But this requires packet reassembly engines on each egress port, which again adds to the design complexity.

Another source of unbalanced traffic comes from the lack of coordination between all the leaf switches. In most multistage fabrics of this type, it is too difficult to coordinate the load distribution across all the leaf switches, so instead, each switch makes independent decisions. So, even with congestion feedback information from the spine switches, several leaf switches may choose the same spine switch at a given point in time, causing temporary congestion.

Load balancing algorithms

In multistage fabrics employing star or fat-tree topologies, efficient distribution (balancing) of traffic across the second stage of fabric devices is a key factor in maintaining full cross-sectional bandwidth throughout the fabric. Uniform load balancing is ideal, but can be difficult to achieve due to the characteristics of data entering the fabric. Variations in frame size, large flows and traffic burstiness all make the load balancing job more difficult.

Several methods can be used to distribute the traffic. A simple method is to send each flow to the next higher switch number in a round robin fashion. The problem here is that each FIC or leaf switch acts independently, and they can become temporarily synchronized, congesting each second stage switch one at time. A better method is to use a hash-based algorithm or a random hash. The efficiency of the load distribution in this case will depend on factors such as the hash algorithm used, the number of different flows and the correlation between the flows. For any given hash algorithm, there will be corner cases where traffic is unbalanced for a given set of flows. It is important, therefore, to select a hash algorithm that has the best load distribution across a wide variety of corner case scenarios.

Traffic buffering

When congestion does occur, there are several actions that the switch fabric can take. The first is to simply drop the frame. In some instances, this is OK as higher layer protocols such as Transmission Control Protocol/Internet Protocol (TCP/IP) will eventually detected a lost frame and retransmit the data. But other applications, like storage, are not as forgiving and require lossless network operation in order to maintain performance and data integrity. Flow control can help to provide lossless operation and will be discussed in depth in the following section. Along with flow control, data can be temporarily stored (buffered) within the fabric, until the congestion subsides. Figure 3.9 shows a star fabric topology using ingress buffering at the FIC.

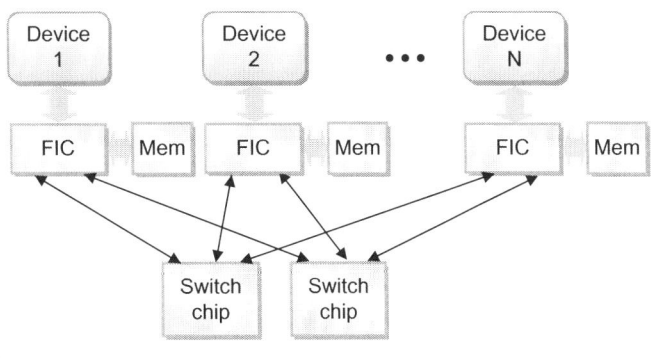

FIGURE 3.9

Star fabric with ingress buffering.

On-chip buffering is sufficient in many network applications and used on many merchant switch chips. In multistage fabric topologies, depending on the expected traffic types and flow control capabilities, on-chip buffering may not be sufficient for maintaining lossless operation. In this case, external buffering will be required. In addition, in order to maintain service-level agreements (SLAs) with the end customer, such as quality of service, traffic management may be required in the ingress FIC as will be discussed after the next section. This also requires external buffering in order to maintain queues for thousands of flows.

As the device continues to send streams of data to the FIC, the FIC uses information such as the traffic class, customer SLA information if traffic managed, and congestion feedback information (flow control) to make a decision on whether to send the data on to the second-level switch. If not sent, it is written into the attached memory until transmission is approved, at which point it is read out of the attached memory. In most cases, to simplify the FIC design, all data is written into the attached memory until it is approved for transmission to the second stage.

One of the challenges here is to provide sufficient memory bandwidth. Most industry standard memory interfaces are living in the old world of parallel busses. For example, a 100G traffic manager may require up to 8 Double Data Rate type 3 (DDR3) memory interfaces in order to maintain full line rate through the memory. At around 70 pins per interface, this means that the FIC needs 500 pins just for buffer memory. Compare that to a 100G Ethernet interface using 25G SerDes and just 16 pins. It is expected that new standards will emerge in the next few years, bringing the memory interface into the modern age.

The size of buffer memory is also an important consideration. The size of the memory depends on factors such as the congestion duty cycles, the incoming traffic rate, the speedup factor in the backplane, the type of flow control used, and the burst patterns of incoming traffic. If traffic management queues are deployed in the external memory, then other factors come into play, such as the number of queues and the minimum size for each queue. As you can see, designing such a system is not easy and one of the important jobs of the network switch chip architect.

FLOW CONTROL

Flow control is a key element in maximizing switch fabric performance while also providing lossless operation. But, effective flow control is one of the most challenging aspects of switch fabric design. Think of flow control as a throttling mechanism, where a switch says, "my buffers are filling up, and I better send a message to whoever is sending me the data to throttle back a bit." This is similar to the stop lights on freeway entrance ramps. Someone is monitoring freeway congestion downstream, and setting the timing on the freeway entrance lights accordingly. Of course it becomes much more complex in multistage switch fabric designs with multiple paths, multiple queuing structures, and multiple traffic priorities. This section will detail several types of flow control and describe the implementation and limitations involved in each type.

Link-level flow control

Link-level flow control is typically used on the link between two chips or two switching systems. Although it provides lossless operation across the link, it can cause reduced bandwidth performance and cause congestion spreading unless other flow control methods are employed in the fabric.

Figure 3.10 shows an example two-stage fabric including a first stage (ingress) switch or FIC and a second stage switch. The egress switch or FIC is not shown, but can also use link-level flow control. Flow control for larger multistage fabrics will be discussed later in this section.

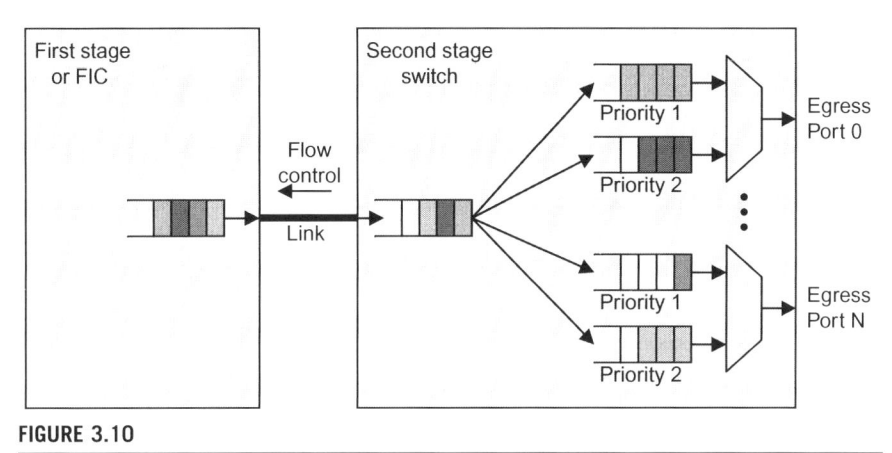

FIGURE 3.10

Link-level flow control.

We will assume a second stage switch that uses two priorities at each egress port but the mechanisms described here can be extended to a large number of priorities using the same concepts. Keep in mind that the egress queues in the second stage switch are also receiving data from other switch ingress ports causing potential congestion.

As discussed earlier, the link between switch chips becomes a precious resource that must be shared by all traffic traveling from the first to the second stage, much like the bridge over a river that cuts through a large city. Without flow control, the second stage switch memory could overflow, causing packets to be dropped. One way to minimize packet drops is to provide overprovisioning (excess bandwidth in the fabric) such that the fabric can absorb bursts of traffic without causing much congestion. But, all of this extra bandwidth can become expensive to implement. Another way to avoid losing packets is to employ link-level flow control as shown in Figure 3.10. In this example, there is both a transmit queue in the first stage and a receive queue at the ingress of the second stage. If the receive queue fills up, a special flow control message is sent to the first stage telling it to stop sending traffic. There are two types of link-level flow control that can be implemented.

- *Threshold based:* The receiving queue sends a flow control message once a preprogrammed watermark level is exceeded. This method is used in the Data Center Bridging standards which will be described later in this book.
- *Credit based:* The receiving device periodically sends credits to the transmitting queue representing the space available in its queues. The transmitting queue will not send data until it has enough credits. This method is used with PCI Express interfaces.

The threshold based method is easier to implement because a flow control message is sent out only when a threshold is reached. But, the threshold must be set such that in-transit frames could still arrive without overflowing the queue. Credit based flow control adds some complexity, but minimizes the need for excess receive queue capacity because the credit number advertises the exact remaining queue size to the transmitting device. But, by sending periodic credit information, it consumes more link bandwidth than threshold based flow control that sends messages only when needed. But what happens if a flow control message gets lost? In this case, a periodic approach is better because the information will eventually get to the transmitter in a following flow control message.

One important concept we need to introduce here is flow control latency, sometimes call flow control round-trip delay. If a threshold is crossed and a flow control message is generated, it will take some time to reach the transmitter. This includes queuing delays when sending the message and processing delays when receiving the message. While this message is working its way back to the transmitter, the transmitter continues to send traffic until it receives the flow control message and can process it. So the receiving queue needs to have enough remaining space to absorb this in-flight traffic. Periodic flow control messages can make this slightly worse, because the credit information or fill level information could have extra latency up to the period of transmission.

One problem with standard link-level flow control is that, if an egress queue on the second stage switch fills up, the receive queue could become blocked even if other egress queues are free. This introduces HoL blocking, which can greatly reduce the link bandwidth utilization. This is similar to the analogy we gave earlier about a single lane bridge crossing the river. The car at the far end of the bridge wants to exit on First Street, but First Street is congested so it has to wait, blocking all the other cars on the bridge. The cars behind this one that want to cross the bridge and exit on other noncongested roads have no choice but to wait. It would be nice to add an additional lane to the bridge like a high-priority bus lane, so that busses can bypass all of the congested traffic.

Now let's introduce priority-based link-level flow control. As shown in Figure 3.11, this introduces priority queues at each side of the link and the flow control message sent back across the link contains the status of each priority queue. Now, if priority 2 traffic is blocked due to egress queue congestion, priority 1 traffic can still be transmitted across the link.

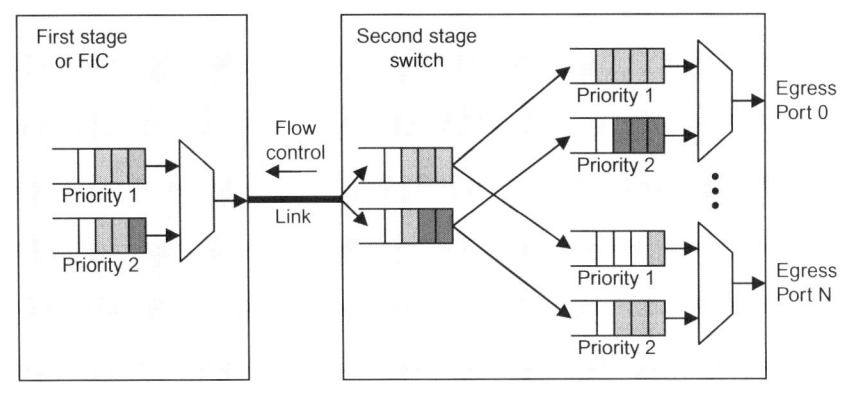

FIGURE 3.11

Priority-based link-level flow control.

This can dramatically improve the link utilization, but does not completely eliminate HoL blocking. For that, we will need virtual output queuing.

Virtual output queuing

In Figure 3.11, one of the ingress priority queues in the second stage can become blocked if only one of the egress priority queues becomes full. In this example, a priority 1 frame intended for egress port N cannot make it through because the priority 1 queue is full for egress port 0. In our high-priority bus lane analogy, if the lead bus needs to exit onto congested First Street, all other busses behind this one will be blocked even if they are not exiting on First Street. Now we have priority-based HoL blocking. So, let's add a lane for each downstream exit to avoid this type of blocking. Keep in mind that there is still only one physical link between stages, but we are adding multiple virtual channels (bus lanes) in this one physical link. Figure 3.12 shows how virtual output queuing works.

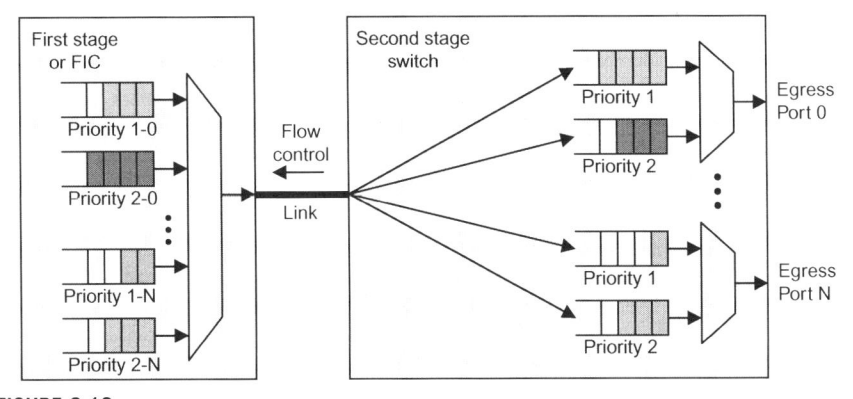

FIGURE 3.12

Virtual output queuing.

In this configuration, the first stage has a queue matching every output queue in the second stage. These are called virtual output queues. Flow control information is sent from the egress of the second stage to the first stage containing information about which output queues are congested. In this way, the first stage will only send traffic to egress queues with available space, eliminated head of line blocking. In general, the different outputs are serviced from the first stage in a round robin manner, with higher priority queues served first. This starts to get into the area of traffic management, which will be discussed later in this chapter.

Multistage switch fabric flow control

Flow control in switch fabric architectures constructed with more than two stages becomes very difficult to implement successfully. This is mainly due to two factors; flow control round-trip delay and ingress traffic management complexity. As the congestion point moves farther away from the traffic source, it can take a relatively long time for the flow control message to work its way back to the source. By the time it is received and processed, traffic patterns can change and other points of congestion can spring up.

End-to-end flow control is ideal in these multistage fabrics because localized flow control methods can cause blocking in the fabric. But end-to-end flow control requires a large number of ingress queues to avoid blocking. Consider that there must be $N \times P$ virtual output queues at each ingress device in a two-stage fabric, where N is the number of second stage fabric ports and P is the number of fabric priorities. Now if we add another stage of N port fabric devices, the number of virtual output queues becomes $N \times N \times P$. In addition, the queue depths must all increase to absorb the additional round-trip flow control delay. At this point, the ingress FIC becomes more of a traffic manager which will be discussed in the next section. Let's look at a few attempts by the industry to standardize multistage flow control.

Explicit congestion notification

Explicit congestion notification (ECN) is an optional feature in TCP/IP networks that provides congestion notification by marking packets that transit parts of the network experiencing high levels of congestion. The receiver of the notification then sends the message back to the source of the marked packet, which then may reduce its transmission rate. As you can see, the flow control round-trip delay is about twice as high as a direct feedback mechanism limiting the usefulness of this feature.

Quantized congestion notification

Quantized congestion notification (QCN) was first introduced around 2008 as part of the data center bridging standards. It provides direct feedback from the point of the congestion to the source but suffers from several issues that have limited its deployment in data center networks. More details on QCN will be provided in a later chapter covering data center bridging.

TRAFFIC MANAGEMENT

One way to minimize the need for multistage flow control is to provide better management of traffic at the source. As we have discussed in the previous section, queuing and scheduling on the ingress side of a multistage fabric can become quite complex, especially when more stages are added. Telecom access systems have dealt with these issues for many years now as they have needed to provide SLAs on a per customer basis including quality of service guarantees for voice, video, and data. Although data center networks do not require the same level of complexity as telecom access systems, data centers can benefit from similar traffic management functions within the data center network. This section will provide an overview of traffic management that can be applied to data center environments.

Frame classification engine

Before traffic is properly managed, it must be inspected and classified. This is done in a classification engine. A classification engine uses a parser to select certain fields in a frame header, and then match those fields to predefined forwarding information. If a match occurs, the frame is placed in a corresponding forwarding queue as described below. If a match does not occur, the frame can be sent to some sort of exception processing engine, which may choose to set up a new forwarding path.

Multilevel scheduler

The heart of a traffic manager is a multilevel scheduler. An example four-stage scheduler is shown in Figure 3.13. Traffic managers are really queue managers in which the queues typically reside in external buffer memory. Ideally, the traffic

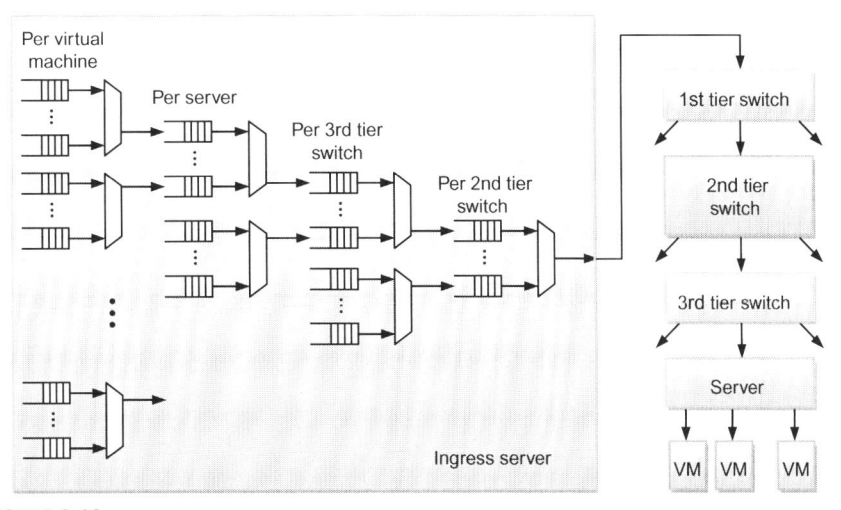

FIGURE 3.13

Example multilevel scheduler for the data center.

manager should exist as close to the source of the traffic as possible. In this example, the traffic manager is inside the ingress server and the buffer memory is simply the main memory within the server. Today, servers rarely include traffic managers, but some have proposed using this technology to provide better data center network utilization along with service-level guarantees. We will use this as an illustrative example of how traffic managers can be employed in multistage switch fabrics.

As can be seen in Figure 3.13, the scheduler has levels that match the number of levels that exist in the data center network. At the first level, the queues represent the final virtual machines and data is selected to be transmitted among the virtual machines within each egress server in the network. At the next level, the queues represent the egress servers within a rack and the data is selected to be transmitted among the servers connected to the third tier switch. At the third level, the queues represent the third tier switches and the data is selected to be transmitted among the third tier switches connected to the second tier switches. At the final stage in the multilevel scheduler, the queues represent the second tier switches and data is selected to be transmitted based among the second tier switches connected to the first tier switch. Priority queues can also be added to this scheduler, but are not shown for clarity.

By constructing a tree of queues in this manner, it becomes fairly easy to assign priorities or weights between queues based on workload requirements or factors such as the bandwidth that has been provisioned between fabric stages. In addition, if flow control is used, it becomes easier to route data around congestion hot spots or failed equipment by reducing bandwidth or even shutting down certain queues within the traffic manager.

There are several ways to select the next data to be transmitted from a group of queues that are connected to the same output in a given stage. Although these methods are used in traffic managers, they also apply to queue selection in other configurations such as virtual output-queued systems that were described earlier. These methods are generally work-conserving, meaning they will service only nonempty queues so that a link will not go idle when there is data that could be transferred.

Strict priority
In this method, each queue is assigned a priority. Nonempty queues with the highest priority are always serviced before queues with lower priority. Typical use cases are for system management traffic, flow control messages, or other time sensitive protocols. But, this method has the potential to starve other queues, unless traffic shaping is also used as described below.

Round robin
In this method, a pointer simply rotates through all of the nonempty queues providing one at a time transmission. In theory, this provides equal bandwidth to all queues, but in practice this depends on the average packet size in each queue. Queues with larger average packet sizes will consume more of the output bandwidth than queues with

smaller average packet size. This is one of the reasons why bandwidth tailoring may be desirable as described next.

Deficit round robin

Deficit round robin (DRR) makes an attempt to provide certain bandwidth guarantees by using a deficit accumulator to determine if a packet can be transferred during a scheduler cycle. A quanta amount is added to each queue's deficit accumulator during each scheduler cycle. If the pending packet size is smaller than the accumulator value, the packet is eligible for transfer. If a packet is transferred, the packet size is subtracted from the associated deficit accumulator. Using this method, each queue can be provided equal bandwidth, assuming the eligible queues are serviced in a round robin fashion.

Deficit weighted round robin

In most cases it is desirable to provide different bandwidth guarantees to different types of traffic. This is done by using different weights for different queues. Weighted round robin is set up to serve some queues more often than others. For example, queue A is allowed to transfer two packets for every one packet queue B is allowed to transfer. But this suffers from the same variable packet size issue as discussed above for round robin.

Deficit weighted round robin (DWRR) is similar to deficit round robin, but can provide different bandwidth allocations to different queues. This can be done in two ways. One is to use different quanta amounts for each queue. For example, lower bandwidth queues will have a slower deficit accumulation. Another way is to use the same quanta for all queues, but to use weighted round robin between the queues eligible for transfer.

Traffic shaping

Traffic shaping can be used to tailor the bandwidth being injected into downstream links. The scheduling schemes listed above also can act as traffic shapers to some degree, but most are designed to be work-conserving so that if only one queue has data in the group of queues sharing an output, that data will be sent without restriction, independent of priority or deficit value. This is why shapers may also be needed. In the case of high-priority management traffic, shapers may also be used to make sure management traffic gets only a certain percentage of the total link bandwidth. In the multilevel scheduler shown in Figure 3.13, shaping is only required in the first stage. There are several ways to shape traffic.

Ingress link-level shaping

In multistage switch fabric architectures, the output of a given stage may not support traffic shaping, but there may be a desire to limit the bandwidth of some types of traffic sent to the following stage. In the second-level switch, incoming traffic can be shaped using link-level flow control. By simply turning on and off link-level flow control at a particular duty cycle, the receiving device can limit the bandwidth from the transmitting device. This can be expanded to support different bandwidth for different traffic classes by using priority-based flow control. This is sometimes referred to as pause pacing. The downside of this technique is that it consumes link bandwidth with multiple link-level flow control messages and in some cases it may be ineffective due to flow control message latency.

Token buckets
A more generalized traffic shaping method that provides higher bandwidth resolution uses token buckets. This is also used for traffic policing to make sure traffic conforms to predefined SLAs. Token buckets operate in a similar manner to the deficit accumulator described above, but provide higher resolution by using smaller tokens down to the byte level instead of larger quanta values.

A typical token bucket shaper may be implemented as a counter that is incremented at a rate proportional to the shaping bandwidth desired. When the counter reaches a value equal to the size in bytes of the next packet in the queue, the packet is transmitted and the counter is decremented by the size of the packet. In this way, the transmitted bytes per second for a given queue will be proportional to the counter rate. In many systems, this type if traffic shaping is used in the egress switch ports to minimize down-stream congestion.

SWITCH CHIP ARCHITECTURE EXAMPLES
Now that we have run through several switch fabric architectures and topologies along with an overview of congestion management, we will next look at some popular architectures used in merchant silicon products. In the period between 1996 and 2004, there were many different merchant switch fabric products proposed (and sometimes even sold) by both startup companies and established companies, mainly for the telecommunications market. By 2005, most of the startup companies had gone out of business and the established companies had shut down their switch product lines. Today, the handful of surviving switch fabric product lines are used mostly in Ethernet networks. In this section, we won't discuss specific products, but will instead describe several popular switch fabric architectures that are still in use today.

Cell-based designs
Several early communication protocols such as ATM and SONET/SDH used fixed sized cells or fixed time slots to transfer data across networks. ATM used a 53-byte frame size, and found some success in telecom networks, but eventually lost out to Ethernet due to added complexity. SONET/SDH systems used time slot interchange switch silicon to reconfigure SONET frames in order to send data to the proper destination, much like a freight train switching yard where fixed size train cars are reshuffled onto different trains. Starting in the late 1990s when Ethernet became

the access protocol of choice, system designers started to propose what they called the "God" box, a switching system that could use a single switch fabric to forward both fixed size SONET fames along with variable sized Ethernet packets. Eventually, Ethernet won out and Carrier Ethernet systems are replacing SONET/SDH systems in most networks today.

Even with this change, some switch fabric designers have maintained cell-based fabric architectures which segment incoming packets into fixed sized cells and reassemble cells into packets in the egress side as shown in the conceptual Figure 3.14. These types of switch fabrics are built using chip sets that include FICs along with multiple central switch chips. The ingress FIC segments the incoming packets into fixed sized cells and adds a small header to each cell with information such as destination FIC, flow ID, and sequence number. On the egress side, the FIC uses this information to reassemble cells back into variable length packets while removing the cell headers. The switch chips can continually update the ingress FICs with their congestion levels allowing the FICs to redirect data flows around congestion hot spots. In some designs, the FIC may also uniformly distribute the ingress flows across multiple switch chips in order to minimize congestion.

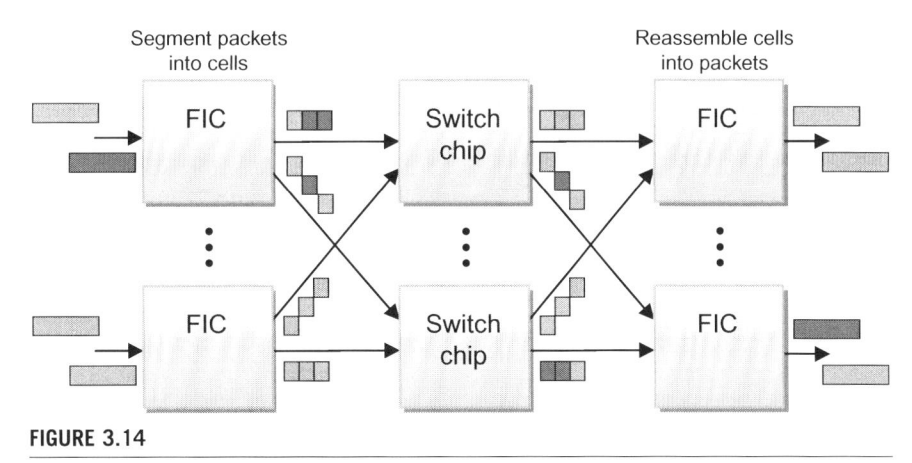

FIGURE 3.14

Cell-based switch fabric design.

There are several advantages to this design. Once in cell form, large packets can be interleaved with one another, reducing periods where a large packet monopolizes a given link which serves to reduce egress jitter. Another advantage is that it's much easier to implement mechanisms such as deficit weighted round robin and traffic shaping using fixed size cells. It is also much easier to distribute data across the switch chips in a uniform manner.

The main disadvantage of this design is complexity. At each egress port, packets must be reassembled at full bandwidth. If the flows are spread across multiple switch chips, they could arrive at the egress FIC out of order, requiring the use of sequence numbers in the cell header. If a give cell fails to arrive within a certain time limit, the associated cells must be flushed from memory and some type of dropped packet error reported. If the missing cell somehow arrives after that, it must be recognized and discarded. All of this also adds latency to the data flow, with the result that most data center switch chip designs today move data around as full packets.

Another consideration that must be taken into account for cell-based designs is the effective link bandwidth utilization. Figure 3.15 shows the effective link bandwidth utilization versus payload size.

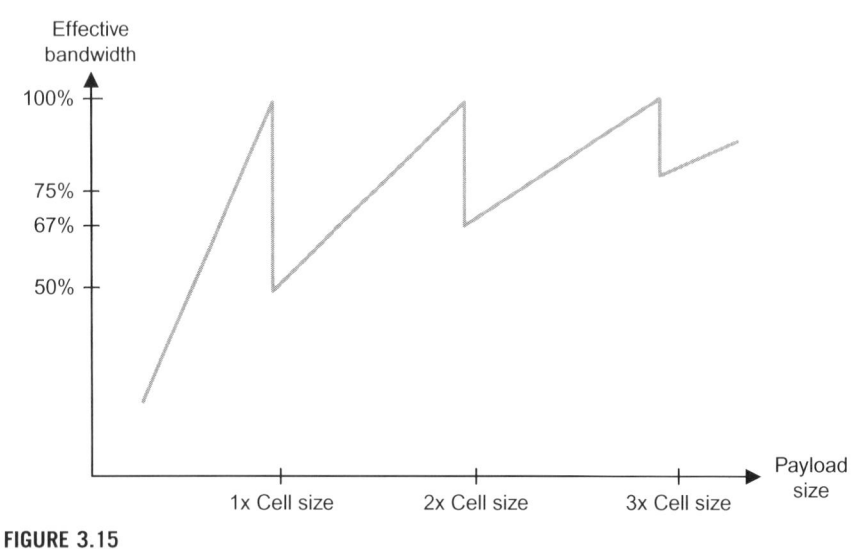

FIGURE 3.15

Effective bandwidth utilization versus payload size.

Because data is transmitted as fixed length cells, if the payload size is not an exact multiple of the cell size, some cells will be partially empty. For example, if the cell size is 64-bytes and the payload is always 64-bytes, the link will operate at 100% efficiency. But if the payload is always 65-bytes, the link efficiency will drop close to 50%. Of course payload sizes constantly vary, but this inefficiency must be taken into account when designing a switch fabric by providing over-speed on the links between chips. Figure 3.15 does not include the packet header overhead which also needs to be taken into account when calculating the over-speed required.

Input-output-queued designs

IOQ architectures were first proposed when designers realized how difficult it would be to design a single shared memory structure that could be simultaneously accessed by all the high-bandwidth ports on the switch. A conceptual view of an IOQ switch chip is shown in Figure 3.16. In order to reduce the memory performance

Switch Chip Architecture Examples

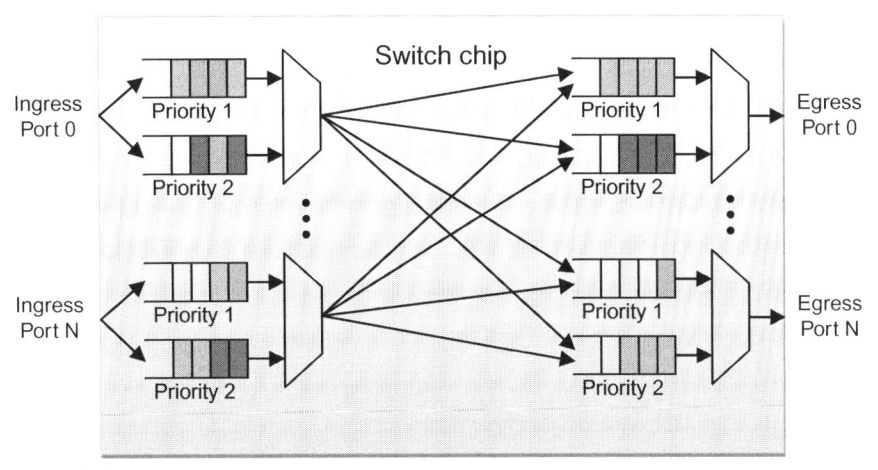

FIGURE 3.16

Input-output-queued switch fabric design.

requirements, data is queued at both the ingress and the egress of the switch chip. For example, if a given output queue is busy receiving data from a given input, another input receiving data for that same output queue can simply buffer it temporarily in the ingress queue until the output queue is available. This greatly reduces the memory performance requirements, but not without some cost.

At the switch ingress, data can be temporarily blocked from moving to the egress queues due to other inputs accessing these same queues, causing HoL blocking. Consider the ingress port 0 priority 1 queue in Figure 3.16. If port 0 egress queue is busy, the ingress queue can be blocked even if port N egress queue is available. This can reduce the overall chip performance in many cases. To avoid this situation, virtual output queues can be established at each ingress port, adding significant complexity to the design. For example, an N-port switch chip would require $N \times N$ virtual output queues on the ingress side for each priority level.

Other factors to consider are latency, multicast performance, and memory requirements. Packets are enqueued and dequeued twice as they work their way through the switch. This, plus the potential for blocking, increases the overall latency even in cut-through mode. Multicast packets must be sent from a given ingress queue to multiple egress queues. This adds to on-chip congestion because an ingress queue cannot be emptied until the frame has been sent to all the required egress queues. This also reduces multicast bandwidth and increases multicast port-to-port jitter. In addition, because multicast packets may need to be stored longer in the ingress queues, or in special multicast ingress queues, in order to minimize blocking of unicast packets, extra memory is required at the ingress. Finally, multicast frames are stored in multiple egress queues requiring additional memory there as well.

Output-queued shared memory designs

Many research papers on switch fabric architectures reference an output-queued shared memory design as the ideal architecture for high-performance switch chip implementations. This is because each output acts like a virtual FIFO in shared memory and all inputs can simultaneously write into this virtual FIFO without blockage as long as the memory is not full. But due to challenging on-chip memory performance requirements, many switch chip designers settle for the IOQ architecture as described above. One successful product line using an output-queued shared memory design is the Intel® Ethernet switch family. Figure 3.17 is a conceptual view of the shared memory architecture.

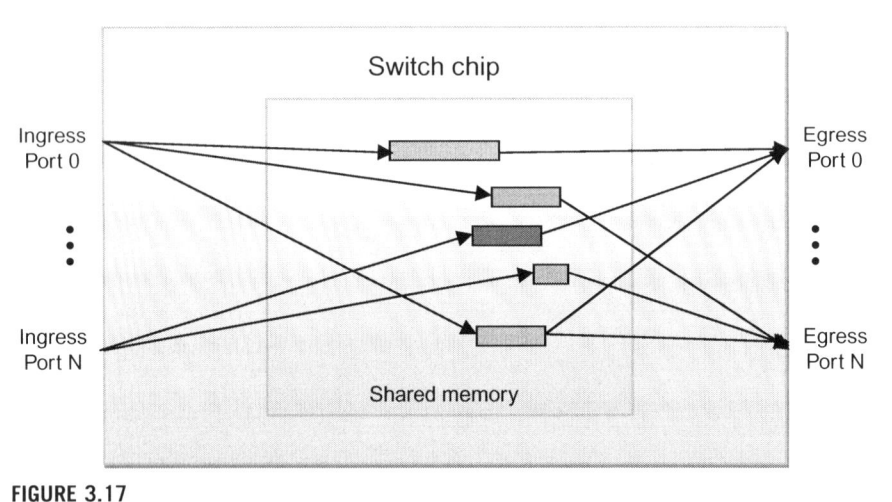

FIGURE 3.17

Output-queued shared memory switch fabric design.

As a variable sized packet arrives, it is written as a linked list into shared memory segments. After a forwarding decision is made, the selected egress port reads the packet out of shared memory and sends it on its way. If a large packet arrives, the head of the packet can start egress transmission before the tail of the packet is written into memory. This is known as cut-through operation, which provides low-latency transmission independent of packet size. As we mentioned in the last section, IOQ architectures can also operate in cut-through mode, but by storing the packet only once, the output-queued shared memory architecture has lower intrinsic latency.

The egress side of the chip provides a lot of functional flexibility when using this type of architecture. Each egress port can independently select packets from memory for transmission and can act like an egress scheduler. Packets can be divided into traffic classes and a list of packets available for transmission can be provided to each egress scheduler. The scheduler can then use mechanisms like strict priority or deficit weighted round robin to select packets for transmission. Traffic shaping can also be applied. Multicast packets can be stored once in shared memory and simply read from memory multiple times for transmission to each requested egress port allowing full bandwidth multicast. Because of this simpler design, less overall on-chip memory is required compared to the IOQ architecture.

Link-level flow control can also be easily implemented in this type of design. Figure 3.18 shows a functional view of link-level flow control in an output-queued shared memory switch.

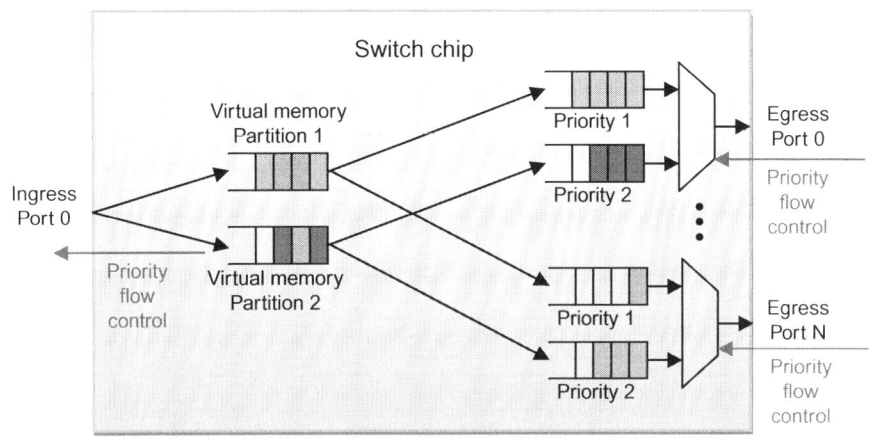

FIGURE 3.18

Output-queued qhared memory switch link-level flow control.

Even though the frames are only stored once, the ingress and egress ports each have a different perspective on how the frames are stored.

From the ingress perspective, the frames are identified as different traffic classes and then associated with virtual shared memory partitions. These partitions are not physical, but can be virtually sized based on traffic requirements. For example, priority 1 traffic can be assigned to one virtual memory partition and priority 2 traffic to another. Each virtual partition can have a separate watermark that, when exceeded, triggers a link-level priority-based flow control message to the upstream link partner. This can easily be scaled to more than two priorities, but we are limiting this example to 2 for clarity.

From the egress perspective, frames are identified as different traffic classes per egress port. As mentioned earlier, each egress port can act as a scheduler providing strict priorities, minimum bandwidth guarantees, and/or traffic shaping. This scheduler also can receive priority-based link-level flow control messages from the downstream link partner and react to them by not scheduling priorities that are currently under flow control. Mechanisms can also be developed to send this virtual egress queue fill level information upstream to the source of the traffic where virtual output queues could be implemented to minimize HoL blocking in multistage fabric designs.

CHAPTER 3 Switch Fabric Technology

REVIEW

In this chapter, we reviewed several basic switch fabric architectures including shared bus, shared memory, crossbars, and synchronous serial designs. Next, we described several multistage switch fabric topologies including ring, mesh, star, and clos/fat-tree configurations. For these topologies, sources of congestion were investigated along with several methods to deal with congestion, such as load balancing, buffering, flow control, and traffic management. Finally, we provided examples of several switch chip architectures in use today along with the advantages and disadvantages of each. The architectures described in this chapter are typically used to build networking equipment for the data center and provide a foundation of knowledge that will be useful in the next chapter, where we discuss how this networking equipment is hooked together in order to create efficient cloud data center networks.

CHAPTER 4

Cloud Data Center Networking Topologies

In the last chapter, we provided a background on the basic building blocks used to design data center networking gear. These components have physical limits that have an impact on how networking gear is designed and how data center networks are configured. In this chapter, we will describe the basic data center network building blocks and how they are connected to form cloud data center networks. We will first introduce traditional enterprise data center networks, from which data center networks evolved. We will then describe the various types of data center network switches and how they are used in the data center. Finally, we will describe how data center networks are evolving from multitiered network architectures to flat data center networks to rack scale architectures.

TRADITIONAL MULTITIERED ENTERPRISE NETWORKS

The first enterprise data center networks connected clients with servers and storage using traditional LAN technology. As corporations expanded their enterprise IT investments and moved their equipment into purpose-built data centers, higher performance networking gear such as routers were employed in order to interconnect large pools of server and storage resources. Enterprise IT managers tend to buy all of their networking gear from a single Original Equipment Manufacturer (OEM) in order to ease the management and support burden for is large set of data center network equipment. Because of this, enterprise data centers tend to have more expensive networking equipment and software from a single vendor with a feature set originally tailored for the enterprise LAN.

In this section, we will describe the cost and performance factors that are driving a change in how these data center networks are implemented and managed. In the following sections, we will describe the various data center networking components and industry trends that are being driven in part by large cloud data center network requirements.

Cost factors

When building large cloud data centers with thousands of racks of servers, cost becomes a key driver. Expenses come not only in the form of equipment acquisition costs, but also in the form of operations and maintenance. Capital expense (CapEx) comes from purchasing the data center facilities, servers, networking equipment and the software. Operating expense (OpEx) comes from items such as electricity, personnel to operate and maintain the equipment and hardware and software maintenance agreements. In this section, we will focus on the CapEx and OpEx associated with the data center networking equipment.

Figure 4.1 shows a traditional enterprise data center network. The servers within the rack are interconnected using a top of rack (ToR) switches containing a large number of 1Gb Ethernet (1GbE) ports that may have been originally designed as an Ethernet LAN workgroup switch. The ToR switches are connected to each other through an Ethernet aggregation switch, similar to a LAN aggregation switch designed to interconnect multiple LAN workgroup switches. These ToR switch uplink ports to the aggregation switches traditionally use multiple 1GbE ports in a link aggregation group or 10GbE ports. As data centers grew larger, aggregation switches ran out of ports, requiring the use of large switch/routers that are typically used to interconnect multiple LANs on large corporate campuses and are similar in some ways to large IP routers used by internet service providers.

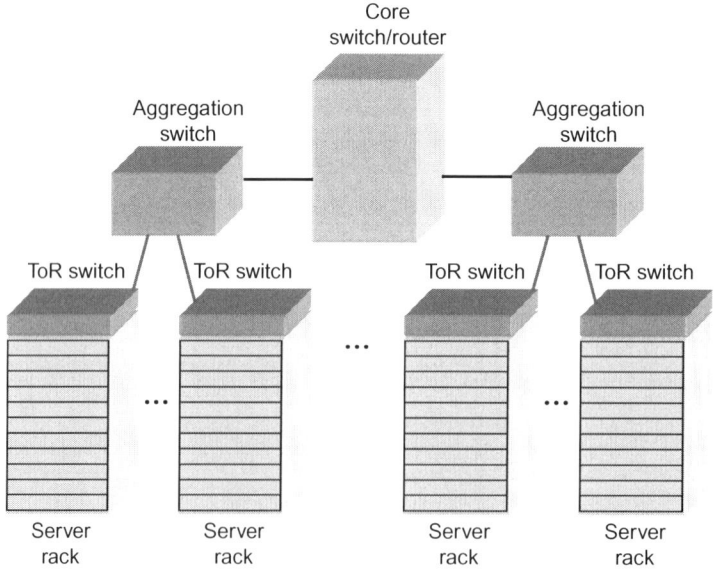

FIGURE 4.1

Traditional enterprise data center network.

One of the key issues with this LAN-based network is the high cost of the aggregation switches and core switch/routers. Although the aggregation switches come from the cost competitive LAN market, they require many high-bandwidth ports and a large number of these switches are required in the data center network. The core switch/routers are very expensive systems that have a large number of layer

3 features designed to support many of the TCP/IP standards such as OSPF, MPLS, IP-in-IP, BGP, VPWS, VPLS and various other IP tunneling protocols. Many of these features are not used in new cloud data centers, adding cost for features that are not required. This is why companies like Google decided to develop their own data center networking equipment at a much lower cost. This also spurred the development of purpose-built data center networking equipment from leading OEMs which will be discussed later in this chapter.

Software is also a key component of data center CapEx and OpEx. Traditional data centers may have separate software for configuring, virtualizing, and maintaining the servers; separate software for configuring and maintaining storage resources and associated storage networks; and separate software for configuring and maintaining the data network. In many cases, they also have separate IT administrators with specialized expertise in these different areas. For some of the same reasons that the networking equipment, such as the core switch/router hardware, is complex, the associated software used to configure and manage this networking gear is also complex, requiring specialized skill sets and a significant amount of time to make changes to the network. Because of the costs associated with staffing different skilled IT administrators to operate these separate software domains, large cloud data centers are now developing their own software or plan to adopt software defined networking which will be described in detail in Chapter 9 of this book.

Performance factors

Not only are traditional enterprise-based data center networks more costly, they have several performance limitations that must be taken into account. These limitations have helped drive new industry standards for bandwidth optimization, congestion control, and efficient data transfer which will be described in more detail in the next chapter.

Traditional Ethernet work group based ToR switches operated at 10, 100, or 1000Mbps. Even today, there are many ToR switches in cloud data centers operating with 1GbE ports connected to the servers. Although these port speeds have kept up with the server performance levels over the years, the emergence of high-performance multicore processors and the desire to transmit both storage and data traffic over the same links has driven the ToR switch server port bandwidth requirements up to 10GbE. Multicore servers that host multiple virtual machines (VMs) can easily saturate a 1GbE link, and, in some cases, operate at peak data rates of up to 10Gbps. In addition, while Ethernet links were operating at 1Gbps in the data center, storage networks using Fibre Channel were operating at 2Gbps or 4Gbps. Once Ethernet moved to the 10GbE standard, storage traffic could operate alongside data traffic using the same physical link while also maintaining these Fibre Channel bandwidth levels. Higher bandwidth also equates to lower latency through a given ingress or egress port on the switch.

Traditional LAN-based Ethernet data center network equipment has been designed without much consideration for packet latency. Core routers, for example, may contain switch chips that use external buffer memory along with store and forward mechanisms where the port-to-port latency is relatively high and the latency varies depending on packet size. In applications like email or video delivery, this latency variation doesn't have that much impact. But many emerging data center applications need low latency networks. These include financial trading, real-time data analytics, and cloud-based high-performance computing. In addition, many web service applications can spawn a large amount of east-west traffic, where the latency of these multiple transactions can build up to unacceptable levels. Consider Figure 4.1, where the packet may need to travel two hops between servers in a given rack, or up to four hops rack-to-rack. This can not only cause high overall latency, but high latency variation and changes in latency as VMs are migrated to different locations within the data center.

Core switch/routers must not only deal with a large number of high-bandwidth links, they must also perform layer 3 forwarding functions which require more extensive frame header processing at very high bandwidth. This adds more congestion to these networks. The traditional Ethernet switch chips used in systems such as workgroup switches or aggregation switches have been designed to drop traffic during periods of high congestion. This could be tolerated because higher layer protocols such as TCP/IP will retransmit lost packets, but at the price of high latency and latency variation. Certain protocols such as Fibre Channel over Ethernet used for storage traffic cannot tolerate dropped packets due to the long retransmission latencies involved. Because of this, data center networks transmitting storage traffic must provide separation of traffic classes and lossless operation for storage traffic. Legacy enterprise networking gear cannot support this, requiring new data center bridging features that will be described in the next chapter.

DATA CENTER NETWORK SWITCH TYPES

Over the years, network equipment manufacturers have settled on a few common types of data center networking gear. The form factor, port configuration, and location in the network of this gear has been driven by several factors. As we discussed in the second chapter, some of this equipment was a carry-over from the enterprise LAN networking gear such as the cloud data center ToR switches that evolved from LAN workgroup switches. As we described in the last chapter, silicon technology has a great influence on how networking gear can be designed and implemented. In addition, factors such as cable length, cable count, and cabling costs also have an influence on how cloud data center networks are architected.

When data travels from a VM within a physical server through the network to another server, or to storage, or outside the data center, it must travel through a variety of network equipment as shown in Figure 4.1. Data traveling to another VM within the same physical server can be routed using a virtual switch (vSwitch) within the server. Data traveling to another physical server within the same rack is routed through the vSwitch and the switch at the top of the rack. Data traveling between racks will be further routed through an aggregation switch or end of row (EoR) switch. If this data needs to be routed to another part of the data center or to the internet, it may also travel through a data center core switch/router. Each of these networking components requires different levels of features and performance. This section will show where these different components are located in the network, and the features and performance required for each.

Virtual switch

The concept of VMs has been around for some time and allows multiple guest operating systems to run on a single physical server. This improves data center efficiencies through higher server utilization and flexible resource allocation. But it also increases the software complexity by requiring switching capability between these VMs using a vSwitch as shown in Figure 4.2. In a virtualized server, the hypervisor is a program that configures and maintains both the VMs and the vSwitch. A network interface device is used to connect the server CPU chip set to the data center network, which is usually a connection to an Ethernet ToR switch. This device may be a network interface card (NIC) or a LAN on motherboard (LOM) device. Although the servers within an enterprise network may have two network interfaces for redundancy, the servers within a cloud data center will typically have a single high-bandwidth network connection that is shared by all of the resident VMs.

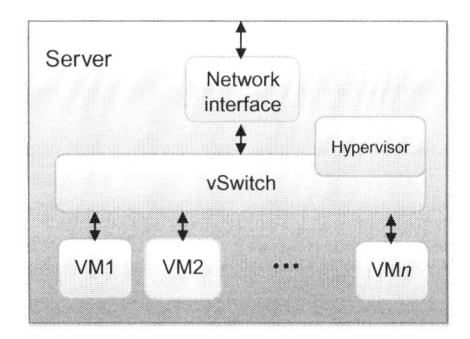

FIGURE 4.2

Logical diagram of a virtual switch within the server shelf.

When sending data between VMs, the vSwitch is effectively a shared memory switch as described in the last chapter. The difference is that the data is not physically moved into and out of shared memory by the connected devices, but instead the data stays in the server's main memory and pointers to the data are passed between VMs. This can provide very high-bandwidth virtual connections between VMs within the same server which can be important in applications such as virtualized network appliance modules where each VM is assigned to a specific packet processing task and data is pipelined from one VM to the next. But data movement in and out of the server is constrained by the network interface bandwidth. This is one reason that 10GbE is used in many of these virtualized servers. In Chapter 6 we will spend more time on the subject of server virtualization as it relates to cloud data center networking.

Another factor to consider is network management. Traditionally, data centers employ server administrators and network administrators. Ideally, the vSwitch would be a seamless part of the overall data center network. But in reality, the vSwitch is configured and managed by the server administrator. This requires tight coordination between the server administrator and network administrator which can increase configuration time as well as introduce errors. In addition, it is ideal if the vSwitch uses the same forwarding rules and capabilities that is used by all of the other equipment in the network in order to provide unified services. This is not always the case, requiring additional coordination with the physical switches. In Chapter 9 we will discuss software defined networking, which can become an important tool in network configuration and orchestration including control of the vSwitch.

ToR switch

The servers within the rack connect to a ToR switch using a star topology as shown in Figure 4.3. Here, every server has a dedicated link to the ToR switch and the ToR switch may forward data to other servers in the rack, or out of the rack through high-bandwidth uplink ports. Due to factors such as multiple VMs sharing the same network connection, 10Gb Ethernet is widely used as the link between the server shelf and the ToR switch in cloud data center networks. A typical rack may contain on the order of 40 or more servers, so many ToR switches contain up to 48 10GbE ports and four 40GbE uplink ports which are connected to aggregation switches. Although this

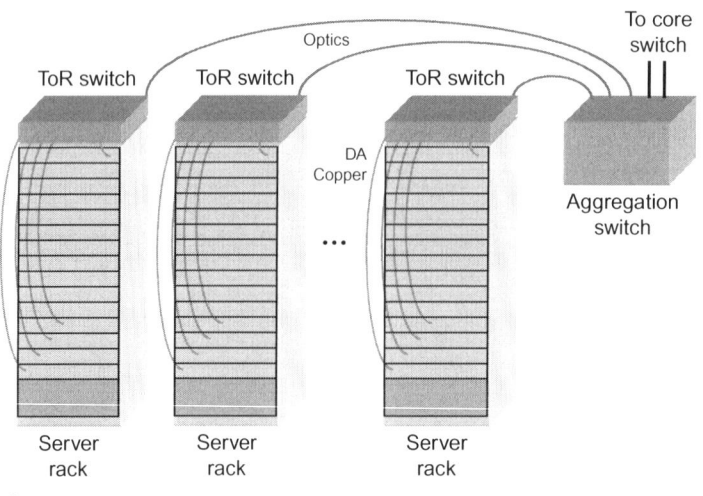

FIGURE 4.3

Top of rack switch feeding an aggregation switch.

is a 3:1 mismatch in server bandwidth (480Gbps) versus uplink bandwidth (160Gbps), data center traffic is very bursty in nature and it is rare for all the servers to be using their full allocation of 10Gbps bandwidth simultaneously.

As we discussed in the previous chapter, switch silicon technology can place limitations on the maximum number of ports per switch chip. In the case of a ToR switch, a single switch chip can support all of the ports described above (48 10GbE plus four 40GbE) using today's technology. In the case of the 10GbE ports, lower cost, direct attach copper cabling can be used for the short distance between the servers and the ToR switches, which is less than a few meters. Optic modules are used for the ToR switch uplink ports as they need to drive longer distances and higher bandwidth to other switches that interconnect multiple server racks. The uplinks may be connected to aggregation switches which aggregate the traffic from multiple ToR switches into a core switch.

Each ToR switch contains a control plane processor that, among other things, configures the switch forwarding tables and monitors the health of the switch. This processor may run layer 2 or layer 3 forwarding protocols or simply process table update commands from an external centralized software defined networking (SDN) controller. Using traditional layer 2 or 3 networking protocols, each switch learns about its environment through exchange of information with other switches and servers in the network. Today, more direct approaches may be used where the network administrator configures and monitors all of the ToR switches in the network. In the near future, this network orchestration work will be performed in a more automatic manner using software defined networking.

The ToR may also act as a gateway between the servers and the rest of the network by providing functions such as tunneling, filtering, monitoring, and load balancing. To enable these features, the ToR needs to inspect packet headers and match various header fields using what are called Access Control List (ACL) rules. The result of a match can produce several actions such as route the packet, tunnel the packet, assign the packet to a load balancing group, count the packet, police the packet, drop the packet, or assign a traffic class to the packet for egress scheduling. By adding this capability to the ToR switch, the functions of the other network components can be simplified, reducing overall network costs.

EoR switch

EoR switches were developed in an attempt to reduce cost by sharing power, cooling, and management infrastructure across a large number of switch components. You can think of these as multiple ToR switches designed as switch cards plugged into a single modular chassis, much like the leaf switches in a two stage fat-tree we described in the last chapter. Other blades in the chassis provide the functionality of an aggregation or spine switch with high-bandwidth uplinks to the core switch/router as shown in Figure 4.4.

FIGURE 4.4

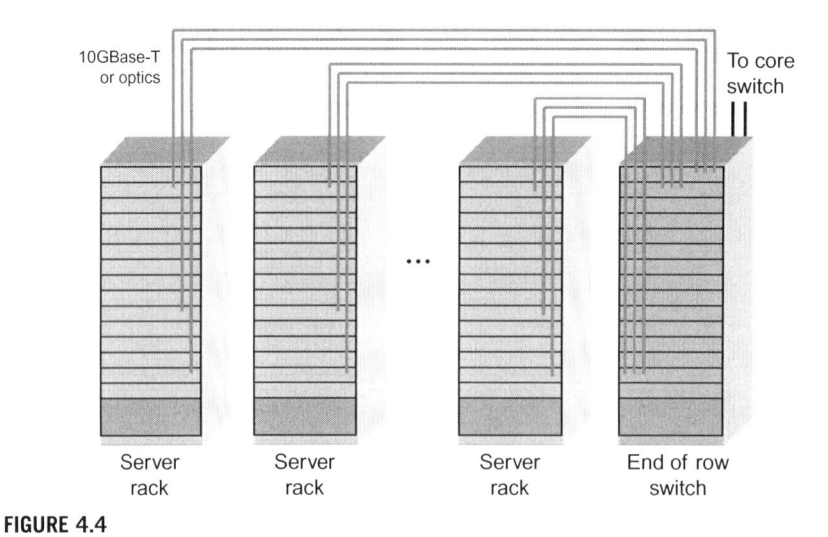

Configuration of an end of row switch.

Cost can be reduced by eliminating separate power supplies, cooling fans, and CPU subsystems that exist in every ToR switch and aggregation switch. Central management processors not only reduce costs, but also provide a single point of management without the need to separately manage multiple ToR switches. In addition, cabling costs can be reduced by interconnecting the switch cards and aggregation cards together through a chassis backplane. But this comes at the cost of additional cable distance between the servers and EoR switches.

In this configuration, each server must be connected to an EoR switch through long cable runs that are typically less than 100 meters. One disadvantage of this approach is that the additional cable length and cable drivers can be more expensive than the cost savings provided by the EoR switch. With legacy 1GbE server connections, this was less of an issue due to the low cost cat5 cabling available. Now that server network connections are moving to 10GbE, 10GBase-T cabling is emerging as a low cost alternative to optical cables when running <100 m. But 10GBase-T switches have higher latency which can impact data center performance.

Fabric extenders

In order to eliminate the need for optical cables or 10GBase-T cables while still providing some of the cost benefits that are available with EoR switches, fabric extenders, as shown in Figure 4.5, were developed. These are sometimes referred to as spine switches and are similar to ToR switches with the exception that they are controlled and monitored through a central controlling bridge. In some ways, they are like a distributed EoR switch.

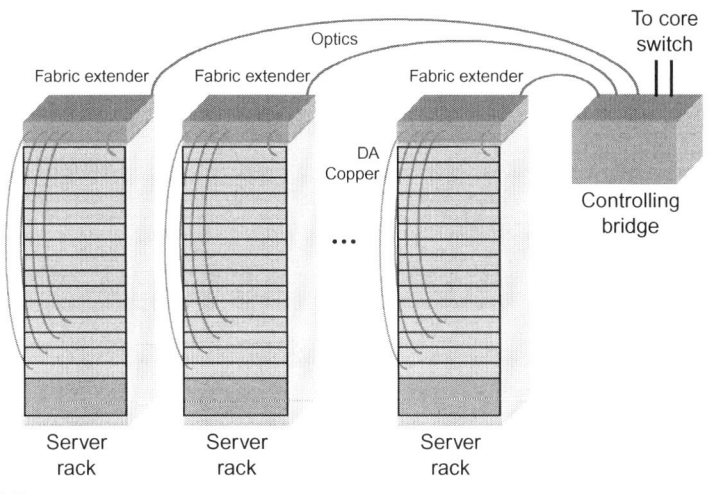

FIGURE 4.5

Fabric extenders acting as a disaggregated end of row switch.

Fabric extenders provide a unified management model while allowing the same cabling topologies used with ToR and aggregation switches. Standard low cost, low latency, direct attach copper cables can be used between the fabric extender and the servers. High-bandwidth optical cables can be used with a much lower cable count between the server racks and the end of row aggregation module which is called a controlling bridge. The controlling bridge also has switch functionality which is much like the second stage spine switches in a fat-tree. Because of this, the controlling bridge is sometime referred to as a spine switch. The entire configuration can be managed through a shared CPU control plane card in the controlling bridge, acting like a single logical EoR switch, easing configuration time and overhead.

Aggregation and core switches

Aggregation switches are typically used to connect a number of ToR switches to a core switch/router. The core switch is at the top of the cloud data center network pyramid and may include a wide area network (WAN) connection to the outside carrier network. Because of the high-bandwidth links and high port counts of these switches, modular designs are employed with two stage fabrics either in a star or fat-tree topology. High-bandwidth aggregation ports are switched or routed to even higher bandwidth uplink ports. In the case of core switches, the uplink interface cards may be designed to interface directly with the carrier network and may include features such as network security and monitoring. These are expensive systems that must meet high reliability requirements. The next section will describe these core switches in more detail.

FLAT DATA CENTER NETWORKS

In the last section we described traditional data center networks using a hierarchy containing ToR switches, aggregation or EoR switches, and core switches. This three tiered approach adds cost, complexity, and latency in large cloud data center networks. In addition, with the large increase we have seen in east-west data center traffic, this approach leads to high-latency variation between servers making data center performance unpredictable. In this section, we will touch on some aspects of data center traffic patterns that influence flat data center network designs. We will then describe the key components in a flat data center network along with the features and performance they provide.

Data center traffic patterns

When you think of servers in the traditional sense, you think of a client making a request to a single server and then getting a response from that server. For example, a user on a home computer could make a request to download a pdf file from a given server. But this has changed dramatically over the last several years as data centers are not only serving data, but also pulling information from a variety of servers and running specialized programs based on user input. For example, a Google map request could spawn some of the following transactions:

- Determine the device type the client is using (laptop, handheld, etc.).
- Send information to a local search engine to match the map address.
- Based on the match, pull up the appropriate map data and send it to the client based on device type.
- Based on the match and the user settings, pull up relative nearby attractions to display on the map and send it to the client.
- Retrieve relative information about the client based on recent web transaction.
- Use this information to identify shopping history and send targeted advertising to be displayed on the client's web page.

As you can see, a single web click can spawn multiple or sometimes even hundreds of server-to-server transactions within the data center. As shown in Figure 4.6, north-south traffic is generally between server and client, while east-west traffic is generated between servers and/or VMs. East-west traffic is also increasing due to improvements in business agility and continuity. Examples include VM migration and storage replication.

FIGURE 4.6

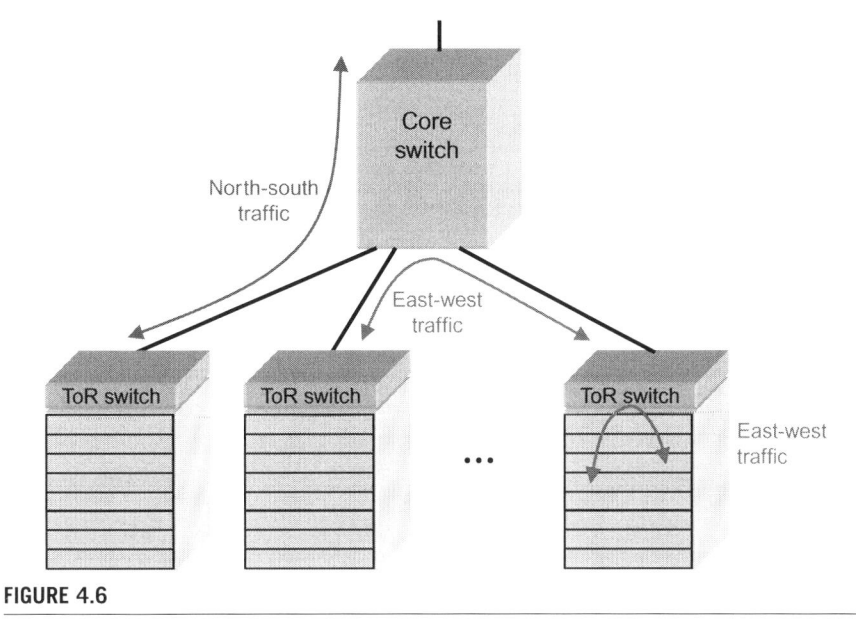

Traffic flow in a flat data center network.

Traditional 3-teir data center networks do not do a good job supporting east-west traffic due to factors such as poor bandwidth distribution, high latency, and high-latency variation. At each tier in the network, the uplink bandwidth should be uniformly distributed across the next higher tier. With a 2-teir network, this is fairly straightforward using traditional hash-based load distribution mechanisms. Although not perfectly balanced in all cases, bandwidth over-provisioning can be used to reduce the probability of congestion hot spots. But when a third tier is added, the imbalance becomes even larger, requiring further over-provisioning of more costly bandwidth and a higher probability of congestion hot spots.

East-west traffic latency can impact data center performance. Although it may take hundreds of milliseconds for data to reach a remote client from a data center through the carrier network, a lot of the response time can be taken up preparing the data during server-to-server transactions, which can negatively impact the user experience. In addition, certain data center workloads lend themselves to server clustering configurations in which the network latency can have a direct impact on system performance. Three tier networks not only have higher latency, but also higher latency variation, leading to both lower performance and unpredictable performance, depending on the network path between the servers. For example, if the servers are all in the same rack, the application performance will be much higher than if the servers must communicate to each other through a ToR, aggregation, and core switch.

Many cloud data centers are moving to a flat data center network for these reasons. Figure 4.6 shows an example 2-tiered flat data center network containing ToR and core switches. We will next describe these two network components in more detail and provide additional information on how they can be tailored for flat data center networking.

ToR switch features

ToR switches are used within each server rack in large cloud data centers. They have links to each server in the rack using a star fabric architecture and high-bandwidth uplinks out of the rack. A typical rack can hold over 40 servers, which are connected to the ToR switch using either 1Gb or 10Gb Ethernet links. Today, most cloud data centers are moving to 10GbE in order to support multisocket, multicore server trays that can host a large number of VMs. Typical cloud data center ToR port configurations are 48 10GbE ports using SFP+, plus four 40GbE QSFP+ ports for uplink connectivity. A simplified top view of a 1U ToR switch is shown in Figure 4.7.

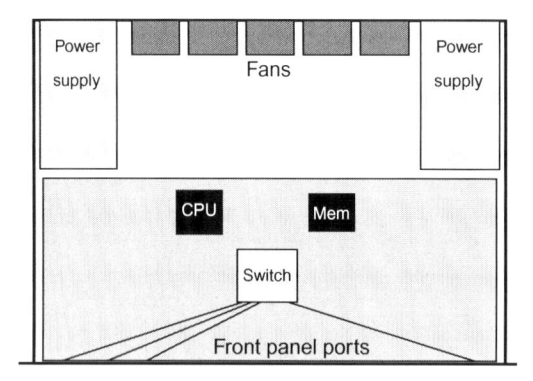

FIGURE 4.7

Major ToR switch components.

This is a single board design with a high port count Ethernet switch chip at the center. A control plane CPU subsystem is also used on the board to run a network operating system and/or monitor and configure the switch along with updating the switches frame forwarding tables. Fans and redundant power supplies round out the major ToR switch components. Most large data centers do not use redundant ToR switches and, in most cases, provide redundancy at the rack level. This reduces the ToR switch cost by eliminating one of the redundant power supplies. In other words, if a single ToR switch power supply fails, the entire rack will be swapped out with a redundant rack. In some cases DC power is supplied throughout the rack, eliminating the need for these types of power supplies entirely.

The ToR switch is a common design in the industry, so network equipment suppliers differentiate themselves by choosing more feature rich switch silicon and/or providing more advanced software running in the CPU control plane. Below is a list of ToR switch features that are critical for today's flat networks used in cloud data centers.

- *Low latency:* One of the key aspects of flat data center networks is low and predictable latency. Because most of the data center east-west traffic must go through two ToR switches, they must have very low cut-through latency.
- *High bandwidth:* When moving from a traditional 3-teir to a flat data center network, high bandwidth is critical, especially in the links between the ToR and core switches. High bandwidth also means lower latency as data moves in and out of the switch.
- *Tunneling features:* In flat data center networks, it is ideal to simplify the frame processing requirements of the large high-bandwidth core switches by moving the tunneling functions to the edge of the network. Some of these functions, such as adding and removing tunneling tags, can be supported by the vSwitch within the server, but, in some cases, these features must also be supported by the ToR switch. We will discuss this topic further in Chapter 7 on network virtualization.
- *Large table sizes:* Data center core switches can simply use tables containing the addresses of ToR switches in the network based on some sort of tunneling label. But the ToR switch itself must deal with addressing at the server or even VM level. This requires the ToR switch to support large address table sizes.
- *Server virtualization support:* In data center networks, there is a blurry line between the features that the vSwitch within the server supports and the features that the ToR switches supports. But together, they must support server virtualization. This will be discussed further in Chapter 6 on server virtualization.
- *Network convergence:* Another common attribute of large flat data center networks is the desire to reduce cost by transporting both server traffic and storage traffic over the same network. This requires low latency, lossless operation which will be discussed further in Chapters 5 and 8.
- *Open software:* The traditional 3-teir data center networks are managed using large software stacks that are over-kill for most cloud data center requirements. That's why we see many of the large cloud service providers developing their own software. This is now changing with the advent of SDN, which is an ideal way to manage and monitor these new flat data center networks. For the ToR switch, this means providing support for management of the forwarding tables and QoS parameters by an outside controller. SDN will be discussed further in Chapter 9.

Core switch features

Data center core switches must be able to forward a large number of high-bandwidth flows in an efficient manner. In a traditional 3-teir data center network, large IP routers are employed but are very costly and have complex features and software that are designed for applications both inside and outside the data center. In order to forward these flows, routers perform deep header inspection at rates up to 40G or 100G requiring expensive network processing units (NPUs), traffic managers, or ASICs. Special software must be created for these devices, increasing the complexity and reducing the ability to upgrade these systems as new data center networking requirements emerge.

To reduce cost and complexity, new data center core switches have emerged with features that target data center applications as shown in Figure 4.8. These are modular chassis with the various cards shown in the figure inserted into the front of the rack, much like an industry standard ATCA chassis and these cards are interconnected through a passive backplane.

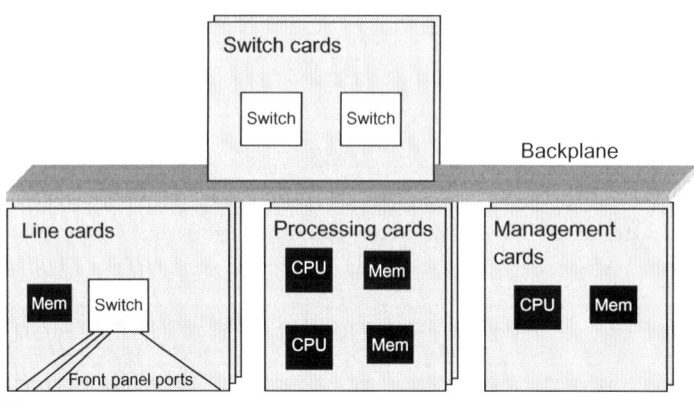

FIGURE 4.8

Modular core switch cards.

This modular chassis example contains a two stage switch architecture that can use a star, dual star, or fat-tree fabric architecture. The line cards contain the first switch stage with multiple high-bandwidth front facing ports. In some cases, packet buffering is used for temporary packet storage during periods of high congestion, or to support traffic management features. The second stage of fabric devices are implemented on switch cards which are connected to the line cards through the backplane. In some systems, specialized line cards are used to connect to the external WAN. In addition, systems may employ specialized processing cards to provide services such as a firewall, load balancing, and WAN optimization. The system may also include redundant system management cards.

In a flat data center network, cost and management complexity can be reduced by implementing simple forwarding rules using various types of forwarding tags. In the second chapter, we described how MPLS labels can simplify the forwarding of traffic in the core of the internet. The same technique can be used in the cloud data center by taking advantage of special header tags available with standard protocols such as MPLS, VXLAN, or NVGRE (which will be described in Chapter 7). By using label switching techniques, forwarding can be done within the core switch by simply inspecting the forwarding tag, much like the post office forwarding letters by looking at only the zip code. In many cases, this can be done within the switch silicon and eliminates the need for costly devices such as NPUs or ASICs.

This also reduces line card complexity and reduces power dissipation, allowing increased port density in these modular platforms.

Given that a single data center core switch supports many server racks, resiliency is much more important than in the case of a single ToR switch. A ToR switch with four 40GbE uplinks many be connected to four separate core switches both to distribute the traffic load and to provide alternate paths in the case of a core switch failure. Within the core switch, data plane redundancy can be supported by using multiple switch cards. Two or more switch cards can be used to provide alternate paths in case of switch card failure. Active-passive redundancy keeps a switch card in backup mode and brings it to life to replace a failed switch card. In most cases, the health of the backup card is periodically monitored to make sure it is available as a replacement when needed. When using active-active redundancy, traffic is sent across multiple switch cards and redirected to the remaining switch card(s) when one switch card fails.

With active-passive redundancy, full system bandwidth must be supported across the active switch cards because the backup switch card is always inactive. With active-active redundancy, either the system must operate with reduced bandwidth during switch card failure, or the bandwidth can be over provisioned during normal operation. For example, if four switch cards are used, either the system must operate with 0.75x backplane bandwidth during a single switch card failure, or the system could be designed with 1.33x oversubscription so that the system operates with 1x backplane bandwidth during a single switch card failure.

It is very difficult to provide lossless operation during a switch card failure without adding latency and expense to the system. For example, packets would need to be stored and acknowledged before removing from memory. Instead, most systems tolerate a small amount of packet loss during failover. For example, higher layer protocols like TCP will retransmit packets if acknowledgments are not received within a given time window. Software failover means that the control plane software monitors the health of the system and reconfigures it during failover. Hardware failover means that there are mechanisms built into the switch silicon to detect errors and update forwarding tables automatically during a failure. Due to longer reaction times, software failover will cause more packet loss than hardware failover.

RACK SCALE ARCHITECTURES

As we have been discussing throughout the previous sections, traditional data center racks contain over 40 server shelves with network connections from each server to the ToR switch. In some cases, redundant connections may be used. The basic server shelf components are shown in Figure 4.9.

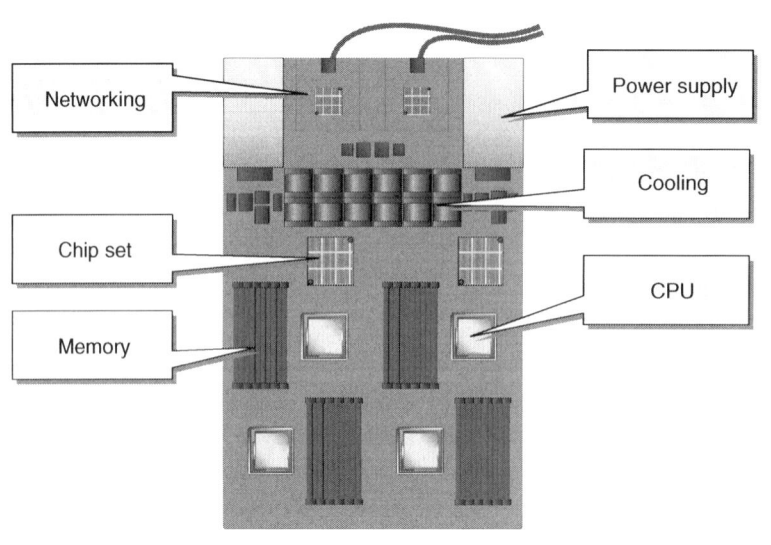

80   CHAPTER 4 Cloud Data Center Networking Topologies

FIGURE 4.9

Traditional server shelf components.

Each server shelf is self-contained with CPUs, chip sets, memory slots, power supplies, cooling, and networking. In some cases, storage modules may also be included. There are several challenges with this type of rack level design.

- *Inefficient power delivery and thermal management:* Assuming a fully populated rack, providing power and cooling on each server shelf is less efficient than sharing power and cooling across the rack. For example, power and cooling designed for peak workloads on a given shelf can be scaled back to support average peak workloads across all shelves.
- *Limited density:* Because each shelf contains power, cooling, memory, and storage, overall CPU density across the rack is limited by these distributed components.
- *Costly upgrades:* Power supplies and fans may last the lifetime of the rack. Networking technology may need to be ungraded every 5 years or so. Memory and storage may be on a 2-year life cycle. But if a data center manager wants to upgrade to the latest CPU technology, which may be on a 1-year life cycle, the entire server shelf must be replaced, making these upgrades very costly.
- *Limited flexibility:* Typically the components and resources on a given server shelf are self-contained and not shared among the shelves. This can limit flexibility. For example, if a given server could use more memory, and the neighboring server is underutilizing its memory, nothing can be done to share this resource between shelves.

Disaggregation of resources

To solve the challenges listed above, data center equipment designers are starting to look at rack scale solutions such as the Open Compute Project (OCP) spearheaded by Facebook. This is sometimes also referred to as Rack Scale Architecture (RSA). The idea is to provide complete rack scale solutions for large cloud data centers. In this model, the OEMs, ODMs, or system integrators would sell complete racks that are preconfigured and tested. The cloud data center administrators would no longer need to buy separate racks, server shelves, and ToR switches and then configure and test themselves. Instead, they simply buy a complete rack. If a rack fails, the entire rack can be replaced.

One of the goals of rack scale architecture initiatives such as OCP is to disaggregate components from the traditional server shelf into pools of resources that can be shared across the rack as shown in Figure 4.10. Here, shared power and cooling are used in order to improve efficiencies and reduce cost. Pooled storage and pooled memory can be used and flexibly allocated among the server shelves as workloads dictate. By not burdening each server shelf with the maximum amount of memory and storage that may be needed and instead providing flexible allocation, the overall memory and storage requirements across the rack can be reduced, saving cost.

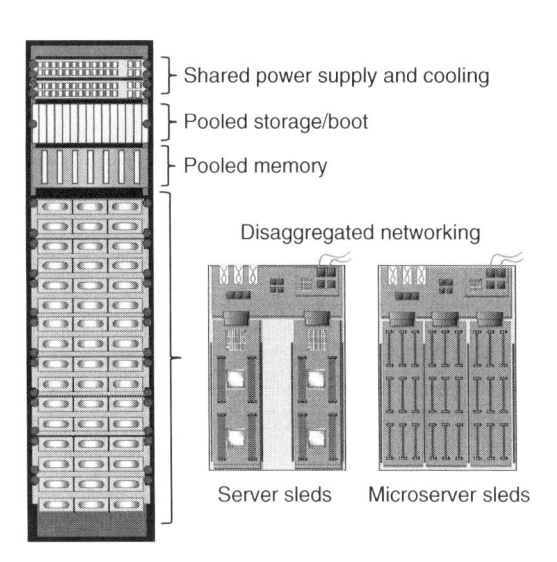

FIGURE 4.10

Rack scale architecture components.

The rest of the rack contains server sleds which plug into a networking board in the back of the shelf. By using sleds, CPUs can be upgraded independently of other components in the rack such as networking devices, providing more timely performance upgrades while reducing cost. In addition, various server types including high-end servers, mid-range servers, and microservers can be easily mixed and matched based on overall workload requirements.

So what does this all mean for cloud networking? Well for one thing, it allows multiple server sleds to share high-bandwidth connections out of the shelf. This reduces cable count and eliminates a large number of NICs in the rack. It is expected that by the time rack scale architectures are prevalent in cloud data centers, 100GbE optical links will be used to interconnect these server shelves and also be used as uplinks out of the rack. This provides a large amount of bandwidth per server and allows the shelves to be interconnected in a variety of ways using rings, meshes, or star architectures depending on the workload requirements within the rack. Figure 4.10 does not show a ToR switch, but for star architectures, a 100GbE ToR switch could be used. In addition, to provide flexible interconnect topologies, an optical cross connect could be used without the need for a ToR switch.

Microservers

Microservers are implemented as small server modules which typically contain a low power CPU and memory. They provide a performance per watt and a performance per dollar savings for certain data center workloads such as first tier web hosting, memcache operations, and cold storage applications. To minimize area, cost, and power, the CPUs are developed using a system on a chip architecture which integrates many of the components seen on a server platform such as IO bridge chips, memory controllers, and network controllers. Figure 4.10 shows example microserver sleds where nine connectors on the sled can host small pluggable microserver modules that look similar to large memory DIMMs. Because of the low power and small area for each module, a large number of these modules can exist on a given server shelf, providing high-density compute resources. But since there are too many microservers per rack to each have a separate connection to a ToR switch, a second tier of switching is incorporated on each microserver shelf.

To connect these microserver modules together and connect them to the ToR switch, the CPUs contain integrated Ethernet controllers with multiple Ethernet ports. Figure 4.11 shows two methods to interconnect these microserver modules within a shelf. The left side of Figure 4.11 shows a three-dimensional ring architecture (third dimension connectivity not shown), which requires six Ethernet ports integrated into each CPU in addition to some extra uplink ports (not shown). Although this topology does not require a separate switch chip, for ring architectures bandwidth must be shared on the ring and multiple hops may be required between CPUs. The configuration on the right uses a star architecture where every CPU is connected to a central switch chip through integrated Ethernet ports. Although this requires a separate switch chip, no bandwidth is shared between CPUs and every CPU is one switch hop away from every other CPU.

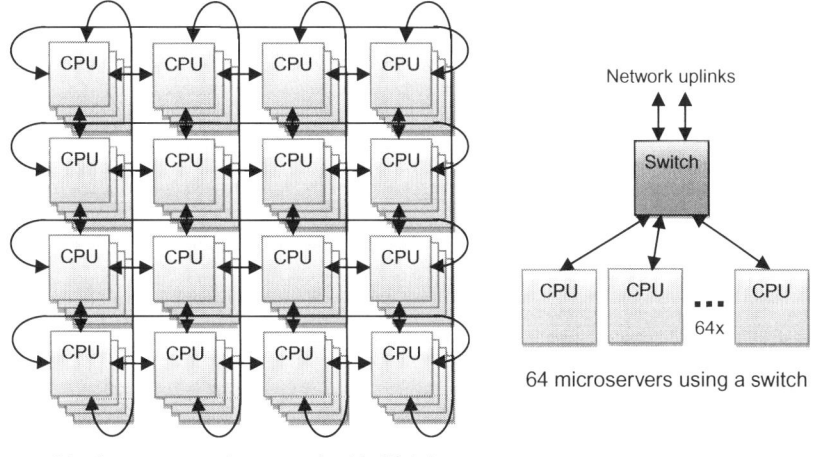

FIGURE 4.11

Microserver fabric architecture comparison.

To connect to the larger data center network, the embedded fabric architecture delegates this function to some of the CPUs which contain additional higher bandwidth CPU uplink ports. The funneling of all of this network traffic through a few CPUs can cause a bottleneck within the embedded fabric. Because the switch uplink port bandwidth in the star architecture can be configured independently of the CPU port bandwidth, it can provide many more high-bandwidth uplinks without burdening each CPU with these types of ports. This means that the star fabric can operate with less congestion than the embedded fabric. In addition, the switch can add features such as load balancing across the microservers from a central point and offer tunneling services without burdening the CPUs with these requirements.

NETWORK FUNCTION VIRTUALIZATION

Network appliance is a generic term for a system that provides various networking services that require deep packet inspection and packet processing. Services may include firewall, intrusion detection, load balancing, network monitoring, VPN services, and WAN optimization. These are typically used in carrier networks or at the edge of data center networks and are built using either modular chassis or other rack-mounted form factors. Some of these services are moving into cloud data center networks and new ways of deploying these services are being developed.

Figure 4.12 shows a traditional modular network appliance with specialized processing blades containing expensive devices such as network processors and/or high-end FPGAs or ASICs.

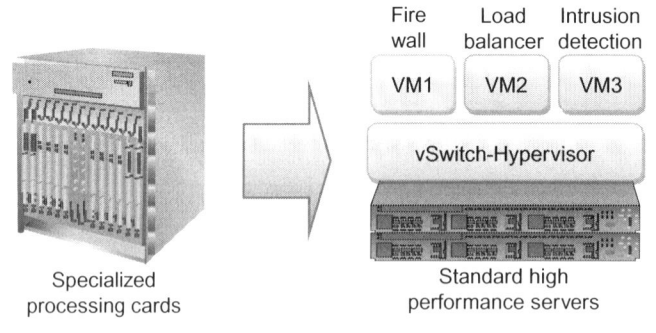

FIGURE 4.12

Moving network functions to standard server platforms.

As data comes into this system, it is distributed across these blades where deep packet inspection is used for applications such as firewalls, load balancing, and intrusion detection. Many of these systems are implemented in an ATCA platform which is an industry standard form factor for carrier networks. A handful of vendors supply specialized processing cards and switch modules that can be mixed and matched within the ATCA chassis. Specialized software must also be developed by these vendors for the unique CPUs, NPUs, or ASICs on these cards.

Data centers also utilize some of these applications for security and efficiency reasons. Firewalls and intrusion detection applications can be distributed throughout the data center to filter incoming data. Load balancing applications can be run within each rack to more efficiently utilize the server resources within the rack. Network monitoring applications can be used to test the health of the network and optimize traffic distribution. WAN optimization applications can be used at the edge of the network to efficiently transfer information between data centers.

A few industry trends are changing the way these applications are being implemented within the data center as data center administrators are attempting to homogenize their compute resources. Not only does this reduce acquisition costs by allowing the purchase of fewer products and higher volumes per product, it reduces maintenance costs and allows more efficient equipment utilization as data center needs change. Another trend is the use of server CPU resources for deep packet inspection applications that previously needed specialized devices such as NPUs due to high-bandwidth processing requirements. Today, multicore server class CPUs can also process these high-bandwidth flows.

Because of these trends, data center administrators are starting to implement these special network applications on standard virtualized servers within the data center as shown in Figure 4.12. This is known as network function virtualization (NFV). In this implementation, a vSwitch is used to move data between VMs within a server. A flow can come into the server, run through a firewall application running on one VM, an intrusion detection application running on another VM, and then be load balanced across other servers within the rack using a third VM, all within the same NFV server. A ToR switch can distribute the load across multiple NFV servers running in parallel in order to maximize bandwidth performance.

The use of standard servers for these applications provides a lot of flexibility for the data center administrator. For public cloud or IaaS services, various network functions can be offered to end customers on demand with little or no infrastructure change. As traffic loads within the data center change, NFV can be moved or expanded at different points within the data center, optimizing data center resource utilization. When combined with software defined networking, this provides a dynamic and agile way to deploy on-demand resources within cloud data center networks. We will provide further details on software defined networking in Chapter 9.

REVIEW

In this chapter, we described various types of networking equipment and how it is interconnected to form cloud data center networks. We also described the recent trend toward flat data center networks and what that requires from networking equipment. We then gave some insights into new data center trends such as rack scale architectures, microservers, and network functional virtualization. In the next chapter, we will dive into some of the new industry standards in data center networking and how they affect the way network equipment and switch silicon is defined.

CHAPTER 5

Data Center Networking Standards

Cloud data center network administrators do not want to be locked into a single network equipment vendor. A robust competitive environment allows them to pick the best vendor for their cost and performance goals, or, in many cases, equipment from multiple vendors may be desired. This requires networking equipment from a given vendor that can efficiently interoperate with equipment from other vendors, not only at the physical interconnect level but at the functional level. This is why industry standard specifications for networking equipment are established.

There are two main organizational bodies that provide industry standard specifications for networking equipment. The Internet Engineering Task Force (IETF) evolved out of a US government–backed organization that started in the mid 1980s. In the early 1990s, it transformed into an international body that develops and promotes internet standards such as MPLS, multipath routing, and TRansparent Interconnect of Lots of Links (TRILL). The Institute for Electrical and Electronics Engineers (IEEE) was founded in 1963 and is one of the leading standards-making bodies in the world today. Relative to this chapter, IEEE work groups have developed a wide range of Ethernet standards along with data center bridging (DCB), the spanning tree protocol (STP), and shortest path bridging (SPB).

In this chapter, we first discuss several physical layer Ethernet standards that are used extensively within large cloud data center networks. The next section will cover the virtual local area network (VLAN) specification that is widely used in Ethernet networks today. We will then discuss DCB, which encompasses a key set of standards for converging storage and data traffic in the same network. Next, various standards for optimizing data center network bandwidth will be discussed, followed by a section on standards for efficiently moving data throughout the data center. Other standards for server virtualization, network virtualization, storage networking, and software-defined networking will be covered in later chapters of this book.

ETHERNET DATA RATE STANDARDS

Ethernet has become the most widely used data transport protocol for cloud data center networks. The main reason is that Ethernet provides a very cost effective high bandwidth link between servers and switches. As was described in Chapter 2, Ethernet beat out several competing network protocols to become the dominant networking technology in local area networks (LANs) and data centers around the world. One could ask, is Ethernet so dominant due to its low cost, or is Ethernet low cost because it's so dominant and produced by multiple competitors in high volumes? The truth probably lies in both statements.

In the 1990s and early 2000s, Ethernet was behind in the bandwidth race. During that time Synchronous Optical Network/Synchronous Digital Hierarchy (SONET/SDH) carrier networks were running at 2.5Gbps and 10Gbps, while storage network protocols such as Fibre Channel were moving from 1Gbps to 2Gbps and 4Gbps. At the same time, 1GbE was just coming into its own. It wasn't until 2003 that companies like Intel started to develop 10GbE network controllers and 10GbE switches didn't start appearing until around 2006. In 2012, 10GbE shipments started ramping into high volumes, including Ethernet controllers used to connect servers to the network and top of rack switches. Because Ethernet now provides both low cost and high bandwidth solutions, it has become the standard transport protocol in data center networks and carrier networks, and is making strong inroads into storage networks with protocols such as Fibre Channel over Ethernet (FCoE) which will be covered in Chapter 8.

10GbE

The IEEE started working a new 10GbE specification in 2002 which has resulted in a series of new IEEE 802.3 standards. As we mentioned above, 10GbE has been around for a while, but has finally started shipping in high volume, and it is having a large impact in cloud data center networks. Before server virtualization became commonplace, individual servers were transitioning from fast Ethernet (100Mbps) to 1GbE speeds as processor performance increased. But with the advent of high-performance multicore processors in the data center, each hosting multiple virtual machines, the processor to network connection bandwidth requirements increased dramatically. In addition, in order to reduce networking costs, data centers started transmitting storage and data traffic over the Ethernet network using protocols such as iSCSI and FCoE. With traffic from multiple virtual machines along with storage traffic, data center administrators started to use multiple 1GbE ports within each server. But today, the price of a single 10GbE interface plus cable is less than the price of multiple 1GbE interfaces and multiple cables, further driving the demand for 10GbE.

40GbE and 100GbE

Up until the 10GbE standard, Ethernet 802.3 standards were increasing by $10\times$ in performance with each new generation. Ethernet specifications moved from 100Mbps to 1Gbps in about 4 years and then to 10GbE in about another 4 years.

It has taken about 10 more years to come up with a 100GbE specification that is useful for data center applications. The reason for this increase in time has a lot to do with semiconductor technology. When the 1GbE specification came out, it leveraged existing 1Gbps serializer/deserializer (SerDes) technology developed for 1G Fibre Channel which was already entering the market. Around the same time, SONET/SDH chips were being developed which incorporated 2.5G and 10G SerDes technology. So, by the time the 10GbE spec was written in 2003, there were already 10G SerDes IP blocks available in various semiconductor technologies.

But this is where things became more difficult. For 100GbE, the choices became running 10 lanes of 10G SerDes, or developing 25G SerDes that could be run across four lanes. Data center top of rack (ToR) switches with multiple 10GbE connections to the servers required high bandwidth uplinks. Using 10 lanes to create 100GbE uplinks did not make sense from a cost point of view, so the IEEE developed an interim 40GbE spec that required only four lanes of 10G. This filled the gap until 25G SerDes could be produced in volume using standard semiconductor manufacturing technology. For cost effective 25G SerDes with good performance characteristics, this required waiting until the 28 nm process nodes were available for high volume production. The IEEE 802.3bj task force is working to produce a $4 \times 25G$ specification that is useful in data center applications (100GBASE-KR4, 100GBASE-KP4, and 100GBASE-CR4). Products incorporating 25G SerDes will start appearing in the market in 2014. As mentioned earlier, 10GbE started ramping into volume production in 2012 including 40GbE uplinks from the ToR switches. It is expected that 40GbE links to the server shelves along with 100GbE uplinks will not start ramping until after 2015. Some are currently proposing an interim step by using single lane 25GbE links from the servers to the ToR switch.

VIRTUAL LOCAL AREA NETWORKS

There are many IEEE specifications related to Ethernet, but one specification that is used extensively in Ethernet networks is VLANs. The VLAN tag format was developed as the 802.1Q IEEE specification. The reason that we are describing it here, is that VLAN tags provide a priority field useful in applications such as DCB and in addition, VLAN ID fields have been proposed as a way to isolate users in data center and carrier networks. We will provide more information on network virtualization in Chapter 7, which covers different network virtualization standards.

As we described in Chapter 2, Ethernet was originally targeted at the LAN. Soon, multiple corporate organizations were sharing a single large LAN, which became more difficult to manage. To solve this, the IEEE developed the VLAN specification, which allows up to 4096 different VLANs to exist in a single physical network. In this way, each organization can have its own VLAN, simplifying network configuration while at the same time providing network isolation. The VLAN tag format is shown in Figure 5.1.

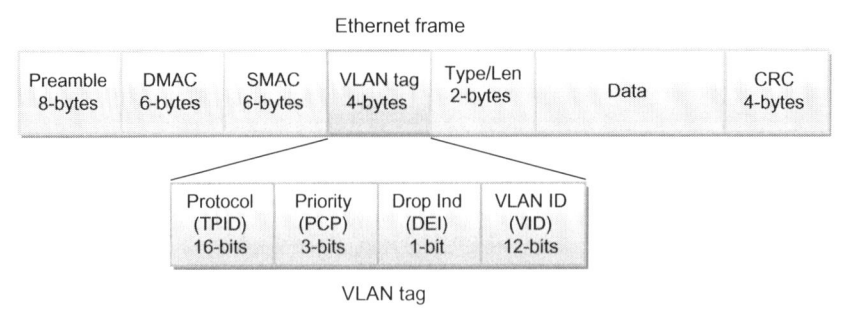

FIGURE 5.1

VLAN tag format.

The VLAN tag is inserted in the Ethernet frame after the destination and source Media Access Control (MAC) addresses and contains 4-bytes of information. The fields are defined as follows:

- *Tag Protocol Identifier (TPID)* This field is set to a value of 0x8100 in order to identify the frame as an IEEE 802.1Q-tagged frame.
- *Priority Code Point (PCP)* This indicates the priority of the frame in order to provide class of service for different traffic types.
- *Drop Eligible Indicator (DEI)* This indicates whether the frame may be dropped in the presence of congestion.
- *VLAN Identifier (VID)* This indicates one of up to 4096 VLANs that the frame may belong to.

This VLAN tag is widely used in Ethernet networks today for associating frames with a particular VLAN and in some cases providing a class of service indicator. Because the VLAN ID acts as a special frame identifier, standards bodies have found other uses such as customer identifiers in carrier access networks and tenant identifiers in data center networks. But because the ID is limited to 4096 values, other labels are used for larger address ranges, as we will see in Chapter 7.

DATA CENTER BRIDGING

As enterprise data centers evolved, separate fabrics were used for data and storage. A server may utilize a network interface controller (NIC) for connecting to the Ethernet fabric or a host bus adapter (HBA) for connecting to the storage network. Large data centers cannot afford to support two separate fabrics and, therefore, send both data and storage traffic across a single unified Ethernet network. Traditional Ethernet switches have been designed to drop packets during periods of high congestion with the assumption that these packets will be retransmitted at the TCP layer. But certain traffic types, such as video and storage, cannot tolerate the high latency variations caused by retransmission time-out values. Because of this, the IEEE has developed several new standards that are collectively known as data center bridging (DCB). Figure 5.2 shows an overview of some of the DCB components.

Data Center Bridging 91

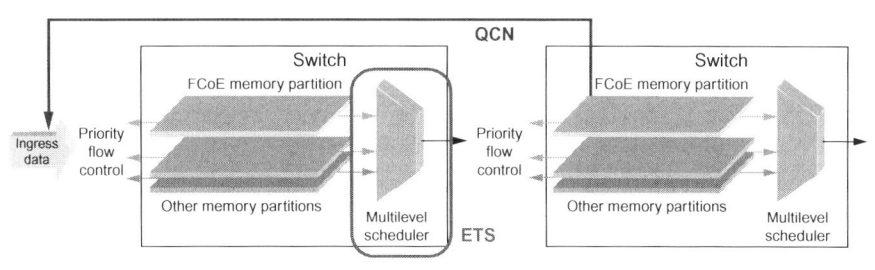

FIGURE 5.2

DCB overview.

Figure 5.2 is a pictorial representation of a device, such as a NIC, sending ingress data into the fabric which consists of two switching stages. Memory partitions on the switch are allocated for certain traffic classes, and, as they fill up, priority-based flow control (PFC) messages are sent to the transmitting device. Multilevel schedulers are employed to provide minimum bandwidth guarantees using the enhanced transmission selection (ETS) protocol. If congestion occurs somewhere within the fabric, quantized congestion notification (QCN) messages are sent back to throttle the source of the traffic. The switches also can exchange information such as the number of traffic classes supported through the data center bridging exchange (DCBx) protocol. In this section, we will provide more details behind each of these standards.

Priority-based flow control

PFC is very similar to priority link-level flow control that we described in Chapter 3 and is used to provide lossless operation for certain types of data center traffic, such as storage. Figure 5.3 shows an example implementation of PFC between switch stages.

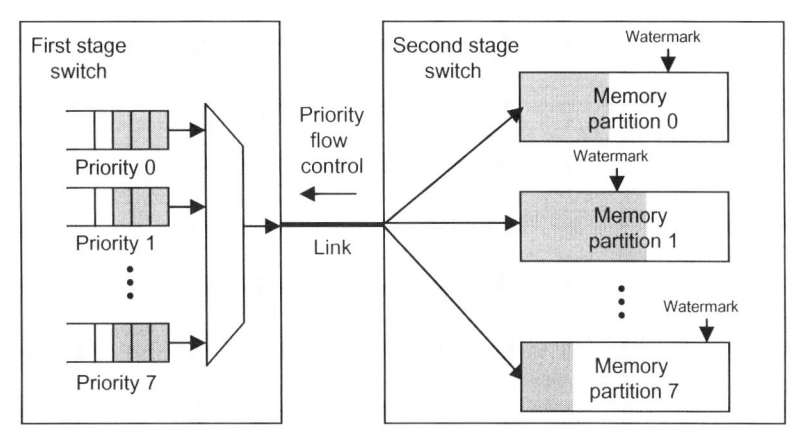

FIGURE 5.3

Priority-based flow control block diagram.

Up to eight priority levels are supported with PFC, but typical implementations may use only two or three. In this example, the second switch stage uses traffic-class-based memory partitions with programmable watermarks. If an allocated memory partition starts to fill up and a watermark is crossed, a priority flow control message is generated and sent to the transmitting switch, which then stops sending frames assigned to that particular traffic class for a specified pause time included in the frame. Transmission is resumed when the pause time expires. This ensures that other noncongested traffic is not paused and, therefore, remains unaffected. Keep in mind that a single memory partition in a shared memory switch may be receiving data from multiple switch ports and, therefore, will need to send PFC messages to all of these ports once a watermark level is exceeded.

Priority flow control evolved from the IEEE 802.3x pause frame which was designed to pause all traffic if a receiving switch global memory started to fill up. The IEEE 802.1Qbb PFC frame format is shown in Figure 5.4.

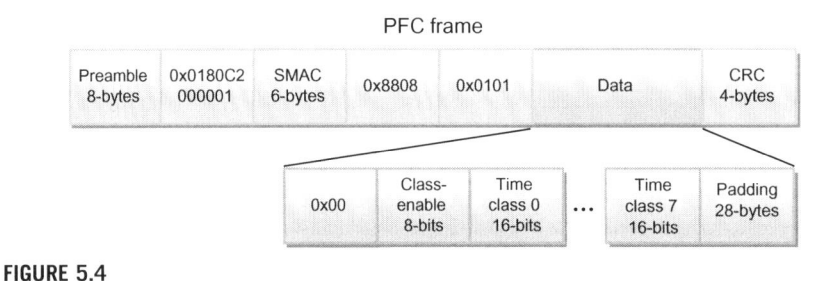

FIGURE 5.4

PFC frame format.

This is effectively a standard Ethernet frame but with some predefined fields and a special payload. The important fields are defined as follows:

- *Destination MAC address:* This field is set to a specially reserved multicast address of 0x0180C2000001 in order to identify the frame as an IEEE 802.1Qbb PFC frame.
- *Source MAC address:* This is set to the MAC address of the sending device.
- *Ethernet type:* This is set to 0x8808 for this type of frame.
- *Class-enable bits:* These bits represent traffic classes 0–7. If a bit is set high, pause is enabled for that class.
- *Class time fields:* For each class-enable bit that is set, these 16-bit values specify the length of time to enable pausing of the particular traffic class. A value of zero tells the sender to un-pause that particular traffic class.

The method in which these values are generated is somewhat vendor and implementation specific. For example, one switch may support eight traffic classes, while the other supports only two. In addition, the pause time and watermark settings depend on the round-trip flow control delay time as described in Chapter 3. The watermark settings must leave enough room in the memory partition so that frames in flight before pause is enabled will still have available memory space. Pause delay times must be long enough so that memory usage levels drop sufficiently before new frames start to arrive. For example, if jumbo frames are being used, or there are long distances between link partners, the watermark setting will need to be lowered and pause times will need to be increased.

Enhanced transmission selection

One way to minimize congestion for certain traffic classes is to allocate and/or limit bandwidth using schedulers and shapers similar to the ones used in traffic managers, as described in Chapter 3. For applications using DCB, the IEEE developed the 802.1Qaz specification known as enhanced transmission selection (ETS). Figure 5.5 is an example of an ETS scheduler that may be found at each egress port of data center NICs or switches.

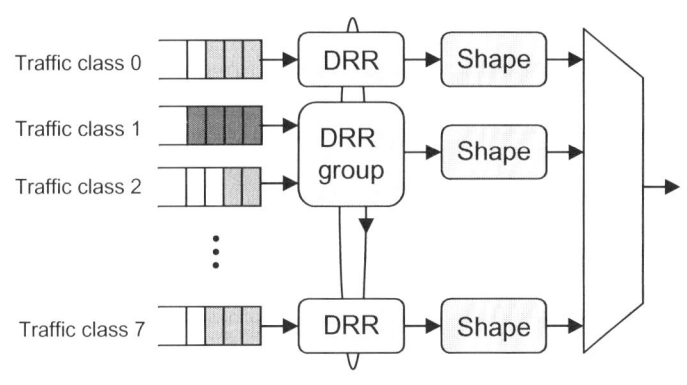

FIGURE 5.5

Example ETS scheduler.

Ethernet frames may be assigned to traffic classes in one of two ways. Various frame header fields may be examined, including MAC addresses, IP addresses, and frame types, to determine to which traffic class the frame should be assigned. This can be done using Access Control List rules which are implemented in a CAM or TCAM memory structure. A second way is to simply examine the 3-bit PCP field in the VLAN tag. Once the frames are classified, they can be assigned to queues where bandwidth allocation and shaping are applied.

In the example above, bandwidth is allocated using a deficit round robin (DRR) scheduler, which can effectively assign minimum bandwidth allocations for each traffic class. These types of schedulers work by rotating through each queue that has data to transmit and then determining transmission eligibility based on the DRR algorithm. For example, a system administrator may want to provide a minimum bandwidth of 2Gbps for storage traffic and 100Mbps for control plane traffic, while all other traffic takes whatever is remaining. If you are allocating a minimum bandwidth downstream, you may also want to make sure the traffic upstream does not exceed this limit using traffic shapers. While DRR makes sure queues are serviced with a minimum frequency, shapers make sure the queues are serviced at a maximum frequency in order to limit the maximum bandwidth. A single DDR scheduler or shaper may also be applied to traffic class groups. The following is required to be compliant with the ETS specification.

- Support for at least three traffic classes.
- The granularity of bandwidth allocation must be 10% or finer. For example, 20% to class 0, 40% to class 1, and 40% to class 2.
- The granularity of traffic shaping must be 1% or finer.
- Support for a transmission selection policy such that if one of the traffic classes does not consume its allocated bandwidth, then any unused bandwidth is available to other traffic classes.
- Support for DCBx which is discussed later in this section.

Quantized congestion notification

In Chapter 3, we showed how link-level flow control can be used to provide lossless operation between devices. PFC is an example implementation of link-level flow control. We also talked about the difficulties of implementing flow control in multistage switch fabrics. In cloud data center fabrics, the source of the traffic is typically a server or virtual machine, and the traffic will flow through multiple stages (ToR switch, aggregation switch, core switch) before it reaches its destination. Even when using PFC and ETS to provide lossless operation and bandwidth guarantees, congestion hot spots can occur in these large multistage fabrics, which can cause unpredictable fabric performance. In an attempt to minimize these congestion hot spots, the IEEE developed the QCN specification 802.1Qau.

Figure 5.6 provides a high level view of how QCN operates in a layer 2 subnetwork. The QCN congestion points are typically located in the second and third switch

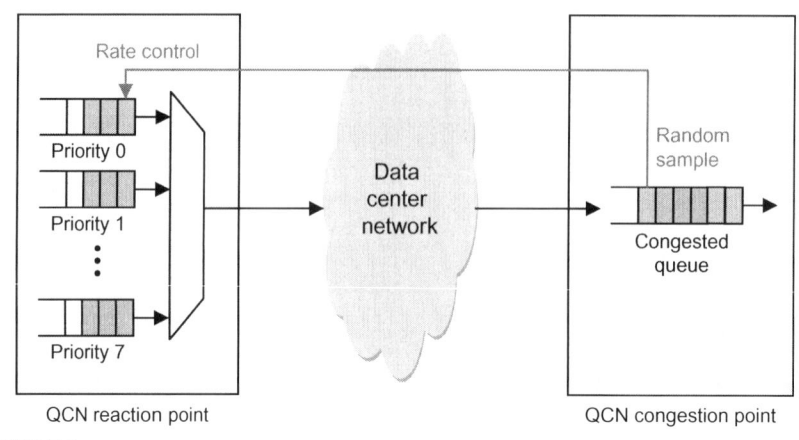

FIGURE 5.6

QCN operation example.

fabric stages and contain functions that periodically sample frames in their queues using a sample period based on recent congestion levels. Keep in mind that each layer 2 frame also includes a source MAC address that can be used as a return address to the traffic source. When a frame is sampled at a given sampling rate, the congestion point:

- Reads the queue length from the switch
- Calculates a feedback value based on the queue fill level information
- Formats a special QCN frame containing the feedback value which is forwarded back to the reaction point using the source MAC address
- Updates the queue sampling rate according to the dynamics specified by the QCN algorithm

At the reaction point, when a special QCN frame is received from the congestion point, the feedback value is used to rate limit the appropriate ingress (source) queue. The rate is decreased based on the feedback value, but then slowly increases again based on mechanisms described in the QCN standard until the initial rate is again achieved.

Although QCN was originally driven in the IEEE standards body by companies like Cisco, it is rarely implemented in data centers today. There are several reasons for this. If you analyze QCN flow control feedback as a control loop, it is highly dependent on factors such as congestion point reaction time, time to send the QCN frame back through the network, and the reaction point queue throttling time. This analysis will show that QCN only works well for long lived data flows, which may not match the traffic conditions within real data center networks. It also requires a lot of simulation analysis and fine tuning based on the network topology. In addition, because frames are randomly sampled, there are corner cases where the source that is throttled may not be the main source of congestion. Also, to get the full benefit of QCN, the rate control should occur at the source of the traffic. In the case of cloud data centers, the NIC in the server is the source of traffic. For efficient operation, the NIC would need to implement one queue for each potential congestion point in the second or third stage of the fabric. This queue structure could look very similar to the traffic manager we presented in Figure 3.13. This adds a lot of cost and complexity to the NIC, so most vendors have not implemented this type of functionality. Finally, QCN only operates across layer 2 subnets which also limits its scale in large data center networks which employ layer 3 tunneling capabilities.

DCB exchange protocol

As you can see by reading this section, the implementation of PFC and ETS require some level of coordination between neighboring devices. For example, PFC requires that link partners understand the number of priorities, or traffic classes, that each other support. In addition to the number of traffic classes, ETS also needs to know the type of bandwidth granularity and shaping granularity that each switch can support in order to provide consistent operation across the network.

DCBx protocol uses the IEEE 802.1AB standard to exchange capabilities and configuration information of DCB features between neighboring devices in order to provide consistent operation across the data center network. With DCBx, link-level discovery protocol (LLDP) Ethernet frames are sent at a periodic rate between link partners that contain the information necessary to properly configure a DCB capable device. DCBx allows data center operators to design their systems using equipment from different vendors as long as they conform to the DCB standards. But some of the coordination and configuration work done using the DCBx protocol will become obsolete once software-defined networking takes hold in the data centers. This will be discussed further in Chapter 9.

IMPROVING NETWORK BANDWIDTH

Large cloud data centers have a lot of money invested in networking systems and cabling infrastructure and, therefore, want to maximize the utilization of this equipment. But the underlying Ethernet layer 2 network has used the spanning tree protocol (STP) for many years to eliminate loops in the network. This leaves a lot of unused link bandwidth that could be used to improve overall network performance. Because of this, several industry standards have been developed to get around this limitation including equal cost multipath (ECMP) routing, TRILL and SPB. This section will provide an overview of these standards.

Spanning tree

Ethernet started life as a simple architecture with transactions across a shared medium. When switches were introduced and these LANs became more complex, a method had to be developed to prevent packets from circulating through these networks in endless loops. To solve this problem, the IEEE developed the STP which is the IEEE 802.1D standard for networks connected using layer 2 bridges or switches. Figure 5.7 shows a spanning tree within a layer 2 network where a subset of links has been selected as active links with the rest disabled but available for backup if needed.

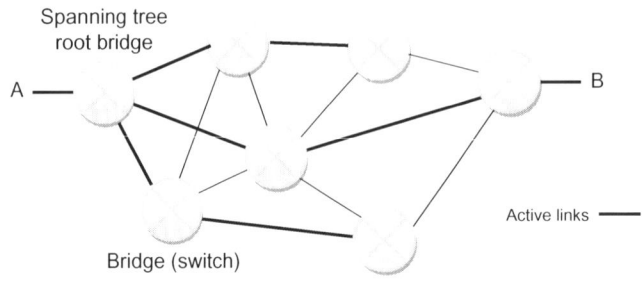

FIGURE 5.7

A spanning tree example.

The STP operates by first selecting a root bridge using the lowest bridge priority and MAC address values. Next, all other nodes on the network find the least cost path to the root bridge by using parameters such as number of hops and link bandwidth capability. Finally, all other paths are set to a disabled mode. When a new bridge or switch is added to the network, the spanning tree algorithm is run again to determine a new set of active links in the network. As networks grew larger, the time to converge on a new spanning tree became too long, so the rapid spanning tree protocol (RSTP) algorithm was introduced as IEEE 802.1D-2004, which obsoleted the original STP algorithm. With the wide deployment of VLANs within Ethernet networks, it became desirable to provide a separate spanning tree for each VLAN. Therefore, the multiple spanning tree protocol (MSTP) was introduced as IEEE 802.1s but was later merged into IEEE 802.1Q-2005.

As we described in Chapter 2, Ethernet equipment in the enterprise LAN was repurposed as data center networking gear, reusing many protocols such as STP in layer 2 subnets. Soon, data center administrators realized that their network contained a lot of disabled links and, therefore, wasted resources. For example, in Figure 5.7, there is only one active path between points A and B even through there are three potential paths that could have been used. Although STP works great in enterprise LANs with arbitrary network topologies that are constantly changing, data center networks are much more structured, enabling the use of more pre-configured networking topologies. This led the industry to try and find a more bandwidth-efficient approach than a spanning tree could provide.

Equal cost multipath routing

Many data centers use some form of layer 3 routing or tunneling between layer 2 domains in the network. When routing data through layer 3 networks, bandwidth can be improved by using multiple paths. The industry has adopted ECMP routing as a way to implement this as shown in Figure 5.8. Figure 5.8 shows one router distributing traffic across three different paths, although each router in this diagram could further distribute traffic across additional paths. Even though protocols such as Transmission Control Protocol/Internet Protocol (TCP/IP) can perform flow reordering at the network egress, due to differences in network latency and other issues, most ECMP

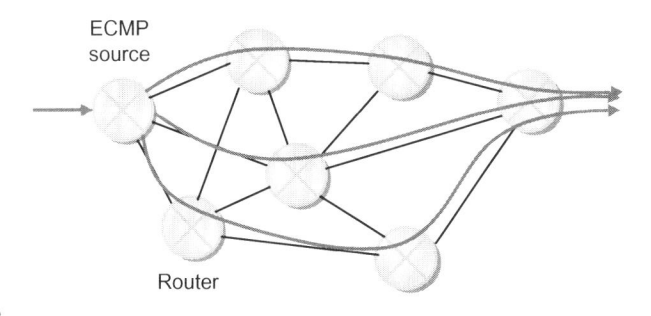

FIGURE 5.8

Equal cost multipath routing.

implementations send a given data flow across the same path, and distribute different flows across different paths. Typically, a hash-based algorithm will be used to determine the router egress port for a given flow. The hash key can be generated from various fields in the frame header such as frame type and address information.

In a data center, ECMP has some limitations. One fundamental limitation is that layer 3 traffic runs over layer 2 subnets. If these Ethernet networks employ the STP, there are still many unused data links throughout the data center. ECMP also has some issues running on systems where the physical and logical topologies of the network are different, for example, when using VLANs or network tunnels.

Shortest path bridging

As we discussed earlier, the MSTP allows a separate spanning tree to be created for each VLAN. The IEEE 802.1aq standard called shortest path bridging is a replacement for STPs, and allows for multiple paths through the network through the use of multiple different spanning trees. To do this, it relies on the capabilities developed for provider bridging (PB) and provider backbone bridging (PBB).

The IEEE has defined PB (802.1ad) as a way to tunnel customer traffic through provider networks using a service tag (SVLAN) for each unique customer. This allows providers to support up to 4096 customers. Due to scaling limitations with Provider Bridging, the IEEE developed PBB (IEEE 802.1ah), which appends customer specific identifiers using MAC addresses along with new service tags and backbone VLAN to the frame. This is known as MAC-in-MAC tunneling.

Shortest path bridging VID (SPBV) adds to the Ethernet frame an additional VLAN tag that can identify up to 4096 paths through the network. An additional specification called shortest path bridging MAC (SPBM) can scale up to 16M versus the 4096 limit using VLAN tags by using MAC addresses representing paths through the network. The IS-IS protocol is used to exchange information between switches which maintain network state information. The ingress switches will encapsulate frames with SPBV or SPBM headers and the egress switches will remove the headers. The paths through the network can be selected using a hash algorithm, and all flows will take the same path.

Transparent interconnection of lots of links

Another method to improve bandwidth utilization in data center networks is to use the TRILL standard developed by the IETF. Here are some of the goals as defined in the IETF charter:

- Minimal or no configuration required
- Load-splitting among multiple paths
- Routing loop mitigation (possibly through a TTL field)
- Support of multiple points of attachment
- Support for broadcast and multicast
- No significant service delay after attachment
- No less secure than existing bridged solutions

The TRILL standard defines RBridges to tunnel packets through layer 2 networks using multiple paths. It uses a link state protocol that allows all RBridges to learn about each other and the connectivity through the network. Both a TRILL header and an outer Ethernet header are added to the native Ethernet frame (that contains an inner Ethernet header). The ingress RBridge encapsulates the frame and the egress RBridge de-encapsulates the frame as shown in Figure 5.9. This figure shows an example network that includes RBridge components in which a packet is being forwarded from end station A (ES-A) to end station B (ES-B). The Ingress RBridge encapsulates the packet and forwards it to the next RBridge using the MAC destination address of RBridge 2. The standard bridges simply forward the packet using the outer Ethernet header. The Relay RBridge acts somewhat like a router, using the egress nickname to determine the next hop for the packet. The Egress RBridge de-encapsulates the packet, which is forwarded through the standard network using the original inner Ethernet header.

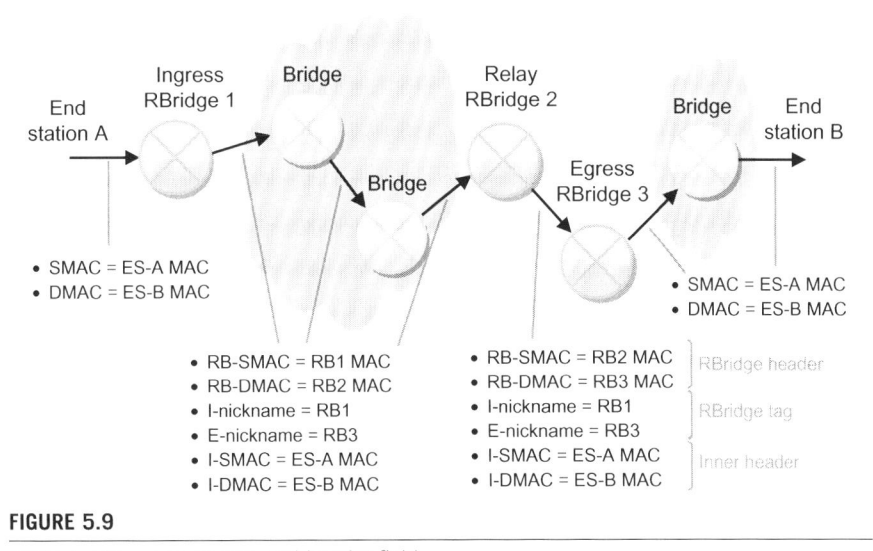

FIGURE 5.9

TRILL bridge components and header field.

Like many networking protocols, TRILL requires that each RBridge maintain state information about paths to other RBridges in the network. There is a lot of debate on whether SPB or TRILL is the best standard for data center networks. Companies like Avaya, Huawei, and Alcatel-Lucent are supporters of SPB, while Cisco and Brocade are backing TRILL. But the industry is starting to embrace software-defined networking as a way to orchestrate the functionality of the network from a central controller including defining the forwarding paths through the network. Because of this, it removes the need for protocols such as SPB and TRILL. More on software-defined networking in Chapter 9.

REMOTE DIRECT MEMORY ACCESS

One type of data transport technology that has several applications in the data center and can improve data center performance is remote direct memory access (RDMA). This evolved from direct memory access (DMA) which is used to improve performance in CPU subsystems. Many CPUs, NPUs, and microcontrollers contain DMA engines which can offload the task of moving data in and out of the CPUs main memory without involving the operating system (OS). One example of this is in the network switch. Let's say that the switch chip receives a management packet that needs to be processed by the attached control plane CPU. The switch can send an interrupt to the CPU, which then would need to access the packet data from the switch memory and transfer it to its own main memory. Executing this transfer as part of the CPUs main processing thread will slow the execution of other critical tasks. Instead, the CPU could send the starting address and packet length information to an embedded DMA engine, which can execute the data transfer from the switch memory to main memory in the background, with little impact on the processor.

Remote DMA or RDMA is very similar, but instead of automating memory transfers between devices on a given circuit board, the memory transfers are executed across the network. For example, a server on one side of the network can efficiently transfer data from its own application memory into the application memory of a server on the other side of the network without the need to write the data into kernel memory first. This is known as kernel bypass. This zero copy approach is much more efficient than requiring multiple data transfers on each side of the network. In most cases RDMA uses an offload engine located in the network controller attached to the server CPU, where the network controller can directly read and write into the CPUs application memory. Today, there are two main competing industry standards for RDMA: Internet Wide-Area RDMA Protocol (iWARP) and RDMA over Converged Ethernet (RoCE).

Data center requirements

Data center performance can be critical in applications such as compute clustering, big data analytics, and financial services. RDMA technology can dramatically reduce latencies in these applications by eliminating the extra memory transitions required between the kernel memory and application memory. The demands placed on data center networks are also changing as the amount of server-to-server (east-west) traffic grows. Some of the changes in data centers that are driving adoption of RDMA include:

- Web applications that can spawn hundreds of server-to-server workflows, with each workflow requiring a rapid response in order to maintain a good user experience.
- Low-latency server-to-server transactions that are required in financial trading and big data applications.

- New storage protocols that are emerging, that can exploit an RDMA-enabled network for significantly accelerated storage performance.
- Virtual machine migration that can be dramatically accelerated in a low-latency, RDMA-capable data center.

These changes are driving cloud data center designers to implement RDMA for certain applications as it provides the right combination of processor offload and low latency to deliver the performance needed for these applications.

Internet Wide-Area RDMA Protocol

In 2004, Adaptec®, Broadcom®, Cisco, Dell®, EMC®, Hewlett-Packard, IBM, Intel, Microsoft, and Network Appliance® formed the RDMA Consortium. Their goal was to minimize the impact of TCP/IP overhead, context switching, and multiple buffer copies when transferring data across Ethernet networks. Today, several network adapters are available that conform to the iWARP standard. They use offload engines to move TCP/IP processing out of software, freeing up CPU processing overhead. Another source of overhead comes from applications sending commands to the network adapter causing expensive context switching in the OS. iWARP solves this by providing OS bypass, allowing an application running in user space to issue commands directly to the network adapter.

Another major area of improvement for iWARP is provided by reducing the number of buffer copies required when data moves from the network into an application buffer. Figure 5.10 shows the multiple buffer copies required when using a traditional network adapter versus the single buffer copy used with RDMA protocols such as iWARP. Companies like Intel also provide direct data placement technology which places data in the application buffer residing in the CPU cache memory to further improve performance.

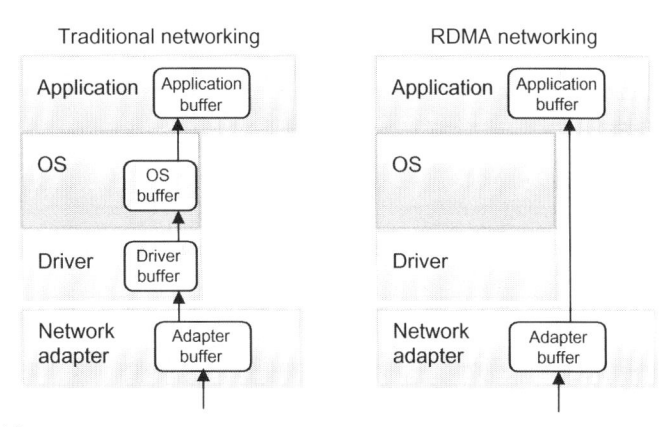

FIGURE 5.10

Eliminating buffer copies using RDMA.

Unlike RoCE described below, iWARP is a layer 3 technology that works over TCP/IP networks and iWARP can eliminate much of the CPU overhead that is traditionally seen in these layer 3 1GbE and 10GbE networks. Many large cloud data center networks deploy RDMA technologies such as iWARP to improve their networking performance.

RDMA over Converged Ethernet

After the iWARP spec was developed, several companies continued to look for better ways to support RDMA. Although iWARP can be run over any TCP/IP network, the TCP/IP protocol adds certain complexity to network adapters including functions such as TCP checksum processing, TCP segmentation, and header split. This additional processing can also lead to higher latency. The Infiniband Trade Association (IBTA) already had a layer 2 RDMA over Infiniband (IB) specification, so they created a new specification that kept the IB transport layers and network layers intact, but swapped out the IB link layer for an Ethernet link layer. They called the new specification RoCE.

There are several applications for RoCE where latency is important such as high-performance computing (HPC) and financial trading, but because RoCE is limited to layer 2, these applications must be confined to an Ethernet subnet. Also, RoCE requires that all the Ethernet switches in the subnet must support the DCB standard, which not all legacy networks support. To get the full performance benefit of RoCE, some vendors are also supporting QCN in the network. As we discussed earlier in this chapter, QCN is not an easy protocol to make work across arbitrary network topologies, and, therefore, has not been widely adopted in the industry. The bottom line is that large cloud data center networks rely on layer 3 tunneling protocols, limiting the usefulness of RoCE in these applications. As of this writing, the IBTA is defining a new layer 3 compatible version of RoCE that some people refer to as route-able RoCE that may overcome some of these obstacles.

REVIEW

In this chapter, we described several types of industry standards that are important in cloud data center networks. We described how the new Ethernet data rate standards have improved data center network connectivity. We also described the VLAN header, which is relevant to many other data center networking standards that are described in this book. Next, we provided some information on DCB, which is key for running converges, storage, and data on the same network. We also described standards to improve data center network bandwidth utilization. Finally, we provided an overview of RDMA as a way to improve application-to-application performance in data center networks. In the next chapter, we will move our networking discussion into the server, where multiple virtual machines must be incorporated into the overall data center network.

CHAPTER 6

Server Virtualization and Networking

The computing power of a single server in cloud data centers has increased dramatically over the years to the point where certain workloads such as web hosting can significantly underutilize the processing power available. This has fueled the push toward microservers for certain workloads but has also spawned the widespread use of server virtualization. Server virtualization allows multiple virtual machines (VMs) to run as independent virtual servers on a physical server. The number of VMs running on a physical server depends on the workload requirements and server capabilities but can range in number from tens to hundreds.

Not all cloud data centers will utilize VMs and some hyper-scale data centers may implement proprietary methods not covered in this chapter. Software as a Service (SaaS) providers may or may not use VMs depending on how their software is written. Infrastructure as a Service (IaaS) providers let their customers make their own choices on how to use the leased hardware resource including the deployment of VMs. Platform as a Service (PaaS) providers will most likely use VMs in order to optimize their server resources in applications such as web hosting.

This chapter will provide an overview of how VMs work along with a key networking component called the virtual switch (vSwitch). This will be followed with a section on PCI Express (PCIe) which provides an alternative to the vSwitch. We will then describe Ethernet virtual bridging standards that were developed to better integrate VMs into the overall data center network. We will wrap up this chapter by discussing VM migration and the associated networking features that can improve this process.

VM OVERVIEW

Initially, host servers within the data center ran one operating system (OS) and, in many cases, one application program (app). As server CPUs became more powerful, these apps were consuming only a fraction of the CPU processing capability, but utilizing multiple apps on the same OS meant that an OS reboot would take down all of the apps running on the host. This led to the development of VMs. A VM is basically a guest OS running on a host server. For example, if you have ever loaded a program on your Apple® Mac computer that allows you to run Windows, you have set up something similar to a VM, and the app that you run to boot Windows on your Mac operates something like a VM hypervisor. The difference is that servers typically host many different VMs using a single hypervisor, each potentially running a different OS as shown in Figure 6.1.

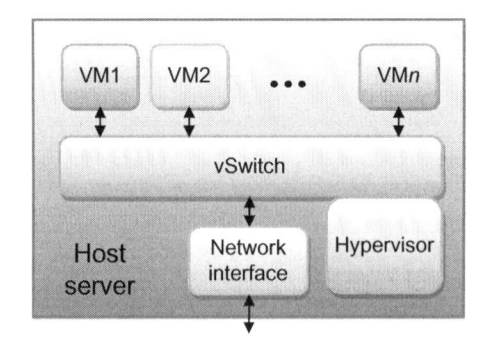

FIGURE 6.1

Logical diagram of a virtualized server.

Multiple VMs are logically connected to each other and to the network interface through a vSwitch, and a connection is made to the physical data center network through a network interface controller (NIC). A vSwitch is similar to the shared memory switch that we described in Chapter 3. A typical cloud data center server may have a 10Gb Ethernet NIC that connects to the server CPU through a PCI Express (PCIe) interface. Both the VMs and the vSwitch are set up and controlled by a hypervisor program that also runs on the server.

VMs allow more flexible allocation of server resources, especially in data centers that are running a large number of smaller applications such as web hosting. By using VMs, server utilization is increased, reducing the overall number of servers required in the data center. In addition, network interface bandwidth utilization is increased with multiple VMs sharing a single network connection. But this also drives the need for high-bandwidth Ethernet interfaces.

Originally, host servers were configured with one network connection per VM. As 10GbE NICs started to enter the market, it became more cost effective to share a single connection among multiple VMs. If you look at the data center network topologies that we described in Chapter 4, many people equate the vSwitch to a virtual top of rack (ToR) switch within the hypervisor, while the NIC provides the uplink ports for this virtual ToR that are shared among multiple servers. In this section, we will provide more information on the operation of the hypervisor while focusing on the network connections to the VMs.

Hypervisors

Hypervisors were first implemented on mainframe computers by IBM in the late 1960s. These were called bare metal, or type 1, hypervisors because they act much like an OS running on the physical hardware underneath. These hypervisors "hosted" what were called "guest" OSs which ran on top of the hypervisor. Another type of hypervisor is similar to the host program running on the Mac OS that was described earlier. This is called a hosted, or type 2, hypervisor that runs as an app on top of an

OS with one or more guest OSs running on top of the app. Other types of hypervisors include kernel-based virtual machines that run as kernel modules in Linux.

Virtualization technology did not find its way into the commodity server market until around 2005 when Unix and Linux systems started to become available. It wasn't until later in the decade that the use of VMs started to take off when Intel introduced x86 with hardware-based virtualization assistance. In addition, companies like VMware® and Microsoft started to introduce virtualization software that was deployed widely in data center installations. We will next provide more information about two of the leading commercial hypervisors in the market today. There are several other hypervisors available such as Kernel-based Virtual Machine (KVM) driven by the Open Virtualization Alliance that will not be covered in this chapter.

VMware

VMware was one of the first software companies to make a big splash in the virtualization market, and they are now one of the largest. They started with workstation virtualization software in the late 1990s and have since moved into the enterprise data center server virtualization market with vSphere™ (also called ESXi). This is a bare metal type 1 hypervisor which allows the VMs direct access to many of the server hardware resources. VMware also provides vCenter as a VM management tool. It provides a technology called vMotion™ that allows the movement of a VM from one server to another and from utilizing one storage device to another while the OS is running. It also provides high availability and load balancing features.

VMware also offers cloud management software called vCloud™ to manage logical pools of compute, storage, and networking resources. They recently acquired Nicira, a company developing software-defined networking solutions based on OpenFlow. These new developments show that VMware is moving toward solutions to help orchestrate and manage all of the key virtual components in large data center networks. We will provide more information on software-defined networking in Chapter 9.

Microsoft

Microsoft has developed a hypervisor called Hyper-V, which is designed for x86 64-bit servers. It is released as a stand-alone version and also with Windows Server OSs. Each server must contain one parent partition along with multiple child partitions. The parent partition creates and manages the child partitions and also handles all hardware access requests from the child partitions. Because of this, it is not exactly like a bare metal type 1 hypervisor but much more like a hosted type 2 hypervisor. With Windows Server 2012, Microsoft introduced live system migration features that allow the movement of a running VM and its storage from one Hyper-V host to another. This release also included features such as Hyper-V Extensible Virtual Switch and network virtualization technology.

VIRTUAL SWITCHING

Multiple VMs must share a single network physical port such as a network interface controller (NIC). One way to do this is to use PCIe single-root IO virtualization (SR-IOV) which will be discussed in the next section. The other way is for the hypervisor to implement a vSwitch in software. In this section, we will describe the vSwitch capabilities provided by Microsoft Hyper-V™ and VMware vSphere along with Open vSwitch (OVS) which is an open software initiative. At the end of this section, we will describe virtual machine device queues (VMDqs) which can be used to accelerate vSwitch operation.

vSphere Distributed Switch

VMware provides a virtual switching capability with their vSphere (ESXi) hypervisor. They call this a vSphere Distributed Switch (VDS) and it allows the extension of the vSwitch domain across multiple host servers as shown in Figure 6.2. Data physically moves between servers through the external network, but the control plane abstracts this movement to look like one large VDS spanning multiple servers. Each VDS can manage up to 500 hosts (servers). With VDS, the data does not move through a parent partition but logically connects directly to the network interface through local vNICs associated with each VM. The logical vNIC to physical NIC command and data translations are performed by the vSwitch.

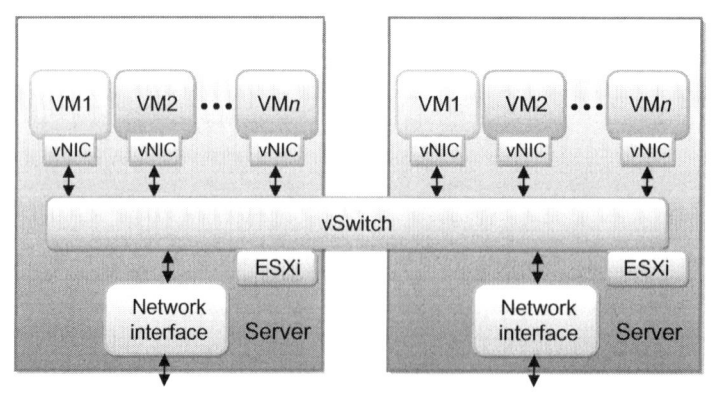

FIGURE 6.2

Logical diagram of a vSphere distributed switch.

VMware has added several advanced networking features to the latest VDS offering including the following:

- *Network traffic monitoring*: Enhanced network monitoring and troubleshooting capabilities
- *Virtual local area network (VLAN) isolation:* Provides network isolation in multitenant environments

- *Traffic shaping:* Provides maximum bandwidth limits to minimize traffic congestion
- *LACP support:* Support for link aggregation control protocol
- *Network vMotion:* Provides a simple way to monitor and troubleshoot when VMs are moved from host to host within a VDS

These features allow the VDS to provide offerings similar to what can be found in a physical network switch. But, like the Hyper-V switch described below, these advanced features require significant CPU processing resources as the number of VMs increase and as the network interface bandwidth increases, somewhat limiting the vSwitch scalability.

Hyper-V virtual switch

The Hyper-V hypervisor uses a parent partition to generate and manage multiple VMs referred to as child partitions. These child partitions communicate to the parent partition through a virtual bus called the VMbus as shown in Figure 6.3. All requests for access to hardware such as a network interface controller (NIC) are made through the parent partition. The parent partition also implements a virtual layer 2 switching function to provide switching between local VMs as well as arbitrating access to the physical network. It also provides a virtual NIC (vNIC) function for each VM that is connected to the VMbus. The vNIC looks like a physical NIC to the VM while the parent partition converts these local VM transactions into function calls to the physical NIC.

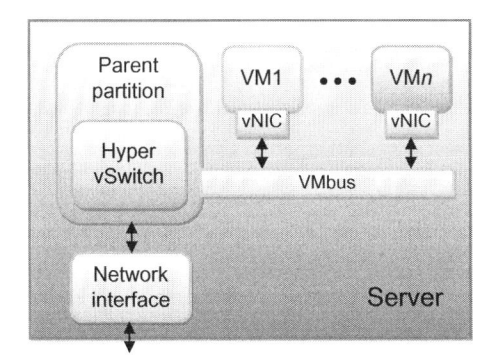

FIGURE 6.3

Logical diagram of a Hyper-V server.

The Hyper-V virtual switch also has three modes of operation; private, internal, and public. Private mode provides logical switching between VMs but no external access to the network. Internal mode is similar, but this mode includes virtual adapters (vNICs) within each VM. Public mode allows communication between VMs and also to the outside physical network through vNICs. With Windows server 2012, Microsoft added additional features in an attempt to provide vSwitch functionality similar to what can be found in physical data center network switches. These include:

- *Port ACL rules:* Access control list rules allow traffic classification and filtering.
- *Network traffic monitoring:* Allows network administrators to trace and monitor traffic in the virtual network
- *VLAN isolation:* Provides network isolation in multitenant environments
- *Minimum bandwidth guarantees and traffic shaping:* Provides minimum bandwidth guarantees along with maximum bandwidth limits
- *ECN marking:* Explicit congestion notification marking for congestion control
- *Network security features:* These include ARP spoofing protection, neighbor discovery spoofing, and DHCP guard protection.

Open vSwitch

OVS is an open source software industry initiative providing multilayer virtual switching capability while supporting standard management interfaces and protocols. It's the same vSwitch used in the OpenStack Neutron plugin and can also run on Microsoft Hyper-V and VMware's ESX hypervisors. Here is a feature list from the openvswitch.org web site:

- Visibility into inter-VM communication via NetFlow, sFlow(R), IPFIX, SPAN, RSPAN, and GRE-tunneled mirrors
- LACP (IEEE 802.1AX-2008)
- Standard 802.1Q VLAN model with trunking
- BFD and 802.1ag link monitoring
- STP (IEEE 802.1D-1998)
- Fine-grained QoS control
- Support for HFSC qdisc
- Per VM interface traffic policing
- NIC bonding with source-MAC load balancing, active backup, and L4 hashing
- OpenFlow protocol support (including many extensions for virtualization)
- IPv6 support
- Multiple tunneling protocols (GRE, VXLAN, IPsec, GRE, and VXLAN over IPsec)
- Remote configuration protocol with C and Python bindings
- Kernel and user-space forwarding engine options
- Multitable forwarding pipeline with flow-caching engine
- Forwarding layer abstraction to ease porting to new software and hardware platforms

Although these various vSwitch offerings provide features similar to physical network switches, in some cases they cannot meet the same performance levels. Because of this, hardware offloads such as VMDq and PCIe SR-IOV may be used in the NIC. These will be discussed in the next sections.

Virtual machine device queues

As the number of VMs increases within the server, the burden of managing all of this traffic within the vSwitch can tax CPU resources, which can reduce server and VM performance levels. To combat this problem, Intel developed VMDqs which are implemented in many of their network controllers to both improve networking performance and decrease CPU utilization by offloading some of the vSwitch traffic management tasks.

Within the network interface controller (NIC), both transmit and receive queues are established for each VM hosted in the server as shown in Figure 6.4. When frames are received from the physical network, MAC address and VLAN tag information in the frame headers can be used to determine the correct destination VM. The vSwitch simply needs to forward the frame to the VM from the corresponding queue. When packets are transmitted from the VM, they are simply forwarded to the associated queue in the NIC. The NIC can then send frames out to the physical network based on various scheduling mechanisms such as round robin, weighted round robin, or strict priority based on service level agreements.

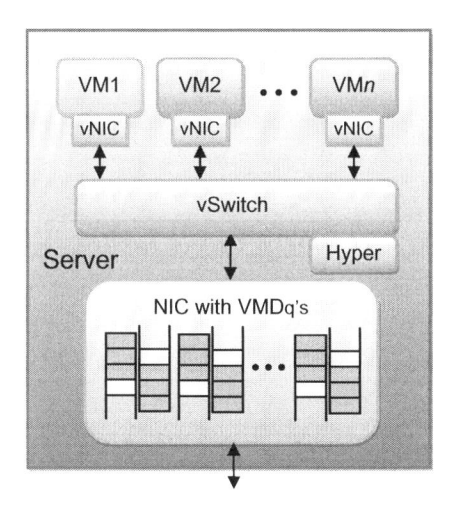

FIGURE 6.4

NIC with VMDq support.

VMs are assigned to cores within a multicore CPU on the server host. In some cases, a single core can burst data at rates over 5Gbps causing potential congestion in the NIC. The egress VMDqs can provide filtering and sorting capabilities to ensure proper egress link utilization under heavy traffic loads. On the ingress side, VMDqs can be used along with a scheduler to efficiently distribute the traffic load across the CPU cores in order to provide optimal performance. In some cases, VMDqs can be used in conjunction with a technology called Receive Side Scaling which is an industry standard mechanism supported by hypervisor vendors like VMware ad Microsoft to efficiently distribute traffic loads across multiple processor cores using a hash-based mechanism. Intel also offers a feature in their NICs called Flow Director which matches layer 2 and layer 3 header fields to determine which core to send particular flows to. This provides a unique association between the core and the client application.

PCI EXPRESS

PCI Express (PCIe) is an interface that you may be familiar with inside your PC. The PCIe interface standard has been used for years to connect peripherals such as graphics cards and network interface cards to the CPU chip set within the PC. This interface standard is also used for the connection between the CPU chip set and the network interface card within the server. Although it has been around for a while, new industry standards have evolved under the PCIe umbrella that provide enhanced functionality and performance when supporting multiple VMs within a server. This section will provide some background on PCIe and describe both the single root IO virtualization (SR-IOV) and multiroot IO virtualization (MR-IOV) standards.

Background

Early computers and workstations used various parallel interfaces such as the ISA or VESA local bus to connect peripheral devices to CPU subsystems. In order to provide a single industry standard interface for its CPU chipsets, Intel started working on what became the Peripheral Component Interconnect (PCI) standard in the Intel Architecture Development Lab around 1990. This work propelled the computer industry to band together to form the nonprofit Peripheral Component Interconnect Special Interest Group (PCI-SIG) in 1992 in order to standardize the PCI interface. Today the PCI-SIG has over 800 corporate members and this standard is widely used in the industry.

The original PCI interface is a 32-bit wide parallel bus operating at a 33MHz clock rate and it quickly replaced the ISA and VESA local bus in most applications. The PCI standard includes bus timing requirements, protocol specifications, electrical specifications, and the physical dimensions of the PCI edge card connector. In some applications, a connector is not used and the bus connects to another device located on the same circuit board. Also, in some cases, the CPU chipset supports only a single PCI interface, so a PCI bridge device is used to expand this single connection to multiple PCI interfaces using a bus-like architecture within the bridge. The host OS enumerates each PCI component on the bus and assigns an address range to each device which can be used by the host to configure, monitor, and communicate with the peripheral. Only one host or root device can be used in this system.

The PCI standard was quickly accepted by the industry, and the PCI-SIG set to work to increase PCI performance levels. There are two ways to increase the performance of a parallel bus; increase the bus bandwidth or increase the bus width. For PCI, this was done in stages as follows:

- 133MBps—32-bits wide at 33MHz (original standard)
- 266MBps—64-bits wide at 33MHz
- 266MBps—32-bits wide at 66MHz
- 533MBps—64-bits wide at 66MHz

The PCI-SIG later introduced the PCI-X standard that not only increased the performance but also improved the fault tolerance of PCI by allowing defective cards to be reset or disabled. The commonly used PCI-X bus standards are as follows.

- 533MBps—64-bits wide at 66MHz (found on older servers)
- 1066MBps—64-bits wide at 133MHz (common implementation)

There are also 64-bit wide 266MHz and 533MHz standards for PCI-X, but these have been rarely implemented and were quickly replaced by the PCIe standard.

As we discussed in Chapter 3, wide parallel busses are difficult to implement in circuit board designs as the bus width and bus frequency increase. These wide busses also consume a large number of pins, taking up area and increasing the cost of integrated circuits. Because of these factors, the PCI-SIG decided to make a significant change by introducing the PCI Express (PCIe) standard in 2004. PCIe can use multiple data lanes, but instead of using single-ended signals between devices, it uses higher performance serializer/deserializer (SerDes) technology with differential signaling. These SerDes can increase performance while easing board layout and reducing pin count. As of this writing, three generations of PCIe standards have been released by the PCI-SIG, each with increased SerDes transfer rates. In addition, various PCIe transfer rates can be supported by using different numbers of SerDes (lanes) as shown in the table for each PCIe generation.

Gen	1-lane	2-lane	4-lane	8-lane	16-lane	32-lane
1	250MBps	500MBps	1GBps	2GBps	4GBps	8GBps
2	500MBps	1GBps	2GBps	4GBps	8GBps	16GBps
3	985MBps	1.97GBps	3.94GBps	7.88GBps	15.8GBps	31.5GBps

For Ethernet network interface controllers, common PCIe interface standards are 4-lane gen2 for 10GbE data traffic (1.25GBps) and 8-lane gen3 for 40GbE data traffic (5GBps). The use of SerDes technology not only increases the interface performance while using fewer pins, it also allows more flexible interconnect topologies with multiple devices connected to the host through a PCIe switch, which logically behaves like a PCI bus. An example PCIe peripheral configuration is shown in Figure 6.5.

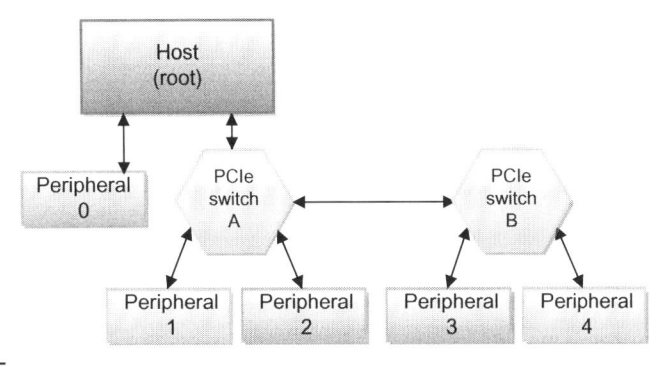

FIGURE 6.5

Example of PCIe peripheral connections.

As you can see, the PCIe switch hierarchy looks like a tree structure with the host CPU referred to as the root of the tree. There are actually three different virtual PCI busses in this example. The host contains an internal virtual bus allowing it to access both peripheral 0 and PCIe switch A. PCIe switch A contains a virtual bus with connections to two different peripherals as well as PCIe switch B. This switch contains the third virtual bus with connections to two additional peripherals. Each peripheral contains at least one physical function (PF) which is connected to the host. We will not dive deeply here into the details of the PCIe protocol; instead, the key take away from this discussion is that any given peripheral can only be connected through the tree to one root (host). This will become important in the next sections.

Single-root IO virtualization

We mentioned above that there can only be a single root host connected to any given peripheral such as a network interface controller. But a single host may be running a hypervisor with multiple VMs that would like to share this network interface. We also mentioned earlier that hypervisors can implement vNICs for each VM, but as network interface bandwidths increase, the vNICs start to tax CPU performance. To provide an alternative, the PCI-SIG issued an extension to the PCIe specification called single-root input output virtualization (SR-IOV). This spec moves the vNIC functionality into the network interface card as shown in Figure 6.6, improving overall performance.

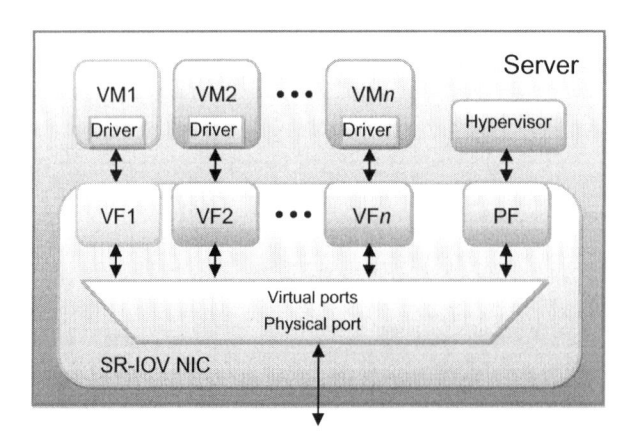

FIGURE 6.6

Conceptual drawing of SR-IOV components.

Instead of having one physical function (PF) like traditional PCI NICs, the SR-IOV NIC contains one PF along with multiple virtual functions (VFs). Each VF has all the features and functionality of a NIC and also has its own PCI configuration space. This allows each VM that is using an SR-IOV compatible NIC driver to function like it's connected to a dedicated NIC. The SR-IOV PF takes care of allocating physical port bandwidth to the virtual ports associated with each VF. For this to work, the hypervisor must also support SR-IOV. Both Microsoft and VMware support this capability as long as specified NICs from certain vendors are used.

The hypervisor communicates to the PF which exposes to the hypervisor the SR-IOV extended capabilities in the PCI configuration space. This allows the hypervisor to configure and manage the SR-IOV NIC including the association of VMs with VFs. SR-IOV capable NICs from different vendors can support different numbers of VFs, so the hypervisor must read this information from the PF configuration space before assigning VMs to VFs. You can think of SR-IOV as a hardware offload of the vSwitch network connections that are implemented in the NIC to reduce CPU utilization and improve performance.

A vSwitch can be thought of as a shared memory switch in which only the memory pointers need to be passed between VMs sharing the same switch. When using SR-IOV, traffic between two VMs within the same server must pass through the NIC PCIe interface before returning back from the NIC. With today's servers connected to a 10GbE NIC, the PCIe bandwidth is limited to around 14Gbps while a vSwitch can maintain transfer rates up to 30Gbps because it is simply passing memory pointers. This performance advantage is becoming more important as the amount of east-west traffic increases within the host servers. Although the vSwitch uses more CPU resources than required with SR-IOV, high-performance multicore processors can easily handle this extra burden. Because of this, along with other factors such as SR-IOV management overhead and resource coordination, SR-IOV is typically used in specific applications where vSwitch CPU overhead and/or latency are an issue.

Multiroot IO virtualization

To reduce cost and improve system flexibility, it would be ideal if multiple CPU subsystems within a chassis could share IO resources such as NICs for networking, host bus adapters (HBAs) for storage, and host channel adapters (HCAs) for computer clustering applications. This was the idea behind the MR-IOV standard developed by the PCI-SIG under the PCIe umbrella.

Figure 6.7 shows an example application for MR-IOV where multiple servers are sharing different IO adapter devices. Each adapter must have special features including support for multiple virtual PCIe interfaces and VFs in addition to a physical PCIe interface and PFs. The MR-IOV PCIe switch must have special functionality to align server transactions to the correct virtual adapter interface. This configuration can be done through a dedicated control plane CPU connected to the switch or through one of the attached servers. Similar to SR-IOV, the trick is to make sure each server driver thinks it owns the resources in each adapter to which it is logically connected.

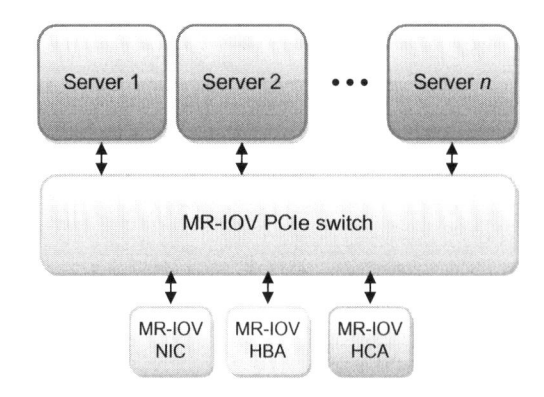

FIGURE 6.7

Example MR-IOV implementation.

MR-IOV has not seen much use in cloud data centers because powerful multicore CPUs that can host multiple VMs need the full bandwidth of the network adapter, so sharing the adapter among multiple CPUs does not make sense. In other applications, it only makes sense where multiple CPUs need to share relatively expensive adapters, which limits the available market. Several companies, such as NextIO and Virtensys, developed IO virtualization systems built on the MR-IOV specification, but both have now ceased operations.

EDGE VIRTUAL BRIDGING

Even though hypervisor vendors have added a lot of networking features recently to their vSwitch offerings, they still lack some of the advanced features that are available in the attached top of rack switch. Because of this, traffic between VMs within the same server may not be subject to the same filtering, security, monitoring, and forwarding capability as traffic that is sent through the top of rack switch. To improve this situation, the industry has been working on some new specifications that are collectively known as edge virtual bridging (EVB). This section will describe two key EVB standards that have been promoted in the industry; virtual Ethernet port aggregator (VEPA) and virtual network tag (VN-Tag).

VEPA

VEPA is a method for providing consistent treatment of all network traffic including VM traffic. This was originally proposed by HP[®] and has since been used by the IEEE as a basis for the 802.1Qbg EVB standard. With VEPA, all the Ethernet frames generated by a VM are routed through the attached network switch in order to provide consistent treatment of all network traffic as shown in Figure 6.8.

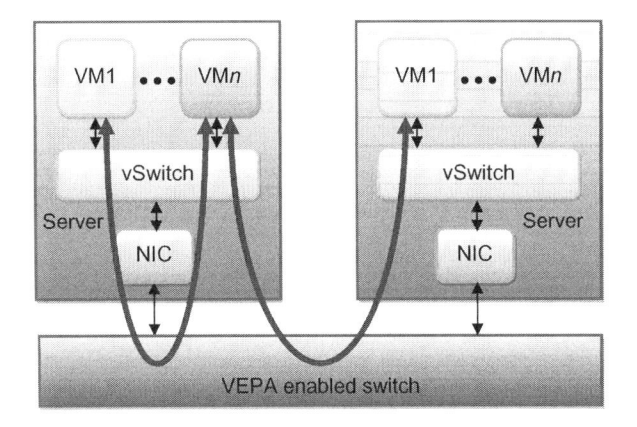

FIGURE 6.8

Forwarding VM traffic using VEPA.

There are two VEPA modes of operation. In standard mode, the hypervisor software must be configured so that all traffic generated from a VM is forwarded to the external switch. For the external switch, this does not require any changes for traffic that is intended for another physical server, but if the traffic is intended for a VM within the same server, the switch must forward the packet back through the same port that it was received on. This is sometimes known as reflective relay, or a hair-pin turn. Because the spanning tree protocol does not allow a frame to be forwarded in this way, the switch may require a firmware upgrade in order to support this. The advantage of this approach is that all traffic is treated in a consistent manner by the attached switch. The disadvantage is that performance may be impacted as traffic that would normally stay within the vSwitch must now be forwarded in both directions through the network interface controller, increasing the bandwidth utilization of this device. The switch must also support a Virtual Service Interface, which makes it appear that the VM is directly connected to the external bridge.

VEPA also supports an optional channelized mode of operation in which all traffic has an extra VLAN tag added to the frame and the VLAN ID represents a channel number. This type of tunneling is also known as Q-in-Q encapsulation. The channel number can be used to isolate traffic from different VMs or different vSwitches within a single physical network connection. The attached switch can also use this channel identifier to provide different service levels to different VMs.

VN-Tag

VN-Tag is also a method for providing consistent treatment of all network traffic including VM traffic. This was originally proposed by Cisco and has since been used by the IEEE as a basis for the 802.1qbh Bridge Port Extension standard. Cisco has been a proponent of the fabric extender concept (using their Nexus 2000 product) that we described in Chapter 4. This approach effectively distributes the line cards of an end-of-row switch to each rack as shown in Figure 4.5.

The controlling bridge configures the port on the fabric extenders as if they were a physical interface on the controlling bridge. To do this, the controlling bridge creates a logical interface for each port in the fabric extender and assigns a tag value. The fabric extender uses this value to add tags to all traffic moving through these ports. Figure 6.9 shows how this concept can be extended to the VMs within a server.

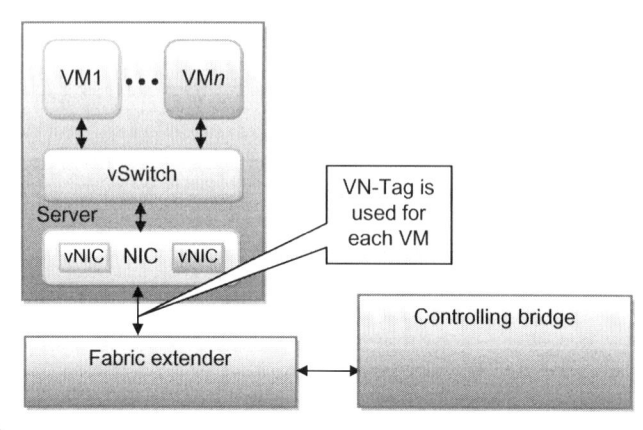

FIGURE 6.9

VN-Tagging.

The use of VN-Tags expands the reach of the controlling bridge into the NIC. A single physical NIC can be configured to contain multiple vNICs each with its own assigned VN-Tag. So now the controlling bridge has extended its reach not just to the external ports of the fabric extender but also into the ports of the vNICs within the server. While the VEPA standard works by extending traffic flows out to the attached switch, VN-Tag works by extending the functionality of the controlling bridge into the server.

Industry adoption

The goal of both VEPA and VN-Tag is to provide more consistent networking policies down to the vSwitch level. In the case of VEPA, hypervisor support is required which in not yet widely available due to the fact that many vSwitch implementations have recently added capabilities traditionally found in the physical networking switches. In the case of VN-Tag, many people still consider it to be a proprietary approach with special hardware requirements such as specialized NICs which has limited it's acceptance in the market. In any case, hypervisor vendors are extending advanced networking capabilities in their vSwitch offerings and advanced network virtualization and tunneling standards are emerging including VXLAN and NVGRE which provide new ways of moving data between VMs which we will describe in the next chapter.

VM MIGRATION

In some cases, a running VM must be moved from one host to another due to failure, maintenance, a performance upgrade, or for network optimization. This is known as VM migration, live migration, or also by brand names such as vMotion from VMware. Most customer applications cannot tolerate downtime while this migration happens. The migration is called "seamless" when the downtime is not noticeable by the end user. There are several ways that the network can impact this migration. First of all, moving all of the current state information from one host to another requires low latency networking with lossless operation. In addition, the network addressing and forwarding must be updated quickly and seamlessly once the migration is complete. In this section, we will discuss VM migration and how the data center network may affect this operation.

Memory migration

Before a running VM can be migrated, all of its memory, storage, and state information must be moved to the new VM, which is configured but not yet running on the new host. The new VM must be configured with the same OS and applications that were running on the old VM. Then all of the storage data, local memory data, and CPU state information must be moved over before the new VM can be started and the old VM shut down. Here are some steps required for memory migration.

Move storage

The first step is to duplicate storage from a hard drive or solid-state drive on the old host to a drive on the new host over the network. This is known as storage migration. This needs to be completed quickly so that only a limited number of storage sectors become stale during the move and the running VM can keep a log of storage sectors that need to be refreshed after the move. To complete this quickly, low latency networking is key. The separation of storage and data traffic using techniques like DCB that we discussed in the last chapter will help improve storage migration performance. In some cases, the running VM may be using pooled storage or storage that is not local to the host. This actually simplifies storage migration as the new VM needs to only learn the address information of the storage location within the network. More information on network migration will be provided below.

Move memory

For memory migration, the hypervisor copies pages of memory from local DRAM on the old VM to the new VM over the network. Some pages may become stale during this operation due to changes, so the copy process may be repeated for some pages during the transition. Again, speed is critical to this operation so low latency networking is important and technologies that we described in the last chapter such as remote direct memory access (RDMA) can help improve the performance during this process.

Move CPU state

Once the storage and memory are moved over, the old VM operation can be suspended while the execution state and register state of the CPU is moved over to the new CPU. Next, the new VM is started up. The downtime is an important factor and it's typically not noticeable if it's less than a second. After the new VM is brought to life, there may still be some clean-up work to do in order to make sure memory and storage are consistent between the old VM and the new VM.

Network migration

Another key factor in VM migration is updating the network to reflect the new location of the VM in the data center. In a traditional layer 3 cloud data center, forwarding of frames to the VM relies on forwarding tables located in each switch. For example, when a frame arrives in a given switch, the switch may inspect the IP destination address to determine where to forward the frame. If that IP address has moved to another location in the network, all of these tables need to be updated in the relevant network switches.

Today, many data center networks are set up to tunnel frames from within the vSwitch or top of rack switch at the network edge. We will discuss this in more detail in the next chapter on network virtualization. The point here is that if this type of tunneling is used, only the tables at the network edge need to be updated. In some cases, a given public cloud tenant may use only a few VMs in the data center so only the edge switches associated with these VMs will need to be updated. In any case, these updates need to be well timed with the VM migration and certain frames in flight may be dropped and retransmitted until the new VM is up and running.

Figure 6.10 shows an example of how the data center network may be affected by VM migration. Let's assume a data center tenant is running applications on two VMs that are located on different data center racks and they are accessing storage on a third rack as shown on the left side of Figure 6.10. This is inefficient and consumes

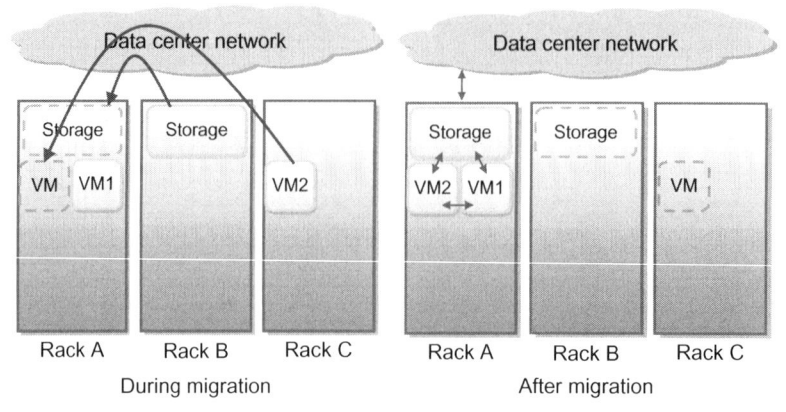

FIGURE 6.10

Network utilization during and after VM migration.

unnecessary bandwidth in the data center network. The ideal situation is shown on the right side of Figure 6.10 where the two VMs reside within the same host server within the rack and the shared storage is also within the same rack. Now the VM to VM traffic runs on the local vSwitch within the server and storage to VM traffic runs on the network within the rack. Only client traffic runs out of the rack, reducing the load within the data center network.

Once the data center server administrator notices this potential optimization, a VM migration process may be initiated as shown in the left side of Figure 6.10. This process of quickly moving storage and server state information across the data center network requires high network bandwidth and may add temporary hot spots to the network. The network administrator must allocate the necessary bandwidth using mechanisms such as data center bridging which we described in the last chapter in order to make sure this migration is completed with minimal downtime. Another factor to consider is that during the migration process, the high-bandwidth NIC operation on the servers hosting these VMs may consume CPU resources, slowing down other applications running on those CPUs.

As you can see from the discussion above, there is critical timing required from both the server administrators and the network administrators to make sure VM migration goes smoothly. A new approach to this is emerging in the industry. It is called software-defined networking and, in conjunction with VM migration software and a central orchestration layer, it can help automate this process and eliminate the human errors that may cause problems. We will provide more information on software-defined networking in Chapter 9.

Vendor solutions

The discussion above was a simplified view of what happens during VM migration. In reality, there are many other moving parts and detailed actions that need to take place. This is where software vendors can really differentiate themselves with VM migration solutions that minimize downtime and maximize ease of use. For example, Microsoft provides live migration capabilities in their Hyper-V product offering which has features to eliminate downtime or the need for shared storage. IBM and Oracle® are two leading server OEMs that also provide tools for live migration. Many of these tools can take advantage of RDMA technology such as iWARP to provide low latency transactions during VM migration in order to minimize downtime.

VMware provides vMotion as well as Storage vMotion as a way to provide live migration between hosts without disruption or the need for shared storage between the hosts. vMotion uses a bit-map to keep track of ongoing memory transactions in order to ensure transaction integrity after the move. Recently, VMware purchased an SDN company called Nicira and now provides their virtualized networking capability under the NSX branded products. It is expected that VMware will expand their vMotion capabilities to include several new network virtualization features that will help automate the VM migration process. We will provide more information on SDN in Chapter 9.

REVIEW

In this chapter, we described VMs and how hypervisors from some leading software vendors establish virtual switches within the host for local connectivity. Next we provided an overview of PCIe and described how SR-IOV can provide an alternative to a vSwitch in the host. We then provided some details on how the physical and virtual switches interact and how the industry is establishing EVB standards in order to unify network functionality down into the servers. Finally, we discussed VM migration and the requirements this poses on the networks. In the next chapter we will complete this story with network virtualization which can allow multiple tenants to have independent virtual networks within a large cloud data center network.

CHAPTER 7

Network Virtualization

Network virtualization is similar to server virtualization but instead of dividing up a physical server among several virtual machines, physical network resources are divided up among multiple virtual networks. This is useful in applications such as multi-tenant data center environments where each tenant can be allocated multiple virtual machines as well as a virtual network connecting these virtual machines. One way to do this is to provide a special label within each frame that identifies the virtual network that it belongs to. Labeling frames and forwarding data based on these labels is sometimes called network tunneling. Tunneling has been used in telecom networks for some time, but these types of tunnels have limitations that make them less useful in virtualized data center networks. This chapter will provide a background on multi-tenant data center requirements along with a background on tunneling techniques used in telecom networks. We will then describe two new industry standards for virtualized data center networks along with example use cases. At the end of the chapter, we will discuss the various tunneling locations that can be used at the edge of the network along with how loads can be distributed through these tunnels.

MULTI-TENANT ENVIRONMENTS

The goal of a multi-tenant public cloud data center is to make the customer experience much the same as if they were using their own private data center. An additional goal of the cloud service provider is to have a flexible allocation of resources so they can quickly adapt to changing needs in order to reduce both capital expense and operating expense. For several years now, virtual machines have been used along with virtual switches to improve server utilization as we described in the last chapter. Attention is now turning to the virtualization of networking resources in a way that maintains a private network experience. Figure 7.1 shows a simplified view of a virtualized cloud data center including the physical servers and physical network components.

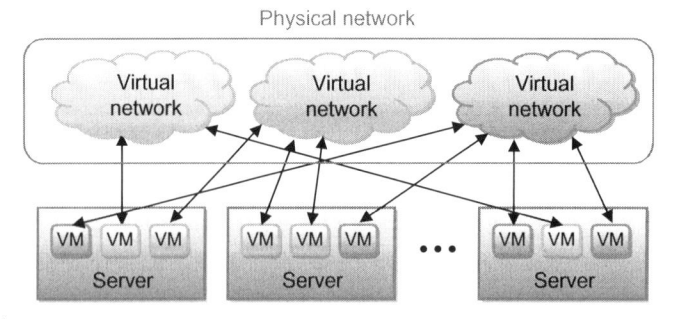

FIGURE 7.1

Logical diagram of multitenant data center.

In this example, the physical resources are divided up among three different tenants. The server administrator allocates virtual machine resources to each tenant that may reside on different servers across the network. The network administrator also allocates virtual network resources to each tenant that interconnects the given tenant's virtual machines. The virtual machine network connections and virtual networks are isolated from each other using special headers that will be described further in this chapter.

Network requirements

Virtualized networking places several requirements on the physical data center network. In many cases, the virtual network is emulating a layer 2 Ethernet network, and all traffic sent or received from the VMs are layer 2 frames that must be tunneled through the data center network without the knowledge of the VMs. To do this, some entity in the server or attached to the server must encapsulate the layer 2 frame with a tunnel header on the transmit side and de-encapsulate the tunnel header on the receive side. The tunnel label, along with other header information, is used to forward the packet through the layer 3 physical network. By using a unique tunnel value (or tag) for each virtual network, separation and security can be maintained between tenants. The number of tunnel values increases dramatically for large data centers which may host thousands of tenants.

One might ask the question, Why not simply use the IEEE virtual local area network (VLAN) tag to identify unique tenants just as it is used to identify different virtual local area networks within a corporate network? The reason for not using this tag is that corporate clients leasing public cloud services want to maintain their own VLAN information to separate different departments just as they would in their own data center. So the tunnel labels cannot share this tag due to conflicts with tenant VLAN information. In addition, the VLAN tag only supports 4096 total values, restricting the maximum number of tenants that a cloud data center can support.

MAC address learning

Because most tunneling endpoints in the network appear as layer 2 ports to the host virtual machines, media access control (MAC) address learning must also be supported through these tunnels. Before we get into the details of these tunneling protocols, let's discuss how traditional layer 2 MAC address learning is accomplished.

When a frame comes into a layer 2 switch, it contains both a destination MAC (DMAC) address and a source MAC (SMAC) address and, in most cases, also includes a VLAN tag. The switch first compares the SMAC/VLAN pair against information in its local MAC address table. If no match is found, it adds this information to the MAC table along with the switch port on which the frame arrived. In other words, the switch has just learned the direction (port number) of a given MAC address based on the received SMAC. Now any frames received on other ports with this MAC address and VLAN will be forwarded to this switch port. This process is called MAC address learning.

But what happens if a frame arrives and has a DMAC/VLAN pair that is not currently in the MAC address table (called an unknown unicast address)? In this case, the frame is flooded (broadcast) to all egress ports except the port it arrived on. In this way, the frame should eventually arrive at its destination through the network. Although flooding ties up network bandwidth, it is considered a rare enough event that it will not impact overall network performance. The assumption is that the device with the unknown destination address will eventually receive the frame and then send a packet back through the network from which its source address can be learned and added to the various switch address tables throughout the network. This can happen fairly rapidly as many network transactions require some sort of response and protocols such as transmission control protocol (TCP) generate acknowledgment packets. These responses and acknowledgments can be sent back to the originator by using the SMAC in the received flooded frames.

TRADITIONAL NETWORK TUNNELING PROTOCOLS

Various tunneling protocols have been used for years in telecom networks. In some cases, this has been driven by the need to isolate different customers as data is transported across Internet service provider networks. In some cases, this has been driven by the need to simplify the forwarding process as data is transported across IP networks. In this section, we will discuss both the Q-in-Q and multiprotocol label switching (MPLS) tunneling protocols that are used in carrier networks. For completeness, we will also describe the VN-Tag that we introduced in the last chapter and how it could be used as a tunnel tag. For each tunneling protocol, we will describe some properties that limit its usefulness for virtualized networking in large cloud data center networks.

Q-in-Q

Within a metropolitan area network, a given service provider may carry traffic for a corporate client that is routed between different facilities in different parts of the city. These corporate clients want their networks to appear as one large corporate network even though they span multiple locations. In order to tunnel client data through their networks, service providers can add a second, outer, VLAN tag as shown in Figure 7.2. This was standardized by the IEEE as 802.1ad and is used in many provider networks today (sometimes called Provider Bridging). Because this is an extension to the 802.1Q standard, it has become more commonly known as Q-in-Q.

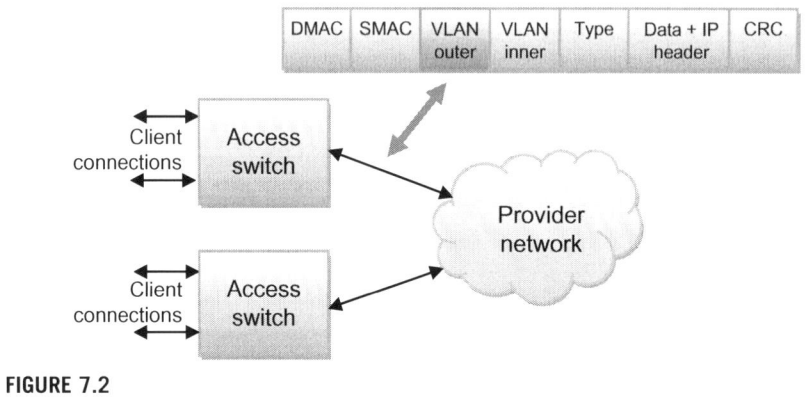

FIGURE 7.2

Q-in-Q forwarding and frame format.

In order to protect the inner VLAN tag for customer use, an outer VLAN tag is added where the 12-bit VLAN ID field is used to identify a given customer. This tag is added and removed by the access switch and is used to isolate traffic in the provider network. All forwarding and learning in the provider network can be done with the MAC addresses and outer VLAN tag. In some cases, the VLAN 3-bit priority field is also used to assign class of service in the provider network. The inner VLAN remains untouched and can be used by the customer for their own purposes. One problem with this technique is that the VLAN ID is limited to 12-bits which can contain only up to 4096 customer IDs. Because of this, it is not very useful for tunneling in large cloud data center networks. In fact, many large telecom service providers use techniques such as MPLS Transport Profile (MPLS-TP) instead; this will be described in more detail below.

MPLS

We briefly described MPLS in Chapter 2 as a way to reduce the frame processing requirements when forwarding frames through a TCP/IP network. In the core of a TCP/IP network, a given switch/router must deal with multiple high bandwidth streams, and matching multiple frame header fields at these high rates can tax the available processing resources. Frame process rates are lower at the network edge where incoming traffic operates at lower overall bandwidth. To take advantage of these conditions, MPLS was first proposed by Ipsilon Networks and then handed over to the Internet Engineering Task Force (IETF) in the late 1990s. Figure 7.3 shows the MPLS label location in the frame header along with the switch and router components in an MPLS network.

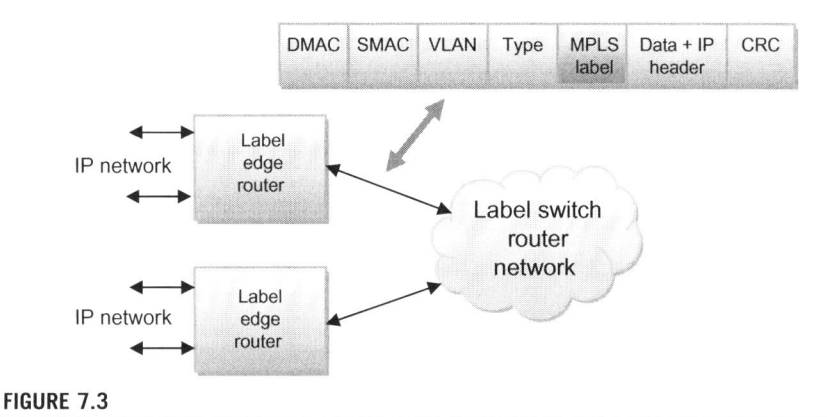

FIGURE 7.3

MPLS forwarding and frame format.

The MPLS label edge router (LER) does the frame match heavy lifting and then adds an MPLS label to the frame as shown in Figure 7.3. This is known as a label 'push' operation. To simplify forwarding in the network core, the MPLS label switch routers (LSRs) only need to examine the MPLS label in order to forward the frame. At the MPLS network egress, the label is removed in what is referred to as a 'pop' operation. It's possible to have a hierarchy of MPLS networks where one network is tunneled through another network by adding additional MPLS labels. In these cases, a LSR may need to examine multiple labels and potentially perform multiple push and pop operations on a given frame,

Since its introduction in the late 1990s, MPLS has found success in many areas. It is used in both IPv4 and IPv6 networks along with Virtual Private Networks (VPNs) and in carrier Ethernet networks using the MPLS-TP. While many people have proposed using MPLS to provide network virtualization and tunneling in the cloud data center, it has not caught on yet and the industry seems to be instead migrating toward protocols such as Virtual Extensible LAN (VXLAN) and Network Virtualization Generic Routing Encapsulation (NVGRE) which are described in the next sections. There are several reasons for this. Some people feel that MPLS is too complex and expensive to implement at the edge of a data center network. In many cases, tunneling occurs within the vSwitch and hypervisor which both consume server processor cycles. Any tunneling protocol implemented here must be as simple as possible in order to minimize CPU overhead. In addition, multicast was not an important requirement for the original MPLS standard. As we will describe in the VXLAN section of this chapter, multicast is an important feature for MAC learning in these layer 2 tunneled virtual networks. In any case, MPLS seems to be as tenacious as Ethernet, and we may find its adoption in some virtual data center networks despite these shortcomings.

VN-Tags

Cisco and other companies originally proposed the VN-Tag protocol which became the basis for the Bridge Port Extension standard called IEEE 802.1qbh as we described in the last chapter. Figure 7.4 shows the VN-Tag location in a standard Ethernet frame and where it is used in the data center network. The VN-Tag contains a virtual interface (VIF) identifier which can be used to forward frames to any type of VIF such as a virtual machine within a server. A single physical network connection to the server using a VN-Tag capable network interface controller (NIC) may, therefore, utilize tags for multiple VIFs.

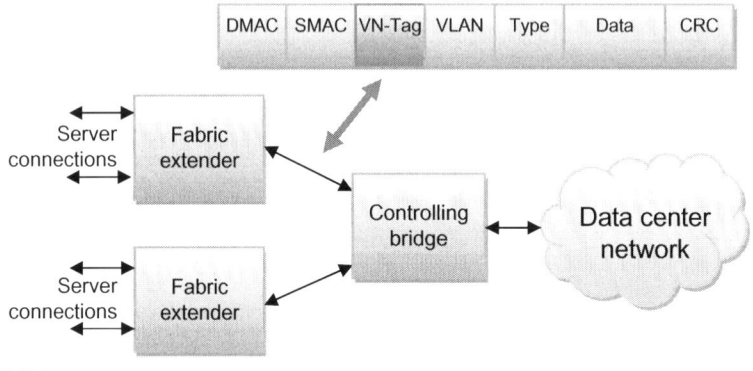

FIGURE 7.4

VN-Tag forwarding and frame format.

Some people may mistake the VN-Tag for a tunneling tag. In a Cisco style network, the controlling bridge at the end of a row is the master of the fabric extenders that sit within the server racks. The controlling bridge makes all of the VIF assignments and the NIC can use these tags to pass the frames to the correct VMs. Because VN-tagging forms a frame that is not recognized by all different types of networking equipment, it is used locally within the controlling bridge domain and may need to be encapsulated further to pass it on through the data center network. Although these VN-tags provide virtual networking features, they are used to identify VMs instead of tenants. Because of this and other reasons, Cisco was a main contributor in the development of the VXLAN standard which will be described in the next section.

VXLAN

The VXLAN specification was originally proposed by Cisco and VMware and now has support from several other leading companies. It's a technique for tunneling virtual layer 2 networks through layer 3 physical networks in large data centers that need to support multiple tenants. In order to tunnel these packets, they are encapsulated using special VXLAN tags. Keep in mind that MPLS is a layer 3 protocol and VXLAN frames may be tunneled through a larger MPLS data center network. The IETF formed a special working group that is finalizing this standard. In this section, we will provide more information on this standard including the frame format and how VXLAN encapsulated frames are forwarding through the network. In the next section, we will discuss a competing standard called NVGRE. As of this writing, both the VXLAN and NVGRE specifications are in draft form in the IETF, and the NVGRE specification is less mature. In this chapter, we will provide information as it is available today. A third tunneling protocol called stateless transport tunneling (STT) has been proposed by Nicira who was recently acquired by VMware. We will not cover STT in this chapter and instead focus on the two main protocols backed by major OEMs.

Frame format

Servers within a cloud data center typically present TCP/IP frames, which are encapsulated with layer 2 header information, to the attached network. In many cases, this header also contains a VLAN tag that the tenant may be using to identify different departments within its organization. From the server's or VM's point of view, it is sending and receiving these types of frames through an attached layer 2 network. The trick here is how to support multiple tenants like this in a large L3 data center network. This is where tunneling protocols like VXLAN come into play.

The VXLAN protocol provides these features by encapsulating these frames with a VXLAN tag along with a User Datagram Protocol (UDP) header as shown in Figure 7.5. Here, the original frame containing MAC addresses and a VLAN tag are encapsulated using a VXLAN header and a UDP header. This entire combination is then routed through the layer 3 network using IP addresses. By using unique VXLAN tags for each tenant, each tenant can use its own pool of MAC addresses while the VXLAN protocol provides isolation between these different virtual layer 2 network domains.

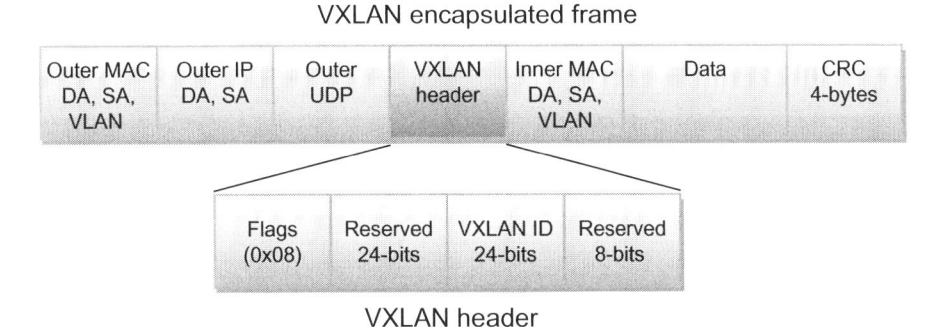

FIGURE 7.5

VXLAN frame format.

UDP is a member of the set of protocols used in the Internet that include TCP. Unlike TCP, which requires acknowledgment frames and can provide error correction, UDP is considered a best-effort protocol with no guarantee of delivery. TCP was designed for the larger internet where connections may be disrupted while packets are being transmitted across long distance telecommunication networks. Within the data center, connections are in a controlled environment, meaning that the likelihood of a dropped packet is much lower. In addition, the original inner TCP/IP header (part of "Data" in Figure 7.5) can provide reliable transmission through error detection and retransmission if needed. Because of this, it doesn't make sense to burden the VXLAN frame with the extra reliability requirements and overhead that is used in TCP. The UDP protocol uses the concept of port numbers. For the VXLAN frame, the source port is provided by the source tunnel endpoint and the destination port is set to a well-known UDP port number.

The point in the network where frame encapsulation and de-encapsulation occurs is known as the VXLAN Tunnel End Point (VTEP). The outer IP addresses are used to forward data through the data center layer 3 network between these VTEPs. These endpoints can be inside the hypervisor, the NIC, or a physical switch, which we will discuss later in this chapter. The VXLAN Network ID (VNI) is a 24-bit value that is inserted in the VXLAN header and can identify up to 16 million unique virtual networks. We will next provide more information on the encapsulation and de-encapsulation process performed by the VTEP.

VTEP encapsulation

The VXLAN Tunnel End Point (VTEP) is the VXLAN encapsulation point and is connected to a traffic source which may be a stand-alone server or virtual machine. For example, the VTEP could be part of the hypervisor in a server platform, part of the network interface device in the server, or part of the attached top of rack (ToR) switch. Figure 7.6 will be used as an example of how a layer 2 unicast frame is encapsulated when sending it from VM2 to VM3 through a VXLAN tunnel.

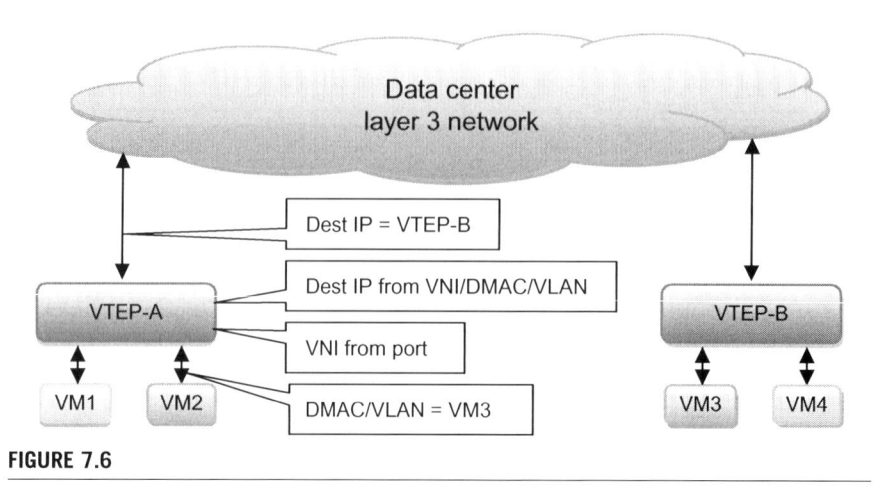

FIGURE 7.6

VTEP encapsulation example.

At the ingress to the network, VM2 sends a frame that may contain a TCP/IP address along with a layer 2 header containing a SMAC address, a DMAC address, and a VLAN tag. The DMAC address is the layer 2 address of VM3 which is part of the same tenant VLAN as VM2. As far as VM2 in concerned, VM3 is part of its local layer 2 network, when in fact it could be in another VM on the other side of the data center.

When the frame is delivered to VTEP-A, the VNI is determined based on information such as which virtual machine the data is coming from. It is assumed that each VM in the network will be assigned to a single VNI and that a given VNI will have all of the tenant's virtual machines associated with it. Once the VNI has been identified, VTEP-A will also examine the inner DMAC/VLAN address and use this along with the VNI to determine that the destination is VTEP-B. The frame is then encapsulated with the VXLAN header containing the VNI, the UDP header, the destination IP address of VTEP-B, and the source IP address of VTEP-A.

If the inner DMAC is an unknown address within this VNI, a MAC address learning process is used similar to what is used within a layer 2 network. To do this, IP multicast addresses are used. Every VTEP associated with a given VNI will join the same IP multicast group. Unknown addresses are flooded to all other associated VTEPs using this multicast IP address in the outer IP destination address field. When a response is received from a destination VTEP, the SMAC from this response frame is used to update the VTEP-A forwarding table, just as it is done in a L2 network. In this way, the environment that the VM is exposed to behaves just like a layer 2 network including address learning.

VTEP de-encapsulation

When the frame arrives at the destination VM, it should appear that the frame arrived from a standard layer 2 network. As shown in Figure 7.7, when the frame arrives at VTEP-B it contains the source IP address from VTEP-A. The correct

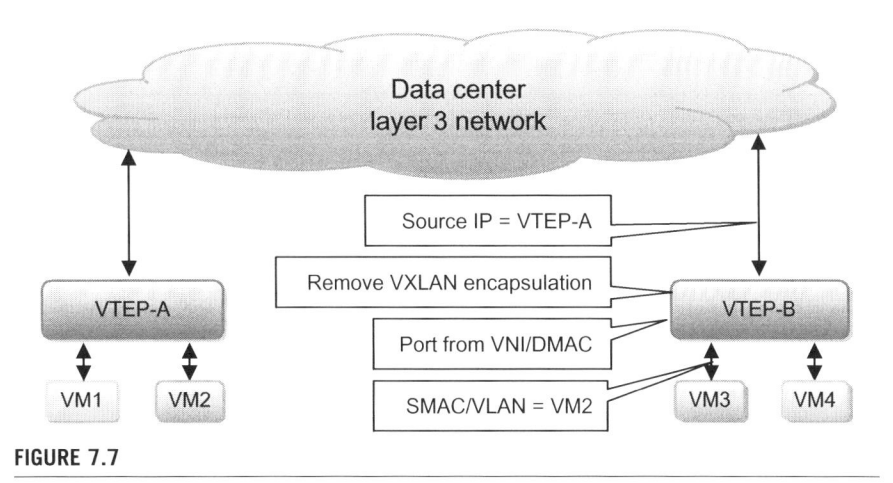

FIGURE 7.7

VTEP de-encapsulation example.

destination VM (VM3 in this example) is determined by examining the VNI and the inner DMAC address. The DMAC is required because there could be two VMs for a given tenant associated with a VTEP endpoint. The VXLAN header, UDP header, and outer IP and L2 fields are then removed from the frame before presenting it to the VM.

For layer 2 MAC address learning, the egress VTEP needs to perform several tasks. When a frame is received, VTEP-B will learn the inner MAC source address and associated source IP address so that it doesn't need to flood response packets later on. In order to receive flooded frames from other VTEPs that have unknown addresses, VTEP-B needs to make sure it has joined the IP multicast group associated with a given VNI. Because a given VTEP may be supporting multiple VMs, each associated with different VNIs, it may need to join several IP multicast groups.

NVGRE

The NVGRE protocol is very similar to VXLAN and was created to solve a similar set of problems that were described in the last section. It is interesting that our industry continues to come up with two competing solutions to the same problem. For example, TRILL versus SPB and iWarp versus RoCE that were described in Chapter 5. Or VEPA versus VN-Tag that was described in Chapter 6. In any case, NVGRE is another IETF standard that is being backed by Microsoft, Intel, HP, and Dell. In this section, we will provide information on the parent Generic Routing Encapsulation (GRE) standard along with an overview of the NVGRE frame format. We will also provide some examples of how frames are tunneled through the network while highlighting the differences between VXLAN and NVGRE. A draft was submitted to the IETF a few weeks before this writing that is a proposal for a tunneling protocol that is a superset of VXLAN and NVGRE called Generic Network Virtualization Encapsulation (GENEVE). It will be interesting to see how this progresses over the next few years.

Generic routing encapsulation

GRE was developed by Cisco as a way to encapsulate a wide variety of different network layer protocols within a generic header that can provide point-to-point links over an IP network. An example application is the secure VPN links that you may use when working at remote locations from your office. When developing a new standard to tunnel layer 2 frames through layer 3 data center networks, Microsoft and others decided to reuse this existing method instead of creating a new header as was done with the VXLAN standard. Although this works well for its intended purpose, there are some limitations which will be described below.

Frame format

The NVGRE frame format shown in Figure 7.8 is very similar to the VXLAN frame format that we described in the last section. Instead of using a UDP header and a VXLAN header, only a GRE header is used, reducing the frame size by a few bytes. The GRE header contains the unique protocol ID (0x6558) for NVGRE frames as well as a 24-bit virtual segment identifier (VSID), that, like VXLAN, can support up to 16M unique tenant subnets. Another difference is that the inner layer 2 header does not contain a VLAN tag, and if one exists, it is removed before the frame is encapsulated. So in this case, the VSID can also be used to segregate multiple virtual network segments for a given tenant.

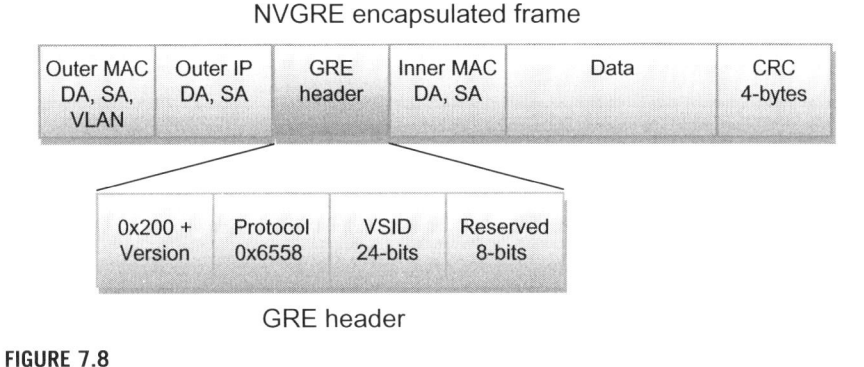

FIGURE 7.8

NVGRE frame format.

NVE encapsulation

The Network Virtual Endpoint (NVE) defined in the NVGRE specification is very similar to the VTEP defined in VXLAN. It is part of the Hyper-V hypervisor from Microsoft and NVGRE is sometimes referred to as Hyper-V virtual switching. Figure 7.9 shows how a layer 2 frame generated from a VM is encapsulated and tunneled through a NVGRE virtual network. In this example, a frame from VM2 has a DMAC/VLAN with the destination address of VM3. As with VXLAN, the VM2 has no idea that the frame is being tunneled, and it thinks that VM3 is attached to its local layer 2 network. Because the NVGRE requires that the NVE remove the inner VLAN tag, the NVE uses the inner VLAN ID plus knowledge of which virtual network the tenant VM belongs to in order to assign a unique VSID. In order to support tenants that want to use multiple VLANs, multiple VSIDs can be supported for a given tenant.

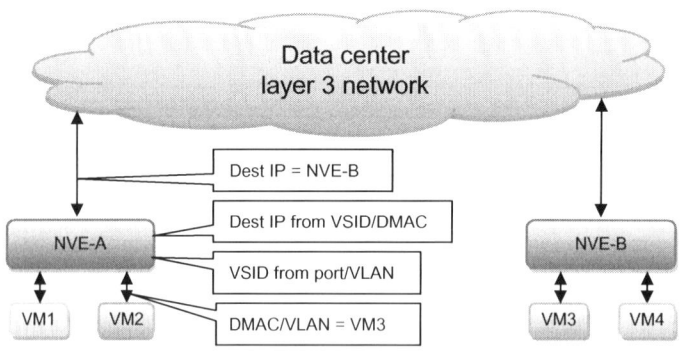

FIGURE 7.9

NVE encapsulation example.

Once the VSID is identified, this plus the inner DMAC address can be used to identify the destination IP address of the NVE associated with VM3. The frame is then encapsulated with a GRE header and the appropriate L2/L3 routing headers in order to tunnel the frame between NVEs. The current version of the NVGRE specification does not define how unicast or multicast address information is disseminated to the NVEs. The specification currently states: *Address acquisition is beyond the scope of this document and can be obtained statically, dynamically, or using stateless address auto-configuration.* This is different from the VXLAN specification that defines IP multicast as the flooding method for MAC address learning, but it doesn't preclude NVGRE from using a similar technique.

NVE de-encapsulation

When a tunneled frame arrives at its destination across the IP network, it is de-encapsulated by another NVE. In the example shown in Figure 7.10, this frame will arrive at NVE-B containing the source address of NVE-A. At this point, NVE-B will

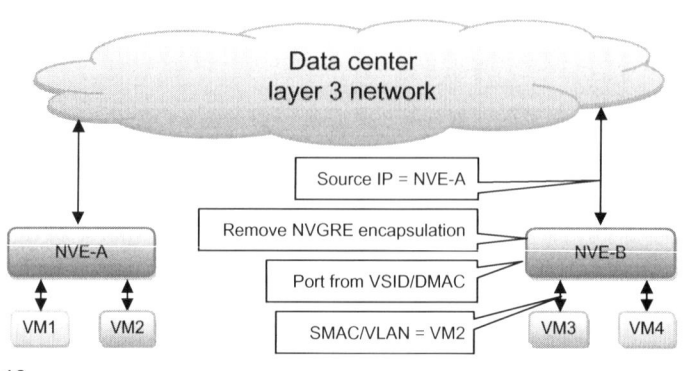

FIGURE 7.10

NVE de-encapsulation example.

use the VSID and DMAC information to determine the destination VM. The DMAC is required because there could be two VMs for a given tenant associated with a NVE. The GRE header along with the outer IP header and outer L2 header are then removed before presenting the original layer 2 frame to VM3.

Although the NVGRE spec requires that the VLAN tag be removed from the original frame, it does not specify how the tenant VLAN information can be tunneled through the layer 3 network. It is assumed that the VSID assigned to a particular tenant VLAN at the tunnel ingress can be used to recreate the VLAN ID and the tunnel egress. It does not suggest how the VLAN priority field is passed through. Maybe this will be covered in a later version of the specification.

TUNNEL LOCATIONS

In the examples above, we made the assumption that the VTEP or NVE tunnel endpoints existed next to the virtual machines in the hypervisor/vSwitch. These are the most common proposals for these new tunneling protocols and it makes sense given that one of the lead authors of the VXLAN spec is VMware and one of the lead authors of the NVGRE spec is Microsoft. But network virtualization tunneling endpoints can also exist at other locations near the edge of the network as shown in Figure 7.11. In this section we will describe three tunneling endpoint locations including the vSwitch, the network interface card, and the top of rack switch.

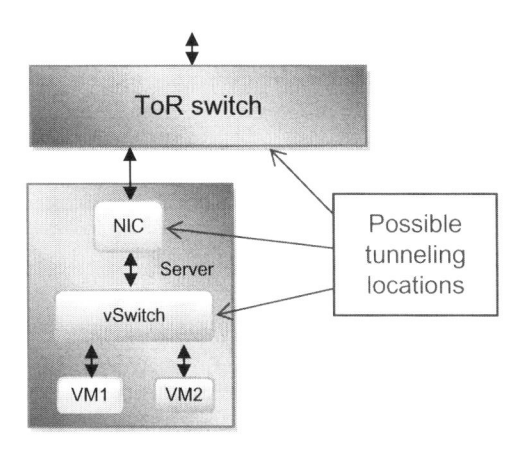

FIGURE 7.11

Tunneling locations in the network edge.

vSwitch

It makes sense to move the tunnel endpoints as close as possible to the virtual machines as this makes tenant identification easier. Today, VXLAN encapsulation and de-encapsulations functions are available in VMware's vSphere hypervisor and NSX software-defined networking products. In addition, Microsoft offers NVGRE encapsulation and de-encapsulation functions in Windows Server 2012. Keep in mind that this type of tunneling consumes CPU resources that must be taken into account when implementing these services.

Another factor that must be considered is the effect tunneling may have on the TCP/IP offload resources in the attached NIC. Today, many NICs have offload features such as large segment offload and TCP checksum offloads that are designed to operate with non-encapsulated packets. For example, large segment offload requires that each new segment generated by the NIC get the same header information. If a NIC is not designed to comprehend the VXLAN or NVGRE headers, it won't know how to replicate them properly. To allow tunneling to work in the hypervisor, these features may need to be turned off, further taxing the CPU resources. Some vendors such as Intel have added large segment offload hardware assist for these tunneling protocols, both improving performance and reducing the CPU workload. There are also cases where technologies like SR-IOV are used to bypass the hypervisor. In these cases, tunneling must be performed in the NIC or ToR switch.

Network interface card

As mentioned above, advanced NIC features such as TCP offloads and SR-IOV can interfere with the ability to provide VXLAN or NVGRE tunneling in the hypervisor. To help this situation, the NIC may provide advanced features that allow them to maintain offload capabilities while at the same time support VXLAN and/or NVGRE tunneling. One example of this is large segment offloads. Many Ethernet networks do not support jumbo frames and have a maximum frame size of around 1500 bytes. If an application wants to send larger chunks of data (for example a video stream), the TCP/IP layer must first divide it up into smaller 1500B frames. This can tax CPU resources and is typically offloaded to the NIC.

The problem is that most NICs cannot deal with a tunnel header added by the hypervisor. They are designed to simply replicate the layer 2 header on each frame segment they create. To solve this problem, NIC vendors have upgraded their large segment offload hardware to replicate the tunnel header along with the layer 2 header so that all segments of a large data flow are tunneled properly through the network. An alternative solution would be to add encapsulation and de-encapsulation resources after the TCP/IP offload functions in the NIC. In addition, if the frame encapsulation and de-encapsulation resources are after the SR-IOV block, frames could be tunneled before reaching the network. But today, few NICs offer this feature, so any data flows that bypass the hypervisor by using SR-IOV must be passed on to the top of rack switch before tunneling into the network.

Top of rack switch

When no hypervisor is used or the hypervisor is bypassed, and the NIC cannot perform tunneling after the SR-IOV block, the ToR switch can act as the tunneling endpoint. Unlike the hypervisor that knows the source VM, in order for the switch to identify the proper VNI or VSID for the tunnel, the switch must use information from the received frame such as the MAC source address from the inner header in order to identify the associated VM. One advantage of using the ToR switch for tunnel endpoints is that traffic intended for other servers within the same rack do not need to be tunneled and can be simply forwarded using layer 2 information, reducing the table size requirements when a large number of VMs for one tenant are in the same rack.

LOAD BALANCING

In a previous chapter, we mentioned that Ethernet uses the Spanning Tree Protocol in order to avoid loops in the layer 2 network. This can leave many unused links in the network, wasting this potential bandwidth. An advantage of using virtual networks is that tunnels use layer 3 forwarding mechanisms that do not have this restriction. In this section, we will describe the technique of using hash-based algorithms for tunnel selection and also a common load distribution mechanism, called equal cost multipath routing (ECMP), used in IP networks. In addition, we will describe how VXLAN and NVGRE can take advantage of these mechanisms along with any limitations they impose.

Hash-based algorithms

Hash algorithms have been around for decades and are used for applications such as table lookups. For example, you can use a person's name and address as a hash key used by a hash algorithm. The output of the hash algorithm will be a pointer into a table where the person's information will be stored. Later, when you want to retrieve a given persons information, you don't need to scan the entire table, but simply use this same hash key and algorithm to obtain a pointer to the person's information in the table. This can greatly simplify the lookup process.

In a switch or router, a similar technique can be used to select a path for a packet to take based on information in the packet header as shown in Figure 7.12. Let's assume that we have a simple switch with one input and four outputs as shown in the figure. For each frame coming into the switch, a header field or multiple header fields can be chosen to form a hash key. Instead of pointing to an entry in a table, the hash algorithm is used to select one of four possible output ports. If a proper hash algorithm is chosen, and frames arrive with fairly random header fields, traffic will be uniformly distributed across the output ports. Another nice feature is that frames belonging to the same flow (for example the same video stream) will always be hashed to the same output, maintaining in-order delivery. The key in networking applications is to find a hash algorithm that provides uniform distribution for common traffic patterns found in the network. As traffic patterns change over time, the load distribution may become less uniform causing congestion points in the network.

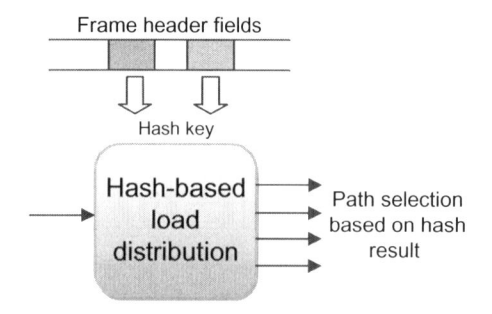

FIGURE 7.12

Load distribution using hashing.

Equal cost multipath routing

ECMP routing is a technique used in IP networks to increase the number of paths and overall bandwidth through the network. In multitenant environments where virtual networks are used, techniques like ECMP can be used to improve tunnel bandwidth and throughput. An example ECMP distribution is shown in Figure 7.13 where the source VTEP or NVE adds the tunneling tag which has information used to help distribute the tunnel traffic across multiple paths in the IP network. What is not shown in Figure 7.13 is that each IP router may further distribute the traffic across additional paths by using the tunneling tag as part of a hash key.

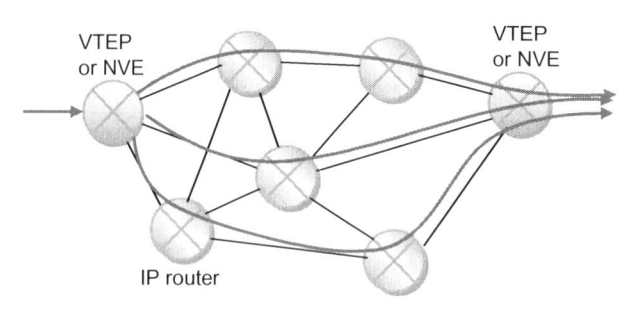

FIGURE 7.13

Equal cost multipath routing from a VTEP or NVE.

When using VXLAN tunneling, the VTEP can use the inner MAC header fields to form a hash key which the hash algorithm then uses to select one of several ECMP paths through the IP network. Typically, the hash key will be used as a random UDP source port number, which is inserted into the frame by the VTEP encapsulation function. Switches and routers in the data center network are designed to use various header fields such as the UDP source port number to form ECMP hash keys. Therefore, the UDP source port field can be used by these switches and routers to select ECMP paths through the network.

As we mentioned earlier, the NVGRE spec is less mature than the VXLAN spec and one issue that has been identified by some people in the industry is that NVGRE does not have a TCP or UDP header. This means that traditional IP routers do not have this information for their ECMP hash key. Some newer IP routers can use the GRE header as a source for their hash key allowing the ability to improve ECMP hashing across the network. The NVGRE draft specification recommends using the full 32-bit GRE field for ECMP hashing. One way to do this is to have the ingress NVE place a random 8-bit value in the reserved field next to the 24-bit VSID field to improve distribution.

REVIEW

In this chapter, we described multitenant cloud data centers and how they can take advantage of virtualized networks. We described traditional methods of tunneling data through carrier networks and challenges that they present in virtualized data center networks. Next, we provided some details behind VXLAN and NVGRE, the two most popular emerging standards for network virtualization in multitenant data centers. In addition, we provided an overview of tunneling locations and also provided details on how traffic distribution can be accomplished using these tunneling protocols. In the next chapter we will provide information on storage networks and how storage traffic is forwarded in cloud data center networks.

CHAPTER 8

Storage Networks

In the last two chapters, we described how virtual machines are used within servers and how they can be interconnected using virtual networks. But there is more to the story. As most computer users knows, storage components such as memory and disk drives are an important elements in any computing environment and this is also true for cloud data centers. The special requirements for connecting servers to storage have evolved as data centers have grown and changed. Because of this, new storage networking standards have been developed to meet these needs.

This chapter will provide insight into how storage systems are implemented in large cloud data centers and how storage data is transported throughout the data center network. We will start by providing a brief background on storage and storage networks followed by a description of several advanced storage technologies. Next, we will provide an overview of storage communication protocols and how traditional data center networks can transport storage and other data traffic using converged networking. Software-defined storage (SDS) will be introduced later in this chapter, and then we will tie all of this together and describe some examples of how storage networking is implemented in large cloud data centers.

STORAGE BACKGROUND

Since the days of the earliest mainframe computers, the requirement to store data has spawned the development of technologies such as magnetic core memory, bubble memory, random access memory (RAM), dynamic random access memory (DRAM), magnetic disk drives, flash memory, and solid-state disk drives. In this section, we will review some of the latest data storage technologies used in cloud data centers. First, we will describe the memory and storage hierarchy used in many data centers today. We will then describe two key storage technologies found in data centers; hard disk drives (HDDs) and solid-state storage. Finally, we will provide information on several methods traditionally used to connect storage to servers including direct attached storage (DAS), storage area networks (SANs), and network attached storage (NAS). Later in this chapter, we will describe how these technologies and methods can be used in real data center networks.

139

Storage hierarchy

The general rule for data storage in computer systems is that faster, smaller memory is closer to the CPU and larger, slower memory is farther from the CPU as shown in Figure 8.1. Data storage that loses information when the power is turned off, such as DRAM, is generally referred to as "Memory." Data storage such as disk drives that retain data when power is turned off is generally referred to as "Storage."

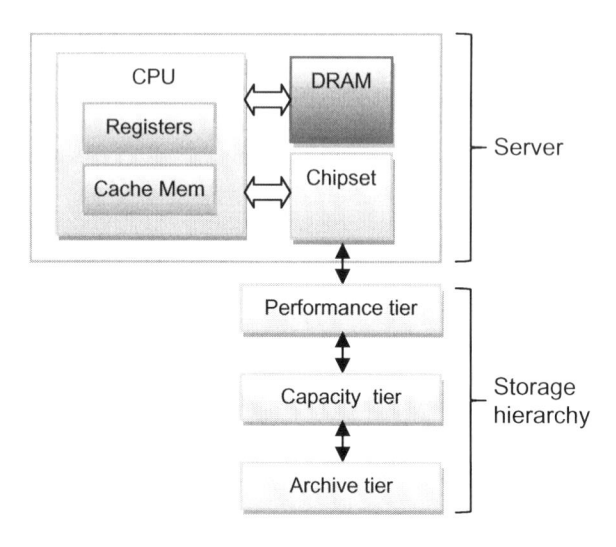

FIGURE 8.1

Data center memory components.

As shown in figure 8.1, the CPU contains registers that are used to store temporary variables and can be accessed within one or two CPU clock cycles. This contains the least amount of memory in the system. Most server CPUs also contain multiple levels of cache memory. These hold most recently used data with the assumption that it may be needed again in the near future. If the data needed by the CPU is in the cache (a cache hit), this speeds up performance because it provides faster access than reading data from external DRAM. If the needed data is not in cache memory (a cache miss), data is pulled from DRAM and also placed in the cache memory. Modern processors may have multiple levels of on-board cache memory with different capacity and performance levels. For example, a first level cache may be dedicated to each processor core while a larger, second level cache may be shared among multiple processor cores.

The CPU uses a parallel bus connection to external DRAM which is the next level in the memory hierarchy. This memory can hold 1000 times more data than what can be integrated within the CPU chip, but has memory access times that can be 100 times longer than the cache memory within the CPU. In some cases, flash memory may also be used on the server motherboard, which retains data when power is removed. The trade-off is that flash memory write cycles are about 100 times longer than DRAM write cycles and flash memory has a limit on the number of times it can be written. More information on flash memory will be provided later in this chapter.

Server CPUs are connected to bridge chips (sometimes called chipsets or hubs) that provide various types of IO expansion ports. An important connection is to external storage devices such as HDDs and solid-state drives. Many external storage systems provide a hierarchy of capacity versus performance. The first tier is the performance tier where most recently used data is stored; it uses faster, more expensive storage technology such as solid-state drives. The next tier is the capacity tier which uses larger storage capacity at lower cost per bit at the sacrifice of lower performance than the performance tier. Data such as old Facebook photos that have not been accessed for a while may be moved to the archive tier containing high-density low-cost storage technology with longer access or retrieval times. Sometimes, the archive tier is referred to as cold storage due to its infrequent access.

Hard disk drives

Spinning magnetic disks known as hard disk drives have been used for decades as non-volatile storage for computer systems. They were first introduced by IBM in 1956 and, by the early 1980s, these drives were the size of small washing machines and could hold around 64 megabytes of data. Today, drives small enough to fit into laptops can hold multiple terabytes (>1,000,000 megabytes) of data. Magnetic tape has also been used for storage, but due to slow access times has been relegated to the archive tier. More recently, Blu-ray disc capacities have increased to the point that they may also be used for data archiving.

Data center applications have driven the need for special disk drive features that may not be found on commercial HDDs for the PC or laptop. A hard disk usually contains multiple rotating platters and an actuator arm with a read/write head that may remind some people of a miniature record turntable. Although the disks are random access, there is a seek time that depends on the rotational speed of the disk along with the reaction time of the actuator arm and the position of the data on the disk relative to the arm. The individual tracks, like the grooves on a record, are where the data is stored using what is effectively tiny polarized magnets. Based on this technology, disk drive manufacturers can make trade-offs between density, performance, and reliability. Obviously, tightly packed tracks lead to higher data density. But the high rotational speeds and actuator arm movements required for high-performance disk drives also require larger track spacing in order to minimize read and write errors. In addition, dozens of drives may be packed together in a storage array chassis, leading to vibrational transfer that also may require larger track spacing for reliable operation. Because of these reasons, HDDs in personal computers may have higher storage density and/or lower cost than HDDs designed for data center applications, but they do not have the reliability and performance needed for these applications. For some high-performance applications, the HDDs may even be "short stroked," which means only the faster access outer sectors of the drive are used.

Flash storage

Flash memory was first developed by Toshiba in the early 1980s and is used today in everything from smart phones to thumb drives to solid-state drives. In traditional semiconductor memory, transistors act like switches with the gate of the transistor turning the switch on or off depending on the voltage applied. Flash memory uses a floating gate that can be programmed to store charge (voltage) that determines if the transistor is on or off as shown in Figure 8.2. Think of this charge like a tiny battery that can maintain this voltage almost indefinitely, even if the chip power is turned off.

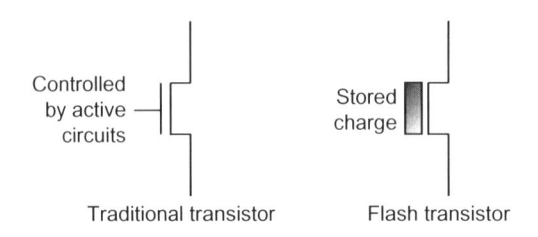

FIGURE 8.2

Standard transistor versus flash memory transistor.

Even though this is a widely used technology, it does have some limitations which affect its performance and longevity in data center storage applications. When writing to flash memory, a single page of memory must first be erased. To write one byte, the entire page must first be moved to RAM where the byte is changed. Then the entire page of flash memory is erased and then rewritten from RAM. This can make the write performance significantly slower than the read performance. This is not an issue when an application needs fast access to semi-static data but can slow down the server performance in applications that are constantly writing new data. Think of your iTunes library on your smart phone where you write a song once to flash memory and then play it back hundreds of times. Even with this limitation, flash memory can achieve higher performance than HDDs. One way to improve performance in server environments is to use a hybrid flash with a battery backup DRAM cache. The server writes at a higher speed to the DRAM cache which then moves this data into flash as a background task when a larger number of bytes can be written simultaneously.

Another issue for flash memory is write endurance which limits the number of times an application can write to a given memory location before those particular transistors can no longer retain data reliably. For flash technology used in the data center, this limit may be somewhere over 100,000 writes. This is mitigated somewhat by the fact that many applications may write data once and then read it multiple times. To improve write endurance, wear leveling algorithms have been incorporated into flash memory controller chips that effectively spread these writes across many different locations, spreading the wear as evenly as possible across the entire flash memory. This can significantly improve the lifetime of flash memory modules allowing them to be used in data center applications. We will next talk about several types of storage architectures.

Direct attached storage

When you are using a personal computer or a laptop, you are using DAS. Generally, this means a disk drive that is directly connected to a CPU subsystem and not shared with any other computers. In the data center, applications such as web hosting use DAS where customers want their own private storage devices connected to their dedicated server. A more common application for DAS in data centers is storage used for booting the operating systems and/or hypervisors although these can also be booted from flash memory on the server motherboard. The problem with DAS is that storage cannot be shared between applications and it creates islands of data in the network.

There are several interface standards that are commonly used for DAS. The standard originally developed to connect hard drives in the IBM PC was called Parallel AT Attachment (PATA). This connects the disk drive to the CPU using the parallel gray ribbon cable that you may have seen if you ever looked inside your older PC. Today, this has been replaced by Serial ATA (SATA), which is the most common DAS standard in the industry due to its wide use in modern PCs and laptops. Another key standard for connecting disk drives to CPUs is called Small Computer System Interface (SCSI) which was introduced in the early 1980s and was used in systems such as workstations and servers. It is considered a higher performance and more reliable interface than ATA, but more complex and costly. It has evolved in recent years into the iSCSI standard for storage transactions across TCP/IP networks and Serial Attached SCSI (SAS) which is commonly used within storage arrays and servers. We will provide more information on the SATA, iSCSI, and SAS standards later in this chapter.

Storage area networks

SANs are specialized networks used in the data center that are dedicated to storage traffic. The most popular SAN standard today is Fibre Channel (FC) which we will describe in more detail later in this chapter. FC requires the use of host bus adapters (HBAs) that are similar to NICs and are resident on the server, along with storage arrays that have FC interfaces. One or more FC switches are used to interconnect multiple servers to multiple storage arrays as shown in Figure 8.3.

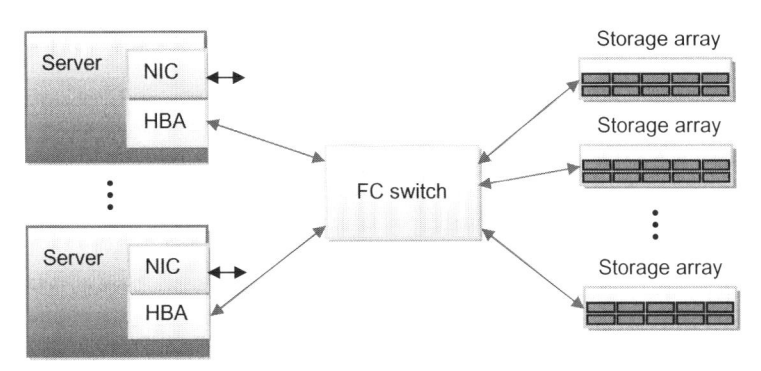

FIGURE 8.3

Simple Fibre Channel storage area network.

CHAPTER 8 Storage Networks

Storage arrays are common in data centers and consist of multiple disk drives within a single chassis. These storage arrays could be built using either SATA or SAS drives connected to a FC interface through a switch on a storage controller board. We will provide more information on this later in the chapter. SAN storage is sometimes called block storage because the server applications deal with storage at the block level, which is part of a larger file or database.

Storage network administrators are extremely concerned about reliability and security. By having a dedicated SAN, they can manage it independently from the rest of the data center and data is physically isolated from other networks for higher levels of security. They also require reliable equipment that has gone through extensive certification testing. Because certification testing is a complex and expensive process, FC networking gear is only supplied by a few lead vendors and less competition leads to more costly solutions. But storage network administrators are willing to accept these trade-offs in order to have a reliable, dedicated network with very high and consistent performance, both for bandwidth and latency.

Network attached storage

NAS has been traditionally used by small to medium businesses within their enterprise networks. This is sometimes called file storage as the applications deal with storage at the file or directory level instead of at the block level, which is referred to as block storage in storage area networks. Figure 8.4 shows how NAS arrays could be connected to an enterprise Ethernet LAN to provide storage to various clients.

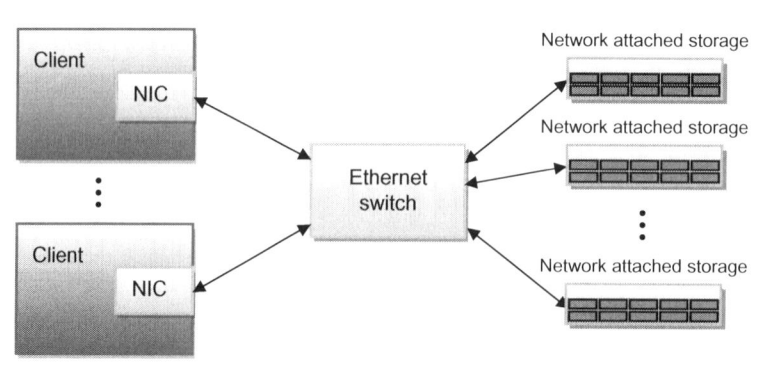

FIGURE 8.4

Network attached storage example.

These storage arrays are similar to the SAN storage arrays described above but have additional processing resources to convert file level data into block level data for storage on the individual disk drives. Later in this chapter, we will look inside a storage array and provide more details on both SAN and NAS applications.

NAS is intended to be a low-cost way to add shared storage for multiple users in the network, but it is not as reliable or secure as a dedicated SAN, and performance is lower due to the fact that storage data is shared with other data on the same Ethernet network. This convergence of storage and data on a single network has been addressed in layer 3 TCP/IP networks using the iSCSI protocol and in layer 2 Ethernet networks through Fibre Channel over Ethernet (FCoE) which was standardized in 2010. Both will be discussed later in this chapter.

ADVANCED STORAGE TECHNOLOGIES

Over the last several years, the amount of storage data from a variety of sources has exploded and data access patterns have changed as client devices have become more mobile. This has generated a significant level of innovation in storage technology with the goal of optimizing performance while minimizing costs. Many of these new storage technologies have an impact on cloud data center networks. In this section, we will provide an overview of some of these innovations and how they may affect networking in the data center.

Object storage and metadata

As we mentioned above, data has traditionally been stored using a file hierarchy in NAS systems or as data blocks aligned to disk partitions in SANs. Unfortunately, finding a particular piece of data in these storage systems can be difficult and can take some time. For example, think of the time you may take to locate a specific photograph from the file system within your laptop. Over the last 15 years or so, this has spawned a large amount of venture capital spending in a new technology called object-based storage.

This is a new storage architecture that treats data like an object instead of a file or a block. Software engineers may be familiar with object oriented programming in which a section of code can be treated as an object and have attributes associated with it. In object-based storage, a block of data is treated as an object which has metadata associated with it. The metadata can be used as a unique identifier across the storage system that can be used to quickly recover the data within the object. Most cloud data centers employ object-based storage including many of the largest cloud service providers. In cloud data center networks, object-based storage can reduce the number of storage transactions compared to traditional block-based storage because data can be more easily located for some applications.

Data protection and recovery

A timed honored way to detect data corruption is to add additional overhead bits as is done with parity protection. When using parity, a single bit added to a data word can be used to tell if any other bit in the word has become corrupt. But it cannot tell which bit has become corrupt or if 2 bits are corrupt. To improve this, most memory controllers within server class CPUs employ Error Correcting Code technology. This uses multiple extra bits to not only detect one or two corrupt bits, but also correct single bit errors. This has become more important as wafer processing dimensions have shrunk to the point where memory cells are more susceptible to single bit errors due to alpha particles. Storage systems have also come up with ways to detect and correct data errors; these are described below.

Redundant array of independent disks

For many years storage systems have used a technology called redundant array of independent (or inexpensive) disks (RAID) for data protection and recovery. In a RAID system, redundant data is generated and distributed along with the original data across multiple disk drives. This allows data recovery in the case of disk failure. It can also improve performance by spreading out the reading and writing of data across multiple disk drives in parallel (called striping). In many cases, a storage appliance, also known as a storage array, will contain multiple disk drives along with a RAID controller as shown in Figure 8.5.

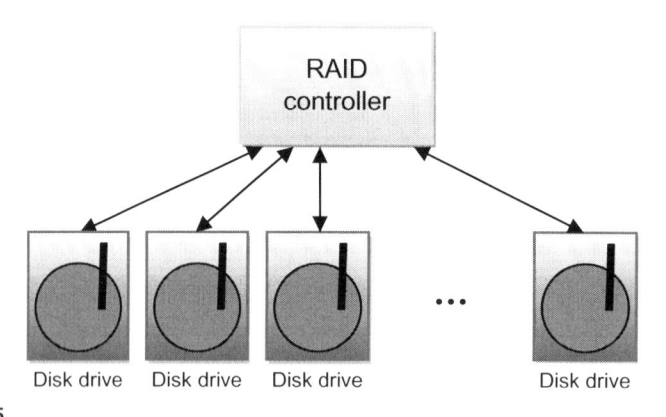

FIGURE 8.5

Storage array using a RAID controller.

The RAID controller is responsible for generating the redundant data and spreading it across multiple disk drives. The RAID controller also presents an image of a single disk to the operating system, allowing software to think it's working with a single disk no matter how many disks the RAID controller is using to create the image.

There are several different RAID implementations as follows:

- *RAID 0*: This stripes the data across multiple drives to improve performance but adds no data protection.
- *RAID 1*: This mirrors the data to two drives. This can improve data recovery time but at the expense of overall data density.
- *RAID 2*: This uses parity and bit-level striping but is not used in practice.

- *RAID 3*: This uses parity and byte-level striping but is not commonly used in practice.
- *RAID 4*: This uses block-level striping with parity stored on a dedicated drive. This has been displaced in the industry by RAID 6.
- *RAID 5*: This uses block-level striping with parity distributed across the drives. The data can be recovered with a single drive failure.
- *RAID 6*: This uses block-level striping with double distributed parity across the drives. The data can be recovered with up to two failed drives.
- *RAID 10*: This uses both RAID 1 and RAID 0 to both mirror and stripe data across at least two drives. This gives the security of duplicating data while improving performance with data striping but at the expense data density.

When a drive fails using RAID 5, the data can be recovered using a technique called data rebuild. This is typically done within the RAID controller card CPU subsystem, but can take some time based on the size of the drives. RAID 6 became a popular choice when drives became so large that, during the long rebuild process, the probability of a second drive failure became statistically significant. Other hybrid RAID techniques are used in the industry, but will not be described here. RAID has the advantage that if the rebuild process is done within the storage array there is little impact on the storage network.

Erasure coding

Large cloud data centers are now implementing erasure coding to provide data protection for their storage systems. This has been driven by the long rebuild times required when using standard RAID with large disk drives and the fact that many large cloud data centers deploy distributed data storage. When using erasure coding, data is expanded and encoded and broken up into small fragments which are stored in multiple places in order to provide data redundancy. If some fragments become corrupt, you can still recover all of the data if you have enough verified fragments remaining. A familiar example of an erasure code is the Reed-Solomon encoding used on CDs and DVDs that allow you to play these discs without error even when they have a scratch.

Erasure codes are ideal for large data centers that may store data on multiple disks within the rack but add traffic to the network due to the extra transport of redundant data to various locations. In addition, there is the overhead of redundant data when data is reassembled from multiple storage devices. In a RAID system, this data reconstruction happens within the storage array and only the final result is seen on the network.

Tiered storage

Storage performance has a significant impact on data center application performance. Using the same justification for adding cache memory in a CPU, frequently accessed storage data is a small percentage of the overall data stored in a network, but keeping this data close to the CPU resources in high-performance storage systems has benefits. On the other side of the coin, there is a lot of data that is accessed infrequently, if at all. It makes no sense to keep this data in high-performance storage, which is very costly. The trick is to determine how to place data in the proper locations which is why modern storage systems generally contain significant computational power.

Figure 8.6 shows an example of three storage tiers that vary in performance, cost, and capacity. Flash memory can achieve higher performance than HDDs but is also more expensive and has a smaller capacity than other types of storage. This high-performance storage tier can be connected directly to the CPU using PCIe cards that plug directly into the server motherboard. In addition, several vendors offer higher capacity flash storage appliances that can sit within the server rack. The middle tier in this example uses SAS HDD storage arrays that are not as high performance as flash, but can provide higher capacity at a lower cost. In some cases, solid-state flash drives can be used to provide higher performance within some of these storage arrays. The bottom tier is where data is archived and is sometimes called cold storage. These devices can be tape drives or Blu-ray drives for longer term archiving, or large arrays of low-cost SATA drives.

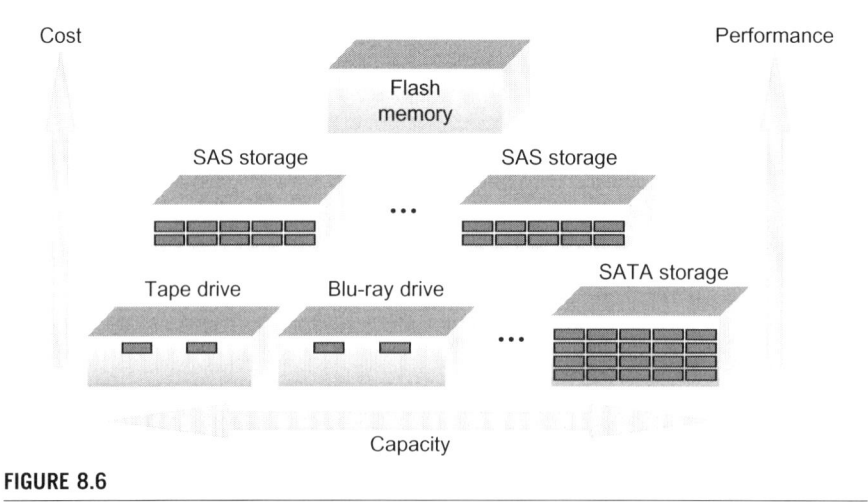

FIGURE 8.6

Tiered storage example.

The key here is to make the hierarchy invisible to the application. For example, you don't want an application running on a server to keep track of how often data is accessed in flash memory and then move infrequently accessed data to a lower tier. Several companies offer hierarchical storage management systems that monitor data and move it between the tiers while at the same time offering a flat storage image to the applications. This can be a complex process in large data centers and this data movement can increase traffic within data center networks. In some cases, data movement can be timed to periods of low data center network utilization in order to minimize the impact. In any case, tiered storage can help optimize the cost-performance trade-off in these large cloud data centers.

Data deduplication

As we all know, electronic data continues to grow at an astounding rate every year, and data centers must keep up by providing large amounts of storage to match these needs. But think about how much duplication of data exists in corporate data centers. For example, someone may e-mail an important presentation that multiple people create a copy of on their own local hard disk. Now when each employee's local disk is backed up to the cloud, multiple copies of the same data will exist across the cloud data center network. This and other types of data duplication can dramatically increase the cloud data center storage requirements.

This is where data deduplication methods come into play. There are two types of data deduplication methods that are used. Postprocess deduplication processes data that is already stored to see if duplicate copies can be removed. This can be done as a background task. The other method, called in-line deduplication, works during a data write process. It looks for similar data already stored on the system and if found doesn't write the new identical data, but instead provides a pointer to the existing data. Postprocessing requires extra capacity to temporarily store data that may be later removed. In-line processing requires real-time data analysis which can slow down activities like data backup. In cloud data centers with distributed storage structures, both of these methods may increase data center network traffic as data is examined and information is exchanged. One advantage of postprocessing, is that this activity can be done during periods of low network activity.

STORAGE COMMUNICATION PROTOCOLS

The industry has developed several standard storage communication protocols that allow host computers to communicate with storage devices. In many of these protocols, the host is called the initiator and the storage device is called the target. Some of these standards have been expanded to support networking features, either within a storage array or within a SAN. In this section, we will describe several of the key storage communication protocols which will also provide the reader some context for the next section on network convergence.

SCSI

The SCSI was first developed in the early 1980s and became a standard protocol for communicating between computers and storage devices. It competed mainly with the lower performance and lower cost PATA interface used in early personal computers. SCSI uses a parallel bus architecture which allows up to 16 hosts (called initiators) and storage devices (called targets) to communicate with each other. The initiator can issue a variety of commands which are responded to by the targets. SCSI commands include Test Unit Ready, Start/Stop Unit, Format Unit, Read, and Write. SCSI is not used any longer but is the basis for other protocols such as SAS and FC which will be described in this section, and iSCSI which will be described in the next section.

SATA

One of the first successful PCs on the market was the IBM PC-AT (for Advanced Technology) which was introduced in 1984. The HDDs in those PCs were connected to the CPU through a 16-bit parallel interface known as the AT Attachment (ATA) interface. This parallel bus can be seen in older PCs as a gray ribbon cable that can connect to multiple disk drives or CD drives using a single cable. In 2003, the serial ATA (SATA) standard was developed which changed this interface from a parallel bus to a serial interface that today operates at rates of 1.5, 3.0, or 6.0 Gbits per second.

To distinguish the older ATA bus from SATA, it is now often called parallel ATA (PATA). The protocols that were used with PATA are mostly reused so SATA is just a change in the electrical interface and cabling. SATA does support an enhanced set of protocols, however. SATA is now the dominant standard for connecting disk drives to CPUs in personal computers and laptops today. A modern PC chipset with multiple SATA interfaces is shown in Figure 8.7.

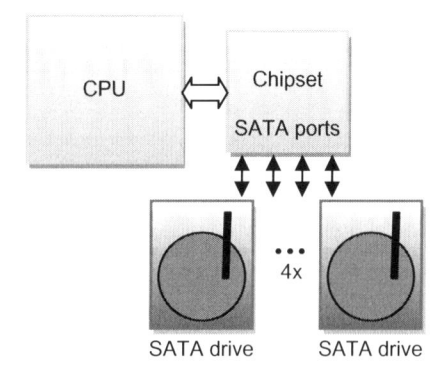

FIGURE 8.7

SATA drives within a PC.

Unlike the earlier ATA parallel bus, SATA cannot support multiple devices connected to a single cable; therefore, the chipset provides multiple SATA interfaces if the user needs to support more than one storage device.

To insure backward compatibility, SATA uses the same command set as used by the PATA standard. In order to support multiple storage devices, the SATA standard defines a port multiplier function, which is what is used inside the chipset in Figure 8.7.

These SATA port multipliers do not form a network but instead provide a tree architecture with only one host similar to the PCI Express topology that we discussed earlier. This is different than SCSI, which can support multiple hosts on a shared bus architecture. In some systems, large port multipliers can be used to support a large number of SATA drives for applications such as archive storage.

SAS

Around the same time PATA moved to SATA, a new standard emerged called serial attached SCSI (SAS). Just like SATA, SAS evolved the SCSI protocol from a shared bus architecture to a point-to-point serial interconnect. Figure 8.8 shows how a SAS expander can be used to support a large number of HDDs in a storage array. SAS uses the standard SCSI command set across 3, 6, or 12Gbit per second serial links and can be used to connect a large number of SAS drives in a storage array. Each port on the expander is assigned a unique SCSI port identifier that is used to address the attached device. Unlike SCSI, which is limited to 16 devices, SAS has a theoretical limit of 64K devices.

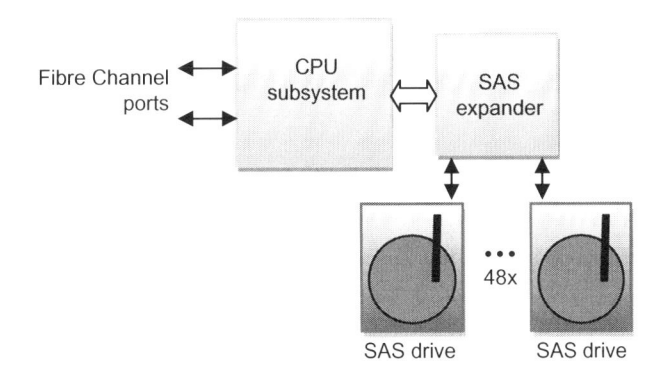

FIGURE 8.8

Storage array using SAS drives.

Some SAS expanders support dual ports for redundancy and also support connections to SATA drives. Another key feature supported by SCSI and SAS but not SATA, is the ability for multiple hosts to share a set of disk drives, which can be important in data center applications. Because SAS uses the SCSI command set, it provides more features and better error recovery than SATA. In addition, disk drives with SAS interfaces are typically designed for data center applications with higher performance and higher reliability compared to SATA drives, which are generally used in PCs. Because of this, SAS is used extensively within storage arrays in the data center, but SAS is rarely used for the network connection between storage systems. For SANs, FC is the dominant protocol.

Fibre Channel

Unlike SCSI, which was first developed within a single company before it was standardized, FC was developed by an industry group and eventually approved as an ANSI standard in 1994. It initially competed with IBM's proprietary serial storage architecture standard, but it eventually became the dominant standard in SANs. It's interesting that the development group decided to use the British spelling of the word fiber. They did this because FC was extended to include copper wire implementations as well as fiber optic cabling and they thought this change in spelling would make that situation less confusing (since then, all the copper implementations have disappeared). Although FC was developed to transport a variety of upper layer protocols, such as IP and ATM, today it is primarily used to transport SCSI.

Like SATA and SAS, FC is a serial protocol. Early FC-based products connected an array of disk drives at 1G bit per second in an arbitrated loop, basically a ring architecture like we described in Chapter 3. Because an arbitrated loop must share bandwidth, it has a limited port count and loop failure can be caused by a single device failure. Because of this, SAS expanders have replaced FC for connecting drives within storage arrays today. But FC has found good success in switch fabric topologies used in SANs and provides serial data rates of 1G, 2G, 4G, 8G, and 16G bit per second using optical cabling. The FC frame format is shown in Figure 8.9. The FC header supports a 24-bit address that can access over 16M ports. The payload can range from 0 bytes to over 2K bytes and the entire frame is protected with a CRC field. Because frame delivery order cannot be guaranteed, a sequence control and sequence ID field is used along with an exchange ID.

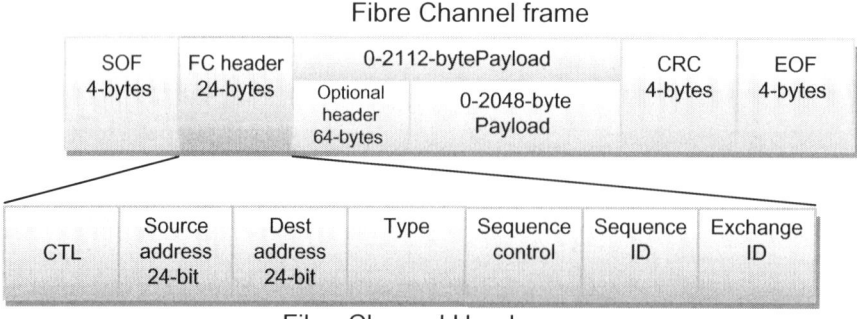

FIGURE 8.9

The Fibre Channel frame format.

There are generally four component types in a FC SAN. HBAs are used in the servers, providing a connection to the FC network. Like the SCSI protocol, the hosts are called initiators. FC switches are similar to the Ethernet top of rack switches we described earlier and make connections to multiple servers and storage arrays within the rack. Directors are large modular switches similar to the end of row switches used in Ethernet networks and can connect to a large number of servers and storage arrays. Finally, the storage arrays themselves look something like the block diagram Figure 8.8 and use a SAS expander to connect the disc drives while the CPU on the storage controller board provides FC target port functionality.

FC supports both connection-oriented and connectionless services between initiators and targets. For connection-oriented service, a connection is first established across the network, data is exchanged, and then the connection is torn down. Connectionless is similar to Ethernet, but the frames may arrive out of order, and the standard defines both an acknowledged and an unacknowledged transport mechanism. FC also includes a rich set of storage network management tools, helping to make FC the preferred choice for high-availability and mission-critical storage systems.

NETWORK CONVERGENCE

Most early computers implemented DAS which initially used proprietary connections, but most computer designs eventually migrated to standard protocols such as SCSI and ATA. Once local area networks appeared, the idea of accessing block storage across a network became attractive. In some cases, dedicated SANs were built. But lower cost solutions can be achieved by transmitting storage protocols across standard data networks such as TCP/IP and Ethernet. This is sometimes referred to as network convergence, where both storage and data traffic share the same network. In this section, we will provide an overview of the requirements that network convergence poses for standard data networks. We will also describe several of the key converged storage network protocols in use today.

Requirements

There are two key requirements when sharing block storage traffic with standard traffic over data center networks. The data transport should be lossless and data should be delivered within certain time bounds. For example, the SCSI protocol, which is the basis for both the iSCSI and FC protocols, uses timeout mechanisms which may attempt to re-establish the connection if an acknowledgment is not received within a certain time period. If the storage data is blocked by other traffic and cannot be delivered within these time bounds, it can significantly impact the system performance.

To improve this situation, TCP/IP provides several quality-of-service (QoS) mechanisms for both lossless operation and minimizing latency throughout the network. These include the following:

- *Acknowledgment frames*: TCP operates by acknowledging each packet that is transmitted for reliable operation. If an acknowledgment is not received within a given time period, the data is retransmitted.
- *Resource Reservation Protocol (RSVP)*: This protocol can be used to request and reserve certain resources throughout the network, such as minimum bandwidth.

- *Differentiated Services (DiffServ)*: This assigns class of service to a packet so that, for example, storage traffic can be given higher priority through the network.
- *Explicit Congestion Notification (ECN)*: When congestion is detected in the network, a flag is set in the IP header which can be reflected by the receiver back to the source, indicating that the source should throttle its transmission bandwidth.

But TCP/IP mechanisms by themselves are not sufficient to provide the QoS requirements demanded by the FCoE community. For Ethernet networks, the IEEE has developed the data center bridging specifications including priority flow control for lossless operation, enhanced transmission selection for minimum bandwidth guarantees, quantized congestion notification for congestion management, and data center bridging exchange protocol for control plane management. Please refer to Chapter 5 for more information on data center bridging (DCB).

Network File System and Server Message Block

The Network File System (NFS) standard was originally developed by Sun Microsystems in 1984. The idea behind it was to provide access to data on remote storage devices in a manner similar to accessing data on a local disk. To do this, they created the NFS protocol which went through several versions but eventually was adopted by the IETF and is mainly used over TCP/IP networks today. NFS uses remote procedure calls from the host to a NAS device in order to read and write data. Most client computer operating systems including Windows, Linux, and Solaris support NFS.

In virtual server environments, VMware supports NFS in its vSphere products in order to provide storage access for multiple virtual machines. Microsoft Hyper-V supports file-based storage using a competing protocol called Server Message Block (SMB) which also runs over TCP/IP and has been included with the windows operating systems since Windows 2000. Microsoft Widows Server 2012 also supports a technology called SMB Direct which can take advantage of the RDMA capability that is available in special network adapters from several NIC vendors.

iSCSI

iSCSI was developed in the late 1990s as a way to carry SCSI commands over TCP/IP networks. As with the SCSI protocol, the client is called the initiator and the storage device is called the target. Although iSCSI has been designed to run over any type of TCP/IP network, including wide area networks, in practice, its performance can be degraded if proper QoS mechanisms such as we described above for TCP/IP networks are not used. In general, it is easier to implement iSCSI within a data center where a network administrator has control over the entire network and can provide these QoS mechanisms. If network isolation is required for security purposes, either physically isolated networks can be used or VLANs can be used for virtual isolation. In addition, data centers supporting network virtualization can isolate tenant storage traffic from one another using VXLAN or NVGRE.

Several computer operating systems include, along with the vSphere and Hyper-V hypervisors, iSCSI initiator functions. In the case of Hyper-V, the iSCSI initiator can be implemented in the virtual machines (child partitions) or in the parent partition. These initiators are the most popular way of implementing iSCSI but can consume a lot of CPU performance, especially when operating at higher data rates. When the server is connected to a 10GbE network, it is common to offload the iSCSI initiator functions to a TCP/IP offload engine (TOE) in the NIC. Some TOEs can offload the entire iSCSI initiator function, while others can offload only the TCP/IP functions. Typically, these offload engines have far more limited compute and memory resources than what is available to an operating system running on a modern server, but in both cases, CPU overhead can be reduced. On the other hand, offloading a segment of an operating system's software stack can lead to a variety of issues, especially when the operating system undergoes a major update.

The iSCSI target is typically a storage array that contains a storage controller CPU board. The storage controller provides iSCSI target functions to the connected network and may also contain a SAS expander for internal connections to the SAS hard drives. In some cases the controller may also provide RAID functionality across the drives. The SCSI standard uses the term logical unit number (LUN) to identify individual drives. So the iSCSI initiator will send commands, including the LUN, to the iSCSI target in order to gain access to one of the drives in the storage array. The controller board can then translate the SCSI commands received to the SAS commands needed to access the individual drives.

FCoE

Many data centers include dedicated FC SANs in addition to their Ethernet data networks. For large cloud data centers, there is a strong financial desire to converge these two into a single network. This was one of the driving forces behind the publishing of the Fibre Channel over Ethernet (FCoE) standard (called T11 FC-BB-5) in 2009 by the International Committee for Information Technology Standards. This standard depends on the IEEE DCB standards for efficient operation, which we described in Chapter 5.

When using FCoE, the FC frame is encapsulated with both an FCoE header and an Ethernet header as shown in Figure 8.10. Keep in mind that the FC frame itself is a transport for SCSI commands much like iSCSI is a transport for SCSI, but instead using a FC transport protocol. The Ethernet header contains an EtherType of 0x8906 to identify the frame as FCoE. A 4-bit version number is used in the FCoE header along with start of

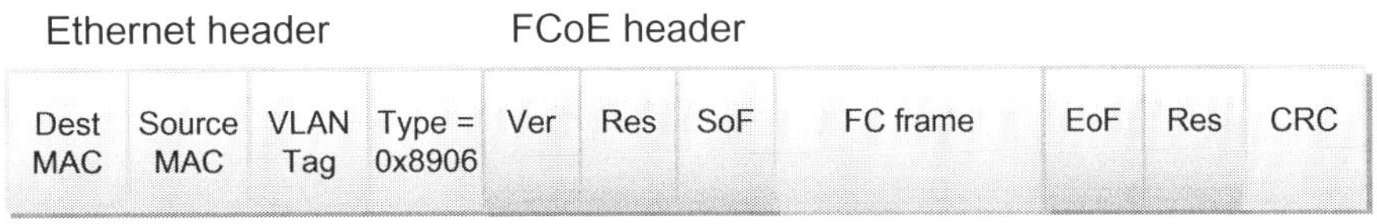

Ethernet header				FCoE header						
Dest MAC	Source MAC	VLAN Tag	Type = 0x8906	Ver	Res	SoF	FC frame	EoF	Res	CRC

FIGURE 8.10

The FCoE frame format.

frame (SoF) and end of frame (EoF) indicators. Reserve bytes are added to maintain the minimum size Ethernet frame when encapsulating smaller FC command frames.

When the FCoE BB-5 standard was issued, it required all FCoE frames to be forwarded through switching devices called Fibre Channel Forwarders (FCFs) as shown in the left side of Figure 8.11. These devices also act as a bridge to traditional FC SANs by encapsulating and de-encapsulating FC frames and providing both FC and Ethernet ports. In the servers, converged network adapters (CNAs) are used to connect to the Ethernet network and can provide the functionality of both a traditional NIC as well as an FCoE HBA by generating and receiving FCoE frames. Special Ethernet switches called Fibre Channel Initiation Protocol (FIP) Snooping Bridges (FSBs) are used which must be connected to FCFs in order for the network to function in a secure and robust manner. The main purpose of FIP snooping is to make sure that only servers that have logged in to the FC network can have access to that network. Snooping is performed by examining certain FC header fields and filtering traffic that is not allowed access.

One of the main industry complaints about the FC-BB-5 standard is that it increases the cost of the network by requiring too many FCFs which are only available from a handful of network equipment vendors. This is because all data must be routed through an FCF and all FSBs must be connected to an FCF. For example, an FCoE storage target connected to the same FSB must have its data routed through the FCF as shown in the left side of Figure 8.11. This increases network congestion and limits the usefulness of FCoE targets. In fact, most FCoE networks have been implemented using FCFs and FSBs with storage targets within the FC SAN.

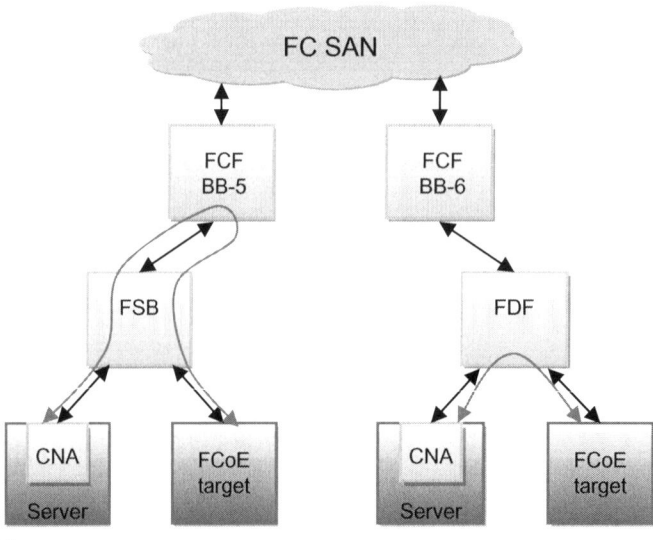

FIGURE 8.11

FCoE network components.

To improve the situation, several leading original equipment manufacturers including IBM, EMC, and HP are promoting a new FC-BB-6 standard that introduces a new type of Ethernet switch called a Fibre Channel Data Forwarder (FDF). With this standard, the FCF still provides FC services in addition to address assignment and FIP processing, but can delegate forwarding to other DCB enabled switches in the network that have FDF capability.

The FDF capable switches provide FCoE forwarding and zoning based on information provided by the FCF. In addition, the FDFs don't need to be directly connected to a FCF, providing for the use of many more lower cost FDF switches in the network compared to the number of FCF switches. In the example on the right side of Figure 8.11, the server can connect through the FDF directly to the FCoE target without the need to be routed through the FCF. This new standard should increase the adoption of FCoE in large data center networks.

Industry adoption

Storage network administrators are a very conservative group because keeping data secure is much more critical than other aspects of data center operation. This is why they like dedicated FC networks which are physically isolated from other networks and use equipment that is certified by a handful of key vendors. Although iSCSI has security features that can be enabled, many companies don't like the idea of their critical data being transmitted on less secure local area networks or public networks. Even so, iSCSI has been a successful solution for cloud data center storage applications where the entire network is controlled by the data center administrator.

FCoE on the other hand has taken a while to gain wide industry acceptance. One reason for that was the lack of Ethernet bandwidth. While FC networks were operating at 4Gbps, Ethernet was still at 1Gbps. Once 10Gb Ethernet became more widely available, companies like Cisco and Brocade started offering FCFs and FSBs with CNAs provided by various NIC vendors. But the lack of FCoE storage targets and the limitations imposed by the BB-5 standard limited the economies of scale that are enjoyed by technologies such as Ethernet. It is expected that the new BB-6 standard will improve this somewhat by opening the market to lower cost FCoE networking solutions. Other factors that will help enable FCoE in the market include the emergence of 40Gb Ethernet which means that FCoE will have a significant performance advantage over 16Gb FC implementations and the fact that storage administrators are getting more comfortable with FCoE technology.

SOFTWARE-DEFINED STORAGE

Storage hardware can take on many forms in cloud data centers, including flash storage in the servers, storage within the server racks, dedicated storage racks, dedicated SANs, and large storage archive rooms. As we discussed earlier, this hierarchy of storage solutions is known as tiered storage and requires a wide variety of storage hardware along with extensive manual configuration to make sure storage is secure, reliable, and provides optimal performance to host servers. In this section, we will provide an overview of software defined storage (SDS) and how it is being deployed in large cloud data centers. We will take a broader view of the software-defined data center in Chapter 9 with a focus on software-defined networking (SDN).

Storage abstraction

One of the key attributes of SDS is abstracting all of the underlying storage nuts and bolts and presenting this abstraction to the application as well as the higher layer orchestration software. In fact, you could argue that storage took the first step toward abstraction with the concept of a LUN in both iSCSI and FC, and SDS attempts to further extend this abstraction. To the application, all of the various tiers of storage are abstracted into a single pool of storage that is tuned for the application. For example, some applications may require more local flash memory for performance while others may require a larger amount of SAS drives for capacity. The pool can span multiple storage arrays from different vendors even if they are spread across the data center. This requires tight coordination with the SDN tools in order to provide the proper storage convergence capabilities across the cloud data center network.

Storage virtualization

In the last two chapters, we described how cloud data center tenants can be allocated virtual machines within a server and virtual networks within the physical network. Storage virtualization can also be used to isolate virtual storage pools for each tenant within the larger abstracted storage pool we described above. This can be done using techniques like zoning within large iSCSI or FCoE storage domains. Also, by using automated policies, a tenant can be allocated various levels of storage performance and capabilities based on workload requirements. In fact, software automation can be a key factor in reducing storage resource allocation times to within hours instead of days.

Open interface

One of the key attributes of SDS is the use of open software interfaces both within the storage equipment and above the storage abstraction layer. By using storage equipment with common open interfaces, the storage abstraction layer can easily communicate with, configure, and monitor all of the storage resources within the data center. By providing a common open interface above the storage abstraction layer, the overarching data center orchestration layer can configure servers, networking, and storage for each tenant in the cloud data center. These virtual resources can then be quickly tailored to the workload needs of each tenant.

STORAGE IN CLOUD DATA CENTERS

Storage is a key component in large cloud data centers. Traditional enterprise data centers may have a dedicated SAN which is physically separate from the data network. This is not feasible in large cloud data centers due to their massive scale. To cope with this scale, data center administrators prefer to deploy basic uniform building blocks that can be easily scaled as capacity requirements grow. Also due to cost constraints, they want to maintain a single converged data center network supporting both storage and data traffic. In this section, we will provide an overview of a few building block strategies used in modern cloud data centers.

Distributed storage

One way to scale storage capacity along with the amount of server resources is to provide storage on every server board. There are actually three types of storage. Boot loader storage holds a small program used to bring up the processor into a state where the bare metal hypervisor or operating system can be loaded and run. This can be a relatively small flash memory device on the board. The hypervisor or operating system can be loaded from a drive on the board or from a shared storage location within the rack. This allows multiple servers to be booted from a single drive. Other storage can exist on each server board and be shared with other servers in the rack using protocols such as iSCSI.

Distributed storage is a good choice for applications such as web hosting, allowing each client to have dedicated server and storage resources on the same board. For applications that require large amounts of storage, dedicated storage arrays may need to be added to the rack. It is also possible to share storage resources between servers within the rack for applications that require a larger amount of processing and storage resources. Storage access by a CPU on a different server card will steal CPU cycles from the local CPU in order to service the request (for example, emulating an iSCSI target). This type of resource clustering also adds additional traffic to the network within the rack. Sharing storage resources between racks can be implemented as long as the additional storage request processing in the server and additional network traffic is accounted for.

Data center PODs

One way to modularize a large cloud data center is to provide basic building blocks containing racks of servers, storage, and networking. These are known as performance optimized data center (PODs) and an example is shown in Figure 8.12. These are similar to shipping containers and are delivered by trucks into large data centers where they are stacked and then connected to power, cooling, and networking. If something fails in the POD, it may be repaired on-site or could be simply replaced by driving in another POD. These can be configured and tested prior to delivery, reducing the burden on the data center administrator. The down side is that PODs are usually built using equipment from a single vendor, which doesn't allow the data center administrator to optimize performance or cost. In addition, a single rack failure requires the replacement of multiple racks that make up the POD, taking down several racks of equipment at a time.

FIGURE 8.12

An example data center POD.

Rack scale architecture

A basic building block that is becoming popular for large cloud data centers is the rack itself. Data center administrators can buy a complete rack that is preconfigured and tested by an outside vendor instead of buying an empty rack and then populating it with servers, storage, networking, and software and then going through a bring up and debug process. Several data center equipment and component vendors such as Intel are embracing this technology and calling it rack scale architecture (RSA). In addition, Facebook has sponsored a new Open Compute Project (OCP) to standardize a 21 inch rack form-factor for large data centers that has gained support from a large number of leading cloud data center vendors. The basic components of RSA are shown in Figure 8.13.

Shared cooling is used to reduce cost by eliminating fans on each server shelf. Shared power can provide DC voltages throughout the rack saving cost through the use of larger shared power supplies instead of individual supplies on each shelf. Modular server sleds allow the easy replacement and upgrading of CPU resources. They plug into a card in the back of the sled that contains network interface components which can aggregate traffic from multiple sleds into a higher bandwidth uplink to the top of rack switch. The network aggregation reduces cable count and the new 21 inch OCP rack improves server density by allowing three-wide server sleds.

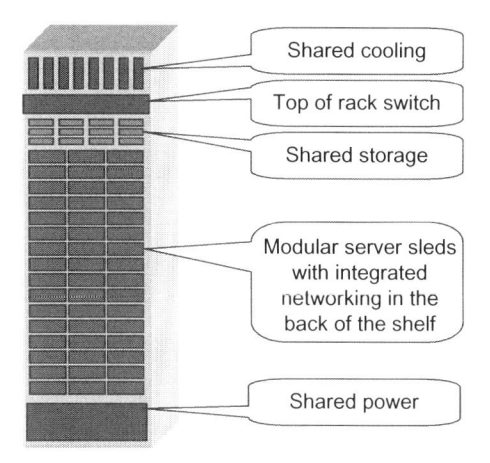

FIGURE 8.13

Rack scale architecture components.

One key aspect of RSAs is the pooling of storage resources instead of providing storage on each server board. This provides several advantages including the ability to upgrade CPU resources without requiring the replacement of the associated storage or rebuilding the data on these drives. It also facilitates the sharing of OS and/or hypervisor boot partitions across all the servers within the rack. Depending on the rack workload requirements, mixtures of solid-state and standard hard drives can be easily interchanged creating a local tiered storage environment. In addition, storage resources can be allocated and quickly reallocated to different servers within the rack depending on workloads. Finally, this architecture lends itself well to data protection mechanisms such as erasure coding where small blocks of data are spread across multiple drives.

REVIEW

In this chapter, we provided an overview on how data storage is implemented in large data center networks. This included a background on storage including some new storage technologies along with an overview of storage communication protocols. Next we discussed network convergence which allows block storage traffic to share a network in large data centers that cannot afford separate storage networks. We also described how software defined storage will improve how storage is provisioned. Finally, we provided some examples of how storage is implemented in large cloud data centers. The next chapter will provide some background and information on the latest industry movement toward software defined networking and the impact this will have on how cloud data centers are configured and managed.

CHAPTER

Software-Defined Networking

9

Up until this point, we have been describing network architectures, protocols, and systems, but we have only touched on how software is used to configure, monitor, and control cloud data centers. There are several applications for control plane software in the data center including software to manage virtual machines, software to manage storage, software to manage the network, and software to manage functions like network security. For network management, software-defined networking (SDN) has become a buzzword within the data center networking industry to the point where people are becoming confused by its meaning. We hope the reader will have a more clear understanding of SDN after reading this chapter. As of this writing, the hype generated by the SDN industry has not been matched by the level of deployment, but it is expected that this will change over the next few years.

In this chapter, we will first provide a background on data center software and how the data center is evolving toward a software-defined data center. We will then provide an introduction to several of the key components in the software-defined data center, including OpenStack and OpenFlow which helps enable software defined networking. Next, we will introduce network function virtualization (NFV) and how this can be used to provide security and improve the performance of cloud data center networks. Finally, we will provide some example SDN deployment models in order to give the reader an idea of how SDN may be used in future data center networks.

DATA CENTER SOFTWARE BACKGROUND

As we discussed earlier in this book, data center networks originally emerged from enterprise networks and used LAN workgroup switches to connect servers within a rack and used large switches and routers to connect multiple racks together. These switches and routers came with proprietary software from the equipment manufacturer and included many features not needed in the data center. Because of this, some large cloud service providers have resorted to developing their own networking software that is tailored to their needs. This has opened the door to SDN with open solutions tailored to the data center that can help network administrators reduce both capital expense and operating expense. In this section, we will provide an overview of traditional data center software along with some evolving data center requirements and describe how the software-defined data center can meet these needs.

Traditional data center network software

Traditional corporate data centers use hardware from large original equipment manufacturers (OEMs) and in many cases mix in servers, networking, and storage gear from several different manufacturers. They may employ a server administrator to maintain the server hardware along with allocating virtual machines and configuring the vSwitches in the hypervisors. A network administrator may configure and maintain all of the networking equipment and a separate storage administrator may configure and maintain storage resources along with the storage area network. All of this requires careful coordination between the administrators.

In the data center network, each piece of network equipment usually comes with software from the OEM that manufactured the equipment. Because this software only runs on a given brand of hardware, the network administrator needs to either buy all the networking equipment from one manufacturer, which can increase capital expense due to vendor lock-in, or run separate network operating systems from each vendor, which can increase training requirements and operating expenses. The network operating systems may also be overburdened with features because the OEM needs to provide software that satisfies a wide variety of customers. Each data center is operated differently, and a given data center network may only use a fraction of these features. This means more expensive software along with more costly control plane (CPU) processing resources are needed to host this software.

Evolving data center requirements

Cloud data centers are different from traditional data centers in many respects. They strive to incorporate a uniform virtualized hardware environment with homogeneous management tools for server, storage, and networking. They also run a limited set of applications across a standard software architecture. Due to the issues mentioned above and the massive scale of these data centers, many cloud data center administrators have turned away from OEM solutions and are using original design manufactures (ODMs) in Asia to build servers, storage, and networking gear designed to their specifications. Due to their uniform hardware environment and the large order quantities, this can significantly reduce capital expense. But because ODMs do not traditionally provide network operating systems, the cloud data centers hire their own software teams or use third parties to develop this software. Google was one of the first companies to do this by developing their own top of rack switch design which was built by an ODM and by developing their own network operating system using a home grown software team. Other companies, like Facebook, are also following this model.

Application programming interface

Before we jump into more details behind the software-defined data center and SDN, we should present a fundamental part of software integration which is the Application Programming Interface (API). In general, an API abstracts much of the low level operational details that exist below the API from the higher layer software. For example, the higher layer software may use an API function call such as *SetPortSpeed*(24, 10), which is used to configure port number 24 as a 10Gb Ethernet port. When this function call is received by the API, it must write to multiple registers in the chip so that port 24 is enabled as a 10GbE port. Using an API function call is easier than directly writing registers and also makes higher layer software much easier to create and understand.

Almost all semiconductor vendors provide some sort of API for their silicon devices and most network operating systems are written using these API function calls instead of accessing registers directly. This same concept also extends to the higher layers in the software stack. For example, a higher layer application may want to configure a certain amount of bandwidth from point A to B in the data center by making a function call to the network operating system such as *SetBandwidthPath* (A, B, 10) which may in turn spawn other API function calls at lower API layers such as *SetPortSpeed*(24, 10) on a given switch chip. In these situations, a northbound API generally refers to an API that is receiving commands from a higher layer application and a southbound API generally refers to an API submitting function calls to lower layer software. An open API refers to a set of common API function calls that are agreed to by multiple hardware and software vendors in the industry to insure interoperability between software layers. OpenFlow is an example open API that we will describe later in this chapter.

Software-defined data center

The ultimate resource management scheme for cloud data center administrators is the software-defined data center. What this means is that a single software interface is used to easily configure the data center at a high level with much less human intervention. For example, a single administrator issues a set of commands to allocate virtual machines, virtual networking, and virtual storage to a new tenant with specified service level guarantees, and it is completed within a few minutes. Today, three separate administrators may need to be notified of the new tenant requirements. Each will access multiple resource allocation tools from different vendors and attempt to coordinate their efforts. This can be an error-prone process that can take many days to complete. Figure 9.1 shows a simplified view of how a software-defined data center can improve this situation.

166 CHAPTER 9 Software-Defined Networking

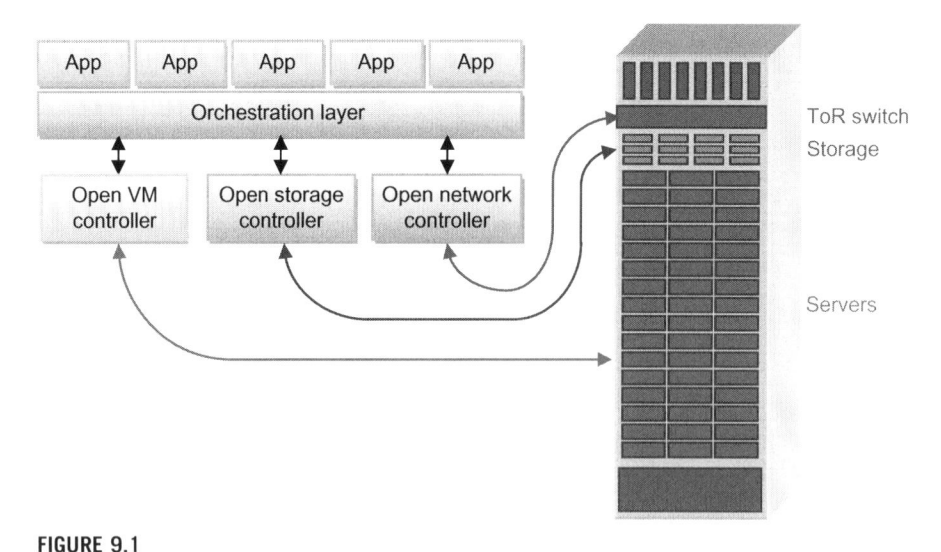

FIGURE 9.1

Simplified view of the software-defined data center.

At the top level is the orchestration layer using software such as the OpenStack cloud operating system. The orchestration layer northbound API can support multiple applications from third parties. For example, an application could monitor traffic patterns in the network and automatically adjust virtual network connections or move virtual machines in order to optimize overall network performance. Another application could allocate certain virtual machines and configure dedicated network bandwidth to move storage data to a storage archive during off-peak hours. In order for this new software-defined data center to configure these various resources, the orchestration layer southbound API sends the appropriate commands to different controller software modules.

Below the orchestration layer, there are dedicated controller software modules for servers, storage, and networking. These controllers translate commands from the orchestration layer into industry standard open APIs such as OpenStack for server virtualization and OpenFlow for networking. Controllers using open northbound and southbound APIs allow for ease of integration with orchestration layers and also allow use of standard high volume hardware from a variety of vendors that support the open API. In this example, the hypervisors and virtual switches in the servers must understand commands from the open VM controller and the top of rack switch operating system must understand commands from the open network controller. For storage, an open storage controller can be used to send commands to configure and monitor the storage resources. By having these controllers communicating with the same orchestration layer, coordination among resources can be guaranteed. In addition, these controllers help expose available hardware resources and features to the orchestration layer. In the next sections, we will provide more details behind the OpenStack and OpenFlow standards.

OPENSTACK

OpenStack is free open source Linux-based controller software that provides an orchestration layer for cloud data centers. In 2010, RackSpace and NASA started the OpenStack initiative and since then more than 200 companies have joined. OpenStack is intended to offer cloud computing services using standard hardware and provides a provisioning portal through a web interface that allows users to provision and manage server, storage, and networking resources. In this section, we will provide more information on OpenStack components and discuss its use in large cloud data center environments.

Networking components

OpenStack uses a modular software architecture consisting of multiple plugin components that can be used to control data center resources. These components are all managed through an OpenStack dashboard called Horizon which allows data center administrators to control all aspects of data center operation from a single interface. OpenStack also includes the Heat project that allows data center administrators to describe available resources using a single template which can be used with configuration applications such as Puppet and Chef. Here are some of the key components related to data center networking. These are being developed by an open software community and are rapidly evolving with regular release cycles.

Nova

Nova is a plugin designed to manage pools of server resources including bare metal servers, microservers, and high performance computing resources. It can also be used to configure and manage virtual machines and has support for several hypervisors including VMware vSphere and Microsoft Hyper-V. It is designed to be scalable and has mechanisms to isolate failures so they can be quickly debugged and remedied. It requires no proprietary hardware and can be easily integrated with third party hardware and software.

Swift

Swift is a plugin supporting object storage which allows objects to be stored across multiple servers in the data center. Swift manages data replication to insure data integrity across the storage cluster in the case of server or hard drive failure. In 2013, the OpenStack development community started an initiative to support erasure coding in Swift to reduce overall storage requirements compared to simple data replication methods.

Cinder

Cinder is a plugin that provides block storage capabilities in OpenStack environments. It manages creation, attachment, and detachment of block storage devices to servers for performance sensitive applications. It can be used with block storage systems from multiple leading vendors and also provides functions like snapshots for storage backup.

Neutron

Neutron (formerly called Quantum) is a plugin for managing data center networking functions. Neutron provides support for flat networks or networks with separate VLAN domains. Floating IP addresses can be used to quickly reroute traffic in case of failure or for applications such as VM migration. Neutron provides a framework for supporting various functions such as server load balancing, firewalls, and intrusion detection. It also provides support for OpenFlow which we will dive into next.

OPENFLOW

OpenFlow was born out of a PhD thesis from Martin Casado, a student of Nick McKeown's at Stanford University. McKeown was well known for his work on switch fabric architectures in the 1990s and he and Casado founded Nicira Corporation in 2007 to provide SDN solutions based on their work at Stanford. Nicira was acquired by VMware in 2012 for $1.26B.

OpenFlow initially started as a way to run experimental protocols on networks alongside standard protocols but was quickly adopted by the data center community as a way to make networking more efficient in large data center environments. More recently, it has also been adopted by service providers as a way to improve the efficiency of carrier networks. This work has now moved under the Open Networking Foundation which is generating the OpenFlow specifications.

The idea behind OpenFlow is to move networking intelligence from a distributed model to a centralized model using a common OpenFlow controller as shown in Figure 9.2. Traditional data center switches and routers learn about their environments through standard data exchange protocols and they each maintain state information about the entire network which is translated into forwarding tables. If a new switch or endpoint is added to the network, this information is propagated to all the switches and routers in the associated networking domain, and they use this information to update their forwarding tables. This adds a level of cost and complexity to each switch in the network.

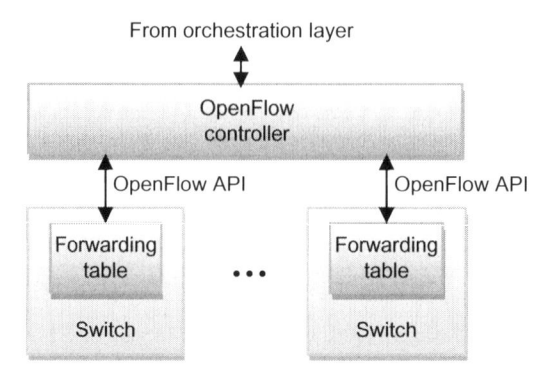

FIGURE 9.2

OpenFlow controller implementation.

OpenFlow changes this by providing a centralized view of the network using an OpenFlow controller. The controller maintains the state of the network and simply populates the forwarding tables within all of the switches and routers in the network. Any changes in the network are communicated to the controller which then updates its centralized state tables. It then uses this information to determine how to populate the forwarding tables within each switch and router that it controls and passes this information to these devices using the OpenFlow API. This separation of a centralized control plane from a distributed data plane is one of the main ideas behind OpenFlow.

As an example, consider the TRILL protocol we discussed earlier in this book. The idea behind TRILL is to take advantage of the link bandwidth in the data center that is left unused by the spanning tree protocol. TRILL operates by broadcasting connectivity information between RBridges. Each RBridge must maintain this connectivity state information. OpenFlow can eliminate this requirement by using a central controller. Because the central controller has a global view of the network, it can update the forwarding tables in each switch, dynamically adjusting connectivity and bandwidth allocation as needs change within the network. This provides more efficient operation compared to TRILL while at the same time lowering the cost of the switches.

Open API

Another key aspect of OpenFlow is the open API that is used between the controller and the networking equipment that was shown in Figure 9.2. An open API allows network equipment vendors to communicate with industry standard controllers and allows the data center administrator to use equipment from multiple vendors, eliminating the software lock-in found in earlier OEM equipment. Figure 9.3 shows how OpenFlow compares to the use of a traditional network operating system.

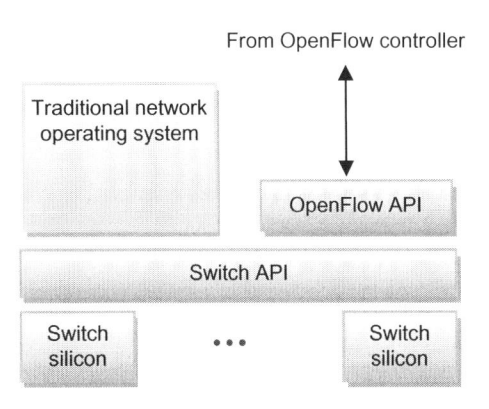

FIGURE 9.3

OpenFlow controller implementation.

A traditional network operating system is written to work with a specific API from a given switch silicon vendor. Some silicon vendors have used this to their advantage by locking in the network equipment OEMs to their specific API which is used on multiple generations of silicon. OpenFlow breaks this lock by using a light-weight OpenFlow API shim layer that simply translates OpenFlow API function calls to switch specific API function calls. But, the switch silicon needs to properly implement these functions in order to take advantage of the OpenFlow features. Many switch silicon vendors today are developing these shim layers in order to be compliant with the OpenFlow standard.

Forwarding table implementation

Forwarding tables are sometimes called flow tables in the OpenFlow standard. These are tables that define how a frame will be forwarded out of a given switch or router in the network. These tables work by matching specific header fields, such as the IP destination address, and when a match occurs, forwarding the frame to a specified egress port. The OpenFlow 1.0 specification defined 12 frame header fields that should be used in flow table matching. They include the ingress port number, the source MAC address, the destination MAC address, the Ether Type, the VLAN ID, the VLAN priority, the source IP address, the destination IP address, the IP protocol, the IP ToS, the TCP source port, and the TCP destination port. It is the job of the OpenFlow controller to populate these matching fields in the switch flow tables using the OpenFlow API.

The OpenFlow specification also requires the switch silicon to implement a multilevel forwarding table as shown in Figure 9.4. Packet header information is passed along to each table stage and then is modified based on action commands from these tables.

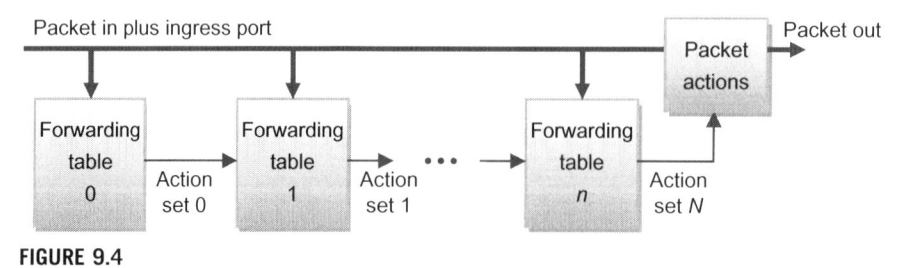

FIGURE 9.4

OpenFlow frame forwarding tables.

Think of this as an if-then tree. For example, using three tables, if header field X matches condition A in the first table, then look at header field Y for a match with condition B in the next table. If that matches, then look at header field Z for a match with condition C in the third table, and if this is a match, modify header field W and send the frame to egress port D. Each table match produces an action set which is used to potentially change the matching conditions in the next table.

This forwarding table could be implemented in software, but software cannot provide this frame matching capability while also meeting the high port bandwidth requirements found in data center switches and routers. Although hardware implementations can provide higher performance, this level of forwarding table complexity has not been easy for switch silicon vendors to implement. Some people have commented that the spec was written by software engineers and not chip designers. Today, some switch implementations meet the OpenFlow forwarding table requirements by recirculating frames multiple times through the same forwarding table pipeline which reduces the overall chip bandwidth capability. For example, if a frame needs to recirculate through the same forwarding table four times, the available bandwidth will be reduced by a factor of four. It is expected that switch silicon vendors will start updating their forwarding pipelines to meet these new OpenFlow forwarding table requirements.

Industry adoption

Several versions of the OpenFlow specification have now been released to the industry and there are several products that are starting to emerge in the market. Google has announced that it has redesigned its networks to run under the OpenFlow standard in order to improve efficiency. Some people consider this a proprietary implementation of OpenFlow because much of the development was done before the latest OpenFlow specs were released. NEC® and HP have also announced OpenFlow support in their networking products. An open source OpenFlow controller called Project Floodlight has been released by a startup company called BigSwitch Networks and has generated a lot of interest in the industry. In addition, Indiana University has opened an SDN interoperability lab to test things like OpenFlow compatibility between products. Although there has been a lot of industry hype and many startup companies jumping on the OpenFlow bandwagon, it is expected that major OpenFlow deployments (not counting Google) in cloud data centers are still a few years away.

NETWORK FUNCTION VIRTUALIZATION

Before data makes its way into the data center network from the internet, it must go through a security check called a firewall. Once inside the data center, data patterns are constantly monitored in order to detect malicious attacks by outside forces. Some data centers also use load balancers to even out server utilization, and network monitoring equipment may be used to optimize data center network performance and/or make sure customers are receiving the level of service they have paid for. In this section, we will describe these functions in more detail and provide an overview of how these functions may be virtualized based on a new industry trend called network function virtualization (NFV). We will also describe how these functions can be orchestrated along with other data center resources in the software-defined data center.

Background

Applications such as network security, network monitoring, and load balancing require deep packet inspection capability which must be performed while maintaining high network data rates. Up until now, this capability has been supplied by dedicated hardware platforms called network appliances that come in a variety of form factors from single board products to modular ATCA chassis. These appliances traditionally use specialized processing chips shown in Figure 9.5.

Depending on the performance requirements, network appliance designers may choose standard CPUs, specialized CPUs called network processor units (NPUs), field programmable gate arrays (FPGAs), or custom designed application specific integrated circuits (ASICs). As can be seen in Figure 9.5, software development costs are higher for NPUs than CPUs due to their unique programming requirements. Both FPGAs and ASICs require extensive logic design and verification, while for the ultimate performance, ASICs also require several years of design and development and millions of dollars in non-recurring engineering (NRE) charges. Because of this, only the largest network equipment OEMs develop ASICs since they can spread the high NRE cost across large product volumes. Some network appliances use mixtures of these products, using the higher cost devices only where needed. For example, CPUs may be used for control plane functions, NPUs for layer 2-3 processing and FPGAs or ASICs for deep packet inspection. But in any case, network appliances are costly systems compared to systems using only standard CPU blades.

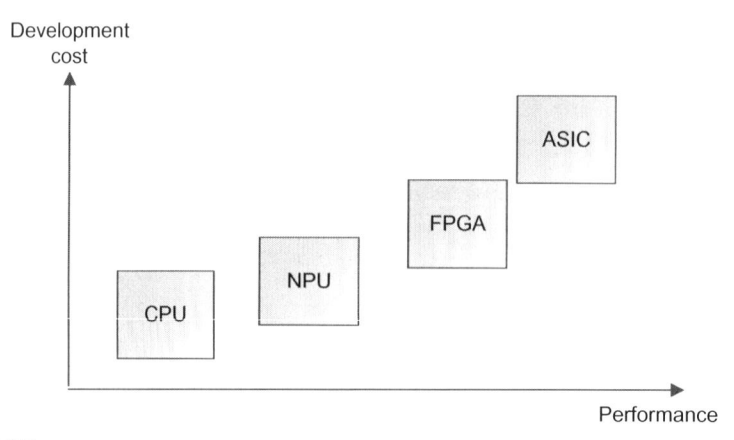

FIGURE 9.5

Packet processing device tradeoffs.

A couple of factors are now changing the way network appliance functions are implemented. For many process generations, CPU performance has been following Moore's law and doubling in density every 18 months which has provided a significant improvement in performance. But NPUs and FPGAs have also kept pace with Moore's law, constantly keeping them in the performance lead for these specific networking applications. Today CPUs have moved to multiple cores and have added some specialized hardware functions that are dramatically closing the gap. Because Ethernet bandwidth performance improvements and therefore the incoming packet rates are not moving at the same pace as processor performance improvements, standard CPUs are now starting to be used in packet processing applications traditionally reserved for NPUs or FPGAs.

Data center administrators require network security, monitoring, and load balancing functions throughout the data center and must constantly install and replace these specialized network appliances to meet their needs. If they could simply repurpose their existing server resources to supply these functions, they could quickly scale network functions based on demand using the software orchestration layer. This is the idea behind the new industry initiative called network function virtualization. Several companies, such as Intel, are behind these initiatives, using their latest multicore Intel® Xeon® processor line and Intel® Data Plane Development Kit (Intel DPDK) to provide network appliance features using standard server resources. We will next describe several key NFV applications that are important in the data center.

Network security

When you think of network security, you may think of a firewall which provides authentication services and protects an internal network from external internet attacks. There are also several other aspects to network security as shown in Figure 9.6. The firewall does deep packet inspection to determine if there are any security threats. Not only are the frame headers inspected, but in some cases the payload will also be inspected. This is sometimes called layer 4-7 processing and may include a technique called regular expression matching in order to detect security threats.

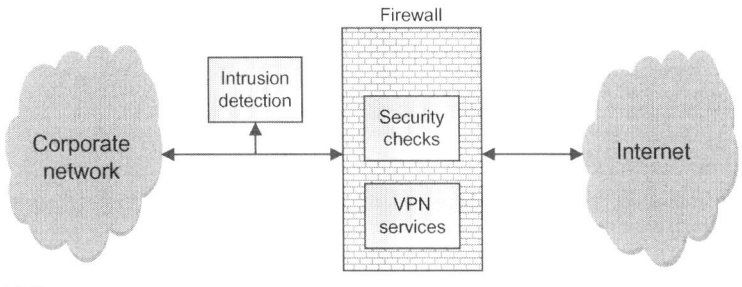

FIGURE 9.6

Main network security functions.

The firewall can also provide virtual private network (VPN) functions which encrypt and tunnel private data through the internet between remote client devices and corporate data centers. Another type of network function is intrusion detection which looks for data patterns or signatures to identify external attacks on the data center that may have slipped past the firewall. A passive intrusion detection system monitors the internal network and then alerts the network administrator of a potential threat. A reactive intrusion detection system (sometimes called an intrusion prevention system) not only detects a threat, it can also program the firewall to block the offending network traffic when it is detected.

Load balancing

As we discussed earlier in this book, data centers are making extensive use of server virtualization. But in some cases the allocation of these virtual machines cannot be adjusted quickly enough to react to the varying usage requirements coming from the network. Load balancing addresses this problem by intelligently spreading the workload across multiple virtual machines. In addition, data centers must be able to quickly recover from equipment failure. This is especially true for applications such as e-commerce where a significant amount of money can be lost during down time. Because of this, both user data and server resources can be replicated at local or remote sites. But idle resources waste money and load balancing can improve this situation by not only spreading the workload across distance resources, but also quickly redirecting traffic away from a resource during failure. Figure 9.7 shows a load balancing system block diagram that can be used to balance loads across servers or virtual machines in a data center network.

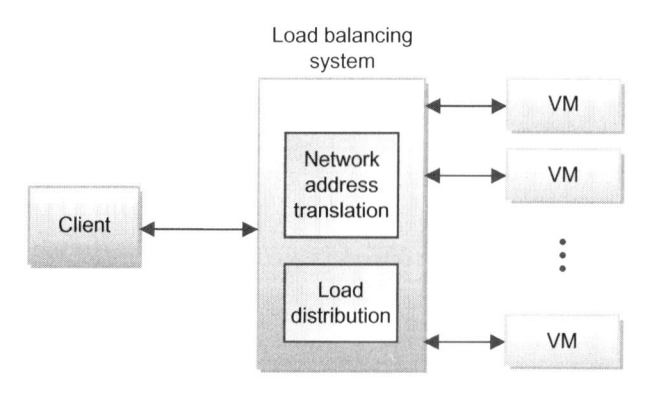

FIGURE 9.7

Server load balancing.

Load balancing is done using network address translation (NAT). Requests come in using the load balancer's IP address. When the load balancer receives a service request, it determines the optimal virtual machine to send this request to. It then modifies the destination IP address to match the VM and sends it for request processing. When the result of the request is sent back to the load balancer for delivery to the client, the load balancer modifies the source IP address to its own IP address. In this way, the client sees the load balancer as a single monolithic server.

The load balancing decision algorithm is an important part of the load balancer operation and can affect the overall system performance. Simple round-robin service distribution may be far from optimal, depending on processing requirements. Also, the health of each virtual machine must be monitored so that a failed VM can be quickly removed from the pool. In some disaster scenarios, the service requests must be rerouted to remote locations. Load balancers can also monitor the CPU utilization of the various virtual machines in order to even out the workloads. For some requests, it is desirable not to load balance. For example, a long-lived connection such as an FTP request must stay connected to the same virtual machine for a period of time. In other cases, such as multiple e-commerce requests from the same client, new requests must be directed to the same virtual machine due to transaction state information. Because of the widespread use of proxy servers, the load balancer may also need to read the packet payload information in order to identify unique clients.

Network monitoring

Network monitoring is similar to intrusion detection in some ways but focuses on network performance instead of network security threats. Performance monitoring can not only detect problems in the network such as slow or faulty network equipment, it can also be used to verify service level agreements for tenants. Special time stamp functions such as defined in the IEEE 1588 standard can be used to monitor network latency. Network monitoring equipment can also accomplish this by sending special packets through the network and measuring the round-trip delay. Connectivity check messages similar to the ones used in carrier networks can also be sent throughout the data center network to continually monitor the network health. Congestion can also be monitored through these same messages which can be used by the orchestration layer to reroute data in order to optimize network utilization and performance.

Implementation

Network function virtualization provides the data center network administrator a large amount of flexibility for providing both optimal service implementation and performance. Instead of providing high bandwidth network security functions at the edge of the data center network, these services can be distributed across the data center, reducing the local bandwidth requirements and providing the flexible control of features that are provided to different data center tenants. For example, providing network security within each rack means that the bandwidth load can be reduced to the level required by the servers in a single rack instead of the much higher bandwidth processing required if a security function is supporting multiple racks. In addition, load balancing functions can be placed close to their associated virtual machines and easily moved and expanded as needs change. Finally, NFV performance can be expanded or reduced by adding or removing server resources, providing an added level of flexibility.

Open daylight foundation

In 2013, the Linux Foundation announced the formation of the Open Daylight Foundation with founding members including several major networking OEMs. The foundation was formed to provide an open source framework to foster innovation in the areas of SDN and NFV. The founding members have committed to contributing source code for the project and some initial source code has been provided by Big Switch Networks®, Cisco, and NEC. The first release, called Hydrogen, will include an open controller along with network overlay support. It will be interesting to see how this initiative will evolve in relationship to other initiatives such as OpenStack. One area of focus in the Open Daylight foundation that is different from OpenStack is support for NFV.

SDN DEPLOYMENT

As of this writing, almost every networking OEM and data center software provider mentions SDN on their web site. In addition, venture capital is flooding into SDN startups, fueled partially by recent events such as the purchase of Nicira Networks by VMware. But this industry hype has not been matched with SDN deployments by cloud service providers (with the notable exception of Google). This is expected to change over the next several years. In this section, we will describe several potential SDN deployment scenarios in cloud data center networks.

Controller locations

One aspect that is not well defined in SDN is how the controller information is transmitted to the switches and routers throughout the network. Figure 9.8 shows an example of how this information can be exchanged. As we have shown earlier in this chapter, the central orchestration controller passes information to the open storage controllers, the open virtualization controllers, and the SDN controllers. Here, we focus on the SDN controllers which use protocols such as OpenFlow to pass information to the various switches and routers in the network. In many idealized SDN or OpenFlow slide presentations, the SDN controller is shown as a single logic function.

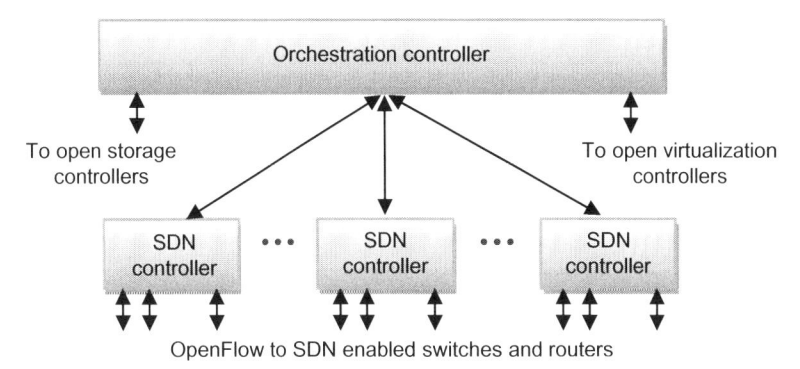

FIGURE 9.8

SDN distribution network.

In fact, there can be hundreds or even thousands of switches and routers in a large cloud data center that must be controlled.

Because a single controller cannot service this many devices, most implementations will require multiple SDN controllers spread throughout the data center. Another question is how data is transmitted between the orchestration controller and the SDN controllers and also between the SDN controllers and the switches and routers. This could be done using a separate lower bandwidth Ethernet network, or could be transmitted in-band through the existing data network. It will be interesting to see how these SDN controllers and SDN data communication will evolve in future cloud data center networks.

SDN at the network edge

In an ideal world, an SDN controller would monitor and control all of the networking equipment in the data center. This would include top of rack switches, end of row switches, and core switches. But it would also include the virtual switches that are part of the hypervisors in the servers. One problem with this vision is that many data centers already use layer 3 forwarding equipment from leading OEMs that do not currently support SDN and they don't want to rip out and replace all of this equipment in order to take advantage of SDN. In order for SDN to work its way into these data centers, implementation must start at the network edge. Specifically, vendors like VMware (through their Nicira acquisition) are providing SDN functionality in the virtualized switch and hypervisor domain as shown in Figure 9.9.

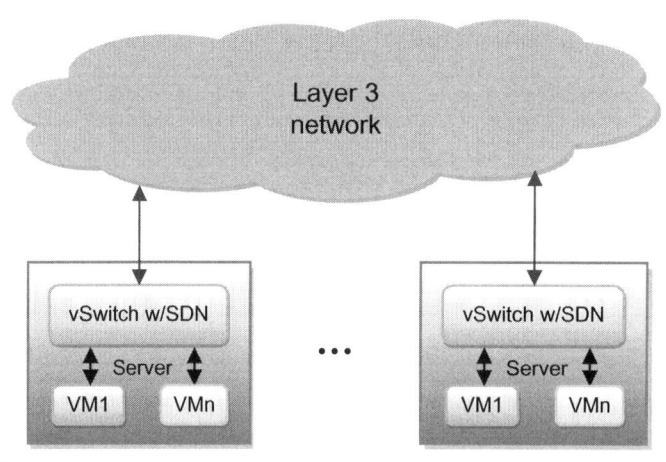

FIGURE 9.9

SDN at the network edge.

This SDN implementation allows tunneling of data through standard layer 3 networks because the hypervisor takes care of the tunneling endpoint functionality. This network virtualization tunneling capability includes support for VXLAN or NVGRE. As an example, VMware introduced their NSX product based on technology acquired with Nicira. With NSX, VMware not only provides this network virtualization support, but also several NFV features such as distributed virtual firewalls, virtual load balancers, network monitoring, and network security. NSX also provides gateway services allowing connections to external networks or non-virtualized hosts. Open interfaces allow NSX to communicate with other SDN controllers using interfaces built on open software standards such as OpenFlow. It is expected that other vendors will soon enter the market, providing a rich ecosystem of SDN products.

REVIEW

In this chapter, we provided a brief background on the current state of data center software and introduced the concept of the software-defined data center. We then provided some details behind OpenStack and OpenFlow which are two key open industry standards used for software defined networking. Next, we described a new industry initiative, called network function virtualization, which is emerging to provide network functions using standard server hardware. We concluded the chapter by providing some examples of how SDN can be deployed in cloud data centers. In the next chapter, we will leave the cloud data center to describe how networks are used in high performance computing applications. Although this is not directly related to cloud data center networks, some of the concepts may find their way into future cloud data center networks.

CHAPTER 10

High-Performance Computing Networks

High-performance computing (HPC) systems are used in several market segments including oil exploration, pharmaceutical research, financial services, aerodynamic simulations, weather forecasting and a wide variety of other scientific applications. Originally these "supercomputers" were designed as higher performance versions of large mainframe computers, but today they are built using massive arrays of off-the-shelf CPUs interconnected through high-bandwidth low-latency switch fabrics. Because these massively parallel computing system designs require a large number of processor racks, HPC systems are typically housed in dedicated data center facilities. The differences between these dedicated HPC systems and the systems implemented by cloud services providers are getting a bit fuzzy for some applications. For example, Amazon now provides compute clustering services for research institutions in its Elastic Compute Cloud (EC2) data centers.

Over time, it is expected that HPC clusters using large arrays of compute nodes interconnected using low-latency switch fabrics, and cloud data centers using large arrays of servers interconnected using Ethernet switch fabrics will start to share certain attributes and even some common technology. The reason we are covering switch fabric technology for HPC in a book about cloud networking is that it may enlighten the reader on trends for future high-performance cloud data centers. In this chapter, we will first discuss HPC system architectures and the movement to massively parallel computing. Next, we will discuss various industry standards used to interconnect multiple CPUs on a single board in these high-performance applications. We will then discuss how these boards are interconnected in large arrays by introducing several HPC switch fabric standards. Next, we will discuss HPC fabric components along with relative performance factors and conclude this chapter by providing an overview of HPC software.

HPC SYSTEM ARCHITECTURES

Originally, most HPC systems were designed using specialized hardware. By the late 1990s HPC system designers started to realize that they could improve performance and shorten time to deployment by using large arrays of off-the-shelf processors. This section will provide a background on early HPC system designs and also discuss some of the latest HPC system architectures based on large compute arrays, also known as massively parallel computing.

Large compute nodes

The original HPC systems were known a supercomputers, and one of the first supercomputers was the Control Data Corporation CDC 6600 designed by Seymour Cray. In 1972 Cray left Control Data to start Cray® Research where he developed some of the most famous supercomputers ever made, including the Cray-1 in 1976 and the Cray-2 in 1985. These Cray computers were constructed in the shape of a circular rack so that the circuit board connectors were close to each other in the center of the ring in order to reduce cable lengths and, therefore, signal propagation delays. Instead of using the larger high-density CMOS processing chips available in the early 1980s, Cray chose to develop processor nodes using circuit boards filled with lower density but higher performance gallium arsenide (GaAs) integrated circuits cooled by a special Fluorinert® liquid. Other companies such as Convex Computer Corporation were also developing high-performance computers throughout the 1990s using large processor boards made with different types of GaAs gate arrays. These high-performance chips made up the functional components of a compute node and were combined on a large board with each system containing several racks of these boards. But the days of designing supercomputers out of a few large high-performance compute nodes came to an end in the late 1990s when new approaches using massive arrays of off-the-shelf CPUs came to the forefront.

Arrays of compute nodes

Supercomputers made out of large arrays of off-the-shelf CPUs started to appear in the late 1990s from companies such as Hitachi and Fujitsu, and this new trend became known as massively parallel computing. Today, all of the top supercomputers in the world use these massively parallel architectures and performance increases each year as the latest high-performance CPUs are utilized. These machines look similar to small data centers with racks and racks full of processor shelves interconnected by a high-performance switch fabric. Some of these machines have been built out of video gaming boards or graphical processing units, but today most of these machines are built using multicore CPUs including the Intel® Xeon Phi™ chip. Each year, the industry releases a list of the top 500 supercomputers in the world based on industry benchmark testing. For example, a recent leading entry in the industries Top 500 supercomputing list from China reached 33,900 trillion floating point operations per second using 3,120,000 processor cores with Intel Xeon E5 processors and Intel Xeon Phi processing chips implemented on 16,000 compute nodes. Connecting these compute nodes together is a challenge which we will discuss further in this chapter.

MULTISOCKET CPU BOARDS

No matter how fast a multicore processor is, the overall supercomputer performance depends on how fast these processors can communicate with each other and to storage. There are two aspects to connecting hundreds of thousands of processing chips together in massively parallel supercomputers. The first aspect is connecting multiple processor sockets together on a single board, which is the subject of this section. In the next section, we will describe how to connect multiple boards together using industry standard switch fabrics to create these massively parallel machines.

HyperTransport

The HyperTransport (HT) Consortium was formed by several companies including AMD®, Apple, and NVIDIA® in 2001 and by 2003 several new products emerged using this new interface standard including devices from AMD and several other companies. That same year the HT Consortium released a specification for multiprocessor communication on a CPU board using an interconnect method which is sometimes called a system bus. This HT bus is a point-to-point connection utilizing 2-32 bits per link and provides up to 51.2G bytes per second of throughput.

An example HT implementation is shown in Figure 10.1. In this example, four CPU sockets are interconnected in a ring structure using HT links. Multiple links are sometimes used between devices to support different traffic types. In this example, two of these processors are also connected through HT links to IO Expanders which are sometimes called Input/Output Controller Hubs (ICHs), chipsets, or Southbridge devices. HT has a limited reach so it is used only within the CPU board and any interconnect between boards uses the ports on the IO expanders.

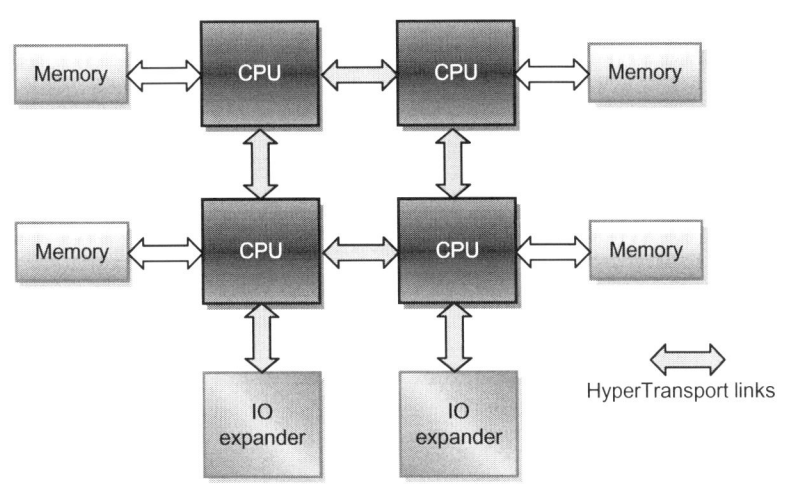

FIGURE 10.1

Example HyperTransport implementation.

HT uses packets to transmit data between devices where the packets consist of multiple 32-bit words. Packets are relatively small and contain a command field along with other optional fields such as address information and data. Because the packet overhead is kept low, high effective utilization of the link bandwidth can be achieved. To transfer data, posted or non-posted writes are used to place data in another processor's memory. Commands are also available to read data from another processor's memory. Although HT is developed by an industry consortium, it is mainly used in AMD multi-socket board designs today.

Intel® QuickPath Interconnect

Intel did not stand still after the HT spec was released and it started working on its own high-performance processor interconnect technology called Intel® QuickPath Interconnect (Intel QPI) in 2004 to replace its long-standing front side bus architecture. The first Intel products to use Intel QPI were their desktop processors which were released in 2008 and later it was used on their high-performance Intel Xeon processors which were released in 2009.

Intel QPI uses a similar architecture to HT as shown in Figure 10.1. The difference is that Intel QPI uses a 20 bit bus which is divided into four quadrats of 5 bits each. Different implementations can use different numbers of quadrants. It used an 80-bit data packet which can be transmitted using four clock cycles across a 20-bit bus. The packet contains an 8-bit link-level header, a 64-bit data payload, and an 8-bit error detection word. Using all four quadrants, the interface can achieve data rates up to 25.6G bytes per second which is twice as high as the theoretical maximum performance of their previous front side bus. Although Intel QPI is available on a variety of Intel processors, it is a critical component in HPC boards which use products such as the Intel Xeon Phi chip.

RapidIO

RapidIO is another processor interconnect technology that was originally proposed by Mercury Computer® and Motorola®. Motorola wanted to develop a standard based on its proprietary PowerPC bus. The RapidIO Trade Association was formed in 2000 to promote this technology as a solution for a variety of applications including the interconnect between boards. Unlike HT and Intel QPI that use relatively wide parallel busses, RapidIO quickly evolved into a serial interconnect technology similar to PCI Express. In fact, in some applications, it competes with PCI Express' non-transparent bridging (NTB) which we will describe below.

RapidIO can scale from supporting a few nodes to supporting thousands of nodes using switches and bridges. RapidIO serial ports can utilize up to 16 lanes providing up to 12G bytes per second of throughput. It is a packet-based protocol supporting both message passing and read/write commands. To support larger fabrics with appropriate congestion control, RapidIO supports packet priority levels along with link-level flow control. Because of the wide 16-lane interface required to achieve high-bandwidth, relatively expensive cables need to be used between boards compared to other technologies such as Infiniband and Ethernet. Because of this, RapidIO has not found much success in supercomputer designs, and even the PowerPC based supercomputers use custom switch fabrics. Today, RapidIO is mainly deployed in applications that use large arrays of digital signal processing boards, although the RapidIO trade association is trying to expand into other markets with improvements to the specification.

PCIe NTB

In Chapter 6 we provided an overview of PCI Express technology and described how it was designed to connect multiple peripheral devices to a single host. Because PCI Express was not designed as a technology to interconnect multiple hosts, the Advanced Switching Interconnect Special Interest Group (ASI-SIG) was started by Intel and several other companies in the early 2000s. Although the ASI specification included standards for exchanging information between hosts using the PCI Express physical layer, no successful products were ever developed and this specification faded away.

One of the leading members of the ASI-SIG was PLX® Technology who went on to work with the PCI-SIG to develop the NTB specification. Figure 10.2 shows how NTB can be used to exchange data between two hosts. NTB is implemented as an endpoint pair within the PCIe switch. These endpoints provide address translation capabilities allowing one host to write into the memory of another host as if it was writing into its own memory space. It also uses doorbell and scratchpad registers to signal interrupts between hosts. The same PCIe switch can provide this capability between multiple hosts while also providing traditional PCIe functionality for connecting peripheral devices such as network interface controllers (NICs). Although NTB has gained momentum in the embedded computing space, it is currently not used very often in the data center or supercomputing markets.

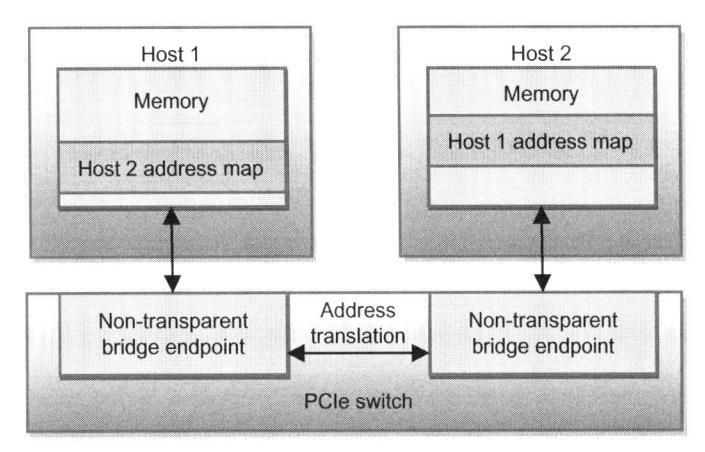

FIGURE 10.2

Non-transparent bridging between two hosts.

HPC NETWORKING STANDARDS

Although there are several workable solutions available for connecting multiple CPUs together on a board, connecting tens or hundreds of thousands of these boards together to create a large supercomputer is a more challenging task. HT and Intel QPI have not been designed for large switch fabric applications beyond the circuit board. RapidIO and PCI Express provide more scalable solutions, but their relatively low per-lane cable bandwidths require wide, expensive cables to reach high link bandwidth rates. In this section, we will provide an overview of several switch fabric technologies that have been used in massively parallel supercomputer installations. Although we will focus on industry standard switch fabric technologies, many supercomputers use custom designed switch fabrics which are beyond the scope of this chapter.

Fabric configurations

The fabric topology can have a big impact on the overall supercomputer performance. The two most popular configurations are the multilevel fat-tree and the 3D Torus as shown in Figure 10.3. The fat-tree is based on the Clos fabric architecture that we described in Chapter 3. In theory, a symmetrical fat-tree can provide full bandwidth connections between all compute nodes. Assuming a 64-port switch, a two level fat-tree can support 2048 compute nodes and a three level fat-tree can support up to 64K compute nodes.

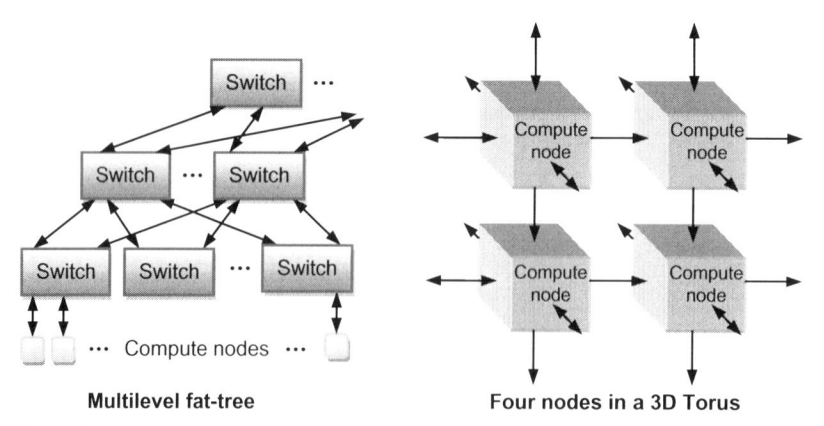

FIGURE 10.3

Popular fabric configurations.

The 3D Torus uses a three-dimensional (3D) array of compute nodes, each with direct connections to its nearest neighbors. If a message needs to be transmitted past a neighbor, the intermediate compute nodes pass the message down the line. At the end of the array, the connection is looped back to the beginning of the array, much like a

3D ring architecture. Although the 3D Torus architecture can save cost by not requiring switches, bandwidth must be shared between nodes in each dimension of the ring. Some supercomputer workloads, such as array processing routines, can take advantage of this architecture, improving performance over a fat-tree implementation. In some cases, a hybrid approach between these two topologies can also be used where local 3D Torus clusters are interconnected through a fat-tree.

Myrinet™

Myrinet™ is a switch fabric technology that was developed by a company called Myricom® for high-performance computer clustering applications. It provides lower packet overhead than protocols such as Ethernet while also providing high throughput and low latency. Compute nodes are connected through a special adapter card to switches and routers using fiber optic cables. The protocol includes features for error detection, flow control, and heart-beat monitoring providing a fault-tolerant fabric design. In 2005, the Myrinet switch fabric was used in over 25% of the top 500 supercomputers but this has fallen to less that 1% today. One reason for this is that Myrinet is a single vendor technology and has been surpassed by multivendor technologies such as Infiniband and low-latency Ethernet solutions.

Infiniband

In Chapter 2, we provided a brief overview of the history of Infiniband. In supercomputing applications, Infiniband has several advantages including low frame overhead, high port bandwidth, and low latency. Figure 10.4 is a pictorial representation of how Infiniband currently fits into the performance gap between high-volume Ethernet and custom switch fabrics in supercomputing installations.

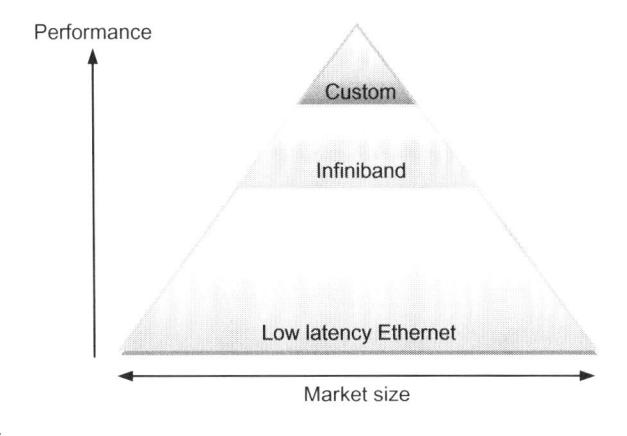

FIGURE 10.4

Fabric adoption in high-performance computing.

Infiniband fabrics use low-latency host channel adapters (HCAs) in the compute nodes and connects these nodes through low-latency switches using 1, 4, or 12-lane cables. Depending on the generation of Infiniband technology, each lane can operate between 2 and 25G bits per second. Because of the low protocol overhead and the use of high-bandwidth links, Infiniband can achieve latencies between compute nodes including HCAs and switches in range of a few microseconds. This is an important factor in HPC applications. Even though there is an Infiniband Trade Association, there are currently only two remaining Infiniband switch silicon vendors; Mellanox who also manufactures Infiniband and Ethernet switch systems, and Intel who acquired the Infiniband business of QLogic in 2012. This is why low-latency Ethernet is used in higher volume supercomputer designs where the performance levels of Infiniband are not as important as the fabric cost.

Ethernet

Ethernet has been around much longer than Infiniband, but it has always lagged in port bandwidth and latency. This changed around 2006 when 10Gb Ethernet switches came on the market and companies like Fulcrum Microsystems offered Ethernet switch silicon with cut-through latencies as low as 300 nS. Since that time, switches with more than 64 10GbE ports have emerged with 40GbE uplinks and low-latency NICs have come to market using remote direct memory access (RDMA) technologies. It is expected that Ethernet will continue to hold a large share of the lower end supercomputer market due to availability of products from multiple vendors and economies of scale driving down cost compared to other high-performance fabric choices. As of November 2013, Ethernet fabrics were used in 42% of the top 500 supercomputers compared to 41% for Infiniband according to the HPC wire.

HPC NETWORK PERFORMANCE FACTORS

Supercomputer designers are always pushing performance levels by using the latest generation CPU technology. But the switch fabric bandwidth and latency can also have a large influence on the performance of supercomputers. There are several key contributors that impact switch fabric bandwidth and latency. In this section, we will discuss key components that impact performance including the HCA and the switch. We will also discuss how the switch fabric architecture can impact overall supercomputer performance.

Fabric interface

For Infiniband fabrics, HCAs are used in supercomputers on the compute node as an interface between the compute node and the fabric. In Ethernet-based fabrics, a NIC is used as a fabric interface. For these devices, bandwidth translates directly into latency which is a key factor in HPC. For example, a data packet will be transmitted with 4 times lower latency when using a 40G port compared to a 10G port. Infiniband has constantly provided higher port bandwidth than Ethernet and is expected to maintain that lead for some time. But Ethernet continues to improve port bandwidth with new 40GbE and 100GbE standards.

Supercomputer performance for a given application can be directly impacted by how long it takes a given compute node to read from or write to the memory of another compute node. As we discussed in Chapter 5, Ethernet RDMA technology can be used to bypass both the operating system and the driver in order to provide lower latency data transfers between hosts. Infiniband is based on RDMA technology and provides a queue-pair construct as a fundamental architectural element. The way this works is that HCA sets up a connection with another HCA by establishing a send queue and a receive queue which are known as queue pairs. Multiple queue pairs can be used simultaneously. Once they are set up, they are accessed by the application layer directly, reducing transmission latency. Queue pairs can be configured independently with different levels of service such as reliable connection, unreliable connection, reliable datagram, and unreliable datagram. Reliable connections utilize completion queues to signal when a transaction is complete. The HCA arbitrates access to the fabric by the send queues and also selects the service order of the receive queues based on service level and priority. Because Infiniband has been architected with HPC messaging in mind, using queue pairs, HCAs generally have lower latency than Ethernet NICs.

Switch

Ethernet switches that are used in HPC applications use cut-through operation in order to reduce latency. In this mode of operation, incoming frame headers are inspected and forwarding decisions can be made in a few hundred nanoseconds. Transmission of the frame can then start before the entire frame is received. Although this eliminates the possibility of checking the frame for errors using the frame check sequence before transmission, most fabrics of this type expect that the fabric interface adapters on the receiving compute nodes will perform this check when the packet is received and flag any errors.

Infiniband switches have less functional overhead than Ethernet switches in that they simply forward packets based on header address information. Forwarding tables simply consist of destination address—output port pairs that are populated during initialization and may be modified if something changes in the fabric. Unlike Ethernet, no routing or address learning features are required, which simplifies the design and allows Infiniband switches to achieve very low cut-through latencies on the order of 100-200 nS. Infiniband switches support multiple virtual channels per port which allow traffic types to be treated differently based on class of service indicators. Both Ethernet and Infiniband switches support link-level flow control with Infiniband using a credit based mechanism compared to Ethernet's priority based flow control described earlier. Today, Infiniband switches are available with up to 32 54Gbps ports allowing the construction of large, low-latency fat-tree fabrics for massively parallel computing installation.

Fabric architecture

The switch fabric architecture can also have a big impact on the overall supercomputer performance. Data congestion points can arise causing latency spikes which can slow down the overall system. In some HPC applications, the data traffic patterns are well understood and the fabric can be designed to accommodate these applications. For example, a 3D Torus may work perfectly fine for some applications, but can cause congestion points for others. Fat-tree architectures require efficient load distribution mechanisms across the second and third levels to minimize congestion. Congestion can be minimized in some cases using the congestion management mechanisms described in Chapter 3. Certain types of traffic can also be given priority through the fabric using link-level flow control and/or minimum bandwidth guarantees. Other solutions include providing excess bandwidth (over-provisioning) which can also reduce congestion levels.

HPC NETWORKING SOFTWARE

Software is an important component in HPC. Massively parallel processing requires tight coordination among all of the computing resources in the array and this is where software engineers spend most of their time optimizing code. A key part of their effort is to optimize the transfer of data between computing nodes through the switch fabric. In this section, we will describe two industry standards that help in this effort.

Message Passing Interface

The effort to develop a standard messaging interface for distributed memory architectures started in the early 1990s and evolved into the Message Passing Interface (MPI) standard which includes contributions from about 40 different organizations. It was quickly adopted by the massively parallel computing community as a standard syntax and a set of standard library routines for use by programmers writing in the Fortran or C programming languages. It soon evolved into the dominant communication model used in HPC today.

MPI implements an application programming interface (API) that includes the syntax and semantics for core library functions that allow various types of communications between routines that may run on individual processors or processor cores. Communication can be between process pairs but MPI also supports gather and reduce operations along with support for graph-like logical routines and various monitoring and control operations. OEMs developing large parallel machines can build upon MPI to provide higher level distributed communication routines to their customers. MPI is considered to be a higher layer protocol that runs on top of lower layer protocols such as sockets and TCP/IP.

Verbs

In 2004, the OpenIB Alliance was formed to provide a Linux API for Infiniband switch fabrics used in applications such as HPC. In 2006, the organization extended its charter to support the iWARP RDMA protocol and at the same time changed its name to the OpenFabrics Alliance. The OpenFabrics Alliance soon released an open software stack called OpenFabrics Enterprise Distribution (OFED) for the Linux and FreeBSD operating systems.

The Infiniband API function calls, known as verbs, make requests to the IB messaging transport services. There are verbs for memory management, address management, queue-pair functions, multicast functions, work requests, and event handling. Infiniband silicon vendors and network equipment vendors provide their own verbs implementation optimized for their hardware features. Although verbs can be used as an alternative to MPI to gain some performance advantages, many MPI implementations use IB verbs themselves. For many applications, programming using verbs can improve performance over using higher layer protocols, such as MPI, due to closer interaction with the hardware resources.

REVIEW

In this chapter, we provided information on switch fabrics used for HPC. We initially gave a brief historical overview of supercomputing along with the evolution of supercomputing architectures into massively parallel computers. Next, we described several standards for efficient communication between CPUs within a single board compute node, followed by a description of several switch fabric architectures used to interconnect these compute nodes to form the large parallel machines. We then provided an overview of several factors that affect supercomputing performance, including component design and switch fabric architecture implementations. We concluded this chapter with a brief description of standard communication software used in these systems. Although supercomputer switch fabric design seems like a departure from the main theme of this book, there are many common aspects that may influence future cloud data center network implementations. In the next chapter, we will explore some of these as we look at future cloud data center networking trends.

CHAPTER 11

Future Trends

Throughout this book we have been discussing the background and current trends in cloud data center networking. Now we have a chance to get a little creative and try to prognosticate where data center networking technology will head in the next 5-10 years. One trend that has already begun is the movement to rack scale architectures. In this chapter, we will attempt to follow this trend and project what these racks may look like in the near future. Another interesting trend involves the switch fabric that interconnects all of the rack scale components together. Today, we have separate technologies and protocols for board-level interconnect, high-performance computing (HPC), storage, and data. Will these eventually merge into a unifying fabric?

Memory technology is also on the verge of some dramatic changes and the line between volatile and non-volatile memory will become blurry as we move into the future. Data center cabling is also undergoing transformations as traditional copper-based solutions are running out of steam and will soon be replaced by low-cost optics for high-performance applications. Finally, as we discussed in Chapter 9, the data center control plane software is evolving into a single point of orchestration covering all aspects of data center operation. This chapter will touch on all of these subjects while attempting to provide a view into the future. Keep in mind that this chapter is based on opinions and educated guesses as to where the cloud data center may be headed.

RACK SCALE ARCHITECTURES

Data center uniformity has many advantages for cloud service providers including the use of common building blocks that can be purchased in high volumes and then flexibly allocated as needed. The designation of the rack as the basic data center building block is one way to achieve this goal as we described earlier in this book. But this new definition of rack scale architecture needs to also support features such as resource disaggregation and distributed switch fabric components. In this section, we will provide some background on the new requirements driving the need for rack scale architecture and some predictions on where this new architectural concept is heading.

Resource disaggregation

In today's cloud data center rack, the components that make up the server shelf may include CPUs, CPU chip sets, CPU memory, network interface cards, disk drives, boot memory, board management controllers, power supplies, and fans. To improve power efficiency, power supplies and fans are now in many cases shared across the rack, but the server shelf itself may still contain all of the other components listed above, most of them soldered to a single board. When a new generation of CPUs comes to market, the data center administrator may need to replace the entire server shelf including components that do not need updating. This increases cost and wastes resources, leading to the desire to disaggregate and modularize these building block components. In the near future, it is expected that the data center rack will look more like Figure 11.1, with pools of disaggregated resources across the rack.

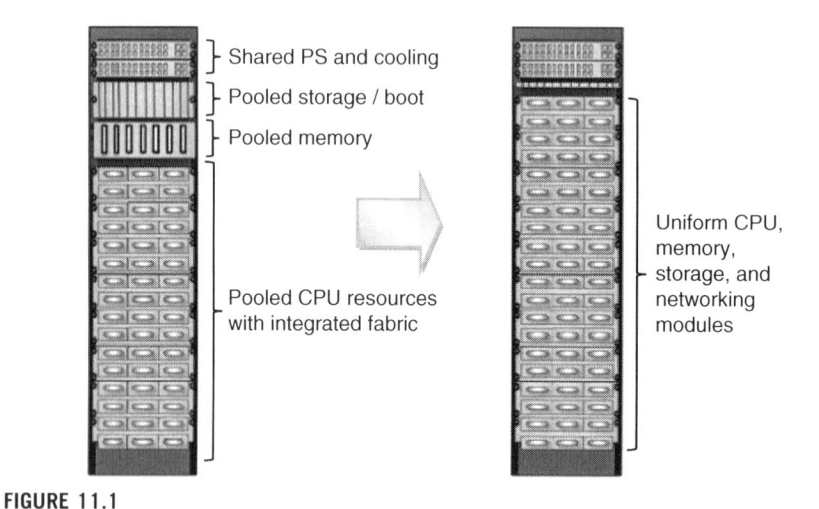

FIGURE 11.1

Rack scale architecture resource disaggregation and evolution.

In this vision, the CPU resources are contained in a pool dedicated modules which include integrated fabric connections. A distributed fabric provides these CPU resources with access to memory, storage, and network uplink ports that are located elsewhere within the rack. The memory, storage, and network uplink resources could be allocated as needed to the various CPUs, providing a very flexible solution.

With a common fabric technology, this could even look like a rack full of uniform slots where each slot could be occupied by a CPU module, a memory module, a storage module, or a network uplink module for the ultimate in flexibility as shown on the right side of Figure 11.1. Imagine a rack using 60% storage modules, 20% CPU modules, 10% memory modules, and 10% networking modules in a storage application. Imagine another rack using 50% CPU modules, 30% memory modules, 10% storage modules, and 10% networking modules in a HPC application. In the rest of this section, we will touch on these various modules and we will dive deeper into the future of memory and fabric technology later in this chapter.

CPU modules

Today, most server CPUs come with chipsets that act as input output (IO) hubs. The reason for this is that CPUs are designed for multiple markets, each with its own IO requirements. For example, a CPU used in a workstation may have different IO requirements than a CPU used in a telecommunication system. In servers, typical IO hub requirements may include a quick path interconnect (QPI) interface for processor communication, PCI Express for peripherals, Ethernet for networking, and Serial ATA (SATA) or Serial Attached SCSI (SAS) for storage. The processors themselves also have DRAM interfaces for local memory. This is starting to change with the introduction of system on a chip (SoC) designs used in applications such as microservers. SoC designs typically combine the processor and IO hub into a single chip to reduce board space, power requirements, and cost.

Future server CPUs may follow this SoC model, which would help to reduce CPU module component count. Instead of local memory, efficient switch fabric technology could be used to connect these CPU modules to a pool of memory in the rack as well as a pool of storage. In addition, multiple switch ports may be included in future server CPU SoCs allowing for a distributed rack scale switch fabric as shown in Figure 11.2. This fabric would allow CPUs to be interconnected in a variety of topologies, including rings and meshes, without the need for an external switching device. An efficient fabric technology could also eliminate the need for special CPU interconnect technology such as Hypertransport or Intel QPI. The important idea here is the use of uniform CPU modules that can be scaled up or down within the rack and can be allocated memory, storage, and networking resources based on workload requirements. The other key point is that they can be upgraded independently of the other resources in the rack.

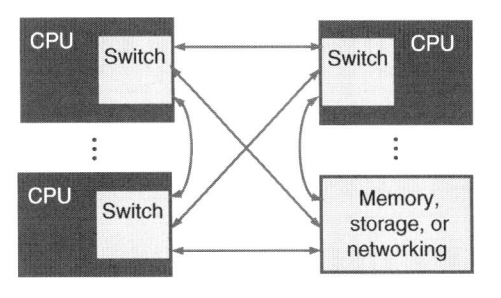

FIGURE 11.2

CPUs with integrated switching blocks.

Memory and storage modules

In idealized rack scale architectures, memory and storage modules could be easily plugged into the rack as needed. On the right side of Figure 11.1, different ratios of CPU to memory to storage could be achieved for a given workload by plugging these modules into a unified rack scale fabric. The problem is that CPU performance is highly dependent on memory bandwidth and latency, while less dependent on storage latency. Because of this, CPUs today use directly connected double data rate (DDR) memory interfaces to DRAM modules, while storage interfaces are relegated to the attached IO hub (chipset) using protocols such as SATA and SAS. Today, many large data centers are using distributed memory caching systems like Memcached to share server memory across the rack or even across the data center using a TCP/IP transport mechanism. But this adds to CPU overhead due to the TCP processing requirements and has performance limitations. To accommodate versatile pools of rack scale memory and storage without these limitations, new interconnect techniques will need to be developed. This will be covered in more depth in the next two sections of this chapter.

Distributed fabric

Initial rack scale architectures will provide distributed networking across server modules. In this case, groups of servers or microservers on a given shelf will be connected to a switch on that same shelf. This switch will also provide high-bandwidth uplinks out of the shelf to an aggregation switch on the top of the rack as shown in Figure 11.3. When using the SoC CPUs with the embedded switches that we discussed above, various interconnect strategies can be used between the server shelves, including ring, mesh, star, or hybrid architectures depending on the bandwidth and latency requirements of the server workloads. In addition, since the sleds on the shelf share the high bandwidth uplinks to the ToR switch, bandwidth can be allocated in a more flexible manner across the sleds.

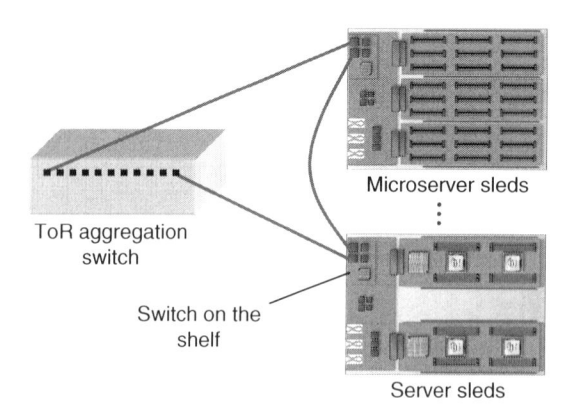

FIGURE 11.3

Example RSA distributed switch fabric showing two types of server shelves.

Projecting into the future, it would be ideal to have a unified fabric for CPUs, memory, storage, and networking so that any slot in a rack could be occupied by any of these resources as shown on the right side of Figure 11.1. In this case, instead of a switch module on every server shelf, the switch modules could utilize some of the slots shown in Figure 11.1. We will provide more projections on what it would take to accomplish this in the "Switch Fabric Technology" section.

MEMORY TECHNOLOGY

In an idealized data center, memory would be uniform, high performance, high capacity, and non-volatile. Today, high-performance memory such as DRAM loses information when power goes away. Flash memory can maintain data between power cycles, but has limited write performance and write durability. Rotating disk drives have high capacity and are non-volatile, but have lower performance compared to solid-state memory. Because of these performance/capacity tradeoffs, CPUs utilize a memory hierarchy as we described in Chapter 9. An ideal solution would incorporate the best features of all three types of storage. In this section, we will describe some emerging data storage technologies that may change the way memory systems are architected. We will also discuss improvements that could be made to the CPU memory interface which has been using the same parallel interface standard since the late 1990s.

Non-volatile memory and storage

As we discussed in Chapter 9, there is a memory hierarchy in data center server systems, with fast, small, volatile memory close to the processor and high capacity, slower, non-volatile memory (storage) further out in the memory hierarchy. There are some hybrid approaches to bridge the density-performance gap such as flash drives using DRAM caches or HDDs with flash memory caches, but these still fit into various positions within the memory hierarchy. If one could come up with a high-performance, high-capacity, non-volatile memory technology, it could dramatically change how storage is used in data center systems.

One example of a potentially disruptive technology is phase change memory. This technology uses localized high temperatures to program the crystalline state of chalcogenide glass in order to store data in memory cells. For example, a low-resistance crystalline state could represent a logic 0 while a high-resistance crystalline state could represent a logic 1. Some researchers at Intel and ST Microelectronics have proposed four resistive states allowing the storage of 2 bits worth of data in a single cell, effectively doubling the storage density. Some people have compared this technology to a variable resistor with memory, called a memristor.

The advantage of phase change memory is that it has the potential to achieve the density of flash memory, but with the read/write performance of DRAM along with reliable operation with up to 100 million write cycles and data retention of up to 300 years. The major disadvantage is that data can be lost when operating at high temperature and the technology is still not very mature. Even so, phase change memory could replace both DRAM and local flash along with hard drive storage within the server rack. It may also replace flash memory in solid-state drives used in the second storage tier. This would allow the use of a single memory interface from the CPU to a uniform pool of storage and memory. But as memory performance increases within the rack, new memory interfaces will also be needed.

Memory interface

Moving memory to a central pool in the rack introduces a new set of challenges. Data transfer rates and latency are key CPU memory performance factors that today are solved using wide DDR3 interfaces to local devices called dual in-line memory modules (DIMMs). Because these interfaces require careful board layout, the DIMMs are positioned close to the CPUs on the server boards. In addition, parallel bus technology like this will eventually run out of performance capability much like it did for PCI which moved to the PCI Express standard using serial interconnections.

But what would happen if we had a clean sheet of paper to design a new memory interface technology that was not restricted to the server board. One choice would be to borrow the 25G serializer-deserializer (SerDes) technology used in the latest generation 100Gb Ethernet ports. Figure 11.4 compares what could be achieved using this technology with existing memory interfaces such as DDR3 connections to DIMMs or PCI Express connections to flash memory.

	4 x 25G Interface	DDR3 SO-DIMM	PCIe Gen3 16-lane
Maximum transfer rate	12.5GB/s	6.4GB/s	12.5GB/s
Latency for 64-bit transfer	0.64nS	1.25nS	0.5nS
Pins required	16	200	64

FIGURE 11.4

Comparison of various high-speed interfaces.

As can be seen in Figure 11.4, this new type of interface could achieve twice the performance with a greater than $12 \times$ pin count reduction compared to DDR3 interfaces and about the same performance and a $4 \times$ pin count reduction compared to the latest PCI Express technology. An additional advantage of the $4 \times 25G$ solution is the use of industry standard 100GbE optical cabling to reduce cost (more on that later), allowing pools of memory modules to be deployed separately from the servers within the rack. Although such an interface does not exist today, it is expected that this type of new memory interface will emerge in the industry, driven by applications such as rack scale architecture. In the meantime, a hierarchical approach may be used with some memory remaining close to the CPU (much like a cache) and other modular memory in the rack connected to the CPU modules using protocols such as Ethernet or Infiniband. As of this writing, new disk drives for the data center have been announced using 1GbE interfaces instead of the traditional SAS interface. It will be interesting to see how memory interfaces evolve to meet future data center performance challenges.

SWITCH FABRIC TECHNOLOGY

Switch fabric technology will become more important as data centers become more distributed and virtualized. The ideal data center switch fabric would allow any resource to communicate with any other resource with high bandwidth and low latency. Today, data centers are converging on high-bandwidth Ethernet as the fabric of choice, but Ethernet is not ideal for all applications. In this section, we will discuss Ethernet limitations along with proposals on how these can be improved for some applications. We will also touch on port bandwidth and the design of modular scalable data center fabrics.

Frame overhead

High-bandwidth Ethernet switch fabrics are now the leading networking solution used to interconnect servers and storage within large data center networks. With the movement toward modular rack scale architectures, some limitations with Ethernet are becoming exposed. As we discussed in Chapter 9, there are various methods for sending storage traffic across Ethernet networks such as iSCSI and FCoE. But for applications such as processor-to-processor transactions in high-performance compute clustering or for communication between the CPU and modular rack scale memory resources, Ethernet is not very efficient.

Ethernet has a fairly large frame overhead when transporting small segments of data. Consider transporting 64-bits of data between two processors in a cluster or between a processor and memory. Ethernet has a minimum frame size of 64-bytes. When you include the frame preamble and the minimum interframe gap, it can take 80-bytes to transport 64-bits of data which is an efficiency of 10%. In other words, a 10GbE link is carrying only 1Gbps of data. One could argue that data can be combined from multiple transactions to improve the frame payload utilization, but this just adds to the communication latency. In contrast, a CPU communication protocol, such as CPI, can transport 64-bits of data within 10-bytes which is an efficiency of 80%.

One way to solve this problem is to develop a more efficient communication protocol within the data center rack. This protocol should have low frame overhead to improve link bandwidth utilization along with high bandwidth and low latency. In addition, it could take advantage of link technologies used in high-volume products such as 100GbE in order to reduce cable costs. It is expected that, as rack scale architectures evolve, new fabric technologies like this will be employed in order to allow memory disaggregation from the CPUs and improve overall rack performance.

Port bandwidth

Switch fabric port bandwidth is an important parameter in new cloud data centers that converge multiple traffic types on single links while at the same time want to maintain high performance and low latency. If the port bandwidth is kept sufficiently higher than the bandwidth required by the servers, congestion can be reduced in the network.

Or, if the port bandwidth is significantly higher than the server requirements, multiple servers can share the same link, reducing the amount of cabling required.

Ethernet port bandwidth has continued to increase by a factor of 10 each generation, but this growth has slowed as the design of high-bandwidth on-chip SerDes has had trouble keeping pace. Today, data center Ethernet switch port rates top out at 40G which utilize 4-lanes of 10G. The next step will increase SerDes rates to 25G providing 100Gb Ethernet ports across 4-lanes. Although the IEEE is looking at developing a roadmap to 1000Gb Ethernet, the most likely next step will be 400GbE. But even this will be challenging as it requires a $4\times$ increase in SerDes bandwidth using process technologies that are increasing in performance by only $1.5\text{-}2.0\times$ with each new generation. This leaves a gap between the desires of data center system designers and networking product capabilities. In the meantime, data center administrators will need to become more creative in optimizing network utilization by localizing workloads and employing better network management using tools such as software-defined networking.

Modular design

Assuming that a low overhead, high-performance fabric technology can be developed for the data center rack, various data center resources could be connected to this fabric, as shown in Figure 11.5. By using uniform modules as shown in Figure 11.1, this configuration would allow resource allocation based on workload requirements. For example, the memory-to-CPU ratio could be configured based on the number of each type of module used. Also, resource could be adjusted dynamically. Today, memory is directly connected to each CPU and the amount of memory depends on the estimated worst-case workload. With the modular rack, memory could be dynamically allocated to the CPUs based on current workload requirements, reducing the overall memory requirements in the rack. In addition, various types of memory and storage modules could be intermixed including DRAM, Flash, and HDDs, and these resources could be allocated as needed to the CPUs.

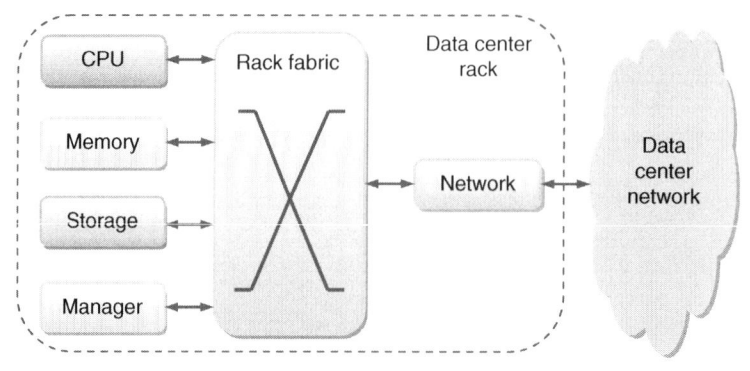

FIGURE 11.5

Modular data center rack.

This new rack will also include some sort of rack manager module for both board-level management and a control plane processor for applications such as software-defined networking. A network module could be used to personalize the rack fabric based on workloads or as a connection to the larger data center network. It is most likely that the larger network will maintain standard protocols such as Ethernet, so these modules will need to act as a bridge between the efficient rack scale fabric and the data center network. This network interface module will be shared among multiple CPUs and more network modules can be added based on bandwidth and latency requirements. We will next discuss the future of cabling technology which is needed to connect all of these rack scale resources together and also to connect these resources to the outside network.

CABLING TECHNOLOGY

The development of cabling technology in the data center is a constant battle between performance, distance, and cost. Performance depends on not only bandwidth but also latency through the silicon physical interface (PHY) devices that transmit or receive signals over the cables. Within the rack, cable distances are only a few meters, but, when sending signals to the end of row switch or to other racks in the data center, this distance can increase to over 100 m. Cost is also a critical factor as tens of thousands of these cables may be used within a cloud data center network. In this section, we will discuss several cabling technologies and attempt to predict where things may be headed in the future.

Copper cabling

For years, Ethernet devices in the data center were connected using the familiar category 5 (Cat5) cables, which support data rates from 10Mb per second up to 1Gb per second. Cat5 cable is low-cost, easy to trim to length, and can be used for connections up to 100 m. When 10GbE started to be widely deployed in the data center, the most prominent copper cable type used was based on the enhanced small form-factor pluggable (SFP+) standard. The SFP+ reach is limited to about 7 m when using direct attached copper cables and around twice that when using active copper transceivers in the cable connectors. For longer reaches, optical cables are used between the racks. But these SFP+ cables are relatively expensive compared to Cat5.

In 2006, the IEEE released a new specification known as 10GBase-T which allows the transmission of 10GbE signals across category 6 (Cat6) cables. These are an enhanced version of Cat5 cables, but are about the same cost. In order to transmit 10G data up to 100 m across the four twisted pairs in a Cat6 cable, special digital signal processing is required within the silicon physical layer transmitters and receivers (PHYs) that are used at each end of the cable. This special processing adds both power and latency to switches that use 10GBase-T. In recent years, the power has been reduced to manageable levels by fabricating these designs with the latest 28 nm processing technology, and in many applications, the latency added is not critical. At this time, 10GBase-T is gaining a lot of traction in the enterprise data center markets where it makes it easy to upgrade from 1GbE equipment to 10GbE equipment using the same cabling infrastructure. Many newly built cloud data centers are sticking with SFP+ cables in the short distances between the servers and the top of rack switches.

For 40GbE, direct attached copper cables using the quad small form-factor pluggable (QSFP) standard can be used for distances up to a few meters. But there is no equivalent 40GBase-T standard, so for longer distances, optical cabling is required. There are some low-cost optical cabling solutions coming to market such as the Modular Optical Cable (MOC) products from Intel, which can provide similar cost to copper for longer cable distances. The next step will be 100GbE using 4-lanes of 25G. At this time, it is not well understood if 25Gb per second copper-based solutions can be used across the height of a rack, so low-cost optical solutions may become an imperative.

Optical cabling

Optical cabling has been used for years in long distance communication networks. It was not until recently that it has been used for high-bandwidth data center connections. Long distance communications networks use single-mode fiber which has less modal dispersion than multimode fiber, allowing it to transmit at higher bandwidth over longer distances. But multimode fiber has lower manufacturing costs and can transmit high-bandwidth signals across data center distances.

At each end of the fiber, electrical signals must be converted to optical signals and optical signals back into electrical signals. For example, the enhanced SFP+ connectors within a top of rack switch in the data center can accept modules that convert electrical signals to the IEEE 10GBase-SR standard using 850 nm lasers over multimode fiber. There is also a 40GBase-SR4 standard for sending 40GbE across four fibers in a bundle using QSFP connectors. The optical transceivers at each end of the cable use more exotic process technologies such as gallium arsenide or indium phosphide and special manufacturing techniques must be used to ensure proper alignment between the lasers and the fiber for maximum optical coupling. Plus, when transmitting 40GbE or 100GbE signals using 4-lanes, this coupling has to be done properly across eight different fibers. Because of this, the cost of sending 10GbE signals up to 100 m using copper cables such as Cat6 using 10GBase-T has been up to 10 times lower than using fiber cables.

As we mentioned above, direct attached copper cables can transmit 10GbE and 40GbE (4 × 10G) signals up to a few meters which is enough for connecting signals across a given rack. But 100GbE cables will need to carry 4-lanes of 25G and copper may no longer be able to meet these required performance levels for even this short distance. To solve this issue, low-cost optical cabling using silicon photonics will start to see use in the data center over the next several years. Silicon photonics uses lower-cost silicon fabrication capabilities and manufacturers such as Intel are using special fiber alignment techniques to further reduce manufacturing costs. By using these low-cost 100G optical cables across the rack, congestion can be reduced by increasing overall bandwidth and/or cable count can be reduced by using a single 100GbE uplink for multiple server sleds compared to using 40G copper uplinks. Fiber cables have additional advantages including smaller size, lower bend radius, and less weight compared to copper.

Wireless interconnect

Some scientists are investigating the use of wireless technology in data center networks. One technique called 3D beamforming is being developed by scientists at the University of California, Santa Barbara using 60GHz wireless transceivers. The idea is that during periods of peak data center bandwidth utilization, high-bandwidth flows could be beamed directly between certain locations in the data center and these locations could be changed dynamically over time without the need to rewire cables.

Other researchers at Cornell University are looking at similar 60GHz wireless transceivers to connect servers within specially designed clusters of data center racks. Instead of using rows of racks as is done in today's data centers, these racks would be arranged in a circle with data transmitted wirelessly between servers within the center of the circle. This is similar to the Cray computers we discussed in the last chapter, as this shortens the wireless distance between racks. They also propose transmitting data wirelessly between rack clusters using similar transceivers. These researchers have estimated that the cost of this type of wireless networking could be as low as 1/12 the cost of conventional cables and switches in data centers with over 10,000 servers. It will be interesting to see how this technology progresses over the next several years.

SOFTWARE-DEFINED INFRASTRUCTURE

In Chapter 9, we provided an overview of software-defined networking and network functional virtualization and how it is all tied together with an orchestration layer. Some organizations are now starting to refer to this as the software-defined data center or software-defined infrastructure (SDI). Not only are cloud data centers starting to embrace this technology, but telecom service providers are considering it as a way to reduce their operating costs. In this section, we will make some predictions on where this technology may be headed in the data center.

Data center automation

The ultimate goal for large data centers is the availability of a central orchestration layer that can be used by the data center administrator to allocate resources, monitor operations, and quickly recover from error conditions. This includes the orchestration of all data center resources including servers, virtual machines, networking, security, and storage. It is expected that this type of centralized control will start to be implemented over the next several years as technologies such as software-defined networking (SDN) and network function virtualization (NFV) become more mature.

Once this centralized orchestration layer is established, it is expected that other types of innovation will start to take place. One area is the use of data center automation running on top of the orchestration layer. Because all data center monitoring information comes back to the orchestration layer, why not automatically use this information to adjust the data center configuration without manual intervention. For example, assume a congestion point starts to develop within one section of the data center network. The data center automation layer could quickly recognize this condition, move virtual machines, and reroute traffic to eliminate this congestion in the fraction of the time it would take a human operator. This would not only reduce data center operating expenses, but also improve data center utilization, which in turn could increase data center revenue. We expect that the development of these types of applications will be the next area of software innovation for cloud data centers.

Network function virtualization

NFV is a new industry term which defines the creation of virtual network appliances using standard server hardware. The main driver is the cost savings compared to the use of specialized hardware components such as NPUs, FPGAs, and ASICs. The first stage of NFV deployments will not use generic servers, but instead will use servers with co-processor chipsets to offload functions such as data encryption and data compression. It is expected that as network bandwidths increase, specialized hardware resources will continue to be used to meet line rate performance requirements. In some cases, these resources will be incorporated in chipsets or within the processors themselves. But this can add expense to the processors that are used in many other applications where NFV is not required. One solution is to use the flexible rack scale architecture that we discussed earlier in this chapter. By using the same low-latency, high-bandwidth fabric required for memory disaggregation within the rack, specialized NFV co-processing modules could be used as needed based on workload requirements. This would allow network administrators to target NFV resources for applications such as security and load balancing where needed within the data center. These modules, along with the other modules we described earlier, could be dynamically reallocated as workloads change over time by the data center software orchestration layer.

Big data analytics

A new buzz word in the industry is big data analytics. The idea is that large cloud data centers such as Amazon and Google gather massive amounts of data everyday that could be analyzed to learn about buying habits, news interests and other useful information. For example, Amazon could use regional buying habits to determine how to stock their regional distribution centers. The problem is that big data analytics can be very compute intensive requiring dedicated data center resources to process a large amount of data which may exist on storage systems across the data center. A technique call MapReduce is used where data queries are mapped across a large number of parallel processing resources and then reduced to useful results. This technique was adopted by the Apache open source project called Hadoop. Future data centers using flexible resource allocation and SDI could allow administrators to re-purpose data center resources as needed to provide this relevant information for their own use or to their cloud data center tenants.

REVIEW

In this chapter, we attempted to provide our vision on where cloud data center networking may be headed in the future. We started by discussing rack scale architecture which could use pools of modular resources to optimize the rack for certain workloads. We then discussed how memory is a key modular component of rack scale architecture with unique performance and interface requirements, and how it may evolve using new memory technology. Next, we described how a specialized, low-latency, low-overhead switch fabric could improve performance within the rack while also providing a flexible and uniform modular architecture. We followed this with an overview of data center cabling options including future directions in low-cost, high-bandwidth optical cabling. We concluded by discussing some future trends in data center software automation and NFV. In the next chapter, we will provide a summary of this book.

CHAPTER 12

Conclusions

There is no easy way to conclude a book on cloud networking without leaving many small avenues unexplored. Even so, we can be satisfied that we met the goal we laid out in the first chapter, by providing the reader with a broad overview of cloud networking technologies. And, as we stated there, this book does not pretend to be a textbook or a PhD thesis, but is, instead, intended to provide the reader with a basic understanding across a wide variety of cloud networking topics. In this book, we attempted to cover topics ranging from the history of cloud networking to the direction in which cloud networking is headed, and everything in between. In this final chapter, we will summarize what we have presented in this book and also attempt to highlight some key points.

TECHNOLOGY EVOLUTION

Semiconductor technology has a huge bearing on what can be achieved in the cloud data center. Semiconductor technology is used to manufacture CPUs, chipsets, DRAM memory, solid-state memory, network controllers, network switches, and physical interface devices. In Chapter 2, we described how mainframe computers using custom silicon chips were eventually replaced by PCs, workstations, and servers utilizing off-the-shelf CPUs from companies like Intel and AMD. We described a similar trend in Chapter 10 for supercomputers which evolved from single monolithic processor boards using custom chips to large arrays of processing nodes using off-the-shelf CPUs. We pointed out that both massively parallel supercomputers and large data centers share the same trait of being composed of large numbers of CPU boards. The performance of these CPUs pace the overall data center performance, but so do the networking connections between these CPU boards.

In Chapter 3, we described how networking technology has evolved to keep pace with CPU performance by utilizing advanced semiconductor technology. As chip-to-chip communications moved from shared busses to shared memory to more advanced topologies, it became clear to silicon vendors that the best way to transmit signals between devices was to use serial connections. But it wasn't until the late 1990s that semiconductor technology progressed to the point where high-quality serializer/deserializer (SerDes) circuits became available for data rates above 1Gb per second. Soon, semiconductor vendors started to produce a variety of high-performance networking devices that exploited SerDes technology. This change ushered in a wide range of new standards and new architectures that we use in large data center networks today.

INDUSTRY STANDARDS

The development of standard form factors and protocols has helped drive the networking industry forward by providing high volume compatible products from a variety of vendors. Throughout this book we have described many of these standards and we also devoted Chapter 5 to several standards specifically developed for data center networking. Ethernet is one of the most important standards developed over the last several decades. Throughout the 1990s, Ethernet was relegated to local area networks while carrier networks were using Synchronous Optical Network/Synchronous Digital Hierarchy (SONET/SDH), storage networks were using Fibre Channel, and most high-performance communication systems were using specialty switch fabric chips from various vendors along with proprietary ASICs. Today, Ethernet standards have evolved to meet almost any market need. Ethernet is now used in LAN networks, data center networks, storage networks using iSCSI or FCoE, carrier networks and high performance computing networks. It is also used within the backplanes of specialized systems such as network appliances and video distribution systems.

Improvement in Ethernet bandwidth was also presented as one reason it has enjoyed so much recent success in these various markets. Ethernet was initially behind in the bandwidth performance race compared to protocols such as SONET/SDH and Fibre Channel until the early 2000s when 10Gb Ethernet specifications were developed. The new 10GbE SerDes also enabled four-lane 40GbE ports allowing Ethernet to meet many carrier network bandwidth requirements while also surpassing what could be achieved with the best storage area networks. Moving forward, we expect Ethernet to continue to be a performance leader in data center network bandwidth.

In Chapter 5, we discussed several other important standards used in large cloud data centers including data center bridging for converging storage and data traffic in the same network. In addition, we covered standards for improving network bandwidth utilization including ECMP, TRILL, and SPB. We also covered RDMA standards for reducing communication latency such as iWARP and RoCE. In Chapter 6, we described several standards used in server virtualization including EVB and SR-IOV, and, in Chapter 7, we discussed some important network virtualization standards including Q-in-Q, MPLS, VXLAN, and NVGRE. In Chapter 8, we covered standards used in storage networking such as SATA, SAS, iSCSI, and Fibre Channel. For high-performance computing applications, we provide information in Chapter 10 on several low-latency communication standards including HyperTransport, Intel QPI, RapidIO, PCIe Non-transparent Bridging, InfiniBand, and MPI. All of these standards help provide the industry with ecosystems of compatible products from multiple vendors, helping to increase the pace of innovation and reduce cost.

NETWORKING

The consistent focus throughout this book was cloud data center networking. In Chapter 3, we described the evolution of switch fabric architectures which has been closely aligned with advances in semiconductor technology. We discussed how multistage topologies can be used to create larger data center networks as long as proper congestion management methods are used, such as flow control, virtual output queuing, and traffic management. In Chapter 4, we described several types of data center networking equipment including virtual switches, top of rack switches, end of row switches, fabric extenders, aggregation switches, and core switches, along with how they can be used to form large data center networks. We also described how flat data center networks can improve performance and reduce core switching requirements.

In Chapter 4, we also described how disaggregated networking can be used within new rack scale products and microservers; which are part of a new industry initiative called rack scale architecture. We also devoted a large part of Chapter 11 to projections on how advances in networking will provide rack disaggregation using modular components. We speculated that specialized, low-overhead switch fabric technologies may be employed within the rack to meet low-latency and low-payload overhead requirements when using pools of memory that are separate from the CPU resources. This type of networking would enable new rack scale architectures where various CPU, memory, storage, security, and networking resources can be flexibly deployed based on workload requirements.

STORAGE AND HPC

Storage is a key component in cloud data center networks, and in Chapter 8 we provided an overview of the server memory and storage hierarchy along with a description of various types of storage technology. We also described several ways to connect CPU resources to storage, including direct attached storage, storage area networks, and network attached storage. Several advanced storage technologies were also presented, including object storage, data protection, tiered storage, and data deduplication. We also described several storage communication protocols, including SCSI, SATA, SAS, and Fibre Chanel. Information on how storage traffic can be transmitted across standard data networks using iSCSI or FCoE without the need for separate storage networks was also presented. We concluded this chapter by providing an overview of software-defined storage (SDS) and how storage is used in cloud data centers.

Near the end of this book, we included a chapter on high-performance computing networks. Although high-performance computing is not directly related to cloud data center networking, there are some common aspects such as the use of large arrays of CPU resources, the use of Ethernet in some HPC networks, and the use of multi-socket CPU boards that are interconnected using HyperTransport or Intel QPI for interprocessor communication. In that chapter, we also provided an overview of HPC fabric technology including Infiniband, which is used in many HPC clusters today. We also provided an overview on HPC fabric interface technology, network performance factors, and HPC software.

DATA CENTER VIRTUALIZATION

Data center virtualization allows data center administrators to provide fine-grain allocation of data center resources to a large number of tenants while at the same time optimizing data center resource utilization. In this book, we covered several components of data center virtualization including server virtualization, network virtualization, and storage virtualization. In Chapter 6, we covered server virtualization, including the use of hypervisors to deploy virtual machines and virtual switches. We described several techniques to provide network connectivity to virtual machines, including VMDq and SR-IOV. We also described several standards used to bridge the interface between the virtual switch and the physical network, including VN-Tag and VEPA.

In Chapter 7, we described how virtual networking will provide data center customers with their own isolated virtual networks within these multitenant environments. We described limitations with several existing tunneling standards, including Q-in-Q and MPLS, and how the industry has introduced new tunneling standards including VXLAN and NVGRE to overcome these limitations. We also described several usage cases for these new tunneling protocols. In Chapter 8, we described storage networks and briefly touched on how storage virtualization can also be used to provide data center tenants with the resources they need. We expect that these data center virtualization methods will continue to grow within cloud data centers and will soon become orchestrated using a software-defined infrastructure.

SOFTWARE-DEFINED INFRASTRUCTURE

The complexities introduced by virtualized servers, virtualized networking, and virtualized storage in multitenant data center environments is adding to administrative operating costs. In addition, the time required to deploy or modify these data center resources for a given tenant eats into data center revenue. In Chapter 9 of this book, we provided an overview of several new initiatives including software-defined networking and network function virtualization which may help improve this. We also briefly described software defined storage in Chapter 8. These initiatives promise to reduce operating expense through the use of a central orchestration layer that can quickly deploy virtual servers, virtual networking, and virtual storage for a given tenant. In addition, this orchestration layer can also deploy NFV features as needed throughout the data center, including such functions as firewalls, intrusion detection, and server load balancing. In Chapter 11, we also described how network automation applications could be used in the future to automatically optimize the location and operation of data center resources in order to maximize data center utilization, performance, and revenue.

CONCLUDING REMARKS

The world has changed dramatically over the last several decades. Working as a new engineer in the 1980s, if I needed a product data sheet, a phone call to the local sales representative would provide a data sheet through the mail within a week. Now, everything is instantaneous. Every day most of us communicate with cloud data centers through our PCs, laptops, tablets, and smart phones. Using these devices, the cloud service providers give us access to various kinds of data including Google maps, Facebook status updates, and eBooks from Amazon. In addition, many corporations are moving their data center capabilities into the public cloud in order to minimize capital and operating expenses. This means that clients who are logged into their corporate network may also be accessing information from the cloud. Many people don't realize that all this information is coming from large warehouses that can contain tens of thousands of servers and that these servers must be interconnected using advanced networking technology.

In this book, we have attempted to provide the reader with a wide background and overview of the various technologies related to cloud data center networking. Some of you may have been overwhelmed by too much detail while others may complain that there was not enough detail presented. For both types of readers, we would suggest searching the cloud for more information on the cloud. Here you will find Wikipedia articles, blogs, white papers, documents from standards bodies, and information from network equipment providers. Some of this information will contain opinions, some will provide marketing spins, but all of it can take you further down the path of understanding cloud networking technology. One thing is for certain, the pace of technology evolution is constantly increasing, so I better stop writing and get this book out before it becomes obsolete.

Index

Note: Page numbers followed by *f* indicate figures.

A

Access control list (ACL) rules, 71
Advanced Research Projects Agency Network (ARPANET)
   cell-based switch fabric design, 17, 17*f*
   circuit-switched network, 17
   IMPs, 17, 18
   NCP header, 18
   packet routing, 17
   packet switching, 18
Aggregation switch, 73–74
ALOHAnet, 24
API. *See* Application programming interface (API)
Application programming interface (API), 165
Application specific integrated circuits (ASICs), 77, 78–79, 83, 84
ARPANET. *See* Advanced Research Projects Agency Network (ARPANET)
ASICs. *See* Application specific integrated circuits (ASICs)
Asynchronous transfer mode (ATM)
   advantages, 22
   circuit-switched technology, 21
   description, 21
   frame format, 21, 22*f*
   NIC card, 21
   packet based networks, 22
ATM. *See* Asynchronous transfer mode (ATM)

B

B-component Backbone Edge Bridge (B-BEB), 28
Big Data Analytics, 202–203

C

Cabling technology
   copper, 199–201
   optical, 200–201
   wireless interconnect, 201
Capital expense (CapEx), 65–66, 67
Carrier Ethernet
   B-BEB, 28
   BCB forwards packets, 28
   CEP, 27–28
   circuit switching to packet switching technologies, 28
   communication, 27
   data centers, 28
   E-LAN, 27
   E-linc, 27
   E-tree, 27
   I-BEB, 28
   I-NNI interface, 27–28
   MAC-in-MAC, 28
   MEF, 27
   MPLS-TE/T-MPLS, 28
   PB and PBB network, 27–28
   S-NNI interface, 27–28
   S-PORT CNP interface, 27–28
   standards, 28
   timing synchronization, 28
Carrier Sense Multiple Access with Collision Detection (CSMA/CD), 25
Cell-based designs
   advantages, 59
   ATM and SONET/SDH, 58–59
   disadvantage, 59–60
   effective bandwidth utilization *vs.* payload size, 60, 60*f*
   Ethernet, 58–59
   fabric interface chips (FICs), 59
   "God" box, 58–59
   switch fabric designs, 59, 59*f*
CEP. *See* Customer Edge Ports (CEP)
Chef, 167
Circuit-switched network
   ARPANET, 17
   ATM, 21
   packet switching technologies, 28
   SONET/SDH, 20
Cloud data centers
   cheap electrical power sources, 4–5
   description, 4
   distributed storage, 159
   driving forces, 31–32
   features and benefits, 15, 15*f*
   flat network topology, 30, 30*f*
   flat tree network, 31
   10GbE links, 31
   hardware and software, 30
   hybrid cloud, 33
   installations, 4–5
   Microsoft®, 4–5
   east-west traffic, 30, 31, 68, 74, 75, 100, 113

211

Cloud data centers *(Continued)*
  north-south traffic, 30
  ODMs, 15
  Open Compute Project, 15
  PODs, 159
  private cloud services, 33
  public cloud services, 33–35
  rack scale architecture (RSA), 160–161
  server connection, 15
  server racks, 4–5
  server virtualization, 5
  service providers, 15
Cloud networking
  convergence, 7
  description, 1, 5, 205
  equipment, 4
  Ethernet usage, 6
  interconnect, 4
  Open Systems Interconnection (OSI) networking stack, 2–3
  packets and frames, 3, 3*f*
  scalability, 7–8
  software, 8
  virtualization, 6–7
Computer networks
  ARPANET, 17–18
  ATM, 21–22
  dedicated lines, 17
  Ethernet, 23
  Fibre Channel, 23
  InfiniBand, 23–24
  LANs and WANs, 16
  MPLS, 19–20
  SONET/SDH, 20–21
  TCP/IP, 18–19
  Token Ring/Token Bus, 22–23
Congestion management
  description, 47
  egress link/queue, 47
  HoL blocking, 47
  load balancing algorithms, 48–49
  traffic buffering, 49–50
  unbalanced traffic, 48
Controlling bridge
  fabric extenders, 80*f*, 85
  spine switch, 73
  switch functionality, 73
Core switches
  active-passive redundancy, 79
  aggregation, 73–74
  fabric devices, 78
  forwarding tag types, 78–79
  label switching techniques, 78–79
  line cards, 78
  lossless operation, 79
  modular chassis, 78, 78*f*
  packets, 79
  routers, 66–67, 68, 71, 72*f*
  server racks and resiliency, 79
  software and hardware failover, 79
Cost factors, data center networks
  CapEx, 65–66
  core switch/routers, 66–67
  LAN-based network, 66–67
  OpEx, 65–66
  software, 67
  TCP/IP standards, 66–67
  ToR switches, 66, 66*f*
CRC. *See* Cyclic redundancy check (CRC)
Crossbar switch
  arbiter interface, 41
  arbitration unit, 41
  architecture, 40, 41, 41*f*
  1Gbps SerDes circuits, 40
  high-bandwidth serial interconnect, 40
  performance, 41–42
  SAR unit, 41
CSMA/CD. *See* Carrier Sense Multiple Access with Collision Detection (CSMA/CD)
Customer Edge Ports (CEP), 27–28
Cyclic redundancy check (CRC)
  frame check sequence, 26

D

DAS. *See* Direct attached storage (DAS)
Data center bridging (DCB)
  DCBx protocol, 95–96
  Ethernet switches, 90
  ETS, 93–94
  fabrics, 90
  PFC, 91–93
  QCN, 94–95
  representation, device, 91, 124*f*
Data center evolution
  cloud data centers, 14–15, 15*f*
  computer networks (*see* Computer networks)
  dumb client terminals, 11–12
  enterprise data centers, 14, 14*f*
  Ethernet (*see* Ethernet)
  mainframes, 12, 12*f*
  minicomputers, 12–13, 13*f*
  servers, 13–14, 13*f*
  virtualized data centers, 15–16, 16*f*

Index

Data center networking
  flat, 74–79
  multitiered enterprise networks, 65–68
  network function virtualization (NFV), 83–85
  rack scale architectures, 79–83
  switch types, 68–74
Data center software
  API, 165
  OEMs, 164
  requirements, 164–165
  software-defined data center, 165–166, 166f
Data center virtualization, 208
Data deduplication, 149
Data protection and recovery
  erasure coding, 147
  RAID, 146–147
DCB. See Data center bridging (DCB)
Deficit round robin (DRR), 57
Deficit weighted round robin (DWRR), 57
Direct attach copper cabling, 6
Direct attached storage (DAS), 143, 153

E

East-west traffic
  latency, 75
  servers/VMs, 74
  3-teir data center networks, 75
ECMP routing. See Equal cost multipath (ECMP) routing
Edge virtual bridging (EVB)
  hypervisor vendors, 114
  industry adoption, 116
  VEPA, 114–115
  VN-Tag, 115–116
End of row (EoR) switch
  cabling costs, 72
  configuration, 71, 72, 72f
  description, 71
Enhanced transmission selection (ETS), 93–94
Enterprise data centers
  aggregation switches, 29
  vs. cloud data center networks, 30–31
  disadvantages, 29–30
  Ethernet, 14
  FCoE, 14
  1GbE/10GbE links, 29
  LAN, 29, 29f
  networks, 14, 14f
  switches, 29
  ToR switch, 29

Enterprise networks
  cost factors, 65–67
  OEM, 65
  performance factors, 67–68
Equal cost multipath (ECMP) routing, 130–133, 136–137
Ethernet
  ALOHAnet, 24
  carrier Ethernet, 27–28
  CPUs, 4
  CRC, 26
  CSMA/CD, 25
  description, 3
  destination MAC address, 26
  development, 24
  Ethertype, 26
  frame format, 25, 26f
  header, 3
  IEEE standard, 24, 25
  interframe gap, 26–27
  jumbo frames, 26–27
  LANs, 25
  layer 2 technology, 2, 3, 5
  payload, 26
  port bandwidth, 25
  preamble and start-of-frame (SoF), 26
  shared media protocol, 25
  source MAC address, 26
  speeds, 25
  transport protocol, 23
  usage, 6
  VLANs, 26
  Xerox® PARC, 24
Ethernet data rate standards
  10GbE, 88
  40GbE and 100GbE, 88–89
  network protocols, 87–88
ETS. See Enhanced transmission selection (ETS)
EVB. See Edge virtual bridging (EVB)
Explicit congestion notification (ECN), 54

F

Fabric extenders
  controlling bridge, 73
  disaggregated EoR switch, 72, 73f
  high-bandwidth optical cables, 73
  unified management model, 73
Fabric interface chips (FICs)
  fat-tree topology, 46
  mesh topology, 44–45
  ring topology, 43–44

Index

Fabric interface chips (FICs) *(Continued)*
    star topology, 45
Fat-tree topology
    architecture, 46
    bandwidth, 46
    load balancing and congestion management, 46
    spine switch, 46
    two-stage fat-tree configuration, 46, 46*f*
Fibre Channel (FC)
    connection-oriented and connectionless services, 153
    FCoE (*see* Fibre Channel over Ethernet (FCoE))
    network protocols, 23
    SANs, 143, 143*f*
    storage traffic, 23
Fibre Channel over Ethernet (FCoE)
    FC-BB-5 standard, 156
    FC-BB-6 standard, 157
    frame format, 155–156, 155*f*
    40Gb Ethernet, 157
    network components, 156, 156*f*
FICs. *See* Fabric interface chips (FICs)
Field programmable gate arrays (FPGAs)
    and ASICs, 172
    Moore's law, 173
Firewall
    and intrusion detection applications, 84
    VM, 84–85
First in, first out (FIFO)
    buffer memory structures, 43
    shared memory, 62
Flash storage, 142
Flat data center networks
    core switch features, 77–79
    ToR switch features, 76–77
    traffic patterns, 74–76
Flow control
    ECN, 54
    end-to-end, 54
    link-level, 51–53
    QCN, 54
    throttling mechanism, 50
    virtual output queuing, 53–54
FPGAs. *See* Field programmable gate arrays (FPGAs)

G

Gallium arsenide (GaAs) technology, 40
Generic Network Virtualization Encapsulation (GENEVE), 130

H

Hadoop, 202–203
Hard disk drives (HDDs)
    SAS, 148, 151
    storage density, 141
Head-of-line (HoL) blocking, 47
Heat, 167
High-performance computing (HPC) system
    compute nodes, 180
    descritpion, 179, 207
    Ethernet, 186
    fabric configurations, 184–185, 184*f*
    InfiniBand, 185–186, 185*f*
    message passing interface (MPI), 188
    multisocket CPU boards, 180–183
    Myrinet™, 185
    network performance factors, 186–188
    verbs, 189
HPC system. *See* High-performance computing (HPC) system
Hybrid cloud, 33
Hyper-scale data center, 1
HyperTransport (HT) Consortium, 181–182, 181*f*
Hypervisors, 104–105
Hyper-V virtual switch, 107–108

I

I-component Backbone Edge Bridge (I-BEB), 28
IETF. *See* Internet Engineering Task Force (IETF)
IMPs. *See* Interface Message Processors (IMPs)
Industry standards, 206
InfiniBand
    description, 23–24
    HCAs, 24
    HPC systems and storage applications, 23–24
    transport functions, 24
Infrastructure as a Service (IaaS), 34
Ingress link-level shaping, 57–58
Input-output-queued (IOQ) designs
    architectures, 60–61
    memory performance requirements, 60–61
    packets, 61
    switch chip, 60–61, 61*f*
    virtual output queues, 61
Interface Message Processors (IMPs), 18
Internet Engineering Task Force (IETF), 18

Internet Wide-Area RDMA Protocol (iWARP), 18, 101–102
Intrusion detection, 83, 84–85
IOQ designs. *See* Input-output-queued (IOQ) designs
iWARP. *See* Internet Wide-Area RDMA Protocol (iWARP)K
Kernel-based Virtual Machine (KVM) Hypervisor, 105

L

LAN on motherboard (LOM) device, 69
LANs. *See* Local area networks (LANs)
Layer 2 header
    components, 2
    switching, 2
Leaf switch
    FIC, 49
    packet reordering unit, 48
    spine switches, 46
Link-level flow control
    credit based, 52
    description, 51, 51*f*
    flow control round-trip delay, 52
    HoL blocking, 52
    losing packets, 51–52
    priority-based link-level flow control, 52, 53*f*
    queuing delays, 52
    receive queue, 51–52
    switch chips, 51–52
    threshold based, 52
Load balancing
    description, 48–49
    ECMP routing, 136–137
    hash-based algorithm/random hash., 49, 135
    microservers, 83
    NFV, 84
    Spanning Tree Protocol, 135
    ToR switch, 71
    traffic distribution, 49
Local area networks (LANs)
    computing applications, 13
    E-LAN, 27
    enterprise networks, 14
    enterprise *vs.* cloud data centers, 28–31
    types, 14
    vs WANs, 16, 21

M

MAC address
    destination, 26
    source, 26

Mainframes
    client terminal connections, 12, 12*f*
    description, 12
MapReduce, 202–203
Memcached, 193–194
Memory migration
    copy process, pages, 117
    CPU state, 118
    storage, 117
Memory technology
    description, 195
    interface, 196
    non-volatile memory and storage, 195
Mesh topology
    description, 44, 44*f*
    fabric performance, 44
    two-dimensional rings/Torus structures, 45
Metro Ethernet Forum (MEF), 27
Microservers
    CPU, 82, 83
    description, 82
    server platform, 82
    three-dimensional ring architecture, 82, 83*f*
Microsoft, 105
Minicomputers
    client terminal connections, 12–13, 13*f*
    definition, 12
    enterprise data centers, 12
    LAN, 12–13
    PDP-8 and PDP-11, 12
Modular chassis, 71, 78, 83
MPLS. *See* Multi-Protocol Label Switching (MPLS)
MR-IOV. *See* Multiroot IO virtualization (MR-IOV)
Multilevel scheduler
    deficit weighted round robin, 57
    DRR, 57
    four-stage scheduler, 55–56, 55*f*
    round robin, 56–57
    strict priority, 56
    tree of queues, 56
    virtual machines, 56
Multi-Protocol Label Switching (MPLS)
    forwarding and frame format, 124–125, 125*f*
    frame processing requirements, 124–125
    Ipsilon Networks, 19
    IPv4 and IPv6 networks, 125–126
    LERs, 19–20, 20*f*, 125
    LSRs, 20, 125
    packet forwarding, 19–20, 20*f*
    tunneling protocols, 19
Multiroot IO virtualization (MR-IOV), 113–114

Index

Multisocket CPU boards
  HyperTransport (HT) Consortium, 181–182
  Intel®QuickPath Interconnect, 182
  PCIe NTB, 183, 183f
  RapidIO, 182–183
Multitenant environments
  flexible allocation, resources, 121
  network requirements, 122
  physical servers and physical network components, 121, 122f
  server administration, 122

N

Network attached storage (NAS), 144–145, 154
Network bandwidth
  ECMP routing, 130–133
  shortest path bridging, 130
  spanning tree, 129–130
  TRILL, 131
Network convergence
  FCoE, 155–157
  industry adoption, 157
  iSCSI, 154–155
  requirements, 153–154
Network File System (NFS), 154
Network function virtualization (NFV)
  appliances, 172
  ATCA platform, 84
  data center administration, 84–85, 173
  description, 83
  firewalls and intrusion detection applications, 84
  implementation, 175–176
  load balancing, 84, 174–175, 174f
  network monitoring, 84, 175
  NPUs and FPGAs, 173
  open daylight foundation, 176
  packet processing device, 172, 172f
  security, 173–174
  server CPU resources, 84
  standard server platforms, 83, 84f, 85
  vSwitch, 84–85
  WAN optimization applications, 84
Networking standards
  DCB (see Data center bridging (DCB))
  Ethernet data rate standards, 87–89
  IETF and IEEE, 87
  network bandwidth (see Network bandwidth)
  RDMA (see Remote direct memory access (RDMA))
  VLANs, 89–90

Network interface controllers (NICs), 4, 69, 82
Network migration
  data center network, 118–119, 118f
  IP address, 118
  network administration, 119
  software-defined networking, 119
Network processing units (NPUs), 77, 78–79, 84, 172
Network stack
  application layer, 3
  data center transaction, 2, 2f
  Ethernet layer, 3
  OSI, 2
Network virtualization
  description, 121
  load balancing, 135–137
  multitenant environments, 121–123
  NVGRE (see Network Virtualization Generic Routing Encapsulation (NVGRE))
  tunneling protocols (see Tunneling)
  VXLAN (see Virtual Extensible LAN (VXLAN))
Network Virtualization Generic Routing Encapsulation (NVGRE)
  frame format, 131, 131f
  GRE, 130
  IETF standard, 130
  NVE de-encapsulation, 132–133
  NVE encapsulation, 131–132
NFS. See Network File System (NFS)
NFV. See Network function virtualization (NFV)
NICs. See Network interface controllers (NICs)
NPUs. See Network processing units (NPUs)
NVGRE. See Network Virtualization Generic Routing Encapsulation (NVGRE)

O

OEMs. See Original equipment manufacturers (OEMs)
Open Compute Project, 15
OpenFlow
  controller implementation, 168, 168f
  forwarding table implementation, 170–171
  industry adoption, 171
  Open API, 169–170
  protocols, 168, 168f
OpenStack (Heat)
  Cinder, 167
  Neutron, 168
  Nova, 167
  Swift, 167
Open Systems Interconnect (OSI), 2–3

Index 217

Open vSwitch (OVS), 108
Operating expense (OpEx), 65–66, 67
Original design manufacturers (ODMs), 15, 30
Original equipment manufacturers (OEMs)
   network equipment, 164
   OpenFlow controller, 169, 169f
OSI. See Open Systems Interconnect (OSI)
Output-queued shared memory designs
   cut-through operation, 62
   forwarding decision, 62
   high-performance switch chip implementations, 62
   Intel® Ethernet switch family, 62
   link-level flow control, 63, 63f
   scheduler, 62–63
   traffic shaping, 62–63
OVS. See Open vSwitch (OVS)

P

PaaS. See Platform as a Service (PaaS)
Packets
   frames, 3
   TCP/IP header, 3
PCI Express (PCIe)
   computers and workstations, 110
   Ethernet network interface cards, 111
   ISA and VESA, 110
   MR-IOV, 113–114
   PCI-X bus standards, 110–111
   performance, parallel bus, 110
   peripheral configuration, 111, 111f
   serializer/deserializer (SerDes) technology, 111
   SR-IOV, 112–113
   switch hierarchy, 112
Performance factors, data center networks
   core routers, 67–68
   Fibre Channel, 68
   layer 3 forwarding functions, 68
   ToR switches, 67
   VMs, 67
   web service applications, 67–68
PFC. See Priority-based flow control (PFC)
Phase lock loop (PLL), 41–42
Platform as a Service (PaaS), 34–35
Priority-based flow control (PFC)
   Ethernet frame, 92
   IEEE 802.3x pause frame, 92, 126f
   implementation, switch stages, 91, 125f
   pause time and watermark settings, 92–93
   traffic-class-based memory partitions, 92
   transmission, 92
Private cloud, 33
Provider backbone bridge (PBB) network, 27–28
Provider bridge (PB) networks, 27–28
Public cloud services
   IaaS, 34
   PaaS, 34–35
   SaaS, 35
   types of services, 33, 34f
Puppet, 167

Q

Quantized congestion notification (QCN)
   feedback value, 95
   IEEE standards, 95
   layer 2 frame, 94–95, 128f
   link-level flow control, PFC, 94

R

Rack scale architectures (RSAs)
   CPU modules, 193
   distributed fabric, 194, 194f
   memory and storage modules, 193–194, 193f
   microservers, 82–83
   power delivery and thermal management, 80
   resource disaggregation, 81–82, 192
   server shelf components, 79, 80–81, 80f
RAID. See Redundant array of independent disks (RAID)
RDMA. See Remote direct memory access (RDMA)
Redundant array of independent disks (RAID)
   controller, storage array, 146, 146f
   data rebuild, 147
   erasure codes, 147
   implementations, 146–147
   striping, 146
Remote direct memory access (RDMA)
   CPUs, NPUs and microcontrollers, 100
   data center requirements, 132–133
   iWARP, 133–135
   kernel bypass, 100
   RoCE, 102
   TCP/IP protocol, 102
Resource disaggregation, RSA
   components, 81, 81f
   OCP, 81
   OEMs, ODMs/system integrators, 81
   server sleds, 81–82
   star architectures, 82

Index

Ring topology
  advantages, 44
  description, 43, 44f
  disadvantages, 44
  FIC, 43
  Token Ring networks, 44
Round robin
  deficit, 57
  deficit weighted, 57
  description, 56–57
Route-able RoCE, 102
RSAs. *See* Rack scale architectures (RSAs)

S

SANs. *See* Storage area networks (SANs)
SAS. *See* Serial attached SCSI (SAS)
SATA. *See* Serial ATA (SATA)
SCSI. *See* Small Computer System Interface (SCSI)
SDI. *See* Software-defined infrastructure (SDI)
SDN. *See* Software-defined networking (SDN)
SDN deployment
  controller locations, 176–177, 177f
  network edge, 177–178
Security concerns, 32
Segmentation and reassembly (SAR) unit, 41
Semiconductor technology
  chip-to-chip communications, 205
Serial ATA (SATA)
  IBM PC-AT, 150
  modern PC chipset, 150, 150f
  port multiplier function, 150–151, 150f
  and SAS, 151
Serial attached SCSI (SAS)
  dual ports, redundancy, 151
  FC-based products, 152
  HDD storage arrays, 148, 151, 151f
  iSCSI, 155
  SANs, 151
Server Message Block (SMB), 154
Server rack, 71, 73, 76, 79
Shared bus
  architecture, 38, 38f
  performance, 39
Shared memory
  architecture, 39–40, 39f
  performance, 40
Single-root IO virtualization (SR-IOV)
  CPU resources, 113
  hypervisors, 112
  NIC PCIe interface, 113
  PCI configuration space, 113
  virtual functions (VFs), 112–113
  vNIC functionality, 112, 112f
Small Computer System Interface (SCSI)
  computers and storage devices, 149–150
  FCoE, 155–156
  iSCSI and FC protocols, 153
  SAS, 151
Software as a Service (SaaS), 35
Software-defined infrastructure (SDI)
  data center automation, 201–202
  NFV, 202
Software-defined networking (SDN)
  data center software, 163–166
  deployment, 176–178
  description, 163
  network function virtualization, 171–176
  OpenFlow, 8, 168–171
  OpenStack, 167–168
Software-defined storage (SDS)
  abstraction, 158
  open interface, 158
  virtualization, 158
SONET/SDH
  description, 20
  framer chips, 21
  frame transport time period, 20–21
  IP traffic, 21
  telecommunication networks, 21
  telephone systems, 20
  time slot interchange chips, 20–21
  transport containers, 20–21, 21f
Spanning tree, 129–130
Spine switch, 46, 48
SR-IOV. *See* Single-root IO virtualization (SR-IOV)
Star topology
  definition, 45, 45f
  scalability, 45
  switch cards, 45
  switch chip, 45
Stateless Transport Tunneling (STT), 126–127
Storage area networks (SANs)
  block storage, 144
  FC and Ethernet ports, 156, 156f
  FC switches, 143, 143f
  and NAS, 144–145
  network administration, 144
  SAS, 151
Storage communication protocols
  fibre channel, 152–153
  SAS, 151
  SATA, 150–151
  SCSI, 149–150

Index

Storage hierarchy
  cache memory, DRAM, 140
  capacity *vs.* performance, 141
  data center memory components, 140, 140*f*
  flash memory, 140–141
Storage networks
  cloud data centers, 158–161
  communication protocols, 149–153
  DAS, 143
  description, 139
  flash storage, 142
  HDDs, 141
  NAS, 144–145
  network convergence, 153–157
  requirement, 139
  SANs, 143–144
  SDS, 157–158
  storage hierarchy, 140–141
  technology (*see* Storage technologies)
Storage technologies
  data deduplication, 149
  data protection and recovery, 145–147
  object storage and metadata, 145
  tiered storage, 147–149
STT. *See* Stateless Transport Tunneling (STT)
Switch fabric technology
  cell-based designs, 58–60
  congestion management, 47–50
  crossbar switch (*see* Crossbar switch)
  description, 197
  fat-tree topology, 46, 46*f*
  FICs, 43
  flow control, 50–54
  high-bandwidth serializers/deserializers (SerDes), 37–38
  I/O circuits, 37
  IOQ designs, 60–61
  mesh topology, 44–45, 44*f*
  modular design, 198–199, 198*f*
  output-queued shared memory designs, 62–63
  port bandwidth, 197–198
  ring topology, 43–44, 44*f*
  shared bus (*see* Shared bus)
  shared memory (*see* Shared memory)
  star topology, 45, 45*f*
  synchronous serial switching (*see* Synchronous serial switching)
  traffic management, 55–58
Synchronous Digital Hierarchy (SDH). *See* SONET/SDH
Synchronous Optical Network (SONET). *See* SONET/SDH
Synchronous serial switching
  arbitration, 42–43
  architecture, 42–43, 42*f*
  FIFO buffer memory structures, 43
  performance, 43

T

TCP/IP. *See* Transmission Control Protocol/Internet Protocol (TCP/IP)
Tiered storage, 147–149, 148*f*
Token buckets, 58
Token Bus, 22–23
Token Ring
  4Mbps and 16Mbps speed, 22
Top of rack (ToR) switch
  ACL rules, 71
  components, 76, 76*f*
  control plane CPU subsystem, 76
  control plane processor, 71
  10GbE ports, 71
  low latency, 77
  network convergence, 77
  open software, 77
  optic modules, 71
  port configurations, 76
  SDN controller, 71
  server virtualization support, 77
  server *vs.* uplink bandwidth, 70–71
  single switch chip, 71
  star topology, 70–71, 70*f*
  tunneling features, 77
ToR switch. *See* Top of rack (ToR) switch
Torus structures, 45
Traffic buffering, switch fabric technology
  buffer memory size, 50
  FIC, 50
  flow control, 49
  on-chip buffering, 49–50
  SLAs, 49–50
  star fabric topology, 49, 49*f*
  TCP/IP, 49
Traffic management
  frame classification engine, 55
  multilevel scheduler, 55–57
  telecom access systems, 55
  traffic shaping, 57–58
Traffic patterns, flat data center networks
  East-West traffic, 74, 75
  North-South traffic, 74
  2-teir network, 75–76

Index

Traffic shaping
  description, 57
  high-priority management traffic, 57
  ingress link-level shaping, 57–58
  token buckets, 58
Transceivers
  GaAs technology, 40
  GigaBlaze® 1Gbps, 42
  phase lock loop (PLL), 41
  serial data, 41
Transmission Control Protocol/Internet Protocol (TCP/IP)
  high-level functions, 18, 18f
  IETF, 18
  iSCS and iWARP, 18
  OSI stack, 2
  transport functions, 19
  types, 18
TRansparent Interconnect of Lots of Links (TRILL), 131
Tunneling
  features, 77
  IP tunneling protocols, 66–67
  MPLS, 124–126
  network edge, 133, 133f
  NIC, 134
  Q-in-Q, 124
  services, 83
  ToR switch, 71, 135
  VN-Tags, 126
  vSwitch, 134
Two-dimensional rings, 45

U

Unbalanced traffic, congestion
  flow-based load distribution, 48
  jumbo frames, 48
  leaf switches, 48
  spine switches, 48
  two-stage fat-tree topology, 48

V

VDS. *See* vSphere distributed switch (VDS)
Virtual Ethernet port aggregator (VEPA), 114–115, 115f
Virtual Extensible LAN (VXLAN)
  frame format, 127–128
  NVGRE, 126–127
  VTEP de-encapsulation, 129–130
  VTEP encapsulation, 128–129

Virtualized data centers
  description, 15–16, 16f
  physical servers, 16
  private data centers, 15–16
  storage, 16
  tunneling protocols, 16
Virtual local area networks (VLANs)
  customer identifiers, 90
  ECMP, 98
  IEEE specifications, 89
  SPBV, 98
  tag format, 89, 122f, 124
Virtual local area network (VLAN) tag, 26, 27–28
Virtual machine device queues (VMDqs), 108–109
Virtual machines (VMs)
  description, 16, 103, 120
  EVB, 114–116
  10Gb Ethernet NIC, 104
  hypervisors, 104–105
  and load balancers, 34
  low-level software functions, 34
  Microsoft, 105
  migration (*see* VM migration)
  operating system (OS), 103, 104f
  PCIe (*see* PCI Express (PCIe))
  physical servers, 16, 103
  SaaS providers, 103
  sending data, 69
  server utilization, 104
  and virtualized networks, 15–16, 16f
  VMware®, 105
  vSwitch (*see* Virtual switch (vSwitch))
Virtual network tag (VN-Tag), 115–116, 116f, 126
Virtual output queuing
  definition, 53f, 54
  flow control information, 54
  ingress and egress priority queues, 53
  traffic management, 54
Virtual switch (vSwitch)
  high-bandwidth virtual connections, 69
  Hyper-V, 107–108
  network interface device, 69
  network management, 70
  NIC/LOM, 69
  OVS, 108
  server and network administrator, 70
  server shelf, 69, 69f
  shared memory, 69
  VDS, 106–107

Index

VMDqs, 108–109
VLANs. *See* Virtual local area networks (VLANs)
VMDqs. *See* Virtual machine device queues (VMDqs)
VM migration
   memory (*see* Memory migration)
   network, 118–119
   "seamless", 117
   vendor solutions, 119
VMs. *See* Virtual machines (VMs)
VN-Tag. *See* Virtual network tag (VN-Tag)
VPN, 83
vSphere distributed switch (VDS), 106–107
VTEP. *See* VXLAN Tunnel End Point (VTEP)
VXLAN Tunnel End Point (VTEP)
   de-encapsulation, 129–130
   ECMP, 136
   encapsulation, 128–129
   NVE, 131

W

Wide area networks (WANs)
   aggregation and core switches, 73–74
   ATM, 21–22
   Carrier Ethernet services, 27
   optimization applications, 84
   and telecommunications, 22
Workgroup switches
   and aggregation switches, 29
   1Gb Ethernet and wireless access, 29
   ToR switch, 29
Workstations, 13, 14

Printed in Great Britain
by Amazon